Encaustic tiles in the Chapel chancel. The school's coat of arms was devised by Hugh Simeon, brother of the first Warden. On the left are the arms attributed to St Edward and on the right those granted to Sir John Simeon Bt. in 1814.

A NEW HISTORY OF
ST EDWARD'S SCHOOL, OXFORD
1863-2013

Malcolm Oxley

Published by St Edward's School, Oxford, 2015

© Malcolm Oxley

The moral rights of the author have been asserted.

Robert Gittings's poem 'September 3rd 1939' is reproduced
by kind permission of The Society of Authors as the Literary Representative
of the Estate of Robert Gittings.

St Edward's School, Woodstock Road, Oxford OX2 7NN
www.stedwardsoxford.org

ISBN: 978-0-9932186-0-6

In memory of my parents, John Oxley (1910-1966) and Rose Hannah Oxley (1908-2002)

CONTENTS

Acknowledgements	1
Preface	3
Prologue	5
1 Beginnings	9
2 New Inn Hall Street	15
3 Simeon	23
4 Before Summertown	28
5 The New Site	34
6 Last Year in Central Oxford	41
7 The New School	47
8 The Chapel	55
9 The Headmaster	65
10 The Parting	74
11 Last Years of the First Warden	80
12 Warden Hobson	90
13 Warden Hudson	98
14 Hudson's School	106
15 Warden Sing	111
16 Sing's School	119
17 In Chapel	126
18 Games	142
19 Domestic Life	158
20 Being a Boy	166
21 Towards War	179
22 Jubilee	191

CONTENTS

23	War	199
24	Aftermath	206
25	Warden Ferguson's St Edward's	216
26	Warden Kendall	230
27	Kendall in Command	237
28	From Strength to Strength	248
29	Thriving in the Thirties	254
30	Kendall's School	262
31	To War Again	275
32	The Ways of Peace	290
33	Schooldays	298
34	Kendall's Closing Years	309
35	The New Broom	322
36	Warden Fisher's School	332
37	Winds of Change	349
38	Centenary	363
39	Warden Bradley	372
40	The Lost Leader?	380
41	Warden Henry Christie	390
42	Warden Phillips	407
43	Co-Education	420
44	Warden David Christie	433
45	David Christie's School	444
46	Epilogue	454
Postscript		463
Sources		467
Index		471

ACKNOWLEDGEMENTS

I thank the Governors of St Edward's for inviting me to write a new history of the school. Its predecessor, Desmond Hill's *A History of St Edward's School*, published in 1962 in time for the centenary the following year, described the first hundred years of the school's life. The present book covers the first 150 years. Approaching the subject with aims and perspectives different from Hill's, I have started afresh, albeit with an uneasy awareness of virtues of his volume that I could not emulate.

I hesitated before accepting the Governors' invitation. Not only was I a septuagenarian but I recalled the state of the school's archives back in 1988, when I had last made use of them, for the exhibition that marked the 125th anniversary. I quailed to think of the time it would take to sort the material even before I could begin working on it. I need not have feared. The present archivist Chris Nathan (*St Edward's School Roll* No. 5045) has brought the archives to order, catalogued them, and made them much easier to use: a mammoth task and a labour of love. He has helpfully answered my queries even when heavily engaged in the preparation of the new *School Roll*. During the research and writing the school has given me every possible help. I am especially grateful for the consistent support of Stephen Withers Green, the bursar, himself no mean expert on the past of his adopted school. In the early stages, when it was hard for me to get to Oxford, he enabled me to employ the services of Dr William van Reyk and then Dr Stella Moss, who worked on sections of the archives, scanned material for me, and made useful suggestions. I thank them both.

Behind the Governors' initiative, and keeping an eye on the author, has been Chris Jones (Roll No. 6564), the 'only begetter' of this book. He has sustained me throughout with encouragement and with a faith in the outcome which I have not always shared. I owe him a huge debt. I was made welcome by Chris and Sara on those visits to the archives when I was not enjoying the equally generous hospitality of Roger and Phillipa Clitherow at their home in Wheatley, which since my retirement in 1999 has become almost a second home for me.

The book draws heavily on written reminiscences, not all of them specified in my text, which over the generations have been deposited in the archives by former teachers and pupils.

The number of these recollections has been greatly increased by the abundant responses to my appeals for personal accounts of experiences of the school. Besides the ones I have quoted, many others have enhanced my knowledge and understanding. So helpful have these reminiscences been that the book has sometimes seemed a collective venture. I am most grateful to those who have written to me.

From an early stage I realized that I would need a reader with both a close knowledge of the school and a keen textual eye. Nick Quartley has been the ideal adviser and guide. With a selfless expense of time, and with the skills he brought to the editing of the school's *Chronicle* for more than a quarter of a century, he has read and checked my drafts, corrected slips and howlers, and answered my innumerable requests for the supply or checking of information.

My greatest thanks go to Blair Worden (Roll No. 5520), one of Britain's foremost historians, who has worked tirelessly, sentence by sentence, on my successive drafts, questioning my hypotheses and proposing revisions in the cause of shape, clarity and succinctness. Without him this book would have been not only very different from the text the reader meets here but far inferior to it. I am most fortunate to have had the help of a friend whom I first encountered in Room 5 when I began to teach at the school in 1962.

If there are mistakes in the book, I alone am responsible for them.

I dedicate the book to the memory of my parents, who, themselves only superficially touched by education, knew its importance and made sacrifices so that I could be more fortunate. They recognized that one of the greatest benefits of education is the widening of human choice.

PREFACE

Like all school histories, this book offers a narrative of events and developments within the institution it portrays. But it also has a broader aim. It seeks to relate the school's evolution to the movements of society at large. The history of St Edward's belongs to a period of great wars and of basic changes in social structure and values. I have sought to place my story within national currents of political, religious, and economic transition.

With that objective I have combined a second one: the recovery of social experience. I have attempted to re-create the 'feel' of school life in successive generations. It is here that the reminiscences of former members of the school have been so useful. Though I have had to bear in mind that individual recollections are not necessarily either typical or accurate, I have been impressed by the frequency with which accounts written independently of each other coincide.

The loyalties that cross the generations of the school's alumni testify to continuities in its character and spirit. The physical heart of the school, the Main Quad, has undergone only subsidiary alterations in its architectural appearance since the 1920s. Much in the earlier history of St Edward's will be recognizable to today's inhabitants of the school: yet at least as much will seem foreign. Initially St Edward's was almost as much a monastery as a school. From the late-Victorian period its values became more secular. Nonetheless, within living memory there were features of the institution – practices of hierarchy and discipline, the preference given to collective over individual aspiration, the instinct to separate the school from the world beyond its gates – that are remote from the principles which guide St Edward's today. In my endeavour to recreate unfamiliar mental worlds I have given more space to the first half-century of the school's existence than to the second; more to the second than to the third.

Three features of detail should be explained in advance. Every pupil at St Edward's is given a number which appears in *The Roll of St Edward's School, Oxford*, the published list of pupils, the most recent version of which appeared in 2013. When former pupils are first mentioned in my text their names are accompanied by their *Roll* numbers. Secondly, until recent times the term 'Assistant Master' was used of all members of the teaching staff below the Warden or Headmaster, however senior. Thirdly, younger readers may welcome a reminder of the divisions of the currency that prevailed until decimalization in 1971. A pound (£) was made up of twenty shillings (s.), which themselves consisted of twelve pence (d.). There were also halfpennies and farthings (quarters). I should also say that in quoting original sources I have occasionally made tiny adjustments in the cause of clarity or syntax, without altering the sense.

PROLOGUE

It is late one evening in April 1866 in the Hampshire village of Hursley. Local worthies are gathered, led by the Lord of the Manor and patron of the church living Sir William Heathcote, Bt. Present too are Charlotte Yonge, one of the most distinguished of Victorian novelists, and George Moberly, about to retire as Headmaster of nearby Winchester College. They were close friends of the deceased vicar, John Keble, whose body was arriving from Bournemouth where he had died a few days before. Keble had been Vicar of Hursley since 1836.

Together with Hurrell Froude and John Henry Newman, Keble had been a leading figure in the creation and sustenance of the Oxford Movement of High Church Anglican revival, which had begun in the 1830s when he was a youthful but distinguished academic. Many regarded him as a living saint. Others saw him as a disruptive and divisive force in the Church of England. In 1833 he had delivered, in St Mary's, Oxford, the university church, a sermon entitled 'National Apostasy'. Its effects still reverberated throughout the country. High Church Anglicans saw the Church of England as a Catholic one: not in the Roman sense, for they rejected papal claims and many 'popish' doctrines, but in an English one. To them the *Ecclesia Anglicana* had a tradition in theology, liturgy and worship which had descended through the High Churchmen of the seventeenth and eighteenth centuries. In the five years before Keble's sermon the rule of the Whigs had placed that tradition under threat. In 1828 and 1829 they had legislated to remove the political disabilities of Dissenters and Roman Catholics, a serious blow to the Church of England's command of society. Representatives of those denominations could now become MPs and might move to regulate the Church of England, even to disestablish it. In 1833 the Whig government, having passed the Reform Act the previous year, offended the Church again by suppressing ten Anglican bishoprics in Ireland. Keble's words in St Mary's lit a torch of resistance to that trend.

The Oxford Movement was more than a protest against Whig policy. It belonged to the general religious revival, High Church and Low, of the nineteenth century, which struck back at the secularizing tendencies of the previous 150 years and reasserted the primacy of faith in the nation's life. By 1866, the year of

Keble's death, the Movement had taken hold in Oxford and in many parishes beyond it. It had acquired a reputation both for sound learning and for its attention to the needs of the poor. Its emphasis on the sacramental presence in worship had wide appeal. But it had suffered painful divisions and incurred keen hostility. Newman had converted to Rome, and the Movement's insistence on its distance from popery seemed belied by the growing element of ritualism in its church practices, which were assailed as crypto-papist. Keble himself had shunned the harsh party spirit of the controversies. He was a simple country parson, who was now to be buried in a simple country churchyard.

Among the mourners was a young man of 19. His name was Algernon Barrington Simeon. He was the second son of Captain Charles Simeon, himself the second son of a baronet. Charles's landowning family were well established but not especially wealthy. They lived in Hursley and were distantly related to the Heathcotes. Algernon would have known most of the distinguished company present. George Moberly had, until the year before, been his headmaster at Winchester.

In the dusk, awaiting the arrival of the hearse, a stranger addressed Simeon. 'Did you know Mr Keble?' he asked. Simeon replied that he had known him from childhood, and added that he himself had attended Winchester College. The stranger went on to introduce himself. 'My name is Liddon – Dr Liddon – and a devoted friend of Mr Keble.' Learning that Simeon was in residence as an undergraduate at Christ Church, Oxford, he added, 'Be sure to call on me at once and regard me as a good friend.'

Thus Simeon met the man who, as he later wrote, 'became a second father to me', and whose influence on him would have a corresponding importance in the development of St Edward's School. At Oxford, Henry Liddon was the driving force of the second generation of Tractarians (the name often given to the adherents of the Movement, after the tracts they published). As Vice-Principal of nearby Cuddesdon he was the shaping influence on that important training college for High Anglican clergy. In the process he acquired an interest in educational matters, which was developed when he became Vice-Principal of St Edmund Hall, Oxford. Later he was a canon of St Paul's Cathedral. His High Churchmanship was controversial, and led to his early resignation from Cuddesdon in 1859. But it was also highly influential, thanks to his attractive personality and his exceptional skills as a preacher and teacher. Undergraduates warmed to his pious, celibate, cassocked, 'Italian-looking' presence. He had rooms in Christ Church close to Edward Pusey, the acknowledged surviving leader of the original Tractarians, whom he greatly admired.

Christ Church produced a host of High Church clergy, including such distinguished figures as Charles Longley and Walter Hooke. The Oxford Movement attracted a controversial group among them. Yet High Churchmanship was only one side of the college's life. Simeon's own recollection of Christ Church, recorded in old age, recalls different and perhaps more characteristic features:

> At that time Christ Church was not a leading college, and there was a great deal too much card-playing, drinking and rowdiness. There were a lot of young noblemen and rich men. In fact my allowance was not sufficient for a Commoner of Christ Church, and I found it very difficult to keep out of debt. But it was some help to be living in the Old Library instead of the Peckwater [Quadrangle] where all the rowdy men lived. There were wine parties almost every night, and we had to give at least two a term. Then followed cards, and often the play was very high, but I generally managed to evade gambling, and played whist for small points .... Ch.Ch. in those days was cut up into sets, and you were bound to join one unless you lived an unsociable life .... There was a musical and literary set .... There was no boat on the river till the following year .... But no one took much interest in it .... I think I was too lazy to row, though often pressed to do so, and spent my time in mere amusement on the river, or sometimes on the cricket ground. The only thing I did in the athletic line was to win the pole-jump. I should have done much better at a smaller college I believe ....

New statutes in 1858 and 1867 dragged the constitution of the college into the nineteenth century, but a handful of Senior Students (known usually as Fellows in other colleges) survived from the old dispensation. Among them was Thomas Chamberlain, nearly twenty years older than Liddon, who had taken only a third-class degree in 1831 but had become a fixture of the college. When Simeon came up to Christ Church in 1865, Chamberlain had already served as vicar of the Christ Church living of St Thomas the Martyr in West Oxford for twenty-three years.

Two years earlier he had founded St Edward's School.

1

BEGINNINGS

THOMAS CHAMBERLAIN attracted admiration but not affection. 'The Vicar was not a man who made many friends,' wrote Simeon, who remembered his 'indomitable will that did not brook opposition'. Just ten years younger than Pusey and nine years junior to Newman, Chamberlain was at the heart of the origins of the Oxford Movement. He thrilled to Newman's sermons in St Mary's, and in Christ Church lived alongside Pusey and then Liddon. Yet he was close to none of those men.

It was Chamberlain's misfortune to outlive his own fame. His great days of parish work started to fade with his health in 1869. He preached his last sermon in his parish of St Thomas's, Oxford, in 1883, forty-one years after his appointment to the living. By then he had moved out of Christ Church, was being nursed by friends, and, in Simeon's words, had 'completely lost touch with the younger generation'. Yet he had made an early and very substantial contribution to Tractarian history. In an Oxford which stressed the theological and political claims of the Movement, Chamberlain put them into practice at parish level. 'What Newman, Pusey and Keble had been doing for the intellectual classes of society, he determined to adapt for his cure of souls in St Thomas's,' observed T. W. Squires in his book *In West Oxford* in 1928. Chamberlain aspired to create the dignified and ceremonial setting, the 'beauty of holiness', to which that theology pointed. The Tractarians traced their roots to the early Church, whose beliefs and practices they sought to revive. That meant choirs, vestments, candles, religious communities – including some for women – and schools.

As a Senior Student of Christ Church, Chamberlain might have had the pick of the college's many church livings. Yet he first served as a mere curate in Cowley before becoming, in 1842, vicar of the unprepossessing and ill-attended church of St Thomas the Martyr. In the past the college had provided no pastoral care in the parish. It had normally left one of its own resident clergy to take the services. Chamberlain changed all that. He knew the history of his parish, which had been dominated in the Middle Ages by the great Augustinian and Cistercian Abbeys of Osney and Rewley. Perhaps he rejoiced to think that the church had been dedicated to

Archbishop Thomas Becket, whose martyrdom under Henry II had foreshadowed Tractarianism's own struggles against a hostile state.

The church itself now belonged to a very different world from Becket's. Though only a few hundred yards from Christ Church and the bustling shopping streets which served the university, this sprawling suburb was Oxford's main industrial area. 'Almost at the very gates of wealthy Christ Church', remembered Simeon, there 'lay (like Lazarus of old) a parish full of sores – neglected, poor, God-forsaken, the haunt of thieves and harlots.' The canal was at its heart, welcoming goods carried from the Midlands on barges which passed, as they entered Oxford, workshops and small factories as well as the dominating printing and publishing world of the Oxford University Press. The more rural parts of the parish around Osney had been industrialized more recently with the arrival of the railway and the houses for its workers. Here was a challenge for the Church. In 1802 there were only ten communicants in the parish and in 1808 weekday services were ended for lack of support. The church building itself was described in a subscription of 1825 as being 'in such a dilapidated state as to render immediate repair absolutely necessary'. The flooding of the Isis in winter repeatedly forced the abandonment of services. In the appeal of 1825, raised for repairs to the building, the population of the parish was reckoned at 2,149. The church had only 221 seats, of which a mere 56 were free to all comers, the rest being rented by those who could afford them. In 1839 a barge was set up on the canal as a chapel, in the hope of attracting new worshippers. It would sink in 1868.

Those who subscribed to the appeal included the Christ Church High Churchmen Longley and Pusey, as well as Newman. But it was with Chamberlain's appointment in 1842 that real change came. He pulled down the galleries, beautified the Chancel, and added a whole north aisle with fine Tractarian windows (1846). In the face of opposition among the wealthier parishioners he ended the system of pew-rents, which had enabled them to reserve seats for themselves. He introduced a choir, which even had girls in it. By 1854 there were Eucharistic vestments, altar lights, the celebration of communion from the eastward position, and the mixed chalice. 'It has been claimed for St Thomas's,' notes Squires, 'that it was the first parish church to revive daily services since the time of Queen Anne.' Bishop Wilberforce's Visitation Returns of 1854 record Eucharistic celebrations 'never less than twice a week', with the congregation 'increasing and the church generally full and sometimes overflowing'.

These changes were achieved during the first fifteen years of Chamberlain's incumbency. They made him possibly the first Ritualist innovator in the Church of England. They accorded with his range of activities elsewhere. He wrote sixteen books, founded the Plainsong Society, edited *The Ecclesiastic* from 1846 to 1867, and gave advice to publishers of Christian works. It was probably Chamberlain who introduced the idea of retreats into the Anglican Church.

With his encouragement his large parish was split into two and the new churches of St Paul's and St Barnabas's built. The building of St Frideswide's in Osney followed. To replace the barge, Chamberlain had the small chapel of St Nicholas erected in Hythe Bridge Street, one of the streets that link the castle area of the city with the suburb of St Thomas's'. With the aid of his cousin, Marion Hughes, he founded the first women's sisterhood in his parish, another innovation with nationwide consequences. He hounded the brothels out of the district. In the great cholera outbreaks of 1848 and 1854 he worked night and day amongst the sick and dying.

There was resistance to overcome. The police advised Chamberlain to use the main road to his church as he walked many times a day to St Thomas's, to avoid the frequent harassment visited on him. He was subjected to oral abuse and sometimes pelted with rotten fruit and stones. On one occasion the police intervened to prevent his being thrown from Hythe Bridge. He seemed unperturbed by all this. 'A Christian is never alone,' he said. Nor was he, for on his way to daily Evensong he was usually accompanied by a posse of Christ Church undergraduates providing muscular protection. Among them, in 1867, was Algernon Simeon.

Though Chamberlain contributed to debates on the liturgy and related issues, he was not an intellectual. Nor was he a particularly good communicator. 'The church was never crowded to hear him preach,' recalled Simeon. 'His sermons were always doctrinal, generally long, and often very dull.' But he did care for education. There was nothing new, of course, about a connection between the Christian Church and Christian schools. By the early nineteenth century, however, the goals of schooling and piety seemed to have become disconnected. Day grammar schools sometimes taught a formal Divinity course, but only in subordination to the demands of the Classical languages. If pupils wished to attend one of the universities, knowledge of Classical languages was essential. Yet although membership of the Church of England was also required, they did not need to know much about its teachings. But the Evangelical Movement of the later eighteenth century, and the general religious revival among the ruling classes in the early nineteenth, brought new developments in the relationship of education to religion. A commitment to the marriage of 'godliness and good learning' steadily took hold in schools, and from 1828 this was particularly associated with the work of Thomas Arnold at Rugby School. This trend became allied to the reaction of early Victorians against what they saw as the moral laxity of the Regency period. A new clutch of Public Schools, meant primarily to attract the middle classes, was founded from the 1840s, almost all with an Anglican affiliation. Nathaniel Woodard, the promoter of several such institutions, described them as 'a mission to the middle classes'. St Edward's would play a part, albeit a minor one, in this national development.

Behind the expansion of middle-class boarding education lay a swelling in wealth and numbers of the professional, commercial and industrial classes. As the landed elite knew, the victories against Napoleon, as well as Britain's status as a world power, had been the achievements largely of those social groups, which, it was widely recognized, had to be incorporated into the ruling structures of the nation. Revivals in religion and education were means to that end. They were not aimed only at the middle classes: the dangerous lower orders were targets too. But whereas elementary education was regarded as sufficient for the working class, the middle class – carefully graded in contemporary descriptions as 'upper', 'lower' and 'middle' – would need secondary education, which had previously catered mostly for the sons of the landed gentry.

How would education and religion be brought together? The few boarding schools of any size and reputation had always possessed their own chapels, but these were chantries, created to benefit the souls of the founders. The chapels of the two leading ancient boarding schools in the early nineteenth century, Winchester and Eton, had not been founded to educate the boys. Boys in such schools did usually attend services, which with their elaborate choirs and liturgies supplied a medieval choreography that had survived the Reformation. But they received no religious instruction there – the headmasters rarely preached. In the many scholarly disputes that have surrounded the reputation of Thomas Arnold at Rugby, one innovation is sometimes missed. He persuaded the Governors to appoint him as chaplain as well as headmaster. He proceeded – through his sermons, his prayers and the inspiration of his presence in the Chapel – to turn the Chapel into a sort of classroom, the central teaching arena for godliness and morals and a counterpart to the equally roomy main schoolroom where the bulk of the pupils were taught their Latin and Greek. When Fitzjames Stephen, the barrister and literary critic, reviewed *Tom Brown's Schooldays* and described Arnold as a 'narrow, bustling fanatic', his son Matthew replied by writing *Rugby Chapel*, which lauded Thomas's Christian example and the permeating effect of his goodness.

The Arnoldian revolution was far-reaching. Chamberlain would have disapproved of Arnold's churchmanship. Arnold represented a moderate, liberal latitudinarian view of what it was to be a Christian and an Anglican, attitudes the Tractarians found wishy-washy and compromising, fearing they might buckle under pressure from the state. But they did agree with Arnold about the need to educate the growing middle class and to couple sound education with sound religion, which meant, for the Tractarians, the new High Churchmanship.

Chamberlain began the pursuit of what Simeon called his educational 'hobby' in Hythe Bridge Street in 1850, when he founded a school named Osney House School for the Sons of Gentlemen. His curate, the Rev. Thomas Russell, was placed in charge. The school was poorly managed and its setting apparently unsuitable. Chamberlain seems to have done nothing to prevent its demise. The girls' school he founded a few years later, St Anne's, which was housed first in Worcester Street and later in Wellington Square near the centre of Oxford, was for a time more successful, largely, one suspects, because Marion Hughes and the sisterhood looked after it. We know even less of two other foundations by Chamberlain, St Scholastica's, 'for the training of school mistresses', and an Industrial Home 'for children taken from evil surroundings'.

At some unidentifiable point before, or early in, 1863 Chamberlain gave the school in Hythe Bridge Street the name St Edward's, after the tenth-century boy king. The most plausible explanation is that Edward seemed to Chamberlain to embody the Victorian ideal of youthful piety. Or possibly Chamberlain was honouring the school of medieval canon law which had stood on the site of Christ Church and been dedicated to the Anglo-Saxon king. At all events St Edward's was the only one of Chamberlain's schools to endure, and that in a re-founded form. It was in that form, in a building in New Inn Hall Street, closer to the centre of Oxford, that it admitted its first two pupils, William Sayer, aged 14, and Edward Becket, aged 10, in April 1863. By August Chamberlain had attracted ten more boys to the school. He later wrote that he had had to work hard to persuade parents to send their sons. Sayer left in 1867, Becket in 1868. Of Sayer's future we hear nothing. Becket was running in a race in the West Indies in December 1873 when he burst a blood vessel and died. There is a poignancy in his premature death, the fate also of Edward, King and Martyr, who was cruelly slain at the behest of his stepmother at Corfe Castle in Dorset in 978.

2

NEW INN HALL STREET

Frederick Fryer, St Edward's first headmaster, was born in 1838, the son of a Gloucestershire country solicitor. At the age of 16 he was removed from the local grammar school at Coleford and sent as a pupil to Osney House School. The school collapsed the year after Fryer's arrival. It had evidently been leading a precarious existence, for Frederick, now aged 17, was acting as second master when it folded. We do not know why Frederick's father had committed him to the care of a busy 53-year-old parson in Oxford. Perhaps Chamberlain's reputation as a High Churchman was spreading. Or perhaps the father supposed that the school's proximity to the university would enable it to draw on local academic talent or make it easier for his son to move on to a degree course – a hope that may have entered many parents' minds down the years.

After the collapse of the school, young Fryer continued to live in the building in Hythe Bridge Street, which acted as a sort of vicarage even though Chamberlain lived in Christ Church. According to Simeon, the vicar paid for the rest of Frederick's education. He went on to St Edmund Hall, where he took a fourth-class degree in Mathematics in 1860, and then proceeded to a curacy in Stafford. By 1863 he was back in Oxford, as a curate at St Thomas's. It was in this year that Chamberlain made an arrangement with Brasenose College to rent a property, 29 New Inn Hall Street, at £95 per annum to house his next St Edward's. The road, which runs parallel to and west of the Cornmarket, now links George Street to Queen Street. The school moved to the property in April 1863. At Osney House Chamberlain had appointed one of his curates to run the school. He did the same now, and made Fryer headmaster at the age of 25.

Evidence concerning the early years of St Edward's is very skimpy. But there do survive some accounts by old boys of their lives in Number 29, as well as Simeon's own recollections and a few pertinent letters. All were composed well after the events they describe, but on one thing they are unanimous: the school building, which was sometimes grandly called Mackworth Hall, was a disgrace. It was little more than a slum, and in photographs of boys, all taken in the playground against the background of the building, it looks nearly derelict. There were rats everywhere. The drains were defective and the sanitation appalling. Friday night was bath night in front of a fire in the boot-room across the playground. Later the tin baths were placed in the passage 'in a through draft'. The water was not heated in the summer months, and in the winter was often so cold that bathing was suspended for weeks. There was intolerable overcrowding, the more so as the numbers – astonishingly, perhaps – grew. Some of the masters slept in cupboards. An oratory was constructed in an upstairs room – an indication of the school's priorities but no help with the problem of accommodation.

The pupils paid £25 per annum, a low fee in comparison with Marlborough College's charge of £50, a more typical figure for boarding schools. In New Inn Hall Street the age for entry averaged around 10 and was never higher than 12. The school attracted 26 boys from April 1863 to the Christmas term of 1864, and 22 more from Easter 1865 to Easter 1866. In the ten years between its arrival in New Inn Hall Street and its move to Summertown in 1873, 250 boys passed through St Edward's. The majority stayed briefly; 161 left after two years, if not earlier, many of them remaining just a term or two. Of the first 105 pupils, 25 are recorded as going on to other schools – sometimes grammar schools, sometimes rising Public Schools such as Marlborough, Bloxham and Bradfield – and there may have been more. The early registers of boarding schools founded in this era suggest that short stays were normal, and that longer ones became usual only as the schools established themselves over the decades, though the data left by the school registers are too incomplete for us to be sure. Radley, established in 1847, had a large number of short-term pupils to begin with, but by the 1860s the norm was a stay of three or four years. The average length of stay at Rossall, which was founded in 1844, increased over the same period, though long stays became usual only in the 1880s. At Clifton, which started a year before St Edward's and had a much higher entry, 35 out of the first 76 entrants left within two years. At Haileybury, another foundation from the same period, 34 of the first 97 boys lasted no more than two years. Things were different at Winchester, where most of the Commoners admitted in 1863–64 stayed for four or five years, and perhaps at other older Public Schools.

Unanswerable questions arise about the early pupils. Why did families commit their eight to ten-year-olds to a boarding school, and in our case to one just starting up in such insalubrious surroundings? To parents of such young pupils the aura of the nearby university can hardly have been a large consideration. Did boarding education, even at an inexpensive school, confer on parents and boys, if hardly the status of an education at Eton, at least an indication of gentility? And what kind of education did parents expect their sons to receive? Did they think of St Edward's as today we would regard a prep school, as a place for the acquisition of learning that would be developed elsewhere at a later stage? Or did they expect their children, while at the school, to build on learning they had already acquired? And what was taught to older boys, such as Alfred Morris (Roll No. 19), son of G. Morris, who on his arrival aged 15 at Easter 1864 was the oldest boy in a school of twenty? When he left the following year was it because of parental dissatisfaction, or had so brief a stay been planned?

What we can say is that the school sought to attract boys from the families of impoverished clergy and of other relatively impecunious professional men. It has been calculated that in 1832 nearly half the parishes of England carried stipends of less than £200 a year, a figure that is unlikely to have altered much over the subsequent decades. Low as the fee of £25 was, it would have been demanding for many clerical families. The Rev. L.W. Stanton had to pay £50 for the two boys who arrived in the school's first term, both of them bearing the names of Orthodox saints: the 13-year-old Cyprian (Roll No. 4) and his 10-year-old younger brother Cyril (Roll No. 5). Both boys were withdrawn after less than a year and both ended their adult lives in Australia in the 1930s. William Stanton (Roll No. 16), the son of a different Stanton, the Rev. W. H., arrived aged nine at Easter 1864. He stayed for more than three years but moved to Marlborough and subsequently to Cheltenham. At Easter 1865, after William's first year at St Edward's, his brother Edward (Roll No. 40) arrived. He stayed until the summer of 1869, when he too left for Marlborough, after which he went on to Woolwich and a military career. The boys' father had paid seven years' worth of fees. Another early pupil, Edwyn Spooner (Roll No. 36), who went on to be a priest, was at St Edward's for two years, left aged 17, and later became an undergraduate at Hertford College, Oxford.

One of twelve arrivals in the Easter Term of 1868 was Irton Smith (Roll No. 97). He had been born in 1856 and was the younger brother by two years of Richard Smith (Roll No. 59), though the two boys overlapped at the school only in 1868–69.

Irton stayed until Christmas 1871, when he left aged 15 or 16. He was a prefect for two years and played in the school's first organized Cricket XI. But he finished his schooling at Newport Grammar School before going to St John's College, Oxford. Perhaps his parents thought the school not up to a preparation for a university education. Only eight of the 90 boys who had entered the school in previous terms went on to university. Irton Smith had a successful clerical career and died in 1933, but not before recording, in August 1930, his recollections of life in New Inn Hall Street.

St Edward's, Smith wrote, was founded 'for the sons of clergy and others desiring distinctive church teaching'. High Churchmanship was not in itself unusual in schools founded around this time, so by 'distinctive church teaching' he may have meant a more extreme High Churchmanship than that practised, say, at Marlborough or Bradfield. Was a Tractarian reputation the reason for the school's capacity to attract pupils to a building which Smith describes as 'extremely dilapidated and insanitary, patched and almost derelict'? He recalls bath nights, and remembers 'one or two housemaids', together with 'Reece', who was 'a sort of scout', and his wife. But no one was responsible for 'health, clothes etc.'. Of the sanitary situation, Smith writes, 'any actual description would not be believed'. Chamberlain himself, when challenged about the conditions, replied that he had endured worse at Westminster.

Irton gives some insights into three other aspects of the new school: religious observances, teaching, and physical exercise. He believed the earlier school, Osney House, to have been founded as 'a sort of choir school'. Certainly singing, which Chamberlain had always incorporated into his rituals, had a large part in the early religion of St Edward's, whose boys attended Evensong at St Thomas's daily. Irton sang in the church choir for four years with at least three other boys from the school. Additionally the pupils sang daily Prime and Compline in the Oratory at New Inn Hall Street, though Terce, which was sung at noon and at which attendance was voluntary, was a service 'to which very few resorted'.

'Teaching, as now understood, did not exist,' Irton tells us. 'We did much repetition in Latin, accidence in Greek and Latin and French.' His words suggest that the curriculum was modelled on grammar school lines and rose above the elementary, though, Smith adds, 'we gathered no idea as to why Latin and Greek must be learnt or any hint as to the literature'. Here he touches on a topic of contemporary controversy. The Clarendon Commission of

1861, which was investigating the practices of the major Public Schools, raised the question whether the ancient tongues, which claimed to train both mind and character, should continue to dominate the curriculum. Ought 'modern' subjects such as French and Mathematics to be introduced, and if so what should be their status? Irton Smith's description can be placed alongside that offered by an advertisement in the *Church Times* in January 1865:

> ST EDWARD'S SCHOOL, OXFORD – The object of this school is to combine careful religious teaching under a clergyman and graduate of the University, with a first class modern education. Day boys are not received. Terms including Classics, Mathematics and book-keeping, Drawing, French, Music, and the elements of Physical Science, twenty five guineas per annum: washing and the use of books, two guineas extra, there is an excellent playground.
>
> Address, the Rev. The Headmaster or the Rev. T. Chamberlain, Christ Church, Oxford.

We must wonder how many of those subjects, other than the ones Smith mentions, were taught in any extensive way.

Fryer, like his successors, faced problems in recruiting teachers. Smith alleged that he relied on employing undergraduates earning pocket money. It is a practice we find in later years, though it could be difficult to arrange the timetable around the teaching they themselves received in college. One undergraduate whom we know to have taught for Fryer was F. W. Davis, a future clergyman who was reading for his degree at Christ Church, and who tells us colourful tales of the appalling food being carved and served by the Reeces and by a boy servant called 'Dirty Dick'. Davis strove to get permission for the masters, who were served 'ill-shaped lumps of meat', to carve their own portions. He condemns Fryer's insistence that the boys eat fat. On one occasion, when the senior boys refused to attend lessons in protest at the food, they were relegated to the lower tables (which indicates that seating was hierarchical) and denied pudding. The episode hardly matched the great rebellions that had broken out in more famous Public Schools, where large numbers of boys lived together with little supervision. But pupils in New Inn Hall Street did sometimes rub the names of those listed for punishment off the board, and apparently got away with it.

Irton Smith was no admirer of Chamberlain. Davis left in 1867 after two years, but other members of Fryer's staff gave longer service. W. M. Martin, another future clergyman, who was there at the start, stayed for ten years. Smith tells us that C. B. Langdon, who later converted to Catholicism, lasted from 1870 to 1874. In any case, inexperienced teachers are not necessarily bad teachers. As the author Kenneth Grahame (Roll No. 107) would observe, their youth can make their teaching more accessible.

Games had little place at Fryer's St Edward's. In schools of the time teachers were hired to teach in the classroom and had only a few supervisory duties, at meals or bedtime. Otherwise they had no obligation to take an interest in their pupils, though some did. In their spare time boys were free to wander at will. Their freedom was as likely to lead to the enjoyment of plants and animals, and to an interest in natural history, as to pleasure in games. Nonetheless, running and swimming were very common. Sometimes there was a degree of organization, either to ensure safety or to add to the fun of runs by turning them into paperchases or games of Hare and Hounds. Games such as football and cricket make much greater organizational demands: they need teams, rules, venues and equipment. When they were played in the schools of this period it was usually at the behest, and under the auspices, of senior boys. Juniors were not usually encouraged to participate. Occasionally teachers who enjoyed exercise took part, but they were more likely to help with the arrangements than to instruct or coach. Competition on the games field, or 'emulation' as it was called, was sometimes regarded as bad for the character.

Smith writes, of his early time at the school, 'We had no cricket or football. We bathed pretty regularly at Parson's Pleasure, an enclave set aside on the banks of the Cherwell.' There were no organized walks, but 'we were allowed to wander'. In 1869, however, Smith helped to organize, and played for, the first Cricket XI, which used pitches on Shotover Hill and Port Meadow. The players competed in their ordinary clothes. The team was photographed sprawling nonchalantly in front of the dining-room window of the derelict school building. Smith would have been about 13, and the rest of the team look young too, but there is an adolescent spirit in their self-conscious, half-truculent, half-raffish poses. There are no teachers in the picture. Such other games as were played were informal. They took place in the playground at the back of the school building, where there were ropes, ladders and exercise bars, and where stumps could be chalked on the walls. Games of fives may have been played there too. Pits were dug in the yard to catch out the unwary, and sometimes Fryer hid pennies and halfpennies in the gravel and turned out the boys to hunt for them in the dark.

Kenneth Grahame arrived in the summer of 1868 with his elder brother Tom (Roll No. 106), nearly two years before Simeon's appointment as Fryer's successor. He was aged nine, Tom ten. Kenneth left as Senior Prefect aged 16, after staying for the exceptional length of more than six years. His recollections, written in old age, convey impressions similar to those left by Smith. The Grahames were a troubled family. After the early death of Kenneth's mother, the father, who took to drink, left his children to be brought up by their maternal grandmother at Cookham in Berkshire. She was supervised – at a distance, from London – by her son John, their uncle. Only for a brief spell were they reunited with their father. Why did the uncle choose St Edward's? The family had no High Church or clerical connections. Perhaps the cheap fees decided him. Not a rich man, he had to educate three boys, for Tom and Kenneth had a younger brother Roland (Roll No. 201), who would arrive at the school in 1873 aged eight. Tom, who had poor health and is unlikely to have prospered in New Inn Hall Street, left after less than two years. By the age of 16 he was dead. Peter Green, Kenneth's biographer, is critical of Uncle John for not sending Kenneth on to university. But that would have meant his staying on even longer or being moved to another school to be prepared for Matriculation. Though Kenneth thrived at St Edward's, it was not until 1879, five years after he had left, that he settled in his job at the Bank of England. Roland stayed for just eight terms.

In 1869 disaster struck the school. The Rev. J. Home had sent his twin sons, John (Roll no. 130) and James (Roll No. 131), to St Edward's. Aged 16, they were the oldest entrants to date. John drowned himself in the Cherwell in his first term, for reasons unknown. It would have been an awkward moment for any school and was perhaps particularly difficult for a religious foundation, since suicide was a sin as well as a crime. Shortly after this episode Chamberlain dismissed Fryer, though whether his removal was caused by the drowning we cannot tell. His dismissal still rankled with Fryer's sister fifty years later. Fryer moved to the Nathaniel Woodard's school, Hurstpierpoint, after which he held five livings before his death in 1881.

How should we judge Fryer? Algernon Simeon knew him quite well. They had worshipped daily together at St Thomas's. Simeon once took a class on Virgil for him, and on another occasion joined him on an expedition to a local park with the boys. But, Simeon writes, 'he was of the social calibre of a national schoolmaster'. The term 'national school' refers to the elementary schools run for the poor by the National Society for the Education of the Poor in the Principles of the Established Church, which had been founded in 1811. Simeon adds: 'The School was managed much on the lines of a national school, though many of the boys were the sons of poor gentlemen and clergymen'. These were damning comments. But were they coloured by the social prejudice of a Wykehamist gentleman? Whatever Fryer's limitations, at least the numbers had increased. Having begun with two boys he ended with nearly fifty. The school faced many problems on his departure, but an inability to recruit boys was not among them.

3

SIMEON

Algernon Simeon was 23 when Chamberlain appointed him to succeed Fryer in 1870. He saved St Edward's and virtually made it a new foundation. He would direct the school for twenty-two years and be a dominant force in its development even after his retirement in 1892.

There were two sides to Simeon. There was the gentleman Wykehamist, and there was the Tractarian convert who was given, in the words of Irton Smith, to 'lachrymose devotions'. His unpublished autobiography describes his colourful career as a pupil at the Winchester of George Moberly, to which he had followed his brother Philip from Twyford Preparatory School. At Winchester it was boys, not adults, who shaped him. His memoir is a tale of fagging and flogging. His solitary encounters with adults were perfunctory. At home he saw very little of his father, who 'liked to be alone'. At Winchester, he writes, the guidance he received from Moberly at the time of his Confirmation in the College Chapel in 1862 'lasted about a minute'. Pupils saw little of their teachers outside the classroom. Algernon, unruly and high-spirited, challenged and wounded a bully and was nearly expelled. He also got into debt. He developed an expertise in the college slang, an asset gratefully acknowledged in 1866 by the Old Wykehamist Robert Mansfield, who drew on it in his *Reminiscences of a Winchester Junior: with a glossary of words, phrases, and customs, peculiar to Winchester College*. The book described some horrendous schoolboy torments of the kind that were being criticized at the time by reformers of the Public Schools.

'I was always ready for a lark,' Simeon remembered, 'especially if there was a spice of danger in it.' With his elder brother Philip he regularly broke such bounds as were imposed, climbing on to and over roofs. He was flogged by Moberly after raiding the garden of a nearby house and being caught by the owner. In his last two years at the college he simmered down, but his was not a distinguished career, in or out of the classroom. Not a team player, he gave up cricket at the first opportunity and preferred trout fishing and swimming. He was made a prefect, but 'while I prevented others from breaking rules, I must honestly confess that

I broke them freely myself and still maintained a reputation for being a bold and ruthless adventurer.'

In 1864, when he was 17, Simeon was at the centre of a dramatic incident at the school. By now he was a strapping, bear-like youth, sporting flamboyant sideburns. In a tradition of clashes of town and gown he led a snowballing expedition against the 'cads' and 'roughs' of the city streets who blocked his way back into school in Kingsgate Street. Moberly appeared 'in full canonicals addressing the mob ... he ordered us home at once. I can't remember what he said except to tell me to pack my things and leave the school that day.' Boys rallied behind Simeon and claimed that if he were expelled they would leave too. He was reprieved.

Though his family were of High Church persuasion and had John Keble as their parish priest, Algernon was not a pious boy. In that he was typical of public-school boys of his time. The preparation for his Confirmation consisted of lectures on the Prayer Book, which were not noticeably informed by spiritual edification. 'I think I had a good deal of religious feeling but it was hidden away. Winchester was not a good soil for it to grow in ... I took no pleasure in religion.' There is no hint yet of the Tractarian convert or of those 'lachrymose devotions'. He tried in vain for a Fell Exhibition at Christ Church, and illicitly lingered on in Oxford for a while after the examination, living it up with his elder brother Philip who was already in residence. Algernon was admitted to Christ Church as a Commoner.

Simeon adapted easily to university life – but he did not warm to his tutors. Dr Brodie failed to interest him in Latin prose and Mr Dodgson (Lewis Carroll), as well as being 'irritable and fidgety', refused to let him 'use algebra when studying Euclid'. There was hunting and a lot of sport but Algernon could not afford to hunt and, he noted, 'I was too lazy to row.' Pole vaulting was his only muscular achievement. He recalled his friends – one of whom was killed climbing back into college after a rowdy night out – as 'a bad set'. Most were richer than he, Etonians and Harrovians.

Yet one of them changed his life. This was the Harrovian Madgwick Davidson, who in Simeon's second year lived close to him in Peckwater Quad. Davidson would get a double First and be a very successful lawyer, but in his first four terms he was a roisterer. Then, in the Christmas Vacation of 1866, he fell under the spell of a London Tractarian clergyman, whose name Algernon does not tell us but who was almost certainly the Rev. Charles Lowder. Davidson and Simeon arrived back in Christ Church early for the Hilary (Spring) Term of 1867, nine months after Simeon had attended Keble's funeral. The two young men talked well into the night, as students will. Davidson had found God – a God of High Church Tractarian ritualism – and signalled his allegiance by announcing an intention to attend Confession. Simeon bowed to Davidson's strong personality and commanding intellect and embraced his beliefs. The religious feeling that Algernon had 'hidden away' was released. Now he remembered the chance meeting with Liddon at Keble's funeral the previous April and the invitation Liddon had given him. He took it up, and brought Davidson with him.

Simeon's closest relationship with an adult male would be with Liddon, who while he lived would be a rock and counsellor to the younger man. 'I poured out my heart to him, and he returned the fullest affection ... We used often to walk together in the afternoons and he was never weary of listening and advising.' The new converts attended the Cathedral for Evening Prayer even on saints' days, 'which no one did'. Their friendship had the cloying character we encounter in closed male Victorian communities; according to Simeon, 'in fact we were never apart.' Soon they were associated with two or three other converts. There were retreats and prayer meetings, often intense occasions, 'with the result that we became very hysterical and I was obliged to go to a doctor'. The emotional pressures on Algernon, the naughty schoolboy transformed into an ardent Christian, were increased by the death of his father at this time.

Liddon, as the former Vice-Principal of Cuddesdon, was well acquainted with religious hysteria. To Simeon and Davidson he proposed a dose of practical Christianity in a parish away from the hothouse of a college. Thus were Simeon and Davidson introduced to Thomas Chamberlain. They were summoned to Evensong at St Thomas's, not to the nave but to the choir where they wore surplice and cassock, a novel experience. It was not a warm first encounter with the vicar. Algernon suspected that Chamberlain doubted their motives. Yet thereafter the two friends never missed Evensong at St Thomas's. They formed the core of the undergraduate 'minders' who accompanied Chamberlain through the streets from college to church, running the gauntlet of anti-popish abuse and missiles. The burly Simeon, hero of the 'Battle of Kingsgate Street' and used to 'roughs', relished it all. 'I was very happy. In spite of the constant petty persecutions we were bound to face, life was full of constant joy and my spiritual nature expanded quickly.' There was work in the parish among 'unruly boys and with the aid of a policeman'. The group kept all the fasts of the Church and contemplated forming a monastic community. They joined a select society, the Brotherhood of the Holy Trinity. It was run by Dr William Bright, then tutor of University College and later its Master, another figure who was to play a large part in the history of Simeon's St Edward's.

Simeon spent the summer in London dockland, where he went to assist Father Lowder as a sort of lay visitor. He found himself standing in for a sick schoolmaster who ran an establishment which Algernon, a careful categorizer, called 'above the ragged school grade, which meant below the level of a national school'. He took one of the pupils back with him, 'a little boy named Tommy', whom he brought 'to Hursley and afterwards to lodgings in Oxford where Davidson and I patronised him and eventually got him a good place as a footman and I heard of him later as a full-blown butler'.

Simeon left Christ Church with only a Pass degree. What was he to do now? He was a gentleman but, conscious of his financial dependence on his widowed mother, needed a job. He does not seem to have contemplated taking holy orders at this stage. His part-time experiences in schools and his religious commitment made private tutoring or school-teaching a possibility, but he 'had neither the inclination or call to the life of a schoolmaster'. He did try his hand in a small church school in Hampshire, only to find that he disapproved of the way the school was run and that anyway he was not paid enough. During the Christmas holidays he looked after two boys in Winchester and successfully answered an advertisement for a teaching post in Birkenhead. He found it 'a wretched place – rather like Dotheboys Hall', though he threw himself into parish work among the Ritualists of nearby Liverpool. He resigned from the school and became tutor to three sons of a Mr Miller, a jute merchant in Dundee. The family he described as 'very pretentious and very vulgar', but the job did introduce him to another circle of Tractarians, this one centring on Alexander Forbes, Bishop of Brechin, who had been one of Chamberlain's curates and was another confidant of Liddon. Forbes was a key figure in the second stage of the Oxford Movement. Soon he made Simeon a lay reader and gave him permission to preach and hold services in his employer's house. Algernon was nudging or being nudged towards the Church. Yet he remained unrooted. He was expecting to move again, this time to the home of Lord and Lady Kinnaird, also near Dundee, to tutor their son Angus.

It was at this point that he received a letter from Chamberlain inviting him to succeed Fryer at St Edward's. How was he to respond? Scarcely equipped academically or by experience to lead a school, he had no firm foundation in his life except his God. He was not even ordained, though we may assume that by now he intended to be, for Chamberlain would not have placed a layman in charge. Simeon consulted Davidson, who now had his First in Greats. Davidson advised against. However, it was Liddon who persuaded Simeon to accept, with the expectation of serving for about five years. So Algernon's brother Philip, who was also seeking a job, took the post with the Kinnairds, while Algernon returned to Oxford as the second headmaster of St Edward's. Only when he took up the post did he learn of John Home's suicide, the event that preceded Fryer's dismissal. Chamberlain had concealed the incident from him.

4

BEFORE SUMMERTOWN

But for Henry Liddon's persuasion, Algernon Simeon would probably not have accepted the post of Headmaster of St Edward's. Simeon shared Chamberlain's Tractarian faith and ideals, and at New Inn Hall Street he gave expression to them. Yet he had a low opinion of the new school and was aware of Chamberlain's shortcomings as well as of his strengths. The job carried all the disadvantages of running another man's institution.

St Edward's was a private boarding school, one of the hundreds that sprang up in nineteenth-century England: owned and controlled by a single owner or a family, such schools were neither registered nor regulated. They might provide a sound education at many levels, or they might merely be child-minding establishments. Many of them did not last, and it would have been a brave man who bet on the survival of St Edward's, for money was short and Chamberlain was unlikely to increase the supply.

Whatever doubts Simeon may have had before accepting, he brought vigour and energy to the post from the start. In 1871 he rented a building two doors down from the school, part of which was used as a new oratory. There Irton Smith recalls hearing Canons Liddon, King and Bright preach. How many schoolboys can have been witnesses to so much High Church distinction? Liddon was already a national figure, in public estimation second only to Pusey in the leadership of the Oxford Movement. Edward King, whose spirituality and preaching commanded a rising reputation, was teaching at Cuddesdon Theological College, which Simeon attended for three days prior to his ordination as deacon in June 1870. Bright, a leading intellectual of the Movement, was now Regius Professor of Ecclesiastical History. The three men would marshal distinguished fellow Tractarians in support of Simeon's St Edward's.

Simeon made changes to the school's worship, on the advice, as he records, of his clerical friends. Chamberlain's inflexible insistence that the boys make the daily journey to St Thomas's for Evensong was a constraint. But Simeon did not always take the boys there on Sunday mornings, as Chamberlain might have liked. Instead he used the little Chapel of St Nicholas in Hythe Bridge Street, and thus, as he recalled, 'had the opportunity of preaching twice to the boys on Sunday'. Boys were made to attend Matins and Prime in the school oratory. Simeon also encouraged them to attend worship at St Barnabas in Jericho.

By now the school's numbers had risen by about ten to nearly sixty. Perhaps parents from High Church backgrounds were impressed by Simeon's work. But his zest and the personal appeal he exerted were not confined to religion. Simeon, in whom we must never forget the boisterous schoolboy rebel at Winchester, described his methods in New Inn Hall Street as 'much more liberal than Mr Fryer's had been'. He encouraged outdoor exercise and impressed the boys by his own prowess. 'In summer,' writes Irton Smith, 'our daily resort to that attractive Paradise "Parson's Pleasure" was enhanced beyond words [by] the effortless energy of this big swimmer and diver, so fine an exponent of the great Wykehamist tradition, and a hero after our own heart.' Simeon negotiated with the university to make a cricket field available out of university term. On other occasions the White House ground beyond Folly Bridge was used. Football could sometimes be played on land close to Norham Gardens, half a mile to the north of the school. It was all rather piecemeal, but it was better than running the gauntlet of the Wolvercote 'roughs' on Port Meadow, as the boys had done under Fryer.

Simeon's great gift was his ability to relate to boys individually. His was a very different style from the one he had experienced at Winchester and in Moberly's one-minute Confirmation talk. Smith describes Simeon's 'whole-souled enthusiasm ... one remembers his grave and penetrating gaze'. Smith's is a subtle portrait of that emotionally intense man, 'anxious and shy, yet often bursting with sudden laughter at our queer ways ... restless and always tearing at his finger-nails till they were raw'. There were limits to Simeon's 'liberal' methods. On one occasion Smith, enjoying the freedom of a walk in Bagley Wood, found a snake. He took it into church to relieve the boredom of the sermon. Simeon caught him. There followed Simeon's 'tearful reproaches ... not omitting his faithful and dignified application for the first time of a true Public School birching'.

Michael Potter (Roll No. 175), son of the clergyman R. Potter, whose brother John (Roll No. 93) had arrived with Irton Smith two years earlier, came to St Edward's at Easter 1872, aged 14, but left within the year and was moved to the Perse School in Cambridge. Later a distinguished biologist, he left memories of his short stay in New Inn Hall Street. The most colourful of them concerns the boys' habit of stealing potatoes from the small cellar where they were kept and of roasting them in the schoolroom fire. One day at mealtime Simeon boomed, 'All those who have taken potatoes, stand up.' Among the boys who rose to their feet were the brothers Sewell, William (Roll No. 138, aged 11) and Henry (Roll No. 139, aged 10), and Michael himself. 'In Simeon's study a chair had been placed for the beatings, six strokes with a switch. One of the smaller boys gave to argue and the Head holding the shirt tail pursued him round the room. The birch would only last for two operations, hence a small supply would be at hand should potatoes be roasted at the schoolroom fire again.'

Michael Potter also describes midnight feasts. Only senior boys could tell when midnight had arrived, for they alone were allowed to possess watches, an ornament fashionably sported in school photographs of the period. During the day, when the bedrooms were out of bounds, boys smuggled food and drink upstairs. Gooseberry wine was popular, and a bottle of alcoholic wine, concealed in a double-breasted jacket, was missed by the normally sharp-eyed Simeon. Kenneth Grahame also left memories of this period, recorded just before he died in 1932. Self-consciously literary in composition, they are less informative than one might hope; but they do remind us of the freedom enjoyed by the Victorian schoolboy outside the classroom. 'During lawful hours we were free to wander where we liked.' Perhaps one can see why some old boys looked back on the days in New Inn Hall Street with pleasing nostalgia. He also remembers walking in crocodile to St Thomas's alongside the girls from Chamberlain's St Anne's School, 'and it felt like the dawn of high romance'.

On the staff was Arthur Cowie, who had been at Oriel with Algernon's younger brother Geoffrey. He had been one of Chamberlain's 'minders' on the walks to church and had regarded Algernon as their leader, always treating him with deference. In 1872, when Cowie was studying for ordination, Simeon called on him and asked him to help out for a week. He stayed for eight and a half years. His presence brought some prestige, for his father was Dean of Manchester. Simeon had an eye for the great and the good. One day from his window in Christ Church he had spotted the Marquess of Bute walking across the quadrangle. With the Marquess was Miss Felicia Skene. 'Little did I guess what a powerful factor in my life this would prove to be.' It was soon afterwards that Simeon joined the congregation at St Thomas's, to which she belonged. But they had not been introduced when Algernon moved into New Inn Hall Street and found she was his neighbour at Number 34.

Felicia Skene was twenty-five years older than Algernon. On her mother's side she was related to Alexander Forbes, the Tractarian Bishop of Brechin who had taken Simeon up. She was a cosmopolitan figure, well educated and well connected. Brought up with the exiled children of Charles X of France, she knew Sir Walter Scott in childhood and in adulthood lived for a time in Athens, where she became a friend of a future king of Bavaria. In 1850 her family settled in Oxford, where she was soon associated with Pusey and Liddon as well as Sir Henry Acland, the distinguished physician and friend of Ruskin, and Benjamin Jowett, the celebrated Master of Balliol College, Oxford. She organized nurses for the Crimea, saved girls from prostitution, and was one the first Prison Visitors. Prisons and prison reform became her chief interest. A prolific author, she wrote travel books and popular devotional works as well as novels.

One evening in 1870 Algernon took a newly born kitten over to Number 34 as a gift.

> Now if I made an impression upon her, which I have reason to think I did, she absolutely fascinated me. She invited me to come to see her every evening, which I never failed to do. She gradually gave me her whole confidence and told me the secrets of her heart. She became as much part of me as it is possible for a woman to become to a man without being his wife. And that close and deep intimacy lasted till she died thirty years afterwards.

Felicia Skene was the *éminence grise* of Simeon, who referred to her as 'Godmother'. She encouraged him, advised him, comforted him. If Liddon was Simeon's intellectual and spiritual support, Skene was his emotional one, even after his marriage. The two can even be thought of as surrogate parents to the eager, pious, easily wrought young headmaster.

Despite their support, signs of stress soon showed in Simeon. He was overworked and consequently unwell. In 1872 Felicia persuaded him to rest at Kennington, a village on the outskirts of Oxford, where she daily brought him pork pies. It was not the only time she would be at hand for a crisis in his life. At the school there was plenty to worry him. The banisters fell off the staircase and the floor of the dining room collapsed into the cellar below. In the winter of 1871–72 a great chunk of the external wall collapsed in a storm, exposing parts of the interior. Though the school was running at a modest profit, the condition of the building required heavy outlay. Yet Chamberlain would not provide the money. Apparently he had lost faith in Simeon and in the school's prospects under him, and had wearied of the whole enterprise. He did agree to a small rise in the fees, but declined Simeon's request, at the outset of his tenure, for the employment of one or more graduates to teach, an essential step if the academic standards were to rise. Simeon's relations with the vicar were increasingly difficult.

A possible solution to the financial problem was a takeover by the Woodard Society, that thriving sponsor of Tractarian schools. But the Society, not for the last time, saw St Edward's as a hopeless case. Simeon consulted an architect about the building, only to be told that 'it was beyond repair and was actually unsafe'. Brasenose College, which owned the edifice, refused to repair it and announced an intention to demolish it. So the school would have to move. The key figure in what followed was Felicia Skene. 'Godmother was, of course, most energetic,' Simeon would remember. 'We talked over possibilities and she reported them to Mr Chamberlain. The upshot was that Mr Chamberlain invited me to take the School into my own hands and do what I liked.' Simeon agreed. He borrowed £300 from the bank, which he repaid from the fees, to buy 'the furniture and fixtures' from Chamberlain. Now the school had to find a new home.

Yet St Edward's, wherever it was housed, could not hope to survive long under any single owner of limited means. To last and thrive it must become a proprietary school, that is, a joint-stock enterprise with trustees or governors whose money and repute would make St Edward's a true Public School. Thus would it join the list of recent foundations, Rossall, Radley, Marlborough, Bradfield, Bloxham, Clifton and so on, which were satisfying the burgeoning demand for 'godliness and good learning'. That was Simeon's aspiration, but it looked a long way off in New Inn Hall Street. Yet if only the money could be found there were great opportunities. As a historian of Marlborough, A.G. Bradley, wrote in 1893, 'The demand has created the supply. New schools upon a large scale have been founded; old ones have been resuscitated and expanded to meet the times. The public school system has found favour in the minds of the entire well-to-do class of the nation, and the scholastic world has risen to the occasion.'

Public Schools needed to be well situated. Some of this era were set in the countryside, though they had to be near the railways or at any rate main roads. Others were in towns with middle-class and commercial populations. Or there were the schools in small, attractive towns, clear of industrial centres, where former grammar schools became the Public Schools of Uppingham, Repton, Bloxham and Oundle. Or a local baronial hall or country house might be taken over, as at Rossall, Marlborough and Bradfield. Rossall apart, there were few new boarding schools in the North until some ancient grammar schools were converted there too, as at Giggleswick and Sedbergh.

Oxford, though it had been partly industrialized, was not the industrial centre it would become with the motor car. But it had the university, which was the capital of Tractarianism and from which Simeon drew his teachers and backers. Keble College was being built on what was then the north end of the city. We do not know whether Simeon looked for a site within similar reach of the city centre. If so, he was unsuccessful. But he was determined to avoid the cramped conditions of New Inn Hall Street. He wanted space where boys could take exercise within the grounds. Eventually he lighted upon five acres to the north of Oxford, in Summertown, which he called 'a miserable dirty little village'. He persuaded the bank to lend him £7,000 to pay the owner, a wealthy clergyman named Bull, who sold grudgingly after months of negotiation. What Simeon needed next was an architect.

5

THE NEW SITE

WILLIAM WILKINSON, the architect of St Edward's, has found only one modern biographer. Few works on Victorian architecture mention him. Yet North Oxford was one of England's most impressive suburbs and he was the most important figure in its development. Coming from a family of Witney builders, he had no formal training. His breakthrough came in 1860 when he secured the post of consulting architect at St John's College, which soon decided to develop its lands to the north and west of St Giles, largely for housing. It is commonly supposed that the freedom of dons to marry and live out of college, which began in 1877, created a demand for genteel housing in North Oxford. Yet that event was only a catalyst in a process that had begun in the 1850s in response to the growth, mostly related to the running of the university, of the professional and middle classes in Oxford. The St John's lands were ideal for development, not just because they were within easy reach of the city centre but also because, straddling a gravel terrace between the Cherwell and the Thames, they offered a healthier environment than the vaporous settings of the other housing projects that grew up in Oxford, around Folly Bridge, Osney and St Clement's. The prospectuses of St Edward's would recurrently describe the school as 'standing on rising ground out of Oxford'.

The expansion of North Oxford in the 1850s began in Park Town. Though several architects contributed to the growing suburb, Wilkinson's practice seems to have designed the streets and spaces of the post-1860 developments and many of the houses. His most glamorous work was the Randolph Hotel on the corner of Beaumont Street and Magdalen Street, which stood as a striking introduction to the Victorian developments to the north. Much praised at the time, it ranks with Cuthbert Broderick's Grand Hotel in Scarborough or even Gilbert Scott's St Pancras Hotel. There were plenty of architects in Oxford, but Simeon went for the best and stuck with the practice thereafter. Wilkinson retained his interest in the commission until well into the 1880s, long after the main work had been done. After his retirement the practice, now in the hands of his nephew Wilkinson Moore, continued to design buildings for St Edward's.

Wilkinson accepted the commission in 1871. In the previous year he had done work for other schools, building a new laboratory at Eton and an addition to the small parish school in Summertown. St Edward's posed a much greater and very different challenge: the creation of a complete, modern school on a virgin site. He made the most of it. At that stage there were few buildings north of Rickett's Lane (later St Margaret's Road), three-quarters of a mile south of Summertown. The new school, partly built on an old turnip field, would stand in more or less open country. Its position had two advantages. First it was healthy, an asset in an age when infections swept through crowded areas and when threats to the health of schoolboys were often fatal. The second merit was at least partly unplanned. The new site stood north of a range of new religious buildings, to which the expanding suburb would in time connect the school. Wilkinson's buildings belong to a superb ensemble of High Church architecture.

Today, looking across Port Meadow from Wolvercote, one can see the spires and towers of some of its achievements: St Edward's, SS Philip and James, St Barnabas and Keble. The Tractarian parish church of St Philip and St James in the Woodstock Road, designed by George Street, had been constructed in 1860. Six years later, under Pusey's patronage, Thomas Chamberlain's cousin Marion Hughes moved her High Anglican ladies' community of the Most Holy and Undivided Trinity into its new building (now St Antony's College), a few yards south of Rickett's Lane. The building of Keble College began in 1867, and in 1869, in the working-class suburb of Jericho, the church of St Barnabas, designed by Arthur Blomfield, was begun. In 1870 another Tractarian women's community was opened, at 52 Banbury Road (now Wycliffe Hall Theological College). Oxford between the Cherwell and the Thames, with its expanding middle-class and working-class population, was emerging as a zone of Tractarian parish work and worship. In 1883 yet another High Church building, St Margaret's Church, again in Rickett's Lane, was added. It was sponsored by William Bright, one of the patrons of St Edward's. Next year Pusey House was founded in St Giles. Much nearer the school, the Tractarian church of St Michael's Summertown was built in 1908, when it replaced the 75-year-old St John's Chapel. Two years earlier the Evangelicals, rivals of the High Churchmen in the religious revival, had built their first church in the suburb, St Andrew's.

Architectural commentary on Wilkinson's St Edward's has been rare and mostly unenthusiastic. Even Sir John Betjeman's praise of Big School (the present library) may be apocryphal, though it may also have contributed to the decision to make him a governor in 1973. Yet the merits of Wilkinson's design are considerable. First there is a striking use of space. The range of buildings on what is now the north side of the quadrangle was extended in the 1880s to form the Quad, which admirers, exaggerating its size, held to be of the same dimensions as Tom Quad of Christ Church, Simeon's college. Despite the architectural expansion the original construction has always commanded the space in front of it. At the west end of the north range, at right angles to it, stands the stately Headmaster's (later Warden's) House. The whimsical, semicircular 'Beehive' (later demolished), also at right angles, linked the range to the original Big School at its east. Chimneys and turrets (now removed) created an exciting skyline, which was accentuated by triangular gables and punctuated by three bay windows. The later additions to the Warden's House, notably his dining room, would be cleverly concealed from most viewpoints, though the effect of Wilkinson's design was to be spoiled by the addition of an extension to the dining area in 1928. The Chapel, with its distinctive lancets and its more expensive stone, a departure from the usual and cheaper red brick and a contrast with the brick and stone facings of the rest of the school, towers over not only St Edward's but the neighbourhood. The Lodge on the Woodstock Road, built in 1879, stands in counterpoint to the new Big School, across the Quad, which was in use by 1881. Big School has fine window openings and a wonderful central grand staircase which rises through an exciting neo-Gothic vestibule. A drawing survives entitled 'Simeon's Dream', which envisages the extension around the quadrangle of the cloister that abuts the Chapel, an aspiration that would persist, though with diminishing hope, through several decades. Had the dream – was it Simeon's, or was it Wilkinson's? – been enacted, the ensemble would have been at once palatial and monastic. Even incomplete and, in places, spoilt by additions, Wilkinson's creation stands with the Randolph as his finest achievement.

The estimates, bills and letters in the school's archives offer a case study of the planning and execution of a large Victorian commission, the largest of Wilkinson's career. A number of the documents were produced by Simeon's disagreements with Wilkinson's firm. They do not show the Warden as a practical man. But then, the whole venture looks impractical. Here was Simeon, in his mid-twenties, with perhaps £6,000 to his name and with little experience of any kind and none in business, arranging the construction of a huge gathering of expensive buildings for a school which, to say the least, was precariously placed and had uncertain prospects. It was a heroic undertaking in a religious cause, and by any objective or worldly test an imprudent one. In Simeon's own words, 'It was a bold venture of faith. From a purely business point of view the prospects of success were not brilliant.'

St Edward's was also a comparatively late arrival on the educational scene. Most Victorian Public Schools had risen earlier, and on a firmer financial and social footing. They too had pious aims and ideals, but they were also businesses. They cultivated well-to-do local supporters and responded to local conditions. Marlborough, which took over the old hall of the Seymour family, was founded in 1842 by the Rev. Charles Plater, who assembled a group of seven from the gentry, lawyers and clergy of the neighbourhood to provide 'a first class education at a low price for the sons of clergymen'. They acquired shares in return for their investment and were given the right to nominate boys for entrance to the school. Larger investors were made governors. When the time came to raise loans, Marlborough was already prestigious. It found it easy to raise £10,000 in bonds in 1844. A further £15,000 followed in 1846 and 1847.

Rossall in Lancashire started in 1844 under the leadership of Canon St Vincent Beechey. Taking over a failing attempt to found a local school by a hotel proprietor in Fleetwood, he soon created a church school which had the local bishop as its Visitor and mustered the support of many nearby gentry and clergy. Investors were entitled to nominate pupils. A council was formed which raised £5,000 at the outset, and a further £1,500 was gathered before building was begun. Cheltenham, founded in 1841, prospered through rich middle-class support in the region. Shares issued at £20 were worth £120 by 1861. Clifton, near Bristol, had the same kind of social backing and was aptly titled 'The Clifton College Company Limited'. Malvern profited from the wealth generated by the spa and health centre, which brought doctors to the area as well as professional men engaged in the Lea & Perrins Company and other service trades. Richard Lea's guarantee of £1,000 ensured the college's successful launch. One supporter was the Tractarian Frederick Lygon (1830–91), later sixth Earl Beauchamp, a Christ Church man, who was to have an important role in the history of

St Edward's. Alliances of well-connected laity with High Church clergy were behind the creation of Radley in 1847, Bradfield in 1849, and of the Woodard schools. Nathaniel Woodard founded no fewer than eleven schools between 1848 and 1890, among them Lancing (1848), Hurstpierpoint (1849), Ardingly (1858), Denstone (1868) and the girls' school Abbots Bromley (1874). Simeon too had High Church backers, of the most distinguished kind. But they were all clergymen: there were no rich laymen to support his enterprise. Oxford's economy was not rapidly growing, as those of Cheltenham, Bristol and Malvern were. The survival of St Edward's in its early decades in Summertown is a remarkable story. It took twenty years for it to acquire the standing of a Public School. It did so both because of, and in spite of, Simeon's vision for it.

In 1871 Orchard's, the builders of Banbury used by Wilkinson, expected to complete the Main Buildings (the block in the north range that from 1930 would be known as School House) by 1 August 1873. They anticipated a cost of £8,659. How were this sum and the other large ones involved to be raised? Simeon had to borrow £7,000 immediately, to pay for the five acres bought from the local clergyman Bull and to set the wider plans in motion. Later, when the estimates and then the bills came in, he had to scratch around for further loans. Scores of letters were exchanged between Simeon's family and their solicitors with the aim of raising further thousands of pounds. Yet he had little security to offer and nothing to mortgage. He was able to acquire some shares belonging to his mother and sister to provide a modicum of security. But he still had to borrow, then and later, often at the high rate of 5%. The debts are recorded in a scribbled summary in his hand. There was a loan from his uncle Cornwall Simeon, whose trustees were approached for £6,500, and who advanced at least most of that sum in 1873. A Mr Guest lent £15,000 in 1880, the Misses Morrill and Miller £3,000 in 1878, and the Rev. R. Sutton the same sum in the same year. Simeon's old friend Madgwick Davidson had to lend £20,000 to pay off Guest and the two Misses.

Wilkinson and his team did all the practical work for the project, not only drawing up the plans but conducting innumerable negotiations with other craftsmen and tradesmen and local property owners. All that preliminary work, including the consultation of 1871, was done for a mere eight guineas. Orchard's was one of seven firms involved in the planning and execution. At this stage Wilkinson's practice had committed itself to an outlay of £12,400. Simeon had to produce £620 to cover 5% interest on that sum.

Members of Wilkinson's practice travelled to Birmingham to negotiate with Messrs Marris and Norton for the furnishings (which cost £502 10s. 12d) and with Mr Skinner for bedroom furniture (£55 10s.).

The bills mounted. Yet Simeon proposed a further expense. Realizing that the Chapel would not be ready when the school moved, he wanted to build a temporary one. Wilkinson estimated the cost at £661 10s. Simeon dropped the plan, naively unaware that the estimate had wasted time and had also incurred its own cost. The time spent even by an assistant on the project added £10 15s. to the bill. Four guineas were spent on exploring with a Mr Eyles the idea of a new altar table, which would have cost £40, too much even for Simeon. True to his priorities, Simeon had made his proposal for a temporary chapel when the school's boilers and water had yet to be arranged.

Negotiations over them, and their installation, stretched on into 1874. By then Simeon had again decided to increase the expenditure on the school's worship. In 1873 he resolved that the permanent Chapel should be longer. This meant new plans, a new survey, new costs. The building, he was informed, would cost £3,500. A further £70 would be required immediately to pay the 2% interest on that outlay, and another ten guineas for the surveying and plans. Simeon nonetheless went ahead, though by 1875 he was asking Wilkinson to make economies on the Chapel 'by certain omissions and reductions in length, height etc.'. The builders, now Messrs Symes & Co., willingly added a cloister joining the Chapel to the Main Buildings at a cost of £300, of which 2½% (£7 10s.) was to be paid immediately. A heating vault for the Chapel cost £145, and again interest on that advance (£3 12s. 6d) was required at once. The design for the organ case cost a further eight guineas. And so it went on.

From the start Simeon complained about costs. In 1874 he challenged a bill that Wilkinson had submitted three years earlier for the design of the new school. In 1878, having alleged that the roofing over the dormitory was inadequate, he withheld payments for it. Wilkinson's manager Frederick Cornwell pleaded for at least £5,000 to be going on with. Simeon also claimed that the charge of £80 10s. for abandoned plans – abandoned through his own prevarications – was excessive, and protested at the surveyor's account of ten guineas for the work and a further ten for correspondence. He tried to offset the mounting costs against reductions on the varnishing of timbers, on cubicle partitions, and on fittings for classrooms and the bathroom, yet his countless and unsubstantiated complaints were those of a man who understood little of the complexity and costs of building projects. In a reasoned letter of April 1878 Cornwell argued Wilkinson's case, reminding Simeon that the Warden had been 'kept informed' of increases which had arisen from his changes of mind and which were raising the costs of the workforce. There were, Cornwell pointed out, four sets of working drawings for the Chapel alone. 'Mr. Wilkinson has ventured to suggest that as working drawings could not be prepared without involving considerable expense you should quite make up your mind on the subject.' To Simeon's complaint that the interest was too high, Cornwell replied that 5% was a normal rate. He reminded him of costs added by a change of the Warden's mind over drainage arrangements and by his attempt to impose deadlines for the completion of particular stages of the project. He enclosed a copy of the rules of the Institute of Architects and pointed out that Wilkinson had scrupulously observed them.

Simeon's protests were unavailing. Wilkinson's firm went on to provide the next stages of the headmaster's project: the building of Big School (which cost £4,229) and the Lodge, and in due course the New Buildings (later Macnamara's or 'Mac's' House). The consequences of Simeon's almost reckless building programme were to dog him and the school for many years. His strengths did not lie in the realms of finance and bricks and mortar, or in relations with other adults. They lay in his charismatic impact on the young.

6

LAST YEAR IN CENTRAL OXFORD

On 15 July 1872 the school, as was customary, celebrated Eucharist at 8 a.m. in the north aisle of St Thomas's, the site also of its daily attendance for Evensong. There followed a procession to Summertown, where the foundation stone of the new building was laid. The masters and boys were accompanied by the choirs of the Tractarian churches St Barnabas and SS Philip and James. Surplices were worn, a banner and cross were carried, hymns were sung. Chamberlain, who was invited to lay the foundation stone, proved uncooperative and cantankerous. 'He expressed strong disapproval of the enterprise,' wrote Simeon, and 'it was difficult, almost impossible, to deal with him.' What troubled the vicar was the realization that it would no longer be practicable for the boys to attend St Thomas's. Simeon talked him out of boycotting the event, but even when he turned up the Headmaster feared what he might say. In the event Chamberlain 'repented and spoke in the warmest tones of my work and asked God's blessing upon the venture'.

After the ceremony the school returned to New Inn Hall Street for its final year. Simeon's head was full of plans. 'Having laid the foundation stone of the buildings, the next thing to be done was to lay the foundation of the system that should educate and train in the knowledge and fear of God future generations.' Simeon's 'idea of school life was that of Winchester,' and he 'proceeded to arrange the School, as far as possible, on public school lines'. Foremost among his goals was the securing of the kind of patronage commanded by the prominent boarding schools. He called on Liddon's help, 'and if he thought the venture foolish he never said so and encouraged me to trust in God and do my best'. Liddon told him that 'something like a governing body must be found with a Visitor'. It was common to appoint a distinguished outsider, often the local bishop, as Visitor, to keep an impartial eye on a school and, in case of internal dispute, to act as arbitrator, much as a medieval bishop had had powers of visitation over religious houses. Liddon persuaded Simeon not to approach William Gladstone, on the ground that the Prime Minister would be too preoccupied by public affairs. A more obvious choice, Bishop Mackarness of Oxford, was also bypassed. He was viewed with suspicion by some

Tractarians, though in due course he would give invaluable if never unqualified backing to Simeon.

Liddon's choice had been the leading layman among the founders of Keble College and was at this time arguably the leading High Church peer of the realm: Frederick Lygon, Earl Beauchamp, of Madresfield Court, Worcestershire (1830–91). In the event no Visitor was appointed at this stage. Not until 1890 would the post be created, and even then, it seems, only by an informal arrangement, which bestowed the position on the Bishop of Oxford. Nonetheless Lygon, who was already a powerful force at Malvern, became one at St Edward's too, even if he was less ready to invest money here. Educated at Eton, and then brought under Tractarian influence at Christ Church, he had a political career under the Tory leaders Disraeli and Salisbury. He had been a Lord of the Admiralty and would become Privy Councillor and Paymaster of the Forces. When a dormitory in the new buildings was turned into a temporary chapel in 1873 it was called Beauchamp, and so became the only space in the school to be named after a living Tractarian.

With Liddon's help Simeon established a body of supporters he called 'Patrons', whom Beauchamp joined. This was scarcely a formal body, and certainly not a governing one. Liddon, King and Bright were, naturally, Patrons. The others were Sir William Heathcote, Simeon's High Church squire from Hursley; the diplomat, another product of Christ Church, Edward Granville, Lord Eliot, later Earl of St Germans; the Hon. C. L. Wood; Edward Talbot, Warden of Keble and later Bishop of Rochester; and Dean Cowie, the father of Arthur Cowie, Simeon's most loyal and best qualified teacher. Talbot and Cowie seem to have played little part, but the rest were stalwart defenders of the school in the face of public antipathy to Tractarianism and of the hostility of Evangelicalism, at that time the dominant religious force. 'We had few friends and many enemies,' recalled Simeon. 'I remember a noted Senior Student of Christ Church, on being asked what was going on in Summertown, replied that it was a feeble attempt to destroy the glorious Reformation.' At the time of the move to Summertown 'the Bishop [Mackarness] ... gave us no support and we felt that we could not put our trust in princes nor in any child of man'. The most influential figure after Beauchamp, and a decisive one in the school's future, was Wood, who was to become second Viscount Halifax and to supplant Lygon as the leading Anglo-Catholic layman of his day. At Eton he had been educated by the poet William Johnson Cory, who dedicated his risqué book *Ionica* to him. As an undergraduate at Christ Church Wood fell under Pusey's spell. In 1868 he became the leader of the English Church Union, a body dedicated to the promotion of Catholic practices and principles within the Church of England. High Churchmanship had produced an imposing list of Patrons.

Of course, the school still had to be run. Simeon's bank book of the early 1870s reveals his frugality as he struggled to keep the school afloat during the construction of the new buildings. He paid little into his own bank account – only £143 between December 1869 and July 1870. He seems to have had to borrow money from Davidson, his undergraduate friend. In 1870–71 he made a number of small payments to Chamberlain, perhaps towards the costs of fixtures and furnishings. But at least the fees came in, for example £729 1s. during April and May 1871.

What, meanwhile, of the boys in New Inn Hall Street, the property soon to be vacated? One thing we know is that a prefect system had been established. We do not have lists of the prefects, but we do learn something of the Senior Prefects whom Simeon appointed. The first, chosen in 1870, was Arthur Chesshire (Roll No. 60), who had arrived four years earlier and who would follow his father into the priesthood. He had arrived at the school aged 14, together with his 12-year-old brother George (Roll No. 61), who left after two years and would later join the merchant marine. The sixth Senior Prefect, appointed in 1873, was the 16-year-old Herbert Harper (Roll No. 141), who was a star in games.

We also discover that there were sporadic matches against such local schools as Cowley College, Northern House and Norham House, the last of which, recorded the school's *Chronicle*, 'played under a disadvantage in using our rules' in rugby. Other communal activities were a Debating Society, breaking-up or end-of-term suppers, and an annual supper and half-holiday on Simeon's birthday. There were prize-giving ceremonies, and the Rev. R. J. Wilson, a Fellow of Merton College, Oxford and later a teacher at Radley, regularly awarded a prize for Latin prose.

The *Chronicle*, that ever-indispensable companion of the school's historian, made its first appearance in March 1873. Like the games it was a boys' project. The 13-year-old Trant Chambers (Roll No. 164), who later had a successful career as a journalist before joining the Australian Civil Service, had brought printing equipment into the school and proposed to publish a paper from the cellar. He got nowhere until more senior and more practical boys took over the project and used Chambers as a figurehead. In its earlier years the

Chronicle voiced the views not of the school's authorities but of its pupils, even if an element of censorship interposed. One or two masters helped in the background, particularly from 1874 to 1878. Prominent among them was the dynamic Irishman the Rev. Ernest Letts. The *Chronicle* belongs to the proliferation of magazines in the schools of the period, as in society at large. The young were aping their elders.

The breaking-up suppers established a tradition of communal festivity that brought the school together with its Tractarian supporters and helped to bond a male community of boys, masters and backers. Even the youngest boys were made to feel part of a club, alongside seniors and masters who would treat them altogether less amicably at other times. The suppers, as reported in the *Chronicle*, were roisterous affairs, at which adults and boys alike let their hair down. In December 1872 – 'our last Christmas in old St Edward's' – Chamberlain, Bright and Wilson were present. After the loyal toast 'no locusts could have effected a cleaner sweep of everything edible'. Masters were called on to stand up, among them Cowie, who was described as Second Master, and three temporary teachers. They were cheered as 'heartily as legs and lungs were able'. Before Simeon proposed bedtime, 'to procure all possible rest before the next day's dispersion', an old boy, Howard Leeds (Roll No. 137), who had been invited back by popular request, proposed the headmaster's health, as other OSE (Old St Edwardians) would be asked to do in subsequent years. Leeds had entered the School at Easter 1870, Simeon's second term, and left four terms later, having been a prefect. According to the first *Roll* it was he who introduced St Edward's to the game of rugby. Apparently he was another of the boys whom the school was not equipped to prepare for university, for he left for Clifton and went from there to New College, Oxford. He would become a priest and army chaplain.

Earlier on the day of the first breaking-up supper, in the Oratory after communion, a new institution was inaugurated: the Confraternity of St Edward, which had Simeon as its Superior. In the previous week he had handed medals to the first seven members, of whom Howard Leeds was the first. The Confraternity was designed with old boys and leaving boys in mind. In the *Chronicle* 'Condiscipulus' described the service: 'It was touching to see these our loved companions kneeling with us in perhaps our last act of united public worship … we had established a bond of union which so long as life lasts might bond us together in the holy tie of Catholic love, faith and practice.' There were rules for the members. They were to remember the school when they prayed or took communion, and to communicate with and if possible to visit the headmaster on St Edward's Day, 20 June (the feast of the saint's translation from Wareham to Shaftesbury, though Edward, uniquely, has two feast days in the Book of Common Prayer, the other being 16 March, the date of his martyrdom). The Confraternity, and the school to which it belonged, were in Simeon's mind akin to the burgeoning Tractarian communities of priests and colleges and sisterhoods. At St Edward's he sought to bring piety together with comradeship and conviviality. Breaking-up suppers, birthday celebrations, old boys' gatherings, the observance of saints' days and holy days, the enjoyment of holidays or half-holidays – all of these would be stimuli to faith and witnesses of it.

Simeon's aspirations for St Edward's are encapsulated in an injunction he included in a set of school rules five years later. Boys were to be

> Christian gentlemen ... that have sworn to fight manfully against the world, the flesh and the Devil and to live in unity and godly love with one another: and as such, they will bravely resist temptation and help one another by all means in their power so to spend their time here, that when they go forth into the world they may be known as true gentlemen, good citizens and faithful soldiers of their common Lord.

In its corporate as distinct from its theological aims, Simeon's High Church ideal was true to the programme of the Broad Churchman Thomas Arnold. Arnold had tried to implement it through pastoral concern, personal contact between masters and senior boys, and by the creation of a responsible prefect class. His vision spread. Rugby School produced many future headmasters, among them James Prince Lee of King Edward's Birmingham and Charles Vaughan at Harrow.

At New Inn Hall Street each boy had a studio photograph taken in a formal pose and dressed in his best suit. We also have group photographs from the period. The school photograph of 1870 pictures Simeon, two masters, and fifty boys. It has none of the formality of the later school photographs and none of their suggestion of adult supervision. There is no uniformity of dress, or standard pose; no attempt even to get the boys to look at the camera. Some senior boys affect dandyish airs or ape adulthood by sporting watch chains, sports caps or velvet collars. One has a moustache. The younger pupils look bored or indifferent. One master rests his arm nonchalantly on a boy's shoulder in what would now be an unacceptable posture.

As the move to Summertown approached, Simeon worried that not just the building but 'the teaching was very inadequate. That was an unceasing anxiety to me. We were getting an indifferent reputation.' There was worse to contend with. In February and March 1873, the year of the move, four cases of acute pneumonia were followed by outbreaks of diphtheria. Felicia Skene 'was up night after night'. The mother of the 11-year-old James Cooper (Roll No. 125) could not get from Suffolk in time because of snow. 'I stayed with him till he died,' wrote Simeon in recalling the details many years later. 'He asked me by writing on a slate (for he could not speak) to receive his confession', that High Church rite. 'I gave him absolution and he died next day.' Another boy had to 'endure a terrible operation from the effects of which he never fully recovered.' Simeon himself was stricken, and himself almost died. The school was sent home early at Whitsun, and with the boys' departure the first ten years of the school's history, and its time in central Oxford, came to an end.

7

THE NEW SCHOOL

THE threat of illness and the likelihood of death haunted all Victorian institutions. Epidemics were common until the 1960s, though with rare exceptions St Edward's was free of the fatalities that afflicted other Victorian schools. To recover from his diphtheria Simeon withdrew, first to the south coast, where he was taken by his friend Madgwick Davidson, and then to Hursley in Hampshire. On his return he lay, temporarily paralysed, at no. 34, where Felicia nursed him. He determined that his new school should have an infirmary and a permanent sick nurse. Felicia found him one, a Mrs Bursey, who lived in the Banbury Road.

Illness, having prematurely closed the New Inn Hall Street site, held up the opening of the new one. There was a further cause of postponement: delays in the building. Simeon had 30 new pupils lined up, whose arrival had to be delayed. Many of the 53 existing pupils arrived at Summertown on 22 August, to find that parts of the school were without doors or windows. There was 'unspeakable muddle and confusion'. The matron was useless. Simeon lived in the servants' hall for the first term. 'I worked like a navvy from morning till night,' he recalled. He had to shop in Summertown village for bread and cheese to feed the domestic staff. 'One boy fell down a hole left by the workmen. Another ran away, but fortunately did not go far before I found him.' Amid the chaos the Rev. W. E. Belson turned up with two new boys, his sons Louis (Roll No. 230) and William (Roll No. 231), aged 13 and 9 respectively. He almost withdrew them on the spot. But by 5 September 26 of the new pupils had arrived.

The building, for all the teething problems and financial constraints, was an excellent educational setting. It was designed to accommodate 135 boys, a number not reached until 1915. A report in the *Oxford Guardian* admired the building, though it could not resist a waspish glance at the school's Tractarian purpose. 'Liberality and taste have been profusely displayed in its design ... for the architecture is aesthetically correct and we believe it is no secret that the Rev. A. B. Simeon, the headmaster, has devoted no less than the large sum of £16,000 towards raising this nursery for Keble College.' Keble, to which four OSE would go up between 1875 and

1882, flew the flag of the Oxford Movement. Simeon would not rest until there was a permanent chapel, a goal not achieved until 1877. Until then the Beauchamp dormitory had to serve.

On Sunday 24 August 1873 the pupils, presumably both the new boys and those already at the school, journeyed from New Inn Hall Street for the official opening of the Summertown site, where Simeon conducted a blessing. They processed, singing and praying, from the entrance to the kitchens, then to the dining hall, then to the Library and schoolroom. Smaller rooms on the ground floor were still occupied by workmen, but the boys, led by Simeon, ascended the 'handsome stone staircase' (which is still there) and visited and blessed Ken, Combe and Keble dormitories and the chapel in Beauchamp. One boy, 'having gone through a little ritual of late at St Nicholas' (Chamberlain's chapel in Hythe Bridge Street), had asked in a letter to the *Chronicle* for incense to be used. The next edition carried an anonymous rebuke to him. Incense was a tender subject at the time. If the boy's lighthearted allusion to its use in Hythe Bridge Street had got into anti-Tractarian hands there could have been unfavourable publicity.

The school's standing would depend not only on its architectural arrangements but on what went on in the classroom. At St Edward's as elsewhere boys were taught in groups. They parsed sentences of classical texts and repeated passages from them to the master. As a pupil mastered these exercises he moved up, irrespective of age, from one form or teaching set to another, until he reached the Sixth Form. 'Dunces' among the older boys were thus in the same class as the brighter young ones. The classes were usually taught in a large schoolroom, the lowest classes at one end and the most senior, which were usually taught by the headmaster, at the other. Successful boys moved up, within and across the groups, while struggling ones moved down. Until what we know as Big School was built in 1881, the name was given to an area (now part of the Common Room) which stood at the east end of the Main Buildings and jutted out at right angles southwards. It had fixed tiers of benches at each end, the Shells (the most junior boys) being placed nearest the door, the Sixth Form at the far end, and the Second, Third and Fourth Forms in between.

These arrangements soon seemed out of date. Schools were beginning to see the virtue of splitting up classes into different rooms. In line with that trend the Fourth Form soon acquired its own room (today used as the Common Room secretary's office) opposite the then Big School. A Sixth Form room followed, though other classrooms had to await the construction of the new Big School. The six prefects were lucky. The 'Beehive', situated on a corridor to the west of the schoolroom, contained prefects' studies 'arranged like slices of a cake'. The other boys had no living spaces outside the classrooms and corridors.

Simeon struggled to staff his school. Below the Sixth Form the teaching was not intellectually demanding. It was within the reach of the undergraduates reading Classics who, as in the New Inn Hall Street days, worked part-time at the school. St Edward's was not the only school in the university towns to employ undergraduates, but the dependence of Fryer and Simeon on them was considerable. Those hired included Arthur Sealy of Keble (1874–76) and, for a year (1875–76), William Hopton (Roll No. 90), the first OSE teacher, who was priested as soon as he took his degree in 1879. If standards were to rise, and if St Edward's were to emulate the Public Schools, it was essential to find full-time graduate teachers. The more impoverished private schools often had to make do with young clergy who aimed to secure a curacy and climb the ladder to a full incumbency with legal tenure and social status, rather than be consigned to a life as a poorly paid schoolmaster with limited preferment. Most teachers at Marlborough, Clifton, Rossall and Malvern were graduates, many of them of high intellectual calibre. At St Edward's the only full-time graduate until 1874 was Arthur Cowie, who worked first for nothing, then for a pittance. Though Simeon frequently encouraged him with praise, he acknowledged during the chaotic move to Summertown that 'Mr Cowie for all his good qualities could not rise to a difficulty of this kind.' Ernest Letts, a BA of Trinity College Dublin, joined the school in 1874. Alfred Legat of Oriel College, apparently a popular and effective teacher, who left a fine collection of photographs of the school and its occupants, arrived in 1875 and would stay until 1880. William Tenant (1876–79), a graduate of Brasenose, came in 1876 and lasted until 1879.

Letts, being married, was provided with accommodation in Grove House in the nearby lane, Middle Way, where he was allowed to take boarders to supplement his living. He taught Mathematics, a subject that was increasingly thought desirable, but Simeon judged him 'not really equipped' for it. Letts also offered drawing lessons and, more valuably in the headmaster's eyes, music. He was indeed the founder of the musical tradition at St Edward's. He ran the choir, to which Simeon looked, together with the organ and bells, for the acoustical dimension of the school's worship. Letts left in 1878, amid recriminations from Simeon, who had handled another adult relationship badly. The only other graduates he could find were two part-time teachers, both of whom stayed only a year. They were clergymen awaiting clerical preferment. Simeon commended the teaching of one of them, the Rev. Robert Hutchison, who in 1874–75 combined teaching with the curacy of Water Eaton and Horton-cum-Studley. He had a First in Mods, but a Third in Greats, from Exeter College, Oxford, where he had graduated in 1868. The other was the Rev. Cecil Tyrwhitt, a product of Christ Church, who in 1875–76 combined teaching at the school with the curacy of St Barnabas. Photographs of the time do not inspire confidence in his effectiveness in the classroom.

Of the few boys who went on to university, most did so within a few years of leaving St Edward's. A rare exception, William Henly (Roll No. 132), who entered Keble in 1875, is stated by the college's *Roll* to have 'stayed up only a short time and [taken] no degree'. Robert Fisher (Roll No. 133) went to Trinity Hall, Cambridge, but not until four years after leaving St Edward's. Even from the great Public Schools only a minority went to university. Many of those who did so thought of it as a preparation for training for the Anglican priesthood. Others, generally the richer pupils, expected to have a good time, whether or not they took a degree.

Simeon voiced repeated concern about the school's academic standards. With no national examinations in these years by which to judge them, we can turn only to the glimpses offered by the *Chronicle*. The contents of the magazine do not indicate high aspirations among the boys. Occasionally the *Chronicle* did publish translations of Horace's *Odes* by pupils. Prize-givings, which for sixth-formers were judged by visiting examiners, offered inducements to pupils. Kenneth Grahame won the Sixth Form Classics prize and the Latin Prose prize in 1874. The examiner that year was the Rev. T. A. Eaglesim, who 'expressed himself satisfied upon the whole, especially with the Divinity. In their Greek Testament translation he remarked that several of the boys had improved unnecessarily on the authorised version.' Speaking at the same ceremony, Canon Bright 'was glad to observe that candour was a distinct feature in the reports of the examination and that praise, where necessary, was qualified with blame'.

The organization of the boys' work clearly had its shortcomings. In March 1875 David Ingles wrote to Simeon settling a bill of £17 16s. 6d for his nephew Roland (Roll No. 201), younger brother of Kenneth Grahame. Roland had joined the school, aged eight, in 1873. Ingles's letter made two complaints. First, the boys had – again – been sent home early. On 23 February Simeon had prematurely ended the term, invoking 'the severity of the weather, and the consequent prevalence of illness, and the frequent outbreaks of hostility among the population of our large towns'. Secondly Ingles, who believed that Roland was under-placed in the school, had asked earlier that the boy be given coaching by Cowie for an examination to get him into Charterhouse, Cowie's old school. Yet Simeon had done nothing, and it now transpired that Roland had missed the exam. Simeon, who did not take criticism well, responded petulantly. Roland, he said, was in reality generously placed in the school and was 'utterly unfit' for the examination. 'It is clear to me,' responded Ingles, 'that the education of St Edward's is so low that if he is to have a chance of doing well at a public school he must go elsewhere.' The boy was withdrawn at Christmas 1875.

We know something of the daily routine of the boys in the early Summertown years. A bell rung by a manservant, known to the boys as a 'guv'nor', woke them at seven o'clock in the winter and six in the summer. There followed three or four minutes for prayer, when boys remained in their dormitories or, if they preferred, slipped into the Chapel. There was then a gap of half an hour, during which they presumably washed and were allowed to talk in the dormitories. A second bell rang to summon the boys to Big School. There, having exchanged slippers for boots, they were called over by a prefect. Milk was available at the foot of the stairs if parents had ordered it, though some may have been deterred by doubts about its purity. There followed a period of preparation for work in Big School, lasting 25 minutes in winter, an hour in summer. A third bell summoned the pupils upstairs to Beauchamp for 15 minutes of Prime, a traditional daily office of a Catholic monastery. Boys carried their prayer books, hymn books and office books with them, as well as their bibles in which they followed the reading. The Oratory, which was never locked, was the only part of the school buildings that boys could enter voluntarily without Simeon's permission.

Breakfast came at last, consisting of porridge, bread and butter. Most boys added to their breakfasts by depositing jam or potted meat with the servants, provisions that were wheeled in on a 'tram' and collected under supervision by the prefects. The prefects had their own separate teapot, while the rest of the school drew tea from urns at the end of the tables. Some parents paid £2 a term extra for meat, eggs or fish. After breakfast there were fines for boys who had failed to change into boots. It was now time for 'spouts', the last opportunity to prepare for the daily ordeal in front of the master. The brighter or more industrious boys briefed the dullards and lazy boys, a system with obvious scope for both intimidation and ingratiation.

The hours between 9 and 11 were spent parsing and construing before the master. From 11 to 12 the choir practised; for the remaining boys there was scope for other musical activity or for drawing lessons. In the summer boys could play informally or, once a bathing place had been 'dug out' in 1876, swim. There was free time from noon to 12.45, when the bell announced dinner (lunch, to us). Boys who arrived for the meal with their hands dirty or their hair not brushed were punished by the prefects. The 'tram' came out again, carrying baskets of bread, private bottles of sauces and pickles, and jugs of beer (a weaker drink than now) served by the guv'nors, two glasses being provided for the prefects and one for the other boys. It was said that half the school preferred water, but beer may have been safer. After lunch there were two more hours of free time, from 2 p.m. in winter, from 4 p.m. in summer. Boys could go anywhere north of SS Philip and James and west of the Cherwell, though they were not allowed to enter shops and were warned against walking by the river or boating on their own initiative (though they were able to use boats provided by the school, among them skiffs at Godstow). Two more hours of work were fitted into the afternoon. Tea, with more bread and butter, was served at 6.15. Meals could be supplemented from the School Shop, at the west end of the collection of buildings we now know as the North Wall, where sweets and other goods were sold from a hatch at the south end. Eggs purchased there would be brought into tea with the boys' names on them, and boiled. All entrances to the school were closed by 6 p.m., after which boys had to wear slippers, an impediment to unauthorized departures from the building. Evensong, at 7 p.m., included all the psalms appointed for the day. There followed two periods of 'prep', divided by a supper of bread, cheese and beer. The juniors then retired to their dormitories, under the supervision of a prefect who brought with him his supper and candles for his work after the gas lights had been extinguished. The seniors retired at 9.30 p.m. and their lights went out at 9.45 p.m. 'No boys may get out of bed, after that, for unnecessary purposes.'

The daily timetable and the rules of conduct were laid down in an array of regulations of a kind that would have been unfamiliar a few years earlier. The *Chronicle* prints three sets of detailed rules, one covering the Chapel, one the Library and one the choir. There were rules against the possession of gunpowder, acids, poison and – after 1877 when the regulations were tightened – catapults. Buying, selling and borrowing were forbidden, as were climbing, carving on property and throwing stones. The lending of schoolbooks was proscribed, as were entry into the shrubberies and unnecessary conversations with servants. From 1877 boys were obliged to make appearances on the games fields, where those who did not choose to play games were presumably required to watch those who did.

Regulations, repeatedly reissued and refined, were one of the means by which Simeon sought to bring St Edward's into line with Public School practice. Another was dress. School colours, neckties and ribbons were worn as marks of sporting recognition. The regulations enjoined black coats, waistcoats, and the types of hat for formal wear. Juniors had to wear the Eton collar. Yet the frequent promulgation of rules is often a sign that they are not being kept. School photographs of the 1870s show that the dress regulations were mostly ignored. Patterns and colours of dress remained various. A piece in the *Chronicle* of June 1876 on the costume and manners appropriate to youth of 'gentle blood' hints at the boys' tastes for the exotic. It recommended, alongside stovepipe hats and black Eton jackets:

> stick-up collars, white pot hats, red neckties, coats with long flaps, trousers about a yard wide at the ankle, checks so outrageous in pattern and colour as positively to dazzle the beholder .... Those who fall into a swagger in their walk think it gentlemanly to suck a toothpick all day and cultivate an obscurity of slang in their converse.

When rules were enforced, boys were at the mercy of prefects. As at Public Schools, which St Edward's imitated here as elsewhere, prefects caned and imposed lesser punishments and ordered junior boys to do fagging duties for them.

Perhaps the presence of several attractive young maidservants, who figure in staff photographs, helps to explain the rule forbidding boys to speak to servants. Sex was always a hazard for Victorian headmasters. In 1871–72 a scandal had rocked Wellington College when three boys, two of them aged 13 and 14, were found to have had intercourse with a 14-year-old serving maid in the holidays at the home of one of them. The oldest boy had apparently contracted a venereal disease. Edward Benson, the headmaster, who was seeking to purify the school, expelled them. Many older men thought it natural and normal for boys to conduct themselves in this manner, and asked why Benson should have taken up an episode that had occurred outside term time and so beyond his jurisdiction. One of the Governors derisively 'indulged in distasteful reminiscences of his Eton days', and his colleagues called on Benson to take the two younger boys back. He stood his ground, mobilized support from other headmasters, and obliged the Governors to back down. The episode reveals a conflict of values and of generations, setting the sober and orderly middle-class morality which Victorian education increasingly fostered against the licence that had marked the previous era and been indulged in the grand Public Schools. The early years of St Edward's were those of the Clarendon Commission and the Taunton Commission, whose reports on Public Schools, in 1864 and 1868 respectively, led to a huge improvement in the quality of the education and an elevation of moral tone.

By 1877 the Chapel was nearing completion and the school was up and running. Numbers had risen to above a hundred. St Edward's was established as a Tractarian community on the outskirts of the capital of the Oxford Movement, most of whose leading figures supported it. To the Tractarian character of the school we now turn.

8

THE CHAPEL

THE Chapel was consecrated on 5 June 1877. The ceremony occurred at a tense time for men of Simeon's faith. Defection to Rome by Newman and others, some of them friends of Simeon, had given rise to a steady reaction against the Oxford Movement, both in the university and beyond it, which took on a new bitterness around the time of the move to Summertown.

The first phase of the Movement, which lasted until Newman's defection to Rome in 1845, was predominantly theological and political. It had emphasized Catholic doctrine and protested against Whig interference in the established religion. But from the 1850s these concerns were rivalled, and sometimes overtaken, by Ritualism, which visibly affected forms of worship. It strove to revive or introduce ritual and liturgical forms of the kind which Chamberlain, who in that respect was ahead of his time, had pioneered at St Thomas's. Ritualism won its most conspicuous successes in the crowded slums of London's East End and in the northern industrial cities. Its success affronted not only Nonconformists but many Broad and Evangelical Anglicans. The English tradition of 'anti-popery' was provoked by the resemblances between Ritualism and Roman Catholic practices. Might not the Movement lead the nation back to Rome and undo the Reformation? Did it not give encouragement to the proselytizing hopes of the Roman Catholic bishops, an office reintroduced to England, in the face of public protest, in 1850? Tractarians and Ritualists insisted that nothing in their worship was incompatible with the Book of Common Prayer. Yet the ecclesiastical choreography of the buildings, the furnishings, vestments, incense, candles, the 'bells and smells' and the whiff of effeminacy provoked fierce reactions in a world where ideals of 'manliness' and 'Muscular Christianity' were commanding growing assent. So did liturgical genuflections and the secret intimacies of Confession.

Simeon knew that his school would be vulnerable to attack. In the early 1870s Evangelicals, many of them advocates of 'manliness', campaigned to secure legislation against Ritualism, an initiative that culminated in the notorious Public Worship Regulation Act of 1874. Proposed in parliament by Archbishop Tait of Canterbury, it split the bishops. It entitled the laity to mount challenges to the liturgical practices and the furnishings of their parish churches. High Churchmen were not the only Anglicans to oppose the Act, for others also resented its invasion of the Church's jurisdiction. But Anglicans could not deter Disraeli, the Prime Minister, who described the Oxford Movement as 'a mass in masquerade'. Liddon and others took the Act to presage the disestablishment of the Church.

In such precarious circumstances it was important that the Chapel of St Edward's should be dedicated by a bishop of stature. Episcopal dedication bestows automatic recognition on a church. The obvious person was the Bishop of Oxford, John Fielder Mackarness, whose earlier lack of support had been lamented by Simeon and whose backing the school badly needed now. He held the bishopric between the tenures of two more renowned occupants, the glamorous 'Soapy' Sam Wilberforce and the erudite historian William Stubbs. Wilberforce had been viewed with deep suspicion by High Churchmen. Though he had helped to found Cuddesdon, it was he who dismissed Liddon as its vice-principal. He had demoted Chamberlain from the post of rural dean. Simeon and his backers seem to have had doubts about Mackarness too. He was sympathetic to the High Church tradition but troubled by the divisiveness of Tractarianism, indeed of all ecclesiastical partisanship. His instincts were conciliatory. Sincerity always commanded his respect, provided it was charitably voiced. He defended Cuddesdon against its partisan opponents, but did not vindicate its own partisan forms of worship.

Mackarness's readiness to attend the laying of the foundation stone of the Chapel on 25 November 1873 strengthened Simeon's hand. It did not commit the bishop to consecrating the building, but it did expose him to criticism. The *Oxford Guardian* alleged that the 'whole ceremony' had 'simply plagiarised Rome ... and our regret therefore is that our respected bishop should have jeopardised his just influence among us by lending the countenance of his person and office to a mere party display'. The newspaper also complained of 'candles, a processional crucifix, and birettas on the heads of the clergy present'. Choral Eucharist – 'at which', wrote Simeon, 'a large number received that most Sacred Pledge of Christian Union' – was held in the Beauchamp chapel, though by no means all the visitors could fit in. In his sermon the headmaster looked forward to 'the power that this building will exercise on future generations'. Then the congregation moved to the building site, where Mackarness and Wilkinson together laid the stone with the trowel that Chamberlain had used to lay the initial foundation stone of the school in July 1872. The Clerk of Works, Mr Cleland, was on hand with a mallet.

To the singing of 'The Church's One Foundation' the gathering moved down the school corridor to the bedecked dining hall. The bishop and Beauchamp spoke briefly, then Liddon at length. Praising his protégé, Liddon spoke of Simeon's 'emptied pockets'. He commended the Chapel, which, he declared, seemed to say 'here we are, and here we mean to be and here we mean to grow'. Speculatively he traced the origins of the school back to the influence of Keble, the parish priest of the young Simeon. Liddon admitted that it would be difficult to recruit good teachers. Yet he argued that, 'in the present day when money was so losing its value', clergymen would appreciate the existence of an inexpensive school for their sons, 'where they would get their heads, their bodies and their legs well looked after, and – what was of much greater importance – their souls'.

Next spoke a parent, the Rev. Whalley, father of Herbert Whalley (Roll No. 155) who was nearly 16 and a prefect. Bright and King also spoke, in a rather bantering tone. Then the Warden of Keble proposed the toast of the masters. He is unlikely to have delighted the boys by his appeal, on a celebratory occasion, for a 'fundamental knowledge of grammar .... If they would begin and learn grammar now they would not fail to be successful thereafter.' The meal finished with a collection for the Chapel. Beauchamp gave a lead by contributing £100, and Liddon, King and Bright donated £20 each. A total of £300 was raised, even though, reported the *Chronicle*, the paper for subscriptions 'did not by any means find its way to all the tables .... The sum required before the building can be entered upon is £3,000.' The estimated total cost was around £5,000, so there was still much fund-raising to be done. By December 1874 the decision had nonetheless been taken to proceed with the building.

Simeon employed the device, which has become common, of publishing a list of the donations received. Heading the list in the *Chronicle* of 1875 was Simeon's mother with £300, followed by Sir J. B. Simeon Bt, a distant relation who gave an unspecified sum. One and two-guinea offerings were the norm, but £30 came from Mrs Combe, the widow of Thomas Combe, the founder and former manager of Oxford University Press's printing house in Jericho. In cooperation with Chamberlain he had founded the churches of St Paul and St Barnabas, and had been a patron of the Pre-Raphaelites. Mrs Combe's donation, which was not her last, was important not only in itself but because it strengthened the identification of the lay elite of the High Church movement with Simeon's scheme. One of the dormitories was named after her late husband.

By November 1876 the building was completed. On the wet morning of the 25th, the date which 'Commem' has marked ever since, Simeon climbed into a large builder's bucket and was hoisted upwards to 'top out' his new chapel. Prayers were said outside. Later in the day an old boys' rugby match was played and thirty-five workmen were entertained to dinner by Simeon. During the meal 'the choir sang "Down among the Dead Men"', and 'solos by Mr Letts effectively appealed to the sympathies of the audience'. Wilkinson was thanked, as were the builders Messrs Symes & Co., who would work for the school again. The customary fireworks ended the festivities. A boy's account of the occasion, composed a week afterwards, reached the school archives in 1992 thanks to the gift of copies of the only letters home to survive from the early period of the school. They were written in the 1870s to Sir Reginald Ogilvy by his 11-year-old son Frederick (Roll No. 348) and his younger brother Gilbert (Roll No. 410). On 2 December 1876 Fred wrote:

> Last Friday there was a display of fireworks but I am sorry to say that I was again ... not well so I had to look at them out of a window. First of all the boys had squibs, crackers, golden rains ... and thats awfully pretty when they all finished then about a dozen rockets went off but then they burst stars as they generaly do and then came some Roman candles and then some more rockets which burnt out and then came down with beautiful stars and then a lot more things but I don't remember them and last of all came a GOODNIGHT. I do not think there is much more to say I send you my best love and to all at home I am your ever loving son, Fred.

The Chapel was finally in use. 'At last! We are in it, we rejoice in it, we are charmed with it! It is delightful!' sang the *Chronicle* of February 1877. 'Acoustically it is perfect ... the altar is elevated as much as anyone could desire ... the bare shell is paradise to us .... On the outside the statue of our patron saint is a real work of art .... The spire is now a well-known landmark and in the distance looks like a twin with St Barnabas as regards general shape.'

Today the building deserves to command as much admiration as any designed by Wilkinson's contemporaries George Edward Street, John Loughborough Pearson, and even William Butterfield. In a clever and consistent use of a form of Early Pointed or Early English style, Wilkinson raised the windows up to a fairly high level and so enabled light to flood in, in defiance of the darkening bulk of the Main Buildings to the west and the impending mass of Big School, which was planned to the south. The concentration of height, encaustic tiled flooring and apsidal shape created a focus for the sacramental chancel. The canopied woodwork at the west end of the Chancel contributed still more to this effect, though it was later removed. Subsequent additions – the Antechapel, the Memorial Chapel, the fixed pews and the memorial plaques – have done little to detract from the consistency and simplicity of the architecture. The bell tower and spire are especially successful; more so, arguably, than those of Street's SS Philip and James. The statue of St Edward, a fine piece of carving which embodies a Victorian ideal of boyhood, deserved the *Chronicle's* praise. Yet there was a lot still to be done. The Chapel had to be furnished, and it would need stained glass, vestments, vessels and frontals, all essential components of the sensory experience of Anglo-Catholic worship.

There remained, too, the consecration, which Mackarness agreed to do. Yet Liddon, in correspondence with Simeon between February and April 1877, argued against consecration. He had likewise opposed, with others, the consecration of the Chapel of Keble College. The act of consecration would require that the building, and the land adjoining it for burials, be conveyed to the Church, in perpetuity, for the sole purpose of worship. But how could this be guaranteed if, as many wanted, the Church were disestablished and its property handed over to the state? Might not the Chapel be put to secular uses and thus be desecrated? There was, urged Liddon, an alternative, which would leave the future of the Chapel under the school's control. Consecration, which entitles a church to hold public worship, is not required for a place of private worship. The Chapel could be made a proprietary or private building, an arrangement which, by virtue of the Private Chapels Act of 1871, would allow any licensed priest to officiate in it, provided he had the permission of the owner.

For once, Simeon did not follow his mentor's advice. A private chapel, he saw, would itself be open to objection: it would be regarded as a secretive cell of Romanism. Consecration, on the other hand, would give the Chapel lasting ecclesiastical recognition. In any case, whether one liked it or not, the laying of the foundation stone by Mackarness had placed the Chapel, and with it the school, within the diocesan framework of the Church.

Alas, in handing over the Chapel for consecration Simeon made a legal blunder. Strictly speaking, the ownership of the building lay not with him but with the mortgagees, who alone would have been entitled to make the building over to the Church. Though this is a thorny issue of ecclesiastical law, it looks as if the consecration carried out in June of 1877 was, and has remained, invalid. Fortunately the worship itself has been legitimate, thanks to the Private Chapels Act. If to us these questions seem arcane, at that time they were alive. In 1892 they would return to trouble the school during negotiations to establish a Governing Body, when counsel's opinion had to be sought. The opinion counsel gave was that the building had never been properly consecrated.

In his correspondence with the bishop over the consecration, Simeon revealed that in the previous year he had taken a bold initiative which would have had fundamental consequences for St Edward's had it come off. He had offered the school and its chapel to Keble College, presumably on the understanding that it would be, as the *Oxford Guardian* had predicted, a 'nursery' for Keble's undergraduate population. In medieval times there had been joint foundations of schools and colleges. Perhaps Simeon had in mind something like the ancient relationship between his own school, Winchester, and New College. Keble eventually refused. The college itself had existed for just six years, and may have felt insufficiently established to take on an additional institution. Or had it examined the finances of the heavily mortgaged school? Whatever the cause, St Edward's would have to manage on its own.

As the consecration drew near, Mackarness displayed his common sense, firmness, and his capacity to defuse ecclesiastical strife. He did not approve of the singing of a hymn after the sermon, but, recognizing that it was a growing practice, did not forbid it. On 2 June, only three days before the great event, he chided Simeon courteously but firmly:

> You will let me give you a word of caution on the eve of your festival. This is a time of suspicion and distrust: do not give any needless offence, or challenge adverse remarks where your purposes may be served by simpler means. In particular let me mention what I hear from my chaplain of a crucifix on a little credence table. I am persuaded that in the use of such a thing you have no motives but those of Christian reverence and piety. However we have not ourselves only to consider in these matters, but the prejudices and scruples of others. I do not wish to speak with authority but rather to trust to your sense of what is due to others – perhaps I may add a consideration to myself – to be careful not to give occasion for strife or offence. I trust that the sun may shine as brightly on you on Tuesday as it has done today.

Simeon heeded the warning. His cooperation had its rewards, for in the years ahead the bishop, though he occasionally criticized High Anglican practices elsewhere, publicly supported the school and privately confronted some of its critics.

On Septuagesima Sunday – the third Sunday before Lent – of 1877, Simeon preached a sermon that was printed in the *Chronicle*. It is one of the few that he preached to the boys to survive more or less verbatim. He alludes to the contribution made to religion by art, which 'sanctifies the precious things of this world to religious uses'. He makes an impassioned plea for 'Ritualism'. Christ's reason for attacking the Pharisees, he says, was not that they had practised rituals but that their rituals had been empty. It was the 'non-observance of the virtues illustrated by [ritual] which He blamed ... The notion that the more homely public worship is, the more spiritual it becomes, is a mistake into which many people have fallen.' Simeon advocates – in front of boys who were allowed only one bath a week – outward cleanliness as a sure sign of inward purity. Then he refers to 'the present crisis in the Church of England ... at a time when the question of the legality of ritual is being argued before the Supreme Civil Tribunal of the land'. This was an allusion to a notorious case in the village of Clewer in the Oxford diocese, where the much-admired Anglo-Catholic rector, Canon Carter, was being prosecuted by Evangelicals under the Public Worship Regulation Act. Mackarness sought to deal with the matter himself in his usual conciliatory way, but by 1879 his opponents, here as elsewhere insisting on the state's jurisdiction over the Church, had tried to deprive Carter of his living by bringing the case to the Queen's Bench. Carter resigned, to be succeeded at Clewer by Arthur Cowie, Simeon's devoted employee at St Edward's.

The consecration was fixed for 31 May, only to be rearranged for 5 June because the earlier date clashed with the university's election of a Professor of Poetry. In the days before the ceremony Simeon received troubling indications of the antagonism it would provoke. Posters hostile to the Oxford Movement were nailed to the school's gates. Then Simeon was told that the Dean of Chichester, John William Burgon (1813–88), a former vicar of St Mary's in Oxford and a theologian, was spreading a rumour that 'Sunday was not recognized in that school'. A preoccupation with observance of the Sabbath was normally associated with Evangelicals, but Burgon, a 'High Churchman of the old school', shared their conviction and concern. Simeon wrote him a characteristically touchy and intemperate letter. It is a 'cruel mistake', he insists, and 'the matter seems already known to several persons .... Sir, I have devoted my whole life and all I possess on earth to the one object of training souls for God in the persons of the boys committed to my care and it seems incredible that you a fellow Christian can have accused me behind my back of teaching them an habitual breach of the Fourth Commandment.' Burgon's reply was no less forceful: 'You have brought a charge against me which I declare to be false and which I require you to retract or else substantiate.' He asked where Simeon had got his information. Simeon blustered, declining to name his sources.

The correspondence went on for about a month, both parties becoming more and more entrenched. Mackarness summoned Simeon to luncheon. He showed Simeon a letter he had received from Burgon, and questioned him about the school's Sunday observances. Simeon 'told him everything as accurately as I could', and admitted to the truth of only one charge: he did allow the boys to bathe on the Sabbath. 'Thank you,' replied the bishop. 'I know how to answer it now: and if anyone attacks you, refer him to me.' Mackarness, Simeon gratefully recalled, 'stood by me through a good deal of obloquy at this time'.

Despite Simeon's difficulties the consecration was eagerly awaited. On 28 May the 12-year-old Gilbert Ogilvie, in a letter that does not inspire confidence in the school's teaching of the English language, told his father: 'The chaple will be open on the 5th of june and I hope you ... will be coming with granpapa to see it becaus nearly all the boys' fathers are coming to see it.' Eight newspapers were invited to send reporters, among them the *Daily Express*, which provided the fullest account. Tickets were issued for the services and for luncheon in 'a *recherché* marquee'. Bills for the occasion, which came to £170, ranged from a butcher's account for £17 to 4 shillings for eggs, and the same amount for 2 pounds of grapes; 4½ dozen bottles of sherry (£5 8s.), 3 dozen of claret (£3), and 18 gallons of cider (£1 4s.) were also bought.

The bishop preached at length, administered the sacrament, and in the afternoon presided over a Confirmation service. Beauchamp, records the *Chronicle*, spoke on the relationship between Church and State, both past and present. This was a central issue for Tractarians, one with a painful and lasting history. Since the sixteenth century the Church of England had been controlled by the state, with the monarch as Supreme Governor. Should the Church draw power and sustenance from that partnership, or should it end its dependence on worldly power and the vacillations of state policy? The partnership had suited Anglicans when Crown and Parliament had been on Anglicanism's side. But the Whig attacks on the Church in 1828–33, and the political enfranchisement of Dissenters and Catholics, had provoked reassessment of the issue by High Churchmen. Keble and, before his conversion to Rome, Newman came down against disestablishment. Fearing what might happen to faith and society under a state freed from Anglican restraint, they had overridden the minority of Ritualists who argued for the liberation of church from state. But they did not want the Church to be at the state's mercy: they wanted it to recover its political authority. So, now, did Beauchamp. His speech presented the Church as the senior partner of the state, which, he said provocatively, 'had grown up under the fostering care of the Church. The parliaments of England had been an imitation of the synods of the Church.'

Simeon had been better prepared for the financial opportunity provided by the consecration than for the parallel chance offered by the laying of the foundation stone in 1873. He composed and circulated an updated list of donations for the Chapel. Beauchamp gave a further £105; five others gave £50 or £25; and there were more than 40 others who donated £5 or £2. The offertory at the service raised £75 15s. 6d. Yet Simeon was unwittingly guiding the school to the brink of financial disaster.

Though he had social pretensions he had inherited little money of his own and had spent it since 1870. His family lent him money, but he had to pay interest on it at 5%. By 1878 he faced an annual bill of £781 to cover the interest on mortgages of £17,200. Costs were rising. Diphtheria and death had forced an outlay of £150 to improve the drains. Then there was the rent of Grove House to accommodate the newly married Letts. Cowie, the best-paid teacher, never got more than £100 per annum, while Alfred Dowling, an unqualified teacher of Art brought from New Inn Hall Street, was paid a mere £15 a term. Even so, the annual cost of teachers' salaries rose strikingly, from £425 in 1875 to £1,225 in 1878. Fees for boarders in the Main Buildings were £75 a year. If boys boarded out, for instance with Letts, the cost might be £80 or more, but Liddon was right: the education was cheap. By the late 1870s rising numbers had produced an annual profit of a few hundred pounds. But far more was needed.

As in the New Inn Hall Street days, there is a contrast between Simeon's inept approach to financial strategy and his attentive supervision of daily running costs. He ran the school single-handedly, acting, in effect, as his own bursar and secretary. All the ledgers are in his handwriting. He dealt with all the staff and tradesmen as well as the parents. He had a punishing schedule. Hundreds of drafts of his letters survive, and every outlay is recorded, albeit in a disordered manner, in his domestic accounts. In 1874, for example, he enumerated the butcher's and baker's bills monthly, the highest totals being around £640 for the butcher and nearly £300 for the baker. In the same year wages for domestic staff generally came to between £12 and £20 per month, though they rose above £23 in February. £1 15s. 11½d went to the County Rate in August, and £8 13s. 7d to the Poor Rate in December.

For all his problems, Simeon had achieved a great deal against formidable odds. The school was functioning. The Chapel, his heart's desire, was in use and had been blessed by the bishop. Soon, however, he would embark on a course that would plunge the school into bitter division.

9

THE HEADMASTER

Simeon's forte was his relationship with his pupils. He placed a value on their individuality that was exceptional in the Victorian world. Many of them testified to his accessibility, his concern and his kindness. None appear to have recorded criticisms of him. Perhaps his tolerance and understanding were informed by memories of his own wild schooldays.

In getting to know the boys he had an advantage over other headmasters in the small size of the school and the closeness of the buildings to each other. He used special occasions to foster a family atmosphere which contrasts with the harsh or impersonal accounts that survive of schools elsewhere. On his birthday in 1876, when he was presented with the coat of arms that remains in the Warden's study windows, there was 'an hour's extra snooze – a good spread at dinner – a whole holiday'. The evening festivities included a fancy-dress performance by the Lower Fifth, which 'passed off with considerable *éclat*'. There were whole holidays, and jollity, on almost every major saint's day, and particularly on St Edward's Day, a great annual event. Old boys were warmly welcomed to such festivities and to Chapel. Games teams, the choir, a brass band, and in due course an orchestra and a new bathing space encouraged communal feeling. So did joint ventures by masters and boys. Photographs of the 1880s show them together on riverside picnics or portray groups of boys in masters' rooms. Though there were beatings and other punishments at Simeon's St Edward's, there were high spirits too.

How sharp is the contrast with Simeon's relations with adults! In 1877 he annoyed Chamberlain, admittedly a prickly man, by seeking to appoint an undergraduate protégé of the vicar named Stevenson to a job at St Edward's. 'Stevenson was and is living in my house,' wrote Chamberlain, 'and is doing certain work for me upon which he lately entered' and which he had agreed not to give up without nine months' notice and until he had taken his degree. 'Under these circumstances you enter into negotiation with him which results in his sending me a shabby notice to leave in six weeks ... I had expressly told you I did not wish him to go to St Edward's.' Simeon had to retreat.

There was further acrimony the following year, when Letts left to take up a minor canonry in Manchester and claimed that he was owed money. The problem had arisen because Simeon had arranged no written agreement to cover the novel arrangement by which Letts looked after boarders in his home in Grove Street. Letts had a choleric side to him, but hitherto had always behaved to Simeon with courtesy and deference. Simeon had conducted Letts's nuptials, and Letts would be present when Simeon himself married in 1883. In the quarrel on Letts's departure Simeon appealed to their friendship, and yet added petulantly that 'you have tried to misrepresent me for some time past to my colleagues at St Edward's, and then by words and statements which are as ungenerous as they are far from the truth'. The correspondence descended into squabbles about who had said what to whom, a familiar pattern in Simeon's contentions. Financial details were disputed. Did or did not Simeon owe Letts money for flowers the master had bought from a tradesman for the Chapel? When eventually, with a bad grace, Simeon sent him £10 4s. 8d, Letts replied: 'The cheque which I now return belongs to me, of that I have no doubt, but I am too proud to receive it in the way you sent it accompanied with reproaches alike untrue and undeserved.' Simeon had alienated the master who had probably achieved more for the school than any other.

Another clash was with the music teacher, Arthur Morris Edwards, who joined the staff in 1876 and whom Simeon dismissed after Edwards, without consulting him, had accepted an offer to work two afternoons a week at the Cowley Military College. 'My letter of engagement,' Edwards wrote in February 1878, 'expressly stated that "out pupils may be obtained" and I have several times endeavoured to realise the permission, hitherto unsuccessfully.' Again there were disputes about money owed or not owed to a master. Though he backed down over the Cowley appointment after Edwards had grovellingly apologized for the 'misunderstanding', Simeon declined to acknowledge his own share of the blame. The musician left in 1879.

On the other hand Simeon won devotion from servants. Mr Bursey, whose wife was hired as the sick nurse, was technically Simeon's coachman but really his factotum. 'He became the most trusted servant that ever lived and I loved him as a brother.' There were no half-measures in Simeon's attachments, to Davidson or Skene or Bursey. Simeon and Bursey collaborated in 1876 in what became known as 'The Battle of Wiblin's Wall', when the belligerence of Simeon's schooldays resurfaced. Workmen helping to build the Chapel had created a gate which gave access to South Parade, the road that runs immediately to the north of the school. Wiblin, a pork butcher, objected that the road was a private one. He filled in the entrance and barricaded it. Led by Bursey, the boys twice tore down the barricades. In response Wiblin dug a ditch across the entrance, only for Bursey and the boys to fill it in with stones that Wiblin had acquired for building elsewhere. The issue nearly came to court, but by 1878 Wiblin had capitulated. Some years later, at a time of particular financial hardship for Simeon, Bursey offered him £80, his life savings. 'I need not say that I did not accept this little present but I never forgot it,' Simeon wrote. After Bursey's death in 1898 an obituary in the *Chronicle* in 1898 ran to three columns. Other servants devoted to Simeon were the carpenter Walter Young, who was appointed in 1883, and Arthur Jeffrey, who was coach-boy, then steward, and by 1890 butler. The son of the cook-housekeeper, Arthur belonged to one of a number of families that have served the school over successive generations.

In assessing Simeon's bursts of irascibility we must always remember the stress of his work. 'The weight of the responsibility that lay upon my shoulders,' his memoir would recall, 'was almost intolerable. I seldom went out in three days and worked hard up to midnight.' This was the background to his approach to Keble College in 1876. Among his anxieties were his own limitations in the classroom. A Victorian headmaster was expected to teach advanced work in the Sixth Form. Simeon 'had to endure the misery of indifferent reports of the VI Form work' and to hear complaints of a 'want of proper organisation'. He tried to pass on much of his teaching to others, but was aware how poor were their own qualifications.

His attempted solution was to be disastrous. In 1877 he decided to appoint a headmaster, who would supervise the academic work while Simeon himself became Warden, in charge of the community as a whole. In seeking a nominee he turned, as usual, to Christ Church. He first thought of Francis Paget (1851–1911), a young Senior Student at the college who had a double First and a brilliant academic reputation. But Paget's father was opposed. So was the college, and so, 'more vehemently', was the great Pusey. Simeon's handling of the matter was typically maladroit. 'I had a long and rather violent interview with Pusey, who declared that a second-rate man was quite good enough for any school. I left him unconvinced.' Pusey never joined the other Oxford Tractarians in giving wholehearted support to the St Edward's project. Paget would become Dean of Christ Church and Bishop of Oxford. 'His prospects,' Simeon later acknowledged, 'would have been injured by leaving Christ Church more than either of us knew then.'

In Paget's stead Simeon found another Christ Church don, the Rev. Herbert Arthur Dalton. He was as well qualified as Paget, and might likewise have made an academic career for himself, with the likelihood of ecclesiastical preferment in due course. He was only 24, a serious and shy young man, who brought his father to the interview. 'I remember,' wrote Simeon, 'how the dear old man said "Let us pray before we talk" and formed our prayer for a wise judgement.' Again the Christ Church authorities, wanting better for their accomplished products, were opposed to the appointment. Yet Dalton chose to exchange so promising a career for a headmastership which was no great catch for him. After his six unhappy years at the school he went on to teach at Winchester, became Headmaster of Felsted in Essex, and ended up as Headmaster of the Harrison School, Barbados. He died in 1928. Did he regret ever having met Simeon?

Dalton became headmaster, and Simeon Warden, on the day in 1877 on which the Chapel was consecrated. The title 'Warden', which would survive the partnership with Dalton, was taken from Simeon's own school, Winchester, the model for much that he did at St Edward's. Simeon followed Winchester in replacing the juniors' desks with the desk-and-storage units which were called 'toys' at his own school and which at St Edward's later became known as 'horse-boxes'. But what would the role of a Warden be? At Winchester the Warden headed a body of Fellows, originally the corps of priests praying for the soul of William of Wykeham and latterly living off the substantial endowments of the college while the headmaster and his usher got on with the teaching of boys. St Edward's had no body of Fellows to head. From the start Simeon's new position was ill-defined. His supposition that he could separate himself from the teaching while ruling over the school was not thought out. Dalton's role was ill-defined too. It was unrealistic to expect him to run the teaching unless he controlled the teaching staff and had at least some authority over school discipline. Clear lines of demarcation should have preceded the appointment. Simeon's characteristic failure to supply them was a recipe for the bitterness that followed.

Dalton went vigorously to work. In December 1877 he reorganized the teaching, creating separate forms for Classics and Mathematics in the Upper Sixth, though the purpose of the initiative is not recorded. In the following June the *Chronicle*, perhaps at his prompting, declared that 'the tone and prosperity of a school depends primarily upon its intellectual level'. He introduced weekly grammar papers and a strict marking system, which he spelled out in the *Chronicle*. He also established three annual scholarships of £30 for boys under 14.

From the outset Dalton failed to hide his low opinion of the Common Room, whose calibre he strove to improve. Of his nineteen appointments between 1877 and 1883, six, including two assistant musicians, were undergraduates, though one of their number, the Art master George Churcher, stayed on after his degree and lasted for nine years, a record at the time. But Dalton did appoint a number of graduates. One of them was his brother Arthur, a product of Clare College, Cambridge, who left after two years to run an East End parish, whence he sent several articles to the *Chronicle* about life among the poor. Another was the Warden's younger brother Hugh, who had a Third in History from Keble. He taught for two years before leaving to take holy orders. Later he became a solicitor and his brother's main legal adviser. Sydney Herington, a graduate of Balliol, stayed for just a year, as did Herbert Ottley, another product of Keble; both men had Thirds in Mods and Greats. Also from Keble, where he had been a contemporary of Hugh Simeon, was James Tibbs, who had a Second in Maths and who stayed two years.

Most of Dalton's other graduate appointments lasted longer. Lengthy service was not common among schoolmasters at this time, when many taught while awaiting work in a parish. Dalton's appointments included the Rev. Edward Shuttleworth, a graduate of St Mary Hall, Oxford, who taught from 1879 to 1883 before going on to parish work; Dr Frederick Iliffe from St John's College, Oxford, a well-qualified organist and music master who taught from 1879 to 1884; the longer-serving Classics teacher, also an accomplished singer, Frederick Jellicoe (brother of the famous Admiral) from New College, Oxford, who was at the school from 1881 to 1890, when he too moved on to a parish; and James Watkins, another product of New College, a career schoolmaster who stayed for six years from 1879 and would later be an Inspector of Schools. The most important appointment was the Christ Church man Wilfrid Cowell, a central figure in the history of St Edward's, who arrived in 1880 and stayed for fifty-seven years.

The *Chronicle* gives the impression of a zestful teaching body throwing itself into a variety of activities, especially musical ones.

Iliffe was a breath of fresh air, organizing concerts and a full programme of varied anthems in Chapel. In the concerts 'all that Mr Jellicoe did was done well'. In December 1881 he sang two solo songs, three duets and two trios. Shuttleworth was scarcely less musical. At an evening arranged by Iliffe 'the Musical Society, owing to Mr Shuttleworth's untiring energy and perseverance, showed to far better advantage' than before. Five boys took part, acting the duel scene from Sheridan's *The Rivals* or playing music. There were musical offerings from Aubyn Trevor-Battye (Roll No. 158), an OSE who had come back to help out at the school, and Robert Tamplin (Roll No. 359), who was soon to gain entry to Keble as the school's first Organ Scholar. Masters involved themselves in games too. Jellicoe played with the boys in the First XI, where his 'bowling was invaluable'. Watkins gave assistance in the rowing and helped revive the Debating Society, in which Dalton also took part. The *Chronicle* recorded fond farewells to Watkins when he announced his departure in 1881, but in the event he stayed for four more years.

But could Dalton's staff teach? Memories of the schoolwork of that period were invaluably recorded in 1932 by Harold Peake (Roll No. 385), who had arrived aged nine at the same time as Dalton and left as a prefect seven years later, after the headmaster's own departure. 'Working conditions,' Peake remembered,

> were not good. The Big School housed all three forms during work hours; it was the only day home for the smaller boys, who had to sit there in cold and wet weather, unless they loafed aimlessly in the prison-like corridor. The room was heated down both sides by hot water pipes, and on cold days we struggled to obtain the places nearest these to warm our hands upon them. The mud, scraped off from our boots upon the legs of the desks, became dust, ascending in clouds around us, so that there is little wonder that our hands were covered with chilblains and our noses streaming from chronic catarrhs. The room was presumably swept at intervals, but was only scrubbed in the holidays and its condition was one which would not today be tolerated for a moment in the most backward of Elementary Schools.

As for the teachers, 'their methods were perhaps old-fashioned but some of them were good scholars: they held the reins of discipline with a light hand and governed by love rather than by fear. They were a kindly lot, perhaps a little behind the times, and in some cases rather eccentric – a few were undoubtedly incompetent.' He praises Cowell's lectures on the Athenian constitution, though 'they were based primarily upon notes taken by him at College lectures'. He recalls Shuttleworth's teaching as acceptable, and regrets the departure of Letts, who was succeeded by 'a kindly but none-too-efficient master, from whom I learnt nothing'. What irked Peake was not so much the quality of the teachers as the methods Dalton imposed on them. 'Though naturally inclined to intellectual studies, and with an insatiable thirst for knowledge, I found no encouragement for either in the regime that was gradually adopted during my first years at school.' Peake was not impressed by Dalton's 'young men fresh from the university, in some cases very good scholars, but all lacking in experience'. The 'new method of ensuring accurate grammatical knowledge' which Dalton introduced is assailed in Peake's complaint about 'schools ... selling themselves slavishly to the ideals of mechanical efficiency, thus sterilising the initiative of a generation of educated Englishmen. The whole lesson was spent on grammatical minutiae so that we had no opportunity of appreciating the beauty of the language or the subtlety of the thought .... As I rose in the school I was subjected more severely to this system of gerund grinding.' Peake 'was naturally very bored with this emasculated and eviscerated treatment of the Classics, on which we spent never less than twenty hours a week'. He remembers 'seven weary years .... French was taught so badly as to be worse than useless .... Our text books were dull and badly written .... Geography was not taught above the Second Form, and I had only one term of it. Considering the way in which it was put before one in those days, this was perhaps as well.' In sum, 'however well we did our work we were unprofitable servants'.

Peake was a clever boy whose interests lay in natural history, in which he would gain professional eminence, and in geology, an enthusiasm he pursued on visits to the claypits south of the cricket field. He made hosts of other expeditions to catch animals and study their habitats. He spent afternoons in the University Museum, where John Westwood, Hope Professor of Biology in the university, offered him guidance. The school's Field Club was largely Peake's creation. He was greatly encouraged in these pursuits by Aubyn Trevor-Battye, but not by the teaching staff.

Peake's comments on the teaching of Classics, a subject he never came to love, touch on a subject of Victorian debate. From Arnold onwards there were those who wanted a new approach to the teaching of the subject, and who would have taken Peake's point about 'gerund grinding'. They wanted to introduce boys to the literary merits of ancient authors and to the contexts in which they wrote. Dalton, whose command of the linguistic side of Classical studies was impressive, did not subscribe to the new approach. Many teachers took a suspicious view of the literary as distinct from the linguistic properties of classical texts, written as they were by pagan authors whose doubtful morals were no models for English schoolboys. In any case the supremacy of Classics was coming under question. Ought not more attention to be given to 'modern subjects' such as Mathematics, Natural Sciences and Geography? Schools were divided on the amount of time they should be given and the status they should be accorded in form-placings and prizes. Geography, if Peake is right, had not got far at St Edward's.

How successful was Dalton in addressing the school's academic standards? If we measure his efforts by the number of pupils proceeding from St Edward's to university the figures are impressive. His six years at St Edward's began in 1877. It seems reasonable to assume that it would have taken about three years for his influence to bear fruit. Between 1880 and 1883, 24 boys proceeded from the school to university, a ratio of the annual pupil population comparable, for example, to that achieved at the established Public Schools Haileybury (27%) and Rossall (20%). Admittedly they all went up as Commoners rather than as award-holders, with the exception of Robert Tamplin, the Keble Organ Scholar (though another of the 24, Arthur Slessor (Roll No. 294) was given a scholarship during his time at Christ Church). Before Dalton's arrival, only four boys had ever gone directly from St Edward's to university. A further 12 were given places there, but only after leaving St Edward's – usually in their early teens – for another school. The transformation wrought under Dalton was long-lasting. In the three years after his headmastership, 1883–86, a further 16 boys proceeded directly to university, and the results remained creditable until the Great War.

One of Dalton's innovations was to expose the school's academic performance to external measurement. In 1882 the Sixth Form was entered for the first time for the Senior Certificate of the Oxford and Cambridge Schools Examination Board, which had been founded ten years earlier. Only two of the twelve boys entered by St Edward's achieved the overall certificate gained by passing Latin, Greek, History, Mathematics and Scripture Knowledge. Next year the school entered 13 candidates, of whom three achieved the certificate. In August 1883 Simeon received the report of Messrs Gross and Lockhart, the Secretaries to the Board. The Board had examined a total of 641 candidates in Latin, of whom 431 passed, whereas at St Edward's only five of the twelve candidates passed. In Greek the Board passed 416 out of 619 candidates, but just two from St Edward's, though one of them, Peake, who so disliked the classics, gained a distinction. In Elementary Maths, where the national figures were 566 out of 693, ten passed, a vindication, perhaps, of Dalton's decision to create two sets in Maths. But in Additional Maths only three passed. At least the school, as befitted the purpose of its foundation, did better in Scripture Knowledge, though even here the eight successes, two-thirds of the candidates entered, were below the national average of about three-quarters. In History, which was taught by Cowell who had read the subject at Christ Church, the picture was reversed. Nine (three-quarters) passed, compared to a national average of about two-thirds. 'It is earnestly to be hoped,' read the report, 'that future candidates will not be satisfied with' the number of certificates gained. An improvement followed, again perhaps a legacy of the influence of Dalton, who left at Christmas 1883. His resignation followed clashes of principle and policy between Warden and headmaster that had brought the running of the school close to breakdown.

10

THE PARTING

Its examination results aside, the school appeared to be in good shape in 1881. There were 109 pupils in the Christmas term, and the numbers were stable. The east and west sides of 'The Meads' were being built on, and 'The Meads' itself was being laid out as the Quad. 'Gradually but surely,' proclaimed the *Chronicle*, 'the whole plan of St Edward's is advancing towards completion.' Big School, though not yet formally opened, had been in use since February 1881, when the celebration of the Warden's birthday was held there. He was presented with a brass coal scuttle and fire irons, and the Senior Prefect, Henry Gill (Roll No. 327), spoke in his praise. Simeon in reply declared that 'they now had a chapel, a school, a library that were worthy of a great public school'. The gathering 'dispersed in happy anticipation of enjoying the usual holiday'. In Dalton's view there were too many holidays and half-holidays.

The schoolroom which occupied the upstairs space of Big School measured 86 feet by 28 feet. Beneath it were housed the Common Room, a classroom, and the Library, whose rules were based on those of the Moberly Library at Winchester. *The Guardian*, a leading Tractarian periodical, fully and fulsomely reported the opening of the building on 9 June 1881. It was a grand occasion, well attended by High Church worthies and supporters. Simeon's speech expounded the priorities of a school founded 'on distinctly religious lines', even if 'the undertaking had been much misunderstood .... There was also a very strong feeling of attachment to the school amongst the old pupils .... With very few exceptions he was able to say that he never lost sight of his pupils.' He then made a bold if elliptically worded claim: that 'the whole history of the school was an apology for the want of a success it was on the point of winning in a remarkable way'. 'At first,' he explained, 'the absence of the materials to work upon and then of masters to make the best of the materials they had, kept them down very much. But now both difficulties have been surmounted.'

The speech mentioned Dalton's arrival, but naturally did not reveal that he and Simeon were already at odds. The clash had a profound and lasting impact on Simeon, who seems never to have recovered his earlier drive and commitment. On Dalton's part there is already a hint of unease, alongside a pledge of dedication, in a letter he wrote to Simeon at the outset of his tenure, in 1877:

> I am not entering upon my new work with any idea of making it a temporary occupation ... but definitely with the intention and hope of remaining in it for a long time ... and so, if any difficulties, now unforeseen, should present themselves, I quite wish rather to overcome them than to flee from them. But I hope and believe there is no need to anticipate such unpleasant things.

He might have been still more uneasy if he had known of the experience of Letts, who on his own departure told Simeon that he felt let down 'after my long service and hard work for you, and the failure of so many of your first inducements for me to come'. Letts had been promised, as Dalton now was, a house where he could take on extra boys, but it had all ended on a sour note.

On 10 September 1877 Warden and headmaster signed a written agreement, which gave detailed attention to financial matters but failed to define the roles of the two men. Dalton was to be paid £400 per annum, plus a £2 capitation fee for every boy received after the first hundred. Simeon committed himself to the construction, across the Quad and facing Simeon's lodgings, of a Headmaster's House, named New Buildings, to be provided rent-free and be big enough to house boys. Until it was built Dalton would live in the Lodge. The Warden was to spend £2,000 on the house, a sum he would somehow have to find, but if the sum should exceed £2,000 Dalton would pay interest on the necessary loan at 5%. Simeon would be responsible for the upkeep of the exterior; Dalton of the interior. Dalton was free to take boarders and charge them for lodging and tuition, on condition that he pay £20 to the school for each of them, though the figure was to be lower until the number of pupils reached twelve.

On 30 December 1880 Dalton married Simeon's sister Mabel. It was after this that hostilities emerged. The Warden seemed taken aback by the match. In the following March he wrote to his new brother-in-law that 'our relations have been unavoidably but seriously altered by your marriage – a condition which I did not anticipate'. His letter was one of a huge series between the two men, the largest collection of correspondence in the school's Victorian records. Sometimes letters crossed the Quad between the Daltons' lodgings in the New Buildings and the Warden's House several times a day. One of Dalton's letters runs to 27 pages.

Simeon's missives of 1881 repeatedly adverted to the marriage. He asked Dalton not 'to discuss me unfavourably with Mabel, without first giving me a full opportunity of explanation'. In turn, he promises not to discuss the quarrel with her. 'Your high principles and keen sense of duty will I am sure never be in any way unduly influenced by your ... tender love to her.'

Dalton had come to St Edward's, and given up his prestigious post at Christ Church, expecting not only to hold the title of headmaster but to exercise the functions. He had supposed, he told Simeon, 'that at least in the course of a few years I should occupy a position, not of course in any way to your exclusion, but as your colleague and coadjutor'. Instead, 'From the first to the last I am kept in the background ... and in dealings of the school with the outside world I am no more than any of the Assistant Masters.' Parents, teachers and pupils indeed saw him merely as one of the teachering staff, so circumscribed was his freedom of action. The issue of days of holiday produced sharp exchanges. In 1878 Dalton had managed to get saints' days reduced from whole to half-holidays. But sometimes the Warden, in Dalton's eyes breaching an agreement with him, would unilaterally announce an extra holiday or half-holiday or agree to a prefects' request for one. Simeon always opposed concessions to teaching at the expense of religious observances. (Dalton's stance points to the future. By the 1960s just one lesson was given up for services on Ascension Day and Ash Wednesday, and other holy days were marked, if at all, only by entries in the termly *Calendar*.) Dalton also contended against other intrusions on the teaching timetable. 'Cricket matches or theatricals,' he complained, 'seriously interfere with the work.'

His disappointment was profound and heartfelt. 'I gave up much and have in this matter lost everything. With a house and income which make it impossible for me to exercise any hospitality; cut off, by pressure of work, from any close intercourse with my former friends, I am yet without any means afforded by my position of forming any connection for myself, or extending my circle of acquaintance, which has been narrowed where I expected it to be widened.' Particular grievances were Simeon's refusal to let him meet parents or correspond with them about the boys' progress, a right Dalton judged necessary to the raising of standards, and the Warden's own practice of discussing the pupils' work with their form masters behind Dalton's back. Dalton was not mollified by Simeon's assurance that in his own dealings with parents he always praised the headmaster's abilities and attributed academic successes to him. The Warden's teaching itself is given a glancing blow: 'I sometimes feel that you might fairly consent to be more guided by my wishes in the carrying out of this work.' Then too there is the question of corporal punishment for failings of work. Who administers it, the Warden or the headmaster? Boys and masters are not sure.

Simeon, himself aggrieved, wrote notes in the margins of Dalton's letters. 'There cannot be two responsible heads.' 'I bear the whole burden of the undertaking and ... I must suffer far more heavily than anyone else in case of failure.' The Warden, who could mix oil with the vinegar, did try to soothe Dalton's feelings. He also took costly practical measures. In March 1881 he added £100 to Dalton's salary and the building of Dalton's new house began. Simeon further promised to reduce the pressures on him so that he would have time to meet his friends. He even proposed to take steps, of an unspecified kind, to 'enlarge the circle of your friends'. None of those gestures addressed the basic problem: the division of power and responsibility. They did, however, buy time, for Dalton responded by withdrawing an application he had put in for the headmastership of Glenalmond.

By the autumn of 1881 letters were once more flying across the Quad. They were shorter and increasingly acerbic, but the issues were the same. By now the clash had moved beyond the school and had extended to its backers. On 28 December 1881 Dalton wrote to Liddon and King seeking arbitration. Would Liddon, so long Simeon's chief male support, back his protégé? Not entirely. He urged Simeon to give Dalton fuller authority in intellectual matters, and added: 'Certainly it seems to me that Dalton's leaving would be a very great misfortune to St Edward's and that much should be done in order to avoid it.' The upshot was a document, undated but clearly belonging to November or December 1882, which constituted the written agreement that should have been made on Dalton's arrival five years earlier. By 1882 it was too late for a formal document to extract either man from his entrenched position. In December Dalton applied for the headmastership of Durham School. Unwisely Simeon mentioned the fact to his brother Hugh, a member of the teaching staff. The indiscretion got back to Dalton, who accused Simeon of suggesting that 'I was deserting you for the sake of my own promotion. I think it is only fair to both Mabel and me that you should not give such an impression.'

The conflict had also reached and divided the Common Room. Matters were brought to a head by a case of indiscipline. The

Sixth Form had been disrespectful to Sydney Herington, one of several inexperienced teachers, who was fresh from Balliol. The masters alleged that the case was symptomatic of a breakdown of order in class. The question whether classroom discipline was Simeon's or Dalton's province had become urgent. It provoked an unprecedented display of independence by the Common Room. On the staff's behalf Edward Shuttleworth asked for a meeting at which Warden and headmaster would be present. Simeon, furious, summoned the masters and vented his wrath on them. After a conciliatory letter from Cowell, the Warden changed his tune. He recalled the masters and laid on the charm. He had, he said lightly, allowed himself to be provoked by unwarranted fears of a 'Republican government'. Now he understood that he needed to support his staff and listen to their views. In his own defence he recalled that 'I have given all I possess' to the school. Indeed he had, and he often said so. He would say it the more plaintively as the financial clouds gathered in the years ahead. He warned the masters against the appearance of division. Competition among three authorities – Warden, headmaster, assistant masters – 'would simply keep up and give undue influence to the idea of a weakness in our corporate unity'.

From outside the school Liddon and King watched these developments with dismay. Reluctantly they told Simeon that, if Dalton got the post at Durham, his departure would be 'better for himself and for you'. He did not get it, even though he was the only headmaster to apply. Fresh issues of dispute now arose. Simeon expressed doubts about the terms on which Dalton should run the new boarding house, and about its practicality. An exasperated Dalton wrote: 'I confess I do not understand why you do now speak so despairingly of a scheme of which you were, until lately, always hopeful. No doubt the house is a risk, but we have always known this; and it is surely late to draw back upon that ground.' In July 1882 new warfare broke out between Dalton and the Common Room. Dalton accused Simeon of listening to accusations made about him by one of the masters, James Watkins. It was on the basis of indiscreet conversations with Watkins, claimed Dalton, that Simeon was making a series of allegations: that Dalton was not at school often enough, especially in the evenings; that he did not undertake his proper share of invigilation; and that even when caning was within his province he either failed to do it or, if he did administer the punishment, omitted to tell Simeon. Finally, Simeon alleged, Dalton had lost the confidence of the Sixth Form.

Senior boys, including the Senior Preferct Arthur Slessor, were drawn into the increasingly undignified row.

Though Dalton stoutly defended himself, he was looking for ways to escape. In February 1883 he put in, unsuccessfully, for the headmastership of Oundle. Simeon refused to let him use the testimonial he had written for his application to Durham. In May, when the issue of Dalton's contacts with parents resurfaced, Simeon brought in Felicia Skene to confirm the Warden's understanding of past agreements. Dalton, despite his failure at Oundle, decided to leave at Christmas. He accused Simeon of spreading the news that he was departing of his own free will when, in Dalton's own view, he had in effect been forced into resigning. He complained to the end. On 3 November he wrote: 'With regard to Mabel I must say that she has not felt your unkindness to be only in not coming to see her, but in your whole bearing towards her.'

Maybe Dalton was the wrong man for the job, but no one could have worked easily with Simeon. The Warden supplied his own, euphemistic account of the episode in the autobiography he wrote for his children and grandchildren in 1913:

> It was in September 1877 that Uncle Herbert came to me with the title of Headmaster. Our relations were somewhat delicate and we both felt that success must depend a good deal upon a mutual trust and unselfishness. His weakness lay in his youth and he made great mistakes and was not very popular. On the other hand he organised the work admirably and put new life into the scholarship. We were very happy together and got very fond of one another and for three years nothing disturbed this harmony of our lives except a certain amount of jealousy amongst the other masters.

The scheme for the boarding house 'did not work as we had hoped and difficulties sprang up between Uncle Herbert and I, in consequence of his being married, which ended at last in their leaving St Edward's in 1883.' Perhaps it is not surprising that Simeon's autobiography ends two pages later. After the conflict with Dalton he had lost heart.

11

LAST YEARS OF THE FIRST WARDEN

On 29 March 1881 Mabel Dalton gave birth to her first child, a daughter, who was christened in the Chapel on 21 April. It was the first christening in the school. Simeon may have been taken aback by Dalton's courtship and marriage of his sister, but he was soon to be married himself. In November 1882 a note in the *Chronicle* revealed that the Warden, who was now aged 35, had become engaged to Beatrice Wilkinson, daughter of the Vicar of Ruyton. They were married there on 16 January 1883. The newly-weds were greeted in Summertown with something of the festivity of a 'Joyous Entry' of the Middle Ages. Summertown was bedecked with triumphal arches and flowers. Simeon had become a sort of 'Lord of the Manor'. Letts attended and Wiblin, the now reconciled pork-butcher, helped to drag the unhitched carriage to the Warden's house. Simeon's ability to charm had not left him.

It was to prove a happy marriage. One cannot help but be glad for him. We have observed his highly strung and easily stressed character and the punishing solitary schedule of the work he had imposed on himself since 1870. Maybe he looked to marriage for a measure of withdrawal from his labours and from his altercations with Dalton. The financial burden, enlarged by the building of Dalton's house and the increase in his salary, seems to have worried the Warden. He approached the Woodard Society again in 1882 to offer the school to them. The Society refused, 'considering that [the school] is saddled with a mortgage of £13,000'.

In his centenary history of St Edward's Desmond Hill, with some justification, describes the remaining eight years of Simeon's time at the school as a 'pause'. Yet these years witnessed one major advance, which again was intended to relieve Simeon's financial burden. He had always wished to appoint trustees or governors and hoped that some of their number would assume collective ownership of the school. Without that constitutional change St Edward's could never really claim to be a Public School. In 1884 he set in train negotiations for such a handover. They took five years to complete, for the complications were enormous. Simeon knew that when he had retired from the Wardenship he would be reliant on a stipend from a parish incumbency. That would mean a fall in income and status for his new family. It was reasonable, as the prospective trustees recognized when he put the point to them, that he should expect an income from the assets at St Edward's which he was about to relinquish. Increasingly Algernon turned to his younger brother, the lawyer Hugh Simeon, for help and advice. Hugh was to be active and supportive in the years ahead, but perhaps not always tactful or wise. From the start he was worried about the feasibility of handing over a mass of debts to trustees, for the whole place was mortgaged, by the mid-1880s, to the tune of £20,000 and more new capital projects were in hand, notably the new indoor swimming bath (situated on what is now the site of the North Wall) and the extension of the Warden's house to make it suitable for Victorian family living. The swimming bath alone cost £1,500. Further expenditure loomed. There was a demand for the extension of the playing fields. James Watkins, before he left, had urged the need for a gymnasium. Such proposals hint at some new and costly educational priorities, to which we will return. In 1886 parents gave £300 for the gym and Simeon had to find another £700 to complete it. There seemed little chance of further capital investment, and little prospect too of the realization of 'Simeon's Dream' of the full cloister round the quadrangle.

The building projects already undertaken were arguably too ambitious. The New Buildings were designed to take up to thirty boys, but they were mostly empty. It was into their vacant spaces that the first science laboratory and other amenities would later be introduced. The Main Buildings of 1873 were meant to house about 120 boys, but that figure was not reached until 1895. It is true that the school's buildings gave ample provision for future expansion. It is also true that they were valuable property, worth much more than the £20,000 for which they were mortgaged. A valuation of 1890, made following the negotiations to set up the governing body, suggested a sum of £34,500, plus £9,902 for the Chapel. Yet Simeon thought the correct figure much higher. He claimed to have spent £60,000 on the school over the years, though typically he gave at least two smaller figures (£45,000 and £50,000) on other occasions. He had undertaken no strategic accounting; there was only his accumulation of detailed lists. Getting at the financial truth was scarcely easier when it came to current outlays and running costs. We have seen that Simeon was good at keeping a tally of such items as the milkman's bill, but his records of bigger items are scattered thinly among his papers. He had conjured a salary from the air to attract Dalton, and had then increased it by £100 in an equally cavalier way to placate him. He was generous to Watkins. In 1883 his salary of £150 a year included 'board and old rooms'. In the following year he was awarded a £50 rise, and after Christmas 1885 his salary was increased to £250. Maybe Simeon was trying to tempt him to stay; if so, he was unsuccessful, for Watkins left the school just at that point. A list of salaries survives for the other masters, who were less handsomely treated. Cowell's many skills are rewarded with only £60 a term, while the next four masters are each paid £50, another £35 15s. 5d, and yet another £32 11s. 6d. The wages bill for non-teachers came to £72 16s. 11d. The total salaries bill for one term in 1883 was £415 0s. 11d, against a fee income of £2,971 0s. 9d. Additional income was raised from the sale of fish at £4 and by charging masters £6 5s. 0d for entertaining guests in hall.

At least the school was running at a profit – but a reduced one. From 1876 to 1882 the annual surplus (once the mortgage interest had been paid) had averaged £2,320, whereas the years 1882–86 yielded an average of only £1,614 a year. The reduction in profit was probably caused by Dalton's salary and those of the new young graduate teachers. There was a slight improvement by 1888, which produced a profit of £1,690, and a stronger one in 1889, when the figure rose to £2,077. Simeon could tell prospective trustees that the school was on a sound financial footing, and that all that was needed was to strike a fair deal over the mortgage and over Simeon's reasonable demands for recompense. No one seems to have considered what might happen if the numbers of boys were to fall and the annual operating surplus were to disappear.

Apart from Cowell and Jellicoe, not a single teacher appointed by Dalton remained in 1883. Simeon was left with the old problem of constantly re-staffing his Common Room and finding suitable graduates. From 1884 to 1892 he made no fewer than 31 appointments, excluding temporary ones whose presence never reached the *Roll*. The 31 were a mixture of graduates and non-graduates. Twenty-two of those staff who were meant to be long-term appointments left between 1884 and 1892, eight of them, apparently non-graduates, departing after one or two years. The high turnover cannot have been good for stability. It was as bad as the New Inn Hall Street days. Probably only D. A. Wynne-Wilson (of Trinity College, Oxford), who served from 1891 to 1904, could be called a real success. Was Simeon missing Dalton? His greatest stroke of luck was to stumble upon J. M. Sing, who was to be a major figure in the school's history and whom we meet for the first time on the 1887 salary list. At first a temporary appointment. Sing was a fine, if rigid, teacher of the Classics, who sustained high standards in the Sixth Form. Among the 31 appointments were four successive organists, one of whom, Cecil Kitcat, died in harness in 1888. He is buried in the Chapel burial ground. More and more it was Cowell, not a great intellect but a good schoolmaster, who was the inspiration behind much in the school.

An appointment which proved disappointing was that of the Rev. Carlton Olive (Exeter College), who took over Dalton's accommodation in the New Buildings and lasted from 1884 to 1887. He was supposed to bring fourteen boys with him to stock the new house, but there were never more than ten there in his time. It was not uncommon for heads or teachers in other schools, on leaving for a new post, to take some of their current charges with them. Simeon handled Olive's failure with his customary clumsiness, and it took ten letters and three additional 'statements' to ease him out. George Sayer (from Trinity College, Oxford), a teacher from 1886 to 1896, kept the *Chronicle* going in some tough times. Simeon called on old boys to help out in the classroom, among them Richard Prioleau (Roll No. 319), who had attended the school as one of three brothers and was now studying for his degree at Christ Church; he taught for over two years. He was a competent games player and became a solicitor. More of a catch was Francis Wylie (Roll No. 310), who had taken a First in Mods at Balliol in 1888 and would achieve the same result in Greats. The school's most eminent nineteenth-century academic, he became a knight, the first Warden of Rhodes House, and a governor of St Edward's.

In 1884, possibly to offer public reassurance after Dalton's departure, the school issued what can best be described as an early prospectus. We do not know how and to whom it was circulated, but if it was a bid to raise numbers it failed. It names the members of the supporting council (which had no formal title before 1889), who are headed by Beauchamp. The list includes Cowie's father, the Dean of Manchester; Liddon, Bright and King from the University; the Hon. Charles Wood; the Rev. A. Gurney of St Barnabas' Church, Pimlico; and Lord Forbes, a powerful figure in the Church of Scotland. The council were all or mostly Ritualists. The document lists the twelve assistant masters, together with Mrs Bursey as sick-nurse and a Mrs Stephenson as matron. The school aspires to provide for the 'sons of gentlemen, at a moderate cost, a first rate liberal education on public school principles, and at the same time to aim at a high religious and moral standard by careful dogmatic instruction and constant personal intercourse with each boy'.

Of the site we are told that 'the substratum is gravel, and the air is remarkably pure and bracing, and suitable for delicate boys'. The need for a healthy environment had been brought home on 18 June 1882, the date of the first funeral service in the School Chapel. It was for William Bates (Roll No. 504), who had died of tuberculosis at the age of 16. The funeral was the occasion for full Tractarian pomp. 'We laid to rest in the consecrated ground on the South side of the Chapel the mortal remains of William Bates; and few of us will ever forget the impression which the solemn words of the Burial Service, sung for the first time in our own chapel, must have made upon all who were present.' Three doctors had ministered to the boy. He died with his mother at his side, who 'had the satisfaction of being with her son some hours before the unconsciousness set in, which never left him until his soul, emancipated from the thraldom of the body, exchanged the darkened room for the bright field of Paradise'. The coffin was covered in a beautiful pall, flanked by six candlesticks which remained lit through the night. His fellow fifth-formers had created a cross of flowers and both the Upper and Lower Schools added a wreath of white hothouse flowers. The service was preceded by a celebration of the Eucharist, for which Iliffe had set the *Dies Irae* and the 'Sentences' – short medieval expositions of Christian doctrine – to music. Six prefects carried the pall. The choir sang the composer Sir John Goss's funeral service, the anthem 'Blessed are the dead which die in the Lord', and the *Dies Irae*. 'The rich and beautiful harmonies sounded as they rose and fell in the still summer air.' William's body rests in the adjacent burial ground together with the ashes of Robert King (Roll No. 6449) who died in 1970, also aged 16. The Bates family bequeathed memorial windows, commemorating Holy Baptism and Confirmation, in the chancel of the Chapel.

The prospectus of 1884 describes the layout of the school, stressing the seven acres of games fields and the outdoor bathing place, where swimming is taught free of charge. 'The ordinary course of a public school education is adhered to throughout the School.' 'The sons of neighbouring gentry,' readers are optimistically told, 'are received as Day-boarders. They are required to be at School by 9 a.m. and to leave at 6.30 p.m. after Chapel.' The boarding fees stood at 75 guineas per annum (65 guineas for the sons of clergy), payable termly in advance.

Additional to the fees are books, clothing, subscriptions 'and such like personal expenses'. It cost two guineas to learn to play the piano, three guineas for the organ, £1 10s. for 'carpentering (exclusive of tools)' and the same for aspiring draughtsmen and painters. Day boys, a useful source of income now as in later times, were charged thirty guineas a year, with an extra ten guineas if they stayed for supper. The prospectus explains that there are three vacations a year. The Easter vacation, which lasts three weeks, always starts on the Wednesday after Easter Day, to ensure that the most important of the Christian festivals is celebrated at school. The Summer break is seven weeks long and the Christmas vacation five weeks.

The academic improvement achieved under Dalton was sustained. Although there was a fall to only one university entrant in 1887, four years after his departure, there were six, and one award, in 1888. Also in 1888 boys who would have been juniors in Dalton's time managed eight Oxford and Cambridge Board certificates, the same number as at Highgate and Rossall and a creditable number, given the small size of the school, which could hardly have expected to match the 24 at St Paul's, 16 at Eton, 12 at Westminster, or 9 at Harrow. In 1889 and 1890, it is true, the figure dropped to five, the number which the Board had judged unsatisfactory in 1883. On the other hand the achievement of eight university scholarships and exhibitions between 1882 and 1892 was creditable, even though three of the awards, to Arthur Slessor, Francis Wylie and E. G. Hall (Roll No. 432), were given only after they had shown their academic capacities at university. The figure was recorded in the national newspapers (*Pall Mall Gazette*, *Daily News* and Jackson's *Oxford Journal*). So the school was becoming known.

By 1889 plans for the transfer to trustees were well under way and Simeon had his eye on a sabbatical term of travelling for himself and Beatrice. His bond to the school was loosening. That year three trustees – Beauchamp, the Hon. Charles Wood (later Lord Halifax) and a newcomer to the support group, Henry Hucks Gibbs (later Lord Aldenham) – became the school's owners, working as part of a governing body of twelve. Simeon was left with total day-to-day control, except that he was obliged to report to the Governors if he wanted to expel a boy. The entry of the Gibbs family into the school's story was a momentous development. They had made their money in South America and later in banking. Henry (1819–1907) was a director and, for a time, the Governor of the Bank of England.

Without his financial reputation and acumen the school would not have survived the years ahead.

These three High Church aristocrats had a touching faith in Simeon. Their trust is surprising, for they were taking over the school's substantial debt, which the surplus in the current account could not conceal. Maybe that was why Lord Forbes, who was to have been one of the owner-trustees, backed out. But Beauchamp and Wood, who had been associated with the school for years, and Gibbs, one of the country's leading bankers, should have known the picture. Beauchamp had at least asked for assurances from Simeon, who in February 1888 agreed that an accountant should look at the books: 'I propose to ask my neighbour and accountant Mr Hawkins to investigate my accounts.' 'He has many years' experience in school matters,' wrote Simeon, 'and has the management of the finances of Radley College, and so I think he would be well qualified for this.' It was a naïve statement. Hawkins later ended up in the courts for financial malpractice, though not for his handling of the money of St Edward's.

On 3 August 1888 Beauchamp, having seen Hawkins's assessment, wrote to Simeon: 'There can be no doubt but that the financial position of St Edward's School is most flourishing and no one can question the propriety of your securing for your family some portion of the large sums you have expended upon the institution.' The Trustees who took over on 24 July 1890 were responsible for buildings and land valued at about £45,000, with mortgages totalling £21,500 at 4½% interest per annum. They had anticipated an annual profit of about £2,000. That estimate assumed that the numbers of boys would continue to hold up. Yet even at the time of the takeover they were dropping. There were 122 boys in Michaelmas 1888, 107 in Michaelmas 1889, 97 in Michaelmas 1890. If the working financial surplus were to be restored, the slump would need to be not just arrested but reversed.

Beauchamp acknowledged that Simeon had spent about £50,000 on the school. To cover this sum, £21,000 was to be raised by mortgage, which would leave a debt to Simeon of close to £30,000. A proposal was made for a public appeal to High Churchmen, but Beauchamp, though no financier, recognized that the agricultural and commercial depression of the period was not conducive to money-raising. Beauchamp recklessly authorized a new mortgage in Simeon's favour of £30,000, to be repaid in three instalments of £333 6s. 8d each year. In addition Simeon would be paid interest at 2% on £20,000, a charge that would decrease as the repayments were made. He would continue as Warden at £500 a year, with everything provided in the house and with free education at the school for his two sons. It was reckoned that it would take thirty years to pay off the new £30,000. The Trustees also accepted the liability for the original £21,500 mortgage. With all this seemingly settled during 1889, Algernon and Beatrice Simeon set off on their sabbatical, leaving the temporarily reinstated Letts as acting Warden. On 24 July 1890 St Edward's ceased to be Simeon's private school.

Simeon tried to tackle the decline in numbers. New Public Schools, like Marlborough and Clifton, sometimes offered to governors, and to parents who might be persuaded to become governors, the inducement of a right to nominate boys to places at reduced fees. The new constitution at St Edward's entitled each governor to nominate two boys whose fees would be reduced from 75 guineas to 55 guineas. If the provision was intended to recruit boys it did not work. The privilege was modified in 1891, when the entitlement to nominations was halved. At the same time, in a bid to stem the fall in numbers, the standard school fee was reduced to £66 per annum. Numerous exemptions made the real figure even lower. All sorts of deals were done with individual governors and parents. Scholarships, reductions for the sons of clergy, the subsidizing of nominees of governors, and other complications had produced twenty different rates of payment, an absurd and divisive arrangement. Four years after the general fee reduction the average fee paid was only £54 7s. for boarders, not much of an increase on the £50 that had been levied in New Inn Hall Street. The fee for day boys was £20 18s. In spite of the fee reductions and concessions the number of boys fell from 100 in 1892 to 80 in 1896.

It looks as if Simeon, having lost constitutional control of the school, was giving less thought to its management. As the Warden's energy declined, Cowell, who was made Second Master in 1886, became the driving force. It was he who produced the first *Roll* of 1890. He was behind the formation of the St Edward's School Society, the old boys' association. His influence and hard work secured the survival of the *Chronicle*. The annual school play was his project. The performance of the play was always preceded by a verse prologue, written by Cowell, and spoken by the Senior Prefect before the curtain rose. The prologues give fascinating glimpses of the happenings and sentiments of the twelve months gone by. In 1890 Cowell records the death of Henry Liddon, who had been Simeon's prime inspiration and his most consistent backer and support:

> The year has passed serenely: yet one cloud
> Has cast its mournful shadow on our hearts.
> One whom this age of ours can hardly spare,
> Whose kindly face taught it true courtesy,
> Whose gentle voice rose calmly through its noise,
> Whose faith stood – rock against its shifting doubts,
> Whom Oxford, England mourns, has passed away.
> Our voice must not be silent. Peace be with him!

St Edward's was Liddon's school as much as Cuddesdon was his seminary. No Warden would have such close ties with a national church leader until the son of the Archbishop of Canterbury became Warden in 1954, and that was in very different circumstances and a very different climate of churchmanship. Liddon's demise was another prelude to Simeon's departure. Obliquely Cowell refers to the new Trustees and Governors:

> Next mark you, now not on one life alone –
> Long be that life! – depends our School's career.
> Firm now she stands, as firm as man can place her,
> That, through the years to come, she still may rear
> Good men and true, to serve our Church and Queen.

Within months Beauchamp too was dead, leaving Wood and Gibbs as sole Trustees and Beauchamp's executors questioning his estate's liabilities in relation to St Edward's. By giving aristocratic backbone to Simeon's scheme, Beauchamp had made it acceptable to many people who might otherwise have been its enemies. He sustained the school's early links with Keble College, of which, together with a host of other High Church organizations and personnel, he had been a founding father. His death was a major loss, which may have helped persuade Simeon to resign. In 1892 came another break with the past, with the death of Thomas Chamberlain. His parting was little noticed by the school, the *Chronicle* being content to print an obituary from the *University Herald*.

In February of the same year Simeon wrote one of his rambling letters to the Council. It prepared the ground for his departure. The school, he wrote, 'is at present standing still to a great measure, and ... I have not the powers to push it forward into a more prominent and useful position'. He rehearses his shortcomings, his Pass degree among them. 'I feel strongly that the Headmaster of a school ought to be the most powerful man intellectually on the staff, and that as well as controlling the discipline and exercising the chief personal influence, he ought to be in the strictest sense of the word Headmaster.' How he must have been reflecting, as he wrote this, on the failed experiment of the Dalton years. A man, he added, is needed 'of sufficient scholarship to win the confidence of the public'. He hints that after his own departure he will be in need of a parish. No doubt he hoped that powerful trustees and governors would find him one. They did, but it took time. Maybe the difficult side of his personality was well known. Eventually Halifax fixed him up with the living of Bigbury in south Devon, where he stayed for ten years. He left a school with falling numbers and an impending financial crisis, but in the coming years never acknowledged any responsibility for its difficulties.

In fact, Simeon only half left. Unable to let go, he was appointed to the new governing body and was one of the three of its members nominated to choose his successor. Both decisions are understandable but neither was prudent. No one was tough enough to 'drop the pilot'. His place in the story of St Edward's was far from finished.

12

WARDEN HOBSON

Sir Cyril Flower (1879–1961, Roll No. 814), a distinguished medievalist and archivist who would become Director of the Institute of Historical Research, arrived as a boy at St Edward's in the Christmas term of 1892 and left in 1896. His first term was Simeon's last. His last term was the first of the Wardenship of the Rev. T. W. Hudson, and the rest of Flower's school career took place under the second Warden, Rev. Thomas Frederick Hobson. Hobson, another product of Christ Church, had taught with success at Radley and Wellington. He was appointed by a committee consisting of Simeon himself, Walter Lock the Warden of Keble, and Francis Paget, Dean of Christ Church. Flower's recollections contain revealing accounts of all three Wardens, and especially of Hobson: 'I remember two farewell sermons when I was a little boy. We felt like an era had ended on Simeon telling us from the pulpit that he was retiring. Four years later it came as a personal blow to many of us when from the same pulpit, with suppressed emotion, Hobson made the bald statement that he was going at the end of term and made it easy for us to infer that he was leaving because he had failed in one of the functions of a headmaster and had allowed the numbers to go down.' Flower adds:

> I think we all regarded him as our Warden and we recognised that a headmaster must be judged by other standards than that of persuading parents. If these stray recollections have a definite purpose it is to put him in his proper place in the picture gallery of Wardens. His faults of manner and temper were obvious; he failed hopelessly with doubting and doting mothers and fathers, but his fine strong character had a profound influence on those who came into close contact with him, and during his brief reign he gave the school a definite shape and spirit of a public school and laid the foundations for his successors.

Hobson was a product of Radley, like St Edward's a Tractarian school. He gained Seconds in Mods (1880) and Greats (1882) at Christ Church, where he also obtained a blue for running the mile and three-mile races. He returned to teach at Radley for six years before moving to Wellington. He was priested in 1887. After his time at St Edward's he became Headmaster of King's School, Rochester. His short career at St Edward's showed him to be a professional both in his manner of teaching and in his approach to school organization and educational ideas. But he arrived unaware of the school's financial situation, with which he was qualified by neither temperament nor aptitude to cope – though he did manage to reduce its running costs by £640 a year. Worse, he was treated badly by his predecessor, and fumblingly by his Governors.

Like Simeon before him he had difficulty in finding and keeping staff. He appointed five men during his brief Wardenship, of whom only two demonstrated any long-term commitment to the school: the Rev. W. T. Kerry, who remained in post until 1890, and P. J. Bayzand, the Drawing master, who stayed until 1911. On the other hand Flower remembers vividly a number of masters who were already there. Cowell, Sing and, in Flower's last year at the school, another future Warden, William Harold Ferguson, particularly attract his attention, but there are also impressions of D. A. Wynne-Wilson, E. H. Montauban, George Sayer, Arthur King-Lewis and the Rev. J. H. T. Perkins (whom Flower remembers as 'Jenkins'). For all its limitations, the Simeon–Dalton era had left Hobson with a group of capable men of character. Flower understood that it is the personal impact of a teacher that makes for effective learning. He saw that Sayer, though not a good disciplinarian or a methodical teacher, made his mark by eccentricity. He would speak in striking parables and metaphors, or would sink into thought so intense that pencils broke in his hands as 'we watched with bated breath. There were rumours of a love affair in the remote past (he was only in his twenties) ... it was said that he used to write "Evangeline" all over his blotting paper. The boys in the Fifth and in his set were genuinely fond of him.' Wynne-Wilson, whose family knew Flower's, frequently entertained boys in his room, where on one occasion 'he maintained the proud fiction that I was one of the editors of the *Chronicle* though he did all the work himself'. He had taken over the supervision of the magazine from Sayer.

Sing he recalls as 'a brilliant teacher and a Classic of the elegance and precision associated with Cambridge'. Yet there is no warmth in Flower's portrait of him. It was for Hobson's teaching of Classics that Flower reserved his heartfelt praise. 'His scholarship was robust and lively – sometimes a trifle too lively for our ease and comfort. He gave Aeschylus, Tacitus and Juvenal a living individuality. It is a tribute to him that we found real interest in working through the Pauline epistles.' It sounds very different from gerund-grinding under Dalton. Hobson took other steps to enliven the intellectual atmosphere. He replaced the last hour of preparation on Saturday evenings by concerts, lectures and debates. Lecturers introduced the boys to science and technology with the help of a magic lantern. With Hobson's encouragement the orchestra became what the *Chronicle* called 'an established fact'.

In his second term Hobson introduced a major organizational change. He began the Set system, which would evolve into the House system. Until now boys had been taught only by their class teachers, who may have had no other contact with them. Now Set tutors were appointed to oversee the intellectual and personal development of boys across the age range. The *Chronicle* barely mentions the innovation, but Cowell grasped its significance and saluted it in his annual Prologue, which explained, this time in prose, that the system 'gives to each who passes through our midst a friend to be his counsellor and guide through all the changes of his life amongst us'. The first four tutors were Cowell, Sing, Sayer and Wynne-Wilson. Later, when sets acquired their own territories, tutors became housemasters. The introduction of the Set system, which was modelled on that at Eton, belonged to a national movement that brought a new esteem, and a new sense of vocation, to teachers. They were to be builders of character and role models.

It was an innovation that had unintended consequences. In time the sets and then the Houses acquired tribal features, turning in on themselves and subordinating the individual to the group. Competition between houses became an alternative focus to loyalty to the school, as well as to the centre of Simeon's vision: the Chapel and the faith expressed in it. When sets were first formed in 1893 the wearing of sports colours and the award of 'colours' to players, a practice already in use for school teams, was extended to Set ones. They carried high status, for although most teachers put the classroom first, boys often had a higher regard for prowess on the sports field, whether for the school or for the house.

A boost to the school was its admission to the Headmasters' Conference in 1894. Membership was recognized as conferring the Public School status that had long been Simeon's goal. Perhaps a new confidence came with it. In 1895 Cowell's Prologue to *Coriolanus* announced:

> An uneventful year has poured away,
> We stand, we live strong life. Within all's well.

Academic improvement was continuing. In spite of the falling number of boys, eight university scholarships and exhibitions were gained in the less than four years of Hobson's tenure, as many as in the decade of 1882–92 and a higher figure than of many larger schools. Two more were won just after Hobson left. All but one of the awards were in Classics, where the combination of Hobson and Sing was very successful. The number of boys gaining the Higher Certificate was rising too. In October 1896 the *Chronicle* claimed that 'the proportion of those gaining distinctions in Divinity to the number of certificates gained, viz. four to seven, is larger than that of any other school'. In the same year seven boys achieved the overall certificate, and there were three distinctions in History and one each in Latin and Greek. By 1897 there were 33 OSE in residence at Oxford and 11 at Cambridge.

On Gaudy Day 1894 Hobson addressed the school and its visitors. The *Chronicle* summarized his address:

> The aim of a school such as St Edward's was to inculcate the idea of Christian manliness. The school was in a sense passing through a period of depression, their numbers not being so large as they should have liked them to be, or what they had been. The school, however, was full of vitality in the best and deepest sense. It was full of intellectual vitality, and he did not think there were many schools of its size in England which, in the course of the academical year, were able to boast four scholarships. Two years ago they were able to say the same thing .... Last year also a large number of boys obtained Oxford and Cambridge certificates.

None of the boys who had been admitted to Oxford and Cambridge colleges, Hobson added, had failed to meet university matriculation requirements.

'Full of vitality', yes, but not full of pupils. The problem already haunted Hobson. He had a second major difficulty: his predecessor. Sometimes Simeon interfered in the daily running of the school. In February 1894, for example, he told the Senior Prefect, Reginald Blyth (Roll No. 661), to ask the Warden for a Full Holiday. No doubt he was anxious to perpetuate the traditional celebration of his own birthday, which fell in that month. Then there was Simeon's attitude to the Warden's Lodgings. At first the Simeon family, which had yet to find permanent accommodation, did not fully vacate them. Even when they did leave they left furniture strewn round the house. Simeon tried to persuade Hobson to buy the furniture for £300, but Hobson, on a salary of £400, was not rich. A single man, he lived simply as Warden and took his meals in Hall to save on domestic costs. 'You see,' he wrote to Simeon, 'I am a poor man and cannot do many things which you have been accustomed to do …. As it is I have to consider every pound, almost every shilling I spend.' No doubt embarrassed, the Trustees and the Council, as the governing body was known between 1889 and 1911, paid for the furniture. There was a similar difficulty over a boat owned by Simeon. The former Warden had his own financial concerns as he struggled to sustain his growing family in Devon.

A letter from Simeon to Hobson in February 1893 opened a more serious issue. 'Will you forgive me for troubling you on a rather tiresome point? I am much puzzled by the great variety in the school fees charged.' Three days later Hobson revealed to Simeon his own problems with the chaotic system of administration he had inherited: 'I cannot find the account book of which you speak anywhere.' In June he wrote: 'As to the accounts I am much concerned.' Simeon's last term had produced a deficit of £363 19s. 9d, 'and I don't see where this is going to be made up at present …. I am afraid the burdens on the school place it in a very critical position.' The sum of £1,200 had to be found annually to pay interest, but because of falling numbers, a yearly profit of just £600 to £900 could be expected. 'The only thing that can save the place and keep it what it is, is increase of numbers …. Had I been fully aware of the state of things … last November, I could hardly have ventured to undertake the task. I understood all that was needed was economy and reduction of household expenses, but I did not understand that the burden of interest on debt was heavy.' Simeon was hurt by Hobson's observation that 'the school is not paying its way nor has it done so since it was handed over to Trustees'. The ex-Warden was anxious to date the slide from modest prosperity to a point after his own departure.

The two men discussed the reasons for the fall in numbers, agreeing that the commercial and agricultural depression of the time was one of them. They agreed too that the school's reputation for Ritualism deterred as many potential parents as it attracted. Passers-by, regarding St Edward's as a hive of papistry, regularly spat on its walls. Hobson believed that there were too many High Church schools. 'We are all,' he declared, 'cutting one another's throats, the supply being greater than the demand.' Tractarian Radley and the Woodard Society schools had better grounds and facilities than St Edward's and could charge higher fees. The father of Harry Ross

(Roll No. 804) threatened to remove the boy 'because Oxford has the name of being relaxing'.

Simeon believed that a man of more mettle than Hobson would have weathered the numbers problem. He is likely to have been disdainful too of his successor's plaintive assertions that parents were put off by his own lack of social status. In Simeon's mind the school needed a mood of confidence, not Hobson's pessimism. 'I am sure you are giving your very best, but may I say that if others should catch the depression that shows itself in your letter, it would be a serious matter.' Yet Simeon himself had been placed on the defensive by the Trustees. After Beauchamp's death Gibbs, with Halifax behind him, did what he could to recover the relative financial prosperity of the Simeon era, though his request to the ex-Warden for proper accounts for the year 1889–90 was not met, probably because they did not exist. What Gibbs did manage to find out alarmed him. Inferring that he and Beauchamp had been duped by 'inadequate and erroneous information', he used his firmness and expertise to secure a thorough and realistic appraisal. Having got the measure of the shady bursar of Radley, Hawkins, he instructed him to inform Simeon that no more payments of interest to him were to be made on the mortgage. Indeed, Gibbs declared that previous payments to Simeon should not have been made, for under the terms of the agreement with him interest was supposed to be paid only if the school had the money to pay it, as it had not. Simeon's brother Hugh, who had drawn up the agreement, could not deny the point. It was, Gibbs wrote, 'extraordinary carelessness' in Simeon to have claimed the money, and 'extraordinary neglect on Mr Hawkins's part' to have sanctioned the payments. A furious Simeon, believing that Gibbs was slurring his character, considered suing the Trustees until his brother restrained him. But Gibbs had grasped the problem and its extent. In this situation, he complained, we 'find ourselves not Trustees at all but absolute owners of, and responsible for, a concern that does not nearly pay its mortgage interest and the interest due to its bankers, the latter debt having been swollen by the payment of sums amounting to £1,300 and more to Simeon, to none of which he was at all entitled.' Gibbs was even said to be considering the sale of the school.

Hobson was caught in the middle between Simeon and the Trustees. The traits of slipperiness and duplicity that had disfigured Simeon's relations with Dalton had reappeared. Hobson accused his predecessor of misrepresenting his own statements to them. It is a tribute to Hobson that he struggled on as long as he did. 'I do not propose to shirk a task because it seems to me difficult beyond my strength.' But by January 1895 Simeon was declaring that 'Hobson has not got the go in him and is not a "strong" man: and therefore I am impatient for him to be moved ... that [the school] will not prosper with Hobson, I have no manner of doubt, and I always said so.' The ex-Warden got his way. In the same month Hobson submitted his resignation to the Trustees. It lay on the table for a moment but was accepted, though he would remain in office for seventeen months. The Trustees, knowing the authority Simeon still commanded, had come down on his side.

To some extent the situation had arisen from the character of the constitutional arrangements made in 1890. The Council was a very occasional and distant body, whose minutes were usually short and insubstantial. Sometimes it could not even raise a quorum for meetings. It could thus provide no check on the Warden, on their fellow governor Simeon, or on the two trustees. Everything was bound to be fixed by Gibbs, Halifax and Simeon. In October 1895 the three men circulated a letter to the Council asking it to appeal for funds: £3,750, they said, might save the school. Two years later this appeal had raised only £355. But a legacy of £1,000 came from Mrs Combe, and Gibbs managed to persuade the mortgagees to reduce their interest rate from 4½% to 4%.

Simeon was determined to choose Hobson's successor. What was needed, he said, was a strong and influential man. He had in mind a certain Sir Edmund Currie, who paid a visit to the school which Simeon kept from Hobson. Currie would not take the job. Next Simeon turned to the agents Gabbitas-Thring, who had a list of 340 clerical candidates for teaching posts. The resulting field of applicants was feeble, perhaps because word of the troubles at St Edward's had got about. Gibbs saw the need for a speedy solution and concluded that only Simeon could provide one. At this point Simeon made another approach to the Woodard Society, which rebuffed him again. So he turned once more to Gabbitas-Thring. The key, he told the agency, was to find a man who could add to the numbers, preferably one who could bring boys with him. Simeon had hoped that Currie would come with fifty boys. It was in a similar hope that the Rev. T. W. Hudson was appointed as third Warden. On 1 June 1896 Hobson finalized his resignation after a 'most satisfactory interview' with Halifax. He went quietly amidst effusions of appreciation by the Council and Trustees, but the dismay of Cyril Flower, who held Hobson in such esteem, went deeper. Hobson was a good and successful headmaster except in one essential respect. A school must pay its way. The fall in numbers was not his fault, but neither did he have a solution to it. Trapped between the despair of the Trustees and Simeon's self-preoccupation, he had no chance.

13

WARDEN HUDSON

Thomas William Hudson was appointed to increase the number of boys, and by doing so he saved the school for a time. Yet we may let Cyril Flower speak again. Hobson's successor 'was a man of charm, urbanity and knowledge of the world; he had a simple piety and simpler tastes. He was fortunate beyond most men, in his wife and children; but he had neither the fine scholarship nor the driving energy of Hobson, who will always be the Warden to my generation of St Edward's boys.' No one paid so devoted a tribute to Hudson.

At Brasenose College, Oxford he had graduated in 1883 in Modern History (Oxford's term for all history later than the ancient world). He was the first of four Wardens to have read the subject. He seems, like so many would-be clergymen of the era, to have entered teaching to mark time while he prepared for ordination and then to have waited for a living. He taught at the undistinguished Clergy Orphan School in Canterbury for a year. When its Headmaster and his deputy were taken ill, Hudson stepped into the breach. He then moved to Newton Abbot and took in private pupils to prepare them for their public schools. He became known for his sound High Churchmanship. In 1892 he became a headmaster, but not in a prestigious or flourishing school: Queen Elizabeth's School, Cranbrook, an old grammar school that took boarders, was described as being in a 'well-nigh death-bed condition'. What made Hudson attractive to St Edward's was his success in increasing the number of Cranbrook's boarders from 11 to 55.

Even before he took over, Hudson wrote disparagingly about Hobson, whom he described as 'sensitive on the point of his dignity, over-fussy, and slow to delegate'. He described the prospectus, which Hobson had published, as 'shockingly inefficient'. At St Edward's he sensed a mood of depression, as had Simeon, and resolved to dispel it. In place of Hobson's doubts he brought a brash confidence. To Simeon – to whom, as to Felicia Skene, he was shamelessly obsequious – he wrote: 'I might say I am accustomed to it. The feeling was exactly the same when I came to Cranbrook, only much worse .... You will say this is rather conceited: but I feel with you the whole business needs confidence, decision and a good heart, and these I shall not fail to bring.' This was just the attitude which Simeon had said was needed. The new Warden was not deflected by grumbles at his appointment. 'I do not think I should worry about what a few may have said, about my bringing boys being the reason for my appointment. People will say something, and if they do not find one subject for criticism they will find another.' As Flower's tribute shows, the boys knew that Hobson had been forced out. There may have been reservations in the Common Room too.

Everyone grasped that Hudson would be judged by one criterion. Could he get the numbers up? The answer was yes. They rose from 82 in Michaelmas 1896 to 100 a year later. Part of this can of course be accounted for by the boys he brought with him from Cranbrook. (During his Wardenship he also contributed five sons of his own to the school's numbers.) Harder to account for is the subsequent rise to a level of 129 in 1898, an improvement sustained for four years. Can it be attributed to the improvements in the national economy at this time? Or were parents persuaded by the Warden's ebullience? Whatever the cause, Hudson must be given his due.

The boys he recruited came at assorted ages. Among sixteen boys admitted at Easter 1897, Leo Tollemache (Roll No. 919) was nearly 18 and his brother Leone Sextus (Roll No. 920) 13; Neville Wallis (Roll No. 921) 17; Athole Murray (Roll No. 924), Clifford Pearce (Roll No. 925) and Edward Hammond (Roll No. 928) were all 16; Algernon Taylor (Roll No. 934), who would stay until 1904, only nine. The rise in numbers allowed an increase in the teaching staff to nine and the reopening of the Keble dormitory. Hudson appointed fourteen men to the Common Room during his eight years as Warden. However, only one of them matched the quality of Cowell or Sing. This was W. H. Ferguson, who had a distinguished career ahead of him at St Edward's but for the present would remain for just three years. Nine of the others stayed four years or less. It was still not a stable Common Room.

To the delight of old boys, three of Hudson's appointments came from their number. Arthur Wetherall (Roll No. 813), a contemporary of Cyril Flower who in old age wrote in Flower's praise, was one of four brothers at St Edward's from a High Church home. He was an undergraduate at Keble, then taught at the school while awaiting his entrance to Cuddesdon. He took holy orders, whereas his brothers pursued military and colonial careers. Christopher Labat (Roll No. 550), another son of a clerical father, taught at St Edward's for eight years. He had entered as a boy in 1883, aged 13, and had had a successful school career. He was an energetic teacher, both on the games field and in the classroom. Previously he had been at Ardingly, a Woodard school, so was one of the many boys who had had only part of their education at St Edward's. After a Third in Mods he took a degree in Theology as a non-collegiate member of Oxford University in 1892. He played rugby for Oxford and for his county, Sussex. He then trained at Cuddesdon and was priested in 1896. He taught at Hurstpierpoint and at Worksop, both also Woodard schools, before returning to St Edward's in 1898 as tutor to Set E. He stayed until 1906, when he left to become Rector of nearby Wytham. The third OSE appointed to the staff by the new Warden was Herbert Wright (Roll No. 702). He had been made a Scholar of the school in 1888, the year he left, and an Open Exhibitioner in Classics at Selwyn College, Cambridge, where he took his BA in 1896. Three blank years precede his appointment by Hudson to supervise Set D. He left in 1903, the year he married. He became Headmaster of Witton Grammar School, Northwich, but died young in 1907. He is buried beside the Chapel.

Of Hudson's other appointments, G. G. Stocks, from St Edmund Hall, Oxford, was the only one to stay long. The school's organist and choirmaster, he served from 1902 to 1912, though the music was at a low point during his tenure. James Sholto Douglas (Roll No. 1155) remembered him with affection as 'very Yorkshire'. He had a sense of humour, for 'one morning when Warden Hudson' – who came of Norfolk farming stock and kept pedigree pigs – 'was absent from Chapel after the demise of one of the animals, a well-known funeral march played us out.' Stocks's namesake, the Rev. W. C. Stocks of New College, Oxford, who was at the school from 1896 to 1902, was also a musician and organist. He was praised in the *Chronicle* for his work in his Set E, on the fields, and on the river. He was one of the few in the group who seem to have been missed when they left. But Douglas did praise T. W. Beasley, the tutor to Set D, as 'a terrific scholar and a man of good humour and also kindly .... He hated beating his house.' Beasley went on to Rossall in 1909.

Cowell's Prologue to *Henry IV, Part 1* in 1897 records the year's academic achievements, all of them by boys left over from the Hobson era. Three Oxford scholarships had been won and nine certificates, six of them with distinction. Cowell's lines celebrate the 200th issue of the *Chronicle*:

> ... the School, which follows ever
> Though at respectful distance, great examples,
> Has once more scored a century ....

He meant that the number of boys had again reached 100. But he was also alluding to the scoring of three centuries in cricket. The lines have more to say about sport, some of it barbed, for the Prologues gave Cowell a chance to comment slyly on school life and policy. His text of 1897 touches provocatively on the activities of the Central Committee of boys and masters that ran the games. Already financed by subscriptions and fines, it had annexed the profits of the School Shop.

> Last, not least,
> That mystic body 'Central', wonderful,
> That hoards subscriptions and grows fat on fines,
> Has laid paternal hands upon 'The Shop'.

Cowell notes a development in rugby too:

> On the field the ordered rivalry of Reds and Blues
> Adds a new zest to football.

He was alluding to the introduction of red and blue shirts for practice games, so that the two teams could tell each other apart. The change, sensible as it obviously was, indicates the growing regulation of pupils' activities and a liking for uniformity. The XV had long played its matches in red and blue striped shirts purchased for them by Simeon, who had come across a reduced offer and bought a job lot. By Hudson's time such casual arrangements were of the past.

Hudson gave a central place to games. With his encouragement the tutors purchased a shield for a gym competition. The Common Room formed its own cricket team, in which Hudson, who believed in 'hearty participation', played. Sliding seats were purchased for the Rowing IV. The VIII raced against an OSE crew. Although the results were not good, a new seriousness had entered the coverage of games by the *Chronicle*, which awarded them ever more space and gave voice to the excitement when school colours were awarded. St Edward's stopped playing Leamington at rugby because Leamington, having beaten a miscellaneous XV from the school, exaggerated the achievement by referring to the defeated team as 'the First XV'. The introduction of lemons at half-time was derided by survivors from a more relaxed era.

The Warden was a notorious caner, often for trivial offences such as 'bouncing a ball'; or a boy might be beaten for failing to learn the Catechism properly. When the young Sholto Douglas, about to be caned by Hudson, protested that he had already been beaten by his Set tutor that day, Hudson replied that that had been only 'with a penny cane', whereas his own canes cost threepence. The Warden's Confirmation classes must have induced more fear than piety, for candidates who did not know their Catechism 'were soundly flogged'. His was an intimidating presence in the classroom. Douglas again:

> His Divinity periods in the Lower Fourth make me wonder why I have any nervous system left at all. The top 15 boys sat on one side of the room, the bottom 5 at the other. Places were exchanged according to the boys' performance in the lesson. If Hudson felt like a bit of exercise a quarter of an hour before the end of the lesson, he would say 'I shall cane all the boys left on the bottom bench at the end of the lesson.' There were bound to be five, and the awful question was which five?

The regulatory tone of the Hudson era is reflected in a new edition of the School Rules, which gave sharper definition to 'out of bounds' areas. The school was to be locked up after tea. Boys were obliged to spend more time within the buildings and were restricted in their movements in the school. They were forbidden to enter any form room but their own, a hindrance to the development of friendships. The boys' Common Room in the New Buildings was available only to the few pupils who already had studies. The rest remained confined to their mixed-age form rooms, where there was no privacy. Freedom to brew tea was restricted to certain times, such as 4.40 to 5.15 on half-holidays. More significant was the growing insistence on uniformity of dress. Dark coats and waistcoats must be worn, together with plain dark neckties, though a telling exception allowed ties carrying sports colours. Photographs of boys in the Hudson era make a contrast to the informality of the poses of earlier years. The boys of the 1890s, individuals subordinated to a group, stand in rows in formal hierarchies. They look serious and manly, spruce and self-controlled, disciplined and seemingly assured of their place in a world confident of Britain's Imperial destiny. The spontaneity of youth is concealed behind solemn, manly postures.

Endurance of painful punishment was judged a test of manliness, a virtue that games fostered too. Alas for St Edward's, its religion came under public attack in the 1890s for its very lack of manliness. The decade produced a fresh wave of anti-Ritualist sentiment. The 'Puseyite' stress on decor, ceremony and choreography brought to mind the decadence of Oscar Wilde, Aubrey Beardsley and the *fin-de-siècle* movement. Hudson, despite his acknowledged High Churchmanship, was steering the school away from its Tractarian identity towards other values. In 1902 the 25th anniversary of an event which Simeon had annually and ardently celebrated, the laying of the foundation stone of the Chapel, passed unnoticed.

Hudson's Wardenship had financial crisis as its background, for the increase in numbers did not resolve the underlying problems. Gibbs, now Lord Aldenham, was determined to address them. The burden of finance and strategy had fallen on him and his fellow trustee Halifax. They had difficulty in replacing their colleague Beauchamp. Only in 1899 did Lord Egerton of Tatton, Chairman of the Manchester Ship Canal, agree to take his place. In the ten years before his death he attended only two Council meetings. The Council itself was suffering depletion: it lost two of its more committed members, the historian H. O. Wakeman, who retired in in 1892, and the Rev. Alfred Gurney on his death in 1898. Canon Bright, with King the last remaining figure of the Liddon group, had died in 1891. King himself, now Bishop of Lincoln, had departed from the Oxford scene. The Duke of Marlborough, who owned the school's games field, was persuaded to join the Council in 1895, but never attended a meeting. Two Council meetings of 1898 were inquorate.

In June of that year, thanks to the increase in fee income, Aldenham was able to announce that the school had paid off the outstanding current interest on the mortgage loan. Yet the bank overdraft stood at £3,000. Tradesmen were being paid by anticipations on the next term's fees. It was a hand-to-mouth existence. Members of the Council, a body which had no financial responsibility for the school, were asked to contribute individually to a relief fund. The initiative yielded a mere £310. St Edward's might now have come to be considered a Public School, but in effect it remained in private ownership, an inadequate financial base. Aldenham believed the school would have to close. He and Halifax saved it by lending £3,000, and later a further £1,000, from their own pockets, sums they did not expect to see repaid. How long could their generosity defer another crisis, given the accumulation of debt and the payments to Simeon?

In 1902 the numbers, which Hudson had dramatically improved, fell away. There were only 115 boys in that year and the next, and 101 in 1904, the last year of his Wardenship. The 21 boys who left in 1903 were replaced by just six. In the Easter Term of 1905 there were only 97 boys. The slump is hard to account for, since amid signs of national economic recovery the intakes of other schools improved quite rapidly at the same time. Perhaps St Edward's suffered in comparison with schools which were providing new buildings and facilities on a scale that was beyond it, or that were making improvements in the curriculum. At all events the figure rose to 107 in the autumn of 1904 and would reach the 120s again in 1907.

From his Bigbury vicarage Simeon offered his usual diagnosis of problems borne by his successors. They must be the present Warden's fault. Simeon told Aldenham that Hudson must go. Again he got his way. Halifax was abroad, and Aldenham, who was stricken by gout and within two years of death, offered no resistance. It made no difference, for Hudson, possibly accepting that he would be unable to reverse the decline of 1903–4, and perhaps keen to do better for his family, had privately decided to leave anyway. He approached his old college, Brasenose, which gave him its richest living, Great Shefford in Berkshire. It came with a house of twenty rooms for his growing family and 100 acres of glebe land. He left St Edward's in the summer of 1904, to farm his pedigree pigs in the Berkshire Downs for a happy eighteen years. The *Chronicle* paid dutiful homage to Hudson's 'geniality, his heartiness and his patriotism that led him to take a keen interest in the school football and other games'. Emotion was reserved for Mrs Hudson: 'We are very, very sorry to say goodbye to her.'

On 18 July 1904 the Trustees and Council unanimously asked John Millington Sing to succeed Hudson. This time there was no approach to Gabbitas-Thring, a move which would have drawn further attention to the school's difficulties. Sing was not in holy orders, which must have raised eyebrows. He was the school's first lay Warden. Charles Gillett (Roll No. 861), his protégé both as schoolboy and schoolmaster, was struck not only by his classical scholarship but by an outlook that owed more to classical Stoicism than to Christian doctrine. But Sing did know St Edward's. He was the figure with most authority in the Common Room, for though Cowell was the senior master it was the more practically minded and politically attuned Sing to whom masters had become accustomed to turn in difficulties. He is known to have been unhappy at the end of Hobson's tenure, either from pessimism about the school's condition or from dismay, which other members of the staff were said to feel, at Hobson's removal. Instead he ruled for nine years as one of the most notable Wardens of St Edward's. Before we turn to the events of his Wardenship we shall try to capture something of the life and atmosphere of the school he inherited.

14

HUDSON'S SCHOOL

SCHOOL prospectuses tell us how schools see themselves and how they want parents to see them. Hudson, who had commented so disparagingly on Hobson's prospectus of 1895, repeated much of it verbatim in his own version the following year, though he gave it a heraldic cover and added several photographs. Thereafter there would be minor adjustments to the document each year until 1905 when, early in Sing's tenure, larger changes were effected to both format and content. One feature of the school that was stressed in the prospectuses was its 'proximity to Oxford', which is 'of great value on account of the facilities which it affords for keeping in touch with University life and thought'. Yet the 1905 version adds a qualifying note, which reflects an ambivalence about the closeness of Oxford that is often apparent in the school's history: 'St Edward's School has no direct connection with any college in the University, and boys are in no circumstances allowed to enter any of the Colleges unless accompanied by their parents or one of the masters.'

The prospectuses affirm the 'purpose' of the school in words that echo the advertisement it had placed in the *Church Times* in 1865. St Edward's aims to provide for 'the sons of gentlemen a first rate liberal education on definite Church principles at a more moderate cost than that of the older Public Schools'. The prospectuses renew the school's assurances about the healthiness of its setting. Matron, the documents add, is close at hand. The dormitories are 'lofty and spacious'. In 1906 parents are informed that 'the drainage system has in recent years been renovated at considerable outlay, according to the most modern principles of sanitation.' The school and its parents had cause to dread the frequent epidemics. In 1901 the 12-year-old Cuthbert Wheeler (Roll No. 991) died of meningitis. He was the second boy to be buried in the Chapel's ground.

The merits of the Set system are advertised. The tutor 'maintains a special interest' in every pupil 'during the whole of his school career'. 'Special care is taken of the younger boys', and, the document claims, 'each boy in the Sixth and Fifth Forms has a separate study', a statement that might charitably be interpreted as intention rather than reality. Parents learn that classes 'seldom number twenty boys' and that 'in the highest and lowest forms ten is an average number'; that very young pupils are accepted; that 'the lowest forms (Upper and Lower Third) correspond to those of a Preparatory School'; and that from the Upper Third a boy passes into either the Classical or the Modern Lower Fourth. Classics were normally for the brighter boys, though some of the independently minded chose the Modern side, which was growing. It offered Maths, French and English and a choice among Science, Latin or German. Until 1905 the prospectuses add that 'Arrangements can be made for teaching Shorthand and Book-keeping.'

Hudson's first prospectus, in 1896, has only one sentence about games, in a section on the attractions of Oxford. It states that matches are played against college teams, and that 'occasional opportunities are afforded to boys of watching first-class cricket and football'. From 1905 the format is changed to provide a whole section on games. The fields and facilities are emphasized, as are the opportunities for 'rational indoor sports'. The days when the playing of games was optional were long gone. 'Cricket and football are compulsory' and 'only a doctor's certificate can secure exemption'. Cricket is coached by F. Reed, a Hampshire professional. Sometimes long walks are organized in place of games. The prospectus mentions evening lectures, concerts and the recently created Rifle Club. 'Definite Church principles' are stressed, as are the 'many beautiful features' of the Chapel, its furnishings and the quality of the music. Yet the handling of the subject is unobtrusive, even evasive. The school's distinctive churchmanship is passed over.

Halfway through Hudson's first prospectus there appears a list of the university awards and degrees won by the school and its old boys in 1892–95. The twenty boys who had won scholarships or exhibitions, or won prizes as undergraduates, or taken their degrees, are headed by Francis Wylie, who had been elected to a full Fellowship at Brasenose in 1891, and Charles Green (Roll No. 768), whose Entrance Exhibition to Trinity College, Dublin in 1894 preceded a distinguished career first as a zoologist and then as a civil servant. The only non-university honour listed was the achievement of Joseph Sandell (Roll No. 649), who would have a successful career in Madras, in coming fifth in the examination for the Indian Police. By 1906 the list of honours had been placed at the back of the document. The five years of 1901–5 had produced eighteen university awards, ten of them scholarships or exhibitions, of which two were choral awards. By now prestige is given to military careers. The 1906 prospectus lists nine entrants to Sandhurst or naval cadetships. A Royal Academy Travelling Scholarship and a Diploma in Education now merit appearances.

The prospectuses state the school's fees and charges. In 1905 the fees were raised from £66 a year – a figure introduced in 1891, which Hudson had not changed – to £84. The charge for boys on reduced fees was now to be £72, and the cost for day boys was startlingly increased from £21 1s. to £33. Compulsory termly charges for extras are listed, among them laundry (one guinea); the use of the gymnasium and indoor pool (both 14s.); subscriptions to clubs and societies ('about' 17s. 6d); and the cost of the prospectus itself (5s.). Separate charges for 'books, clothes etc.' are to appear on the termly bills. Parents are advised to provide 'pocket money, journey money and the like'. Extra commons at breakfast can be had for £2 2s. per term. Private tuition by a master for a special examination is available at £5 a term. From 1906 a further 10s. a term was levied to subsidize the *Chronicle*. So the fee of £84 was far from inclusive. Yet the proliferation of charges, which can be seen from the early 1890s, reflects the growing scope and improved facilities of the education that parents were buying. The only surviving termly bill from the period, that of Harold Rogers (Roll No. 689), who left in 1895, charged £16 for extras, about two-fifths of the total: this included charges for the swimming bath, the rent of his study, clarinet lessons, and 'theatricals'.

What did boys of the late-Victorian and Edwardian period do with their lives? Most did not go to university. For example only four of the fifteen entrants at Christmas Term 1900 did so, three to Oxford or Cambridge and one to Sheffield. Among the rest one became a farmer, one an engineer who emigrated to Canada; one worked in insurance; one joined the Indian Army; one the home army. Of fourteen boys admitted in 1906 two went to Oxford or Cambridge and one to King's College, London. Of the others nine made army careers, three of them in India; one went into mining in Canada; one was a businessman who emigrated to the USA.

Simeon had founded, in his own devout image, the Confraternity of old boys, who returned to the school for worship and festivities. In 1892 there appeared a very different association of old boys, the St Edward's School Society. It committed itself to 'preserving the traditions of the School and encouraging the spirit of unfailing loyalty to its interests'. The 'traditions' and 'loyalty' the founders had in mind centred not on Simeon's religious vision but on secular values of manliness, athletic endeavour and group loyalty. The association had begun as the informal Old St Edward's Club, which from 1884 held a roistering annual dinner in an Oxford hotel. We learn that OSE cricket and football clubs had been established for 'some years' by 1890, when they were 'in a flourishing condition' and when their members received the right to 'wear OSE colours and receive a copy of the School *Chronicle* for five years'. Henceforth the dinner was to be held in November.

A circular of 1892 announced, not very sensitively, that 'there seems to be no further use for the Confraternity. Membership with the Club will produce the desired result more effectively and to maintain the two seems not only superfluous but to be more likely to lead to division than to union.' The Elizabethan Club at Westminster and the Cheltonian Society at Cheltenham were the models for the new enterprise. But the initiators had jumped the gun. As they apologetically admitted, in the face of grumbles from some local OSE, they were portraying their school society as an Oxford-based club. Nonetheless the Society was granted recognition by the school. Two figures dominated its early history: Cowell, who was soon named as treasurer, and who as editor both of the *Roll* and the *Chronicle* would help bind alumni to the school; and Harold Rogers, an up-and-coming local architect. By 1899 they had got a full set of rules passed. The Warden, as president, was to nominate the officers.

The guinea subscriptions, managed by Cowell, placed the Society on a sound financial footing, but it took time to grow. By 1893 only 20 had joined, 'a miserable percentage out of 600 or 700 past members of St Edward's', as the first secretary, Alexander Doull (Roll No. 716), an undergraduate at Oriel College, remarked. Cowell received the guinea subscriptions and in that year, when membership had crept up to 45, he kept £38 in the bank. Doull was succeeded by Walter Kitcat (Roll No. 767), another Oriel undergraduate. Members were urged: 'use your influence to persuade any more old boys to join'. Also in 1893 the Society broke new ground by publishing, in its second annual Report, a summary of the school's events in the preceding year, a practice that would be enlarged in subsequent reports. The reports have much to say about the school's sports results, a certain amount about academic honours or the school play, and nothing about the Chapel.

Membership stood at 55 by 1896, and would soon rise further. The Society received two boosts in that year: the arrival of Warden Hudson, whose vigour and athletic proprieties appealed to the old boys and who gave the institution wholehearted support; and the appointment of Harold Rogers, at that time another Oriel undergraduate, as the third secretary. He would hold the post for twenty-five years and sustain the organization. It was he who expanded the Report and made it annual.

The dinner of 1896 was held at the Holborn Restaurant in London, a sign that the Society had reached beyond its Oxford base. It was a typical late-Victorian feast. Soup, turbot and fried smelts, Grenadin of Veal and Pears, and Chicken sauté were offered as entrées. Then came 'Removes' of Saddle of Mutton and York Ham, followed by the 'Roast', Pheasant Barde. The sweets – apricots, jelly and ice pudding – preceded cheese and celery. A toast to Church and State was followed by one to Simeon, 'The First School Warden', who still commanded intense loyalty, and who in attending had overcome whatever reservations he may have had about the Society's attitude to the Confraternity. Then came 'The Old Boys' and 'Floreat St Edward's'.

By overseeing the *Chronicle* over the years and producing fairly frequent editions of the School *Rolls*, Cowell kept the school and its old boys in touch. The *Chronicle* carried an OSE section, where those attending Gaudy were faithfully listed. Cowell would have liked the links of school and alumni to be stronger still. In an open letter of 1906 he apologized for the fact that lack of time on his part, and the expense of printing costs, would prevent the inclusion of extensive biographical details of OSE in the next *Roll*. We too have cause to lament this omission. Fifty-four diners mustered for the Society dinner at the Trocadero; 130 letters of regret had been received. Kenneth Grahame, already a well-known author even though *The Wind in the Willows* would not appear for another two years, presided, and Simeon sat down to dine with Hobson as well as Hudson. These dinners were covered in detail in the *Chronicle*.

15

WARDEN SING

John Millington Sing was born in the year that Thomas Chamberlain founded St Edward's School. He was a product of Thring's Uppingham. Edward Thring (1821–87), the creator of the Headmasters' Conference, was possibly the greatest and most influential of all the Victorian headmasters. During his thirty-two-year tenure of the headship from 1855 he transformed Uppingham from a small grammar school into a thriving Public School. No one better exemplifies the moral seriousness of later nineteenth-century education. Reacting against the wretchedness and unhappiness of his own education at Eton, Thring believed passionately that pupils brought up with sympathy in decent surroundings would become better citizens than those produced by the old Public Schools. The energy and talents of boys must be given scope for fulfilment. That meant games, for Thring was of the muscular school of thought, but he was also convinced that a school should foster intellectual and artistic interests. The curriculum, too, should be widened. Uppingham's workshops and music were legendary. Thring, who wrote much on educational theory, took a modern psychological approach. He wrote in 1858 that 'Many a boy whom we must put at a low level in school redeems his self-respect by the praise bestowed on him as a games player, and the balance of manliness and intellect is more impartially kept.' Uppingham had its chapel, but it was not among Thring's priorities.

Sing was a Classical Scholar who had held an award at Christ's College, Cambridge. He followed Thring in the eclecticism of his educational interests and commitments. He would strive to give the boys of St Edward's the variety of skills and talents he had encountered at Uppingham, and which was now a widespread goal for the nation's boarding schools. With Sing's ideals went a shrewd business head. He was a down-to-earth manager and a clear-sighted realist. Inspiring more respect than affection, he does not come over as a warm man. His blue eyes were famously piercing. In sharp contrast to the emollient Cowell, he could seem fanatical and spartan, insisting on high standards and not suffering fools gladly. Few pupils were close to him, though he won the personal devotion of his star pupil Charles Gillett, who taught at the school for five years from 1904, the year Sing became Warden, and who wrote a memoir of him.

Sing's appearance was tweedy and unmistakably Edwardian. His droopy moustache belongs to a later era than the sideburns and whiskers of the Victorians. 'His own violent delight in violent exercise and his rooted conviction of its indispensable virtues was indelible,' wrote Gillett. He immediately introduced 'School runs' and 'School walks', excursions Gillett remembers as 'more numerous, more regular and more gruelling than those of earlier days', which 'reduced dreadfully the number of afternoons (even, and especially, Sunday afternoons, when he would often arrive himself to set a merciless pace to laggards) when a boy could concentrate properly on doing nothing.'

Sing made fourteen appointments to the staff, five OSE among them, during his nine-year tenure. They were men of calibre and commitment, even though only two of them stayed a long time, the Drawing master H. E. W. Phillips, who taught from 1907 to 1934, and the Director of Music, W. K. Stanton, whom he appointed for a year in 1912 and who would return, after Sing's departure, to serve from 1915 to 1925. Three, J. G. Bussell (Roll No. 972), L. F. Cass and J. B. Partington (who taught for a year from 1913), all vigorous and popular figures in the school's sports and its military training, were killed in the war in 1915. Gillett, with whom Sing judiciously chose to share the Classics teaching, was the only appointment with scholarly credentials. When he left the school in 1909 it was because of ill health. Though he had a distinguished career ahead of him in other walks of life, he had wanted to have a full career as a schoolmaster.

So did all Sing's appointments, a pattern that signals the rise of the professional schoolmaster. When the others left St Edward's it was to teach at other schools. The Rev. B. Heald taught at St Lawrence College, Ramsgate and at Epsom College before becoming Headmaster of Midhurst Grammar School. The Rev. H. Lucas proceeded to Denstone and then Lancing, Bussell to Marlborough, A. J. Weller to Shrewsbury and then the Inspectorate of Schools, G. M. Sergeant to Marlborough, E. G. N. Kinch to missionary schools in Burma, the Rev. B. Hope (Roll No. 1000) to Radley, L. F. Hervey (Roll No. 1021) to Brighton and then Droitwich. The movement of teachers across the Public Schools, and the making and renewal of acquaintances at sports fixtures and other out-of-school activities, would gradually foster camaraderie among men conscious of working within a single system and holding common educational ideals and assumptions relating to the development of boys' characters, not merely of their minds. Few members of that professionally self-sufficient world were trained to teach, or joined the Assistant Masters' Association, let alone a trade union.

Games were essential to their vision. But games need games fields. Here was a basic problem which it took all Sing's shrewdness to resolve. The school was no longer on the edge of an agricultural village. Summertown, which could now be reached from central Oxford by tram, had joined a commuting and service economy. Red-brick housing now lined and joined the Woodstock and Banbury Roads close to the school. The playing fields of St Edward's and of Keble College next to them were the only green space between St Giles and Upper Wolvercote. The St Edward's fields belonged to the Duke of Marlborough, that inactive member of the Council, from whom the school held them on recurrent – and burdensome – seven-year leases. The current lease was up for renewal in 1908. Marlborough's agent R. L. Angus was urging his employer to develop the fields for housing which would complete the red ribbon development. As early as 1902 he had warned the school that such development might occur. Sing knew that if it did St Edward's would have to close. Its increasingly suburban setting, which distinguished it from the rural environments of some of its competitors, was disadvantage enough. But the playing fields had become indispensable. In the days when exercise had been merely a pastime, when boys had rambled or gone paper-chasing in the green spaces and woods or on the riverbanks of the area, the fields had mattered less. Sing knew how much had changed. 'I have never concealed my opinion,' he wrote to the Council, 'that it will be impossible to carry on the school if the cricket ground' – the term used to cover all the fields immediately opposite the school and down as far as the canal – 'is taken away.'

From 1902 to 1908 Angus kept the school guessing. His aim was to provide access to other lands of the duke, further from the Woodstock Road, by driving a roadway behind what is now Corfe House. This would destroy a school pitch as well as Hudson's pigsties. As often happened, matters were complicated by Simeon's interests. Simeon had purchased Field House, as Corfe was then known, for himself. He had leased it to the school but now proposed to sell. Aldenham had to persuade him to change his mind. In 1905, by getting Simeon to re-lease a 15-foot strip of land, he enabled the school to construct a roadway, later known as the Avenue, which would avoid the pitch and the pigs. But the danger that the lease from Marlborough would not be renewed remained. In the same year Sing, in despair, secretly visited another school, which was about to close but whose identity no one has ever discovered, with a view to moving St Edward's to its site. Not even the Trustees were informed.

How could the duke be won over? Sing matched a grandee against a grandee. He approached not Aldenham, whose peerage was tainted by banking, but the landed Halifax, whom he asked to intervene with Marlborough. Halifax sent the duke an adroit letter explaining that 'the cricket ground is a matter of life and death to the school'. He wrote of the sacrifices that had been made 'on behalf of a school which has done, and is doing, really well, and is supplying a great want – I refer to the class of boys educated and the cost of the education – which no other school as far as I know exactly supplies'. Perhaps, Halifax suggested, Marlborough might seek a second opinion? He suggested that the duke consult the school's Visitor, the Bishop of Oxford. Marlborough appeared to melt. He would, he replied, not sell the lease for the moment. If he did decide to sell, he would offer it to Aldenham. But the reprieve was temporary, for soon the duke, or his agent, had second thoughts. At the start of 1908 Angus abruptly announced that the lease of the fields would henceforth be yearly. The school would have to live under an annual threat of disaster. Again Halifax approached the duke, this time together with the Bishop of Oxford and a cohort of aristocrats headed by Lord Hugh Cecil and Lord Jersey. At last Marlborough relented. He agreed to sell the land for £6,822, a very fair sum. He even led the subscription list for the purchase. Sing himself gave £250, over half a year's salary, while the Society and the Central Fund gave £700. By 1910 the fields were secured. It was a crucial success.

Sing had been less fortunate in another matter of property. Under Hudson a strip of land behind New Buildings had been acquired, perhaps to keep suburbia at bay. From 1906 Sing sought to secure 1½ acres east of the Chapel in what was known as Wiblin's Field. The price was hard to assess and agree. On the one hand there was at this time a general expectation of a fall in land values. On the other the arrival of the trams seemed likely to raise their local level. Wiblin wanted £800. In 1906 he settled for £500, but the uncertainty of the land market made it hard to raise a loan. Eventually one was agreed, only for the lender to reduce it by £200. Sing turned to the ever-generous Aldenham, who wrote out a cheque for that sum. Then Wiblin raised the price and the school backed off. Only in 1918 did it secure the field, which would be vital for future development. It is now occupied by the Maths Centre, Cooper Lodge and the Cooper Quad, and the Art and Design Centre.

Between 1904 and 1907 three masters left: Wynne-Wilson, who married and left to be Headmaster of Gresham's in 1904; Labat; and the Rev. R. M. Tuke, who taught at the school for four years from 1903 and was tutor of Set B. In 1905, when numbers were so low, Set C, whose tutor Wynne-Wilson had been, had to be dissolved. Its boys were redistributed and the Set was not reconstituted until 1909. So acute had the financial difficulties become that it proved difficult to scrape £50 together for the enlargement of the carpenter's shop. The numbers of boys did rise to 120, but flattened out at a little under 120 thereafter. Welcome as the rise was, it did not solve the underlying problems. It was against a sober background that Aldenham, the man who more than any other had kept St Edward's going, died in the summer of 1907. It was a mercy for the school that his younger son, Vicary Gibbs, MP, who succeeded him as trustee, proved equally shrewd and committed.

Nonetheless, Aldenham's death exposed the precariousness of a school dependent on private owners. His executors were reluctant to continue his guarantee of the mortgage. They set their face against any increase in the current debts of the school from its present sum of £2,500. Had it not been for Vicary they might have pulled out altogether. Sing knew that an element of joint-stock ownership was needed, as it always had been. Whereas Simeon had relied on the shady Hawkins for financial counsel, the school was now advised by Oliver Williams, a very capable solicitor. He, Sing and the Trustees proposed that the public be offered debentures of £50 each in an issue of £18,500. These would pay 3% a year, provided the school made a profit. The scheme would reduce the £20,500 mortgage, provide the money still due for the playing fields, and leave a margin for current use. But would the public take up such an offer? Assertions that sympathizers with the school's churchmanship would rush to subscribe did not impress the hard-headed Vicary Gibbs. The debentures were not offered. Gibbs took a different course, which revealed not just his realism but his generosity.

What he did was to persuade his late father's executors to buy £4,000 of the proposed debentures to free themselves of the old obligations of the trusteeship, which were handed over to him. Halifax, generous as ever, bought £5,000. Of the £9,000 thus raised, £8,000 was to be used immediately to reduce the mortgage to £12,500 and thus its annual interest to £500. Gibbs saw that the mortgage was the school's millstone. His plans, however, ran into trouble on the Simeon front. Sing took endless trouble in handling his predecessor. He wrote more than a hundred letters to Hugh Simeon as the ex-Warden's adviser. With masterful diplomacy he persuaded Algernon to accept £5,000 in debentures in lieu of his worthless second mortgage. Now the former Warden suddenly asked for another £1,000, in lieu of the mortgage's arrears. Gibbs was furious, as his father had been in the face of similar conduct by Simeon ('bosh', the father had called it). Simeon was demanding income from his own failed investment. Gibbs warned that if Simeon's demands were met his father's executors would withdraw their offer. Sing's long association with Simeon placed him in an embarrassing position, for he could hardly take sides with Gibbs against him. He stated that Simeon's claim should somehow be satisfied.

A more fundamental disagreement between Gibbs and Sing soon emerged. Sing had doubts about Gibbs's scheme. He feared that Gibbs's 'overriding commitment to the reduction of the mortgage', understandable as it was, would leave the school unable to meet other pressing financial needs. He was bent on improvements to a school that had been starved of funds. Oliver Williams's scheme had proposed that a new mortgage of £4,000 be taken up to pay for the playing fields and other improvements. That recommendation was adopted. But under Gibbs's scheme any profits would go to the debenture holders and towards the mortgage. Gibbs's proposed measures would thus reduce the old mortgage but would not address the problem of the outstanding new one. Sing announced that he would resign if the scheme were implemented. The struggle lasted for months. Halifax and Gibbs knew that if Sing resigned the school would collapse and close. It was Halifax who, with renewed generosity, broke the deadlock on 25 October 1910. His debentures of £5,000 were converted into an outright gift, which reduced the school's annual interest charges by £150.

In the light of that move, Sing agreed to stay. Yet serious challenges persisted. A total of £680 would have to be found annually for the repayment of money to the Prudential Society, which held the mortgage on the fields, and for interest on the bank overdraft. The mortgage was to be reduced by thirty annual payments of not less than £416. If profits were made, an additional sum of £270 would be paid to Simeon as debenture interest and a maximum of £1,336 to the Aldenham executors. Any remaining profits, and any gifts of money, would be devoted to the reduction of the overdraft. In case there was no profit or times worsened, provision was made that the payment of the £270 to the debenture holders (Simeon and the Aldenham executors) could be suspended. The school was annually to repay £1,379, the working annual surplus at the time the arrangement was made.

In terms of the balance sheet it seemed that little if anything had been gained. Yet there had been two important steps forward. First, the mortgage, though it remained a heavy commitment, no longer overshadowed the school. The threat of foreclosure on it had been removed, the mortgage itself had been lowered, and repayments would reduce it further. Secondly, one outcome of the 1911 settlement was the school's acquisition of 'Articles of Association', which were submitted to the Council early in the year and then approved by the Board of Trade. The school had in effect become a limited liability company. Sing had more financial crises to face, but he had staved off the threat of closure at a decisive moment in the school's history. The stabilizing arrangements he had achieved made St Edward's more securely recognized as a Public School.

Yet in the same year, 1911, a new crisis arose. 'There seems to be no end to the bother which St Edward's gives,' wrote Vicary Gibbs. Halifax's donation of £5,000 was intended to contribute to the purchase of the duke's land and so reduce the mortgage burden. But that arrangement was based upon the assumption that the Prudential Insurance Company, which held the mortgage, would recognize the fields as part of the collateral. It refused to do so. Halifax had already paid £3,000 to the duke on the assumption that, in helping to buy the land, he was reducing the mortgage. Hugh Simeon, who cheekily suggested that Gibbs should put up more, was brusquely rebuffed. Algernon simply said 'I don't understand much about it all – you can hardly expect it.' Again the Gibbs family came to the rescue. Vicary persuaded his sister, the Hon. Edith Gibbs, to sign a new contract with the Duke of Marlborough. She paid £6,822 to the duke who, in turn, refunded Halifax's £3,000. The school paid Edith £2,822 and an annual ground rent at 4% on the remaining £4,000. So again the school had been rescued – but Edith Gibbs now owned the playing fields. After a year's negotiation, and having secured the agreement of the Board of Trade, Vicary Gibbs, who was Chairman of the National Provident Institution, transferred the mortgage from the Prudential to that body. Would St Edward's have survived without the expertise, generosity and, almost above all, the patience, of the Gibbs family?

16

SING'S SCHOOL

WE have been watching the school's responses to developments within it and in the outside world. They are tellingly reflected in the *Chronicle*. Here we shall set two years of the publication beside each other: the six issues of 1878, and the five of 1910. In both years the magazine ran to eight pages.

A conspicuous difference between the two years is in the treatment of games. In 1878 they are already a prominent feature. Editorials discuss prospects for coming seasons, a subject which is occasionally combined with requests for financial contributions to sustain the teams. But games mix freely with other topics. In February 1878 two columns are devoted to the previous Christmas examinations, two more to an essay on 'The Eastern Question' by an anonymous old boy, and two to Football and Athletics. There are three poems, one in Latin, though another is not an original composition but a hymn lifted from the hymnal. The deaths of the 21-year-old OSE Herbert Cunningham-Grahame (Roll No. 207) and the 18-year-old George Cornish (Roll No. 178) are recorded within black borders. There are two prescient letters, one asking for a Committee of Games, a suggestion later met by the establishment of a Central Committee, the other for a regular school play, which Cowell's productions were to provide. At the end there is a miscellany: an anecdote about a horse, a puzzle, a chess problem, and a few scrappy notes headed 'Gossip' which scarcely merit their title. Athletics and Fives are covered. So is the Library. In the April issue Football, Athletics, Fives and Boating occupy nearly seven columns, but there are also two translations of passages from Euripides and Virgil, more animal anecdotes, and other material away from the athletic world.

The July 1878 issue of the *Chronicle* introduced what would soon be the familiar practice of printing the scorecards of the cricket matches. Together with comments on the matches, they occupy nine columns. There are two columns on Boating and Aquatic Sports. The anonymous old boy reports again, this time on the Congress of Berlin. The 'Gossip' lists the names of boys who have earned the right to join the Boat Club by swimming a designated distance over the previous month. The departure of

Letts is recorded. There are some notes on the achievements of old boys, another feature that would be expanded in later issues. The Chapel figures too: 'The sermon at Matins on Sunday has been discontinued, and in its place the Litany is sung. There is now only one sermon on Sundays and, though the change seemed unpopular at first, we are inclined to think it is a good one, and hope that we are endorsing the opinion of the majority.'

The July edition supplied the first instalment of a potted history of the reign of Edward the Martyr, which continued over the next six issues. The November number announced the school's decision on a sensitive subject, the annual commemoration of the consecration of the Chapel on 5 June, a date that fell inconveniently close to St Edward's Day on the 20th of the same month. The solution was to celebrate St Edward on 18 March, the anniversary of the death that made him a martyr: a fitting outcome, for 20 June was merely the date of his translation from Wareham to Shaftesbury. But what, asked the editors, if 18 March fell in Holy Week, for Easter was always celebrated at school? As the *Chronicle* asks that question we feel the directing hand of authority. The supervision of the magazine by masters had increased over the years. Here the *Chronicle* is being used to reassure boys about the niceties of the liturgical celebrations. If the anniversary of Edward's death should fall in Holy Week, it explains, the observance of the royal day could be moved. Boys and parents are told that the revision of the calendar will not threaten the traditional full day's holiday on 20 February (Simeon's birthday), 'and the services in Chapel will be the same as usual'. So in future there are to be three commemorative days: 18 March (St Edward), 5 June (the consecration of the Chapel) and 25 November (the laying of the Chapel's foundation stone).

In October the Prize-Giving and the accompanying speeches occupy nearly six columns, Football and Cricket five. There is a hefty four-column piece on the West Country. The 'Carmen', which has just been introduced as the school song, is printed, alongside a hymn with a militaristic refrain:

> We joy to fight the battle,
> The battle of our Lord.
> His name our Tower of Refuge,
> Himself our sure Reward.

The last editorial of the year, in December, describes the celebrations on 25 November. There had been Eucharist at 8 a.m. At lunchtime Simeon toasted the school 'without any accompanying speech'.

'Carmen' was 'sung by the Glee Club making the rafters ring'. At 8 p.m. came a concert of songs and readings, during which the 'walls, hung with festoons and flags, gave a festive appearance to the whole'. The report of the concert, which gives attention to individual performances, evokes the Victorian middle-class tradition of self-entertainment. Cowie, returning to the school, preached a sermon, which the *Chronicle* prints in full. The issue also carries a letter from a former teacher, R. Hutchinson, who seeks contributions to a fund to supplement the stipends of lowly paid clergy.

The second of our two years, 1910, saw the death of King Edward VII. A poem honours him in the May issue:

> Let them salute the dead, the living chief.
> Silence the voice of faction! Let the watch
> Peer with keen eyes into the mists ahead ....
> Let the stern gunners man their mighty guns.
> Pass round the ancient watchword 'Duty'.
> Then, with stout heart, each at his post,
> Forward! For God and the King!

The royal death was a blessing to the editors, who, evidently short of content, filled further space by printing the Proclamation of the Accession of George V. In June the purchase of the cricket field, 'removing all uncertainty and misgivings on this all important subject', was celebrated. Editorials, which had become briefer since 1878, were now on the way out. After the July issue there were none for several years. The requirements of sustained continuous prose had evidently become too taxing. In place of the editorials came random collections of 'Notes', most of them snippets of school news and many of them aimed at OSE rather than pupils or parents. Ten columns carried analyses of every cricket match, but only eight were given to the rest of the sports. The *Chronicle* had become addicted to batting and bowling averages and other sporting statistics. They appeared together with character sketches of the leading sportsmen.

No one would claim that the *Chronicle* has been a great force for schoolboy literary life. Mostly it has been dull, a mere 'chronicle' in fact, though the routine character of its coverage of facts and events has benefits for the school's historian. Yet the early issues, in the 1870s and early 1880s, were more varied in coverage than their successors. God and the Chapel, sermons, pious speeches at prize-giving, as well as puzzles and anecdotes, supply the spice of variety.

Thereafter the steady shift towards the priority of sport gives a more monochrome feel, especially from the late 1880s. Less is conveyed of the range of boys' interests and accomplishments, and less space given to examination results or to scholarships and prizes. Even the reports of Gaudy and Commem have shortened. On the other hand, in the Edwardian period there is increasing space for the Officers' Training Corps (OTC), whose Inspection and Shooting Cup and annual camp are prominently covered in July 1910. The magazine voices the new military enthusiasm of the period in and following the Boer War. It stresses the obligations of duty, the virtues of tradition and patriotism, and the ideal of the manly all-rounder.

It is not that there were no versatile boys. One of them was Cyril Bleadon (Roll No. 1182), Senior Prefect in 1909. He was a classic Public School all-rounder, singing in the choir, captaining the XI, acting Coriolanus. He went on to Christ Church, joined the army, and in 1922 was priested. Yet the *Chronicle* gives no indication that boys of his kind existed. In 1910 it did not record a single society of the kind a boy such as Bleadon might have eagerly joined. In any case the *Chronicle* was of limited interest to the boys. More and more it was a vehicle for OSE news and, together with the Society and OSE teams, a means of binding past and present. That was a priority of Cowell, who for twenty years was in charge of every issue of the *Chronicle* and directed the boy editors, of whom there were usually three.

In 1911, during the financial crisis, Sing arranged an inspection of the school. It was conducted by four inspectors from the Board of Education on 25 and 26 July. Much of the report is statistical. It states that Sing employs nine regular and three part-time teachers, who look after 107 boarders and twelve day boys. It confirms that the boarding fee remains at £84. Of the 121 pupils inspected, three were aged nine, eight under 11, five under 12 and six under 13. So twenty-two boys were still at what we would call the prep school stage. Seventy-six per cent were aged 12–16, and 11% were over 16. There were fifteen under-14-year-olds, a further twenty-two under 15, twenty-eight more under 16, and twenty-one more under 17. Only eight were 17 and five 18 or over. 'The School,' as the Inspectors put it, 'is one offering prolonged education.' The headache for Sing was the 13% of boys aged between 9 and 12, an anomalous minority but one which the school, in its financial plight, could not afford to lose. It did, it seems, manage to hold on to them. In the years 1909–10, for example, only four 13- and 14-year-olds left. The youngsters were placed in a Lower or

Upper Third Form, 'constituting a Junior Department with the curriculum and aims of a Preparatory School'. The Inspectors noted that in the lower forms, where the ages ranged from nine to 14, all subjects except Latin were taught in one classroom by one teacher, who managed every subject except French and Arithmetic. Reminiscences of old boys contain painful memories of the bullying to which the arrangement gave rise. There were academic drawbacks too. How, as the Inspectors asked, could a History textbook be found that was suitable for the entire class? The junior curriculum included Religious Knowledge, English, History, Geography, Latin, French and Arithmetic. This syllabus the Inspectors called 'narrower in scope than is usual', for there was no Drawing, Nature Study, Manual Work or Physical Exercise (other than Military Drill) or Singing, subjects which 'add variety and interest to the Curriculum'. The Inspectors, perhaps the kind of men who like skills and pastimes to be schoolroom subjects, seem either to have discounted or to have been unaware of the extracurricular life of the school. The boys may not have been formally taught Physical Exercise or Singing but they all played games, many of them took drill, and a substantial number sang in the choir.

The Inspectors were critical of the teaching of English and Geography. Indeed 'generally the teaching, though patient and sympathetic, does not reach a high level of skill'. They remarked on the low salary rates for the staff and the poor classroom conditions, a reminder of the severe constraints under which Sing was working. In the lower school, complained the report, not enough time was found for English grammar, and boys were not even introduced to the great works of English literature. The History syllabus was not planned, and one teacher, instead of getting his pupils to read a textbook, relied solely on his own lecturing. In Geography, too, there seems to have been no planned syllabus. Mathematics left something to be desired, especially in algebra and geometry, where 'No class gave the impression that they were really being drawn out ... they develop too little intellectual consciousness and are still capable in the second Set of making really bad blunders.' The standard of attainment in Maths seemed below that demanded for entry to Sandhurst, and 'it does not cover the ground required by Woolwich'.

Other findings of the Inspectors are more positive. The Science is praised, even though 'there is considerable interference with the efficiency of the work owing to the shortness of the laboratory periods. In many cases the notebooks show unfinished experiments.' There is a tribute to the Classics teaching, which 'is in the hands of men of scholarly attainment and vigorous teaching power'. It was noted that 10–14 hours a week were spent on Latin and Greek, and that the school was organized with a view to the Scholarship Examinations at Oxford and Cambridge. The Inspectors questioned whether it was appropriate for Latin to be taught to the youngest boys, but to Sing it was axiomatic that an ability to cope with the Classics syllabus was a test of a school's status.

Of course, he knew that only a proportion of his charges would go on to university and that the less able boys would have to be content with modern subjects. Yet the results achieved at Oxford and Cambridge were a yardstick of Public School attainment. Again the school's record holds up well. The thirty-two awards won between 1883, the year of Dalton's departure, and 1907 may seem puny beside those of larger and more prestigious Public Schools. Between 1886 and 1900 alone St Paul's achieved 270 awards, Merchant Taylors' 230, Winchester 146 and Eton 142. But there were 1,000 boys at Eton, 600 at St Paul's, 500 at Merchant Taylors', and 400 at Winchester. The numbers at St Edward's hovered around 100. Besides, those famous and long-established schools had large numbers of closed scholarships at the ancient universities. The 230 awards by Merchant Taylors' included 196 closed ones. Between 1886 and 1900 Radley won 28 university awards compared to the 19 of St Edward's, but Radley too was a larger school; it had 258 boys in 1908. Throughout the 1890s St Edward's achieved results comparable with those at Thring's Uppingham, where, in 1881, he had been one of three boys to win scholarships to Cambridge in the same year.

The Inspectors had a suggestion. 'In view of the large proportion of boys who go on to the universities, an endowment providing the School with a certain number of Leaving Exhibitions would be of very special benefit to the School.' It would indeed, but the school had more pressing financial concerns. Its own scholarships and exhibitions, of which usually between four and seven were awarded each year, had to be found from current income, for there was no scholarship endowment fund.

The report praised the dormitories but remarked that 'the addition of bathrooms is desirable when funds permit'. The OSE Sholto Douglas recalled that 'the majority passed through the School without even knowing where the bathroom was located'. At least some of the rooms were looking more presentable, as a result of refitting and redecoration which Sing had instigated. With some success he tried to separate teaching areas from living areas. By now most boys had acquired the privacy of the famous 'horse-boxes'. Rooms also acquired new names, which reflected the Imperialist spirit of the time. The classroom of the Shell became 'Canada', that of the Upper Third 'Jamaica', the Upper Fourth 'Natal', the Lower Fourth 'New Zealand', and the Fifth and Sixth 'Ceylon'. Upstairs an older Tractarian vocabulary persisted. The boys, like their predecessors, slept in Combe, Ken, Beauchamp and Keble. Later, when new buildings were added to the school, the nomenclature was less expressive, as, perhaps, was the school itself. 'New Buildings' (1882) would be followed by 'Memorial Buildings' (1925) and the 'New Hall' (1975).

The Inspectors produced some thorough figures on the social origins and the futures of the boys. They described an overwhelmingly middle-class school: 112 of the 119 boys were of 'the Professional classes', though five had 'Wholesale Traders' for fathers. Twenty-two boys lived in or near Oxford, 94 were from the rest of England, three from outside the country. The geographical spread was typical of a Public School. Though 85% of boys had been to a school before they came to St Edward's, the remainder had been privately educated. The report reveals that since the school's inception 130 pupils had become clergymen and that about the same number had entered banking and trade. Ninety had joined the army and military police and 46 had taken up careers in education. In the spirit of the time the Inspectors pay homage to the ideal of military service, noting that 'the detailed *Roll* and the Obituary [section] reveal a long list of men who have served with distinction, both in the United Kingdom and in its Dependencies'.

The curt final sentence of the report reads: 'There is a service regularly, morning and evening, in the School Chapel.' The school's religious life, a life without which it would never have been founded, was of minimal interest to the Board of Education Inspectors. To it we now turn.

17

IN CHAPEL

Wilkinson's Chapel stands in a position in the school where it cannot be ignored. It asserts itself not just by its situation but by its Gibraltar and Bath stone facings, which contrast with the red brick around it. From its elegant tower and spire the young sainted martyr, King Edward, looks down across the Quad. When Simeon arrived from New Inn Hall Street he brought with him the ideal of a medieval college. He wanted to re-create the structures of a Christian community that he had known at Winchester and Christ Church. Simeon's aims were not just Christian. They were to a degree monastic, or at any rate collegiate. So there would be cloisters, to link buildings which, as at Winchester and Christ Church, were designed for the liturgical round – the processional singing of services by the choir, in accordance with monastic practice – as well as for teaching. The first part of the cloisters to be built linked the Main Buildings with the Chapel's original entrance, 'a deeply recessed and moulded doorway' to the north-west corner of the Chapel, now the entrance from the vestry passage, which is the old cloister with its formerly open arches blocked in. The great staircase to the dormitories, now the Apsley staircase, enabled the boys to descend to prayer at day and night in the manner of monks in the Middle Ages. The services in Chapel were faithful to medieval practice too, for although Victorian High Churchmen of the age gave a renewed emphasis to the Eucharist, it was the medieval daily offices – Matins, Prime, Evensong and Compline – that predominated in the school's Chapel. Later the cloisters would be extended to the new Big School, but they never reached beyond it. So a Quad that was intended to be monastic and enclosed has remained open. Shortage of money, which thwarted 'Simeon's Dream' at the time, does not altogether explain the subsequent failure to fulfil it. Later Wardens and governors had different visions of the school. The failure to complete the Quad symbolizes the school's journey in spiritual matters from Simeon to Sing, and indeed beyond.

It is difficult for us to reconstruct the mindset, emotional and intellectual, which motivated such men as Simeon and his kindred spirits. Yet without the attempt, and unless we capture, if only in outline, the spirit of the Oxford Movement which animated them, the early religion of St Edward's will seem to us merely quaint, not its lifeblood. Simeon's background and his life at Christ Church had made him a disciple, albeit not the intellectual equal, of the leading members of the Tractarian Movement in Oxford, Liddon, Bright and King. He had been plunged into the struggles that Tractarianism had provoked. Before Simeon's arrival in Oxford, Tractarians had been attacked or sniped at in a succession of controversies provoked by their sermons, by moves to award posts or honours to their sympathizers, and by the opposition of Keble, Newman and others to the erection in 1840–42 of the memorial in Oxford to Cranmer, Latimer and Ridley, martyred Protestant divines of Queen Mary's reign.

The Tractarians were at odds not only with the world but with themselves. They were split by arguments over the question whether certain traditional Catholic doctrines were compatible with the Thirty-Nine Articles. In 1845 came the bombshell of Newman's conversion to Rome and the divided reaction to it. Those controversies weakened the Movement, in Oxford and in the wider nation. Yet other developments brought it strength. It established working-class roots. It was in London's East End, in the company of Charles Lowder, that Simeon and Madgwick Davidson had found their God, and it was in the parish of St Thomas's in Oxford that their fervent service of him had begun. It was advances into working-class parishes, and the reactions they provoked, that obliged Simeon to give physical protection to Chamberlain in Hythe Bridge Street, and that led to attacks on Ritualists at St George-in-the-East in London, where Chamberlain's own ritualism paralleled that of Lowder at St Barnabas', Pimlico. Simeon also encountered the working-class dimension of the Movement in the work of Alexander Forbes at Brechin. But the Movement did not confine its energies to the working class. It had also, in Woodard's words, its 'mission to the Middle Classes'. This was the role of the new public schools such as Radley, Rossall, Marlborough, Bradfield and, most impressively, the Woodard schools such as Lancing and Hurstpierpoint. It was the aim of St Edward's, too. Through Chamberlain's cousin, Marion Hughes, who led the sisterhood in St Thomas's parish, the school was also linked to another leading aspect of the Movement's work: its encouragement of communities of women.

Looking back during a Gaudy speech in 1900, Simeon reflected that less than a century earlier people had regarded the Public Schools as

> about the worst place they could send their sons .... They knew very well in times past religion had almost ceased to have a real influence in schools and it was because men felt this so strongly that efforts were made some half century ago to build new schools, in which, more distinctly than had been before, the principles of Christian truth should be pressed forward and kept before the minds of the scholars .... They meant to show that the Church of England was something real, and that they wished to bring up their sons in full communion with the highest principles of the Church.

Simeon was endorsing the aspiration of Arnoldianism to 'godliness and good learning', but he was also giving the movement a corrective Tractarian slant. Arnold had looked to devotion and spirituality to replace the vice and disorder of the old Public Schools. He wanted the teaching of the pagan Classics to be associated with a broader training, which was to be essentially religious. The Tractarians shared that ideal but interpreted it differently. The difference is encapsulated in the words of the sermon, one of his best, delivered by Bishop King at Commem on 12 June 1895. He titled it 'Ideals of School Life'. Speaking of the old Public Schools of the last generation he said, 'Many moral and religious boys, doubtless, came every year out of them: but morality and religion were hardly the aims of the system and the notions of the latitudinarian and political economist respecting the relation of Church and State had almost found a counterpart in the relation of the master to the boys in our public schools. The instinctive feeling, though it would not have been formally confessed, was that good scholarship, not good morals, was the legitimate aim of the schoolmaster', who 'had little to do with the boys' consciences'.

The word 'latitudinarian' was a glance at the spiritual shallowness of Arnold's liberalism. Yet, for all the differences, the educational ideals of Arnoldianism and Tractarianism were essentially the same. In both movements the Chapel was to be at the centre of a school's life, promoting proper worship and its partner morality. When Chamberlain laid the St Edward's foundation stone he hoped that the school would have a part in a wider revival of the Church and its message. On 24 July 1872 the *Oxford Guardian* unsympathetically recorded a statement by Chamberlain of his aspiration for the future of the school, which he foresaw 'making roads for the great army of God which would advance ... like a settler in Australia who went forward and cleared the bush leaving it for his children to build up a community'.

Beauchamp and Halifax were the two most active laymen of the High Church Movement, while the friends and governors of the school were a list of Tractarian heroes. In 1894–96, while Lord Aldenham was tackling the serious financial crisis under Sing, Halifax took part in negotiations for reconciliation between the Roman and Anglican churches. St Edward's, we have to remember, grew up against a background of fierce controversy, in which some of its leading supporters were attacked as crypto-Catholics and even, for the comfort they gave to the foreign power of the papacy, as traitors.

Not all Ritualists gave their blessing to the school. Sir William Heathcote, Simeon's old squire at Hursley, politely avoided close association with it. More significant was the refusal of Sir William Herschel, scion of a famous family of astronomers, to join the new Council. He had learned of the overtly religious character of a document of 1889 – 'The General Scope of the Trust' – which defined the aims of the revised governing body that would eventually be set up in 1890. The opening clauses of the text encapsulated the creed of the Oxford Movement. The first declared that the school had been 'founded to the Glory of God and the furtherance of the faith in Christ as it was held and taught by the Primitive Church before the division of East and West, and hath been received by the Church of England'. These historical references would not have pleased Anglicans of uncompromisingly Protestant inclination. But it was the second clause that especially upset Herschel. In draft it had already committed the school to holding its services in accordance with the Book of Common Prayer in perpetuity. But Liddon had persuaded Simeon, ever his faithful follower, to insert the words 'unless through God's mercy, the use of the First Prayer Book of Edward VI, or of some other equally Catholic form of liturgy, should be restored by lawful authority'. This was a minefield. The Edwardian Prayer Book of 1549 was nearer to Catholicism, both in language and rubrics, than the 1662 version, the one that was in present use. Liddon's words 'or some other equally Catholic form' were even more explosive. They revealed the extent to which men of Liddon's mind had departed from liturgical orthodoxy. They also highlighted a Tractarian dilemma, for as the law stood the only means of altering the liturgy was through the state in parliament, to whose authority in such matters Tractarians had always objected.

These controversies were given a nervous edge by the general crisis of faith, and the advance of secular values, which characterized the later nineteenth century and which exposed divisions within the High Church Movement. In 1889 Liddon preached vehemently at St Paul's Cathedral against a collection of essays, edited by Charles Gore, entitled *Lux Mundi* (the Light of the World). The volume accepted novel critical approaches to the interpretation of the New Testament and argued that 'the catholic faith' should enter 'into dialogue with modern intellectual and moral problems'. All the contributors were Tractarians. Although Liddon was dead by 1890 when the document establishing the Trust came into effect, the document aligned St Edward's with an old-fashioned side of the Movement of which it was a part.

Secular principles, among them the belief in 'manliness' which was now so powerful a force in the school's life, had become the predominant ones of society. In the school's early period many of the boys' parents were High Church clergy or else laymen in sympathy with their ideals. By the Edwardian era the proportion of them was diminishing. Would their attitudes survive the new mental climate or would they be forced to adapt to it? The place to seek an answer is the Chapel. By looking at what happened to the building, to its furnishings and equipment, to the worship and the music, we can watch the modification of Ritualism and its adjustment to the secularizing trends of late-Victorian and Edwardian England.

Ritualism was not a set of unified practices. Though Ritualist clergy were at one in trying to bring the Eucharist back into prominent and frequent use, the forms of worship they favoured varied. There was variety at St Edward's itself. Until Bishop Mackarness asked Simeon to have it removed, the Chapel had a credence table – a small side table always found in Roman Catholic churches – on which the communion vessels were placed before they were brought to the altar. And yet the plaintive request for incense in the *Chronicle* of 1877 went unanswered. Incense was never a lasting feature of worship at St Edward's and the Chapel never acquired thuribles to burn and distribute it. The design of the new Chapel accorded the Eucharist a primary role, as we shall see. And yet Mackarness told Simeon of his concern that the boys were not offered the sacrament often enough, and were having largely to make do with Matins and Evensong, where hymns or sermons predominated. Simeon assured him that all a boy who wanted to attend Eucharist needed to do was to put his name down for it. It is not hard to understand why Matins and Evensong figured so prominently in the school's calendar of services, for the whole school could attend them, whereas many boys would not yet have been confirmed and so would have been unable to take the sacrament.

Because of the liturgical emphasis of the Chapel, there were not as many sermons as at other schools. Lawrence Eyres (Roll No. 1256), who was a boy at the school from 1907 to 1911 and a master in 1920–21, remembers the absence of Sunday morning sermons. Were two sermons on a Sunday too much for St Edward's, too suggestive of the Protestant emphasis on 'the Word' in preference to the sacrament? Most of the preaching seems to have been done by visiting clergy. In New Inn Hall Street Simeon had preached twice on Sunday. Had he not done so, Chamberlain would have required the boys to make the journey to St Thomas's to hear two sermons there. But in Summertown Simeon appears to have preached only rarely, in sermons – some of which were subsequently printed – to mark such special occasions as gaudies, anniversaries and the departure of eminent members of the school. In other Anglican schools, where the churchmanship was broader, the headmaster's weekly sermon was a central device of moral education. The sermons of Charles Vaughan at Harrow, and of Benjamin Kennedy at Shrewsbury, loudly denounced sin and warned of the perils of the sinful soul. They denounced lying, thieving and dishonesty. In more coded terms they condemned 'impurity', a euphemism for masturbation, and 'beastliness', a noun betokening homosexual activity, itself an adjective that seems to have entered the language in 1897. The boys of St Edward's, whose religion was less easily reduced to injunctions of morality, were evidently spared such insistent fulmination.

Having given top priority, at a great financial cost, to the building of the Chapel, Simeon had to pay for its use. Ritualism was expensive. It required lavish architecture and lavish furnishings. It demanded choir stalls and canopies, patterned and tiled floors, stained-glass windows, an organ, bells, vestments for the clergy, altar frontals which had to be changed with the liturgical seasons, vessels for the vestry, robes for a choir, an organist, choirmasters and other musical costs, and surplices not only for the choir but for the congregation. In the 1870s boys who joined the choir had to provide their own cassocks and surplices, though the school was ready to pay parents ten shillings for a boy's robes when he left. The school's financial difficulties were for long a restraining force on the ceremonialism of its worship. When boys entered the Chapel in the 1870s they would have been struck by its bareness and coldness, which were not at all what Simeon had envisaged. The walls still had damp plastering, the widows were plain, and the canopies had yet to be installed, though the stalls, choir desks and fittings were ordered in June 1877. 'There was no organ and no money for one,' recalled Simeon. 'Two alms bags sewn by the Sisters from Wantage and a stole seemed to be the sum total of gifts so far .... A violet super-frontal is much needed, also a piece of point lace to edge the fair linen cloth.' A series of appeals was launched in the *Chronicle*: 'if anyone has some money to spare we are in great need of a pulpit, a very exquisitely carved oak one will do .... We are sure some Old Boy or other kindly disposed person must want to erect a handsome memorial to his grandmother or someone, and this is just the opportunity ... others may safely be allowed to fill in some of the windows with really handsome stained glass.' Simeon solicited donations in a sermon on 'the necessity of making our lives consistent with the exterior beauty and purity of the building'. 'Therefore let the House of God be richly adorned, for it is His dwelling-place: let the vestments of the priests blaze with gold and jewels, for they are His servants: let the altar be radiant with light' – Cowie had given six tall candlesticks – 'and flowers, for it is His throne.' Boys were given collection cards to try to raise contributions from prosperous relatives. From the proceeds every boy was to be provided with a surplice. 'The effect, we are sure, will be very nice,' said the *Chronicle*.

We shall never know how most of the boys felt about the role of religion in the school's life. Many of them, as sons of clergy, were well used to being in church. But even they may have balked at having not only to attend Chapel services but to learn the Catechism and Psalms 120–123 by heart; get to know the Book of Genesis closely; and, in the Sixth Form, to learn Old Testament history from the Pentateuch and to study the Epistles to the Thessalonians and Galatians in Greek. There are hints that the choir was not attracting many boys in the 1870s. Perhaps they were deterred by the detailed rules that governed its members. Extra pocket money, in lieu of a Tuesday half-holiday, was introduced to attract membership. Even boys who joined the choir were not always keen to stay. There was introduced what the *Chronicle* in February 1876 called 'a new and wise rule requiring three months' notice before leaving' the choir. The arrangement 'will also save great annoyance at the commencement of the term', when presumably there had been sudden shortages. An organ made by Vowles of Bristol was installed in October 1877, but, says the *Chronicle*, 'IT IS NOT PAID FOR'. Even after further appeals, and when Simeon had given £100 to pay for the organ case, there was still £450 to be found. But gifts came in steadily during the 1870s, among them a set of banners to hang against the bare walls, a corporal (a cloth placed on the altar at the Eucharist), and hangings for the lectern and pulpit. The Consecration of 1877 was followed by donations of a lace cloth for the altar, a Processional Cross, an alms dish of polished and beaten brass, and a set of markers for bibles.

If the *Chronicle* is to be trusted, the services were improved by Frederick Iliffe's arrival as choirmaster in 1879. At Gaudy on 25 November Stainer's *Magnificat* and *Nunc Dimittis* were sung, together with Iliffe's own new Commem anthem, the whole occasion tending 'to promote among us a reverent and beautiful worship'. Subsequent issues of the *Chronicle* list the music at Sunday services and on special holy days. The lists – equivalent of those of games fixtures – reveal a firm attachment to the great Victorian (then 'modern') composers such as Wood, Stainer, Ouseley and Sterndale Bennett. Summer Term 1883 is typical, with sung services on thirteen Sundays and Ascension Day, and also at the service of celebration on 5 June when Hopkins in F was sung together with Stainer's *Sing a Song of Praise*. There was admirably little repetition of service settings or anthems. March 1879 saw the hanging of the new bells by Taylor of Loughborough at a cost of £297 14s. 9d. Meanwhile the master Frederick Jellicoe was heading up an Organ Fund. It had raised £18 11s. by December 1882. Most of the donations were from fellow teachers, and he himself gave £1, as did Cowell, Shuttleworth and Vaughan, a generous sum given their small stipends. Generous too was their offer to fund a Choral Scholarship to the tune of £37.

The biggest change to the Chapel, and the most signal act of its beautification, was the addition of the stained-glass windows from 1882, nearly all of them by C. E. Kempe. Those in the chancel furthered the sacramental role of the sanctuary. The Bates family provided two of them (depicting Baptism and Confirmation) in memory of their son William, and the Eucharist window was provided by one F. Noel. The Simeons commemorated their marriage by donating windows devoted to Holy Matrimony and the Burial of the Dead, the latter acting as a general memorial to boys who had died at the school. The Ordination window had to wait until 1897, when its installation marked Queen Victoria's Jubilee.

Old boys and present pupils gave the central lancet window of the Crucifixion. Absolution and the Visitation of the Sick, which completed the set, were given in memory of a publisher, Thomas Roberts – perhaps the OSE of that name (Roll No. 329) who died in 1891 aged 29 – and of Cyril and Wilfred Wilkinson (Roll No. 260 and 399). Wilfred, who died in 1886, aged 19, was one of six brothers to attend St Edward's. These windows, still the glory of the building, embody the spirit of High Church worship of the period in their enthusiastic acceptance of the full set of seven sacraments, a position viewed suspiciously by most Protestants. There are four windows in the nave, one of them to Felicia Skene, the rest to old boys: one to Robert Tamplin, hero and victim of a fire at the Theatre Royal, Exeter; one to Joseph Sandell of the Indian Police, who died in 1908; and the last to Alfred Spurling (Roll No. 870), the first among the seventy old boys serving in the South African War to be killed in it. Gifts of windows were welcome, though there was a potential problem. Might too many individuals want to be commemorated in Chapel? What if war fatalities mounted?

Let us make a tour of the Chapel as it was in 1888, for in that year we have a helpful description of it by the OSE Harold Rogers. Passing through the main entrance from the cloister (now the vestry) we enter the most westward ten feet of the building, which formed the Antechapel. Above it was the gallery with the organ. The Antechapel was separated by a glazed oak screen from the Chapel proper, with gates to give entry. The vestry was east of the tower, and formed part of its base. Set against the screen on either side of the aisle were two long oak stalls, canopied at the aisle end. Another two long stalls, provided with arms, were in front of them, and a further four seats, with arms on both sides, were placed in front of this second row. The old communion rail from the Beauchamp dormitory chapel fronted all this seating. The Warden used the south side seat with his family, the masters the seating on the north side, with the canopied portion reserved for the senior master. Cowell did not occupy it, for he sang with the choir. Two sacristans, some senior boys and any visitors occupied the front seats with the arms. On the north side the front seats were occupied by the butler, the matron and the cook, and on the south side sat Mr and Mrs Bursey (the Warden's coachman and the sick-nurse) and Mrs Bursey's maids from the New Buildings. Bursey acted as a verger, wearing a black gown with silver mountings. Rush-bottomed chairs occupied the rest of the nave, facing north–south in the monastic manner in three blocks of three rows on each side of the aisle. The front row had some light book desks, which had survived from New Inn Hall Street. On Sundays, at both Matins and Evensong, the maidservants, gloved and bonneted, sat in the back rows. Some of the servants attended the early Eucharist, and most attended with Simeon and his family at 9 a.m. on Wednesdays, when a special household service was held. The boys sat in school order, the lowest forms in the front row starting from the west and ordered in ascending seniority to the prefects in the back row of the centre block.

This seating arrangement seems to have survived until 1890, though thereafter the monastic north-south orientation was abandoned and the chairs were turned to face eastwards and set in rows of six and seven. The maids still sat at the back, but now the boys were in front of them, still arrayed in order of seniority down to the juniors near the front. Prefects sat on the aisle chairs, no doubt to keep order. There were only five or six feet to spare between the front row and the four narrow chancel steps.

For High Churchmen the restoration of the chancels of churches to their proper sacramental place was essential. Wilkinson had met their demand. The east end was well and truly defined, and was elevated from the nave by the steps. The sacramental end of the building received further emphasis from a low oak screen, canopied stalls, and desks with carvings of Moses and St John the Evangelist. The lessons were always read by masters in holy orders. The choir seats had no front desks, so eight trebles on ther side had to accommodate their service books and music on their seats. The boys with broken voices were ranged behind them, and spare spaces at the back were occupied by the 'baby choir' of probationers and by any singers resting from a cold. The south canopied stall was for the Warden when he was officiating and not using his west end seat. The choir stalls were very close to the base of the five steps that led up to the altar. In Rogers's disapproving words, they gave the altar 'a very perched up appearance'. In 1913, in his capacity as an architect, Rogers would be largely responsible for their reduction in number and height.

Simeon had not minded the cramped impression, for to him the 'perched up appearance' was essential to the sacramental significance of the altar. Early twentieth-century worshippers had different priorities. Rogers, disapproving again, noted that behind the altar there was a reredos of three shelves 'for the numerous ornaments then in vogue'. On the top tier stood Cowie's six massive brass candlesticks and the crucifix. There were a further eight candlesticks on the lower tiers, where candles were lit for a variety of occasions and services. There were also brass vases for flowers, and yet more single and branched candlesticks were added for special occasions, when, wrote Rogers, 'the candle-power was very considerable'. Though Rogers was himself a Tractarian, whom we shall later find coming to the defence of the school's Tractarian tradition, he was of a generation not drawn to the sacramental intensity of its predecessor. His alterations of 1913 got rid of the reredos. They also widened the altar so that it could at last accommodate an imposing frontal, dating from around 1750, which had been given in 1887 by Sir Coutts Lindsay to commemorate the confirmation of his son James (Roll No. 608). The building was lit by naked gas jets grouped in sixes. They generated massive heat, as there were no ventilators. The sacristans enjoyed racing each other to ignite their six jets first. The back of the reredos obscured the lower part of the east window. I list below, with brief elucidations, the services which Rogers recorded.

Sundays
9.00 a.m. Voluntary Holy Communion with hymns at the Offertory, during Communion and after the Blessing. A sacristan served.

11.00 a.m. Matins followed by the Litany and attended by those boys not at the early service.

7.00 p.m. (or 7.30 p.m. in summer). Evensong. A full sung service with the Magnificat and Nunc Dimittis, an anthem, two hymns and a sermon, all lasting 60–70 minutes.

Weekdays
Prime for about 15 minutes between preparation and breakfast including the day's set psalm, antiphons appropriate to the season, and a hymn.

Evensong: Sung to the end of the Third Collect and with a hymn.

Red Letter saints' days
During early morning preparation the Eucharist was celebrated before breakfast and Prime was observed as usual.

Evensong, both on the eve and on the saint's day itself, began and ended with a hymn sung as the choir processed in and out.

Other services (until 1892)
Compline replaced Evensong on the first evening of term.

Ad Itinerarium, a service to prepare for the journey home, replaced Prime on the last morning of term. Boys whose voices had broken but were not in the choir joined the back rows of the choir on that morning in place of the masters who normally sang there.

(Rogers's comment on this arrangement has a shaft of irony that brings home the mixture of formality and indulgence in Simeon's running of the school: 'The masters found it discreet, I fancy, to be absent from an occasion when the bounds of reverence were apt to be exceeded.')

On the second evening of term the prefects were formally admitted to their office, kneeling at the altar rail at a special service from the office book at which the Warden presided. Similar arrangements applied on the last night of term, when the Office of the Confraternity was said and those elder boys who were leaving received their medals from the Warden as they knelt before the altar (though this practice was discontinued in 1892).

Holy Week
Palm Sunday: Matins was preceded by the singing of 'All Glory, Laud and Honour'.

For the next four days there were early celebrations of the Eucharist. The choir sat in the nave as their surplices had gone to the laundry to be crisp and clean for Easter Eve.

Good Friday: Services, at 7.00 a.m. and 9.00 a.m. and Matins at 11.30 a.m. followed by a series of short addresses and hymns. At 2.30 p.m. there was a special office including the 'Reproaches' – a rarefied Tractarian service observing the crucified Christ's rebukes to his unfaithful people – which lasted until 3.00 p.m. Evensong and Compline followed.

Easter Day: 7.00 a.m. A Eucharist for the choir and servants, followed by breakfast for the choir. At 8.00 a.m. there was a Choral Celebration of the Eucharist which the whole school attended. The Warden celebrated, flanked by two sacristans who wore scarlet cassocks. Matins and Evensong were held as usual, for it was imperative that the office be never omitted.

Choral celebrations
There were two more of these each year, on 5 June and November 25, the two Gaudies. At the summer one, which parents attended, there were special prayers and processional hymns and a sermon from a distinguished visitor.

On the last evening of the Winter Term, anticipating Christmas, the altar was vested in white, special psalms were sung, and there were carols after the service.

Occasionally there were addresses to communicants after a saint's day or Saturday Evensong. The bishop administered Confirmation in May or June.

Rogers tells us much more. Boys wishing to communicate wrote their names in a book in the Antechapel the evening before. On Saturday evenings, Sundays, saints' days and eves and in the evenings, the whole school wore surplices, loose, open-fronted and unbuttoned. Masters buttoned theirs and wore their hoods. Sacristans whose duties took them into the Chancel wore cassocks and surplices, though later the rules which had allowed no boy ever to enter the Chancel without a surplice were relaxed and sacristans were allowed to wear either a cassock or a loosed surplice. In the 1880s there were white, red and violet frontals for the altar and a white lace one for Advent and Lent. There were also white, green, violet and red chasubles, some of which are still in the Chapel vestry, including the fine red altar cloth designed by Kempe and worked by the Sisters of St Thomas's in 1883. The red chasuble with angels playing musical instruments worked by the Sisters of St Mary's House, East Grinstead, was given to the school ten years earlier.

Simeon's regime was modified by his successors. Hobson abolished Prime and shortened Matins and Evensong in January 1893, and reduced the number of Good Friday services. Some services were made voluntary, among them preparation for communion and Compline on weekday evenings in Lent. Hobson's changes were not radical, but they are indicative. As we have noticed, there was a fear that the demands of religious observance made of boys in High Church schools might be unpopular among prospective parents. Warden Ferguson was to introduce further relaxation when he dropped the rule that the school must always celebrate Easter at school, whatever the date on which it fell.

Criticism of its religious practices from outside the school had continued. In September 1885 a copy of the Office Book reached the *English Chronicle*, which went to town against this 'great red pile ... intended for a school and that, too, of the very highest Puseyite type. It is all part of a "ritualistic Conspiracy" confirmed by the Office Book. Even the many-headed educational monster which Canon Woodard has set up has developed nothing like it.' Particularly to be condemned was the apparent practice of Confession: 'The Book contains a "Form to be Used in Confession" employing at its start precisely the words of the Roman Confessional .... Here the very innermost recesses of the poor boy's heart are to be laid open to the prurient gaze of his "Spiritual Father", of whom – rather than from God and his Son – he is made to ask penance, counsel and absolution!' The paper calls the school a confraternity, alleges that prayers are said for the departed, and claims that the role of priesthood is being outrageously elevated. In support of the last charge it quotes an Ember Hymn, which, it alleged, was used in the Chapel:

> The priests of the Most High,
> A band of kingly race,
> From Christ the Great High Priest
> Unbroken lineage trace.

'Surely the force of blasphemy can no further go.' The report decries the vestments as a 'royal wardrobe, which shall furnish a goodly store of gorgeous vestments wherewith they may meet the King when he comes 'neath sacramental sign'. The frontals are condemned, and 'your true Ritualist never hesitates to run up a heavy ecclesiastical tailor's bill .... This is not the voice of Christ, it is the voice of Anti-Christ.' The service of Ad Itinerarium, adds the *English Chronicle*, presumes to refer to 'the ministration of angels'. Even the use of the Chapel vestry comes under attack. As the choir don their cottas and cassocks, the priest, in a separate recess, 'repeats certain Latin prayers before a crucifix while he puts on the various articles required for the celebration of MASS'. The accuracy of these charges is, alas, impossible to assess.

We have noted the rapid and thorough advance of games, competition, team values and 'manliness'. These were not by themselves bound to undermine Ritualist worship. There was no conscious move to modify the old values, let alone an abandonment of them. Yet changes of attitude there were. Some of them were to be expected. The intensity of Simeon's vision was unlikely to be matched by his successors. To him the Chapel 'must always remain ... the centre of my love: this dreadful place where we have so often met God face to face ... the image which of all others I shall delight to take out'. The words are from his farewell sermon of December 1892 when, in an emotional reverie of recollection, he seeks to 'look at and dream over the [sight] most sacred and lovely to me': 'the touching sight we have so often witnessed here, the crowds of white robed boys, which fancy depicts as angels, kneeling before God's throne on earth'. The abandonment of the Confraternity, which had occupied so prominent a place in Simeon's hopes, was symbolic, as was the removal of its place in the Office Book. Simeon's approach had come to seem rather cloying, rather personalized, and rather ostentatious. Its following had narrowed. The OSE represented a much wider constituency than the Confraternity. A diminishing number of boys were products of the rectories of England who intended to replicate their fathers' careers. More and more leavers looked to the new freedoms of the Nineties, or to worldly success in the professions, in the armed forces, or to the opportunities of public service in an Imperial universe. It was not that the Oxford Movement itself had become disreputable. Crown patronage was bestowed on High Church clerics, for whose social work there was general admiration. Many of their liturgical innovations, notably those involving candles or providing for more vestments and more communion services, were adopted by non-Tractarian churches. Yet the more extreme Ritualists, with whom St Edward's tended to be associated in the public mind, aroused suspicion and hostility.

And so the fervour seemed to go out of the Chapel. The failure of the school authorities to notice or commemorate the 25th anniversary of the laying of the Chapel's foundation stone belongs to this pattern. A plaintive letter which appeared in the school *Chronicle* in June 1900 enquired 'why we allow our Patron Saint's Days to pass absolutely unnoticed .... In our Office Book we have a St Edward's Day hymn. Why not use it? Why are we never told anything about him? It does not redound to our credit that we have let the observance of these festivals fall through.' Now and for decades to come, the services spoke more of the togetherness of the community than of a devotional ideal. Simeon's vision of holiness yielded to the hearty singing of popular hymns. Chapel attendance was an act of allegiance more to the school than to God. Morality, which the Oxford Movement had been eager to teach, was being separated from the spirituality which was the Movement's light, yet which now had a less wide and less intense emotional appeal than the winning of games and the winning of wars.

We return to Bishop Edward King's Commem sermon of June 1895. King was one of the Ritualists to be rewarded with a bishopric. Though never free of controversy, he was the most saintly and intelligent of his Tractarian generation. The analysis offered by his sermon was acute. 'Schools,' he said, 'can and should teach that "manners makyth man". Yet self-knowledge, self-mastery, self-culture, all this and far more might be included in the motto, without reaching that higher level of morality which distinguished Christian from Heathen Ethics'. He explained that what the High Church schools had achieved, unlike the broader Arnoldian ones, was to ensure that sacramental Catholic Christian values undergirded the morality of their communities and indeed all the education the schools offered. Was not that achievement under threat? Were not work and games now being given a higher value than the spirituality that should motivate them? King's words belonged to a nationwide debate about religious education which did not focus solely on the Public Schools. There were questions about the denominational forms that religious education should take in the new state schools, and even about whether they should teach religion at all. In face of such developments there was a growing fear that children from all classes might lack basic Christian knowledge. Liddon had said, 'We none of us probably adequately comprehend the degree of ignorance or half-knowledge, vague, baseless, meaningless, in which multitudes of our educated classes grow up. They have never had a month's real and serious teaching about the rudiments and first principles of the Christian revealed truth.'

It was not only religious knowledge that was under threat. Touching on another danger, King proceeds to sensitive ground: 'There might be an imperfect tendency of other bonds of Brotherhood which made their School, their "House", their "Home" as important centres of loyalty as the Chapel', and so carried 'that virtue to the excess of a vice'. Those 'other bonds' were secular ones. It was, King was intimating, dangerous to limit the values of a school to the secular claims of group loyalty and of patriotism. For 'the House to be sought is the House of God'. Yet King, having advanced these criticisms, half retreated from them. Perhaps, he tactfully conceded, there had in the previous generation been 'some failure in consequence of a reaction from the general intellectual teaching' in favour of 'the personal spiritual training of individual souls, but now we believe that true balance is being obtained'.

The Boer War brought home and heightened the changes that had troubled King. In 1903, after so many wounds and deaths, and so much heroism, had been recorded, a decision was taken to line the nave of the Chapel with oak panels to which plaques to honour the dead would be attached. At a stroke the character of the Chapel had been altered and its appearance transformed. Henceforth it would be a kind of mausoleum, a monument to dead Old Boys linking the youth of the present with their dead school heroes and uniting both in a building dedicated to loyalty, patriotism, Imperialism, and the virtues of struggle and sacrifice for the group. The founding ideal of the school as a nursery of the soul had been supplanted.

18

GAMES

Much the longest poem in the early *Chronicles* was written by Herbert Harper (Roll No. 141), one of two brothers at St Edward's in the 1870s. He was Senior Prefect and captain of the earliest Rugby XV of which we have a record. Entitled 'The Football Match', the poem differs from the other verse in the magazine not only in its length but in its subject matter. Apart from the occasional piece of translation, most of the poems were brief celebrations of nature and its seasons. They carried such titles as 'Morning', 'Arise the merry morn has come', and 'Evening'. 'The sun went down behind a cloud/ But all around his radiance shed', reads one. Herbert's poem, an account of the XV in action, fills a whole column. It describes a match against Northern House on 4 March 1873, played on a pitch off Norham Gardens, for this was before the school had its own playing fields. Selections will convey the spirit of the poem. The other boys named in it are Russell Bencraft (Roll No. 182, aged 15), George Dickinson (Roll No. 189, aged 17), and Charles Preedy (Roll No.167, aged 17 or 18 and one of six brothers at the school).

> For they are all St Edward's lads, and on this very day,
> The fourth of March at half past two, it was arranged to play
> A game of football fierce and rough ....
> Who've come to see St Edward's fight and bravely win the day ...?
> The 'Northern heroes' hove in sight, singing right merrily
> 'Ho ho' they thought 'what tiny chaps! We're twice as big as they.

A florin is tossed and Herbert loses the call.

> And so the 'Northerns' won the toss, and had their pick of goal.
> And fifty other boys there stand, against the field of play,
> While a burning thirst for vengeance filled each brave Edwardian's soul.

Herbert kicks off. The ball is caught by an opposition half-back who

> Then charging like a warhorse, through the forwards burst his way
> Till he met that plucky Bencraft, who like a tiger on his prey,
> Springs on his back and brings him down with a cry unto the ground ....
> Aha, there's plucky Dickinson, he's got the ball at last,
> And now while rushing onward, the entangled mass he's passed;
> But now the 'Northern' captain has caught him round the waist!
> And now's the time St Edward's the 'Northern's' strength to taste.
> But no! You are not beaten yet, there's Preedy – dear old soul! –
> Has got the ball and touched it down behind the Northern goal.

Herbert converts the try. St Edward's has scored three goals.

> So we will leave what is untold for history to tell,
> While we'll rejoice for evermore, that St Edward's fought so well.

The game being played was different from the one we know. Though rugby teams were normally 15-strong the rule was not invariable until 1891. The *Chronicle*'s account reveals that in this game only nine a side were fielded. Another difference is that touching the ball down did not, as now, earn a team points. It simply provided an opportunity to kick for goal, and on this occasion Harper's kicking secured a victory by three points. What of the spectators? If there were fifty of them, as the poem tells us, then most of the school was either playing or watching. Did the spectators attend of their own accord, or was pressure put on them? If the latter, the pressure would have come from the boys. For although, in this infancy of organized games, members of the staff sanctioned them and sometimes took an interest in them, it was the boys who arranged the fixtures.

Herbert Harper's fondness for games and his evocation of boyhood enjoyments are authentic. Such enthusiasm was the stuff of school sporting stories in books and boys' magazines in the decades that followed. But it was not universal. One of those probably in the crowd was Kenneth Grahame, then aged 15 and later Harper's successor as Senior Prefect. Though he too would play in the XV he was a much less conspicuous member of the team. His preoccupations were different. Walking and observing were the key to his childhood, as they were to many others in the nineteenth century. His early years, spent by the Thames in Oxford and Berkshire, were marked by the love of nature and its 'magic' that we find in his *Dream Days* and in *The Wind in the Willows*, a book which has behind it long unsupervised walks during his time at St Edward's, on which he watched and absorbed the natural world. Of course he was a sensitive soul, of literary bent, but many other boys used their spare time in similar ways at a school which took no real responsibility for their lives outside the classroom. In 1913 Grahame wrote an essay for the *Chronicle* entitled 'The Fellow That Goes Alone'. It compares his own experience to the early years of St Edmund of Abingdon, whom his imagination places among lush water meadows in the town. 'Especially,' writes Grahame,

> we should envy him his white vision in the meadow: for which he should be regarded as the patron saint of all those who of set purpose choose to walk alone, who know the special grace attending to it .... For nature's particular gift to the walker, through the semi-mechanical act of walking – a gift no other form of exercise seems to transmit in the same degree – is to set the mind jogging, to make it garrulous, excited, a little mad maybe – certainly creative and super sensitive .... Then gradually everything seems to join in, sun and wind, the white road and the dusty hedges, the spirit of the season, which ever that may be, the friendly old earth that is pushing forth life of every sort under your very feet or spellbound in death like a winter trance.

What would Harper have made of these reminiscences? By the 1870s scorn was beginning to descend on free spirits such as Grahame. They had freedom – but a freedom that was coming under threat at St Edward's as at the older Public Schools. It was not only solitariness or wandering that was frowned on. It was spacious, uncontrolled leisure. Liberty, it was feared, could become licence. After all, not all boys, if left to their own devices, spend their time observing the seasons and their changes, or studying birds' eggs or fossils. Many Victorian boys, if they were rich enough, preferred beagling, riding to hounds and a variety of blood sports, activities that had acquired a bad name in high-minded quarters. They were held to encourage gambling and to lead to the bashing up of locals and the seduction of their daughters. Arnoldianism went to war on such abuses. Its disciplines and proprieties, imposed through a reform of the Prefect system, a greater emphasis on the Chapel, and a more rigorous imposition of the Classical curriculum, were geared to a sterner moral outlook. But something more was needed. If morality were to be instilled, the traditional disorderliness of the communities of boys had to be overcome. A means had to be found of organizing pupils en masse.

Unruliness was not confined to old aristocratic schools like Winchester and Eton. It affected the new Public Schools too, especially as their numbers grew. Marlborough experienced 'The Great Rebellion' of 1851–52 when, having wreaked damage outside the school, the 'rebels' more or less took over the college, 'trashing' it, as we would now say, and defying the headmaster and his teachers in spite of mass floggings. It was a salutary lesson for all headmasters in these new Public Schools, who saw the need to look beyond the philosophy of 'godliness and good learning' if the new middle classes were confident that they could entrust their sons to a boarding school. George Cotton, the headmaster appointed at Marlborough after the riots, has been credited with having introduced organized games to solve the problem of control, but the methods he employed were to be found across the schools. A new breed of headmasters (some of whom had been masters under Arnold at Rugby) gradually moved towards first the recognition, and then the facilitating, of team games. The result, slowly but surely realized, was a profound shift in conceptions of the formation of character. In essence, the games field took over from the Chapel. This was happening in both the new and old Public Schools at the time when Chamberlain and Simeon were pioneering their own school. The cult of games emerged in the decade following the move to Summertown in 1873. In those years the generation of enthusiasm by pupils themselves gave way to compulsion. The organization of games grew, and with it the competitiveness that flourished with the Set system.

We start with the voluntary beginnings. Why was it that, at St Edward's as elsewhere, boys started, with little adult encouragement, to choose to spend their free time playing games which required the disciplines of organization and training? Why did ramblers become athletes; why did 'messing about in boats' give way to river-racing; and why was larking around with racquets replaced by fives and tennis? What had become of 'the fellow that goes alone'? Or what was the experience of, say, a boy who entered the school after being privately tutored, or who came from a small family and who sought, in the larger community of St Edward's, to preserve his own individuality or develop his own hobbies?

Such a boy was Harold Peake, the son of the Rev. J. Peake, whose recollections of St Edward's we have already met. He entered the school in September 1877 at the age of nine, and left in 1884, aged 16 and a prefect. Just after him came his brother Walter (Roll No. 411), who was born in 1869 and also arrived aged nine but who left in 1883 aged only 14, when he was moved to Marlborough. Later Walter went to Sandhurst and proceeded to a successful army career. It would be good to know why both boys were removed prematurely. Marlborough was more expensive, so the answer can hardly lie in the agricultural depression that was putting school fees beyond the reach of many clergy. Was Walter unhappy? Certainly Harold was at first, for he tells us so in a memoir composed in 1932: 'I was left alone at St Edward's, a rather shy little boy, far from robust and not yet ten years of age. For the first fortnight I was utterly miserable, and, though in time I managed to tolerate the conditions with a certain amount of stoicism, I was never really happy during the seven long years that I spent there.' How much did the pressures of collective sport contribute to his unhappiness? 'Most men's memories of school life', he recalled, 'are filled with recollections of the games in which they took part and which overshadow all other activities.' But Harold had a 'weak herd instinct' that had made him disliked. 'I played games only from a sense of duty and felt a distinct relief at their termination. I had always rather wander in the country around, observing nature in her varied moods .... I have never been able to rouse any enthusiasm for running after a ball but I have lived a full life of enjoyment and have never lacked for interest in any part of the world to which my travels have taken me.'

So Peake is one of Grahame's 'fellows that go alone'. His memoir shows him as an outsider in relation not only to games but to the classroom, where he remembers the instruction boys received as being inimical to real observation and thinking. 'Since my earliest childhood I had been interested in Natural History and this interest increased as the boredom with more orthodox occupations grew deeper.' In the late 1870s it was still possible to avoid games, at least for most of the time. His memories take us into the fields around Wolvercote village and to the disused railway cutting nearby. He watched and collected insects, bred larvae, and dug for pupae. Butterflies became a consuming passion. He wrote to Lord Abingdon – who thought his correspondent a master of the subject – to get permission to walk in Wytham Woods. In wintertime he turned to geology and hunted for fossils. Soon he was making visits to the University Museum and consulting with dons. 'Most of the masters disapproved and would have preferred that I remain to watch the matches. They were not sure that my activities were not subversive of school discipline. The Headmaster [Dalton] gave me a serious talking to about expending too much interest on what his classically trained mind shrank from calling "hobbies".' Only one full-time master, that exceptional figure Cowell, was sympathetic to Harold's interests. Peake praises Cowell's productions of plays, his supervision of the *Chronicle*, his organization of concerts, his support for the choir. It is a tribute that confirms Cowell's sometimes single-handed role in the development of a range of activities away from both the classroom and the playing fields.

Peake was fortunate to be taken under the wing of the young OSE Aubyn Trevor-Battye. Trevor-Battye had been at the school for only two years, from 1871, and had left eleven years before Peake. Ten of those years, Peake tells us, Trevor-Battye spent 'shooting and studying bird life'. He was no academic high-flyer, for at Christ Church he kept failing 'Smalls', the examinations to qualify for residence. Yet he had many talents. While he was studying for his passes Simeon employed him, nominally as his secretary. He helped with the *Chronicle* and wrote for it. He organized concerts, sang in the choir, and acted Mark Antony, Shylock and Wolsey in Cowell's productions. 'Battye and I,' recalls Peake, 'soon became fast friends, and he always treated me with a degree of equality quite unexpected considering the difference in our age and status.' Here is a relationship reminiscent of earlier Victorian education, which had seen easy and sometimes intimate relationships between boys and adults that would have been frowned on in later years. Aubyn was a free spirit, another goer-alone. Together he and Peake formed the Field Club and established a museum for Natural History objects. Accounts of the two young people figure frequently in the *Chronicles* of the early 1880s. Aubyn, having got his BA in 1886, went on to become a distinguished explorer and a writer of adventurous travel books.

A decade earlier Harold would not have felt an isolated figure, or been subjected to the demands of conformity that the rise of sport would bring. The change was far-reaching. As early as 1873, when a cricket First XI had barely been created, letters in the *Chronicle* asked why no Second XI had been formed; complained that 'the grass on the Meads does not look very promising'; and wondered why boys who had showed they could swim a required distance should not be allowed to set up a rowing club.' A further letter in the same year, which asked whether there might be a 'uniform' for the cricket team, hints at the rise of the taste for sartorial distinction in games and for the uniformity of clothing that marks a team's solidarity. A letter of April 1874 complained that the development of cricket was being held up by the lack of a pitch. From 1875 the names of boys with rugby colours were painted on shields hung in the dining room. Rowing would follow in 1888, cricket in 1890.

The growth of 'colours', both school and Set, followed a rising trajectory of team spirit, hierarchy and formality. From time to time old boys, who had their own array of sports clubs, applied pressure on behalf of school games. There was a plea that a race for old boys be held on Athletics Day. But in 1876 it was pressure from boys that secured the appointment of a professional cricket coach, Alfred Merritt. The *Chronicle* is peppered with requests from pupils for more games and better facilities. Remarking on the Athletics Day of March 1874, one writer offers a confident generalization about the worth of games:

> We are not going to enter upon the question of their abstract value or desirability: among Englishmen there can be no doubt on the subject. We have got bodies to be trained as well as minds. No sane person, we imagine, would take an absence of enthusiasm about athletics and field sports for a sign of intellectual or moral vitality in a school .... We are concerned with ordinary members of society, not with prize pupils and philosophers; with athletes if you please, not brainless bipeds .... Our business is to systematise both activities, bodily and mental, mental and bodily.

Such sentiments reflected a national trend. The development of organized games for middle-class children was part of a social revolution in which the appeal of sport hugely expanded, not least because sport was reduced to order. Sport became palatable not only to the aristocracy and to the working class but to the expanding stratum of society in between, which tended to be more restrained and conventional. The games that had been popular before the Victorian period, versions of football, cricket, boxing, racing on foot and in boats, had been fundamentally lawless. Over the nineteenth century they acquired rules. Team games not tamed by rules can become dangerous mêlées, encouraging drink, violence and riot. The rich had their own violent and unregulated games, as the Eton Wall Game testifies, but it was working-class disorder that the authorities feared. The Industrial Revolution had brought large groups of working-class men together. Quelling a village riot after a spontaneous unregulated game was one thing: controlling such gatherings in a city, with next to no police force, was well nigh impossible.

Rules were the answer – and money was the key. Rules and order are more easily constructed if money controls them. Money found another means of establishing control: the organization of gambling, which spread among all classes. Horse-racing, a rich man's sport because of its costs (horses, training, courses, jockeys, grooms, etc.), attracted the lower classes by the prospect of a flutter and became a well-regulated sport which crossed social boundaries. Boxing likewise won wealthy backing and attracted working-class gamblers, and eventually the Queensberry Rules would give it respectability too.

The new public mood of seriousness, which cleaned up the old Public Schools and informed the foundation of new ones, also came to associate morality with exercise. Walking (climbing by the Alpine Club, for example) and Swedish drill (gymnastics on bars and ropes) became highly popular among those with the leisure and freedom to pursue them. The same spirit came to Oxford University, and to St Edward's. Warden Sing was a restless walker. And there are all those long walks, intense with feeling or conversation, taken by Oxford men, such as the expeditions that took Matthew Arnold to Boar's Hill, with its view of the 'dreaming spires', and Gerard Manley Hopkins to Binsey and its poplars. But walking, while by no means always solitary, was not ordinarily a team game or a magnet to the competitive spirit. Competitive team games came to seem gentlemanly when young men at the old universities took them up.

The organizational practices of the well-off were soon followed by the lower orders. In industrial towns and cities, manufacturers were behind the founding of football clubs, which became professionalized as players from working-class backgrounds took to the game and as the railway system increased the scope for fixtures. The legalization of professionalism in soccer in 1885 was a demonstration of a working-class identity. Yet it was middle-class schools and universities that formed and settled the rules of sports. The rules at Rugby in 1845 allowed the handling of the ball, whereas those at Eton in 1849 forbade it. Rules devised at Cambridge in 1873, which banned the use of hands, were adopted by the new Football Association in the same year. Clubs and schools that disliked this sport took up the game we now call Rugby Union, which would later split into its Union and League forms. Associations were founded: the Amateur Athletic

Association in 1866, the Rugby Football Union in 1871, the Lawn Tennis Association in 1888. While the upper and middle classes generally retained their control of the games, the football teams of the industrial towns of the North and Midlands, often based on pubs, could escape it. In the other major sports, gentlemen not only retained control but did much of the playing. Cricket was developed and controlled by a landowning class, who established the game on an old rural base and owned the facilities. The Marylebone Cricket Club succeeded in devising generally accepted rules in 1835, and, with some reluctance, professionals – 'Players' – were admitted alongside the amateur 'Gentlemen'. The Public Schools took to cricket once they had fields for pitches and could contemplate hiring a professional coach, as St Edward's did in appointing the cricket coach Merritt. Rowing, the alternative summer team game, had the social appeal of offering days at the river. The first Henley Regatta was held as early as 1839. The sport was adopted at Eton and Westminster, and the universities soon followed.

Headmasters of the large Public Schools realized that games, and the enthusiasm of so many boys for them, provided an opportunity to manage the pupils and keep them occupied between work and sleep. Boys of all ages and aptitudes could be marshalled into teams. The esteem of games and of the 'bloods' who shone at them strengthened existing hierarchies and was in turn enhanced by them, for the captains of sport, and owners of colours, tended to be prefects. New arguments for the virtue of sport emerged. It was said to channel competitiveness and violence into healthy courses while promoting the manly virtues of physical fitness, which itself was proclaimed to be an antidote to vice. How often was the taking of exercise, and of cold showers after it, contrasted with the temptations of the sedentary boy, content to read or draw or talk, whose idleness also depleted the team and so let the side down!

Yet it took time for games to become compulsory. A mental change was needed, for boys' freedom in the use of their leisure hours had been taken for granted. Compulsion had extended only to the spheres of Chapel attendance and the daily timetable in and out of the classroom. Harrow was probably the first major Public School to make games compulsory, and it was several years before its decision was fully enforced. At Lancing, a Woodard school, rugby was compulsory every day by 1888, but cricket was obligatory only three days a week. At Uppingham in the following year games were compulsory only three days a week.

At St Edward's, too, compulsion was introduced in the 1880s. Competition between the new sets helped to embed its practice. In two respects St Edward's was not typical. It was small and it was poor. Inter-school fixtures, which are essential to the status of games, demanded a pool of boys to draw on. By the 1880s the number of boys at St Edward's hovered, as we have seen, around 100, of whom quite a few were of prep school age. The school's fixtures, most of them with Oxford colleges, were often played with under-strength teams. Secondly, games are expensive. They require fields that have to be maintained and prepared by a labour force. Other facilities were needed, too. In 1886, even though, as Simeon said, 'times were very bad', parents gave £300, and Simeon himself £700, to provide a gymnasium and to pay an instructor, 'Bill' Adams. In 1888 the indoor swimming bath was being built. Its rectangular formality was designed with a mind to the swimming races that were impracticable in the outdoor 'bathing place', the great kidney-shaped construction which, in 1876, had been dug by boy volunteers working under Ernest Letts. Apparently the shape of the outdoor pool was to have been oval but was modified so as to skirt an ash tree. Its original wooden lining was subsequently replaced with concrete, and a reconstruction was initiated in 1896. The outdoor pool was built for leisure, not for competitive sport, and its relaxing character would later be enhanced by the development of gardens around it.

The year 1875 marks a step forward in the development of games. An article in the *Chronicle* of April encapsulates the zest for them. Evidently written by a keen senior, it discusses the principle of compulsion, noting that it is being tried in football but is thought less appropriate to cricket. In a tone of exhortation often adopted in the *Chronicle* by senior boys advising junior ones, the author voices the hope 'that a little more zeal and energy may be exhibited than seemed to be displayed last year'. It was in the same year that the school for the first time used a cricket pitch in the area where the XI now plays. The XI drew up rules, 'confirmed by a meeting of masters', which required members to pay subscriptions: six shillings for the Upper Game, four for the Middle Game, and 2s. 6d for the Lower Game. The most senior prefect in the XI was automatically to be captain. Only the Upper Game might use the new pitch, and the rest must continue to make do with the Meads, whose shortcomings occasioned so much complaint. The captains were to run all the games, though they must 'pay deference to the advice or judgement of any master exerting himself in the interests of the club'. More specific rules follow. A boy treasurer will administer the subscriptions, which are to be audited by Simeon and published in the *Chronicle*.

The arrangements for the organization and financing of cricket belong to a common pattern in the Public Schools of the time, when clubs and societies were a thriving practice. The XI's rules reveal the extent to which the running of games was left to the boys, with the school providing distant supervision. They also indicate the school's answer to the problem of finance: if the boys wanted games, let them at least largely meet the costs. Simeon had paid for the new ground from his own pocket, but the boys and their supporters had to find the money for a pavilion. Supportive friends and parents gave money towards the £38 needed to make a start on the building, Simeon contributing ten guineas. In February 1876, when the cricket accounts were published, they recorded boy subscriptions amounting to £19 12s. 6d. They also reveal that the cricket club was subsidizing the rugby football: three guineas had been spent on footballs and six shillings on touch flags; £13 was put towards the pavilion. At the same time the School Shop account revealed a surplus of £17 4s. 4d. Boys eager for the subsidizing of games would soon be eyeing the Shop's income as a potential source.

But it was rugby, not cricket, that dominated the columns of the *Chronicle*. The reports of rugby matches, and descriptions of individual players, became fuller. Of Kenneth Grahame in the XV it was said: 'A useful forward: always upon the ball, lacks weight and strength'. Other players lacked them too, for three members of the team were under seven stone and the heaviest was only 10st. 12 lb. Some rugby fixtures in the 1880s were still played with fewer than 15 men. In 1883 Bromsgrove School, one of the most regular of the school opponents, refused to field more than 12 players. The number of inter-school fixtures grew slowly. Rugby School's first fixture was not held until 1867, and the University Club, whom St Edward's played, dated only from 1871. A match against St Paul's College, Stony Stratford, was played 'upon their swamp'. Since Oxford colleges were the most frequent opponents, there must have been significant weight differentials. A few masters played for the XV and no one seems to have objected. The edition of the *Roll* produced in 1890 recorded that in 1878–79 two masters had played in six matches and 'probably in five others'. They seem to have made a difference, for in that season 11 of the 14 matches were won. Only in 1883, however, did the *Chronicle* first give the names of playing masters. They were J. K. Watkins, the Rev. E. J. Vaughan and C. S. Knight. The first match against the OSE was as early as 1875, but not until 1884 was a regular OSE club set up, and it had to be re-founded in 1887. Largely a local team, it played against the school and against Oxford colleges. The OSE Cricket Club was founded in 1885.

Between 1873 and 1897 there were only six seasons when the school won more rugby fixtures than it lost. The number of games played against Oxford colleges may help to explain the imbalance, but Stony Stratford, Leamington College and Bromsgrove all recorded more wins than losses against St Edward's, where enthusiasm seems mostly to have exceeded skill. Only occasionally did the school field a Second XV, despite frequent requests for one. The occasional junior fixture was played. The XV coached themselves, though during his Wardenship Sing would referee matches and senior games. Probably the Rev. C. L. Labat, appointed in 1898, was the first master to coach the juniors. By 1905 adult coaching had become a regular feature. By that time, too, the fixture list had been reduced. The XV of 1905 was run by Charles Gillett, who was described by the *Chronicle* as introducing 'scientific forward play of the modern kind'. John Bussell (Roll No. 972) succeeded him in 1910. Coaching by masters improved the results. In 1908, after thirteen years of losses against Bromsgrove, the school's oldest rivals, came victory at last. Over the next five years St Edward's would beat Bromsgrove nine times in eleven matches. The rise in standards placed the school on rugby's national map. A striking number of OSE played first-class rugby football in the decade before the Great War.

Rugby and other games entered the school's bloodstream. The standing of St Edward's, as of other Public Schools, was to a large degree measured by its games results. Within the school the team ethos had acquired ever more repute. In three long articles in the *Chronicle* – which are beautifully written – Gillett argued that the members of a successful team require not only physical prowess but intellectual qualities. Brawn and brain were therefore allies. Gillett, a clever Classicist and himself a distinguished games player, answered to the new Public School ideal, as a man wholesome in both body and mind.

Cricket developed alongside rugby, but it cost more to operate, which is probably why the XI took the initiative described above. A cricket pitch requires the careful attention of groundsmen, while the employment of professional coaches, which had become an accepted practice in this otherwise rather aristocratic sport, posed financial problems. Alfred Merritt, the first such coach, was paid £16 for eight weeks' work in the summer of 1876 and a further £2 for an extra engagement. He also submitted a bill for £12 11s. 6d for acting as groundsman. Costs rose further, for a year later his coaching stipend was £28 and his additional bill £12. A boy servant was paid 8s. 6d for work on the grounds in 1875, a sum cut to 7s. 6d in 1876, when a man named Burborough was paid £9 2s. 'for rolling'.

In the same year the account secured a donation of £20 from the School Shop. Sport was to build a close relationship with the Shop, which was soon making annual donations. The costs of games rose in parallel with the enthusiasm for them. By 1878 there was a separate balance sheet for the fives court. Subscriptions were demanded, £3 17s. 6d being raised for the Christmas Term. By 1880 the growth of athletics had produced a separate Athletics Account. The involvement of masters seems to have come about more quickly in cricket than in other games. Dalton and Jellicoe both played in the XI from time to time, though they do not appear in the published lists of team members, and the practice of masters playing seems to have ended in 1883. Jellicoe belonged to a new breed of graduates, who brought both academic and athletic accomplishments to the job. He was a 'blue' and a Hampshire county player. The XI had a lean spell in the 1880s. In 1882, for instance, it averaged fewer than 60 runs per innings, a low figure even for that time. In 1883 only three members of the team had a batting average of over six. But the team was much more successful in the 1890s, when cricket had better results than rugby. A number of the players of that decade would return in later years to play for the OSE against the school. The XI's successes are succinctly described in one of the essays by Derek Roe (Roll No. 4623) that form appendices to Desmond Hill's *History* and recount the school's sporting record. The *Chronicle* amply recorded the XI's achievements. Cricket tends to attract aspiring writers and lovers of lists and statistics. Though it was rugby football that particularly enthused the editors and readers of the *Chronicle*, cricket, with its statistical preoccupations, took up more space. Results were tabulated, scorecards reproduced, batting and bowling averages given. As in the reports on rugby, thumbnail sketches of the players described their strengths and weaknesses, sometimes with self-conscious turns of phrase.

Again as in rugby, the school's opponents in cricket were often colleges from the university. As in rugby, too, the school most commonly played against was St Paul's, Stony Stratford. In 1877 the match against Bloxham provoked a crisis. With St Edward's six runs short of winning and with six of its wickets standing, the Bloxham captain led his men from the pitch, using the drizzling rain as an excuse, though it had been drizzling for most of the match. An hour and a half later, in spite of remonstrations, Bloxham would not carry on the game, 'and so', reported the *Chronicle*, 'it remains by the written laws of cricket a drawn game, but by those unwritten laws which should regulate the conduct of gentlemen, and more especially of schools, a manifest victory.' There was no attempt by authorities of either school to intervene in what was still the boys' game. By the turn of the century they would not have stood back from such a confrontation.

Cricket's monopoly of summer sport came under challenge. Boys had long enjoyed 'messing about in boats', and in 1877, with the help of Letts, a Boat Club was formed, with 25 members. A contract was made with Bossom, the boatbuilders, for the hire of boats. The cricketers opposed the club, reasoning that in a small school the removal of 25 boys from the pool of potential cricketers would be disastrous. There was reluctance too to admit boaters to the Central Committee, which decided sports policy. Boating was not cheap, a point made against it in 1879 when a levy of an extra shilling was placed on sports subscriptions. It was also a hard activity to discipline, for it offered the chance to get away from school and misbehave. Boats were taken out and damaged by 'idle loafers'. Boys rowed in IVs and sculls, but many of them saw the activity as an amusing pastime rather than a serious sport. In some years during the 1880s there was no rowing at all. There were constant complaints about the quality of Bossom's boats.

In rowing, Sing saw an opportunity to enhance the school's status. But he was anxious to protect cricket, and was also insistent that boys be kept from the river until they were 16 and until they could swim. So he moved cautiously. Only in 1888 was a race against another school – St Mark's School, Windsor – organized, when St Edward's lost by 22 seconds. Eventually annual Bumpers – the boat races where crews aim to bump boats ahead of them – were established. They were followed by a race against another school in June and by Summer IVs in July, a pattern that lasted until the Great War. The school competed at Marlow Regatta, and bought a second-hand eight for £10 in 1893. The sport, like others, was assisted by the growing popularity of inter-Set competitions, which equalled school matches in the length of coverage in the *Chronicle*.

By the 1880s the sports clubs were part of the Central Committee of senior boys and masters, which would manage the sports finances, and therefore largely dictate sports policy, well into modern times. The committee published its own annual accounts, so that boys and masters, who between them supplied most of the money, were able to ensure a degree of accountability. This arrangement no doubt suited the school, which, by keeping the finances and organization of sport at a distance, could escape some of the responsibility for decisions and be spared some time-consuming administration. Yet the notion that the boys ran the games themselves was increasingly a fiction – a convenient one, for it was still the boys who were funding them. Boys' subscriptions in the 1880s usually totalled between £20 and £30 per term, while the Common Room paid a subscription fixed at £4. Fines imposed by prefects for misdemeanours usually topped £2, and the sale of football cards by boys brought in a little more than £1. Second only to the income from the subscriptions were grants from the takings of the School Shop, usually around £10 a term. Boys who bought goods from the Shop knew they were subsidizing the games.

From these various sources a total of £121 4s. was raised in the school year 1880–81. The largest expenses were contributions to the wages of the cricket coach (£24 3s.) and ground staff (£9 18s.). Cricket materials cost £22, footballs £4, printing £2 4s. At this stage the Boat Club cost just £6 4s. Inevitably the sums rose as the games developed. By 1912 the boys' subscriptions stood at £168. The levy on masters, however, was now only £3 10s. By this time their most significant contribution to games lay in coaching, not financial support. The *Chronicle* had now joined the Shop in helping to finance the sports, providing £6 1s. 2d alongside the £55 provided by the Shop. Fines still figure, amounting to £2 16s.11d, and there is now a dividend of £3 10s. 2d from the Midland Railway stock, for the committee had entered the stock market. Earlier in the year it had sold £200 of Midland Railway's 2½% preferential stock. Cricket now cost £70 11s. 11d and boating £54 1s. 4d, of which £5 19s. went to Bossom and £16 10s. to Salters, another provider of boats. A total of £7 10s. 5d was spent on footballs, and £2 15s. 6d on the replacement of lost balls for fives. Hockey now makes an appearance, £1 16s. 1d being spent on the purchase of sticks. A new gymnasium rope cost £1 10s. 9d. Tennis nets accounted for £2 12s. 6d and hurdles 19s.

6d. It cost £9 15s. to empty the outdoor pool. These expenses left a surplus large enough for the committee to donate £200 towards the purchase of the fields from the Duke of Marlborough. The pool was the one which Letts and the boys had dug out. A 'bathing place' redolent of idle sunbathing in country houses, it did not accord with the new spirit of regulation, to which other outdoor activities gradually succumbed. The old Hare and Hounds paperchases, in which the fast runners had scattered litter across the countryside and left the slower boys to catch them, had given way to an annual steeplechase. There had been no team spirit in the paperchases, which had tended to be subverted by the taking of short cuts or to degenerate into rural strolls or mischief-making. The steeplechases were a team event and an inter-Set competition.

By the time of the school's Jubilee of 1913, games had arguably become the main instrument for the building of moral character. Gradually sport had been taken over by the masters. Their initial involvement had arisen when boys found there were adults who shared their enthusiasm, especially among graduates from the universities where sport was developing. With time, masters became not athletic partners of the boys but their controllers, their role contributing to the integration of sport into the institutional life of the school. Such masters as Labat, Gillett and Bussell took their activities as coaches to be every bit as important as their work in the classroom, because in their eyes academic achievement and sporting prowess were complementary accomplishments of an English gentleman.

19

DOMESTIC LIFE

For the opening years of the twentieth century the school's archives have a rich source: a series of domestic account books. In conjunction with other evidence they show St Edward's as a domestic organism, to be fed, cleaned and serviced. They also remind us that the school belonged to a wider and more complex society.

On 17 September 1912 the Oxford carrier Mr C. Rooke opened a new account book headed 'Young Gentlemen's a/c'. Two days later Christopher Bird (Roll No. 1291) alighted from his train at Oxford station, to return for his penultimate term. Christopher, born in 1899, had joined the school in the summer of 1908, and was planning to leave, aged 13 or 14, to become a midshipman in the Royal Navy. His elder brother John (Roll No. 1286) had left in 1909, aged 16. Their father was a High Church cleric, the Rev. J. Bird. On that first day of term Christopher was one of forty-one boys carried by Rooke from the station to the school.

The service was not cheap. All but four of the boys were charged a shilling, but for some reason Christopher and two other boys, Rupert East (Roll No. 1325), who was about the same age as Christopher, and the 17-year-old Bernard Penny (Roll No. 1237), paid only 6d., while Claud Green (Roll No. 1245), later Senior Prefect, who left two years later, was charged 2s. Any luggage that arrived apart from its owners, and had to be taken to the school separately, was charged at 3d. a box. Over the next eighteen days six boxes belonging to Cyril Peach (Roll No. 1349), aged 17, were transported, so that the boy's father, the Rev. P. H. W. Peach, had to foot a bill of 2s. 6d for the transport of boy and luggage. Henry Holdcroft (Roll No. 1395), aged 15, paid 1s. 3d for a box and 6d for the delivery of his bicycle. Perhaps the three boys who paid sixpence for their transport were less heavily laden than the others, for three boxes later arrived for one of them, Bernard Perry, and one for another, Christopher Bird.

In 2010 it cost me £7 and a small tip to take a taxi from the station to the school. I followed the same route as those forty-one boys, along Hythe Bridge Street, past Chamberlain's still surviving small chapel, into Beaumont Street with its Regency buildings and up the Woodstock Road, which had been newly asphalted in 1912 and was being dug up again in 2010. What feelings or sensations touched the boys on the same journey? Though account books are apparently dry matter, they give glimpses of human experiences and occasionally even allow us to catch something of their mood and texture.

Carrying boys and their luggage was not Rooke's only service to the school. On 2 September 1913 he was paid 6d to carry washing to Mrs White, the laundress, and another 6d to transport some carpets. He often conveyed mattresses, carpets and chairs to the school, and occasionally delivered spirits and oils from the firm of Wyatt's. From the station he delivered two hampers of chickens on 25 September and, at a charge of £2, ten cases of wine on 20 October. From September to December 1913 the school paid £2 3s. 5d to Rooke for such work, and a further £3 6s.7d for the 'Young Gentlemen's a/c', i.e. for carriage of their luggage. The document recording these payments was signed by Rooke over a 1d. postage stamp and then, on 4 November, endorsed with the company rubber stamp of Cash, Stone & Co., Chartered Accountants.

Like other financial documents of Sing's tenure, the records of this transaction give an impression of regularity and business sense far removed from the administrative disarray of the hand-to-mouth regime of Simeon. Yet Simeon himself left, on disorderly scraps of paper, evidence which affords glimpses of the school's domestic arrangements in his own era. From 1888, in despairing attempts to impose order on the day-to-day finances, Simeon, probably with the help of Hawkins, kept drawing up rough balance sheets at the end of the school year, often in pencil, in the hope of making sense of the deteriorating financial situation. I give the expenses for two selected years.

	1888	1890
Interest	£910 9s. 10d	£533 0s. 4d
Upkeep of clock, organ, telephone	£23 1s. 0d	£7 0s. 0d
Fire Insurance	£29 9s. 9d	£26 9s. 9d
Butcher	£729 11s. 8d	£504 5s. 2d
Baker	£103 14s. 2d	£182 5s. 10d
Coals, coke, wood	£181 7s. 9d	£162 3s. 4d
Milk	£49 13s. 9d	£12 2s. 0d
Beer	£161 0s. 9d	£123 1s. 6d
Jam	£40 3s. 4d	£1 3s. 4d
Poultry & Fish	£53 8s. 2d	£65 8s. 11d
Grocer	£447 14s. 1d	£372 4s. 7d
Gas	£88 19s. 9d	£76 14s. 1d
Water	£18 19s. 9d	£26 18s. 9d
Laundry	£259 7s. 2d	£159 6s. 0d
Prizes	£39 18s. 10d	£29 4s. 6d
Library & *Chronicle*	£69 15s. 6d	£75 4s. 0d
Newspapers	£10 6s. 7d	£17 16s. 2d
Examinations	£106 15s. 6d	£28 13s. 6d
Salaries	£1,131 10s. 0d	£933 10s. 1d
Wages	£920 7s. 7d	£600 6s. 0d
Tailor	£326 15s. 0d	£306 10s. 9d
Bootmaker	£88 5s. 3d	£42 15s. 3d
Books & binding	£211 5s. 11d	£206 15s. 7d
Chemist	£21 0s. 11d	£22 13s. 6d
Dentist	£6.16s.5d	£8.18s. 6d
Cash allowances to boys	£44 17s. 2d	£119 5s. 4d
Journey money	£185 9s. 6d	£75 0s. 0d

[The last two items would have been claimed back on parental bills.]

Not all the figures are easy to explain, but there is a clear pattern of reduced expenditure as a result of the decline in numbers over those two years, from 120 pupils in 1888 to 97 in 1890. There are sharp reductions in milk (a drink anyway not popular with the boys) and jam. Less meat is eaten, more bread. The laundry bill, a labour-intensive cost, is reduced by £100. The achievement of a reduction in examination costs, by nearly three-quarters, is a mystery. Masters' salaries were pared, probably as a result of the departure of Jellicoe and of the young OSE Richard Prioleau (Roll No. 319), who left to join the Inner Temple. They were not replaced. The wages bill suggests that there were a number of redundancies among the servants and ground staff.

If the figures illustrate the financial strain, they also give us a picture of the school's daily costs and requirements. As we would expect, food and drink take up much of the annual outlay. The figures would have included the feeding of the Warden and of living-in masters. Butcher's meat far exceeds poultry and fish, while much more beer is drunk than milk. A lower proportion of expenditures goes on the services of gas, water and fuel than it would now. The high cost of tailors' and bootmakers' bills can be attributed to the cost of the labour involved and to the rough treatment of clothes and boots worn by boys. Bills for those items were presumably passed on to parents. Reading these lists we understand why the school palmed off the bills for games on to the boys. The Chapel also seems to have been funded separately, largely by an ever-open appeal fund. Donations to it are often registered by the *Chronicle*.

The account books of the early twentieth century give us fuller evidence of the school's dealings with local tradesmen. The ever-careful Sing produced a summary of principal tradesmen's accounts from 1904 to 1910 and, in a few cases, beyond. We can begin with the account with Gibbard, the butcher. In September 1904, a bill of £241 11s. 11d was settled for a twelve-week term with a hundred boys to feed. That scale of expenditure did not change over the years up to 1908, even though the length of the terms varied from 11 to 18 weeks and boy numbers ranged from 90 to 127. The costliest term for butcher's meat exceeded the figure for September 1904 by only eight shillings. The cheapest one incurred a bill of £193 13s. 10d. The far smaller poulterer's bills submitted by Mr Kinch ranged, in the same period, from £8 3s. to £16 17s. Parker the fishmonger sent bills ranging from £9 19s. 10d to £23 4s. The termly bill for the fruiterer, a mere £10, is no more suggestive of a healthy diet than the low expenditure on fish. Wine (presumably for entertainment by the Warden) and beer from Phillips ranged from £14 9s. 4d to £29 5s. 3d. Mineral waters narrowly exceeded £2. Mrs White usually submitted termly bills for laundry not far in excess of £70, quite a saving on Simeon's earlier laundry costs. Gas and water costs were lower too, gas costing £60 or more in the winter terms and water never exceeding £13 a term. Occasionally there were big items of expenditure, among them the £63 0s. 5d for new boilers in January 1905 and the £45 9s. 3d for 'alterations to the kitchen range and heating apparatus' a year later.

The precision and order of Sing's accounts contrast not only with Simeon's methods but with the rather jumbled bank book kept by Hudson in 1900, where payments to masters in August (£35 to Wright in July, £50 to Cowell, and £48 6s. 8d to Wynne-Wilson in

August) rub shoulders with a portion of Bursey's wages of £15 2s. in September, and in October with the £3 annual subscription to the *Church Times* and an ironmonger's bill of £30 3s. 2d. Payments to the teaching staff are staggered across the months. Hudson made payments of £50 to himself and sometimes to leading teachers such as Cowell and Sing. In 1911 the Inspectors noted that masters had no written contracts and were paid in accordance with gentlemen's agreements between them and the Warden.

One of the traders with whom the school dealt regularly was the general blacksmith, A. Plowman, who operated in South Parade and whose account book for 1905 survives. His frequent tasks for the school, all of them small, take us into the world of a long-lost trade. Where there are boys there are repair jobs. The mending of one bedstead with a new leg cost £2, and four more bedsteads had to be repaired in September, evidently a rowdy time in the dormitories. The repair of a horsebox cost £3 0s. 6d for six bolts which presumably held the structure together. The grinding of a scythe, a reminder that the games fields needed maintenance, cost 6d. A new hoe blade cost £2 and a hay fork was repaired for 3d. A new lawnmower chain cost 5s. 6d. Horseshoes were supplied, as were 'pig rings' for Hudson's prized herd.

At least until recent times, the food at St Edward's has rarely attracted praise. In the decades around 1900 it seems to have been very basic, with little variety and with dietary gaps. Boys supplemented their diet with hampers brought from home, with extras paid for by parents and placed on the 'tram' in Hall, and with purchases at the popular School Shop. The water seems to have been reasonably safe and the cholera threat was withstood, even though other illnesses were common. In 1911 a dairy in Summertown, Edmonds, supplied milk at a shilling a gallon in 1911. In July the daily order varied between two and four gallons a day. Occasionally cream was purchased, but the whole dairy bill for the month was only £6 18s. 11d. S. E. Hall was the long-standing baker to the school and we have his account book with Sing for the same year. His bill for the first week of May, when term had yet to start, was £3 6s. ½d. The separate sum of £1 13s. for flour perhaps suggests that some baking was being done in the Warden's house. The costs naturally rose as term got under way, and the bill for the whole of May amounted to £23 6s. 4d. Rock cakes and buns cost 3s. 6d an order, but most of the money went on 103 loaves, which cost £1 1s. 10½d. Each day's delivery was carefully recorded by Hall and later endorsed by the watchful

Sing. Boys may not be the most reliable judges of school food, but their comments are not heartening. Charles Jotcham (Roll No. 545), who arrived in 1883 aged 11, described the fare as 'terrible and nauseating'. Philip Merivale (Roll No. 1027) more delicately called it 'not intrinsically attractive'. He sadly remembered the time, after the first few days of term, when hampers brought from home had been exhausted. No wonder boys dashed to the School Shop immediately after lunch to fill out with a penny 'stodger', a form of doughnut, or, if they could afford it, an iced cake for 1½d.

Mr and Mrs Bursey were the presiding figures of the domestic staff until well into the 1890s. Henry died in 1898, but his wife carried on working as sick-house matron until 1903. She worked in a corner of New Buildings, where she supervised some young female servants, whom we met earlier in the Chapel. Long service is often a characteristic of schools, and not only amongst the teaching staff. Instructor Adams, who ran the gymnasium from 1886, served for twenty-two years before retiring with his champion fox terriers. He lived until 1928. Scivyer, the head gardener appointed in 1878, served for thirty-four years and retired with a pension from the School worth 10s. a week, a standard figure introduced by the Governors in 1912. Mrs Jeffrey, the housekeeper, died three months after her retirement in 1903. Her son Arthur, who started as coach boy in 1890 and graduated to become steward and butler, was to serve until 1946. When today a pupil climbs to the raised platform at the end of the Library, he or she is standing on the stage built for Cowell's productions by Walter Young, the legendary school carpenter from 1883 to 1920. The Shop, which was presided over by an old lady called Mother Blencowe, was later managed by a Mrs Johnson and her daughter Lizzie, whose father had served for sixteen years as butler and porter. Lizzie was an appreciated figure, for if approached courteously she would prolong the Shop's opening hours after 'dinner' to make sure that everyone was served. She arrived in 1910 and did not leave until 1943.

These names remind us of the importance of the female element in this male environment. A key figure was Matron Bishop, whom the boys knew as 'Popper'. Miss Bishop's room was just beyond the Hall on the right as one approached the dormitory staircase. She greeted the pupils at the foot of the stairs as they appeared for breakfast, no doubt to check their cleanliness and appearance and perhaps to persuade them to drink a glass of milk, a beverage boys tended to shun unless they could take it with them to make cocoa in the form rooms, where they lived and were taught. She also served at breakfast, 'carrying four, sometimes five plates of porridge and distributing them with the ease of an expert card-dealer', as Harold Rogers remembered. Richard Butler (Roll No. 1154) remembers her boxing his ears, though she could barely reach them. William Jackson (Roll No. 693) recalled: 'Mother Bishop was a good old sport and very kind to me.' She kept a fire in her little room at the time when the school was largely unheated and sometimes allowed boys to warm their hands on it. She retired in 1910.

Some servants were accorded the status of taking part in the procession of the Warden and masters into the Hall for dinner. Miss Bishop, Miss Piper (the cook) and Walter Young were usually there, together with four maids. We have already met the 'guv'nors', the male servants who awoke the boys in the morning, though later they would be called 'Johns'. Maids were known as 'Annies'. Sing, perhaps troubled by the patronizing tone of this slang, tried to suppress it, but it was still in use in the 1960s. We have all too few photographs of the servants. That of 1876 with the then matron, Miss Edwards (whom we see at the far left of the front row, looking pleased with herself), is one of the few. We note the freshly pointed bricks of Wilkinson's building and the spruce servants' uniforms. Surely these nubile young ladies cannot have escaped the boys' attention. Yet, though we have accounts, whether real or invented, of boys seducing the maidservants in other schools, I have encountered only one piece of evidence (to be mentioned later) of any such exploit at St Edward's.

We have occasional evidence for the wages of servants, though they seem often to have been paid in a random, hand-to-mouth manner. Sergeant Adams was paid £41 3s. 2d in July 1900, and £44 8s. 8d at the next recorded payment in December. In that same year Bursey received £22 10s. 6d in June, £15 2s. and £24 4s. in September, with a final £6 2s. 6d in December. We cannot be sure that these entries for 1900 represent the total wages paid in the year to those two very senior employees. In any case some recipients, like Adams and Bursey, were also housed and fed free. Arthur Jeffrey is paid £27 12s. 6d in August, a further £4 4s. 6d in October, and £8 9s. 11d in December. Realistic comparisons between such wages and national ones are hard to make. In 1885 the Scottish economist and statistician Sir Robert Giffen estimated that 50% of all adult male workers earned less than £1 5s. a week, while a decade later Charles Booth reckoned that another 30% earned between £1 5s. and £1 15s. a week. In the Wages census of 1906 the average wage of skilled workers was £2 a week. But such figures conceal a host of regional and occupational variations. There are also problems in interpreting the school's accounts. Hudson's outgoing account book for 1900 mingles masters' salaries with servants' wages; however, we cannot assume that all of those named in the book whom we know not to have been teachers were servants. Despite these difficulties, there is one generalization which can be sustained: that from 1879 to 1900 wages at St Edward's were earned against a background of falling prices.

In the account books and ancillary materials we have glimpsed the domestic life that was the school's essential infrastructure. Next we move to the lives of the boys.

20

BEING A BOY

WHAT was it like to be a pupil at the school before 1914? The archives, and especially the *Chronicle*, tell us about the boys' achievements and activities in games, plays, poetry, debates and society activities. Rules, notices and so on give us glimpses of the daily round. But what of the inner feelings of the hundred or so boys, stretched across a wide age range, who lived and worked in and around Wilkinson's buildings? Reminiscences, a chief source for us, have their limitations, among them a tendency towards benign distortion and the filtering out, conscious or unconscious, of unhappy memories. Some recollections, like those of Harold Rogers, survive from people who devoted much of their adult lives to the school's welfare and did not dwell on its past deficiencies. Old men sometimes like to think of the bad times of youth as tests and shapers of character on the path to manliness, a perspective that is especially pronounced in retrospective accounts of the school in the period leading up to the Great War. What they may forget is the distinctiveness of boyhood. For boys are not just men in the making. They have their own, self-sufficient lives, about which masters know a great deal less than they may suppose.

Periods of history have their distinctiveness too. 'The past,' as L. P. Hartley wrote, 'is a foreign country.' To us the punishment of boys by other boys, through beatings, fines, detentions, the writing of lines, or the setting of humiliating tasks, is foreign indeed. Yet it was taken for granted until around the time of the school's centenary half a century ago. Victorian and Edwardian new boys, if their families knew anything of the Public School world, would have arrived expecting a pecking order, fagging and beatings. They would have been prepared for cold, hunger, loneliness, intimidation and bullying. Some of these things they may already have encountered at prep school. Or they may have experienced, in their genteel homes, a degree of discipline and subordination that is also remote from our experience. They would have been brought up in a world of nurses and governesses, which allowed only fitful and infrequent closeness between boy and parent.

In 1913 Arnold Lunn wrote the best Public School novel there is, *The Harrovians*. It was followed in 1917 by the 17-year-old Alec

Waugh's novel *The Loom of Youth*, which is set in 'Fernhurst', a very thinly disguised Sherborne, the school Waugh had recently left. Both books caused outrage. Though the two writers loved their former schools, they were critical of some of their characteristics. Especially they noted the excessive time given to games, the importance attached to them, and the hierarchies among the boys that games created. Lunn and Waugh disliked the dominance of the 'bloods' of the games fields. As the bloods tended to be prefects, it was generally they who ran the fagging system and administered harsh beatings. The two authors turned aside from the violence, and from the rituals of conformity, to the forbidden subjects of school life: to schoolboy attachments and passions, sometimes sexual, which they portray as sources of damaging unhappiness. The books, one of them published in the prelude to the Great War and the other during it, seemed stabs in the nation's back, the scribbling of traitors. They provoked ripostes. Such novels as Martin Browne's *A Dream of Youth* (1918) were written to refute Lunn and Waugh. The distinguished schoolmaster Edward Lyttelton asserted that Waugh's novel was 'uniformly dull, occasionally unpleasant, and, in my judgement at least, almost wholly untrue'. Yet it was a best-seller, written by a boy who had just left school, and composed with an apparent honesty whose very naïvety was part of its appeal.

Boys at St Edward's would surely have seen in Fernhurst an image of their own schooldays. Yet St Edward's produced no such novels. So where do we turn for evidence of the experience, as distinct from the regulations and conventions, of the life of the school in the first half-century or so of its existence? The reminiscences, for all their varying degrees of distortion, are normally our most revealing source. We have already met those of Harold Peake, Philip Merivale, Harold Rogers, Cyril Flower, Sholto Douglas and Charles Gillett. There are others too, among them the recollections of Charles Jotcham, William Jackson (Roll No. 693), and those of the editor of the hand-produced *Common Room Magazine* of 1892, Charles Green.

Occasionally we have a source free from the hazards of retrospect, though it can carry its own problems of interpretation: the letters boys wrote home. Herbert Moss (Roll No. 503) joined the school, aged 16, in January 1882. On 27 March his father, C. B. Moss, wrote to Simeon in terms of vigorous complaint: 'I enclose you two bits of letters from Bertie .... I may tell you: that this sort of thing has gone on ever since the poor boy went, that he has hated the whole thing, and been <u>persistently</u> and <u>brutally</u> <u>bullied</u>, from the first week, even until now.' Here are some of the things Bertie had written to his father. 'We have just come out of church and the fellows have been strangling me with the cord of the blind guillotining and just before church they [beat] me with a stick and threw one of the hollow tennis balls like the ones we used to play with at me and they stung most awfully and then a fellow came up to me and hit me with the knob of a stick on the elbow. I am very unhappy as you may imagine my head aches so from the guillotining and I feel sick from the strangling. Do you think I could leave at Easter? I cannot work properly with my head in such a state and my back is constantly bruised. I was caught doing work out of school on Thursday and have not had any peace since. I have had my books taken away.... I have also been put in a basket on the lockers where it is just balanced and if I move ever so little it will go over and them fellows shoot paper and throw shots at me. The V Form has always been noted for their bullying so I was very unlucky getting up here .... The fellows seem to pride themselves on "giving Moss hell" and hell this whole place is to me.'

On 29 March Mr Moss wrote to Simeon again. 'I think it would be better to remove Bertie at once as it is evident to me that the 5th Form are hypocrites.' He asks to withdraw his son without paying the term's notice. In a further letter on 1 April the father recalled that on his own first visit to the school he had been concerned to learn that the Head Master, as he calls the Warden, did not sleep on the premises, and had wondered whether bullying might thrive in his absence. In fact Simeon slept in the adjoining lodgings, which communicated with the boys' dormitories. Every letter from his son, Moss told the Warden, had 'complained of bullying, misery and persecution, until the one I sent you – which spoke of pistols, being strangled etc.'.

Simeon at first responded defensively to Mr Moss's charges, stressing that the dormitories were supervised by prefects and that he himself was close at hand at night-time, though he did not address the allegation of daytime bullying. But on 3 April Simeon went on the attack. 'Unless your son is playing a double part and telling me one thing while he tells you another (which I cannot believe) your letter is quite unintelligible to me. He entirely denies having said anything about "pistols" and while he admits that he has exaggerated his troubles in his letters to you, he also says that you have taken a much more serious view of them than he intended to convey. This charge of bullying rests upon very scanty facts which are so trivial that very few boys would think of complaining about them.' Simeon was firm. He would not allow the boy to leave without a term's fees, a concession that would be an acknowledgement of the truth of the accusations. The father immediately backed down, replying on the next day: 'I quite forgot to say that I had a letter from Bertie' – presumably written after Simeon had seen the boy – 'saying the bullying had ceased and he was quite happy.' Yet Bertie left at the end of the summer term and completed his education at St Michael's College at Tenbury in Worcestershire.

What are we to make of this exchange? Had Bertie exaggerated, even invented? If there was truth in his accounts, did Simeon really consider the boy's treatment 'trivial'? Was Mr Moss looking for a chance to get off a term's fees? 'Bullying', the charge Bertie levels, is always a problematical word. Boys accused of it may be baffled ('Couldn't he see it was just a bit of fun?'). One boy's torture is another's 'ragging around'. The word 'bullying' is now used more widely than in the Victorian age. Schools were violent places, meant to toughen boys up. Outside the classroom, where there was little adult supervision, assertive adolescents were free to test their mettle. Prefects could beat more or less at will. So physical exchanges, of one kind or another, were commonplace. Yet boys did sense that there was a line to be drawn. In Thomas Hughes's novel *Tom Brown's Schoolboys* such acts of torture as the roasting of boys over open fires affront boys' own feelings of decency. Yet there was also a code of uncomplaining endurance, even in the face of what must often have been terror. The imperative of 'not telling', unusually broken by Bertie Moss, hid most of what went on from the authorities, and hides it from us too.

Harold Peake, who wrote that he had been 'born without the due allowance of the herd instinct', was ill suited to the collective conformities of relationships among the boys. Peake, the lover and observer of the natural world, remembered his time as a junior boy as boring and cheerless. He had spent much it in a 'dismal passage', a 'long and dreary brick corridor ... more suited to prison than a school'. He hated the form rooms where the boys otherwise lived and were taught. The only escape was the Meads where, in good weather, impromptu games could be played. 'We all enjoyed building circular huts from the dried grass' when the Meads had been mown for hay.

When Big School was built in 1881, the old schoolroom was redesigned. Harold returned at the start of term to discover that the middle part was now allocated to his Shell form. Its name had been fixed on the door lintel, but 'we lost no time in mutilating this', which hardly suggests firm discipline. Though Harold's brightness brought him rapid promotions up the school, he remembers receiving 'no encouragement' from 'the regime' for his intellectual interests and thirst for knowledge, though he does emphasize an improvement under Dalton. It is to the school's credit that Peake, in spite of not being a games player, became a prefect.

Much the saddest letter I have encountered in the archives was written, some time in the late 1950s or very early in 1960, by the retired priest Charles Jotcham, who died in 1960 in his late eighties. It was written to Bill Veitch (Roll No. 2258), a master at the school. Jotcham had been at the school for three years, from 1883 to 1886. He begins with the bullying. 'It was the order of the day. Every Sunday afternoon I and others were made to fight to amuse the bigger boys and there was no let-up until one or the other drew blood. The prefects were set to watch over our games and heaven help any boy who came away with clean knees .... In every way the prefects made life hell for the small boys .... But the worst thing of all was the appalling immorality of the big boys with the small boys. It is still to me the worst of the horrors of my memory. Our parents in those days did not believe in giving their own sons some necessary and useful knowledge of the "facts of life", so we were left to learn them for ourselves .... I give you a specific instance of the kind of moral rottenness. There was a young girl, nurse to the housemaster and one night three of the older boys seduced her. I have never forgotten this and it has often, even now, made my heart sick for that very nice girl who was such a friend to me when I was laid up for some weeks. Fortunately my father moved me away and it was like a precious relief from Purgatory. I never told him what had happened and I have never before this mentioned it to anyone. I was too ashamed.' The memory rings true — maybe truer than that of his contemporary Bertie Moss — but, as always, we wonder how typical are the memories contained in a single recollection. Cruelty and unhappiness are more likely to be recorded than their absence.

Harold Rogers was very different from both Peake and Jotcham, both as a boy and as a man. In adulthood he lived near the school and to a large degree built his life around it. In 1937 he was Mayor of Oxford. He was the school's chief architect, designing War Memorial Buildings (now Tilly's), the Sanatorium, and the Cowell Gates (at the main entrance on the Woodstock Road), and making the alterations to the Chapel that we noted earlier. The pillar of the St Edward's School Society, he made it an influential force in the school's life. He had arrived at St Edward's at the age of eleven, though he would have come a year earlier had he not been struck down by measles. Brought up in Richmond in Surrey, he first attended a small local day school for boys and their sisters, where the teachers had 'no educational qualifications'. Games, held on Saturday afternoon, were voluntary, and included rounders as well as some sort of cricket and 'some very elementary football' with a round ball and 'no hands allowed'. So he had had none of the toughening experience of boarding prep school life known to most of his contemporaries.

Harold's father was a quantity surveyor in the City, six of whose cousins went to Harrow and four to Charterhouse. But Harold's mother was a High Church devotee who had read about St Edward's in the *Monthly Packet*, a Ritualist periodical edited by the Simeon family's neighbour, the novelist Charlotte Yonge, who attended John Keble's funeral. Charlotte sang the praises of the school, of its High Church backers in Oxford, and especially of Simeon. Harold's parents made a choice between St Edward's and the Woodard Society school Hurstpierpoint. On 24 April Harold arrived at St Edward's with his mother; having cast his old knickerbocker suits aside, he was now equipped with a play-box, a portmanteau, suits, Eton collars, boots and indoor shoes. Mother and boy were given morning tea by the Simeons. Mrs Simeon was arranging the Chapel flowers in the drawing room, and the pious Mrs Rogers remarked of the geraniums, 'There you see, red for St Mark.' Young Violet Simeon asked Harold if he knew any hymns, 'and I odiously replied "Yes, and I know some psalms as well".' Lunch with the family followed. Were all new boys and their families accorded such a capacious welcome? Certainly Simeon captivated both mother and son. Harold was taken into Oxford for the afternoon, on the tram that started at the end of St Margaret's Road. He returned to report to the butler, Duncan, and was led down that dismal corridor to Matron's room.

Sixteen boys had been entered for the Easter and Summer terms of 1888. Rogers, whose memory was phenomenal, remembers when each arrived and left. One among them, Felix Blakiston, who like several others arrived during the course of the term, is not recorded in any of the editions of the *Roll*. Felix was withdrawn with illness after a fortnight, his bed immediately filled by his brother Alban Blakiston (Roll No. 699). All fifteen boys who arrived alongside

Harold were older than he, no doubt an intimidating prospect for him. Three were already 16, six were 15, one 14, three 13, and two 12. The spread of ages was typical. In the Christmas term of 1888, the term after Harold's arrival, the other boys' ages ranged from 10 to 18. The integration of so diverse an intake into the community must have been a challenge.

Matron's room was gloomy. 'I was not feeling hilarious myself, but my companions seemed to be in the depths of despair.' Term began with exams to place the new entrants, and Harold, who had done no Greek, was placed in the lowest form with four of the other new arrivals, three of whom were aged 15 and one 12. So he had to work alongside older boys. But he may have had no difficulty keeping up, for, as he recalls, 'there were some heavy passengers in the two lowest forms whose progress was, to say the least of it, slow'. In the unyielding atmosphere of the boys' world the Warden's lodgings provided what, to the younger boys at least, must have been welcome intimations of humanity. 'Some small boys were occasionally asked to the Warden's House for tea and on some afternoons – in the winter before Chapel – the Warden would have any of the Lower School who cared to attend into his large Drawing Room and read to them, Stevenson, Ballantyne and other such authors.' Sometimes Mrs Simeon read, and her readings were very popular, conveying as they no doubt did something of the air of domestic family life starkly absent from the form rooms and dormitories down that corridor from the Lodgings. In the Summer Term every form was entertained to strawberries and cream in the Warden's garden 'with plates and sugar'. When Harold needed an oculist, Simeon took him down to Oxford in his own carriage. Harold also recalls the famous Warden's birthday parties on 20 February, when sausages were served for breakfast and the school had a half-holiday.

Even though Rogers was at the school only for Simeon's last four years, his recollections give us our most vivid impression of his methods. They convey the warmth, the pastoral attentiveness, and the sense of presence and personality that made Simeon so attractive to boys and parents. 'It will be gathered that his attitude to the younger boys was paternal, most of us loved him – his nickname, "The Wolf", being a term of endearment without any predatory implications.' Though in other respects keen to reproduce the character of his own school, Winchester, Simeon realized something that Winchester had not: that masters must spend time among their charges, not just to discipline them but to get to know them and nurture them. 'In his velvet dining jacket and carrying an impressive bunch of keys, he would go round the dormitories and the Shell Form Room during second Prep and talk to the Matron if he met her on her round of the small boys, and talk to one or two of the boys at their prep work.' Rogers describes other occasions when Simeon would come into the form rooms both during and after lessons. The Warden personally presided at the handing out of pocket money, so that he met every boy once a week, levying any disciplinary fines from the sums deposited by parents and no doubt keeping an eye on the maintenance of good order and behaviour. On the last morning of term Simeon saw every boy and handed him his money to get home. He would quiz him about his journey and his plans for the holidays, and make sure the boy was not exaggerating the rail fare so as to get cash to settle debts, a common practice, according to Rogers.

Harold gives descriptions of punishments. Fines seem to have been the most common of the penalties imposed by prefects. They could be exacted for untidy hair or dirty collars or unbrushed boots. Masters handed out detentions for bad work. Canes were carried by the prefects and sometimes used to punish talking or ragging but, in Rogers's time, not very often. The carrying of canes by all prefects other than the Senior Prefect and the captains of games was dropped soon after Harold's arrival. There does not seem to have been anything like as much beating at Simeon's St Edward's as there was after his departure. William Jackson, who like Harold joined the school in 1888 and who was the 12-year-old in the group, did remember that 'the prefects were allowed canes and used to use them to practise with during Call Over' (the time of day when boys were assembled and their presence checked). He also states that boys talking in the dormitory were told to stand in basins of cold water. But on the subject of punishments there is no evidence to support Jackson's reminiscences, which date from the 1950s. The memoir of Charles Green, who arrived two years after Jackson, never mentions punishments. 'There was,' he writes, 'no oppressive tradition ... to regulate such matters as, for instance, the way in which a lower school boy must wear his cap.' Green's assertion chimes with the informality of the photographs of the time and the disregard for sartorial uniformity that they display. It was the inexorable growth of team spirit and of the ideal of muscularity that produced more formality of clothing, more rules and regulations, and, in all probability, more and severer punishments.

Rogers was a meticulous little boy who enjoyed making lists

and recording minute information; fortunately for us, for he supplies all sorts of nuggets of information that would otherwise be lost. Each boy had a printed calendar of the term, listing saints' days, the preacher and anthems for the Sunday services, the games fixtures and so on. Opposite each calendar page was a blank page on the right, headed 'Memoranda', which the boys were left to fill. Whereas the surviving calendars of other boys are devoid of annotation except for the occasional notice of an upcoming examination, Harold's are packed with it. His pages for Easter Term 1881 begin by listing all the teachers and giving the titles of their degrees and their university colleges. Next comes a list of the XV. To the printed account of the daily routine he adds details such as the time of breakfast on Sundays and saints' days. All choir practices, which were usually held three times a week, are recorded. On Monday 26 January he notes the first use of the new Office Book in Chapel. He invariably names the celebrant at communion, and adds the name of the preacher when the calendar does not print it.

Twice a week Harold is required to attend classes in the Gym run by Instructor Adams. He lists his drawing lessons, though we do not gather how far they prepared him for his career as an accomplished architect and draughtsman. He makes drawings in his calendar, among them ones of animals to illustrate the song 'The Frog He Would a-Wooing Go'. Rogers did not get on with his Maths teacher, the Rev. Arthur Hall, even though he boasts of being in the first division of the subject. On Thursday 29 January Mr Hall is 'called home' and the 13-year-old Harold writes 'Joy, joy'. On Hall's return a week later Harold laments: '*Dies Irae*, oh misery, oh wretched day'. The pages give us glimpses of encounters with other masters. 'Sunday 8th Feb. Spent the afternoon with "Jelly" [Jellicoe]'. In learning the organ Harold seems to have got on with the organist, for many times he writes 'Brewed [tea] with Mr Carter (org)' – the abbreviation 'org' being used to distinguish Mr Carter from a full member of the teaching staff, the Rev. J. O. H. Carter. In the fifth week of term Harold's copy of the calendar records two brewings with Carter as well as a Confirmation lecture on Renunciation. Harold was much involved in both the Chapel and the music. 'Song prac[tice]' and 'Glee prac' appear from time to time. On the whole holiday of Simeon's birthday on 20 February 'the concert was a great success'. Harold spent the morning walking to Yarnton with Hubert Marsham

(Roll No. 683), the son of a clergyman and the youngest of four brothers who attended St Edward's.

Rogers's surviving entries cover the following term too. Sunday Confirmation classes continue, one of them on the subject of 'Revenge'. There are more walks. On Ascension Day, 7 May, he takes a morning walk with Alban Blakiston to Yarnton and an afternoon one with Frank Loscombe (Roll No. 755) to Wytham. In recording the second walk he writes and underlines 'Lost Purse'. The next day was one of liberation: 'Mr Hall left. Mr Fowler' – R.C. Fowler, who left later the same year – 'came'. On Sunday the 10th Harold has tea with J. O. H. Carter, though brewing with the organist seems to have ceased. On Monday 11 May we read 'purse found' and 'planted mustard'.

The memoir of Philip Merivale, who would become a successful Hollywood actor, has a self-consciously stylish tone. He has none of Rogers's interest in preserving a record. He remembers his years at the school, 1899–1904, as ones when nothing much happened, 'with not a single addition to her buildings, not one change in her institutions'. His is not a cheerful account. He describes a world dominated by games, at which he did not shine. He remembers runs which were imposed simply for the sake of it or when floods ruled out cricket, which he portrays as an elitist game. 'You are born to it or not and if you are not you are simply a helot to wait upon your masters and a helot you will always be .... If any dissentient voices were raised they were quickly stifled.' Philip conveys his sense of relief in reaching the rooms in the New Buildings, which provided some of 'the dignity of privacy'. Provision had been made for studies and a Common Room (precursor of the day rooms) had been created in the new building. The noise was intense. Yet it was not 'the predominant element of that atmosphere, or if it were, its claims were boldly challenged by dirt. There were no ceilings to the studies, which facilitated the disposal of rubbish, waste-paper or the fragments of a "brew". You simply threw everything against the end wall, from which ... it fell into the end study, which seems to have been always empty.'

Perhaps the greatest legacy of the fitting out of a common room and studies in the New Buildings was the 1892 *Common Room Magazine*. The room was well suited to the production of this hand-produced publication, in which Rogers, at the age of 15, was heavily involved. His copies of 'Volume 3' survive. We learn from the first surviving edition, that of Sunday 21 February, that the previous two issues have been bound in two volumes and are available for inspection. The main article of 21 February, an anonymous discussion of the modern schoolboy and his education, concludes: 'above I have spoken of bullying which [goes] on amongst boys; but it's well known that masters [are] nearly as bad if not worse'. The magazine describes the Fourth and Fifth Form supper of the previous summer, which was held in rooms made available by the Warden:

> The services of two members of the Lower School were secured as waiters .... The festive board creaked under the weight of a goodly show and nothing occurred to interrupt the harmony of the meeting, the greatest hilarity prevailing throughout. There were toasts to Church and Queen, *Floreat St Edward's*, Leaving Boys, the Captains of Football and Fives, to boating prospects, the Magazine and the Common Room itself. A few songs were given by members of the company before it became necessary to adjourn for tea.

In the next issue, of March 1892, the editors get tough with their readers. 'You must remember that [the *Common Room Magazine*] is intended to be a boys' paper and solely kept up by the boys of the New Buildings. But this cannot be unless you contribute. We don't want to mention names, but there are some of you who have plenty of wit but will not muster enough energy even to write a column for the C. R. M.' Schoolboy editors down the ages will recognize the feeling. Few contributions matched the originality and humour of the drawings with which Rogers enlivened the magazine. They form a series of 'Types of Beauty', which present the caricatured heads and shoulders of not very attractive females. By July 1892 he had become a co-editor.

The *Common Room Magazine* carries only two poems. Here is one of them, an offering of Public School stoicism.

To the School Bell, 6.30 a.m.

I hear the bell at half past six,
And, washing, rub my eyes.
The other bells all follow soon,
And soon, too, I must rise.
In winter time how hard it is
To get to prep in time,
To go across the frozen quad,
Mid snow, and cold and rime!
And, if you're late, your fate it is
To do a hundred lines,

Or, if in the Sixth Form you are,
A sixpence goes in fines.
But still it seems you have a fate
Which all the others share.
And so, of course, as best you may
You have to 'grin and bear'.

Another memoir, that of Sholto Douglas who was at the school from 1903 to 1909, conveys the hardening both of attitudes and of punishments in the Hudson era. A scholarship, as he soon realized, was a handicap, as it placed a small, clever boy – he was 11 – in the company of less bright ones. In his first year – Hudson's last – he had to choose between 'being beaten in the "Boot Room" by bigger boys whom I had gone above in Form, or being beaten by my housemaster for slacking at work. The latter hurt far less than the operators in the boot room.' Douglas seems to have been less of a conformist than Harold Rogers. He was beaten by a school prefect for 'popping jam pots etc,'. He and Michael Nethersole (Roll No. 1212) were discovered by Sing 'shaving an antique piece of beetroot with a safety razor. He was not amused.' Sing as Warden was not the flogger that Hudson was, but, with his 'moustache bristling', he could dish out punishments. The end of a period taught by him often saw a good proportion of the form being made to stand on the benches. Others were 'led away to execution with impositions and gatings'. Sing more or less forced Douglas to go to Confession at St Margaret's. He also told him loudly to 'stop that filthy noise' as he sang in Chapel, and instructed a reader who had pronounced the name of 'Timotheus' wrongly to write it out 500 times. Boys were required to hand in Greek and Latin exercises for Sing on a Saturday, but sometimes failed to finish them and had to make clandestine visits to his study to retrieve them on the Sunday, complete them, and secretly return them. The precaution was wise, for work came back from Sing 'looking like one of Turner's sunsets', so heavy were the red-inked corrections.

Douglas gives an account of one of his greatest japes. He and other 'toughs' who were not yet prefects made a huge candle out of the little ones that were used in their studies at night. They boiled them down in kettles and poured the resulting mass into a 7 lb biscuit tin, with a piece of rope as a wick. They then removed the sides of the tin, and hoisted the great candle up to the beams of the roof, 'where it burnt merrily, from time to time dropping a pat of grease about the size of a small fist, with the result that not only were our clothes all spattered with grease but the floor of the room was covered, so were our books'. Sing arrived in the Common Room 'in a fine fury, his moustache sticking out in all directions'. The offending boys were made to live in the boot hole for a time. 'While we were down there the drains burst, and floods were added to our crowded and unsavoury misery.' A deputation to Sing on their behalf got the answer, 'I don't care as long as it makes them uncomfortable.'

Douglas's recollections have one mystery. He tells us that 'the great Chapel demonstration' occurred after his time. I can find no other reference to so dramatic an event, or to any other sensation or scandal of the kind that enlivens the narratives of other Victorian and Edwardian Public Schools. 'Thank God for the Chapel at S. E. S.,' exclaimed Douglas, who proves to have had his high-minded side. 'Arising from this the moral tone of the School was excellent. In my 6 and ½ years there was [only] one "row" (I was in hospital at the time and I don't know much about it) but I heard tales of inquisitions, birchings and a grisly public "sacking".' In a letter to Desmond Hill after the publication of Hill's *History* in 1962, Lawrence Eyres, a boy at the school from 1907 to 1911, wrote that 'moral offences of the first magnitude were simply unknown in my time'. Talking to fellow undergraduates about their own schools, he had discovered how exceptional St Edward's appeared to be. 'How much of the credit for our code of decency is attributable to Sing is known only to the Almighty. I expect the fact that a high percentage of my schoolfellows were clergymen's sons had something to do with it. We others did not regard as freaks the minority who went periodically to Confession.' Yet Eyres's letter also hints at a different picture. He remembers that a boy was deservedly expelled in 1905, though he does not say why. Then comes a startling remark. 'In my last term [in 1911] Bickley [George Bickley, Roll No. 1229, Senior Prefect] and I had to investigate a revolting incident in which a master was involved. (He prudently left the country before the police could deal with him, and Crockford [the *Clerical Directory*] knew him no more.)' It is striking to find such an incident, presumably sexual, being dealt with by boys. Or perhaps there was more to the case than Eyres knew. Like so many reminiscences of St Edward's, his letter arouses more curiosity than it can satisfy.

21

TOWARDS WAR

THE years leading up to the Great War, exhausting for the shrewd and hard-working Sing as he faced critical problems at St Edward's, were a time of crisis in the world outside, for Britain and its Empire. After the culmination of the colonial wars in the occupation of the Sudan, and then the wake-up call of the Boer War, there had come the Balkan wars and the growing strain in relations with Germany. The state had turned to the Public Schools to provide leaders in the colonial services and the armed forces. The ethos of St Edward's merged with the ideals of Empire, patriotism and service. In a poem in the *Chronicle* in July 1913 we read:

> Wherever the English race has spread,
> Wherever their flag has flown,
> Whenever the field has been piled with dead
> And the battle bugle's blown,
> To islands basking in sunny seas,
> To deserts swept by the icy breeze,
> To mangrove thickets and coral keys,
> St. Edward's has sent her own.

The refrain after each verse reads:

> A School that plays for the sake of the game – a simple and manly code.
> The School that's proud of her name and fame,
> With honour her only goad.
> The School that faces the Berkshire Hills,
> The School that braces up nerves and wills,
> And every heart with affection fills,
> The School of the Woodstock Road.

As manliness advanced in schools, so were they militarized. The process is mirrored in the *Chronicle*. We noticed earlier the contraction of the range of voices in the magazine. In the 1870s the titles of articles include 'A Chat about Cornwall', 'A Trip to Clovelly', 'Snakes', 'Punch and Judy', 'The Cuckoo', 'Stories about Whist', 'Omens', and 'Rollright Stones, Oxfordshire'. In the 1880s there was a growing emphasis on games, now a major feature of the magazine, which carried lengthy reports of matches. Yet there remained contributions on a wide range of topics: 'From London to Leith by Boat', 'On Nothing', 'The Schoolboy and Hawks', and so on. There are frequent poems, although the quality was variable and the number declined from 1883. Books acquired by the Library, usually on Cowell's recommendation, are assiduously recorded. It is probably in the mid-1880s that the *Chronicle* comes closest to achieving a balance that gives room to sports reports, creative writing, and reports of society meetings, especially of the Field Club and the Debating Society. When the *Chronicle* of that decade looks out to a wider world, its overriding interest is in High Churchmanship in action in London's East End. In the March 1881 issue an article headed 'An Evening in the East End' describes a visit by boys to a small school run by the Friendly Society, where evening classes are held for thirty local factory girls. 'Free and independent, they yield readily to gentleness and good breeding.' The author of the article, teaching a girl how to hold her pen, learns that she had never attempted to hold one until the previous week. There is a patronizing air which reminds us that working-class areas may have seemed as remote as darkest Africa to boys from St Edward's.

A. E. Dalton, Herbert's brother, a priest in Poplar, submitted two long pieces to the *Chronicles* of March and April 1882 which likewise convey the foreignness, to the middle classes, of the life of deprivation they describe. 'Just lately I have come across a case in which a family of nine sleep all in one room .... You see us then with about 9,000 working people ranging from the respectable mechanic who earns from £2 to £2.10s. (and does not spend it all in the public house) down to the casual labourer who but too often cannot find for his family the common necessities of life .... Another drawback to East London work ... is that there are no gentlefolk at all, and so no one to associate with. But this has its advantages too, for the multitude of the work demands all the time that can possibly be given to it.' The school gave money for work of this kind from time to time, but its commitment ran dry during the 1880s. The decline runs parallel to the loss of fervour in the Chapel.

From the late 1880s more and more of the *Chronicle* is taken up with the old boys: their games, their Society and their adult doings. OSE reporting back to the *Chronicle* show no interest in the slums of Britain, but a great deal in lands abroad. In November 1879 an anonymous OSE, prefacing an exotic description of Tangiers as a town full of mosques, turbans and veiled women, notes that 'travels and adventures in foreign lands have a peculiar charm for schoolboys'. Other accounts by OSE describe life in California. Such reports made boys aware of the school's far-flung participation in the world: a participation which had little to do with the religious ideals of the school's foundation, even though Imperialism and militarism sometimes had their religious dimensions. The *Chronicle* reflected a national preoccupation with foreign affairs that was boosted by the new popular press and by the expansion of literacy from the 1870s. In 1880 the Sixth Form took the *Illustrated London News*, *The Standard*, *Field* and *Punch*, publications which would have connected the boys to the concerns of the nation. The Third Form took the *Graphic*, *Funny Folks* and *Boys' News*, while the Second Form read the *Daily News*, *Fun* and the *Union Jack*. Articles in the *Chronicle* from 'a casual correspondent', an anonymous OSE, in 1878–79, under the title 'Passing Events', introduce boys to the cosmopolitan world of London. There is an interest in the theatre, especially the arrival of the Comédie-Française at the Gaiety Theatre: 'all London is flocking to see them'.

These publications cover more earnest subjects, too. There are attacks on Charles Parnell and Irish nationalism, while an approving reference to the Liberal *Daily News* encourages interest in 'the gallant defence of Rorke's Drift', that brave feat of resistance to Zulu warriors in 1879. Old boys evidently thought it their role to steer boys towards such subjects, a view which seems to have had the approval of the school authorities. Boys who were used to reading schoolboy novels of derring-do in the Empire – especially in the Zulu War – warmed to such encouragement.

Charles Commeline and his younger brother Archibald (Roll Nos. 63 and 64) had entered the school in 1866, when Fryer was headmaster. The careers of the two boys indicate the two faces of St Edward's in the late century, the one Imperialist in sentiment, the other Tractarian. Archibald represents the school's High Churchmanship. An academic clerk at Magdalen College, priested in 1882, he was a vicar-choral of York Minster and hospital chaplain, and then for twenty-six years vicar of Beaconsfield. Charles chose the Royal Engineers and rose to the rank of colonel by 1902 after serving in South Africa from the Zulu War to the Boer campaigns. Mentioned in despatches, he was a true Imperial hero. He joined the school aged 11 and left it aged 15, but he was clearly attached to it, for as a lieutenant he wrote three long letters to the *Chronicle* in 1879 describing in exciting detail his role in the Zulu War.

They read like a novel by Henty and must have been thrilling for St Edward's boys. He traces the early reverses of the war from the time of the disastrous defeat of the British forces at Isandlwana on 22 January, when he was himself in the region. His first letter, in February, has such sentences as: 'We met crowds of our native troops hurrying away in full retreat, some few being wounded and all looking very weary and sheepish at meeting our little company going the other way. In fact the fellows had made a very early bolt for it, leaving the white men to their fate.' In June the editor's space in the *Chronicle* is given over to Charles's second letter. He is serving in Natal with John Chard, the hero of Rorke's Drift, having been sent there to record any damage to the mission station:

> I shall take my man with me to look after my horse when there .... This is a country where nobody walks but black men .... The whole country seemed utterly deserted by man and beast, but at one burnt kraal we came upon two wretched old Zulu women, who had been left there without food or shelter to starve, but of course we could do nothing for them. This heartless treatment of the aged is quite the custom of the Zulus and I believe of all barbarous nations.

The colonial wars, and above all the Boer War, had made the schools not merely admirers of Imperialism but participants in it. The transformation took time. In spite of Commeline's letters, the school of the 1870s was not obsessed by the Imperial adventure. Nor was it much interested in current political questions. The Debating Society confined itself to such motions as 'In the Opinion of this House the execution of Charles I was unjustifiable' (carried by 11 votes to 9) and 'Lord Dunraven's action [in refusing to race again in his yacht after a quarrel with the New York Yacht Club] was justifiable' (carried by the same margin). The nearest approach to politics was the motion that 'This House deplores the advanced condition of women at the present day, and earnestly hopes they will never have a vote at parliamentary elections' (carried 12–11). Imperial matters were not debated for the first time until April 1896, when the Society tackled the motion that 'In the opinion of this House Dr Jameson's Act [the Jameson Raid, a bungled private-enterprise invasion of the Transvaal, undertaken the previous December with Cecil Rhodes's covert backing], as far as we know, was justifiable' (carried 10–5). The Boer War helped direct the Society towards wider military and political issues. Debates of

1901 discussed the ancient and modern methods of warfare and a proposal to adopt conscription (lost 14–3).

Yet, at least for a time, the Imperialist cause was not universally admired. When on 1 December 1890 the Society debated the motion that 'This House approves of the War and of the causes for which it has been undertaken and the way in which it has been carried out', the *Chronicle* recorded that 'P.C. Underhill [Percy, Roll No. 897], who was presiding, found it sometimes a difficult task to keep order.' The motion passed by just two votes (14–12). What provoked this dissent? Was there unease among the boys, and perhaps their parents too, at the shift in the school's culture away from Tractarianism, a movement which had its misgivings about the Imperial adventure? The tension between Tractarian and Imperialist enthusiasms emerged in the speeches at Gaudy on 5 June 1902. There was a sermon by the Rev. Starkey Coles, Principal of the High Church establishment Pusey House. After lunch the toast of 'The Preacher' was proposed, and the virtues of Pusey House extolled, by the Rev. F. V. Bussell (father of John Bussell, Roll No. 972). Coles, replying, reminded everyone of the ideals of Charles Liddon, that grandee of the Oxford Movement, and of their influence on St Edward's. The Warden of Keble, Walter Lock, toasted 'The Army and the Navy'. His speech was a rearguard action on behalf of the Ritualists of Liddon's and Simeon's generation. It was, he said, hard for the clergyman and the head of a college to propose a toast to the army at a time when it was emptying the colleges, and when undergraduates – some from St Edward's among them – who had intended to take holy orders were instead enlisting in the army or leading the troops. Perhaps sensing the bitterness of his words, Lock drew back. He voiced the hope, perhaps not too confidently, that the motives for fighting for one's country were compatible with the values that led men to become priests; and that even if the participants had impure motives the war would purify them.

Yet unease about Imperialism was a diminishing sentiment. Warden Lock was out of step with his audience, for the Gaudy was held just after the relief of Mafeking. Once the clergymen had had their say the gathering turned to uninhibited celebration. A glee was sung to mark the victory. Then the OSE Captain Arthur Slessor, acting adjutant to the Volunteers in Oxford, spoke. He applauded the 'intense interest' aroused by the Boer conflict of 1899–1902 and the renewed enthusiasm for the army it had brought, and 'was sorry they had not a cadet corps at St Edward's'. In the absence of conscription, he explained, volunteers were essential. So he urged 'the boys of St Edward's when they left to go to the Varsity or wherever they found a Volunteer Corps to join it and learn how to shoot'. While the prospective ordinands of Keble were rushing to the colours, the boys of St Edward's could hardly be expected to resist the military ardour of the day. The relief of Mafeking and of Ladysmith was marked by bonfires and holidays, and when Pretoria fell the whole school, joined by most of Summertown, celebrated around a bonfire by the outdoor pool after Chapel.

The ardour was fanned by the *Chronicle*. Old Boys, most of them anonymously, showered the editors with exciting tales of the fighting on the Veldt. Columns of the magazine recorded the military movements of seemingly every one of the seventy OSE in the services, often with accounts of their actions or extracts from lengthy letters. Particularly vivid were letters written in the summer of 1900 by Herman Agnew (Roll No. 795), who served in South Africa together with his brother Percy (Roll No. 796): 'Suddenly about 1.25 p.m. we heard firing all around our rear and the Major was at once sent for; he ordered us all to fall in and take the kopje. As we started bullets were flying all round and [a name blanked for security reasons] was hit through the fleshy part of the thigh .... Went up an awfully difficult hill – about 20 of us all told arrived at the top. We dismounted and [blanked name] who was within 3 yards of me was shot through the neck. I went to him but he was unconscious. I hooked my reins over my right arm and prepared to fire but my horse got a bullet in her rear fore-leg and became unmanageable .... I felt another bullet pass under my nose and then another struck my bayonet belt, breaking the buckle.' Herman was killed in action on Christmas Day 1902 'while trying to save the guns'. Percy was wounded in May 1900, but survived. The prologue to Cowell's production of *Julius Caesar* paid tribute to Herman:

> vision rises first, of that dark camp ...
> On which the foe broke in with shot and shell,
> (Oh Christmas bells dream-heard!) the wild alarm
> And one still form by a disabled gun ....

Agnew was one of three OSE who died in South Africa, the others being Alfred Lund (Roll No. 274), who had been born in the year of the school's foundation, and Alfred Spurling (Roll No. 870). Nine OSE were wounded. Warden Hudson presented the school with a Union Jack in tribute to the fallen and the injured.

The OSE at war were *Boy's Own Paper* heroes, none more so than two old boys who were the embodiment of the 'manliness' of late-Victorian and Edwardian England: Beverley Ussher (Roll No. 783) and John Bussell. Beverley, one of three brothers, left the school in 1898, aged 19, after seven years there. He had been a prefect, sung in the choir, played for the XV and the XI, appeared in Cowell's productions, and been a capable athlete, a career he crowned by winning a place at Wadham College, Oxford. Whereas his father had entered the Church, Beverley took a university commission in the Leinster Regiment. He fought successfully in the Boer War, was promoted to lieutenant in 1902, remained in the army, and was made captain in 1910. The second figure, Bussell, would have struck a special chord with the current boys, for he had only left in 1900, aged 17. Readers of the *Chronicle* would have remembered him as a prefect and for his athletic prowess. There was a moment that became famous in the school when, while waiting at St Edward's to join his regiment, he abruptly shed his military uniform and donned his Set colours to win the mile and secure the cup for his Set. Warrior and athlete had become one. Two days later he sailed for the Cape, where he participated in more than thirty military engagements. He returned as a master in 1908.

As with the rise of games, so with the school's engagement with the war, change came after pressure from boys. Demands for a Rifle Club were supported by letters in the *Chronicle*. Both Hudson and Sing seem to have been unenthusiastic. Maybe they were conscious of the doubts behind the Warden of Keble's speech. Maybe they thought that, once established, the club might be difficult to remove. They would have considered the expense, and also the likely stretching of the school's timetable. Would time for games have to be given up to sustain the club? Yet schools were under national pressure to produce fighting men and officer material. Lord Haldane, Secretary of State for War, had long complained of a shortage of officers in Britain's small army. Lord Roberts, everybody's hero of the South African War, wrote to schools in 1904 encouraging the formation of rifle clubs and cadet corps. The following year Sing relented and the Governors agreed to the establishment of a 'cadet corps or rifle club', terms that seem to have been interchangeable. Sixty-five boys rushed to join the club. A master whom Sing had just appointed, E. A. Jermyn from Worcester College, arrived full of enthusiasm for the Corps and was put in charge of it. All boys of 15 or over were compelled to join for two years. There was weekly drill, and two rifle ranges were built. Yet Jermyn soon left for India, and the appointment of the gym instructor Adams in his place suggests a lack of enthusiasm for the project in the Common Room, though Adams was a safe enough pair of hands.

By July 1906 'skirmishing is improving noticeably', even though drill was limited by the demands of cricket and rowing. The War Office sent drill rifles, and OSE donated money for small-bore rifles. Soon the school was participating in local and national shooting competitions, so that shooting, which according to the *Chronicle* was 'rather a good game', took its place alongside the other sports. Candidates could win a Rifleman's Certificate, or compete for silver and bronze medals presented by the National Service League for combined skill in drill and shooting. In 1906 Sing made what proved to be another short-term appointment, that of the Rev. B. Heald, who had been one of the volunteers from Keble whose departure the college's Warden had regretted. For two terms he led the club with 'able superintendence'.

More than three columns of the *Chronicle* of April 1906 are given over to an account of a field exercise. 'Some of us felt a little nervous .... As we were only furnished with the more necessary portions of military equipment it seemed a little doubtful to the most sensitive of our number whether the denizens of Summertown would take in good part our little game of soldiers.' Adams, having left a rearguard on the left bank of the Cherwell to command the fords, led an advance guard against an imaginary enemy as it retreated towards the village of Elsfield. Sections 1 and 2, screened by trees, 'kept up a withering fire on the enemy's position', and Heald provided a pontoon made from a punt for sections 3 and 4 to cross the water. The exercise continued with fearsome attacks, though the *Chronicle* has some measured criticism of the tactics employed. The magazine's report self-consciously echoes despatches from the Boer War.

The Rifle Club, which had its first inspection in 1906, had its own accounts. By the end of 1905 the committee was subsidizing the Rifle Club with a loan, and OSE had given £15 3s. 6d to the fund, the largest contribution to its coffers. As in other sports, boys paid a subscription. The club raised £41 to finance its first year, whereas over the same period St Thomas's Church Mission Clubs, financed by the school's Mission Account, collected only £29 16s.9d, to which boys contributed a mere £6. Meanwhile 'the Drill Book begins to oust the popular literary periodical *The Monthly Magazine* from its established position as light dinner-table literature'. The first Inspection of the Rifle Club followed. The *Chronicle* acknowledges the roles of Jermyn and Heald in furthering the club, but still no other master is associated with it. The two young men belonged to a generation more committed to the new Imperialism than their elders in the Common Room. In that context 1908 was a key year for both the Rifle Club and the school.

Wars tend to enhance the power of the state. The pressure exerted by Haldane and Roberts, the award of military certificates and prizes by outside bodies, the holding of inspections by regular army adjutants – all of these developments reflected a trend towards external involvement in the school's life. A significant moment was the passage of the 1907 Territorial and Reserve Forces Act, which in the following year implemented the 'Haldane Scheme'. All Public Schools were invited to form an Officers' Training Corps. Government money was promised; field days were to be subsidized; commissions were to be offered to young schoolmasters willing to command the new contingents. The award of the new 'Certificate A' would give a cadet 200 points towards the Sandhurst entry examination. It would enable him to join the Special Reserve and to draw, even while remaining in civilian life, an emolument of £30 a year. Schools could hardly decline to join a scheme that had patriotic sentiment and boys' enthusiasm on its side. Participation in the Officers' Training Corps (OTC) became as essential a mark of a real Public School as sports teams and colours or awards in the Classics. With a new confidence the Rifle Club requested and was granted a half holiday on 9 July 1908 for a special Field Day in and around Yarnton, when one half of the contingent attacked the other half with the aim of capturing a wagon, only to be thwarted by the defence mounted by Oswald Blencowe (Roll No. 1130), the Senior Prefect and later a schoolmaster, who would perish at Gueudecourt on 7 October 1916.

The national mood that produced the Haldane Scheme eventually permeated the Common Room. No masters were present at the Field Day of 1908. But in that and the following year Sing made three significant appointments, again of young men fresh from university. They were John Bussell from Brasenose College, Oxford, Arthur Weller from Worcester College, Oxford, and Leonard Cass from Emmanuel College, Cambridge. All three were made Set tutors. Armed with their new Haldane commissions, they converted the Rifle Club into the OTC, a move delightedly reported by the *Chronicle* in December 1908: 'It is not often that a new Act of Parliament has an obvious effect on one's everyday life.' That was indeed an unusual experience for the Edwardian age. The measure presaged the blizzard of controls by Westminster and Whitehall that would hit twentieth-century society and twentieth-century St Edward's. A thin wedge had been inserted into the independence of the school, which had accepted the state's money and entrusted masters who were agents of the state with the running of the OTC.

Field days and annual inspections acquired the same status in the school's calendar as its games fixtures. In July 1909 came the first military promotions for the boys. The elevation of eight boys to positions ranging from colour sergeant to corporal was published in the *Chronicle* in the same manner as the award of games colours. The OTC Accounts of 1909 show receipts of £161 3s. 2d, of which the bulk came from the War Office. The Central Committee's loan to the Rifle Club had become a full grant of £13 0s. 2d to the OTC. Camps were held and their activities reported in the *Chronicle*. By 1912 there was a Military Week, which in that year was held from 26 February to 2 March, with Weller, Cass and Bussell in charge. At the Inspection, Major Percival from the War Office gave the school a good report, in spite of some less than burnished boots. But he pointed out that even though the government was spending £87,000 a year on school cadet corps the expenditure had resulted in very few take-ups of commissions. His words intimated that state pressure would increase. In October 1912 there were 63 boys over 15 in the OTC, out of 120 boys at the school. By April 1914 the number had swelled to 73. A sergeant-instructor named Cunningham was given a permanent appointment to introduce greater professionalism. Yet the leadership of the OTC in the Common Room suffered depletion. Bussell moved on to Marlborough in 1913, and Weller left in 1914 to be head of a grammar school. So the OTC entered the war short of officers.

In 1912 Public School cadet units received another letter from Lord Roberts, who had been Britain's Commander-in-Chief from 1900 to 1905. 'You have had great advantages as British Public Schoolboys and as British citizens you will have even greater privileges. What do you mean to give your country in return? It is in the power of every one of you to give personal service, that is, deliberately to work for our nation, as well as for yourself; but personal service means some sacrifice of self.' Public School boys were used to the ideals of loyalty and of putting the team before the self. Now they were being acclimatized and organized for the big test, which would come in 1914. The school would meet it. In November 1914 the *Times Educational Supplement* announced that St Edward's, with three others, 'headed the list of all the schools in the country with 100% enlistment in the OTC of those eligible'.

I have indicated that the military component of education merged with, and was nourished by, the muscular, competitive values that the schools had already adopted. Militarization had another consequence too. In April 1903 the *Chronicle* reported that

> the panelling of the Chapel is a "fait accompli". The work has been going on for two or three weeks without interrupting, and as we write, it has just received its finishing touches. The panelling is of oak, it covers the walls of the whole nave to a height of about eleven feet and is stained a shade or two darker than the rest of the woodwork. It would be impossible to exaggerate the gain to the Chapel which results from this comparatively simple addition .... There remain to be added the memorial tablets and we hope that they may be in place by Gaudy Day.

The panels, which now clothed the plain painted walls, were the school's memorial to the OSE who had died in their country's service, and whose names were recorded on five brass panels attached to the panelling at the north-west end of the Chapel. An OSE Memorial Fund, set up to help meet the cost, was supervised by Sing. By April 1903 the Fund had topped £96, and contributions continued to come in. In March 1903 a new window by Kempe on the south side of the Chapel, representing 'Hope', had been unveiled in memory of Alfred Spurling, a hero of Mafeking who was killed in action at Rietpoort in November 1901. His brass plaque joined those dedicated to William Clarke (Roll No. 525), a victim of the 1895 Matabeleland War; David Osborne Jones (Roll No. 559), who died in the Tirah Campaign of 1897; and Herman Agnew and Alfred Lund, the other two victims of the Boer conflict. Group memorialization of this kind, a response to the intense patriotism of the day, was a new phenomenon. In a sense the old boys had taken over the Chapel. Old boys and present ones joined, as team brothers, to honour the fallen, especially those of them they had known. The Spurling window, a classic form of remembrance of a member of the family that had paid for it, represents an older method of commemoration alongside a new one more collective in spirit.

The decision to commemorate the dead in Chapel was significant. Some other schools adopted different courses. They listed the dead on a cloister wall, or set up a Calvary cross, or put up a building for a secular purpose and dedicated it to the fallen. After the Great War St Edward's would adopt the second and third of those courses, but as additions, not alternatives, to the honouring of the dead in Chapel. Even when the chapels of other schools paid tribute to the dead the memorials were normally a less conspicuous presence, though Charterhouse built a whole new chapel as a war memorial. At St Edward's the plaques left large areas of vacant oak, an ominous hint, perhaps, of the attrition to come. Simeon's Chapel had been a vehicle of Ritualism, a liturgical space whose furnishings and music stressed the sacraments and the beauty of holiness. Now the building was not merely a place of worship. It was a reminder of military sacrifice, and a place of pilgrimage for OSE.

22

JUBILEE

In 1912 Sing decided to leave St Edward's, though he stayed until the summer of 1913 in order to see the school through to its Jubilee. He announced his decision in an extended letter, which he sent to parents on 2 June 1913, just over a month before the celebrations. He had been at St Edward's since 1887, longer than anyone except Cowell. Throughout his time the school had been in financial difficulty, which he had done much to allay. He was worn out. Possibly he had been a poor delegator, though there were few people to whom to delegate, for masters, with the outstanding exception of Cowell, passed through the school at a fairly rapid rate. 'I have been at St Edward's for 27 years in all,' he told the parents, 'and though I am beginning to feel the strain of heavy work, I should be loath to leave it, were I not confident – with an unusual degree of confidence – that Mr Ferguson [Sing's successor] will manage the School wisely and well, quickly winning the respect and affection of boys and the trust of their parents.'

As at the time of Sing's own appointment there was no wide casting of the net for a successor. William Ferguson was apparently the only candidate. In 1896, at the age of 23, he had been, as Sing's protégé, Warden Hudson's first appointment to the Common Room. He had stayed for three years before moving to Bilton Grange Preparatory School for a further two years. After that he was priested. Yet he always saw himself as a professional schoolmaster, and he had gone on to serve the Woodard foundation of Lancing for thirteen years. There was one other teacher whom we might expect to have been a candidate to succeed Sing. Wilfrid Cowell was rumoured – only rumoured – to have been offered the job in 1904, before Sing himself was given it. Yet there is no sign that he was considered now. Perhaps he was judged to lack, or knew himself to lack, the administrative and financial skills which the Wardenship required. In any case a very long-serving member of staff can seem so much part of the fabric of a school as to make it difficult to see him as its leader. In many respects St Edward's was Cowell's school. He was the keeper of its memory, preserving its growing archives and perpetuating its life through the series of *Rolls* he edited. Yet he seems a figure set apart from the currents of an age that brought sport and muscularity and manliness to the fore.

In a special Jubilee number the *Chronicle*, amid the usual plethora of games reports, and alongside a report of a lecture to the OTC and a list of Certificate 'A' successes, momentarily resumed some of the variety that had characterized its contents in earlier years. There were poems and original essays. Literary compositions were sent in by OSE, among them Aubyn Trevor-Battye and Kenneth Grahame. The same issue recorded a brave motion of the Debating Society, that 'in the opinion of this House Sports and Athletics are carried too far'. The motion, proposed by Ronald Halcomb (Roll No. 1360), who was to have a successful career as a soldier, was lost by 29 votes to 6. One of the poems, written by Bernard Nunn (Roll No. 771), who had left in 1885, had a military theme. A keen member of the military Reservists, and now a colonial administrator in Malaya, Nunn reminded boys of the school's duty to the world, in verse printed in the *Chronicle*, which proclaims, admittedly in crude lines, the umbilical tie of the present boys with OSE, living and dead:

> We're sons of St Edward's, we rule and we fight
>   In our country's dominions afar,
> We ranch and we plant and we teach and we write
>   Under each his particular star.
> Yet, though we all know of the strength and the verve
>   Of your Home-guard [the OTC], it's perfectly plain –
> We're your Training as well: if you want the Reserve
>   We are eager to come out again! . .
> We're sons of St Edward's, those buildings of red
>   The Quad and the Chapel are ours,
> We dream of them living (though some of us dead,
>   Even they in their graves are still yours);
> And we're ready if danger or doubt should befall,
>   We are only repaying a due,
> To come out in support, yes, though distant the call,
>   If we ever are wanted by you!

The most substantial and significant piece in the issue, entitled 'Harvest', analyses the school's achievements to date. It was written by the man best qualified to write it, Cowell. For him St Edward's was what it had been for Simeon: a religious community. He proudly recorded that 150 OSE and 21 masters had been ordained, though his hope that 'this proportion of ordinands be maintained' was not to be fulfilled. He also tells us that fourteen boys had joined the Royal Navy as sailors and that three of the ordinands had become naval chaplains. The Navy commanded huge public esteem, as the school's photograph of Warden Hudson's children, which shows them in the familiar garb of sailor suits, reminds us. Yet until recently those seeking a naval career had had to join during boyhood. It was the army, fearful of a shortage of officer material as of manpower generally, that set the pace in recruiting Public School boys. Cowell calculated that the school had contributed 72 former boys to the Army List. We might think it an impressive tally, but Cowell suggests a reason why it was not higher. He noted that officers were badly paid and reckoned they needed a private income of £100 a year to sustain their role. 'The families from which we draw our boys are not as a rule wealthy. A very considerable proportion of them, for example, are the families of the clergy.' In Cowell's judgement the country ('or the Government – the two are not synonymous nowadays') would not secure enough officers until it paid them properly. 'We should hear nothing about the scarcity of officers, was it otherwise, and their quality would rise rather than fall.' There was evidently a radical streak in Cowell. The Army had made entry to the officer class dependent on wealth to keep inferiors out of the messes, but, as he grasped, its social exclusiveness had produced a damaging shortfall of leaders.

Cowell counts the numbers of old boys in other careers: 60 in medicine, 42 lawyers, about 35 in various branches of education, 20 civil servants and about 30 who either were explorers or belonged to the worlds of literature and the arts. Might OSE have been better represented in that capacious last category? Perhaps too the figures exposed the weakness of modern and scientific studies at St Edward's. Yet there was a creative side to the school's life, of which Cowell, inside and outside the classroom, was himself the inspiration. It was he who had spotted and encouraged the interests of Aubyn Trevor-Battye and of Arthur Mace (Roll No. 743), the eminent archaeologist and the intellectual force behind Howard Carter and the Tutankhamun discoveries. Cowell then turns to the 250 OSE who live abroad, often serving in the forces, or farming across the Empire. Finally he comes to 'gentlemen at large – a dangerous sort of wild beast', by whose wastrel tendencies he seems embarrassed. But 'it is a negligible quantity in the total of our results. The OSE are almost without exception workers.'

And so the Jubilee Commemoration arrived on Sunday 6 July 1913. The first of two days of celebration was almost wholly set aside for Simeon. He presided at the Eucharist in Chapel at 8 a.m. A Choral Eucharist followed at 11 a.m., when the celebrant was a schoolmaster-priest, currently teaching at the school, Lawrence Harvey (Roll No. 1021). Simeon preached on Psalm 77: 5, 'I have considered the days of old, the years of ancient times.' He places the school where he firmly believes it belongs, in the Tractarian tradition which guided his life. He lists the chief supporters and benefactors who influenced him and who had been the inspiration of the school. They range from Keble, Liddon and Chamberlain to Beauchamp, Aldenham and Halifax, to Mackarness, King and Bright, to 'Mrs Combe of the Press' and to 'Godmother' herself, the late Felicia Skene. Of those names only Halifax was still alive. The address was a roll of honour, not to the soldiers named on the Chapel panelling but to soldiers of Christ.

If the Sunday was Simeon's day, the celebrations of Monday saluted the school itself. Again the Chapel was the centrepiece. A massive procession of dignitaries was led by the Bishop of London, Dr A. P. Winnington-Ingram, and the Bishop of Oxford, the liberal Tractarian Charles Gore. After a lengthy bidding prayer, Winnington-Ingram preached. The bishop was himself a Tractarian, but never a dogmatic one. A keen sportsman, and an eager champion of Empire and of the military spirit, he would have approved of the games culture at St Edward's and of the rise of the OTC. If the coded allusions of his sermon mean what they appear to mean, his was an extraordinary address, the more so for being delivered in Simeon's presence on the day after such homage had been paid to the leading figure of the school's history. The bishop's text was the third verse of the Epistle of Jude, who exhorts his fellow believers 'that ye should earnestly contend for the faith which was once delivered unto our saints'. The founders and initial supporters of St Edward's, the bishop indicated, had in one sense been admirably true to Jude's injunction. They 'had to fight' if they were to 'break through the apathy about Church teaching, which was far stronger then than today'. Yet in the bishop's hands Jude's words become not so much an injunction to zeal as at least a half-warning against it. Where Simeon's sermon had lauded the Victorian soldiers of Christ, Winnington-Ingram indicated that their 'earnestness of conviction', indeed 'fanaticism', had 'carried them away', or at least had given that impression to 'men of the world', whose complaints 'we were bound to notice', and among whom the 'religious controversialists' of that generation 'had not earned a very good reputation'. For the ideals of a school, the bishop implied, will prevail only if it commands the respect of conventional opinion outside it, to which it must accommodate itself. Like it or not, it mattered 'what men of the world thought'. If intemperance of zeal had been a failing in the school's early years, so much more would it be now, when 'we are in a world of greater compromise with the Word', and when a more measured and less controversial approach would be better fitted to secure improvements in the Church. The preacher's points were shrouded in elaborate biblical analogies. If the congregation grasped their meaning, there must have been some sharp intakes of breath.

The visitors were served luncheon in Big School, which was 'filled to the last inch'. The tables were four abreast instead of the usual three, and above 260 guests were seated. The 120 boys and an overspill of OSE were fed in the dining hall and came into Big School for the toasts and speeches. Sing made a characteristically low-key and self-effacing speech, which praised everyone from Simeon to the servants and included a special tribute to Cowell, who 'has devoted great gifts to the School's service for the best part of forty years'. Sing described the purpose of the school as the preparation of good churchmen and good citizens, a judicious characterization if one lacking the fervour of the statements of purpose of the 1860s and 1870s, which had dwelled exclusively on the mission of boys to do God's work in the world.

Then the 74-year-old Halifax, who had already proposed the toast 'Floreat St Edward's', rose a second time, to praise the retiring Warden. The Council, he declared, felt 'incapable of expressing the whole of the gratitude they felt to Mr Sing'. It was an emotional speech, for Halifax knew better than most what the school owed to Sing, not only as Warden but earlier as a master. As Warden he had restored the numbers, raising them above a hundred again. He had secured the games fields. In the running of the school his presence and influence had been ubiquitous. He had also been choirmaster for fourteen years; had set up the Central Committee and its funds; had organized the new Boat Club; had acted as treasurer to innumerable appeals and funds; and had run Set B, the most successful of the five Sets both academically and athletically. (Cowell had been in charge of Set A since 1893.) Amid all those demands Sing, before and after he became Warden, was an outstanding (if old-fashioned) teacher of Classics in the Sixth Form. Before his arrival in 1887 only three boys from St Edward's had achieved Classical Scholarships. Between 1887 and 1907, 23 such honours were won, a considerable achievement. Over his whole time at St Edward's, from 1887 to 1913, there were 41 awards overall (including Choral ones) at Oxford and Cambridge, 17 of them in the nine years of his Wardenship. His devotion to St Edward's ran deep. Like Simeon he remained a presence around the school for many years after his retirement, but unlike him he did not interfere. He stood in briefly for Ferguson when the Warden was ill in 1925, and was a governor from 1927 until his death in 1947.

The last speaker at the lunch was Ferguson himself. 'He said, the *Chronicle* tells us, that he 'regarded St Edward's as his home. He owed to Mr Sing a debt of gratitude he could never repay. He also owed St Edward's a debt for teaching him many things about his profession. There was an atmosphere about the place which gripped everyone who came in contact with it .... It was a living witness of the great principle for which the Church had been fighting – they could not separate religion from education.' Ferguson's background placed him firmly in the High Church movement, and he was devoted to its liturgical practices. He would have known of Simeon's school since childhood, when he was a pupil at Magdalen College School. He had been organist at Keble and was an accomplished church musician in the Tractarian mould. So why had he left St Edward's after only three years as a teacher? Had he found the methods of Hudson, who was not always liked in the Common Room, uncongenial? The school of Simeon and Hobson had been small – too small, perhaps – but it had been cosy. Everyone knew everyone else, and Simeon and Hobson had won high praise for their gifts of translating their Christian ideals into pastoral care and of nourishing the spirit of fraternity. Hudson was different; less approachable by boys, readier to punish them. He had seemed to care more about raising the number of pupils than about their individuality. Whatever the reason for his previous departure, Ferguson would attempt to reinvigorate the previous ideal of a Christian family. Many boys would remember him with affection.

The Jubilee, which ended with a garden party, was commemorated by poems in the *Chronicle*. The best of them was written by Edwin Stonex (Roll No. 1351), School Scholar and a prefect, who would go up to Oriel in 1914 with a Classical Scholarship he had won under Sing's tutelage.

SES

Martyr'd Boy-King, look down and see
How young and old are meeting here,
To keep in this our fiftieth year
The joyful feast of Jubilee.
The young come in with doubts and fears,
With timid step and wandering eyes,
But, ere they leave, they gain the prize,
The ordered strength of ripening years.
The fathers love again to pass
Within the walls they held so dear.
May all their sons who sojourn here
Learn true *'Parentum Pietas'*.

The last line invokes – with the two Latin words in reverse order – the motto that was given to the school by Simeon's brother Hugh during his time on the teaching staff in 1879–81. Its meaning (literally 'the piety', or 'sense of duty', 'of the parents') has perplexed succeeding generations.

On 30 September 1913 Sing, accompanied by his spinster sister who had long kept house for him, sailed in the SS *Grotius* on a cruise round the world. On the same day Ferguson, the fifth Warden, took up office. There were 117 boys in the school, a number that would rise spectacularly during his tenure. Ferguson's commitment to the Tractarian ideal, and his record as a housemaster at Lancing where he had won warm admiration for his relationships with his pupils, made him seem an ideal appointment. Among those pupils was W. K. Stanton, whom he had taught the organ and of whom he was a lifelong friend. Stanton had worked temporarily at St Edward's in 1912. He now returned as organist and choirmaster, and would stay until the end of Ferguson's tenure in 1924. The Warden made him Tutor to Sing's 'star' Set B.

The cost of the Jubilee had drained most of the working surplus of 1913 and there were recurrent shortages of money. In 1914 Gaudy had to be skipped to save funds. Ferguson, with Halifax as his confidant, resolved to tackle the financial problem. Yet the two men made what could have proved a serious misjudgement. Early in his Wardenship Ferguson proposed that an appeal for £5,000 be made to the kinds of churchmen who valued the place of St Edward's in the High Church revival of yesteryear, who appreciated the school's contribution to the education of the clergy, and who could be expected to welcome the chance of a retrospective salute to the Simeon years. 'Without being in any sense an ecclesiastical seminary,' declared the draft of the appeal document, 'the school has as a result of its tone and training produced over the last fifty years a succession of earnest workers who have entered the ministry with the very highest motives, and have been at all times ready and willing cheerfully to endure hardship and to face poverty.' Boldly the manifesto asserts that 'in the school the Church possesses a very considerable asset. The question therefore arises – could not the Church make still more effective use of this instrument which lies ready to its hand?'

There being few rich parents, it was perhaps understandable that Ferguson and Halifax should look to a core market, even if it was shrinking. Of the 132 boys in the school in October 1914, 44 were the sons of clergy, 16 of them in Cowell's Set. Yet the catchment area was too small and was itself insufficiently endowed. An appeal so clerical in character, which recalled the failed proposal of 1911 to tempt High Church sympathizers with offers of debentures, was unlikely to enthuse prosperous men of the world among the OSE, such as Rogers or the rich and successful barrister Edmund Brewer-Williams (Roll No. 366). Rogers had welcomed the demise of Simeon's Confraternity and built up the more secular Society at its expense. Ferguson's vision for the school was essentially Simeon's, even if it lacked the power and intensity of the earlier man's aspirations. He was sympathetic to Simeon's ideal of a semi-religious community. The realistic Sing, genuine as his faith was, would not have embarked on an appeal of the kind proposed by Ferguson and Halifax.

Fortunately perhaps, the proposal was not put to the test. War was declared while the appeal document was being printed, and the project was instantly shelved. Without it Ferguson could only try, like his predecessors, to make do with limited resources. There was, however, one bright development. As war approached, the boys' numbers increased. On Sing's departure in 1913 there were 112. The next year there were 132. The surge continued during the war until in 1918 there were 168 boys. Comparable schools such as Malvern and Radley, though also expanding in the same period, did so less impressively. The exceptional growth of St Edward's is hard to account for. Perhaps the school's embrace of military values, chiming as it did with the national mood, helped. But the trend would long outlive the war, and in time would turn St Edward's from a small school to a substantial one.

23

WAR

THE effects of the Great War on the daily life of the school were quickly apparent and were profound. The flocking of senior boys to the colours reduced the average age of the prefects by nearly eighteen months. In games, fixture lists shrank. Few of the Oxford colleges whom the school normally played retained teams. In the school's own teams 16-year-olds took the places of 18-year-olds. Though food rationing was not introduced until 1918, St Edward's had to adjust to shortages and to the threat to the nation's supplies. Rowing was halted in 1916 on the ground that the sport encouraged eating. There were 'meatless days'. Margarine, a recent invention, sometimes replaced butter. The fields were put to agricultural use. On some days rice replaced potatoes, though junior boys helped lift a local potato crop and eventually enough potatoes were grown on the lower fields to last a year. Oats were grown there too. As in earlier times, hay was mown in the Quad. After its acquisition in 1918, Wiblin's field to the east of the Chapel produced vegetables. In June 1915 the *Chronicle* recorded that 'following the example of His Majesty King George, the school has given up alcohol for the period of the War'.

The war made almost a clean sweep of the Common Room. Of Ferguson's first seven appointments none lasted beyond 1919. At least five masters left for the front, including Leonard Davies, who was said to have been a popular tutor of Set E, and who was killed in Flanders in June 1916. J. B. Partington, who had taught in 1913–14, fell in February 1917. Frank Barnes (Roll No. 1022), appointed in 1914, was instantly made tutor of Set B, but by 1915 he too was at war. He had been a useful addition to the staff, despite his unpromising record as a boy, when he had been dismissed as a prefect for smoking and other misdemeanours. Ferguson made numerous appointments during the war, most of which lasted a very short time. There was a similar pattern in other schools. Ferguson did manage to hold on to three men appointed in 1917–18: the Rev. J. W. Griffiths, who stayed until 1927; W. M. W. Shackleton, who remained until his death in 1926; and that long-lasting appointment, B. G. Segar. But for at least the greater part of the war Ferguson probably relied heavily on Stanton and on N. W. Hammond, who was appointed in 1914 and stayed until 1919. He ran Set C and the OTC, and seems to have been a colourful character.

From the outbreak of the conflict the OTC's rifles were kept in the relative security of the Town Hall cellars. But they had constantly to be brought back for use at the school, where most were housed again by 1917. The OTC was training young men only weeks or months from military service, who knew that success in the Corps could lead to an immediate commission when enlistment came. Boys next in line to be called to the colours wore white bands round their caps. The OTC became a central feature of the school's life, at the expense of time spent in the classroom and on games. The process is penetratingly observed in the articulate memoirs of the successful journalist Patrick Lacey (Roll No. 1604), who joined the school, aged 13, in the Christmas Term of 1916 and became an OTC sergeant. He recalled that the school 'was now an integral, important and active part of a vast military college and machine for the manufacture, as quickly as possible, of cannon fodder fit to lead other cannon fodder in a business preoccupying the whole country's effort and attention.' By 1917 there were seven parades a week. The rapid turnover of officers from the Common Room was a problem, and in 1917 Instructor Adams was called back from retirement. For a brief time cadets walked the 15 miles or so to Didcot (for there were no trains to get them there) to unpack and stack camp stores from Woolwich.

Wartime legislation required the turning off of lights, with the result that people kept bumping into each other in the Quad. Headlong collisions were staged to annoy the masters. A temporary aerodrome was erected on Port Meadow, where there were frequent plane crashes, some of them close to boys walking there. Planes, of course, were something of a novelty. Lacey recalls the thrill of a small boy's proximity to them, and the occasion when an OSE war hero, Louis Strange (Roll No. 1215), flew his plane across the Quad and between the Chapel tower and Beauchamp dormitory, a presage of the school's later association with daredevil aviators. Boys broke bounds to visit the airstrip and enjoy the airmen's 'illicit generosity', presumably gifts of drink and cigarettes. Lacey remembers Ferguson's moving announcement in Chapel of the death in a flying accident of 'a popular prefect who had left under a cloud about six months before and had redeemed himself instantly and magnificently'. This was almost certainly Bernard

Carter (Roll No. 1421), who was killed while flying 'on special duty' in Anglesey on 7 November 1917.

The solemn announcements of the war dead accentuated the Chapel's new role as a mausoleum. 'A single ghastly day,' Lacey recalled, 'added eight names to the roll of honour around the Chapel's walls, and the carpenter had to give up trying to make finished plaques in pace with the casualty lists.' Within four years the walls containing the space for plaques had been filled to capacity. Brass ones had to make way for the less expensive oak. The announcements of deaths must have been chilling for senior boys, those closest in age to their slain former fellows and who would soon join the forces. Perhaps, alongside dread and resignation, they experienced a determination to make the most of what was left of a youth likely to be shortened. Lacey, one of the younger boys, recognizes that the dangers of war seemed less immediate to them, though he recalls the 'slightly envious awe' with which they regarded contemporaries when news arrived of the death or injury of an elder brother. He records deaths that particularly affected him, among them those of the former master Leonard Davies, who fell in Flanders in June 1916, and John Ley (Roll No. 1428), whose death in France in December 1917 was announced after he had been reported missing. Touchingly, Patrick remembers how Ley, his senior by four years, had twice saved him from bullying in the Shell. On a different note he recalls a visit to the school by Cecil Pogue (Roll No. 1540), 'a laughing typhoon of a boy' whom the war had made 'a serious-minded officer of tanks'.

Lacey's memoir conveys two strong impressions of the effects of the war on the school. The first is of the atmosphere of militarism. The colonial and Boer wars had nurtured military preoccupations, but nothing to match the new experience. There was also a change of tone. In the *Chronicle* the Kiplingesque tales of the earlier conflicts had given way to spare but moving accounts of the fighting. The immediacy of the conflict was brought home when officers recuperating from wounds or shell shock were seconded to the Corps. Lacey remembers how the boys drilled, took part in grenade practice outside the Armoury, and issued 'blood-curdling gurgles and shouts as they bayoneted sacks'. The bayoneting took place on an evocative spot, the lawn beside the Chapel burial ground.

The second impression, though it is hard to test, is of a fall-off in discipline in Set and school. Lacey argued that 16- and 17-year-olds who were thrust prematurely into privilege and power made poor prefects, and that Ferguson, in no position to pick and choose, had to 'take them as they came'. Continuity was lost when whole groups of prefects left at the same time. The result was a 'cheerful state of irresponsibility'. One Senior Prefect, Rupert East (Roll No. 1325), held the post for just ten days before leaving for the war. His successor, Alexander Tod (Roll No. 1530), was just 17, though Lacey acknowledged that he was 'old for his age' and, because he caned often and 'with a breathtaking bang', effective. Tod left as the war was drawing to a close and became an Indian Army cadet. Lacey describes teachers struggling with discipline too. 'There were no competent young masters, and [only] a few really hefty boys, to take a directly instructive share in the School's organised or unofficial and sometimes unlicensed recreations. The rabble had to look to it and each boy to fight for himself.' Lacey acknowledges Ferguson's problems in filling vacant posts, and describes the stand-ins as 'gallant triers'. But he remembers that all but two or three of the teachers, who were 'old regulars', could be 'ragged' and that many lessons were pandemonium. The effect on standards of work was seen in the 'gaping voids on the Honours Boards' that Ferguson had placed on the walls of Big School.

Lacey finds a further explanation of the failure of discipline in a development the school would have faced even without the war: shortage of space as the numbers expanded. Overcrowding in the form rooms, where living and teaching still went on, produced misbehaviour he describes as 'pretty heavily charged with clumsy climactics', whatever they were. There being too few baths, the outdoor pool was in effect used as one, though boys tried to avoid that insalubrious experience. The water became dirty; mud from the field was plastered along the borders; towels got sodden and filthy. 'When all is said and done,' declares Lacey, 'our daily round in those days had a concentrated grimness ... that lent itself pretty exclusively to the survival and pleasure of the fittest'.

The memories of Oswald Shuffrey (Roll No. 1579), who attended from 1916 to 1920, are no more cheerful. He describes his early years at the school as 'pretty miserable'. He started in the New Zealand day room in the New Buildings, a room lit by gas lights which were inadequate for reading. It was impossible to 'do anything worthwhile in the day room. We ran around, shouted and fought.' 'Hell' was the name given to the lavatories for New Zealand, 'rows of booths resembling telephone boxes. We were not allowed doors, I presume for some inscrutable moral reason.' He slept in Ken, his ablutions being confined to an early-morning icy wash and a weekly bath. Eventually he became a day boy. He also made friends with Serbian refugee pupils who had been taken into the school by Ferguson as part of St Edward's support for the nation's allies. Shuffrey records frequent beatings by prefects 'for sins such as being a minute or two late for games, talking in Chapel. This did not mean that one had actually spoken, but if one turned towards one's neighbour, and a prefect considered that you might have spoken that was enough. I was only beaten once by a prefect. The crime was "ragging" in the quad. There were fights and much bullying.' Shuffrey remembers that two women were employed as temporary teachers, 'one young and attractive whom we adored, one old (to us that meant over 35) and ugly, whom we treated abominably'. The young Classicist – though the *Roll* did not record her presence – was Miss Sylvia Richards, who had a First from Girton College, Cambridge. Shuffrey's second tutor in Set D was George S. Duncan, known to the boys as 'shit Duncan'. The year before Shuffrey left, Duncan's place was taken by Arthur Macnamara, the future housemaster, 'a splendid fellow'. Shuffrey's best teacher was Cowell, 'the most remarkable character ever to be on the staff of St Edward's'.

Shuffrey's account, like Lacey's, indicates a decline of discipline in the war years. Yet much of what the two memoirs describe would have been familiar to pre-war generations. It should also be recorded that when Desmond Hill's *History* was published in 1962 Lacey's contemporary, Bob Mortimer, who was then Chairman of the Governors and Bishop of Exeter, wrote to Hill declaring Lacey's description to be overstated. Yet he does allow that 'we can take Lacey seriously' and himself acknowledges a succession of failings of the wartime school. He admits there was ragging of teachers such as M. W. M. Shackleton (who taught from 1917 to 1926), B. M. Goldie (in charge of Set E from his appointment in 1915 to his departure in 1919) and E. M. Clerk (employed only in 1919), who was so susceptible to the treatment, in which Mortimer himself joined during Clerk's sixth-form lessons, as 'to be in the *Decline and Fall* class'. Mortimer concedes that Ferguson had to 'scrape the bottom of the Gabbitas and Thring barrel'. He also remembers that 'during the last two years of the War there were, I think, three "rows" which ended in one or more expulsions', though he adds that 'we only heard of these rows. We had no personal experience of the matters involved.' But Mortimer, an intellectually exceptional boy and one of the few winners of a university award, does defend the standard of teaching. He praises not only Cowell (as Shuffrey did) and Hammond (whom Lacey also admired) but also Duncan.

At the end of the war Cowell recorded in a private document the sacrifices and glories of the conflict. He reckoned that at least 620 OSE had been involved, 'every available man, except one "conchy"'. They had fought in all the services on virtually every front. Cowell counted 19 DSOs (two of them with bars), 50 MCs (three with bars), 2 DCMs, 4 DFCs and 3 AFCs. Other distinctions included a KCIE, a CB, and 18 OBEs. There were awards by foreign powers too, ten French, six Belgian, two Italian, one Russian and two Egyptian. A total of 132 OSE had been mentioned in despatches. The toll was terrible: 117 old boys had died, many of them aged only 18, and three masters. Cowell calculated that at least 119 others had been wounded, 23 of them more than once. The oldest to have died, Harry Hopton (Roll No. 98), was aged 60. He had been in New Inn Hall Street with Fryer, Chamberlain's first headmaster. The youngest was probably Wilfred North-Cox (Roll No. 1306), who had entered the school in the Christmas Term of 1908 aged 11 and had left aged 14. He was wounded in March 1916 and died in Newcastle.

Of the First World War battles it was the Somme that claimed most lives, especially the first day, 1 July 1915, when within hours almost 20,000 soldiers died and nearly 38,000 were injured. Grouped at the back of the Chapel on the south side are the five plaques of OSE who died that day. The first plaque was for Thomas Haughton (Roll No. 1170), aged 25 and one of three brothers at the school. James Hyde (Roll No. 1302), a clergyman's son, was 21 and had a younger brother at the school. John Craig (Roll No. 1324), who was only 20, was killed in the famous advance by the Ulster Brigade towards Thiepval, where he fell. The other two had enlisted as privates in 1914. Eric Hobbs (Roll No. 1383), who died aged 21, was the youngest of three brothers at St Edward's. He was a private in the Royal Fusiliers before being commissioned in 1915. Harold Williamson (Roll No. 1370), who was 20, joined the 9th London Reserve and at the Somme was a Second Lieutenant in the 6th North Staffs.

At Winchester, where Sing was teaching temporarily to fill in for an absent master, the former Warden knew how many of the boys from his own time at St Edward's had perished. There were sixty-two of them, including two who had arrived in his penultimate term as Warden. He wrote personally to every family who had lost a son. The replies are haunting. Dorothea Bussell, John Bussell's wife, wrote to Sing in a vein characteristic of the letters:

It is a terrible thing. I feel as you do that everything seems altered and meaningless. But there was splendour in his death as in his life, and we all share something of it, don't we. It may be that I delude myself because I haven't the courage to look the facts in the face ....'

John had been the classic Victorian schoolboy, sportsman, schoolmaster and priest. Now the mental world of his upbringing had been broken. Public Schools that had absorbed the values, and adjusted to the priorities, of Imperialism, patriotism and martial ardour would now have to adapt to the war's legacy.

24

AFTERMATH

THE Chapel bells were among the first in Oxford to ring for the Armistice on 11 November. According to the *Chronicle*, 'Summertown, busily engaged in beflagging itself, was listening anxiously for them all the morning.' In 1917 the Prince of Wales had sponsored the idea of War Memorial funds to commemorate the fallen. It was an original concept, meant to tie communities to perpetual remembrance of the current sacrifice. With the same intent St Edward's resolved to add to the individual plaques in the Chapel a collective memorial on which the names of the dead would be listed. The Calvary which stands in the Quad to the south of the Chapel (and which was moved some yards in 1954 when the Memorial Library was built) was one of the thousands of memorials that went up throughout the country. Designed by the OSE Harold Rogers, it was dedicated at Commem in 1919 by the Archdeacon of Oxford, the Ven. T. H. Archer-Houblon, a leading High Church figure, a governor since 1902, and a member of a clerical family which had long been associated with the novelist Charlotte Yonge and her circle. The service was held in an interval between Cowell's production of *Twelfth Night* and an OTC march-past. 'All the arrangements were perfect,' reported the *Chronicle*. In 1922 an opening was made in the cloisters to give access to the monument, and windows were installed for its view. In the same year Sing returned to unveil the stone panels in the cloister which recalled the dead of the war. It was in 1922, too, that the individual panels in Chapel were completed. They were a special concern of Cowell, who had appealed personally to relations of the fallen for the money and had made his own financial contribution.

The Calvary was expensive. It was built at a time of sharp price rises and scarcity of money, when the school needed new buildings and facilities to meet the increase in boy numbers. Yet was the Calvary, even in straitened times, a sufficient tribute to the fallen? Might not funds be set up, it was asked, to educate sons of killed OSE at reduced rates? More ambitiously, might not the dead be honoured by the fulfilment of 'Simeon's Dream', through the completion of the cloisters around the Quad? A minority of OSE were very committed to this long-established plan. They were strongly represented on a committee to receive donations for the Memorial Fund, which amounted to £8,000 by 1922. Thereafter the money was slow to come in, despite annual appeals by Ferguson at the OSE dinners. The proposal to build additional cloisters was soon abandoned.

Instead the school decided in favour of a more practically minded building project. The school was short of accommodation, of science labs, of classrooms for the growing Modern side. Cowell initially opposed any expenditure from the fund on functional buildings, no doubt on the ground that the school would be using the wartime sacrifice to meet needs that had arisen independently of it. He was overruled. Instead the decision was taken to construct Memorial Buildings, which were opened in 1925.

The Spanish flu of 1918–19, which killed more people than the war, hit the school, but there were no fatalities. St Edward's was 'islanded for six weeks' and nearly everyone, from the Warden downwards, was taken ill. Most of the servants were struck down, and Miss Richards, the temporary Classics teacher, joined a team of lady volunteers to help out with nursing and domestic chores. Eight senior boys acted as hospital orderlies. Other pupils went home. Evensong was still said daily in the Chapel even though there were no clergy to officiate. Despite interruption by the virus, pre-war aspects of the school's life were soon resumed. Sports fixtures were restored; yet the impact of rising costs was seen at once on the river, where, reads the *Chronicle*, 'the cost of boats has trebled and the price of boating clothes, even when they are obtainable, is prohibitive and their quality deplorable'.

The war had almost emptied the Common Room. Restoring it to normality was far from easy. N. W. Hammond moved to King Edward's, Birmingham, in 1919, and George Duncan left in the same year. After the war, as during it, there were some transitory appointments, but others stayed much longer. In spite of low salaries Ferguson succeeded in establishing a loyal teaching staff that would be the foundation of the school's success under the next Warden, Henry Kendall. The long-term appointments made by Ferguson were joined in 1920 by Arthur Tilly, whose arrival (and perhaps that of others) was delayed by the slow pace of demobilization, and by the Rev. K. Menzie and P. B. Whitrow. A. F. Yorke started in 1922, W. S. Dingwall, A. W. Guest and Gerry Segar in 1923, H. G. C. Mallaby, J. M. D. ('Henry') Gauntlett and L. H. Ovenden in 1924. All these men were committed professional schoolmasters. Only two of them, Macnamara and Menzies, were priests. By 1925 Ferguson had added two more clergymen, but the proportion of them on the staff had gradually dropped. Half of Hudson's appointments were in holy orders; a third of Sing's; only four of the twenty-nine teachers appointed by Ferguson.

For all the difficulties, the numbers went on rising. There were 199 boys, all but eleven of them boarders, in September 1920, 213 the following year, 216 in 1922, 229 in 1923, 236 in 1924: an 18% increase over four years. Simeon's buildings had been designed for about 110 boys and, even after the addition of the New Buildings, the pressure on space was obvious. In a letter to parents of April 1920, Ferguson wrote that the existing number of boys 'absolutely exhausts our accommodation', and urged parents to alleviate his plight by giving as much notice of a boy's removal as possible. Makeshift adjustments were made to cope with the population increase. A 70-foot hut was purchased from the wartime aerodrome on Port Meadow to provide a new changing-room, the old one being converted into the Canada day room. The old gym was converted into an armoury, an indication of the continued importance of the OTC, which remained compulsory for those boys, 147 of them, who were over 15. It was increased from two to three platoons in 1920. The building of more huts where Tilly's now stands (though they were later moved to the position of what was for long Segar's House) freed space in the New Buildings, but they had to house the two science laboratories. An old games/box-room and an engine-room were converted into a day room for the Remove, and a further hut was added for the day boys.

These improvisations were costly, but Ferguson was not content with them. He embarked on a large, long overdue and very expensive programme of renovation, intending to bring the boys a measure of physical comfort. In 1923 a new furnace for some central heating and hot water was acquired at a cost of £2,000, and electric light was installed in Big School, the Chapel, the cloisters and two classrooms. Big School was extensively renovated, panelled on the east side, and newly heated. It accommodated a new Bechstein piano, a purchase reflecting the Warden's musical interests. The main staircase of Big School was given the undergirding that survives today. The dining hall acquired new panelling as well as shelves to display games cups, which stood between the shields with the names of teams. Down the decades the cups and shields would be a much more visible presence than the honours boards in Big School.

The early 1920s saw the dormitories Combe, King and Ken

refurbished and decorated, as was the Lodge. Washrooms and bathrooms, though delayed by a workmen's strike, were installed in the Main Buildings, and a bathroom and WC in the Hollies, the oldest of the school properties, a house in South Parade which currently housed masters. In the New Buildings the unhygienic Common Room and studies, where the *Common Room Magazine* had been founded, were torn down and the Ceylon day room, which accommodated thirty boys, established in their place. In 1922–23 a new pavilion was built, the first new building to be raised since the 1880s. This was financed partly by the profits of the School Shop. Games had regained their exalted place among the school's priorities. One of Arthur Macnamara's first tasks after his appointment in 1919 was to supervise the levelling of the lower field, which had been ploughed up during the war, to restore space for sport.

Changes in the Chapel indicated a deeper preoccupation of Ferguson: the renewal of the school's worship. The walls were repainted, the organ cleaned and tuned; and new seating resulted from a request that each boy donate a chair with his name on it. The alterations to the altar steps proposed by Harold Rogers, which sacrificed elevation to a clear view of the East window and the creation of more space around the altar, belong to the early 1920s. The *Chronicle* commented that the effect of the changes to the building 'is all to the good, though not all the alterations have escaped criticism: that however was inevitable and fully expected'.

Not every refurbishment planned by Ferguson could be implemented. Money could not be found for new lavatories in the Main Buildings. Yet at least the school must have looked spruce and its inhabitants were better provided for. In 1921 there came a more ambitious step. The leasehold of Corfe House was secured for £2,500. The Memorial Fund was raided for £1,000 and the rest was raised by a mortgage paid off a year later. Perhaps the use of the Fund for the project helps to explain why subsequent donations to it were disappointing. Eighteen boys and four masters were put into the house. Other accommodation was provided by Mrs Dore, mother of Hayward Dore (Roll No. 1270) who had been killed in the war. A major supporter of the school, she took sixteen boys, free of charge, into her home, Bishopstone, at 195 Woodstock Road, an arrangement which lasted until 1924. The 'Dorians' saw themselves as something of an elite. Thirty-four boys now lived outside the Quad, and had to cross the road from Corfe or Bishopstone to reach it.

In 1923 Harold Rogers secured the first of several lucrative architectural commissions from his old school and designed the Sanatorium. It catered for the almost annual visitations of illness, from flu to chickenpox and from mumps to measles, though the building opened too late to tackle the three epidemics of 1924. In designing the 'San', which retained its original use for seventy years, Rogers took the advice of Thomas Rayson, FSA. Innovatively, the planning allowed for the accommodation of twenty boys and for the separate treatment of three simultaneous infections. But the San lacked isolation facilities and was naturally far too small to house all the victims of mass epidemics. Later, when such epidemics had become scarce, the building seemed too big. But at least, like the laboratory huts, it freed space in the New Buildings, where the sick had hitherto been tended.

The Memorial Buildings were much the most ambitious of the post-war projects. They catered for thirty boys in two dormitories and housed five masters. In addition a day room, a library, two classrooms, an art room and six music rooms were provided. Until the completion of the building in 1925 the accommodation had an improvised feel, which attracted the occasional parental complaint. When in January of that year Peter Rawlinson (Roll No. 2070) wrote to his mother that he had been placed in the Armoury to live and sleep for the first half of term, the boy's father, Leo Rawlinson, town clerk of Leamington Spa, wrote to Macnamara, his tutor in Set D, to say that his son was 'very much upset about it. Practically all last term Peter had a cold. He is not a strong boy and we are very much afraid that his health will suffer if he remains where he is.' Leo's concern was not unreasonable, for two boys had recently died of illness at the school. Macnamara hastened to explain that the Armoury was heated, and that in any case the Memorial Buildings, where Peter would live, would soon be finished, but the father was 'disappointed that my letter has not had the desired effect .... I have no desire to be unreasonable but I cannot help feeling uneasy about the boy's health.' Perhaps spartan conditions would have caused less concern to Victorian parents, who had been readier to accept stern stuff.

Ferguson's initiatives extended to other aspects of the school's life. He attempted to enliven Sundays, first by the introduction of a lecture or debate between 8 and 9 p.m. for the Upper School, and secondly by an open invitation to OSE to supper in the Warden's lodgings after Evensong, from 6 p.m. The second step was aimed to tie old boys not merely to the school, to which so many of them anyway gravitated, but to the Chapel. In response to a Board of Education Inspection Report at the end of Sing's tenure the new Warden changed the regime of conventional gymnastics to 'Swedish drill', with its emphasis on ropes and bars, though he did not know that he was about to lose Sergeant Cunningham, who was in charge of gymnastics and would have supervised the change. Ferguson was as attentive to the day-to-day running of the school as Sing had been, though he had more help. Just as Sing's sister had acted as his housekeeper and hostess, so Ferguson was aided by his own sister. She was a married woman, who moved into the Warden's house with her husband, B. W. Machin, and their children. The family paid for their board and accommodation, but in the staff shortages of wartime Machin was soon making up the numbers. He taught the Fourth Form, refereed games, and eventually took over the OTC. More importantly he became Ferguson's de facto secretary, dealing with much of the day-to-day correspondence until his departure for a living in Leicestershire in 1921. Yet there was sadness ahead. Mrs Machin died on 31 December 1918 and was buried in the Chapel graveyard. Her daughter took over the role of hostess but left to marry in 1921.

The expansion of the number of boys brought a reorganization in the structure of the teaching and the curriculum. 'Middle Remove', a new Third Form, was created, though intermittently it would disappear and then be revived. The Modern and Classical sides were now divided into separate Removes, and there was a comparable demarcation in the new Upper and Lower Fourth Forms below them. The changes reflect a gradual swing away from the Classics to the Modern side, a development bemoaned by Cowell among others. In earlier times schools had earned their academic reputation by the teaching of the Classics. Other subjects such as History, Modern Languages and Sciences, which were judged less testing of their students, had seemed intruders. The shift to Modern subjects helps to explain why awards at the universities in the prestigious Classics were no longer the strong point they had been in Sing's time. The rate dropped slightly after Sing, and such awards as were now achieved were as likely to be won in other subjects. Between 1916 and 1925 there were nine open awards at Oxford and Cambridge, four of them in Classics, two in Mathematics, one in History and two Choral Scholarships. There was a disconcerting drop in the number of other places won at universities, and disappointment at lower levels too. In 1922 only one Higher Certificate was achieved. The truth was that standards had declined as the numbers of boys had risen. Real as the virtues of the staff appointed by Ferguson were, intellectual edge was not among them. Perhaps, too, there had been a decline in the average intellectual capacity of the boys, of whom Ferguson said, in an unguarded moment, 'I've taken anything in trousers, so long as they can pay the fees.'

Unfortunately the income from fees was of diminishing value in the severe economic conditions of the post-war world. The era of stable or even falling prices for consumables, from which the pre-war school had benefited, was over. Prices rose sharply from the outbreak of the conflict to the end of 1920. The Reith Index and the Phelps-Brown Scale record an increase of about of 250% between 1913 and 1920. In 1916 alone there was an inflation rate of 29%. It is true that in 1920 prices fell back, though not to their pre-war level. But wages, which had also soared during and immediately after the war, did not. Always a main element of the school's expenditure, they made still greater demands on its budget during the programme of building and physical repair. In 1920 a bricklayer's rate was 235% greater than in 1914, and his labourer's 300% greater. Over the same period the wages of salary earners, from whom the school's parents mostly came, no more than doubled. Clergy won nothing like that increase.

Nor did schoolmasters, whose salaries were very low by the standards of the professional classes. The masters were housed in cramped conditions and, unless they had private means, would have found the financial burdens of marriage hard to contemplate, as the very high percentage of bachelors on the staff until the Second World War testifies. At least priests had benefices and, with them, houses suitable for a family. Yet teachers' stipends, exiguous as they were, made increasing demands on the school's finances. Cowell was the highest paid. In 1916 his salary had been £180, while those of his colleagues had ranged from £130 to £145. In each case a further £75 had been estimated for the meagre board and lodging. When Tilly joined the staff in 1920 he was paid £307. Stanton's salary rose from £133 6s. 8d in 1915 to £245 in 1925. Cowell, offered the same sum, declined to accept more than £210. In 1924 the minimum starting salary was raised to £200, a figure that remained unchanged until 1947. Ferguson's own salary increased disproportionately, from the miserly £300 in 1916 to £750 in 1924.

In 1924 the school submitted to the Board of Education some figures which we can compare with the lists of expenditure in 1888 and 1890 that we looked at in Chapter 19. Other figures, most of them from 1916, can also be used. The full-time teaching staff, which had increased over the years to teach the growing number of boys, were together paid £1,131 in 1913, £1,351 in 1916, and £4,075 in 1924, when £82 was also spent on visiting and occasional teachers. Wages of the rest of the school's employees amounted to £920 in 1888, were reduced by the wartime diminution of the labour force to £757 in 1916, but stood at £2,104 in 1924. Not only had expenditure increased but financial management had become more complex. By 1924 Ferguson's friend and colleague W. K. Stanton was in effect acting as school secretary, work for which he was paid an additional £50.

In that year, just before he left, Ferguson named Walter Dingwall, whom he had appointed to the Common Room in 1923, as the first bursar, a job Dingwall would combine from 1927 with the posts of housemaster and teacher of history. It seems remarkable now that St Edward's and schools like it managed so long without a bursar. Accountants had to be appointed too, in 1925: the firm of Cash, Stone & Co., for whom the OSE William Bayford Stone (Roll No. 769) acted. From 1925 to 1940 there was now a new burden, a teachers' pension scheme, which cost the school £884 in contributions in that year together with a capitation fee of £221. Rates, taxes and insurance, which had cost £415 in 1916, were £484 by 1924. Over the same period the cost of repairs had risen from £335 to £4,415, that of furniture replacements from £176 to £780. Fuel, lights and water costs, which amounted to £410 in 1916, rose to £982. Expenditure on the boarding of pupils had grown from £3,020 to £7,790. In 1924 £2,640 went towards the building of the Sanatorium. Books and stationery cost £123; the movement of the hutted laboratories and equipment £585; printing, advertising and postage £169; porterage and other sundries £137; the visits of the Sunday lecturers £51; the tuning of the piano £15. Only £3 was spent on the Library.

The overall financial picture was on the face of it not unhealthy, in spite of the rapid inflation. The fee income, £8,733 in 1916, had swelled to £26,737 eight years later. There was £2,228 in the bank, whereas there had been only £121 in 1916. The sum of £9,000 was paid back in capital in 1924, though interest, which had risen to 5½% in 1917, still amounted to £790. Welcome as the financial improvement was, the school was still running to keep up. It was in any case questionable whether the surge in boy numbers would continue, for the aftermath of war was not a prosperous period for families of the kind to which St Edward's looked for its recruits. Yet continue it did. In spite of the strains on genteel income, and in spite of the state's mounting appetite for taxation, this was a period of growth in the Public Schools. St Edward's retained a base among clerical parents, who are likely to have looked to it for an upbringing that not only held to the school's religious ideals but protected their children from the secularizing trends evident in education provided by the state, a sentiment which some lay middle-class parents may have shared. Yet the ecclesiastical identity of the school, while it might help sustain the numbers, was by itself unlikely to increase them. Rather it was diluted by them, for any increase would raise the proportion of boys from non-clerical backgrounds. What enabled St Edward's to keep up with the numerical rise in more prestigious schools was its low fees. Together with those of the Woodard school Denstone they were the lowest we find in a sample of 30 Public Schools. They stood at £90 in 1920, a very cheap education even when the habitual 'extras' had been added to the bill. In the same year Radley charged £165 (and was in financial difficulties), Marlborough £126, Malvern £123.

For all the advantages of low fees, Ferguson needed to raise them. He did so over two years by means of surcharges, which had been introduced during the war at £6 a head and were now substantially increased. The total charge (extras aside) accordingly rose to £120 in 1921, £125 in 1922. It was a big rise, but low relative to prices. Other schools that charged much higher fees likewise imposed large increases around the same time. Between 1920 and 1922 Radley's fees rose by a further £10; Malvern, having roughly increased the fees by half in the previous years, raised them by a further quarter, to £156; Marlborough's rose to £145. Denstone and Bromsgrove, schools in the same income bracket as St Edward's, increased their fees too. Parents seem to have viewed Ferguson's increase with understanding. He did not oblige those who had entered their sons at one level of fee to transfer to the higher one, but more than half of them agreed to do so. St Edward's has an enduring history of low fees, which would work to the advantage of its numerical intake in the decades ahead. Even in 1945 they stood at only £145.

In March 1919 the Governors decided on a bolder solution to the school's difficulties. They succeeded, where their predecessors had failed, in an approach to the Woodard Society. The school's financial position, vulnerable as it was, was not quite as precarious as the pessimistic Ferguson supposed, and it is questionable whether the move was necessary. But finance was not the only reason for the initiative. Ferguson and like-minded figures would have seen it as an opportunity to reaffirm, and to give protection to, the school's founding purpose in a secularizing world. Ferguson was an admirer of the Society, a sentiment confirmed by his time at Lancing, the senior Woodard establishment, and it is conceivable that his attitude was among the reasons for his appointment as Warden. Anxiety about secularism had been increased by the recent exertions of H. A. L. Fisher, the Liberal who had become President of the Board of Education in 1916, and who was an adversary of denominational schools. He hoped to persuade Public Schools to offer free places to working-class boys at elementary schools in return for some government grants. S. R. James, Headmaster of Malvern, described the Public Schools as 'the roost which may next be attacked'. To St Edward's the Woodard connection seemed to offer a refuge from state intervention.

Ferguson and Sing, who was Bursar of the Southern Division of the Society, were the driving figures behind the approach to the Woodard Society, perhaps in association with two of the Governors, Archdeacon T. H. Archer-Houblon and Walter Lock, the Warden of Keble, who were members of the Southern Division Chapter. It took a year for the Society, which had rejected previous approaches from St Edward's, to reply. But at last the Provost of Lancing, Canon E. M. Lance, who had studied a confidential report on the school and communicated it to the Society, told Ferguson that the Chapter had 'decided unanimously to take you over ... you personally will be welcomed with open arms'. The association of the Society and the school, which was formally implemented in 1921, might have been a transformative event, though the school has preferred to forget what proved to be a temporary alliance. On paper the arrangement transferred large powers of strategy and direction to the Society; in practice the powers were limited and rarely, if ever, used. When the association was dissolved after only six years, in 1927, its termination was not even recorded by the *Chronicle*.

25

WARDEN FERGUSON'S ST EDWARD'S

PERHAPS few pupils at St Edward's who have sung the popular hymn 'O Jesus I have promised to serve thee to the end' have noticed that it was composed by Warden Ferguson, who set to music words written by one H. C. Bede in 1868. Ferguson had been organ scholar at Keble and President of the University Music Society. At St Edward's he was eager to promote the music, and was assisted by his friend and *éminence grise* W. K. Stanton, a very effective choirmaster. The choir gave outside concerts and Sir Hugh Allen, Head of the Royal College of Music, said 'he had never heard any school sing better'. Internal concerts are frequently reported in the *Chronicle*. There were solo performances on the violin or piano of pieces by Bach, Brahms and Debussy, as well as songs and folk songs written or arranged by the modern musicians Roger Quilter and Cecil Sharp.

Sometimes the musicians had to share an occasion with a troop entertainment given by gymnasts under the direction of the ubiquitous Company Sergeant Major Merry, the stalwart of the OTC who conducted all the frequent military drilling and also cut the boys' hair. He served the school from 1910 to 1963. In April 1920 some rather feeble sketches were performed to raise money for the tennis club. One of them, 'Diamonds', was described in the *Chronicle* as 'wanting more rehearsal', though the future bishop Bob Mortimer played his 'unpleasant part with intelligence'. There was a concert of pieces by Sullivan, only the lightest of them taken from the Savoy Operas. Three concerts in June and July 1920 were performed by thirteen boys, and three prizes were given for 'good service at these and previous concerts'. Oswald Shuffrey won the violin prize in this, his final year. The Director of Music at Balliol College Oxford, Dr Walker, wondered 'whether at any other educational establishment on the face of the globe, headmaster and music master can be observed exchanging, conducting and accompanying activities in the remarkable and most successful fashion normal for many years at St Edward's'.

Respected as the music was, it was organized games that appealed most to boys. In 1919 these were fully reinstated, their revival being marked by a traditional paperchase in March. An athletics contest planned for the same month was delayed by snow until April, but the *Chronicle*, which gave the event three columns, judged it a success, 'considering that most of the competitors had done no serious running for three years'. Rugby resumed, with matches against depleted college teams at Oxford which were awaiting the demobilization of undergraduates, and to which the school sometimes lent players. Yet nearly all these games were lost. In the period 1919–24 there were few rugby matches against other schools (three in 1919, four in 1920, three in 1921, five in 1922 and 1923 and six in 1924). The school played Bromsgrove in each of those years and lost every time except once, when it drew. There were also matches each year against King Edward's School, Birmingham, and fixtures against Imperial Service College in 1922 and 1923. Against schools other than Bromsgrove, St Edward's did better, winning seven matches and losing six between 1922 and 1924. One member of the team in 1919 and 1920 was John Eardley (Roll No. 1512, always known as Bill), who would return as a master in 1926.

Cricket against Bromsgrove was not renewed until 1926, though before then there were occasional games against Denstone, Bedford Modern School and the Oratory. Most cricket matches were played not against schools but against Oxford colleges, local clubs, the Old Boys, gentlemen's clubs and the Heythrop Hunt. In 1922–24 there were 13 wins, 9 defeats and 16 draws overall. Against schools there were four wins, two defeats and one draw. Such improvements as occurred in sports results probably reflect the influence of recently recruited young masters, among them Arthur Tilly as rugby coach. Ferguson was a keen cricketer, sometimes to be seen batting on the fields, and the game was given encouragement by the revival of the OSE Cricket Week in 1920. In 1922 the XI won just four of its 12 matches. Only two of them, one won, the other lost, were against other schools. The introduction of Colts colours gave stimulus to younger cricketers, Douglas Bader (Roll No. 1983) being one of the earlier holders. Competitions between sets in cricket and rugby continued to attract as much interest from the *Chronicle* as school matches. Bill Eardley figured again in the revived Boat Club. By 1920 there were eleven crews to compete in the bumping races, though the races were hit by measles in 1923, floods in 1924, and by both floods and illness in 1927. Successes at Marlow Regatta were few.

Despite his personal enthusiasm for cricket, Ferguson's interests were more cultural than athletic. The Sunday evening lectures he inaugurated included an address by a distinguished parent on his experiences as Food Controller during the war. 'He was an admirable lecturer,' piped the *Chronicle*, 'and he held his audience from beginning to end.' The lecturer, father of William Clynes (Roll No. 1638), was the Rt. Hon. J. R. Clynes, a famous or infamous trade union leader and a prominent Labour MP, who in 1922 would almost pip Ramsay MacDonald for the Labour leadership. More conventional guest speakers were Commander Wild, who spoke on Shackleton's Antarctic Expedition, and Captain Gwatkin-Williams, who talked on 'Prisoners of the Red Desert'. Their performances were much enjoyed. But there was criticism too, including one of the most hostile articles to appear in the earlier *Chronicles*. Boys 'sit bored and weary on Sunday evenings, enduring gentlemen who see fit to undertake tasks beyond their powers'. And why has the school to endure so many talks on birds? 'Can we ever discover wherein lies the attraction of Greater Black-Backed Gulls and their lesser brethren?' How can the vast subject of astronomy be covered in an hour and a half? Would not time with a history textbook tell one as much as one needed to know about the French Revolution? Though the editors distanced themselves from the article, it points to a newly critical spirit at work in the post-war world.

In May 1919 the *Chronicle* announced an adjustment of its own pages to the return of peace. During the conflict, as it observed, the bulk of the magazine had properly been given over to news, especially military news, of OSE, and to their promotions, injuries and deaths. But the primary obligation of the *Chronicle*, observed the editors, was to record developments within the school, a responsibility which the virtual monopoly of its pages by old boys had in truth usurped. More of a balance was now achieved, though the OSE still figured prominently. The magazine was shorter in the early 1920s, an unoriginal period in its history. Sport, whose coverage had been much diminished by the war, resumed its prominence. The latest War Memorial donors were listed, alongside the contributors to another appeal, this one for an altar cross in memory of Miss Bishop, school matron from 1886 to 1912, who among her many contributions to the school's life had helped take care of the Chapel and its fittings. In October 1919 Ferguson had to plead with OSE for £38, which brought the total up to the £100 needed.

Cowell's school plays had been suspended in wartime. Ferguson encouraged their revival, with one performance usually being set aside for the general public. The plays resumed in 1919 with *Twelfth*

Night, in which Bob Mortimer (who would also play Ferdinand in *The Tempest*) was Viola and Bill Eardley Antonio. Cowell's Prologue was a masterly tribute to the war dead. The *Chronicle* tells us that the revived Debating Society 'carried out a revolution – fortunately bloodless – of an oligarchical character, involving a strict limitation of numbers, and the exclusion of noisy spectators, who do not contribute to the debates'. Mortimer, prominent here too, expressed conservative views. He proposed, unsuccessfully, 'That Labour was not fit to govern', but successfully opposed a motion favouring recognition of the Bolshevik government in Russia, maintaining that 'Bolshevism meant trouble and disorder and it was our duty not to give Bolsheviks freer opportunities. To do so was contrary to British traditions.' 'It was,' judged the *Chronicle*, 'perhaps the best speech the House has heard from him.' His career at St Edward's displayed a versatility of talent and achievement of a kind which had been familiar in the pre-war decades but was now becoming altogether less common. He scored a century before lunch against Bloxham, was Captain of both hockey and tennis, Sergeant-Major in the OTC, head of his Set and then Senior Prefect. He won an Exhibition to Keble, where he would achieve Firsts in Mods and Greats. He went on to further academic distinction and to the bishopric of Exeter, and became the acknowledged Anglican expert on ethical questions.

The year 1923 was the 50th anniversary of the move to Summertown and the 60th of the school's foundation. So Commem, held in the second weekend of September, was a grander occasion than usual. The OSE celebrated by defeating Radley and enjoying a dinner at the Clarendon Hotel in the Cornmarket. In Chapel there was the usual range of services, where the aged Simeon gave a blessing from his stall. There was a supper in Hall, an 'At Home' in the Library, and a concert. On Monday a formal gathering in Big School was addressed by the Dean of Winchester, W. H. Hutton, who had written devotedly on that hero of the Tractarian movement, Charles I's Archbishop of Canterbury, William Laud. His speech echoes anxieties we have encountered on more than one other commemorative occasion. 'As time goes on, some of the old schools, we cannot deny it, have lost the clear intention of their founders; they are not pre-eminently schools for the making of the servants of God in the Church of England.' There was a danger of religion 'falling into the background'. But the dean derived hope from the new association of St Edward's with the Woodard Society and from the religious idealism that had propelled the move. Now the school's future is 'secure, because we know that it will carry out the truest ideals of the Country to which we belong and of the Catholic Church of Jesus Christ our Lord ....' He continued:

> I believe that there is coming back – slowly, yet coming back – a feeling among Englishmen that no education can be true education which is not founded on religion .... This school I believe in no sentimental way, but in downright truthfulness of life, has known the religion of Jesus Christ, which means the Incarnation, and the Crucifixion and the Resurrection, the life of God on earth lived for man that he might know himself to be a child of God and inheritor of the Kingdom of Heaven. I believe the religious teaching here has been real and thorough in a sense it has not been in many other Public Schools, and the worship too in the Chapel has been a more intimate part of life.

Was this wishful thinking, and would his audience have sensed it to be? How wide could the appeal of such language be in the increasingly secular society that had emerged from the carnage of the Great War and that faced 'the morbid age' of the 1920s?

Hutton's claim to have witnessed a godly community at St Edward's hardly squares with the memories left by John Castleden (Roll No. 2044) of his time as a new boy in Christmas Term 1924, when he was placed in Set E under B. M. Goldie. Castleden's recollections of the school cannot be ascribed to bitterness. They are those of a conventional man whose memory dwells affectionately on sport, inter-Set rugby, athletics, cross-country races and bumpers. His bed, he remembered, stood between those of 'two bigger boys', of whom 'the older being aged 16 had entered the School as a cathedral chorister from Exeter after his voice broke. Both boys proceeded to bully me intending to show how much stronger they were. I spent a pretty miserable first term.' Castleden found that boys were discouraged from making friends outside their own Sets, a convention that would harden when the Sets were converted into Houses under Kendall. But he was able to get round it, for the juniors in Sets C and E shared a table in the dining hall, where he struck up a friendship with Philip Swatman (Roll No. 2075), another ex-chorister, who had been at Salisbury Cathedral; perhaps Ferguson's impact on the music was drawing singers in. In his second term John made another friend, this one in his own Set, Cecil Dexter (Roll No. 2079). After leaving school John became a chartered accountant, Philip a solicitor, and Cecil a member of the Stock Exchange before joining the Bank of England.

Like most boys, the three did not proceed to university. Only 12 of the 56 boys who left in Ferguson's last two terms did so: nine of them moved on to Oxford, one to Bristol and two to London. The adult careers of half of the other 44 leavers are unknown. Of those whose futures we do know, just two became priests, a much smaller proportion than in earlier days. Of the first thousand boys to attend the school, between 1863 and 1898, 143 were ordained; only 73 from the second thousand (1898–1923); and 46 from the third thousand (1923–35). A mere seven of the 44 leavers of 1924–25 were sons of clergy. Three of the 44 became accountants, three solicitors, three teachers, two soldiers, two bankers, two farmers and two surveyors. Three went into estate management or valuation. One became a colonial administrator, another a colonial policeman.

John Castleden's reminiscences are one of several sources which give us a feel of the post-war school. At least he escaped one fate awaiting most new boys. They were placed in Ceylon, the notoriously tough large day room in the New Buildings. One such boy was Geoffrey Meadmore (Roll No. 2033), who was in Set C under the Rev. J. W. Griffiths. Meadmore's arrival in the Summer Term of 1924 was 'one of the most harrowing experiences a young boy of thirteen can undergo ... yet how little was done to cushion the effects'. He particularizes three horrors. First there was the traditional song or monologue to be delivered by each of Ceylon's new boys in front of the seniors, 'a terrifying ordeal'. Secondly every boy was forced to fight in a boxing contest, which was 'guaranteed to strike terror'. Thirdly he remembered 'that charming boy who at the table in the dining hall emptied the contents of my newly purchased bottle of pickled onions on to my plate'. Meadmore recalls beatings 'with the cane as everyday occurrences either from masters or from prefects'. He remembers Arthur Tilly as a sadist and 'arch exponent of that mental sickness'.

Generally, Tilly was not kindly remembered. The distinguished clergyman Robert Newhouse (Roll No. 1860), the first of three brothers and a contemporary and lifelong friend of Geoffrey, composed his own memoir in retirement in 1996. He warned that his own reminiscences might be too prim, Meadmore's too scurrilous. Yet he broadly agrees with his friend about Tilly, who 'coached, criticised, reviled and very occasionally praised ... he was not universally popular'. Yet when Robert faced failure in Maths for his coming School Certificate, Tilly gave him free extra tuition and the boy was 'gratefully astonished to discover, in due course, that the fiery little martinet of the classroom not only had a sense of humour but could for an hour, in his own room, become patient, encouraging and almost, if never quite, benign'.

It is on the masters that Robert's memoir concentrates. In April 1921 he entered the bottom of the Third Form under William Shackleton, 'Shack' to the boys, who 'never had a chance'. His class 'ranged from mild unruliness to bedlam. Booby traps were laid and waste-paper baskets caught fire; one boy filled his mouth with sherbet powder to simulate a fit.' Shackleton died of double pneumonia in 1926 and the boys contributed towards an especially large wreath, 'in token, I like to think, of belated regret'. It was in intervening to restore order during one of Shackleton's lessons that Arthur Macnamara uttered his immortal remark, 'If you carry on with this noise you will hear more of it.' John Fletcher (Roll No. 1684) was one of a number of OSE to recall other utterances of Macnamara that entered the school's folklore. 'Sit round square.' 'I know who you are. What's your name?' 'You've got to learn to disobey.' Macnamara, who had a raffish air and sported a two-stroke motorbike, had many fond admirers. Fletcher remembered how well-turned-out he was, how good-humoured and kindly.

As a rule Robert Newhouse thought well of his former teachers. In the 1990s he still knew the 'tables of principal parts of Greek' taught him by the 'genial clergyman' Ken Menzies. B. G. 'Binks' Segar taught French lessons solely in French, drew legendary cartoons on the blackboard, and kept forgetting to set prep. The ageing Cowell (whom Newhouse calls 'Poif', one of his many nicknames) is remembered as 'a dedicated teacher who could inspire something of his own love of English and the Classics in us, so that learning became interesting'. Not that Cowell's teaching methods were very modern. He would make the Shell forms face inwards rather than in the usual rows, the top boy sitting on Poif's right and the bottom on his left near the door. If a boy was unable to answer a question correctly, the question was passed down the form to the left until someone got the answer right and exchanged places with the original defaulter. Robert, having been moved to the bottom after a minor error, was restored to his original place after giving a correct reply.

Geoffrey Meadmore's memoir is indeed less respectful than Robert Newhouse's, though it can be tantalizingly short on detail. How we would like to learn more about Warden Ferguson's 'receiving his come-uppance in the notorious night rioting [in 1925?] by the pupils over the imposition of some disliked measure of discipline, to rhythmical chanting of "Boots", his uncomplimentary nickname'. Meadmore tells us of one boy who was frequently beaten and who devised 'rope bags, a pair of trousers reinforced by a coil of thin rope, which he hastily donned before presenting himself for the expected punishment'. We also learn that boys summoned to the 'Beehive', where the prefects were based, to fag for them would evade the imposition by hiding in the enormous bush at the centre of the Quad known as 'The Jungle'. But Geoffrey admits that fagging taught him to clean shoes, cook eggs and prepare toast. He had 'an enduring memory of Christmas terms toasting muffins at the big log fire in the Library under Big School used as a dressing room for the Shakespeare play, and being made up by "Binks" Segar'. Meadmore left in 1929 from the History Sixth. His memoir ends: 'The final irony of my own stint at St Edward's is that twice-a-day Chapel and religious brain-washing of every kind only succeeded in converting me from a potential agnostic into a committed atheist – which was not at all the intention of its founders. On the other hand they might have been well pleased that I had derived so much of lasting good from my years there.'

Meadmore recalls the performances on stage, during his own first two terms, of Laurence Olivier (Roll No. 1885). The actor, who on his own later admission was known as 'that sidy little shit Olivier', sought to reduce his exposure by adopting an English pronunciation of his surname. Can we trust Meadmore's recollection that Olivier's 'acting abilities in the school plays' were 'already enough to make him a legendary figure'? Bob Mortimer remembered Olivier's big success at the school, his Puck in an 'open stage' production of *A Midsummer Night's Dream* in 1923, as 'by far the most notable performance', though he also found it 'a little too robust and jovial'. Not all the tributes were retrospective. A parent, reviewing the performance in the *Chronicle*, described it as 'distinctly original which set the audience thinking'. Olivier wrote subsequently that he had not been happy at St Edward's, and his contemporary Stephan Hopkinson (Roll No. 1897) has told me the same thing. Yet on the occasions when the actor performed at the New Theatre in Oxford, Macnamara was always invited backstage after the show to meet him. Towards the end of his life Olivier was grateful to successive Wardens for staving off enquiries from would-be biographers.

John Fletcher is one of many whose recollections describe the perils of Ceylon. His account exposes a problem inherent in the layout of the school. The sets were not separated by geography. Tutors (the future housemasters) had to supervise scattered flocks. In spite of the loyalties fostered by inter-Set games it could be hard to instil a sense of unity. There were consequences for discipline too, for the most immediate wielders of power were not the prefects but the day-room presidents, an arrangement open to abuse. 'Natal', recalls Fletcher, was 'famous by reason of the "'having in'" of boys for rebuke or humiliation. 'These "have ins" were always after Sunday morning chapel. And the president of Natal would hold court on anyone who had offended his residents by "guffing" [cheek], refusing to "face off" [avert his eyes from a senior boy]', or who was 'in any way considered to have behaved in an unacceptable manner. On one occasion the President named Hyde [Edward Hyde, Roll No. 1602] actually had in Havergal [Henry Havergal, Roll No. 1600] of Jamaica, though Jamaica was senior to Natal, in the same way that New Zealand was senior to Canada, and Canada to Ceylon.'

The last of the retrospective accounts of the Ferguson era for us to consider is the most informative and well written. It was published in 1982 as Chapter 4 of *Of This Our Time*, the autobiography of Sir Tom Hopkinson (Roll No. 1709), brother of Stephan (Roll No. 1897), John (Roll No. 1642), and Paul (Roll No. 815). These sons of an archdeacon all had distinguished careers. Tom himself became a famous editor of *Picture Post*. He described Ferguson as 'an excellent headmaster ... a dignified, awe-inspiring but humorous and warm-hearted man'. Yet in Hopkinson's account the Warden's personality makes little impact on the daily life of the boys. Tom recognizes the school's musical renown, 'but otherwise it was more like a penal settlement for young delinquents than a place of education'. Trying to keep warm, fed and washed was a major preoccupation. A small boy's life was dominated by eight or ten prefects, their 'bummings' (beatings), and by the fagging. He too endured Ceylon and the bullying there. Another inhabitant of it was Edmund Norris (Roll No. 1712), who arrived in the Easter Term of 1919 with Tom. Among boys before whom, in Tom's words, 'the worst offence was to be weak or rather to show weakness', the fatherless Edmund 'could not stop his lower lip from trembling. In this society he was a foredoomed victim, and if he haunts his tormentors as much as he has haunted me who did nothing to protect him, they will have paid sufficient penalty already'. He was withdrawn by his mother after two terms.

For Tom himself the school became more tolerable as he moved up it. He lived first in Field House and then in the main buildings. He tells us how boys set mole traps on illicit nights out, skinned the animals, cured the pelts with salt purloined at mealtimes, and sold them at tenpence each to a local tailor for making waistcoats. He was not himself among the mole-hunters, but it was on a nocturnal excursion with a different purpose that he was caught by Arthur Tilly. Tom was attempting to deliver a love letter from Brian Moody (Roll No. 1694), star of the XV and the XI, to the Warden's niece, 'a radiant beauty glimpsed only once a week in Sunday chapel', who was not immune to Brian's charms. Tom owed Brian a favour, as the older boy had secured a place for Tom to beat the cymbals in the OTC band, a post Tom had craved not because he had any liking for the Cadet Corps or any love or talent for music but because the band, with the choir, enjoyed a special half-holiday. He was not a pious boy, despite his family background. He remembers that the devout Bob Mortimer made dormitory prayers last a full two minutes as the boys knelt on cold, hard floorboards. By the time Tom left, 'discipline had become a part of me and I conformed automatically, like a circus horse'.

We are fortunate to have, alongside these retrospective accounts, a bundle of vivid letters from the time, written by and to Cyril Keller (Roll No. 2031). He arrived at the school in the Summer Term of 1924, the same term as Geoffrey Meadmore, and was placed in Set D under Macnamara. We hear little of his father, A. H. Keller. Neither, it seems, did Cyril, all but one of whose surviving letters are to his grandfather, about whom we otherwise know nothing. The exception, an undated letter to his mother, reveals that 'I do not know your address up North.' She had in fact sent more than one letter, as well as two tins of sardines, which he declared 'jolly fine'. Yet he has to explain to her that 'We break up on July 26th, so it won't be any good your coming to SES.' The letter describes the squalor of Ceylon and adds: 'I have had my first caning. A boiler room is to be built on the site of the old rears [lavatories] and as the new ones are not ready some temporary things have been put up under a wooden shed and we just have some dirty Woolworth pails which are never emptied and we call it Wembley and I wrote up "rodeo stables" and "Giant Switchback" and old Mac came to inspect them and he saw it and asked who did it so he gave me 4. Everyone else is writing home about these disgustingly filthy rears because they are perfectly unbearable.' A postscript, hinting perhaps at a craving for maternal contact, asks her to 'send me some snapshots'.

It was the grandfather who took an interest, indeed a close one. He addressed to the boy two typed lists of questions, to which Cyril was required to fill in the answers. The first, sent in Cyril's first term, asks: 'Do you like the Food and what consists Breakfast of?' Answer: 'Bread, porridge, sausages (or bacon and eggs).' The grandfather offers to send 'whatever you like to have of your own', and adds 'I have some bloater paste. Do you like your school?' Answer: 'Very much better than B. H. [Beaumont House, his prep school].' 'Do you feel quite at home?' Answer: 'As much as possible without you and mummie.' 'Are you quite well and free of colds?' 'I have belliake every day,' answers Cyril in his 13-year-old's spelling, 'and so does everyone else from eating so much. Everyone eats in class because there is no time between works [lessons].' Evidently breakfast had become more generous since the frugal meal of the Simeon era. By the time of the second questionnaire Cyril is indicating an adolescent's understandable distaste for these inquisitions. 'Have you got your cricket bat yet?' 'I wrote and told you on a postcard.' 'Why did you get 600 lines?' 'I don't know.' Then comes the sole allusion to the boy's father. 'Why did you say you had thanked your daddy for the magazine as he had not heard from you since he sent it???' 'I have written as I told you before. Do not bother to send these question papers. I have answered most of the questions previously.'

The letters offer glimpses of Macnamara, who in March 1925 writes a letter to Cyril's father which indicates that the boy has developed a crafty streak. 'There has been a mild epidemic and Cyril has been a not very ill victim. He has spun the story that boys who have been ill are to be sent home early, a useful rumour to put about. This was quite unauthorised .... The ruling is that only boys who are in a low state of health, and are obviously delicate, shall be allowed to go. Your boy is rapidly picking up again and is now getting about as usual .... So I think, if you don't mind, it will be better for Cyril to wait and come back at the ordinary time. The epidemic has been of a very light type and we have no extreme cases.' As Cyril gets older his irritation with the grandfather becomes more marked, though affection and gratitude still accompany it. 'You are perfectly misled in thinking I do not read your letters because I am only too pleased to get them. Very, very many thanks for the priceless rug, which is warmer than the other one .... Every time you write to me it is the same thing – you think I don't work. I can't understand why. Surely you don't judge whether I work hard or not by the holidays? You think my holidays are long because you compare them with what you had when you were at school.'

Cyril's letters have a good deal about food. He reports during his first term that 'The Brazil nuts were delicious, none of them had any contents except one and that was mouldy, however enjoyed that. I have made a jelly in a jam jar and am going to eat it when it is properly set.' At the start of his second term 'I feel awfully fed up – the buildings are not finished and there are so many new boys that some of the old boys have been put into the armoury and I am among the latter.' The discomfort of the arrangement, recorded by other boys too, continued, for the completion of the Memorial Buildings was delayed by industrial disputes and a strike. In February 1926, when the 15-year-old Cyril has become senior enough to be allowed a cushion or 'sit-a-pon', his grandfather sends one, 'which I received intact the other day. What is it stuffed with? It makes it a pleasure to sit down now that I have that instead of the hard boards with splinters in!' Yet in the same month the boy voices revulsion at his lot. 'I am so absolutely fed up with this hole now it is so beastly monotonous: the same people and the same things over again. Mac is going to give a lecture with lanternslides tonight. I am coming to the conclusion that this place is not what it seems like. One does not get a moment's privacy or peace here like one does at other schools. Everyone shouts and chases about, when anyone else wants a bit of peace he can't get it. This is alright for a while but it tends to go on forever and one is bound to get fed up.'

In October of the same year 'They have started making everybody have cold showers in the morning again now, I am sure I will get 'flu soon.' In January 1927 'It is so cold I can't feel my feet. The rooms do not seem to be heated at all.' There are nonetheless moments of cheerfulness or high spirits. In another letter of January 1927 he reports that a ring has been rigged up in Big School for boxing, which 'was jolly exciting', and describes 'appallingly, disastrously ghastly thunderstorms, some of the chaps were so frightened that they howled. A! Ha! I did not. I have got something rather ghastly to tell you. You know that rather big tooth in the top row at the back of my mouth; well two pieces (which are enclosed) have broken off. This leaves a nasty hole in the side so shall I have to wait till next holidays? It is very unadvisable to go to the school dentist because he is very bad. You see he knows we can't go to another man so he doesn't care what he does.' Ill health is a recurrent theme. 'I have awful pains in my neck and ears,' relates an undated letter, 'and come over dizzy every 10 minutes. The queer thing about it is that my temperature is only 99 and they won't let you go to bed unless it is about 100. I have had to leave off everything and wear an overcoat and that is all. It is jolly disgraceful not giving me proper attention, and I am not the only one .... Two other people are in this form-room with their glands sticking out about 3 inches.'

Despite Cyril's reports, the atmosphere of the school was praised by the Board of Education Inspection of 1921. The academic performance was not. Ferguson himself was commended for his hard work as a teacher and manager and for his understanding of boys and their needs. But the Inspectors criticized the teaching on the Modern side, and, while acknowledging the school's achievement in raising numbers, noted that the absence of any academic criterion of selection had allowed in a good many pupils who were unequal to the school's curriculum. The school's Articles of Association indeed had no clause stating a minimum standard for admission. All the document had done was to note that 'the practice up to the present has been to examine boys at entrance with a view to placing them in the most suitable form'. Applicants were supposed to take Common Entrance, the national test for Public School entry set up in 1904, but probably no one was ever turned away.

In 1924 Ferguson suddenly announced his impending departure to the Governors. He had been chosen as the next Warden of Radley. The Chairman of the Governors there, Archdeacon Archer-Houblon, had been a governor of St Edward's since 1902 and was almost certainly the instrumental figure in the appointment. Ferguson would be a success at Radley, whose historian describes his Wardenship as 'the beginning of a great resurgence' at the school. He used the same methods there as at St Edward's: the expansion of numbers and a building programme to accommodate it. But why did he take his new job? Radley was a richer and larger school than St Edward's, but its facilities were no better and it had no higher a record of achievements. In some ways his time at St Edward's had not been happy. There had been the disruptions and difficulties of the war and the obstacles to post-war reconstruction. There had been the deaths of his sister and of his brother Arthur Ferguson, to both of whom he had been close. Perhaps he was influenced by the decision, announced the term before Ferguson announced his own intention, of his friend the invaluable Stanton to leave to become Precentor of Wellington College.

Ill health had dogged Ferguson. In 1921, after Stanton, who himself had so many duties, had returned from an illness of several weeks, the Warden in turn had to take ten days' rest. He was ill again after announcing his departure, Sing holding the fort in his absence. Were Ferguson's illnesses related to the stress that the job inflicted on him? He was a congenital worrier, especially about the school's financial difficulties, which his mind perhaps exaggerated. When appointing masters he worried about whether he could offer them security of tenure. 'You've no idea of what a parlous condition we are in,' he once wrote. Perhaps the strain had become too much.

The Governors recorded Ferguson's achievement: 'the School has increased in size, in public esteem and in material prosperity. More than all are the Governors thankful for the atmosphere of religious sincerity which they believe to be characteristic of this school.' The *Chronicle*, which hailed his 'winning friendliness and wide-minded tolerance, great patience and determination', had 'no doubt' that under him 'the reputation of the School, long unjustly obscured, has spread very widely, not merely in Oxford but far afield. Three former headmasters have stated that he is "the best schoolmaster in England", what more can be said?' In later years men would speak of the benign atmosphere he had brought to the school, the sense of community, and the spirit of informality and friendliness which St Edward's has regarded, sometimes perhaps a little complacently, as its characteristics. Gerald Segar, whom Ferguson had made Head Prefect in 1915 and whom he would later appoint as a master, wrote of Ferguson's arrival: 'The new Warden surprised us by the friendliness of his approach; his charm of manner put one straightway at ease, and an interview in the Warden's study was more a friendly chat than a strained ordeal ... [he] seemed to walk by our side, full of sympathy and understanding, ready to help us on.' Such tributes have the ring of truth. Yet, when set beside the letters of Cyril Keller and the reminiscences of other OSE, they leave us with a question which might equally be asked of many a benign Public School headmaster. How was it that a man so true to his pastoral ideas presided over what, at least to a later age, seems the primitive and sometimes brutal way of life among the boys?

26

WARDEN KENDALL

THE appointment of the 36-year-old Henry Ewing Kendall to succeed Warden Ferguson was announced in February 1925. He took over the office in the Summer Term and held it for twenty-nine years, during which time 3,129 boys passed through the school and eighty new masters were appointed. His domination of St Edward's was total. It was unmistakably Kendall's school, and the Thirties in particular became retrospectively known by boys who were there at the time as 'the Golden Age of St Edward's'. OSE and masters of the period have told later generations time after time of his greatness.

Yet he was appointed only after another potential candidate had declined. Sing would remember that he himself 'and another governor paid a formal visit' to the 39-year-old Rev. Charles Gillett, a Fellow of Peterhouse (the Cambridge College). A former Scholar of St Edward's, he had been appointed by Sing as a master and had taught at the school, from 1905 to 1909, with acclaim both in the classroom and on the games field. Sing recalled that the two governors 'spent two hours trying to persuade him to accept the Wardenship, but in vain. Insofar as it is the Warden's duty to be guide, philosopher and friend to masters and boys alike, he would have been ideal .... He was a deeply spiritual man, and a fine presence, was a good athlete, a first-rate scholar and the finest preacher I have ever heard .... He was idolised by the boys as an Assistant Master and would have been idolised as Warden.' Gillett was indeed the obvious choice. He belonged to a clerical family and had impeccable High Church credentials. As a boy he had been Sing's finest academic pupil and had starred in plays and in both the XV and the XI. He won his Scholarship to Queen's College, Oxford, and though he missed a First his intellectual accomplishments were highly respected. After teaching at St Edward's he had held a curacy and a chaplaincy at Liddon House, the religious centre for 'educated young people' in Kensington. He was priested in 1914, was Vice-Principal of Westcott House, the High Anglican college in Cambridge for training priests, in 1921–22; held his Fellowship at Peterhouse from 1922 to 1932; and from 1933 to 1946 would be Principal of

Chichester Theological College. He was a governor of St Edward's from 1927 to 1947. As the sixth Warden of St Edward's he would have been a catch.

When Kendall was appointed in his stead the *Chronicle* indicated its regret at Gillett's refusal: 'Mr Kendall is at present a stranger to us, and herein is, for us, an unusual thing, for our last two Wardens were known and loved and honoured long before they were appointed.' Why did Gillett decline? In a letter to Desmond Hill in 1962 the OSE Lawrence Eyres (Roll No. 1256), who had taught at the school in 1920–21 and known Sing well, gave two plausible reasons: recurrent ill health, which might have made him hesitate to accept what he had seen from Sing's and Ferguson's years to be a heavy burden; and a lack of financial expertise, 'which would have bothered him'.

Once it was clear that Gillett would not stand, the job was advertised. The Governors set up a sub-committee of four, Sing and Ferguson among them, to scout for candidates. Sing wrote what proved to be a decisive letter to Canon Sawyer, Headmaster of Shrewsbury, asking if there were members of his staff whom he might recommend. In reply Sawyer gave the names of three clergymen whom he vouched to be 'in complete sympathy with the spiritual ideals of St Edward's': T. A. Moxon, J. O. Whitfield and H. E. Kendall. Sawyer put Moxon and Kendall ahead of Whitfield. Both men were keen to be headmasters, and both had shown an interest in the headship of the new, experimental foundation of Stowe, though in the event Kendall did not apply and Moxon withdrew from the shortlist after taking exception to the Low Churchmanship of the enterprise.

Moxon, wrote Sawyer, had a 'brilliant degree'. The same could not have been said of Kendall. All previous Wardens had been Classicists, as Moxon was, but Kendall's Second was in History, which like other 'Modern' subjects was deemed inferior. Kendall's accomplishments as a teacher of French were, acknowledged Sawyer, limited. Nonetheless, Sawyer came down on Kendall's side. 'He is intensely real, and is the greatest spiritual force we have at Shrewsbury, even greater than Moxon, and that is saying a great deal.' Perhaps it was, though Eyres, who had himself briefly taught at that school, recorded that Moxon 'was rather disliked by his colleagues at Shrewsbury (including me)'.

In his concern that St Edward's should make a wise choice, Sawyer let slip a telling observation. 'The future of St Edward's ... and schools like [it], which provide a first-rate public school [education] for the less wealthy, seems to me to be of supreme importance. They are the schools who are drawing from the best class socially at the present time.' Shrewsbury was one of the great Clarendon Commission Public Schools – the prestigious schools chosen for inspection by the Commission for its report of 1861. Yet here was Sawyer commending schools on the educational rung below, whose pupils in turn tended to be from the corresponding social rung. Behind his statement lies the feeling of the time that the ruling class was not what it had been before the war. In the age of the 'flappers', the Roaring Twenties, and of the epicene hedonism of Maurice Bowra's Oxford, a school such as St Edward's, with its upright and morally conventional games players, might foster a dependable genteel solidity. The school, suggested Sawyer, needed a man who held a 'balance between enthusiasm and originality on the one hand, and sanity and conservatism on the other'.

The sub-committee interviewed Sawyer's three candidates and concurred with his choice. Kendall was unanimously elected by the Governors on 25 January 1925. His salary of £500 was to be enhanced by a capitation fee, up to a ceiling of 100 boys, for every boarder above the number of 150. He was in some ways a surprising appointment. Though he was a High Churchman, whose religious position was evidently acceptable to Canon Lance of the Woodard Society, he had no links to the Oxford Movement. Shrewsbury, where he had been educated and where he had returned to teach in 1913, had no Tractarian tradition. Possibly there were those who welcomed the break with Tractarianism, for there are hints that Ferguson's piety had been a little stifling. (Geoffrey Meadmore, admittedly no churchman, remembered him as 'excessively pious'.) In comparison the new Warden seemed a man of the world. He had won an OBE for his work in the war, when he had served as a naval chaplain on board HMS *Alsatian*, the flagship of the 10th Cruiser Squadron from 1916 to 1918, and then, in the last stages of the conflict, at the RN barracks at Shotley and with the Northern Patrol. After the war he returned to Shrewsbury. Sawyer's support for him is some tribute, for Kendall had been a controversial figure at the school. Sawyer explained that he himself had founded a House 'on new lines viz. a limited Hostel system. Kendall in fact is in charge as Housemaster, gets a salary, and runs it with the help of a lady Matron. Everybody prophesied disaster.' The old boys had viewed the initiative with suspicion and 'The Governors would have nothing to do with it, so

I financed it myself.' The whole endeavour was a huge success and made Kendall's reputation.

His achievement at Shrewsbury belongs to the development of the House system in the Public Schools. In their early stages most schools had only one boarding House, which the headmaster directed. As numbers grew, the practice arose of allowing masters or even local women to provide accommodation, which they ran for their profit. By such means the schools could expand their numbers without incurring the costs of accommodation. Gradually the arrangements were formalized and the homes turned into Houses, which divided large numbers of boys into manageable units. The arrangement also advanced the ethos of competition and group loyalty. In many schools housemasters ran their Houses with a large degree of autonomy, charging their pupils for the costs and collecting the income. In effect the housemasters were barons running fiefdoms under a headmaster-king, who would hesitate before confronting them. Sawyer, financing a new house from the centre, was doing something different. At St Edward's Kendall adopted the same model. Hitherto the school, pinched for money as it was, had had to make do with sets, whose boys usually lived not under the immediate supervision of the housemaster or the prefects but scattered across the school. There had been some embryo versions of the housemaster system, as when Simeon placed Ernest Letts in Grove House or, later, put Dalton in charge of New Buildings and permitted him to derive additional income from his charges on a per capita basis. As teachers provided with school property, they had a more significant role than mere landladies would have had. But there had been nothing on the scale of the system that Kendall introduced.

In the lodgings, where a tradition of family support had been established, Kendall's sister-in-law, whose husband had been killed in the war, arrived with him to keep house. He took up office in time to receive an encouraging report from the school's financial watchdog the OSE Bayford Stone, who was Secretary of the Society from 1923 to 1928 and its treasurer thereafter. He was one of the new governors appointed in 1927 and later became an active member of the Executive Committee. In 1928 he was put in charge of the newly established Endowment Fund. At the outset of Kendall's tenure he reported an annual working profit of £5,000. There were 242 boys, and 55 more were promised for the coming term. The immediate problems facing him were ones of space, which Ferguson had energetically tackled but had not overcome.

As fast as new areas for accommodation were created or adapted, so boys arrived to fill them. The result was a jumble. Too many boys lived and worked together in the same room; there were thirty or forty in Canada, the former changing-room. Cleaners struggled with the conditions. Osberton House, on the corner of Osberton Road, had been taken over in order to squeeze in another twelve pupils, and a marquee had been set up by the north side of the Chapel for extra changing-room space. Seven forms were taught in huts. Four had their lessons in Big School, and when functions were held there the disruption was enormous. One form was taught in the Lodge. The boys could no longer fit into the dining hall, and some ate in Corfe. It is true that the Memorial Buildings were at last in use, but they had to fulfil a host of functions, from classrooms to laboratories to music rooms.

On his arrival Kendall found on his desk a hard-backed exercise book marked 'Warden. Private', which had been left for him by Ferguson. Much of its information is practical, concerning the structure and running of the school, but it also introduces Kendall to subjects of contention within the community. Ferguson recalls differences over the allocation of rooms and boys in the Memorial Buildings. 'If, when you have had time to take everything in, you feel dissatisfied with the arrangement, you can alter it.' There are also observations on standards of behaviour. 'Ever since I came I have had to wage constant warfare against the spirit of destruction which was firmly ingrained in the School. The place was in a very bad state of affairs ... even now the boys are far from what they ought to be. I don't think there is a single thing in the school that has not been repaired.' Ferguson then explains his policy with respect to the sets and the appointment of their tutors, which he has made on the basis of merit rather than seniority. 'On the last occasion I passed over two men. Were I staying on I should appoint Menzies to the next tutorship vacant. I think he is a good influence both within the School and among the staff.' Already, Ferguson explains, Menzies was responsible for most of the Divinity teaching, not least for expounding Church History and the Prayer Book to 'a crowd of small boys'. Kendall would not share his predecessor's admiration for Menzies.

Ferguson then records complaints by the tutors 'that I do not summon them into counsel more often'. That was because 'I have often got better results from private discussions. And also the rest of the staff is a bit touchy about the position of tutors.' Kendall notes in the margin that at Shrewsbury 'we have housemasters' meetings whenever necessary and I find them very helpful'. Ferguson records that prefects may cane to a maximum of six strokes, punishments which have to be recorded in a book. He notes too that 'As boys may wear unregulated clothes on week days there is always a tendency to burst out into imitation of the undergraduate. I will not allow the very light-coloured balloon shaped grey flannels nor bizarre jumpers.'

It was in the realm of clothing that Kendall decided to make an immediate mark. He chose headgear, an almost universal feature of the dress of the period. Hitherto boys had worn an assortment of hats, bowlers among them. On 20 March 1925 the School Shop received a letter from Battersby & Co. Ltd of Falcon Square, London, offering to supply a school boater at 42 shillings a dozen. Kendall probably already knew the firm, whose factory was in Stockport, through family connections. Boaters – 'bashers' – were introduced in his first term as Warden. They were to be worn whenever boys left the school grounds. Boaters, which would survive until the 1960s, distinguished the boys from the world outside. Boys did not like them, either then or in the generations to come. They belonged to Kendall's drive for uniformity of appearance and conduct, a goal which had been pursued long ago by Hudson and which Kendall revived for a new generation. The wearing of distinctive headgear in the outside world also hinted at a tendency towards the introversion of what I shall call 'the boy-centred commonwealth': a community, that is, which throve on self-sufficiency, not on interaction with or responses to the adult community outside.

Kendall handled the reaction to 'bashers' with characteristic adroitness. He flattered three boys who had complained about them by inviting them to accompany him in his car to a rugby match at Iffley Road. They turned up impeccably arrayed in their new hats. In a speech at the first OSE Dinner after Kendall's appointment, the school's most distinguished living soldier, Brigadier-General Francis Carter (Roll No. 243), remembered that fifty years earlier, when he was a prefect, Warden Simeon, who had earlier beaten him three times, had taken him bathing in the Cherwell. It had been a comparable exercise in the management of boys. Simeon and Kendall alike understood how to introduce them to a milieu of gentlemanly adult bonhomie while keeping them in their place.

The core of the staff Kendall inherited from Ferguson was his great asset. In Arthur Tilly he had a firm disciplinarian and an accomplished games coach, who, despite the evidence of his unpopularity with the boys, was regarded as the most influential of the masters by many of his colleagues. One of them judged that 'he really ran the School'. When Kendall introduced Houses he was able to appoint Macnamara, Menzies, Whitrow, Yorke and G. H. Segar as housemasters. In the classroom Whitrow (History), Yorke (Science) and B. G. Segar (French) were all remembered as accomplished teachers, even if not as high-powered ones. Walter Dingwall was a talented administrator. The first five years of Kendall's Wardenship saw the arrival of Jack McMichael, Bill Eardley, Eric Reid, Edward Manning, 'Bim' Barff and Stanley Tackley. Their loyalty to Kendall would be unshakeable. So would that of long-serving appointments of the 1930s: Maitland Emmet, Leslie Styler, Hubert Beales (Roll No. 2433), Roger Northcote-Green (Roll No. 2231) and Jack Tate.

The stability, solidarity and conviviality supplied by all these men offer a striking contrast to the early years of the school, when the teaching staff had fluctuated so much. Poorly paid and for the most part poorly housed as these men were, they made St Edward's their life. Only a minority of them married: McMichael, Whitrow, Manning and Barff. Was there, together with the merits of long and devoted service, a danger? Might it breed unthinking or complacent conservatism? The question would become pressing towards the end of Kendall's Wardenship, which the Second War had unexpectedly prolonged. But in 1925 the condition of the school – its staff, its rising numbers, its reasonable financial health, which we will consider shortly – emboldened the new Warden to embark on policies more fundamental than the inauguration of boaters.

27

KENDALL IN COMMAND

KENDALL'S aims were clear from the start. In July 1925, at his first OSE dinner, he made a characteristically succinct statement of policy, for he was never a man for prolixity or jargon. 'The members of the School are increasing so rapidly that we must be prepared for the new demand. In future the Sets are to live together, grouped around their tutors.' Kendall always managed the old boys and their influential Society adroitly. His short speech began, 'I have the distinction of being the only Warden [here] who has not caned Mr Stone', and ended with a tribute to the loyalty and support of the OSE. He needed their money. 'I may mention,' he told them, 'that we are handicapped by an absence of scholarships for boys leaving school for the universities.' By December ten OSE had raised £50 for that purpose. The speech voiced disappointment that the school was not represented at Henley Regatta – as old boys would have liked.

On the same occasion Kendall announced the purchase of 'an estate of ten acres called Apsley Paddox, which includes a house for fifty boys and a ground for three football fields'. Apsley Paddox was the name of a Regency mansion and its ten acres of land stretching between the Banbury and Woodstock Roads. The purchase, achieved in a period of rapid residential building in the area around and north of Summertown, was a masterstroke, a credit to the school's estate agent, Brooks's. Admittedly there was a drawback, in the ensuing geographical widening of a community which had derived coherence from the concentration of its buildings round the Quad. Yet the opportunity was too good to miss, and Kendall seized it. The decision may have been encouraged by the knowledge that Sing, energetic as ever in his retirement, had recently become Bursar of the Southern Group of Woodard Schools, and would be in a position to answer any doubts about the expenditure on the Society's part. In fact the Society had limited control of the school it had taken over. Nor did it have much responsibility for its debts, which the acquisition was likely to increase. The amount of £9,250 was set aside towards the purchase of the property, which in the event was secured for less. Even after adaptation and refurbishment Apsley Paddox cost only a little over £11,000. A few years later the sale of the frontages on the Woodstock and Banbury Roads recouped £7,000. The remaining grounds of the Paddox were kept as an asset in the hope that land prices would rise or in case the school needed to build more. To the north of the Paddox the rash of suburban building continued. The construction of Davenant Road, just south of the roundabout where the Woodstock Road joined the bypass, had been begun during the war, which halted it. Now it was resumed. The road, observed the *Chronicle*, 'is now nearly filled with houses of strangely varied suburban types. The frontages on the Woodstock and Banbury Roads are rapidly filling up.' Two impending new occupants of Davenant Road were the now retired Simeon, ageing fast at 80, and his wife. The couple had bought a newly built house and were awaiting its completion.

The purchase of the Paddox launched Kendall's programme. Set E, now named Apsley (though for administrative convenience the sets also retained their former letters on their conversion into Houses), was moved en bloc to the Paddox building. Set C moved to Field House (the future Corfe House) and took that name. In the Main Buildings there was now space to allow Set F, which became Tilly's, to be installed on the first floor, while Set A, now Cowell's, had its day rooms on the first floor and its dormitories on the second. With Houses came housemasters. B. M. Goldie, the tutor to Set E, was not appointed to Apsley, and instead left the school to resume his former career as an examination coach in Oxford. The Warden himself nominally took charge of the new House, but the housemaster in all but name was the 28-year-old Gerry Segar, a former Head of School, who would later have his own House. He had had a distinguished war, after which he had taken a mediocre degree in History at Exeter College, Oxford, where he had played rugby for the university's second team. After two years of teaching at St Ninian's, Moffat, he returned to St Edward's in 1923, only two years before being entrusted with Apsley. J. W. Griffiths, who had been appointed in 1918 and was by now the longest-serving master other than Cowell, moved with Set C into Field House. He left to run a parish in 1927 and was replaced by Walter Dingwall, who was housemaster for ten years. In the same year Tilly moved into the Main Buildings with what had been his Set, but Kendall tactfully persuaded Cowell, who had been a tutor since 1883 and whose name was given to his Set, to retire from the role and take the eminent and undemanding post of Second Master. In 1925 Cowell's House was given to Freddie Yorke, who in his three years at the school had established himself as a popular and versatile schoolmaster with an evangelical enthusiasm for the teaching of science. The House simultaneously moved into the Main Buildings, where it remained for five years before moving to Field House, which it would occupy for six years before the new building which has subsequently accommodated it was finished.

Thus far the process of reallocation had been neat. But there were three more Houses to accommodate: Sing's, the former Set B; Macnamara's, hitherto Set D; and a newly created House, which was allocated the letter G and named after its first housemaster, Menzies (whose pastoral gifts the departing Ferguson had pressed on Kendall). Sing's took over most of the Memorial Buildings and was given to Philip Whitrow, who had succeeded Stanton as Set B's tutor. Macnamara's and Menzies's shared the New Buildings (later named Mac's). No more new Houses would be created at St Edward's until Corfe was inaugurated in 1982. Those established by Kendall had much stronger identities, and commanded stronger loyalties, than the sets before them. They became the centres of the life of the boys, who except for the prefects (and they only rarely) never entered other Houses. The change was reflected in, and promoted by, the reorganization of the Prefect system. Hitherto there had been eight or ten prefects, whose writs ran across the school. Now each housemaster supervised a team of House prefects under a head one. The School prefects remained, consisting of the Heads of Houses and a small number of sporting 'bloods', but though they supervised the House prefects their role diminished as the identities of the Houses strengthened.

From the start, sporting competitions were more frequent and more keenly fought between Houses than under the Set system. The *Chronicle* of April 1926 lists a Head of the River cup, a Sports cup, a Senior and Junior Football cup, Senior and Junior Cricket cups, a Sculling cup, the Garnett cup for long distance swimming, a Junior Squadron cup for swimming, a PT Shield, Senior and Junior Fives cups, two Diving cups, a Junior 100 yards Swimming cup and three Shooting cups. House colours succeeded the old Set ones. Another innovation was 'Standards', the protracted annual athletics contest which measured the performance of each boy, and the average performance of his House, in running and jumping, with ignominious and sometimes punitive consequences for boys who did not reach the required level. A significant advance in the House system came in 1929, when the tables in the dining hall were divided up among the Houses, whose members thus sat together. In due course there would be House singing competitions and House plays.

Transformative as the introduction of the Houses was, history and geography conspired to set limits to its impact. At other schools the Houses were gradual growths, responses to pressures of numbers. Pupils were scattered throughout a town or suburb under the supervision of men who, though appointed by the headmaster, ran their communities more or less independently. The Houses at St Edward's were created in one swoop, by Kendall's diktat. They were also, despite the extensions of the school to Field House and Apsley, confined within a smaller space. Since the school's inception the Warden, from his vantage point in the corner of the Quad, had been a towering presence. Wardens had controlled or involved themselves in almost every aspect of school activity. The creation of the Houses did not end their hegemony or greatly modify it, even when the numbers of boys swelled rapidly. By force of personality Kendall and in due course his successor Frank Fisher dominated the school. When, as late as 1988, the then Warden David Christie and his wife moved from the Quad to a house in the Woodstock Road (while retaining reception rooms and his study in the old lodgings), the feeling was voiced by generations of boys and masters that St Edward's would never be quite the same again.

There was nothing outwardly authoritarian about Kendall's style of government. His despotic power was gently wielded. He had legendary qualities of conciliation and pacification. Problems were minimized, oil poured on troubled waters. He did not need to bully his housemasters, for he had appointed conscientious, conservative men, sometimes of limited talents, of whose support he could be sure. He knew they would not strike out on their own or try to introduce policies or practices outside the norm. Perhaps it was because Apsley was relatively distant that Kendall nominally reserved the housemastership for himself, though, lying so far from his view, it did uniquely acquire some measure of independence and individuality, a characteristic which puzzled the rest of the school and was mourned by the House's inhabitants when, by now named Field House, the building was sold in 1963 and the House was brought on to the main site.

Kendall soon achieved another important acquisition of property. In earlier days the school had escaped the reappropriation of the games fields by their owner, the Duke of Marlborough, by buying them from him. His successor, feeling the post-war pinch like many great landowners, and urged by his advisers to sell property in the vicinity for housing development, hinted that St Edward's might like to pre-empt such a move by making an offer, at the market price, for 'the land around your school'. From 1927 to 1929 the school acquired land from him which would bring its property right up to Wolvercote. More than a quarter of the new property lay near the canal. St Edward's bought 15 acres in 1927; 4½ acres north of the Avenue on a 30-year lease in 1928; and in 1929 a further 15 acres beyond the canal and 11 more on the school's side of it, all land which the school had previously rented. In 1928 the ground rent of Corfe House and its cottages was purchased, and the levelling of Avenue and Corfe Fields produced the appearance it has today.

Overall, the school's freehold land increased from 25 acres to 97 in the decade from 1924. The expansion not only provided new space but strengthened the rural aspect of the school. By the summer of 1926 six cricket pitches had been contrived. 'But we want seven,' beseeched the *Chronicle*, which asked for House nets too. Kendall had a different purpose in mind. Hudson, we recall, had kept his own pigs. Stanton, possibly inspired by the school's agricultural improvisations during the war, had envisaged a commercial farm for the school. Now the new field was husbanded with cows and pigs. Kendall's likely aim, self-sufficiency in foodstuffs, was not achieved, but the animals did yield some commercial gain.

There seemed no limits to Kendall's enterprise. Early in his tenure he provided electricity for Corfe House, raided the Corps funds to build a new armoury, doubled the OTC subscription, and started a new School Shop. Then, in 1927, emboldened by Brooks's valuation of the school property at the healthy sum of £107,300, he resolved to free St Edward's from its ties to the Woodard Society. What benefit, he asked, had the school derived from an association into which it had entered from a fear for the survival of Public School education, and of St Edward's in particular, that had now passed? Larger social issues had diverted public hostility from private education, while growing religious indifference had taken the sting from the doctrinal contests that had subjected St Edward's to antagonism. In any case the Society, mindful no doubt of the school's past financial crises, had been unwilling, when the merger was negotiated, to take on 'certain mortgages and charges' on the school property. Furthermore the school's Articles of 1911, which had defined St Edward's as 'an Association limited by guarantee and having a capital share', conflicted in a number of ways with the

Statutes of the Woodard Society. There was a logistical difficulty too, for it was hard to arrange Governors' meetings which both the school's and the Society's representatives were able to attend. The truth was that St Edward's had never been properly integrated into the group of Woodard schools.

The extraction of the school from its commitment was dextrously handled by Kendall. He negotiated behind the scenes with the Chapter and cooperated with the Woodard trustee Chief Justice John Sankey, who would soon be Lord Chancellor. It is probable that Bayford Stone played an important part in the background. Kendall's political antennae were as sharp as ever. As a believer in close ties between schools and their old boys, he took note of feeling among the OSE in favour of a break from the Woodard connection. No old boy was more devoted than the influential Stone, who seems to have taken over the role among the OSE once exercised by Harold Rogers. The Woodard Society did not resist the divorce and may even have welcomed it. As a result, the school's Governing Body was reconstituted. Tactfully, three Woodard representatives, Lance, Sankey and Walter Locke, were appointed to it. Archer-Houblon, a member of the Governing Body since 1902, and Canon Kidd, the newly appointed Warden of Keble who now joined it, also preserved the link with Tractaranism. The appointments of Stone, Gillett and Francis Wylie, and the continuing presence of the ubiquitous and seemingly indispensable Sing, ensured close ties to the OSE. An inspired appointment was the Hon. G. H. B. Gibbs, of the Aldenham family which had saved and sustained the school in the past and which was now to be associated with it for another generation. Kendall, whose influence is manifest in the appointments, would exercise an ever greater influence on the composition of the Governing Body, so that the school's personality and policies became barely distinguishable from his own. By January 1927, when he was barely two years into his Wardenship, he was in complete command.

The *Chronicle* published its 400th issue in July 1925. It contained letters of congratulation from the five previous Wardens. There were prose and verse from distinguished OSE, among them Kenneth Grahame, Harold Peake (now a prominent anthropologist), the naval historian Geoffrey Callender (Roll No. 775), and the archaeologist Arthur Mace (Roll No. 743). Sing contributed a memoir on OSE football. A letter from Cowell urged that the new music rooms in the Memorial Buildings be named after the past music teachers Stanton, Shuttleworth and Jellicoe. The issue exudes a sense of well-being and of happy continuity between past and present. A series of articles described the school 'Fifty Years Ago'. One of them related chance encounters between the author and other OSE during the war and across the world, which had produced 'a pleasant and useful intimacy'. Readers were urged to 'take in the *Chronicle*, write to it and for it: wear the OSE colours and be worthy of them!' The anniversary issue was selective in its memories. It did not recall the school's founding spiritual purpose. And while it hailed successful and reputable OSE, it overlooked the one by far best known to the public, Arthur Devereux (Roll No. 600). He had been hanged on 15 August 1905 after the bodies of his wife and twins were discovered in a trunk in a furniture depository in the Harrow Road.

The *Chronicle*, which after the war had mildly protested at the virtual monopoly of its pages by OSE news, still gave many columns to them. The magazine remained an essential link between the school and its alumni, though the OSE supplemented it with an annual Year Book, which summarized news and achievements of the school. The generosity of old boys was crucial. Next to paying for its own games and fixtures, financial support for the school was the main concern of the St Edward's Society. In December 1925 the Annual Meeting noted that £15 had just been donated to the Boat Club for the purchase of a new Four, £40 5s. 6d towards the deepening of the outdoor bath so that diving competitions could be held there, and another £30 from twenty-five old boys for the Memorial Fund, which OSE had kept open. Many gave small sums many times over. Another OSE fund raised money for a fourth edition of the *Roll*. The Boat Club was essentially the creation of the OSE. In 1926 the Society quickly found the £200 to acquire the river frontage south of the Trout Inn, and two years later a fund for a boathouse had reached £550. Money followed for new boats, which saved the £160 a year that had still been needed for hiring. Former pupils were not automatically members of the Society. Those who joined had to pay a guinea's entrance fee and an annual subscription, and there was a separate subscription for the *Chronicle*. In 1925 the Society had 715 members. By 1931–32 the number had risen to 1,150, though admittedly 'of this total, 97 are known to be deceased'.

Commem in December 1925 brought the opening of the Memorial Buildings. It was a lively gathering in bitter weather. On Saturday 5 December an OSE dinner started the weekend's festivities at the Clarendon Hotel in Oxford. Sunday saw a combination of Chapel services, the Sung Eucharist attracting 180 guests as well as the 270 adults and boys of the school. Kendall had created two rows of additional seating, with more in the organ gallery. After the service there was a parade of the OTC, whose members had attended the service in uniform. In spite of the cold an ailing Simeon looked on as General Godley, GOC Southern Command opened the building with his staff in attendance. A slab was erected above the entrance, with a laurel and oak and the words 'Alumni Alumnis 1914–1918' inscribed on it. Beneath it was placed another slab, which was left blank after discussions of the design had faltered. A march-past followed, after which came Evensong in Chapel. Then there was supper in Hall, followed by carols in the Warden's House. The celebrations ended on Monday the 7th with a performance of *Twelfth Night*, another production of the play by Cowell, who this time used Roger Quilter's settings of 'O Mistress Mine' and 'Come Away Death'. The annual survey in his customarily skilful prologue recorded the arrival of ninety new boys, the acquisition of Apsley, Bob Mortimer's First and other achievements of OSE at university; and, of course, the new Houses:

> So Sets grow into Houses and alas!
> Old Boys must learn a new topography
> Lest unaware they tread where they should not.
> For one room 'in its time plays many parts'.

The missing feature of the Commem was the rugby match, cancelled because of frozen pitches. Kendall would have been sorry, for games, at school and House level, were essential to his vision of the school's development. They would bind old boys to St Edward's, enhance its reputation in a middle-class society that admired amateur sportsmen and, above all, promote those virtues of loyalty and healthy competition that had long been the appeal of games to the Public Schools. Kendall aimed to improve the facilities and the coaching. He also hoped to end the tradition of playing Oxford colleges, perhaps because true Public Schools play their matches against one another, perhaps because interaction with the more cosmopolitan world of undergraduates was not something he cared to encourage. But the change took time, for travel to away matches was expensive. It cost nearly £12 to hire a bus for a fixture outside Oxford. Kendall expected almost all his staff to teach games, and to combine, as the boys were meant to do, a healthy mind and a healthy body – one reason why the word 'schoolmaster' was preferred to the narrower 'schoolteacher'.

Only occasionally was a professional coach to be seen, as when Tom Hayward was recruited from Oxford University's cricketing staff.

Success came early for Kendall in both rugby and cricket. The increase in boy numbers helped. So did the growth of junior teams, which nourished talent. So too did the excellence of the coaching. The main coach in both sports was Tilly, who was assisted in rugby by George Mallaby. In cricket he was aided by Macnamara and, from 1926 to 1937, by the former Oxford triple blue and Warwickshire player Edward Hewetson, a fine schoolmaster who was said to have been one of the fastest bowlers in England and who had achieved the rare distinction of having hit the ball out of the ground at Lord's in a Varsity match. He has been called the architect of the school's successes in the sport. Only one school, Denstone, defeated St Edward's at rugby in 1925, and none did so in 1926 or 1927. The leading player of those three years was Douglas Bader. In 1927 the *Daily Telegraph* wrote that the 'powerful' XV 'rates very high amongst the schools', publicity that must have delighted the Warden. After a drop in 1928, which was blamed on the exceptionally hard ground in the autumn, the success was resumed. Between 1929 and 1938, 36 school rugby matches were won, one drawn, and only nine lost. In cricket this was, as Derek Roe has written, the school's 'heroic age'. In the twenty-eight matches against other schools between 1931 and 1938 there were no defeats and just four draws. Bader, captain in 1928, topped the batting averages, and many would recall his haul of six wickets against a club side fielding eight members of the Authentics Cricket Club. Rowing was slower to take off, largely for financial reasons. Kendall personally donated three cups for House rowing, and in 1931 appointed as the leading coach Maitland Emmet, whom Desmond Hill described as 'laying the foundations on which our post-war successes were built'. Other rowing coaches appointed were Trevor James in 1926, Roger Northcote-Green in 1936, and Mark Tindall in 1937. The St Edward's of Kendall was renowned for its games. There survive excellent sets of team photographs of the inter-war years, in which square-jawed, serious, impeccably kitted young men with cropped hair gaze confidently outwards. These regimented gladiators are a world away from the lounging young men of the informal pictures from the Simeon era.

This was not an era of high intellectual attainment. The Inspection of 1926 examined 293 boys (sixteen of them day boys), who were taught by 22 masters in 13 forms. It may have come at an unfortunate time, for Kendall was carrying out a minor but unsettling reorganization of the form structure, one purpose of which was the restoration of Latin as a compulsory subject on the Modern side. The report was critical of the school's work. It noticed that no one seemed to fail Common Entrance, though the report is at least evidence that it was being sat, whereas the Inspectors' Report of 1921 had implied that it was not. The report of 1926 describes most of the teachers as young and inexperienced. Kendall is praised for his energy but advised to devote more time to teaching methods, syllabus construction and guidance to the teachers. Those were not his forte. Insufficient time, noted the report, was given to science, because so many boys concentrated on two languages (usually Latin and German) in order to qualify for Responsions (an examination taken by undergraduates in their first year which tested the work they had done at school) even though a minority of the boys were likely to take them. In spite of that priority the school's record at the universities 'admits of improvement'. In the past three years (1924–26), observed the report, only thirty-three boys had gone to Oxford and Cambridge and only three open awards had been won there. Those years were not unrepresentative, for there were between nine and eleven annual admissions throughout the 1920s, and three was the average number of awards in the 1920s and 1930s. Yet St Edward's did well enough in the classroom to appeal to parents who wanted for their children not an academic hothouse but a school which, amid the variety of activities they hoped it would offer, would not let its brighter pupils down. To judge by the school numbers, the formula worked.

As Kendall's regime entrenched itself the school projected a glow of content – and with it perhaps a whiff of self-regard. At the Summer Gaudy of 1933, following Ferguson's example a decade earlier, Kendall took advantage of the 70th anniversary of the foundation, and the 60th of the move from New Inn Hall Street, to proclaim the school's achievements. A Diamond Jubilee number of the *Chronicle* recalled the building programme of recent decades and noted the sporting exploits of St Edward's. Yet 'it is not for these [a man] loves his old school ... but for the confident morning of his friendships'. It was true that 'much can be measured and much can be defined: the extensions of the School can be marked down, its successes counted, its benefactors praised. But no catalogue of achievement, and no record of gratitude, will by themselves bring back to a man the full joy of the enchanted time.' What a contrast to the Jubilee number twenty years earlier, in 1913, where poetry and prose had addressed the school's obligation to public service and the contributions that patriotism and Christian manliness can make to a world of Imperial expansion and military challenge. The Britain of the 1930s, enduring economic decline, industrial unrest and political uncertainty, was a different and less confident society. The *Chronicle* turned away from it. In its perception, the growth and happiness and friendships of the individual are the institution's sufficient and proper goal. 'The gift given to a man by his school is himself. Out of him there came that nameless and vital spark which gave life to the common day and won back life from it ... and the power of a school is to nourish the vital spark that is lighted in the dawn of life.' As at other Public Schools, the virtues of loyalty, tenacity and honour now seemed commendable not as preparations for the outside world but as preferable to it. Well might OSE during the Depression, and in the war that followed, look back nostalgically on those insulated boyhood certainties.

28

FROM STRENGTH TO STRENGTH

By the beginning of 1927 there were 326 boys at St Edward's. The school was bursting at the seams. The purchase of Apsley Paddox in 1925 had done something to reduce the pressures of space, but nowhere near enough.

There were 200 boys to feed, and a dining room designed for 120. Overflows had to be provided, in Canada and in an old box room. In other schools, Houses ate separately, in their own buildings. At St Edward's this happened only in Apsley (later Field House), which at mealtimes preserved something of a country-house atmosphere. Boys heard rooks in the woods and had to walk down Middle Way into Summertown to reach the school. As late as the mid-1950s the housemaster, Bim Barff, and his wife Renée, attended by a uniformed maidservant, would dine by candlelight in front of the boys. A pupil of that time, Ian Dunn (Roll No. 5325), remembers that 'Being geographically apart from the main school intensified the sense of belonging.' Yet the food was only marginally better than in the rest of the school, where it was poorly controlled and where the portions of the juniors tended to suffer from inequitable distribution. The rooms where the boys ate, Ferguson had lamented, 'are very untidy ... owing to the crowds: the waste of food is deplorable.' From 1928 boys could turn for sustenance to the new School Shop, which stood immediately to the north-east of the Chapel, facing the Main Buildings. The building, now the Bursary, was designed by Harold Rogers and run as a profit-making concern.

The building of the Shop and of the new Armoury behind Big School opened up the old playground area north of the Chapel. The old Armoury was now used for gymnastics and for a vast changing-room. The small transforming chamber of the Oxford Electricity Company was turned into an outpatients' waiting room for the Sanatorium. A fire escape and gallery, paid for anonymously by the Warden, were soon added to Big School, which now housed a portrait of Cowell and where, in 1928, the Public Schools' Physical Training Shield, won by the PT squad of the OTC under CSM Merry, was proudly hung. The tradesmen's gate from South Parade was opened up. In the Chapel, where Kendall had already created new seating, a more radical step was taken in 1928 with the replacement of chairs by the pews we see today. The width of the aisle was reduced and the Victorian tiles of the floor gave way to the small oak blocks that still survive. The tiles seem to have passed unlamented, though those in the chancel, which remained, now seem an asset of the building. Six windows were given openings to improve ventilation, and a door was created at the north-east corner to create a separate entrance.

Those measures of containment were not enough. New buildings were needed. Kendall submitted a hugely ambitious series of proposals to the Governors and their Executive Committee. One was for a new boarding house, and for Memorial Buildings – that hotch-potch of accommodation and classrooms – to become a self-contained boarding house. The year 1929 saw the building of a science block, a classroom block, the subway under the Woodstock Road, and a transformation of the eating arrangements. The Governors were initially attracted by a proposal of Harold Rogers for a new dining hall, projected north from the old one to the edge of South Parade, and for a new dormitory overhead. The existing dining hall would be converted into day rooms. The scheme would have disposed of what Desmond Hill called 'a succession of utilitarian excrescences' behind School House and leave the façade facing the Quad unchanged. The scheme was abandoned, perhaps as an ambition too far. The decision seems to have piqued Rogers, who anyway had his doubts about Kendall, and who now brought his role as the school's main architect to an end. His successor for the next twenty years, Brook Kitchin, favoured a style that may never find its admirers. He designed the additions to the dining hall made in 1929, the science laboratories and 'The Workhouse' (later 'The Work Block') in 1931, the new pavilion of 1933, additions to the Chapel, and the Cowell's and Segar's Block erected in 1936.

For financial advice Kendall could turn to Bayford Stone and Lord Aldenham on the Governing Body. He had the astute Dingwall as bursar until 1932 (when Dingwall gave up to devote more time to his House). Yet the Warden himself was the driving force in the taking and implementing of the main financial decisions. He was every bit as skilful here as in his management of boys and masters. In March 1928 the Governors were persuaded to authorize the building of the subway, the laboratory block, and the extension of the dining hall into the Quad. A total expenditure of £14,000 was envisaged, a sum eventually exceeded, in the way of building projects, by £8,000. Here Kendall played a strong card. A friend of his family, William Goodenough, was Chairman of Barclay's Bank. Through him, and by pointing to the school's operating profits and to the existing assets that could be offered as security, the Warden secured a loan of £18,000 on 1 August 1928. Goodenough was made a governor of the school the following year and brought additional financial expertise to the Board. Kendall struck a further deal with Barclay's for the creation, for five years from 1929, of scholarships for the sons of staff and pensioners of the bank. They would be worth £80 a year, almost two-thirds of the fees of £125. The scheme was designed to attract boys from what, at the time of Kendall's appointment, Canon Sawyer had called 'the best class socially at the present time'. Goodenough would remain a governor until 1951, and the relationship between Barclay's and St Edward's would long endure. The school became the leading one in the bank's national scholarship scheme.

After protracted problems of excavation the subway was opened in June 1930. The inauguration of the Science Block, as the laboratory block came to be called, and of the extension to the dining hall followed in October. Freddie Yorke planned the interior arrangement of the Science Block and made it a huge success. Kitchin's obtrusive 'mock early Tudor' extension of the dining hall, though it temporarily solved the problem of numbers, damaged Wilkinson's original conception, breaking the Victorian Gothic façade of the Main Buildings and spoiling the relationship between the building and the rest of the Quad. Perhaps Rogers's plan to build north would have been better.

The increase of traffic on the Woodstock Road, and thus of the danger to the boys crossing it, had made the subway a pressing necessity. There had been opposition to its construction by Oxford's city fathers and by the providers of water, gas and electricity, whose lines the subway disturbed. Resistance was eventually overcome, and the Lord Mayor ceremonially opened the subway with the City Engineer in attendance. Distinctive as it is, the underpass was the least obtrusive of Kendall's building schemes. Yet it had far-reaching consequences. Linking the Quad to the games fields, it brought the two sides of the school's life closer together, bypassed the suburban sprawl between them, and enhanced the rural aspect of the school's character. Increasingly, the school was becoming a self-contained community. The gates to the Lodge, firmly shut, kept the outside world at bay. In 1932 hedging was removed from

THE VICTORIAN SCHOOL ASSEMBLED

New Inn Hall Street c. 1870. In contrast with later group photographs there is no uniformity of appearance or dress. At least two senior boys sport moustaches. Kenneth Grahame sits at the feet of the Headmaster, Simeon.

1899. Warden Hudson sets the tone of solemn and disciplined formality. Every boy wears a uniform and looks at the camera.

EARLY LEADERS

Thomas Chamberlain, the founder.

Frederick Fryer,
the first headmaster
1863-70.

Herbert Dalton,
headmaster 1877-83.

Henry Liddon, Tractarian
and the main influence on
Simeon.

Frederick Lygon,
sixth Earl Beauchamp.

Charles Lyndley Wood,
second Viscount Halifax.
He and the Tractarian
Beauchamp generously
supported the school from
an early stage.

Henry Hucks Gibbs,
Lord Aldenham, another
important source of
support, as his family
would continue to be.

THE FIRST WARDEN: ALGERNON BARRINGTON SIMEON

As a Sixth Former at Winchester, 1865.

With Felicia Skene, c. 1875.

With his family.

In his vestments in 1927, the year before his death.

WARDENS

Thomas Frederick Hobson, 1893-6.

Thomas William Hudson, 1896-1904.

John Millington Sing, 1904-13.

William Harold Ferguson, 1913-25.

Henry Ewing Kendall, 1925-54.

Frank Forman Fisher, 1954-66.

Richard Alan Bradley, 1966-71.

Charles Henry Christie, 1971-8.

John Christopher Phillips, 1978-88.

David Christie, 1988-2004.

Andrew Frederick Trotman, 2004-11.

Stephen Charles Ion Jones (2011-).

THE CHAPEL

1877.

Painted by James Elder Christie in 1892, when the original canopies and raised altar survived.

The west end, 1896.
Seating in the gallery would be added later, as would the ante-chapel.

c.1918. The original tiles still remained. The first of the Great War plaques have been installed.

THE TAMPLIN WINDOW

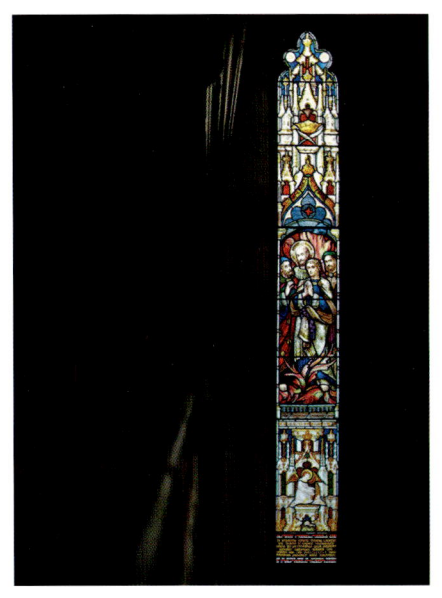

The window, installed in 1888, was a memorial to Robert Tamplin (Roll No. 359), who as Organ Scholar at Keble College was the school's first pupil to win a university award.

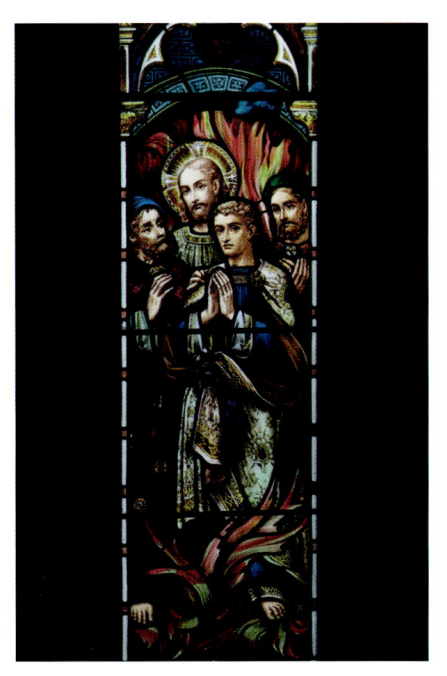

The Three Holy Children in the Burning Fiery Furnace.

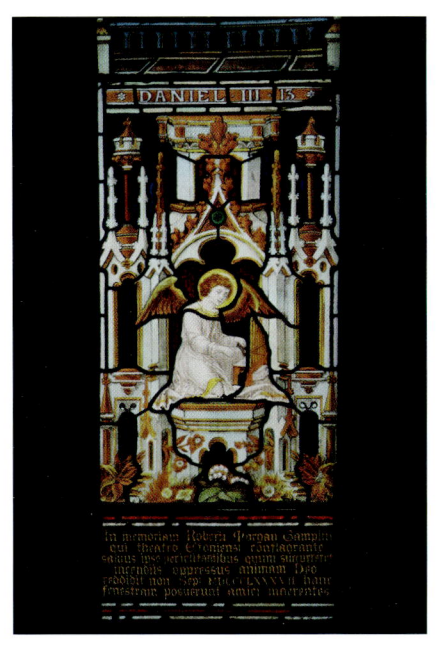

Detail: the dedication.

THE SOMME PLAQUES, COMMEMORATING FIVE OSE WHO FELL ON 1 JULY 1916, THE FIRST DAY OF THE BATTLE.

Photographs by Casper Sunley (Roll No.12756)

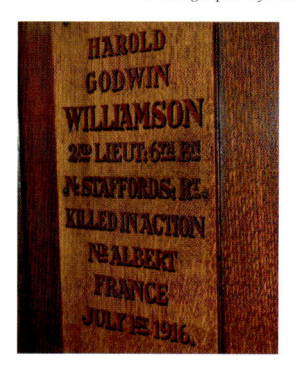

Harold Williamson (Roll No. 1370), aged 20, the fourth of the five OSE Second Lieutenants to die on that day. He had played in the XV and the XI.

Thomas Haughton (Roll No. 1170), aged 25. He was part of the famous Ulster Division advance on Thiepval.

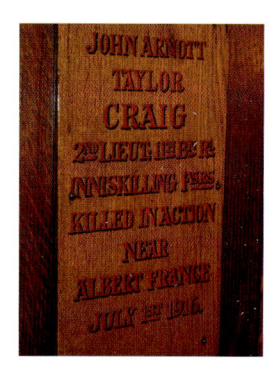

John Craig (Roll No. 1324), aged 22. He had left St Edward's in 1912 and entered the Belfast linen trade.

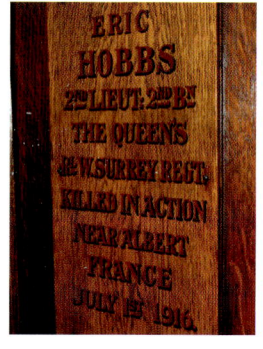

Eric Hobbs (Roll No. 1383), aged 21. His brother Thomas (Roll No. 1088), a farmer in Canada who fought in the Canadian Expeditionary Force, died of wounds in 1918. Another brother, Ernest (Roll No. 1087) a priest, died in 1948.

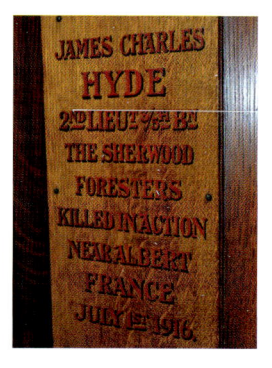

James Hyde (Roll No. 1302), aged 22. His younger brother John (Roll No. 1425) was just too young for the war, became a solicitor after attending Cambridge, and died in 1965.

THE COMMON ROOM

1875.

2004.

MASTERS

Wilfrid Cowell, 1900.

Arthur Macnamara, 1934.

Arthur Tilly (taught 1920-51).

Pat Brims (1936-72).

Three genial masters:
Myles Arkell (1955-90),
Derek Henderson (1950-61),
Brian Gale (1951-84).

Five Sing's Housemasters: left to right Philip
Whitrow (1924-31), George Mallaby (1931-6),
Eric Reid (1936-40), Leslie Styler (1940-7),
Stanley Tackley (1947-65).

Three Housemasters of Menzies and - the House's later name – Segar's: Henry Gauntlett (1950-55), Kenneth Menzies (1925-35) and Gerry Segar (1935-50).

Four more Segar's Housemasters: David Wippell (1985-97), Mervyn Evans (1964-73), Malcolm Oxley (1973-85), Andrew Wright (1997-2007).

Duncan Williams (1948-84).

Peter Church (1950-87).

Fran Prichard (1952-87).

Joe McPartlin (1963-98).

BURSARS

Capt. R.S. Thursfield, a former naval officer, held the post 1932-6.

Hubert Beales (Roll No. 2433), bursar 1946-75, previously a Maths teacher.

John Armstrong, Housemaster of Apsley 1955-69, Second Master 1969-75, bursar 1975-87.

Lt. Col. David Bramble, bursar 1987-98, the second retired officer from the armed services to hold the post.

Stephen Withers Green, bursar since 1998, with Warden David Christie.

GOVERNORS

The Governors gather for a meeting in 1948.

1971.
Warden Henry Christie stands at the right.

The Governing Body in 1963 together with Archbishop Fisher (*sixth from right*) and Douglas Bader (*eighth from right*).

David Conner, Chaplain 1971-80, Governor 1983-94.

Catherine Repp, 1992. A life scientist and university administrator, Repp was the first female governor of St Edward's.

EVENTS

Celebrating victory in the Boer War, 1902. Walter Young, a long-standing member of the domestic staff, stands at the base.

The Jubilee Lunch, 1913. Big School is filled to overflowing.

The opening of the Memorial Buildings (now Tilly's), at Commem. 1925. Kendall is at the right.

Four prelates at the Centenary: *left to right* Noel Hudson (Roll No. 1145, Bishop of Ely), Harry Carpenter (Oxford), Geoffrey Fisher (Canterbury, Frank Fisher's father), Robert Mortimer (Roll No. 1608, Exeter).

The 1997 intake, with the first thirteen-year-old girl pupils.

INTERIORS

The Beauchamp Dormitory, 1873. It served as the chapel until 1877.

Wilfrid Cowell's sitting-room in the Lodge, *c.* 1900.

Big School, 1920.

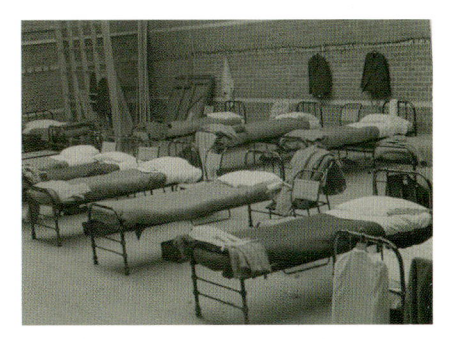

The old gymnasium (now part of the North Wall) in use as a medical ward during a 'flu epidemic, 1957.

The New Hall, 1975.

Jubilee House, 2013.

EXTERIORS

The artist of this water-colour, painted c.1880 and the most familiar and attractive view of the school, is unknown.

Corfe House (originally named Field House), 1902.

The Beehive, 1931, the year of its demolition. It housed the prefects' studies.

Big School (now the Library), c.1980.

The Cooper Quad, 1988, named after the benefactor Graham Cooper (Roll No. 2656), Senior Prefect in 1937 and Chairman of the Governors 1973-85.

The view across the Quad, by Nicholas Sutcliffe (Roll No. 9510), a pupil 1991-6.

To the west of the Woodstock Road, recently photographed.

The North Wall Arts Centre, 2006.

The Ogston Building, where Life Sciences are taught, in 2009.

The Martyrs Pavilion, 2009: the most recent of the five pavilions.
Photographed by Gilbert McGarragher.

The Quad, 2013.

NURSES

Miss Bishop, c.1895, who served 1886-1912.

Kay Puxley, nurse to Cowell's and Segar's 1949-70.

Jane Haddock, nurse to Tilly's and Mac's 1973-97 and mother of four boys at the school.

Violet Davies, nurse to Cowell's and Segar's 1979-2001, was the last state-registered nurse to be appointed.

SERVANTS

1876.

Henry Bursey in 1894, four years before his retirement as the Warden's coachman, butler and factotum, positions he had held for 24 years.

Walter Young in 1902, the year of his retirement as the school's carpenter after 37 years.

Arthur Jeffrey, 1930. He served from 1890, starting as a coach boy and finishing as the Warden's butler.

Marion Gierlicki, the Warden's steward and chauffeur 1948-95.

The Beasley Family at the Boathouse.

NEW PUPILS

In the early years each new boy submitted an individual photograph, for which he posed in a studio in his best suit. Charles Commeline (Roll No. 63), photographed in 1866 aged eleven or twelve, would serve in the Zulu and Boer War campaigns.

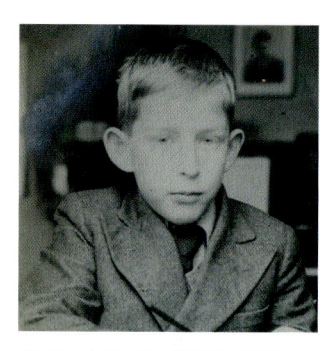

Peter Blake (Roll. No. 3025), 1935, aged 14. His elder brother (Roll No. 2839) was also at the school, as his grandfather (Roll No. 413) had been. Peter served in the RAF and was killed in 1941.

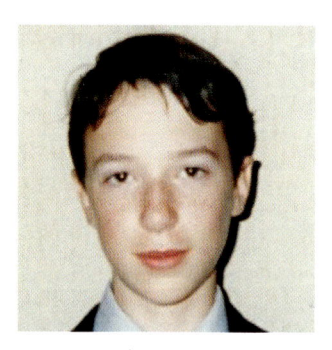

Thomas D. Appleby (Roll No. 9543), 1992, aged 13. His father (Roll. No. 5654) and three siblings (Nos 9385, 10446, 11449) were also at the school. Thomas attended Nottingham University and became an analyst of trade investment and commercial strategy.

Georgina Pelham (Roll No. 8765), daughter of an OSE (Roll No. 4836) and sister of a Head of School (Roll No. 7972), arrived at St Edward's in 1986, aged 15. She gained degrees at Oxford and the Courtauld Institute, is an art historian and conservator of paintings, and in 2014 became the first female President of the St Edward's School Society.

Philippa Warner (Roll No. 10970), and Polly Badham-Thornhill (Roll No. 10965), 2001, both aged 13. Pippa is a renowned actress and Polly is a teacher.

FORM GROUPS

The IV form in 1874 with its master Arthur Cowie (taught 1872-80). Because pupils moved up the school on the basis of academic merit rather than age, senior boys languished in junior forms. The youngsters wear boaters but older boys sport bowlers and, in the case of Cecil Tyler (Roll No. 171), a watch chain. Tyler, one of four brothers to attend the school, is shown here in the last of his three years in the form.

Wilfrid Cowell with his Shell Form in 1899. Again the ages are mixed.

John Todd with the History Sixth, 1965.

Shell O, 1988.

The Geography Sixth Dinner, 1994. The Head of Department, Garrett Nagle (1986-) is in the centre, Joe McPartlin on his left (1963-98).

PUPILS AT WORK

Certificate Examinations in Big School in 1933.

A class in 1959 with the Art Master, Lawrence Toynbee (1947-61), in the art room above the Memorial Library which had been opened five years earlier. Art was a hobby rather than an examination subject.

Class taken by Warden Fisher.

Chemistry lesson, 1964.

A recent Economics class. Jeremy Mather (2011-) teaches James Coker (Roll No. 12304) and Moora Heil (Roll No. 12949).

DAYROOMS

The New Buildings (later Mac's), c. 1890.

Natal, the Apsley day room, 1919. The space is now part of the Senior Common Room.

Mac's junior day room, 1930.

Segar's senior day room, 1959.

Prep, 1964, supervised by a prefect.
The other boys occupy their 'horse-boxes'.

PUPILS RELAXING

By the Cherwell, c.1895.

Formally dressed by the waterside.

Tea with Warden Sing.

The Camera Club, 1900. The school's archive amply illustrates the Victorian enthusiasm for photography. Many of the pictures were taken by the masters Wilfrid Cowell and Arthur Legat (taught 1875-1980).

The Tuck Shop, 1902.

Skating on Port Meadow, 1940.

Members of Menzies House, *c.* 1930, in the standard baggy trousers of the period.

The School Morris Men, 1980, an extra-curricular activity run by the Physics teacher Tony Snell (1965-96).

The Jazz band entertains Summertown, 2000.

Mathilda Littlehales (Roll No. 12365) and Oliver Knight (Roll No. 12874) in front of the old Cowell's and Segar's building, *c.* 2012.

EATING

The Dining Hall seen from its west end, 1894. Masters as well as boys ate there.

Before the meal, 1938. Boys sat by Houses with their House sports trophies on shelves beside them.

OSE Dinner, c.1960.

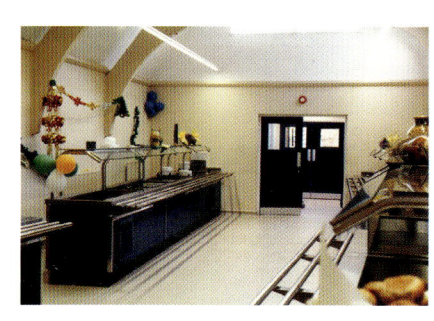

The new kitchen servery, 1995.

The Dining Hall, 2010.

SPORT

Cricket XI 1869, at New Inn Hall Street.

Bumpers, 1948.

The undefeated First XV of 1960.

The first ever undefeated First XI, 1968.

The First VIII of 1977.

The Girls Hockey XI of 1988.

THE SECOND WORLD WAR

Douglas Bader (Roll No. 1983).

Guy Gibson (Roll No. 2755). Drawing by William Rothenstein.

Arthur Banks (Roll No. 3203).

Adrian Warburton (Roll No. 2718).

Alec Cranswick (Roll No. 2846).

Tom Hankey, the only master (1936-9) killed in the war.

THE CADET FORCE

Field-Marshal Lord Roberts inspects the Officers' Training Corps, 1912.

The March Past outside the Warden's lodgings on the opening of Memorial Buildings, November 1925.

Air Cadets at Camp, 1951. Warden Kendall looks on.

The pupil pilots who staged a fly past for the Centenary celebrations.

Fly past by the Battle of Britain Flight, a Lancaster and a Spitfire, 1993.

Bethany Reed (Roll No. 12570) and James Chainey (Roll No. 12472) accept the Cadre Trophy from the inspecting officer, Lieutenant-Colonel Robin Sergeant (Roll No. 8779), Commanding Officer of the First Battalion Coldstream Guards, July 2013.

MUSIC

Edward Manning (taught 1927-63) conducts the orchestra.

The Brass Group led by Peter Corlett (1954-89), 1979.

The School Quartet, 1897: *left to right* Cyril Flower (Roll No. 814), Warden Sing, the future Warden W.H. Ferguson, and Harold Ridsdale (Roll No. 833).

Flautists in the Concert Band, 2013: Flora King (Roll No. 12701) and Celia Hodgson (Roll No. 12685).

Choir Practice, 1954.

The Chapel Choir, 1993. The sixth figure from the left at the front is the Director of Music, Anthony Kerr-Dineen (1992-2008).

DRAMA

Cowell's production of Shakespeare's *King John*, 1905. Samuel Haughton (Roll No. 1135) is the boy Arthur, Theophilus Heale (Roll No. 1101) Hubert.

Jean Anouilh's *Thieves' Carnival* (1962).

Irving Berlin's *Showboat*, 1998: the last production by Malcolm Oxley (taught 1962-99).

Arthur Miller's *A View from the Bridge*, directed in 1999 by Nick Quartley (1975-2006). Robin Giles (Roll No. 10040) is Marco (*centre*).

Stephen Sondheim's *Into the Woods*, 2011, directed by Lucy Maycock (2000-), Director of Drama.

The Wind in the Willows, 2013, also directed by Lucy Maycock. Theodore Smith (Roll No. 12614) is Toad.

THE GRAPHIC ART OF THE FRENCH TEACHER
B.G. 'BINKS' SEGAR (TAUGHT 1918-55)

Henry Kendall.

The Lord Mayor arrives to open the new subway, May 1928.

The Mayor searches for the subway.

'Summer Camp'.

Walter Dingwall (1923-37).

Charles Mather (1946-76).

the Quad area and replanted at the south of the First XI pitch to shield the school fields from the Keble fields.

On 14 November 1930 Kendall and Stone submitted to the Governors a crystal-clear analysis of the school's 'Buildings, Land and Finance'. It summarized the achievements of the past years, which it boldly categorized merely as Phase One. Since 1920 the school had spent £89,786 on land, buildings and equipment, of which a little more than half, £46,000, had come from profits on the fees. The cost of the next phase was estimated at £65,000. It would have included the purchase of Northern House, the special school owned by the local authority, the first of many initiatives for its acquisition which were never formally pursued.

In March 1928 Simeon had died. His coffin was borne in state from Davenant Road to the burial ground he had created by the Chapel. The question how to commemorate him provoked a long-running controversy. Rogers proposed a recumbent effigy. Having been told that there was no space for one in the already congested main area of the Chapel, where anyway the tribute might have looked dated and theatrical beside the austere plaques of the fallen, he proposed the creation of a separate chapel in the corner of the building used as a vestry and tower-base. The effigy would be at the centre. The chapel went ahead, but without the effigy. Dalton, Simeon's old colleague and adversary, died in the same year. An era was passing, for Hobson had died in 1925 and Hudson would follow in 1929. In the same year Cowell, now aged 74, gave up his Classical Shell and the supervision of the *Chronicle* which he had exercised for twenty years, though he carried on teaching. Walter Young, carpenter for forty-six years, retired with the present of a gramophone and on a school pension. He would live for another twenty-seven years, a rare link with the distant past, when he had been one of Chamberlain's choirboys at St Thomas's.

In 1929 the waters were ruffled by the abrupt resignation of Sing as Chairman of the Governors, a post he had held since the time of the withdrawal from the Woodard Society in 1927, and in which he had safeguarded the school's interest with his customary skill and care. He and Kendall were contrasting figures: Sing austere, punctilious, scholarly, cautious, a little distant; Kendall buccaneering, warm, emotional, optimistic, and perhaps with a touch of the maverick. It is a surprise to find the two men holidaying together on a brief Mediterranean cruise at Easter 1929. Sing's letter of resignation, worded with characteristic restraint, came after their return. 'It is not to be thought either by you or anyone else that I am in disagreement with your policy for the School, either in the past or as outlined for the future.' He acknowledged the rising numbers and the building projects as marks of Kendall's success. Yet 'it is perhaps true that I for my single self might have been content to make haste more slowly'.

It is hard to say how much Sing's departure owed to his concern about the pace of Kendall's programme or its attendant financial risks, and how much to irritation at the dynamic Warden's impatience with protocol. In 1929 Kendall, as always setting a high priority on the cultivation of the old boys, had decided to tell the assembled OSE at Commem about the next stage of his development plans even though they had yet to be brought before the Governors. Sing, already on the point of resignation, was not consulted. Having learned of Kendall's intention he told his fellow governor Francis Wylie (Roll No. 310): 'Well, I think I had better know nothing about it. I have to be away [on the day of the next Governors' meeting] and perhaps that is as well.' Wylie, an elder statesman anxious to keep the peace, reported to Kendall: 'He is evidently a little nervous as Chairman of the Governing Body of seeming to discuss proposals with Old Boys of which the Governing Body have never heard, which is perhaps natural. But he showed no sort of resentment (though I should not go so far as to say that he exactly "approved"!) – and he does not wish to be mixed up with it himself.' Bishop Southwell, Provost of Lancing, succeeded Sing as chairman, which indicates that the withdrawal from the Woodard Society had not damaged relations with it. Southwell held the position until 1934, when Kendall's close friend A. B. Emden, Principal of St Edmund Hall, Oxford, took over.

Kendall's financial operations went from strength to strength. He saw that the mortgage and overdraft from Barclay's, which together amounted to £13,250, were needlessly low. In 1930, with the advice of the Aldenham family and of Stone, he redeemed them and instead borrowed £33,000 from the London Life Assurance, at 5½% and on the security of the school's main buildings and its land. In 1930 the Aldenhams, generous as ever, exchanged the debenture that was owed them for £2,400, which was only 60% of its value. The Governors demonstrated their gratitude for Kendall's work by increasing his salary and his entertainment allowance. His energetic reach extended far beyond the school. Regional dinners for OSE were founded. In 1935 the record of the Northern dinner noted that 115 of the 896 boys to have entered the school in the last ten years had come from Merseyside, the Kendall family's base. Links he formed with preparatory schools in Cheshire and the Wirral would be maintained until the 1970s. Another of Kendall's initiatives was to create associations with the armed services. In 1930 he secured the establishment of a bursary, awarded twice a year, for sons of naval officers. There would be comparable arrangements with the other services.

How much he had done! By 1930 he had recovered the school's independence, created a new House programme, achieved dominance of the Governing Body, charmed and mobilized the old boys, attracted yet more parents, increased the school's sporting facilities and reputation, established a cadre of loyal and energetic teachers, won the affection and respect of the boys, and acquired virtually unlimited control of the school. The 56th annual OSE dinner at Oxford's Clarendon Hotel on 7 December 1929, attended by a record number of 148, among them William Goodenough and fourteen of Kendall's staff, must have seemed like a royal court assembled. In the chair sat Harold Graham-Hodgson (Roll No. 1223), the King's radiographer, who would soon be a governor and have a Physics prize named after him. He remarked on the progress of the school, which he attributed to 'the vital energy of the Warden'. There was a great deal more energy, and a great deal more progress, to come.

29

THRIVING IN THE THIRTIES

THE 1920s were a buoyant period for the Public Schools. In spite of left-wing criticism they grew in numbers and self-assurance. Between 1918 and 1930 Harrow increased its numbers from 552 to 661, Oundle from 350 to 565, Clifton from 680 to 775. New schools, some of them progressive or experimental, were founded: Rendcomb in 1920, Summerhill in 1921, Stowe in 1923, Dartington Hall in 1926, Bryanston in 1928. The expanding middle class, for all the taunts in *Punch* at the nouveaux riches, knew that a Public School education was the route to esteem and success. In his book *Equality* in 1927 the Christian Socialist historian R. H. Tawney pointed out that in Britan all but four of the 56 bishops were from Public Schools, all but 39 of 161 County Court judges, all but 27 of 99 directors of banks, and, even in industry, all but 37 of 94 directors of the main railway companies. The esteem of the Public Schools extended to classes that had no hope of access to them. Grammar Schools imitated them in their systems of prefects and punishments and their attitude to games. Children of all classes devoured comics with Public School settings, taking the *Gem* and the *Magnet* – where they could follow the misadventures of Billy Bunter – or reading the innumerable novels that were set in Public Schools or related the exploits of their old boys.

Scholarships offered by the schools or by the army or banks enabled men in modest professional posts to send their sons to boarding school. Even without scholarships an increasing number of parents could contemplate the cost of private education. Prices fell by around 27% between 1920 and 1922, and the decline continued, albeit at a lower rate, until 1933. Falls in costs of food and transport were especially marked. The standard of living of most professional employees rose significantly through the 1920s, for although salaries fell the drop was far smaller; only about 12%. It helped schools' budgets that their teachers' stipends fell more than most. In the 1930s the basic salary of masters was £200, with built-in increments of £15, a lower total than in Ferguson's time but higher in relation to prices. Kendall had the rates adjusted for individuals when it suited him. The low fees of St Edward's gave it a competitive advantage. In 1930 it was operating at a surplus on a basic fee of £133. Of comparable schools only Bedford (£129) and Denstone (£130) charged less. Rossall's fees were £144, Bradfield's £150, Cheltenham's £162, Malvern's £165, Oundle's £170, Clifton's £173, Lancing's £174, Marlborough's £185, Radley's £185 and Rugby's £201.

The distinctive achievement of Kendall's regime was to defy the Depression, which ended the post-war security of other schools, where numbers fell away after the Wall Street Crash of 1929 and Britain's abandonment of the Gold Standard in 1931. Malvern dropped from 577 in 1930 to 430 in 1939. Harrow, having peaked at 675 boys in 1928, suffered a loss of 22.5% between 1931 and 1939. St Edward's, despite dips in 1933 and 1940, generally sustained its growth. Even before the Depression it did better than most schools. There were 260 boys in the Michaelmas Term of 1925, and 351 by 1930. The trend would last, the figure rising to 339 by 1943 and 449 by 1948. The school's recruits came mainly from the lay professional classes, from families in banking or accountancy or the services. The proportion of sons of clergy had greatly declined. The 55 new boys of Christmas Term 1930 included only eight sons of clergy, and just one of the 55, Thomas Packer (Roll No. 2590), himself a clergyman's son, would enter the Church.

In 1930 Kendall, with Stone at his elbow, was planning the next stage of building. He wanted to improve the rooms and facilities of the houses and to ensure that there was space for every one of their members to live and sleep there. The Library needed improvement, which it would long be denied, but the main challenge was the classrooms. To the dismay of prospective parents, some classes were still held in huts adjacent to the Memorial Buildings. The 'Workhouse' replaced them in 1931. It was opened by the Warden of New College, H. A. L. Fisher, who as a government minister had been the terror of the Public Schools in 1919. Even so, the huts survived, resituated beside the Armoury behind Big School, where they would accommodate Geography, Carpentry, Music practice and Vehicle Maintenance in the years ahead. They were not demolished until the 1970s. The 'Workhouse', set back a little from the Quad and less aesthetically intrusive than Kitchin's extension to the dining hall, was to prove a very successful building.

Another initiative addressed the problem of overcrowding in the Chapel. Here the school called on the services of Harold Rogers, even though he was no longer its principal architect. He converted the south-west corner of the building, where the vestry had been, into a memorial chapel for the fallen of the Great War. It had been furnished by 1934 and had a screen facing north into the nave, as it still does. But where would the vestry be placed? Until now the entry to the Chapel had been an elaborate Early Gothic door at the north-west of the building. It led from the cloister, which itself led into School House and then to the staircase to the dormitories, which had the manner of a monastic night stair. Now that High Church feature was lost. The cloister was enclosed and the former approach to the doorway became the vestry. The question of a new entry to the Chapel was left to Brook Kitchin, who provided 56 new seats by bringing the old Antechapel into the body of the nave and added a new Antechapel or porch to the west end with two doors into it, north and south. The project was completed in 1931, when the new Antechapel was dedicated by Bishop Southwell. As in Kitchin's extension of the Main Buildings, improvement and enlargement came at an aesthetic cost – a heavy one, in the Chapel's case. There were piecemeal improvements elsewhere in the school. Kitchin added the small anteroom to the Warden's House by his study entrance. Four tennis courts were laid out in 1929 and six squash courts in 1931. The gallery of Big School, to which Kendall gave £350 anonymously, was built in 1932, and a boatman's house was erected in 1935. At the same time some of the old huts were moved to the fields to house the headquarters of the newly formed Scout Troop.

Brooks's now valued the school's property at £154,525. In 1932 the mortgage, which Vicary Gibbs had transferred from the Prudential to London Life, was increased to £50,000 at 5¾%. It was paid in two years and nimbly replaced by a loan of £60,000 at 4¼% from the University Chest. In his first decade Kendall had spent £99,453. Of that sum, £11,218 had been contributed by the OSE, the OTC and the profits of the Shop, which between 1919 and 1947 contributed a handsome £10,693. The Endowment Fund, essentially an OSE project, had raised £6,615 by 1926 and was to stand at £20,500 by 1947, an increase achieved with guidance from Stone and through wise investments by successive bursars, Dingwall and, from 1932, R. S. Thursfield. The St Edward's Society had contributed more than £3,000 in gifts and donations, had bought and set up the rowing facilities, had given the new pavilion, and had generated £8,000 for scholarships. It had contributed £9,377 to the War Memorial Fund in 1919–23, and between 1939 and 1947 would raise £9,499 for the Second World War Memorial Fund.

In 1931 there was a geographical reorganization of the Houses. Apsley House and Sing's House moved into the Main Buildings, which had previously been occupied, in haphazard arrangements, by Cowell's and Tilly's, which now moved to buildings of their own. Tilly's went across the Quad to the Memorial Buildings, which it has occupied ever since, and Cowell's across the road to Field House, which in turn moved to Apsley Paddox, where it would remain until 1964. In the Main Buildings, which were now renamed School House, Apsley and Sing's lived semi-separately, a clumsy but not unsuccessful arrangement. The squeezing of Apsley and Sing's into the building was the reason, or pretext, for the demolition of the 'Beehive', which Kitchin's extension replaced.

Kendall harboured larger ambitions. He wanted the erection, at an estimated cost of £16,869, of a single building to hold two houses which, in contrast to Apsley and Sing's, would be clearly separated. An alternative plan was to build a single house for fifty-six boys, which might cost £5,000 less. The school went for the bolder scheme. Kendall's friend A. B. Emden, Principal of St Edmund Hall, Oxford and Chairman of the Governors from 1934, threw his weight behind the Warden's ambitions. The sale of the road frontages of Apsley Paddox for £7,000 (a move which followed the pattern of the school's withdrawal behind the world's frontiers) raised money for the new building, and £5,500 was diverted from the Endowment Fund. The new building, which stood to the east of Big School and the 'Workhouse', was designed by Kitchin and completed in 1936. It was divided between Cowell's, which moved after its five-year occupancy of Apsley, and Segar's, whose move left Mac's, which had hitherto shared with Segar's, in sole occupancy of New Buildings. The eventual cost of the Cowell's–Segar's block was £25,064. Viscount Sankey, a governor, opened it. The building, well planned and constructed, was tidily arranged into dormitories and day rooms. There was, however, no provision for married accommodation: Kendall expected housemasters to be married to their Houses. But in 1931 Philip Whitrow, Housemaster of Sing's, had announced that he was getting married. Another housemaster, Walter Dingwall, did the same in 1937. Whitrow had to give up Sing's, there being no married accommodation in either its old or its new home, and was replaced at the time of the move to School House by the unmarried George Mallaby. But the transfer of Field House, still then based in what we know as Corfe House, into

Apsley Paddox, where there was room for married accommodation, enabled Dingwall to move there with his bride.

Together with the 'Workhouse' the Cowell's–Segar's block, which lay out of sight of the Warden's lodgings, to a degree shifted the geographical emphasis of the school towards the Oakthorpe Road, where an exit had to be created to enable the new buildings to be connected to the main drains. The school had owned a house in the road since 1895. Number 42 was purchased in 1931, a move which started the gradual acquisition of most of the properties on the north side of the road. In 1937 Emden bought the house and rented it to the school for £40, a sum he donated to a fund for OSE who went up to St Edmund Hall. Later he gave money for work on the Chapel roof and donated a field, Fair Close, for the boathouse. When the school rented out the field he asked that half the income be given to the fund for OSE at his college. The houses in Oakthorpe Road accommodated masters, as did houses that Kendall also acquired in Stratfield Road, Woodstock Road and Grove Street. Accommodation for the teaching staff was increasing. So, as Kendall had to accept, was their tendency to marry. On the Paddox site two new houses were built in 1928 to house married masters, E. P. Hewetson and the Rev. C. W. Sowby. The extraordinary building programme was completed in 1937 by the erection of a new boiler house, extensions to the kitchen extensions, and a wooden isolation block by the Sanatorium.

Buildings were the outward and visible triumph of Kendall's Wardenship in the 1930s, but there was a triumph of spirit too. Above all he generated confidence, which persuaded governors to spend large sums of money, parents to send their sons, old boys to give. Boys would look back on their time with an intensity not shared by any other generation of pupils, with gratitude and happy memories. Derek Henderson (Roll No. 3367), one of three Roman Catholic brothers in the school between 1933 and 1944, remembers how impressed his father had been by Kendall, by the sense of well-being and unflappable competence he exuded. His accomplished manner projected a set of values. What were they?

When in 1974 I was introduced to Ernest Bigland (Roll No. 2295), who was at the school from 1927 to 1930 and had just become a governor, he asked me, 'What's your game?' It took me a moment to grasp that he was not questioning my integrity but enquiring which sport I preferred. He had been a Silver Goblets finalist at Henley in 1933, had had a most distinguished Second World War, and was a powerful force in Guardian Assurance. He shared his rowing interests with his younger brother Anthony (Roll No. 3388). His own twin sons Robert (Roll No. 4681) and John (Roll No. 4682) followed him at St Edward's in 1951, and Robert's daughter Emma (Roll No. 8287) was among the early girl entrants to the school.

Between the wars the phrase 'the Public School type' came into common use. It could be derogatory and a caricature, but it also conveys an ideal, one to which Ernest Bigland's question points. It was tested in the Second World War and proved suited to it, most conspicuously in the personality and achievements of Douglas Bader, a hero of the games field as a boy and amid the demands of war so brave, so confident, so inspiring a leader, so dauntless before even the most formidable obstacles. Public Schools aspired to teach character, male character, of a particular kind. Its marks were integrity, endurance, courage, stoicism in adversity, loyalty to a group, the subordination of the self to the common good, acceptance of the rules of the community, conformity to its customs and values. The hierarchy among the boys taught the exercise of responsibility at the top and the acceptance of subordination at the bottom. Games were not the only generator of collective spirit, but the individualism and dissent associated with literature and the arts were not trusted. No doubt some boys reacted against those mores, but the inter-war world knew nothing of the cult of the 'teenager', nothing of a dissident counter-culture.

Kendall encouraged anything that promoted group loyalty and identity. House colours and cups multiplied; the system of School and House colours assumed a Byzantine complexity; OSE bought school scarves, blazers, ties, cufflinks. Collective feeling was expected to foster friendliness. 'You will never lose anything by being friendly with the boys,' Kendall told Cedric Sowby when appointing him to the staff in 1928. He himself spoke lightly and informally to them, taking care to know their names and interests and, as they grew older, giving them the impression that he was taking them into his confidence. Prefects, sacristans and librarians were made to feel valued members of an establishment. On the Central Committee team captains worked with masters and felt they were helping to shape policy. Kendall played on sentiment, too. In a letter for circulation to old boys in 1934 he voiced 'pride in your efforts to rise superior to these hard times', 'gratitude for all your affection and help to the School', and the hope that, in 'your lonely jobs in the Colonies, or South America or Sarawak or Palestine or Costa Rica or goodness knows where', his letter might prompt 'some memory of your own time at St Edward's; it may be a glimpse of the outdoor baths on a summer afternoon, or the sunset over Wytham, the Rugby XV struggling against odds, the shouts and excitement of bumpers, the last Sunday in Chapel'. 'The present generation,' he assured his readers, 'are bringing to their life here the same vigour and good humour and simplicity which have meant so much to you all, and which are standing you in such good stead.'

Not every facet of school life flourished under Kendall. Though pieces of creative writing appeared in the *Chronicle* they were undistinguished and never numerous. Societies fared a little better, even if as usual their fortunes fluctuated. Four met through most of Kendall's tenure (the Debating Society; the Scientific and Engineering Society; the Literary Society, which Bill Eardley sustained; and the Camera Club), and others prospered from time to time. But only eleven meetings of the Debating Society were reported between 1925 and 1933, and ten of the Scientific and Engineering Society. The Thirties did see the start of the Musical Society (1934), as well as the Field Club (1935) and the Arts Society (1939). But Kendall showed no great interest in music and did little to foster or extend it. The concerts, under Lionel ('Bertie') Ovenden who was Director of Music from 1924, were fewer and less ambitious than in the era of Ferguson and Stanton, and many of the performers were OSE or other visiting adults. Though Ovenden could be a difficult man, Alan House (Roll No. 3369) remembers him as 'kind, good and friendly' and recalls that he 'always had time to talk to us who sang in the choir. Perhaps at St Edward's he was never given the accord and recognition which were his due .... He strove to keep musical culture alive often under rather alien circumstances.' Sowby recalled a visit to the Chapel by Sir Hugh Allen, a Professor of Music in Oxford. After the service 'the organist showed him out, obviously expecting some expression of congratulation. Sir Hugh's only comment was "Never saw a better behaved congregation. Good morning."' There was decline in the drama, too. When the long-standing Shakespeare productions ended with Cowell's death in 1937, the rich dramatic tradition was severely weakened. Kendall seems to have had few if any intellectual or cultural interests.

In March 1947 the manager of A. E. Turner and Son, clockmakers of George Street in Oxford, wrote to Kendall to mention vacancies for the training of 'intelligent boys of good appearance and address for a skilled trade with good prospects'. Kendall tersely replied,

'I am afraid there are no boys at this school for the posts you offer.' He had other ideas for his pupils. His many surviving letters of recommendation for boys applying to businesses, the civil service, the armed forces or the universities tend to commend standard virtues in standard phrases. On behalf of Eric Wynne Davies (Roll No. 3078), who applied to the Civil Service Commission in January 1939, Kendall wrote: 'He is a sound and trustworthy boy, fit for responsibility, of a healthy moral tone with plenty of courage, and he has an influence for good among his friends.' It was Kendall's ideal.

30

KENDALL'S SCHOOL

WILFRID COWELL, who celebrated his 80th birthday in the autumn of 1936, died on 5 September 1937. He was the first assistant master of the school to be accorded a portrait. Paid for by money raised by the St Edward's Society, it is the most successful of the portraits, most of them of Wardens, that now hang in the Library. It was painted by Edward Newling (Roll No. 1236) and captures Cowell's avuncular presence. Cowell's was the last body to be buried in the ground by the Chapel. By any standards he was a remarkable schoolmaster. As a teacher he had run the Shell from 1880 to 1928 and Set A from 1893 to 1925. He had acted as de facto Second or Senior Master from 1886 to 1925. From 1880 to 1887 he taught all the French in the school, except in the Sixth Form, and marked 400 compositions every week. For two years in the 1880s, before a science teacher was appointed, he taught the subject to the Shells, manufacturing his own equipment.

Cowell was Librarian from 1883 to 1928 and produced forty-five plays, productions remembered for their quality and for their prologues, those nimble commentaries on the current life of the school. He sang in the school choir from 1880 to 1907, never missing a choir practice. Often he sang solos in concerts, and found time to sing in three major choirs in Oxford. As well as supervising the editing of the *Chronicle* he wrote extensively for it. He compiled the school lists for 1904 to 1927 and the address lists from 1914 to 1926. He set his famed annual General Knowledge Paper from 1893 to the year before his death. The first four *Rolls* were all either his own work or based on his records. He sustained the Field Club and Debating Society when time allowed, and voiced some bitterness when other masters who had taken them over let them slide. He claimed to have attended Chapel 25,000 times. To it he gave the Sanctuary Lamp and the prayer books and bibles that are now placed in the Chancel pews. He bequeathed his pension fund and a further £1,000 to the Endowment Fund, and in his lifetime gave handsome gifts to it as well as to the Field Fund and the War Memorial Fund. He helped shape the St Edward's Society and was its treasurer from 1893 to 1928 and vice-president in 1928. Its constitution of 1922 was largely of his making. He preserved a fine set of documents and photographs which makes the archives for his period the best part of the school collection.

Sing's tribute in the *Chronicle* observed that

> it was of supreme value to the School to have within its walls one firmly fixed and respected person who seemingly would go on for ever .... My own Head Master [Edward Thring] would tell us to be 'Jack of all trades but master of one'. This is exactly what Cowell was – in the world of learning and the arts. His multifarious interests included scholarship, French Literature, Greek Scripture, Italian and Dutch pictures, gardening, photography, music and fringes of Natural Science .... It was in English Literature and particularly English poetry that he was acknowledged master.

He took a 'useful share' in the coaching of crews on the river but 'he could say with the author of *Ionica* "I cheer the games I cannot play"; yes and also criticise shrewdly'. The 'author of *Ionica*' was the late William Johnson Cory of Eton, who had inspired enthusiasm and affection in his pupils, Lord Halifax among them. Few schoolmasters of the early twentieth century can have shared Cowell's breadth of interests and culture. In his last years, living in the upper rooms of the Lodge, which he had occupied for fifty years, he kept open door, as he always had done, to the boys. In his memory his devotee Harold Rogers designed the wrought-iron Cowell Gates, which were opened in 1939 by the Princess Royal, another coup by Kendall among the great and the good. Because of the growth of motor traffic, that gap in the Woodstock Road had replaced the Lodge as the main entrance.

Cowell was not a man of limitless tolerance. In the year of his death Oswald Shuffrey, who had been a boy under Ferguson, was appointed Senior Language Master at Ardingly, a Woodard school. When an undergraduate at Christ Church he had intended to be ordained in the Anglican Church, but he had converted to Catholicism. In old age he remembered that the headmaster of Ardingly 'was, of course, an Anglo-Catholic clergyman but saw no reason why he should not appoint me to the language post. A few years later Ferguson came to preach .... The headmaster naturally invited me to dinner presuming that we should wish to meet. That evening however he came and told me, with much regret, that Ferguson did not wish to see me.' In the previous year Shuffrey, undergoing a tonsil operation in the Acland Home in Oxford, discovered that Cowell was also in the hospital. But

Cowell 'told the Matron that he did not wish to see me', for 'Cowell would have nothing more to do with a boy who converted to Roman Catholicism .... What I have recounted of Ferguson and Cowell may seem bigoted and small minded today. Whilst I was naturally offended and sorry I realise they were absolutely devoted to their beliefs. They believed that it was of paramount importance to defend those beliefs at all costs in a world in which already not only the laity, but certain well known clergy, were beginning to waver. Additionally, the Tractarians and their heirs were always sensitive to the accusation of being crypto-Papists.'

If St Edward's had to a degree been secularized since its early era, religious sensitivities survived. They created difficulties for Kendall. In 1928 the 14-year-old Charles Michie (Roll No. 2414) entered the school. The son of Presbyterian parents, he had not been confirmed. Charles's parents told Kendall, as a courtesy, that they expected the boy to take communion in the Chapel, as members of the Presbyterian Church of England who had not been confirmed were allowed to do in Anglican services elsewhere. The boy told Kendall that he shared their wish. 'Sixty six years later,' Charles writes, 'I can still recall the horrified silence that greeted my utterance; unwittingly I had really put HEK on the spot! As a result he referred the matter to the Bishop of Oxford, who in due course decreed that the only way I could receive communion was by converting to the Church of England. I was given no explanation that I could follow, and as a very immature 14-year-old, I just did not understand what had hit me. My parents were very upset but short of removing me from the School there was nothing that could be done about it. Until I left in 1932, like everyone else, I had to attend Chapel (to which I did not object at all), but when it came to the Eucharist I had to leave God's house.'

Kendall did not want to discriminate against prospective pupils on religious grounds. What put him 'on the spot' were the sensitivities of the school's ecclesiastical constituency. This was a touchy time for High Churchmen, who were angered in 1927 by parliament's rejection – to them a symptom of the creeping secularism of post-war society – of a new Prayer Book, which would have allowed for a more sacramental form of the Eucharist as an alternative to the service prescribed in the Prayer Book of 1662. In November 1930 Kendall received an indignant letter from Harold Rogers:

> From the *Chronicle* I learn that a boy has gone (apparently directly from the School) to St Peter's Hall [in Oxford, which had been founded two years earlier as a Low Church Evangelical college], and that the Gaudy is fixed for Advent Sunday and the OSE Dinner for a vigil; these last are confirmed by your invitation which I have just received. I rub my eyes and ask 'Is this St Edward's or any other Public School?' No, I ought not to say that for I don't think the date for Commem would have been selected by any of them. You must forgive me for writing but I have been very much troubled, and as these things are bound to be talked about I feel it only frank to register my respectful protest directly to yourself.

The boy in question was Gerald Solomon (Roll No. 2182), who came from an Evangelical family and as a priest would be a distinguished Chaplain to the Forces from 1942 to 1963. He sent his twin sons to St Edward's. Kendall replied to Rogers:

> He was a boy who came from an evangelical home, of a very deep piety, who intends to be ordained .... It would be a poor day for St Edward's if such a boy were discouraged here, or even if any OSE, whatever his great services to the School, should feel it necessary to criticise him, a fellow OSE, for taking this step with the full approval of his housemaster, a devout Catholic [the Anglo-Catholic Arthur Tilly] and of myself.

In his emotion Rogers had muddled Commem with Gaudy. Commem, traditionally held on the Sunday closest to 25 November, the anniversary of the laying of the foundation stone of the Chapel, had in recent years been observed in December. Kendall moved it back to November, but in 1930 not far enough. The Gaudy was fixed for Sunday 30 November and the OSE Dinner, to be held in the Randolph Hotel, was arranged for the previous evening. Kendall received another protest, this time from Warden Kidd of Keble College, a powerful force in the High Church movement, who had been a governor since 1927. 'I want to ask you,' wrote Kidd, 'whether there has been some oversight in allowing the dinner to be arranged for the Vigil of a Saint's Day and to suggest, as a governor of St Edward's, that this should be carefully avoided in future. It is bad for the principles which St Edward's was founded to maintain.' In Keble, Kidd added, dinners on any Saturday evening were forbidden 'because they are bad for Sunday morning worship'.

Kendall was angered by Kidd's epistolary 'pinpricks'. He 'makes a great mistake if he thinks I am interested in anything but the real religious side of work among boys'. In reply, the Warden pointed out that the OSE dinners had been held on Saturdays, and attended by members of the Governing Body, for many years. If Kidd objected to them he should either have raised the point before joining the Governing Body or taken it to his fellow governors. Kendall consulted Henry Southwell, formerly Bishop of Lewes, now residentiary canon at Chichester. The bishop thought Kidd's points absurd and came to Kendall's rescue. Kidd's protest about the feast of St Andrew rested on a technicality which, the bishop was able to report, the Warden of Keble had got wrong. Southwell told Kendall with evident pleasure, and with no less pleasure told Kidd, that even in the Prayer Book of 1928, which parliament rejected but many High Churchmen adopted, the eve of St Andrew is not a vigil. The canon had also consulted the Bishop of Truro, who himself had impeccable High Church credentials but lacked Kidd's inflexibility. 'I understand the Warden's [Kidd's] dislike of a Saturday dinner as a whole,' replied the bishop, 'but yours seems very safe and quite justifiable "ecclesiastically".' Southwell for his part could see a case for Kidd's demanding standards being imposed on parish priests or religious communities, but 'this cannot apply to schools'. The spat did not impair the merriment of the dinner, which was attended by 155 people, among them Sing, Ferguson, two governors, fifteen members of Kendall's staff, and the offended Rogers. Bob Mortimer, now a powerful Oxford academic who had recently been a Select Preacher to the University, reported in the *Chronicle* that one of Kendall's jokes had been lost amid the 'malignations of the champagne cork' which 'landed in the midst of the youngest section of the party, who at once became helpless victims of uproarious hilarity'.

After Kendall's death members of the Common Room would speak of him with a reverence that far exceeded the usual nostalgia, under any Warden, for the reign of his predecessor. He had created a close-knit gentlemen's club, most of whose members were unmarried, though the married men sometimes complained about their pay. Before joining the staff Cedric Sowby had heard Kendall described as 'an earthquake'. He continued:

> When I arrived in 1928 he was more like a volcano in full and joyful eruption. During the whole of Kendall's twenty-nine years as Warden, the governors realised their good fortune, listened to his imaginative plans, provided him with money and left the rest to him … while the Old Boys were always enthusiastic and ready to

help him .... He selected his staff with great care and trusted them. He earned the complete loyalty and trust, co-operation and affection of his staff and was seldom, if ever, let down .... With Henry it was 'The School, the School' all the time .... He always succeeded in giving the impression that he had not a care in the world and always had time to talk if we went to ask for his advice. He never played the part of the over-burdened titan or the ruthless butcher, and I do not remember any member of staff being dismissed in the five years I was there. Kendall would probably have felt such an action to be a reflection on his own powers of selection and leadership. St Edward's justly had the reputation of being a happy place, and in Kendall's time never lacked excellent candidates for the staff, since they were certain of interesting work and of professional advancement if they wanted to go further.

As Sowby pointed out, many of them went on to headmasterships. A. D. James proceeded to Christ's College, Brecon in 1931, Mallaby to St Bees in 1935, Hewetson to a prep school, L. A. Wilding to King's School, Worcester in 1936, Dingwall to Hurstpierpoint in 1937. In 1933 Sowby himself became Warden of St Columba's College at Rathfarnham near Dublin. In the years after the Second World War Canon W. A L. Vincent would leave to run Christ Church Cathedral School in Oxford and Roger Northcote-Green (Roll No. 2231) to be Headmaster of Worksop. It is an impressive list for a small staff, a tribute to the reputation Kendall had established for the school and, perhaps, to his powers of networking.

In 1937 the Inspectors reported 'a striking improvement ... since the last report on the development of the Sixth Form Work'. They noted that in the last three years 82 boys, 31% of the leavers, had gone on to university, whereas the figure for the corresponding period before the previous report, in 1926, had been 28. Ten scholarships and exhibitions at Oxford and Cambridge over the past three years, and another four in the present one, was also an improvement. The report noted that in 1933–36 twenty boys had gone to Service colleges and ninety-eight into business. There was no problem, the Inspectors explained, of boys leaving prematurely. The report describes the average age of departure in 1935, 17½, as 'exceptionally high'. Of the seventy leavers in 1935 one was aged 20, fourteen were aged 19, twenty aged 18. There were eighteen 17-year-olds, fifteen aged 16, and two aged 15. The Inspectors record that in 1935 twenty-two boys had achieved the Higher School Certificate, though puzzlingly the *Chronicle*, whose facts and figures do not always concur with those supplied by other sources, gives a total of only fourteen. The Inspectors' figure of 142 passes in the Basic Certificate, a pass rate of 38% compared with 15% in 1925, looks encouraging but is again much higher than the *Chronicle*'s figure. Improvement in these examinations should have been expected, for universities and employers were giving more attention to them, while the numbers of university entrants were increasing too. But at least Kendall was able to sustain the school's reputation for providing, within a rounded education of character, an adequate academic record.

The Inspectors did have some tactfully worded reservations. Of Kendall's practice of leaving masters to their own ways in the classroom they observed: 'While complete uniformity is clearly undesirable, for the individuality of the teacher must be preserved, it is obviously essential that each Master should know how his own subject is being approached by his colleagues.' 'The Masters possess adequate but not strong academic qualifications.' Three of the 23 masters teach very well, while the rest achieve 'a general level of competence. As a team they are extremely conscientious.' Kendall's attempts to raise the academic profile of his staff had limited success. Three of them had Pass degrees, one an Oxford Fourth, several more Thirds. Yet Kendall did recruit two very successful Classics teachers with Firsts, Leslie Styler in 1931 and Pat Brims in 1936.

Sowby's memories usefully supplement the impressions of masters left by boys. He recalled the devoted industry of Walter Dingwall, who as well as his duties as bursar and housemaster taught History, Maths and English and was a captain in the OTC. He founded the Public Schools Bursars' Association. A shrewd player of the stock market, he left some £1.95 million when he died, in his 91st year, in 1990. He privately helped Douglas Bader's family to pay the boy's fees. From Sowby too we get a portrait of Arthur Tilly, who befriended Cedric, his wife Mary, and their little girl Rose Mary, to whom Kendall stood as godfather, and who named her doll after Tilly as 'Arthur Dolly'. The reputedly fierce Tilly melted in the Sowbys' company and spent holidays with them. Cedric himself built a house with four living rooms and five bedrooms on the Paddox site for £1,150. 'There we resided in comparative affluence with two maids, on an income of £450 a year.'

A vividly remembered teacher was Henry Gauntlett, 'The Grocer', a science graduate of London University, whom Ferguson had appointed in 1924 and who would be Housemaster of Segar's from 1950 to 1955. His teaching was praised, especially in his early years. Hubert Beales called him 'a mischievous little cockney and practical joker'. He had a practice of setting light to colleagues' newspapers in the Common Room. At the start of one term he read out a list of boys: Walker, Rider, Hunter, Going, Leeper, Hopper, Jump. He once sent Kendall an 'Application for Holiday' form requesting absence for forty days on full pay from 22 February 1939, and stating that he had 'arranged for the performance of his duties by The Head Warden [with] attendance by Donald and Terry' (apparently members of the domestic staff). In the 'approved' section he gave the initials of A. B. Emden, Chairman of the Governors. On the 23rd Kendall replied: 'I do not quite understand an application for leave of absence on full pay received from a Mr. Gauntlett. There was a gentleman of that name on the staff of the School but he left us finally on 22nd Feb. this year with the full approval of the Governors, Staff, Domestic Staff, boys and Donald and Terry.'

Happy and harmonious as Kendall's relations with his staff normally were, there was one serious exception. In 1935 he precipitated the resignation from his housemastership of Ken ('Father') Menzies, who had served in the school for fifteen years and been Housemaster of the former Set G. 'The sudden removal of a Housemaster,' as Graham Cooper (Roll No. 2656) recalled, 'was obviously a major event in the School .... I was head of the house at the time and was sad about the change because it was a happy house. I remember going to the Warden to make representations about the change. Perhaps this was an impertinent thing to do, but Kendall did not tick me off and just pointed out that it was his responsibility to do what he thought was right.' Edward Moberley (Roll No. 2958) remembers that when Menzies announced his departure to the House 'we couldn't have been more stupefied. Nobody spoke for a long time.' Thereafter 'the cheering at house matches continued to be for Menzies till it was stopped officially'.

Cooper writes: 'The surprising thing for me now, and at the time, is that I know so little background to the event. Obviously I was a favourite of the Warden and had a friendly if distant relationship with Menzies as head of the house. Neither of them had given me any hint of trouble of any kind either in the House or between themselves.' Mystery surrounds the affair. The sympathies of Menzies, a Scot, were with the High Church tradition which Kendall had confronted over the Commem of 1930. Moberley, who kept in touch with Menzies for the rest of the former housemaster's life, wrote that 'he belonged to the School's Anglo-Catholic roots' and had told Moberley that 'once the Catholic faith was fearlessly taught, but now the god of athletics *regnat in excelsis*'.

However, it was a particular episode that occasioned Menzies' departure. It involved Moberley himself. A new boy whom he had been asked to befriend turned on him with 'two other chaps', one of whom had been Moberley's own best friend. Menzies, discussing the matter with Moberley, asked 'Do you think a good punch on the nose would be the best thing?' There followed a fight, which was reported to Menzies. He wielded his cane and told the other two boys not to associate with the new boy. A term or two later the 'chap who had caused all the trouble left'. In later life Menzies confided to Moberley that he had wanted the troublemaker to leave immediately, that Kendall had refused to agree, and that Menzies 'felt himself with no honourable alternative but to resign his house. An attempt was made to get him out of the school .... But Ken [Menzies], a Freemason, appealed to Lord Sankey on the Governing Body as a fellow mason to stand by him. Lord Sankey intervened in some way and Ken was able to continue as an ordinary assistant master until 1946.' Nevertheless, Gerry Segar, that safe pair of hands, was moved into Menzies' house, which was now renamed Segar's. Only a dormitory (subsequently a reading room) retained Menzies' name.

Moberley says obscurely of the episode that 'the trouble did lie at a graver level'. Possibly there was a sexual dimension. Schools tend to hush up such matters, partly to protect the reputations of boys in later life, partly to conceal trouble from the outside world. The publication of Robert Graves's *Goodbye to All That* in 1929 had drawn unwelcome public attention to the mutual endearments of boys at Charterhouse, and tales reached Oxford of the effeminate vices practised by former Public School boys at nearby Garsington Manor. As far as the evidence allows us to say – for most old boys' reminiscences are reticent on the subject – St Edward's appears to have experienced nothing out of the ordinary. In 1932 Kendall, having learned of a letter written by one boy to another, asked Gerry Segar to investigate. Segar made the recipient open it and read it aloud to him. 'It's just a lot of slop – nothing evil,' reported the housemaster, though the letter-writer had been 'getting quite "goofy"' and was trying to arrange a meeting in the holidays. The mother of one of the boys was told that the other was not advisable company. Peter Camp, who arrived at the school in 1931, recalls that 'certain young boys were supposed to have sex appeal and got labelled "college tarts" (a "lush" was a later piece of slang for these boys). There was a general rule "older boys mustn't associate with younger boys" – bad for discipline, and there was that ... er ... other angle. To a large extent I feel most of these sex problems stemmed from lack of female company.' John Moreton (Roll No. 2686), who arrived the term after Camp and would be a distinguished diplomat and a governor of the school, also remembers the phrase 'college tarts'. 'There were, of course, romantic friendships between older boys and good-looking younger ones', but Moreton 'never came across any physical misbehaviour nor would this have been easy given the communal living arrangements and full timetable. If discovered it would mean expulsion.'

Interest in the female sex could not be excluded. Boys got hold of *Film Fun*, *Razzle*, and other savoury magazines, though when they learned that the authorities had got wind of the material they would get a day boy to leave the offending material on a bus on the way home. Macnamara, on discovering that sex manuals were being passed round, 'got more and more worked up'. As he told the boys: 'There's a lot of undesirable literature circulating .... If you've seen any of it ... Forget it all! Forget it all!' Pin-ups were nonetheless allowed in Mac's, provided they had the housemaster's signature of approval. Camp remembers the 'Annies' (maids) as 'nice looking girls. One – ah! yes! I remember, just like Greta Garbo. But the domestic staff were kept well segregated and were not even allowed to pass across the Quad.'

Other memories of Kendall's regime are supplied by the Norwegian Theodor Abrahamsen (Roll No. 2835), who was at St Edward's from 1933 and left in 1939 as Head of School and with a cap for the English Public Schools XV. He would be arrested by the Gestapo in 1943, and spent two years in Buchenwald concentration camp, until 1945. Later he was a headmaster in Norway. He remembers that Kendall 'always imitated my accent in a friendly manner showing that he noticed me and that he seemed to care for me'. Abrahamsen praises the teaching of Pat Brims and of Eric ('Peggy') Reid. On the other hand he could not 'remember a single inspiring master before I reached the Sixth Form', and thought the teaching in the lower forms 'extremely poor' – 'The School seemed to depend so much on its sporting reputation that scholarship was of minor interest.' Successful sportsmen 'were quite simply a privileged class'. Yet he considered all at the school in Kendall's earlier years 'a most privileged group of schoolboys. In fact I am surprised that no biography of this Warden has been written', though Abrahamsen acknowledged that the Warden may have stayed in office too long. Kendall invited the boy to his house in Hoylake on Merseyside as well as to his holiday home in Mevagissey in Cornwall, and took him to his club and to the theatre in London. 'I was later myself a headmaster ... and know full well how much time is spent in running a school and that individual pupils are more in the hands of their teachers and that a headmaster is on the outskirts. Not so with Henry Kendall. To him the individual boy came first.'

John Moreton, too, remembered that 'the ethos of the school ... was essentially games-oriented. In retrospect I have often regretted this, but I did not do so at the time. There were certainly other things on offer – Debating Society, Literary Society, the Kenneth Grahame Society – but they did not carry much weight.' And like Abrahamsen, Moreton stresses the personal links between the boy and adult worlds:

> I must not overlook the value of holiday visits and reading parties organised by masters, no doubt involving some self-sacrifice on their part. There were the famous 'reading parties' with Warden Kendall at Mevagissey .... With Leslie Styler there was a working holiday afloat in the Fowey estuary: he also took me to stay with his parents in Shipley. 'Peggy' Reid invited me to stay at his parents' home in Perthshire where his father was a bishop and introduced me to the famous course at Gleneagles. All these visits were formative and confidence-building.

On one occasion Moreton, having dozed off in a sermon, 'woke up suddenly, half-conscious that something was over', and 'started clapping'. Fortunately 'I heard no more about it. When I was a school prefect I reported a boy to Warden Kendall for some minor offence .... He gently suggested to me that there was sometimes virtue in flexibility and discretion.'

Moreton describes the practice, remembered by many OSE, of deliberate misbehaviour that would be punished by a beating and so spare a boy 'a "goody-goody" reputation'. Peter Camp, after 'beginning to be teased' for not having been beaten in his first two or three terms, 'had to do something about that. Thus "flicking paper in Day room" – 3 strokes, followed by "noisy in dormitory" – 4 strokes'. Anthony Diamond (Roll No. 2848), who got six strokes from the head of Mac's for reading a 'thriller' in Prep, remembers that 'it was quite a source of pride on being caned for the first time, to display the weals to one's mates'.

Ronald Perkin (Roll No. 2615) writes: 'I had the doubtful privilege of holding the record for beatings for some years .... I know that on three occasions I was beaten quite unjustly, but, in spite of this, I hold no strong views on the subject.' Beatings administered by the Head of School (the Senior Prefect) were announced ahead in Hall. The miscreant was summoned to High Table and then sent upstairs to receive the punishment. Silence fell as the assembled company listened for the strokes and perhaps the cries of the offender, who returned to his place at table trying to look nonchalant. Arthur Macnamara was famous for his distaste for beating boys. John Bell (Roll No. 2293) recalls that 'he would just administer three strokes with a cane as painlessly as possible, and then possibly invite the boy to tea on Sunday, cutting a doughnut with his OTC sword!' In old age Macnamara told Bell that when Henry Kendall left Shrewsbury to come to St Edward's as Warden, Shrewsbury masters had said 'God help St Edward's on account of his beating prowess'. In 1927, in Bell's first year, some of the Mac's boys were temporarily located in the Main Buildings. Bell was in a noisy dormitory, which was warned by Kendall to stop talking after lights out. When they persisted the prefect was instructed to give the Warden the names of the offenders. There were at least twenty-four of them, and at intervals over two days Kendall gave each four strokes.

Being beaten by Kendall was a common experience. Late in the Warden's tenure David Corlett (Roll No. 4443) was reported for smoking. Boys were beaten in 'the ante-room which you passed through to get to his study from the Quad (now the Warden's Secretary's office). Perhaps the worst part of the whole business was that as the condemned man you had to prepare the ante-room. Curtains had to be drawn, doors locked so that nobody entered from the Quad, and the door to the study was also locked to prevent Warden Kendall's sister, Katie, who lived with him, from bursting in! After the punishment (6 strokes) he sat down at his desk and had a pleasant chat.' OSE recall, perhaps not always reliably, that Kendall would assume that any boy who came to see him had been sent for misbehaviour, and would cane him. Occasionally the Warden, and he alone, used not a cane but a birch. Peter Camp remembers that, birches being short-lived and expensive, a birching was discreetly entered on the school bill as 'Extra Tuition – 7s. 6d'.

The mixture of bonhomie and violence in the Warden's relations with the boys was not universally admired. Geoffrey Meadmore, admittedly writing in retrospect in a period when attitudes to corporal punishment had changed, acknowledged that Kendall 'undoubtedly lifted the reputation of the School to incredible heights and was responsible for a great deal of worthy innovation', but added that 'although amiable enough and a great character [he] was to my mind also (it is of course sheer heresy to say so) a sanctimonious old humbug – an opinion no doubt stemming from the time when I suffered a birching at his hands (with Matron standing by with an iodine-soaked pad, the application of which was more painful than the birching) for some trivial offence'. 'How', asked Meadmore, could a grown man in a dog-collar 'behave thus to a fellow creature?'

The dominant subjects of old boys' reminiscences of the period, other than the beatings, are fagging and the initiation rites of new boys, which in Mac's, recalls Camp, 'knocked out of them any "guff" or conceit'. Alan House remembers that a boy's arm was broken when he was tossed aloft in a blanket which was then withdrawn. Fags could be sent to warm the toilets of the prefects, who liked to linger in their defecations, reading their mail or swapping gossip with their peers in neighbouring cubicles. 'There was considerable lack of privacy,' remembers House, 'all bathing being done in the nude and there were no doors on the toilets.' At night enamel jerries [chamber pots] were provided, 'the contents of which', according to House, 'froze on a few occasions'.

Alan House entered the school in the summer term of 1939. Four months later the nation would be once more at war.

31

TO WAR AGAIN

THEODOR ABRAHAMSEN observes of his experience at St Edward's in the 1930s that 'a boarding school at that time was very much an isolated island with little interest among the boys for what went on in the wider world, even in England .... We were not even allowed to go into Oxford or anywhere else on our own. Our world in term time was within the School.' This was Kendall's boy-centred commonwealth. Wirelesses were not allowed in the Houses, even if the world of light entertainment penetrated the Rag Revue of 1936, when singers and a band and tap dancers performed selections from *Top Hat* and *Anything Goes* and a close-harmony rendering of 'Misty Islands'. The St Edward's of the 1930s produced no conspicuous rebels against the establishment, though John Berger (Roll No. 3484), who was to be so radical and so distinguished an art critic, was a pupil from 1940. No OSE seems to have joined the International Brigade in Spain.

The Debating Society did occasionally discuss politics. In February 1933, a month after Hitler came to power in Germany, it carried by 23 votes to 6 the motion that 'Absolute Monarchy is the best form of Government.' Arthur Tilly, proposing it, declared that 'democracy was unfit for the complicated task of governing the modern state, since in technical matters the majority was always found to be in the wrong'. The President of the Society, Alfred de Denne (Roll No. 2396), spoke on the same side: 'The ordinary man found no inspiration in party politics, but could gain confidence in the vigorous action of one man, like Mussolini or Hitler ....' In October 1935, on the other hand, in one of the few debates held that year, Tilly proposed the motion that 'Italy is unjustified in her action against Abyssinia.' It was carried by 36 votes to 7. Other motions of the Thirties debated the existence of ghosts, the view that 'a line must be drawn somewhere', and the proposition that 'Great Britain can never become an A1 nation without physical training for all', a motion supported by Philip Whitrow who 'asked the House to think of Hitler's youth movement and the wonders that it had done for the German people'.

Politics made another appearance in a debate of October 1936 on the motion that 'the Government has ample justification for its policy in Palestine'. The President, Dudley Bell (Roll No. 2647), spoke against. He displayed a cartoon from the *Evening Standard* and 'went on to denounce the Jews, morally, facially and utterly. The wrong type of Jews,' he said, 'had returned to Palestine after the War.' Graham Cooper, Head of School and a future Chairman of the Governors and benefactor, 'objected to the personal element' of Bell's speech, which 'had been nothing but personal insults and anti-Jewish propaganda, both quite irrelevant'. That was the last political motion until well into the war. Although debating was popular enough for a Junior Debating Society to be formed in November 1939, the school's debates suggest disdain for the moral condition of the outside world. When, in December 1937, the Debating Society considered the question whether the theatre was superior to the cinema, speakers portrayed the mass entertainment of the cinema as morally undermining. The vote was tied, 39–39. In January 1938 the House debated the motion that 'the British race is decadent'. Scorn for transatlantic vulgarity, plutocracy, canned food, jazz and song was elicited by a motion in March 1940 that 'it would have been better for Europe if Columbus had never discovered America'. Against the tense international background of March 1939 a majority of 42 agreed that 'Assistant Masters are insane'. Serious contemporary issues were debated only after the start of the Blitz. In December 1940 a motion that 'This House is in favour of immediate reprisals for the bombing of civilians' was defeated by 32 votes to 15. By that time there were air raid shelters in the Quad.

On the outbreak of war the poet and Cambridge don Robert Gittings (Roll No. 2267), who had left in 1930, submitted a poem to the *Chronicle*:

September 3rd 1939

Eating an apple from an English tree
With autumn at our feet, we are at war.
It might be madness from a martian star
For all the evidence that eyes can see –
Wasps at their prey of plums, intent as we,
But wiser in their limits – calendar
Of ripeness everywhere but us, who are
Seasonless, reasonless, mortal and unfree.
No words can put this right. Our proper place
Is now our proper selves. The only hope

For man is still man though mankind be cursed.
Horror may slash the earth's and every face
With hate; yet, if we fill our harmless scope,
We, the last Adam, need not be the worst.

What were the thoughts in that fateful month of the masters who had seen active service in the Great War and lost family or friends in that terrible slaughter: the Warden, B. G. Segar, Arthur Tilly, Ken Menzies, Philip Whitrow, Freddie Yorke, Aubrey Guest, Gerry Segar, Henry Gauntlett, Jack McMichael? The Great War was the most important fact of their lives. It had been meant to end wars, but now advances in weaponry and air power threatened a still higher death toll, especially among civilians. Every day Kendall's generation worshipped in amid the plaques on the Chapel walls, or passed the carved names of the fallen in the cloisters, or used the Memorial Buildings. Now they had to watch young men again leave school to go to war.

There were 392 boys when war broke out, 68 of them new boys. The school was larger than it had ever been. Only three boys were withdrawn on the outbreak of war, and numbers would continue to rise during the conflict. In September 1940 there would be 80 new boys. And yet the war brought a fundamental change in the character of Kendall's Wardenship. It blunted its dynamism. The building programme had to be shelved. There was a change in the character of his reign, too. Hitherto he had shaped events: henceforth he responded to them. When the war ended in 1945 he was near the conventional retirement age of 60, though he stayed on to guide the school through the post-war privations.

The school's condition in and after the Second War is reminiscent of the improvisations of and after the first, when Ferguson was Warden. In 1939 five masters left for their military units and had to be replaced. From that year there was a diminution of the domestic staff, which left much of the cleaning and catering and of the maintenance of the fields in the boys' hands. The blackout required a complete reorganization of the timetable to make maximum use of the daylight hours. Because the Chapel had no curtains Evensong was brought forward, first to 5.22 p.m. and then to 4 p.m. Bursar Thursfield's burdens now included the issuing of identity cards and ration books and the preparation of lists of names for national registration. Shades of the prison house drew in during the war. As well as the darkness of blackout there was the silence of the Chapel bells at waking-up time or for services. The bells were rung to celebrate El Alamein, but not by boys, for none had been trained to ring them.

There was no patriotic rush to the colours as there had been in 1914, and no opportunity for one. The holding of Certificate 'A' in the OTC, which was soon to be renamed the Junior Training Corps (JTC), entitled boys to register for service, but only when they were 19. They were not called up until they were 20. In 1939 there was a full rugby season despite bouts of flu and German measles, though the times of matches were brought forward so that the away team could get back before blackout. There was a prestigious new fixture against Wellington, whom the school beat by 11 points to 8. The following term there were nine First XI hockey fixtures, and matches in squash, boxing and rugby sevens. Wartime restrictions reduced the frequency of the *Chronicle* from the six a year issued in 1940 to five in 1941 and only three in 1942. A 'rationed' issue of October 1940 ran to eight pages instead of the usual 15 to 20. In 1941 two issues were combined. In the wartime issues, less of the material was written by boys. Even as the magazine contracted, its OSE section, already large, expanded. There were lists of OSE on active service, and of the dead, the wounded, the captured, the missing, the decorated. Obituaries of the fallen were printed. Even so, the reporting of School and House games remained the most prominent features.

With Brims, W. R. Hartley, Tom Hankey, Northcote-Green and Beales gone to war, Kendall had to scour Oxford and beyond for stand-in staff. OSE recalled that most of them were poor teachers, though Kendall was lucky to secure the services of Norman Whatley, a former headmaster of Clifton. The Senior Tutor, named Houghton, of St Peter's Hall, the Evangelical college whose recruitment of a boy from the school had horrified Harold Rogers, joined the staff, and soon the Master of that college, the Rev. Thornton-Duesbery, was giving two sermons in the Chapel. There were shortened Commems – 'pocket Commems', Kendall called them – and Gaudies, with curtailed entertainment. The butler Arthur Jeffrey, presiding at his 50th Warden's reception at Commem, was toasted. There were no plays and few concerts, though masters from Radley provided a show for four years. But OSE dinners survived the outbreak of war. Roger Northcote-Green arranged one at Aldershot soon after reporting for military duty; Hubert Beales another in Richmond in Yorkshire.

In December 1939 the *Chronicle* listed 338 OSE in the forces. The following month its editorial made a revealing observation. It noted that though the early stages of the war – the 'phoney war', as the period would be dubbed – had had a limited practical effect on the school, it had made it conscious of its involvement in a wider society, for the war 'has brought in its tracks such disturbances and excitements as even we have participated in'. The editorial described blackout regulations as the most irksome intrusion: a boy 'with a large piece of sticking-plaster over the bridge of his nose is a timely reminder of the perils awaiting the unwary walker. And what of the boy who set out to cross the Quad from Tilly's to Chapel and arrived at Segar's?' Soon boys would be expected to help farm some of the school fields and to work on farms in the holidays. Stanley Tackley led five camps in the West Country, where boys manufactured pit-props. Freddie Yorke took plum-picking expeditions to the Vale of Evesham. Kendall himself, with Henry Gauntlett, led harvesting trips to Ross-on-Wye, the largest consisting of sixty boys.

Ten shillings was added to school bills to cover air raid precautions and equipment. The *Chronicle* noted the frequent visits by young OSE 'of all kinds of ranks and all sorts of uniform .... Perhaps they do not understand all that these visits mean to us and how much we at School think about them.' The bond between past and present which had been so powerful in the Great War and its aftermath was being reasserted. In March 1940 the deaths were announced of Humphrey Pearson (Roll No. 2591), killed in the RAF, and Colin Murray (Roll No. 3062), a naval cadet drowned at sea at the age of 18, of whom Freddie Yorke wrote: 'He arrived from his beloved Border as a very small boy, intensely patriotic and devoted to the sea. His life belongs to the freedom of the seas.' Henceforth each OSE war death was marked by a short obituary in the *Chronicle*.

The pace of war quickened with Dunkirk and the fall of France and then the invasions of Denmark and Norway. Boys trained on Field Days and in OTC training camps performed useful functions. Ninety boys enrolled in the Local Defence Volunteers under the leadership of Yorke, Gerry Segar and Gauntlett, who thus donned uniforms in a second war. The Volunteers manned Port Meadow and the boathouse area to warn of possible parachute landings, and later performed roadblock duty. Segar, to public indignation, set up a barbed-wire checkpoint on the bypass, presumably to intercept the Germans. Though Prep and Public Schools near the south coast moved north, Oxford was thought to be safe, even though the Morris Motors radiator factory across the road from St Edward's was on the Luftwaffe's hit list. Kendall was ready to offer space to Prep Schools near the coast and responded sympathetically to an appeal by Tonbridge. In the end he chose to accommodate St Bede's, Eastbourne, while Eastbourne College moved to Radley. The Headmaster of St Bede's, Kenneth Harding, an active OSE (Roll No. 1189) who had played rugby for the Barbarians and cricket for Sussex, arrived with his seventy charges in June 1940. They occupied Corfe House and parts of School House. The evacuation was a great success, and many 'Bedes' stayed on at the school for their secondary education. Malvern College, which evacuated to Blenheim Palace, used the school's laboratories.

On 26 May 1940 the 31-year-old A. S. (Stephan) Hopkinson (Roll No. 1897), whose elder brother Tom we encountered in Ferguson's school, preached in Chapel. He had been the intellectual star of his year, a scholar of the school, a winner of prizes and a voracious reader, who in 1927 had won a Classical Scholarship at Wadham College. He was a remarkable man who led a varied life. In 1930 he went to South America to work in the oil industry, returned in 1935 and in the same year got married and was ordained priest. He worked in deprived industrial districts, served as a curate in Putney, and was successively Vicar of Barrow, of Battersea, and of St Mary Woolnoth and St Katherine Cree in the City of London. Later he was a prebendary of St Paul's, an industrial adviser to the Bishop of Chelmsford and an Anglican adviser to ATV. In his eighties, when he had ostensibly retired, he did some teaching and pastoral work for Winchester. Before his death he remembered his visit to preach at St Edward's. The gist of his sermon was that while Fascism was an evil ideology, to be utterly resisted, there was no reason for unthinking hatred of the Germans. The Christian should hate the sin but love the sinner. As they left the Chapel Henry Kendall voiced his disapproval of Hopkinson's argument. He blamed the German nation, not Fascism, for the havoc Germany had brought on the twentieth century. The preacher made a mental note not to return to his old school in a hurry. Then a smartly suited OSE, ten years younger than Hopkinson, approached him and thanked him for his sermon and its sentiments. He introduced himself as Guy Gibson, at that time an undecorated Flying Officer (Roll No. 2755).

Those conversations signify a change of outlook with the passage of a generation. It was the plight of Kendall, who had known the carnage of the Great War, to announce to the boys, often tearfully, the deaths of their former schoolfellows in the second war. In the previous era, that of the late-Victorian Anglo-Catholicism of Simeon, Christian imperatives of love, compassion and mercy had not been tested by the bitterness and destruction of war. For its part Hopkinson's and Gibson's generation had grown up only in the aftermath of the Great War.

One early death was that of Paul Cooke (Roll No. 2474), a model product of Kendall's school. He was killed, aged 24, while directing the fire of a Bren gun section in Belgium as second in command of his Company. A school prefect in Segar's, he had represented the school at rugby, cricket, athletics, boxing, hockey and swimming and was a sergeant in the OTC. At Oxford, where he read Law, he played rugby and cricket both for the university and for Trinity College. He toured South America with the English Rugby Union in 1937 and played twice for England in 1939, by which time he had begun a promising career in Barclay's Bank. Letters by him to his parents, informally punctuated, survive from his schooldays. He describes a 'terrific game in a quagmire we lost 5–3 to Marlborough' and recalls the film shown in Big School 'about the world's largest volcano, that was followed by a film of the building of Sydney Harbour Bridge and we had a Krazy Kat comedy which was jolly good'. In an undated letter which almost certainly belongs to November 1933, when he was nearly 18, he notices that 'the Remembrance Service', hitherto a separate occasion, 'has been fitted into the usual Eucharist service – a mark of a long trend in the school's religious character'. He ponders his future. Should he go on to university? 'Everyone' has told him that 'I should be a fool not to', but it would cost £900–£1,000 and 'I'm not especially drawn to the varsity'. An alternative is to read for articles in Law at home, which would allow him good holidays 'and a fair amount of sport'; or he could go into the Bank, 'where for the next five years I should be a complete nonentity, have bad holidays and yet be on the way for a good sense job'.

Meanwhile there is the question of whether he should stay on at school. 'I'm not doing much work but I think the House is a bit the better for my presence, although it's I who says it.' In May 1934 boys from the Bermondsey Boys Club in east London, which the school had supported since the 1880s, are back for rounders and he is active in the Scout Troop. 'I have been reading the lesson this week, Hebrews of all things. It is awfully hard to make it sound sense.' He inveighs against the 'priggish sermon', 'of the worst possible taste', by Canon Crum of Canterbury, who had preached on 28 October 1934. 'Not content with talking trash, his voice, which would have made him a famous comedian, he used in such amazing ways that people were openly grinning.' On another occasion the Warden took Cooke by car to the university rugby ground in Iffley Road and sat in the stand with him. For most of his time his housemaster was Ken Menzies. In 1941, after Paul's death, Menzies replied to a letter from Paul's mother, who had sent some snapshots. 'I do myself remember the day so well and how Paul won the day [in a game played by the school at Iffley Road] for us. He was always so loyal and devoted to his House and I know how much the rest of the boys loved and respected him.' A university don had told Menzies 'that he regarded Paul as the best fellow the School had ever sent them'.

Like Sing before him, Kendall kept in touch with the families of his dead boys. The emotion of Sing's letters of condolence had been restrained by a certain aloofness. Kendall's can border on the sentimental. So it was in the case of Cooke:

> There never was a boy more loved and respected by his school friends, juniors and masters and his love and respect was earned by his simple goodness and unswerving character. I know the War will take its toll of our best boys and this is most true in the case of Paul. Looking back on fifteen happy years here I always think of Paul as one of the boys I am proudest to have had here in the School. He seems to typify all that has been good in this time, and once this shock is over, I know that he will always seem to be present with us here forever and that he will always call out and expect the best that is in us.

His death was reported in the *Chronicle* in July 1940, in the issue that announced Guy Gibson's DFC, details of which 'will be published when they are available' (though they never were). Guy Charter (Roll No. 3214) recalls the announcements in Chapel of the deaths of OSE, some of whom he knew. 'A particular friend, Sydney Harrison (Roll No. 3231), was in the same house as me [Mac's] and he spent nearly all his four years at the bottom of the School. He said what is the point of working? I shall not survive the War. He joined the RAF and after training in Canada he was reckoned to be such a good pilot that they made him a flying instructor. However he took a Tiger Moth up on a weather flight, flew into a thundercloud and it was so turbulent that the aircraft broke up. Why he could not open his parachute we never knew.' He was 21.

By 1942 Lower Field 1 and the Canal Fields, about 22 acres in all, had been ploughed and sown with wheat. Near the piggeries each house had an allotment, on which boys worked before and after games. The plots raised 5 tons of potatoes and 3,000 cabbages between 1942 and 1945. Games were not unduly affected by the agriculture, for Keble College let out its fields to the school. In the carpentry workshop boys helped to make metal aero-parts, which earned £360. The sum was paid into the new War Memorial Fund, which the Governors launched in 1943. They had long-term plans for the money, among them the extension of Big School to the east, so that the Victorian building would serve as a grand façade and entrance hall – a scheme which, much later and in a much modified form, would be effected by the building of the New Hall. The Fund, which stood at £8,414 in 1946, rose slowly, to £11,334 in 1948 and to nearly £19,000 by 1955. 'The scheme', Kendall wrote in 1944, 'may seem an ambitious one, but then it has much to commemorate and cannot be too ambitious for such a purpose', which though 'hard to put into words is meant most sincerely. The boys we commemorate were young, and life at its best, as they knew it, was largely bound up with their years at School. They found here a place for friendship, for happiness and for faith.'

Yet the scheme would struggle in the post-war world, when the middle classes, whom the aftermath of the Great War had treated relatively kindly, expected to be hard hit by socialist privations. OSE were not markedly more generous than their forebears had been after the Great War. In any case the local authority, in the post-war spirit of austerity, refused licences for new buildings. Ten years after the return of peace the only fruit of the Fund was the Memorial Library, of which the foundations were laid in July 1953 and which was opened on 5 June 1954. The building has been put to a succession of uses over the years. In 1945 the school did receive the greatest bequest it had known, from Edmund Brewer-Williams (Roll No. 366). Amounting to £34,000, it was the last substantial bequest for a generation. The role of the OSE was changing and diminishing. The earlier Memorial Fund, the controversial project launched after the Great War, had been largely led by OSE. Now the school itself, under Kendall's leadership, was in charge, even though the St Edward's Society launched the appeal jointly with the Governors. The OSE would remain a powerful social organization, especially on the sporting front, but they became less important to the school's finances and therefore wielded less influence on the direction the school took. After the war, full-scale Gaudies and Commems would return. In July 1946, 105 OSE diners gathered for the Gaudy in London, with Douglas Bader, who had been freed from Colditz the previous year, in the Chair. At Commem of the previous year 180 OSE had gathered at the Randolph in Oxford for the first OSE dinner since 1938.

The Brewer-Williams bequest would help to redeem the final debentures owed by St Edward's, a move which strengthened the school's control of its assets. Its income had been boosted by the imposition of a 30 shilling surcharge on bills since 1941. In September 1945 there was an increase of £5 a term in the fees. Yet even now the fees stood at only £168. Kendall, with good advice from Goodenough and Stone, had positioned the school astutely for the economic difficulties of the post-war years. In 1944 he had persuaded Barclay's Bank to help the school repay the mortgage to the University Chest by providing a loan at lower interest. At the same time the Bank also increased the value of its scholarships. Paul Cooke had been the first recipient of a Barclay's Scholarship. At Gaudy in 1942, where Cooke's memory was honoured, the prizes were given by the Chairman of the Bank, Edwin Fisher. It was a characteristically adroit arrangement by Kendall, that subtle knitter of communal emotion with financial realism or opportunism. The lists of prize-givers in Kendall's time, as of the preachers he chose, illustrate his gift of networking. It was always combined with ideals of service, as when he acted as an honorary chaplain to HQ Home Forces and served on several Admiralty selection boards.

When Jack Tate was called up to the Navy in 1943 he was the ninth master to leave for the war. Like Ferguson before him, Kendall had to keep the teaching going amid all the uncertainties and improvisations which wartime brought. Between 1939 and 1945 he appointed twenty-one masters. Two of them proved long-standing appointments. John Alexander, an Austrian of formidable intellect, the only 'First' appointed by Kendall other than Pat Brims and Leslie Styler, would build up the school's reputation in Modern Languages. From 1941, when he was put in charge of the teaching timetable, he became something like a de facto Director of Studies. Jack Scarr, who was invalided out of the war and taught from 1942 to 1980, would be a memorable teacher of Spanish and produce a long succession of well-remembered school plays. Only eight of Kendall's other wartime appointments stayed long enough to earn an appearance in the *Roll* of 1992. The remainder served for just a few terms at the most. One OSE recalls that 'the standard of the teaching was appalling. Sometimes local clergy came in thinking they could "teach" without any preparation. Sometimes senior boys took classes because no one else was available.' He praises Styler, Yorke, Gauntlett and Whitrow for keeping the show on the road, but while he appreciated the Warden's strengths he writes: 'To be honest, I don't think Kendall was interested in a deep understanding of teaching, though he was a good judge of character. Games players came first, teachers second.' Anthony Lowe (Roll No. 3242) has favourable memories of Styler and Brims and also of Tom Hankey, who had been appointed in 1936 and taught largely in the Sixth Form. He was killed in Burma in 1944, the only Common Room fatality of the war.

The most detailed account of school life during the war has been left by Antony Barrington-Brown (Roll No. 3482), who was at St Edward's from 1940 to 1945. As a boy, he says, he had realized that 'war had deprived the School of those who might have become "young Turks" as the older and more traditional masters retired'. For him Ken Menzies, who taught him Greek, was both the most successful and most eccentric of the masters. 'He pranced around the room declaiming, emphasising each point by waving a sort of miniature totem pole with a kneeling figure at the top. He would approach boys at random and thrust the baton at them with the word "catch-hold!" We would grab our end and he would saw it back and forth chanting principal parts of verbs etc.... The knowledge seemed to flow from him to us down his magic rod. He never threw it on the floor so we never discovered if it would turn, like Aaron's, into a serpent.' He had been using it since 1920. The only other master praised by Antony is Yorke.

It was to members of the ancillary staff that Antony really warmed. Taking a special interest in science and enjoying making things, he forged a bond with the lab technician, Walter Dunn, 'a gnome-like figure ... with a strong sense of his own indispensability and the dignity of his position. Like that of a butler in a grand house, he ran the department.' The friendship lasted until Walter's death. Antony also enjoyed the company of 'Long Earnie', the boiler man, and of Reg Barson, the woodwork instructor, 'who taught me the rudiments of cabinet making which I have continued ever since .... George Schoons came in from Morris Motors to teach "mechanical drawing", from whose teaching I benefit to this day. I feel I would meet any of these with as great a pleasure as any of the teaching staff if I had the chance today.'

Antony is one of the few OSE to express a dislike of Kendall, whom he thought a bully and whom he remembered treating the music master, Lionel Ovenden, 'with contempt even in front of the boys'. Walter Dunn confided to Antony an account of the Warden's unsympathetic treatment of Willy Weeks, a master appointed in 1935 who had an extravagant wife. When Weeks appealed to Kendall for a pay rise he was told to get a grip on himself. In 1945 Dunn arrived one morning to find Weeks in the gas cupboard, where he had gassed himself. Dunn himself seems not to have been a conciliatory character. He took exception when George Burton, a top university scientist who had taken Jack Tate's place, ordered new and, in Dunn's eyes, needless apparatus at great expense. Burton died of a brain haemorrhage within weeks and the boys were left with another temporary science master, the Polish Dr Prag, known as Tooley. Tales of Tate's own teaching abound down the decades. He was much loved but forever mocked. Japes were endlessly repeated. One wartime double period on 'Light' became a legend. Each pair of boys had a light source consisting of a tin box containing a wooden block with a bulb-holder and two large screw terminals which served wires leading to a 110-volt socket under the laboratory bench. If the block were lifted an inch the terminals would touch the tin and the room would be plunged into darkness. Cheers and chaos followed. Dunn was called to mend the fuse. Tate's service in the Battle of the Atlantic may have seemed a lesser ordeal. For a time he was commanded by his former pupil Midshipman Brian Jones (Roll No. 3267). After the war Tate did more than anyone since Cowell to build up and organize the development of the school's archives.

There also survive the wartime memories, beautifully laid out with accompanying drawings, of John Lambourn (Roll No. 3840), who entered the school in 1943 having already lived on the site as a member of the contingent from St Bede's. One of the very few boys to take Art as a subject, he was supposedly allowed to draw in Prep, but prefects were always confiscating his drawings. With many others he recalls punishments for not 'facing off' from senior boys. Twenty press-ups were the usual consequence of 'guff' towards prefects or day-room presidents. Juniors were tossed in blankets. A long-standing unofficial regulation, which would persist until the early 1960s, required new boys to keep their jackets fully buttoned. One button could be undone in their second term, another in the third. The 'bashers' (boaters), which were useful for hiding 'ice-creams, fish and chips etc.', would be floated in the canal to make them look suitably worn, another practice to persist until the 1960s. Offences for which boys were beaten included 'crossing in the passage, [avoiding compulsory] runs in rainy weather, running [rather than walking] to the School Shop, skiving during school matches, talking in Prep, wearing dirty shoes in chapel, walking in front of the cricket screens'. It was endless. 'Rules included no hands in pockets in the Quad, no walking on the Quad grass, no use of hair oil or Brylcreem, and no social visits to other houses or day rooms. Seniors just one term above regularly forced one to recite or sing on an upturned bathtub in the nude and flicked by wet towels.' Compulsory attendance on the touchline was another long-lasting practice. I recall a beating of a quite senior boy in the autumn of 1962 for practising his oboe when he should have been watching the XV.

Lambourn's memoir conveys the enclosed, even sealed character of the school. Boys needed permission to walk into Summertown and a chit from the Warden, given only for strong reasons, for more distant outings. Kendall used requests for chits as opportunities to talk to boys, though many found the meetings daunting. Still, boys managed to break the bounds, as Lambourn recalls. 'There were night time escapades in the small hours. A popular one was tapping the MCR [Masters' Common Room] beer barrel. One outing resulted in our changing names and numbers on houses in the Woodstock Road (letters slid in a frame were popular and easily altered).' There were breakouts on Sunday evenings when boys got up to pranks in Summertown and even met girls, 'chatting them up and at nine o'clock [we] rushed back, safely arriving in time for Dormy. So ended a happy evening, to be repeated several times, the boredom of Sunday lock-ups overcome!' Lack of money restricted such outings, but John recalls clandestine outings to the cinema in 1944, when he saw *The Sky's the Limit* and *Girl in Overalls* at the Ritz, *Hangmen also Die* at the Regal, and *Sailors Three*, with Tommy Trinder, at the Scala in Walton Street. 'One boy turned around in the interval to ask for a light for a fag only to find that he was addressing his housemaster!' What Lambourn mostly recalls, however, is the sheer boredom of free time.

A series of punishment books which survive from the war support Lambourn's recollections of the penalties meted out to boys. Geoffrey Keith (Roll No. 3240) was Senior Prefect in the Easter Term 1942 until he left in the summer. He heads his book 'Justitia Regat' ('Let justice rule'). He beat thirty-one boys in his last two terms, though he did go six weeks without beating anyone. Other beatings were administered by the Warden, masters, and other prefects. Four strokes, the most common penalty, were given for such offences as skating without permission on Port Meadow, throwing snowballs, eating in the Library, ragging in the tea queue or going round it twice, going on to the fields before Sunday Eucharist, and misbehaviour during grace in Hall. One boy got four from Geoffrey for missing Sunday Chapel. Another got five for the evidently graver offence of jumping out of a window. Geoffrey was killed in Italy on All Saints' Day 1943, when he was leading his platoon of Gordon Highlanders. He was 20. His successor as Senior Prefect was David Street (Roll No. 3256), who kept the beating book going from September 1942 to March 1943. He beat sixteen boys. Four strokes remained the norm, though six were administered for 'exploding a homemade bomb in the box room' and for being in Summertown or Oxford without a 'basher'.

A total of 1,360 OSE served in the war, of whom 155 were killed. Twelve masters and fifteen other staff served. One master, Tom Hankey, was killed. Much has been written on the astonishing number of war heroes who were products of the school. As in the First World War, the upbringing offered by St Edward's had forged the courage and commitment shown in what everyone saw as a just cause. The *Roll* states that 161 decorations were awarded to OSE, and that 127 were mentioned in despatches. *The Chronicle*'s figures are rather different, but likewise impressive. The contribution made by a handful of heroes in the RAF is legendary. The feats of Douglas Bader and Guy Gibson have acquired particular celebrity through the films *Reach for the Sky* and *The Dambusters*, but they were not alone. Among the last OSE killed in action was Arthur Banks (Roll No. 3203). A sergeant pilot, he had been shot down in Italy but had survived to join the local partisans, only to be tortured and killed by the Germans, aged 22. He was awarded the George Cross posthumously. He was, wrote Kendall, 'constantly on the alert for the zestful love of worthwhile things'.

When news of the D-Day landings arrived in June 1944, the Governors were in session. They promptly suspended their deliberations and joined the school in Chapel for a service of intercession before lunch. But victory took long to come. At Commem on 2 November 1946, All Souls' Day, a special memorial service was held for the dead. Kendall's forceful and emotional address, recorded in the *Chronicle* in the following month, emphasized the place of religion in Public School life and the purpose of the Chapel, which teaches that 'it is the quality of service that counts'. There were three reasons, he told the boys, for their presence in Chapel that day. They were there to honour the dead, 'to acknowledge our personal pride and thankfulness for our share, both at home and at school, in their affection and their upbringing', and 'to witness that all is well with them'. 'Whatever may be the pattern of the texture of this School in years to come,' he added, 'it will be forever shot through with the fine thread of the gold of their sacrifice and of their love.' In 1945 Harold Rogers designed for the Chapel a three-arched oak screen as a memorial to the fallen of 1939–45, anonymously paid for by Macnamara as a tribute to his old pupil John Simmonds (Roll No. 3253) who had been killed in action in 1943. SS George, Martin, Aldhelm and Edward surmounted the arches. The screen closed off the Memorial Chapel. By 1949 it had been joined by a tablet which recorded in gilt the names of the dead of the Second World War. In 1950 windows were inserted behind the back pews to commemorate the school's founder, Thomas Chamberlain, who had been curiously omitted from past memorials, and Sing, who had died in 1947, leaving £3,700 to the school.

The issue of the *Chronicle* that reported Kendall's sermon also carried an article, written in the wake of the bombings in Japan, entitled 'The Rise of the Atomic Age'. At home, where Britain's economy was on its knees, a socialist government had been elected with a massive majority. Fears ran through the Public Schools. Would they now have to face another kind of conflict?

32

THE WAYS OF PEACE

David Thomas in Tilly's (Roll No. 3863) wrote this letter home:

Tuesday 8th May 1945. 8.30 p.m.

Dear Mummy and Daddy,
   So it's all over at last; not a bad birthday present!! We had a half hour chapel service at 1.45 and were then allowed down town between 2.45 and 5.45. It was very hot .... The houses all the way in had flags .... Carfax was packed and no traffic could get through. A Yank had got hold of a ukulele and there was singing and dancing all through the town. We managed to find a cafe and had an awful tea (1/6d each!) .... There were lots of flags out at school and red, white and blue blankets and rugger shirts hanging out of the windows. I'm writing this in the half hour reading prep we've got before we go up to Big School to have a Sing-Song. At 10-45 we got into the Quad to see the chapel floodlit. Bed at 11-15. Tomorrow we get up at 8-45!!, one and a half hours later than usual!! There were lots of rags and processions by the students in Oxford. There is no extra day on Gaudy but on the hols, as the petrol is coming back on June 1st. Do you think you'd be able to come up to Gaudy in the car? I've just had to make out a rota for the VE holidays for fags!!
   Wednesday. I felt awfully tired today. After all the singing last night we were allowed in the Quad until 11.30. . .Then we had a dormi brew. Cold baked beans and sardines eaten with fingers. The pres {prefects} even joined in. It was half past two before we went to bed. Tilly was awfully annoyed at all the shouting but nobody bothered about him. Fortunately he didn't come into our dormi .... Tomorrow is Ascension Day. It's a half hol and in the evening we're going to be allowed to listen to ITMA [*It's That Man Again*, Tommy Handley's popular radio comedy] and then the P.M.'s speech ....

With love from David.

Despite the relief and rejoicing there was no optimism about the school's future. The *Chronicle* voiced a subdued mood. In filling in the trenches on the playing fields and dismantling the air raid shelters 'we will, perhaps quite unconsciously, slide into the ways of peace again', but 'let us remember that the time has not come when we may once more take Mrs Beeton's best-seller from the depths of the kitchen cupboard and blow the dust off it after its wartime seclusion. We cannot yet pull up at a wayside pump and call upon the garage mechanic to "Fill her up"!'

In the Common Room, Brims, Emmet, Northcote-Green, Tate and Beales were soon back, though Emmet had been ill for a time on return from Burma. By April 1946 it was clear neither W. R. Hartley, who taught Modern Languages, nor another master who had left for the war, the art teacher T. L. B. (Tom) Huskinson, would return. Reid did, but not until 1953, for he had been recruited by the War Office in 1945 (where he was rumoured to be involved in espionage). There was a vacancy in the School Shop, for Miss Lizzie Johnson, who had arrived at the school as the daughter of servants in 1887 and had run the shop for thirty-three years, had retired in 1943, and Kendall's niece Susan, who had filled in for her for the next eighteen months, left when her husband returned from the war. The boys from St Bede's went back to Eastbourne. Thursfield, the bursar, left, and St Edward's also lost the services of Frankland West who had been school doctor since 1925. Two long-serving masters, Lionel Ovenden and Ken Menzies, retired in 1946. Ovenden, whose health had collapsed, had kept the music going since the halcyon days of Stanton, but concerts were occasional and relied much on imported adults, among them Henry Gauntlett's brother Ambrose, a professional cellist, and the professional tenor Arthur Cranmer. Only a few boys learned instruments and there was no real orchestra. In the Gaudy Concert of 1948, two years after Ovenden's departure, what passed for the orchestra consisted of only eleven boys, and six adults who were brought in to supplement them. The performance of the Chapel Choir and Choral Society under Ovenden does not seem to have been distinguished. Edward Manning, having previously sung at the school as another of the adults brought in for concerts, had worked as a visiting music teacher since 1927 and was given charge of the music in 1946. He tried to raise the level of instrumental playing, but under Kendall (to whom he was devoted) there would be no significant advances in the cultural life of the school.

Menzies, the other departure of 1946, can be seen as the last of the Tractarian priests in the Simeon tradition, a survivor from the days before the cult of muscularity. In Kendall's time, even before his resignation from his House, he seems something of an outsider, whose personality and interests moved beyond the school. He created and tended the water gardens, liked angling, and sustained a quiet commitment to Classics. He published a book, *Addresses to Christian Minor*, which consists of impressive sermons he had given at St Edward's and is the only collection of its kind we have for the school. It contains a number of oblique glances at Kendall's Wardenship, among them a remark in the preface about headmasters who, instead of providing instruction in theology from the pulpit, invite ecclesiastical grandees to preach at Sunday Evensong.

The choice of replacements both for long-serving staff and for the many temporary appointments of wartime would be critical for the school's future. In 1945 Kendall himself was approaching 60, though his grip on the Governing Body ensured that he would be able to choose his retirement date. In 1948 he was given a sabbatical term (his second, for he had had one in 1937), and it was privately agreed with the Governors that he should stay at least until he was 65. Arthur Tilly, his right-hand man, was in declining health and died in the Sanatorium in 1951. It was an ageing Common Room. There were seven survivors from Ferguson's time, B. G. Segar, Macnamara, Whitrow, Yorke, Guest, G. H. Segar and Henry Gauntlett, while McMichael, Eardley, Reid, Manning and Barff had been early appointments of Kendall. Four of the housemasters, Yorke, Tilly, Macnamara and Gerry Segar, had been in post since the Twenties. Even the youngest housemaster, Barff at Field House, had been at the school since 1927 and had run his House since 1937.

In 1945 Jack 'Crasher' White became one of the first post-war appointments to the Common Room. The word 'crashing' now betokens a bore, but White's nickname derived from his spirited performances as a Tourist Trophy motorbike rider before the war. Lively, cantankerous, militantly left-wing and with no commitment to the school's religious life, he was a breath of fresh air, not just in the Biology Department. When he and I visited Cambridge for an OSE dinner in the early Sixties and I tried to take him into King's College Chapel, where Evensong was about to be held, he remonstrated: 'What? You think I'm going to go in there and me a bloody atheist?' He stayed until 1964, though he was a somewhat detached figure, his life centring on his smallholding in Steeple Aston. White offered no games, but Charles Mather, a historian who also arrived in 1945, had skills on the river. There were more appointments in 1946. The OSE Bill Veitch, a dazzling games player, had a proud war record though a dubious academic one. The clergyman Tom Williams remained until 1957. Desmond Hill was to reshape the rowing, write the Centenary *History* of the school, gain the admiration of many boys, and incur the envy of some colleagues by his nonchalant style and his sports car. OSE recall him arriving late for class under Kendall's more vigilant successor Frank Fisher and climbing in through ground-floor windows in the Work Block, saying 'I don't want the little man to see me.' He was a lively communicator whose irreverence charmed the boys, several of whom gratefully recall the arm signals and oral cluckings with which, as he dictated the passage set for the O-level French dictation paper, he illicitly indicated the accents to be put on the words. He was one of several whom Kendall reportedly asked, as they left his study after being appointed by him, 'Oh, by the way, what do you teach?' In 1961 he left to become the *Daily Telegraph* rowing correspondent. Lawrence Toynbee, a practising painter and a skilful teacher with a useful sideline in sport, came to teach Art in 1947. Like Jack Scarr he was a Roman Catholic, as was Derek Henderson who joined the staff in 1950. Scarr was told later that his faith would preclude his being a housemaster, and Henderson expected to be passed over on the same ground. John Dizer, a master appointed in 1951, announced his conversion to Catholicism at the time of the arrival of Frank Fisher, who after consulting the Bishop of Exeter asked him to leave. Whether Scarr's and Dizer's faith was the real or only reason for the passing over of the one or the dismissal of the other it is impossible to know.

In 1947, when Styler left to become Chaplain of Brasenose, Kendall appointed, at first on a temporary basis, Mervyn Evans, a Classical Scholar of Hertford College back from the war. He too was married. A thoughtful Liberal with no interest in games, he would make most of his many contributions to the school in intellectual and cultural activities and would invigorate the ailing societies, of which there were only four after the war. He and John Alexander represented a commitment to the exercise of the mind in a community much more enthusiastic about that of the body. Kendall's remaining appointments reflected the Warden's athletic priority. Stewart Pether, a product of Magdalen College School in Oxford, who had blues in hockey and golf, arrived in 1946 to teach Geography. Duncan Williams (at the school from 1948 to 1984), Peter Church (1950–87), Derek Henderson (1950–61), Bob Arundel (1952–64) and Francis ('Fran') Prichard (1952–87) were all able games players with an interest in coaching. Convivial and cooperative in spirit, devoted to their charges and responsibilities, conservative in spirit, they would show a strong commitment to St Edward's, to the Public School ideal, and to Kendall. They brought with them the air of men who had known the wider world of war. From their number would come the dominant figures of the Common Room in an era extending well after Kendall's retirement, when they kept his spirit alive. Frank Fisher would have a limited number of vacancies to fill in his early years.

John Brewer (Roll No. 4236), who arrived at the school in 1947, recalls some of the teaching staff in verse:

> If and when you pass your GCE,
> With emancipated glee
> Choose your Sixth.
> Don't choose Stew
> For there's too much work to do.
> It's too technical with Joe and Jim Grow.
> Brim's too grim; and we ban the Doctor's fate
> And you can't associate with Jack Tate.
> We suggest that the History Sixth is best
> That the History Sixth is best, for a rest.
>
> (Stew = Stewart Pether; Joe = Peter Church; Jim Grow = Henry Gauntlett; the Doctor = John Alexander)

Reputedly the veteran Philip Whitrow, Head of History, was not best pleased.

Kendall had appointments to make to housemasterships. In 1947 Tilly and Macnamara gave up the Houses that bore their names, and Styler left Sing's. Yorke retired from Cowell's in 1949. How would those men be replaced? Tackley, who had arrived in the Common Room in 1930, and Emmet, who had been appointed in 1931, took over Sing's and Tilly's respectively, but there was a shortage of younger candidates for the other Houses. In the event Brims and Northcote-Green, who had taught at the school for only three years before being called to the war, took over Cowell's and Mac's. In other Houses Kendall probably hoped to replace Segar and Eardley by younger men when they became available. But in 1950, when Segar retired, the Warden felt constrained to appoint the veteran Henry Gauntlett as a stopgap. Not until 1952, when Northcote-Green left Mac's to become Headmaster of Worksop, did Kendall feel ready to appoint a post-war arrival, Charles Mather.

As bachelors, Emmet, Tackley and Brims could be given housemaster's quarters in existing accommodation. But the age of bachelor teachers was receding. In December 1946 the *Chronicle* announced Northcote-Green's engagement to Joan Greswell, Matron of Field House; his appointment to succeed at Mac's, where fortunately there remained the married accommodation that Herbert Dalton had occupied as headmaster, was announced at the same time. In 1955, a year after Kendall's departure but in accordance with a decision taken in his time, nine acres of land which looked down on the school fields from the back gardens of houses in Blenheim Drive, part of the property acquired from the Duke of Marlborough, were sold to help pay for married quarters so that Bill Veitch could become Housemaster of Segar's. Gradually bachelor housemasters became the exception rather than the norm. In 1973 there would be mild disapproval and maybe a measure of shock when I was appointed to Segar's, the first bachelor to be given a House since 1955, when John Armstrong took over Apsley. He subsequently married the house nurse.

In 1946 the Governors agreed to the appointment of the Maths teacher Hubert Beales, a former pupil of Kendall and a keen admirer of him, as bursar in succession to Thursfield. Amid the grim economic circumstances of the post-war years, which brought rationing and controls on investments, Kendall continued to keep a close eye on finances and to draw on the advice of Bayford Stone, who remained close to the school until his death in 1952. Kendall, whose dominance of the Governing Body was such that he virtually chose its composition, had persuaded the Governors that their number should include representatives of the Church, the academic world, the services and business; they would then possess a range of connections to and knowledge of the wider world. If some of them were old boys, so much the better. Charles Jenner (Roll No. 1158) became a governor in 1944. He was Bursar of Radley, and in 1949 became Bursar of St Edmund Hall, Oxford, where Emden, Chairman of the Governors of St Edward's, was principal. The academics were well chosen. They included Sir Roger Mynors, Corpus Christi Professor of Latin Language and Literature at Oxford; B. H. Sumner, the Warden of All Souls; Sir John Masterman, Provost of Worcester College and a figure with many influential contacts in public life; Sir Arthur Norrington, President of Trinity, who had comparable influence; and Philip Landon, a Fellow of the same college and a close friend of Kendall for more than twenty years. The services were represented by Air Chief Marshal Sir Roderick Hill and Admiral of the Fleet Sir John Cunningham, the First Sea Lord. The appointment of Andrew

Gibbs in 1948 not only renewed the link with the Aldenham family but strengthened the connection with Barclay's Bank, which until 1951 was also represented by Sir William Goodenough. Gibbs would be an influential governor until his retirement in 1983. Perhaps Kendall's most important nominee was Bob Mortimer, who was appointed in 1947, two years before he became Bishop of Exeter. A man of distinctly conservative outlook, he was already a major academic as well as a rising star of the Church. He loved his old school, became a good friend of Kendall, and was the natural choice as chairman when Emden retired in 1951. Mortimer would be chairman for twenty-two years and was especially influential after Kendall's retirement.

The numbers of boys continued to grow. There were 465 in 1949. The fees had to rise, for retail prices soared by 26% between 1946 and 1950 and by another 30% in the next five years. In 1947 the Governors reluctantly increased the fees from £168 to £175, still a remarkably low figure. There were further rises: to £186 in 1949, £230 in 1951, £263 in 1953, £275 in 1954. In December 1946 Kendall announced that a variable surcharge would be levied from the following term. The initial sum was to be £3 a term (£2 for day boys), but the Governors retained the option of increasing it to £6 (and £3). Parents were given the choice of declining to pay the surcharge, but only about 6% did so. There was another surcharge, of £9, in 1952.

Few realized that inflation, and the fee rises that met them, were indications of economic revival. In the post-war years, under the Attlee government, the Public Schools feared that the contribution their old boys and their values had made to the winning of the war would be overlooked in the socialist fight against privilege. Radical change was in the air, not least in education. The 1944 Butler Act ensured universal free secondary education. It laid down a national model of Grammar Schools, Secondary Modern Schools and Technical Schools. It began Direct Grant Schools. These were old Grammar Schools, often financially weak. The scheme was meant to reduce the temptation for them to go independent. Might not potential Public School parents be attracted to the new state system? The Fleming Report on Public Schools of 1944 proposed that they should accept a proportion of pupils who would be paid for by the state or by local authorities. Many Public Schools were sympathetic to a proposal that might assure their survival and assist their intakes. Others feared it would lead to a growing number of state-funded pupil and perhaps, as the state's grip accordingly became tighter, lead to abolition. Many opponents of the Public Schools also disliked the scheme. Some thought it would weaken the new state system by allowing Public Schools to drain off the best pupils. Above all there was the question of cost. Would not taxpayers and ratepayers be aggrieved to find themselves subsidizing children at Public Schools? Neither central government nor the local authorities wanted to meet the bill.

The Fleming Report was never implemented. The Labour Government, preoccupied with more urgent and critical economic issues – the American loan, the flight from sterling – did not place the Public Schools high on its agenda. Well before Kendall's retirement, Churchill was back in power. For the moment there would be no more talk either of assisted places or of abolition. But the Public Schools had not given a good account of themselves during the period of alarm. Attacks on their social divisiveness, and the extent of hostile comment by influential commentators, took them aback. The Governors and Heads of some schools took note to be better prepared if, as seemed all too likely, the threat should recur.

At the Gaudy of 1950 Kendall's twenty-five years at the school were celebrated. Emden, nearing retirement as Chairman of the Governors, offered fulsome praise, as the *Chronicle* reported. Over the quarter-century, he said, there had been 'great material progress – the numbers for instance had increased from 230 to about 470 – there had also been a steady growth in prestige. The Warden had steered the School through the difficult war years, and was noted for his confidence and persuasion. Besides this there was his own presiding, inimitable personality. *Jubilate Deo* was expressed in all that he did. He had a sense of humour and through it a sense of proportion, which he communicated to the School itself. He was a "beloved captain of a very solid ship".' Kendall was 64. How long would be stay at the helm?

33

SCHOOLDAYS

Smells! How they can define or recall experience. When Charles King-Smith (Roll No. 4606) visited the school in 2009, fifty-four years after leaving it, he was struck by the absence of smells. Where was the cinnamon scent of penny buns in hall, the aroma of lunchtime cabbage which persisted at teatime, the fierce chemical smells in the labs, the whiff of the formalin that preserved Crasher White's dogfish? In King-Smith's time the odour in the changing room from each boy's two rugby shirts, one pair of shorts and single pair of socks, all normally unwashed, 'was truly pungent towards the end of term'. Many boys avoided the compulsory daily cold shower by a token rinsing of the hair. Water for the weekly baths served a procession of users. 'Early bathers warmed the water slightly for later arrivals, but there was a slow build-up of curly hairs in the bath.'

Antony Barrington-Brown (Roll No. 3482), who was at the school from 1940 to 1945, makes an observation which could equally well be applied to the years after it:

> I do not think it is an exaggeration to say that life at the School was dominated by two elements: fear and conformity .... The whole of life was beset by rules, disciplinary and social – all unwritten. As a new boy one was terrified of breaking a rule of which one was not conscious. As time went on one either learnt the rules by experience, or observance became part of normal behaviour. Ultimately some could be circumvented or broken.

Here was the rough end of Kendall's 'boy-centred commonwealth', where status was rigidly defined by seniority and its observances. The 'facing off' rule was outlawed only in the 1960s and was covertly imposed even thereafter, for boys themselves were defenders of harsh conventions, which, as at other Public Schools, the authorities hesitated to challenge. Crossing an unmarked line across the floor of the day room, or looking in the direction of the president or vice-president's horse-box, was punished by 20–30 press-ups or by the more exacting 'crow-hopping', which required a boy to squat on his haunches, with the Bible in one hand and a complete Shakespeare in the other, and hop up and down the day room. Post-war variations on this exercise were known as 'the Belsen Bounce'. In Tilly's, perhaps the fiercest of the Houses, boys 'having the wrong attitude' would be summoned from the Junior to the Senior day room early on a Sunday morning while the housemaster was at communion, to be pelted, bullied and kicked, or made to crow-hop to the jeers of the tormentors. 'One dreaded getting the instruction "Don't go to Communion tomorrow",' recalls David Vaudrey (Roll No. 4436), who arrived in 1949.

Punishments and other conventions and rituals varied from House to House, so that practices recognized by OSE of one House may be unfamiliar to products of another. Yet there was a high degree of uniformity too, and very similar conventions obtained at other Public Schools. Punishments by the Warden and housemasters were relatively infrequent. Most rules, many of them unofficially created by the boys themselves, were enforced, rigorously and vigorously, by prefects and day-room presidents. Vaudrey recalls being reproached by other boys for not meting out punishments when he was president of his day room. There was a range of arcane rules about the buttons and pockets and flaps of a jacket. In the Quad, boys were not allowed to put their hands in their pockets or walk more than two abreast. Humiliating ordeals awaited new boys. David Watkin (Roll No. 4296), who arrived in 1947, survived the initiation ceremony by tunelessly singing the first verse of the Welsh national anthem in Welsh. Oral new boys' tests, conducted by the prefects after the first three weeks, required knowledge not only of rules and customs but of the geography of the school and its slang, and the names and nicknames of masters. The required vocabulary included 'chaosing' (disorderly conduct), 'chimneys' (compulsory long runs), 'the Crystal Palace' (the lavatories at the west end of the indoor pool, a favourite site for illicit smoking), 'fug' (the Junior Training Corps, later the Combined Cadet Force or 'CCF'), and 'rears' (toilets). Chris Phillips (Roll No. 4533), a new boy in Field House in 1950, remembers that 'in the first three weeks at the School we were obliged to recognise every other boy in the House by name and their "house order", the school song, the sacristans, every cricket, rugby, athletics and boating "colour" and their initials, every master and his initials and of course landmarks such as the Jungle, Crystal Palace, etc.' Each new boy was allotted a mentor from his day room, who prepared him for the test and was punished if the new boy failed it and so had to retake it. I encountered resistance when as Housemaster of Segar's I ended the test in Segar's in 1973. It persisted in other Houses after that date.

The House prefects ran the fagging system. All boys fagged at least for their first few terms, and some had additional duties as the personal fag of a particular prefect. There were messages to carry, errands to the Shop to be run, baked beans on toast to be cooked, shoes and boots and CCF kit to be cleaned and polished, desks to be tidied, malefactors to be fetched for interrogation or punishment, lavatory seats to be warmed for the prefects. Each boy had a weekly quota of faggings to complete, though it was reduced with seniority. Bells wired from the prefects' study to the junior day room would summon the fags, who in one House at least were divided into cadres, some answering a ring of one bell, some two, some three, some four. The first boy to shout 'I'll go' answered the call. On Saturday afternoon a boy short of his quota would stay in his day room hoping anxiously for the bell. In Apsley the bell-ringing acquired a new name after Alec Cranswick (Roll No. 2846), the RAF Pathfinder, had come to speak at the school and provoked merriment by referring to the operation of releasing a bomb as 'squeezing the tit'.

Fagging was justified as character training, a view many older OSE would still hold. Prefects who exercised the responsibility of power had earlier experienced subordination to it. Some OSE remark that the more intelligent of the prefects were the more humane ones in their treatment of fags. There were some generous tips at the end of term. The Prefect system had long seemed a training in leadership, of the kind demanded by public service in the Empire or Commonwealth or the services or the Church. With time, however, the hierarchical and disciplinary basis of the ideal of leadership would lose its force. Pastoral and communal ideals of guidance would replace it. When that happened the traditional character of the prefect system, and the fagging system too, began to look dated.

Other than in the Chapel, in the classroom and on the games fields, the House prefects were the dominant presence. They would set lines, up to 100 of them, in the form of conjugations from *Kennedy's Latin Primer*, or require boys to carry out wake-up calls in the early morning, or impose extra runs. Sometimes boys were made to learn and recite a psalm. Or there was drill, usually of half an hour, conducted by Sergeant-Major Merry, who led mass PT for the school in the Quad every morning break. The Head of House caned, a ritual preceded by coded indications of the fate of boys summoned to the prefects' study. 'We'll see you later' meant either that a beating was being considered or that the housemaster's permission (rarely, if ever, refused) would be sought for one. At the subsequent summons the weightily intoned words 'Go away' meant that the offender or offenders would be beaten. The sentence of doom was accordingly known as 'getting the go away'. 'You may go', on the other hand, meant that mercy had prevailed. The normal time for beatings was during the silence of evening Prep. The normal place was a dormitory above, where furniture was cleared for the event and where the boy, having removed his jacket, was made to bend down to clutch the bottom rail of the end of a bedstead. Barrington-Brown remembers climbing 'the thirty stone steps in Apsley. You could hear a pin drop in the day room below; the sound of hesitant footsteps crossing the wooden floor above.' In the formal exchanges before the offender was told to bend over he was offered the right to appeal to the housemaster, but it was rarely if ever exercised. After the beating, at which another prefect was present, the Head of House customarily said 'Well taken', and the victim was expected to answer 'Thank you'.

Barrington-Brown reckons he received 21 strokes at St Edward's, which he thinks was below the average. David Vaudrey remembers the occasion when five boys, of whom he was one, playfully pulled away the wrapped bath towel of Peter Pugh (Roll No. 3965), their dormitory prefect. In came the Head of House, Roger Neville (Roll No. 4063). Vaudrey remarks,

> I have often wondered why he laid into us so hard. We went up to a dormitory in alphabetical order so I suffered increasing dread as those before me staggered back looking shaken .... I remember being rather ashamed that I had let out a gasp on receiving each of the last three strokes (of six) .... When I met Neville years later, watching a cricket match, I did not think I should bring up the subject. In the summer [around the bathing pool] one could see who had been beaten recently by the rows of linear bruises across the bottom.

A later victim of Neville's vigour was Anselm Kuhn (Roll No. 4556), who also remembers that a boy a year below his own, Grahame Dangerfield (Roll No. 4634), who would become a wildlife expert and a television presenter, was so often caned 'that we lost all count of the number of beatings'. Alastair Dunn (Roll No. 4907) states that 'the discipline would be considered abuse today'. Barrington-Brown is more forgiving: 'In these politically correct times corporal punishment is regarded with horror and seen as both cruel and degrading; we must not ascribe the feelings of today to those of years ago.'

There were fewer school rules than House rules. School prefects were responsible for their enforcement and the Senior Prefect caned for breaches of them. Among them were leaving the grounds without a 'basher', walking in front of the sightscreens other than between overs, 'chaosing' in the outdoor baths, and, most seriously, missing or being late for Chapel, which could be punished by six strokes from the Senior Prefect during supper. Housemasters occasionally wielded the cane, usually for such offences as not handing in work or for misbehaving in class. Barrington-Brown resented a beating by his housemaster Leslie Styler ('Uncle Ned' or 'Mickey' or 'The Count') for sending a message to a friend in the San by means of the internal staff post, though he knew he did not have too much to fear, since Styler was 'not much good with the cane'. Anyway, if sometimes the punishment seemed unfair, 'we were quite philosophical about such a thing bearing in mind the sins we had got away with'. Beatings by the Warden, whose severity and accuracy with the cane were renowned, were often for particularly heinous offences: lying, smoking, excursions to Oxford and other breaches of bounds, and what was called 'moral turpitude'.

Undetected escapes from the grounds were a coveted achievement. The Segar's Navy Club was founded in 1948 when Anthony Sparrow (Roll No. 4020) found a tin advertising 'Navy Club Cigarettes 10 for 6 pence' in a ditch on the lower fields in 1948. A founder member was John Michael Owen (Roll No. 4064), who recalls the meals eaten in the House on Sundays and, more excitingly, in the Friar Bacon pub on the bypass near the Banbury Road roundabout. The club's minutes recorded the gift of a bottle of British sherry, which was served in chipped enamel egg cups. On one occasion there was cold roast pheasant, with disastrous digestive results. At a feast in the House Gerry Segar made an unexpected entrance. He was plied with non-alcoholic drink, only for the booze and cigarettes to reappear after his departure. 'We still meet,' writes Owen in 2013. Even after sixty-four years, 'minutes are kept and the old formalities observed'. 'It is an understatement,' he reflects, 'to say that our fellowship has been happy and lasting. It has been hilarious.'

John Lambourn (Roll No. 3840), in Sing's from 1943, remembers that Sunday night lock-up was the best time for an outing into Summertown to 'chat up' the local girls. A Sing's boy, disguised with side whiskers, horn-rimmed glasses and a pork-pie hat, managed to drink in the Red Lion with masters a stone's throw away, and on another occasion attended Henley Royal Regatta in the same disguise and mingled with the Eight undetected. One of Lambourn's friends was Bob Marsh-Allen (Roll No. 3904), 'Maude' to his friends, who had a huge pair of binoculars which supposedly came from a captured U-boat. From the senior dormitory he could – or so he claimed – see people alighting from buses on Hinksey Hill. Once, closer at hand, the glamorous Joan Northcote-Green, the former matron of Field House, came into view by Mac's. Then a shift of the binoculars revealed her husband viewing the boys through his own mini-binoculars and noting down their names. Lambourn's other memories include a description of the great freeze of 1947. 'This term had been exceptional in its succession of circumstances. The fuel crisis. The food crisis (bread was now rationed). Burst pipes everywhere ... record temperatures below zero.' That summer John and his friends were photographed on the lower fields during Sunday evening lock–up by a local girl named Doreen, who was enamoured of Bob.

Defiance of rules always carried excitement. Feasts in excavated spaces beneath the day-room floors were facilitated by the improvisation of ingenious and perilous electrical devices for lighting and heating. Nocturnal bathing, which often meant dodging masters on a night stroll, was common. Vaudrey remembers one venue for smoking, the small shed behind the Work Block where tuck boxes were stored. Tuck boxes, where sauces and sweets that defied the austerity of the period could be locked away, allowed a rare sense of private possession. Another escape from the crowd was the Science Block, which Anselm Kuhn remembers as 'almost a world apart .... Walter Dunn was almost revered by us VI Formers', and the boys had their 'first taste of taking part in scientific activity' there. 'In this sanctum, Jim Gauntlett and Freddie Yorke somehow became more approachable; there was a beginning of a feeling of "we" rather than them and us'. The friendliness of Dunn the lab assistant was matched by that of the ex-army NCOs, Merry and Sam Tero, who was PT instructor from 1948 to 1952 and RSM of the CCF from 1952 to 1962. Many OSE remember humane conversations with Merry as he administered his 'short back and sides' haircuts. Few masters ever seem to have made friendly human contact.

An activity which took boys legally out of the grounds was rowing. Kuhn, who took refuge in the science labs, found 'one other world apart', the Boat House at Godstow.

> I would say this was close to 'magical'. As one came down the gravel track one was met by two noises. The first the endless thundering of the weir at The Trout, the second the wild shriek of the peacocks. Before reaching the boathouse one had to pass the Beasleys' cottage

and this too, a scene of rural domesticity, was so utterly different from the highly organised atmosphere of the School. 'Pop Beasley' and his son Geoff seemed to work so well together and struck a good note with us boys, perhaps not unlike NCOs in their dealings with officer cadets. Like the Science Block the whole place was filled with a sense of purpose, a hive of activity.

Many OSE are grateful to the Beasleys for the friendly gestures and the human touch. Boys were required to reach the river on foot. Some enjoyed the run, but others took illicit short cuts or used bicycles.

Single sculling, a contrast to team games, gave a sense of individual liberation, as did Jack Tate's Sailing Club. Even masters could unbend in the riverside setting. Desmond Hill lent his special sculler to boys and, when negotiating special meals for his crew, was sure to have half a pint of bitter included. Grenville Collins (Roll No. 5235), who entered the school in 1956, remembers that on Saturdays in summer crews often could not get back in time for Chapel. 'Oh dear. What a pity!' Desmond would say. 'Why don't we drop into The Trout and have a quick couple of halves of beer. So we did.' 'Desmond Hill,' writes Collins, 'was a truly wonderful man. I owe him much. He taught us Chaucer in breathtaking terms. It was mesmeric stuff for young schoolboys. Here was a man who drank First Growth clarets, owned a blue metallic Healey sports car and was his own man, unafraid of anyone or anything. We adored him; being in his class was like being at home. He was so different from the other members of the staff .... Desmond hinted that he did not much care for them either. Perhaps his secret was that he treated us like adults and not children.' As for the other masters 'very few of them ever laughed'.

Guy Charter (Roll No. 3214), who came to the school in 1937, remarks that 'apart from the Housemasters and masters involved in coaching games we saw very little of the staff outside classes'. The same was true for the post-war generation. Housemasters seem to have entered the boys' part of the building only occasionally. Once Tilly, having heard noise in a dormitory, merely put his head round the door and barked 'Send someone down.' So a luckless victim among the offenders 'volunteered' for a beating in his pyjamas. Few boys sought out contact with their housemasters. In Cowell's, Pat Brims was kind and conscientious but shy. 'Mr Emmet,' writes Vaudrey, 'was an amiable man but a little cold. I was never taught by him so I never got to know him. He could be brusque.' When

Vaudrey wanted to get Henry Gauntlett, one master whom boys did find approachable, at least when he was in a good mood, to take a passport photograph for him, Emmet told him that the master 'wouldn't want to photograph your ugly face'. 'He may not have meant anything by it,' remembers Vaudrey, 'but it pained me at the time.' On one occasion Emmet entered the Junior day room and 'harangued us for visiting the surgery unnecessarily, which he said "was a sign of a weak house". I think he was proud of presiding over a tough house.' In the surgeries nurses such as Elsie Matthews and Kay Puxley offered a rare touch of solicitude. Kuhn writes: 'The idea that there was at least one surrogate mother on the scene meant a great deal – just to know that she was there and accessible.' Several OSE remembered the improvement in atmosphere when married men became housemasters, and fondly recalled the presence of the wives of Northcote-Green, Barff and Veitch.

Housemasters offered few restraints on boys' treatment of each other. Giles Hunt (Roll No. 3622), who left in 1945, writes that his housemaster Bill Eardley 'had little or no grip and there was some appalling bullying – I am deeply ashamed at having joined the throng who really beat a boy up badly because he was a German Jew, [an] evacuee from Nazism'. Anselm Kuhn has a 'very bad memory. In our Day Room there was one boy, a not very prepossessing chap. He had a limp, he was not very bright, he was somewhat lacking in social graces and, coming from Sheffield, he had a northern accent. For years and years this boy was teased unmercifully. I was not among the main tormentors but neither can I claim total innocence. Looking back, that this boy survived such unrelenting torment is little short of miraculous. By the same token, one wonders that it was allowed to continue as it did. This was bullying of a horrific order.'

OSE who recall their boyhoods in the post-war age almost invariably remember the frequency of services in Chapel. For the best part of a century from the move to Summertown there were morning and evening prayers on all weekdays and, on Sundays, a voluntary early morning communion, a compulsory Choral Eucharist at which the congregation did not communicate, and compulsory Evensong. OSE remember that though almost all boys were confirmed few chose to attend the early communion service or the communions arranged during the week. The Chapel had become more instrumental in promoting conformity and discipline than in advancing faith. The wearing of surplices by the congregation, the symbol of collective devotion which had been revived after the Great War, was ended by Kendall. Boys appeared in their Sunday best, in blue suits, stiff clean white collars and gleamingly shined shoes, though there were exceptions to that last requirement. It was maintained that the main duty of the sacristans was to spot dirty shoes. 'To this day,' writes Geoffrey Gover (Roll No. 4041), 'at reunions, I still rub the top of my shoes on my trouser legs on going into chapel.' Prefects patrolled the Chapel to ensure attendance and proper turnout, and announced a variety of punishments as offenders left the building. But OSE recall with pleasure the hearty singing of the hymns and the weekly Congregational Practice (the rehearsal for Sunday hymn-singing, a practice which continued into the 1970s). Old boys who rarely go to church attend Chapel at special Gaudies to sing 'Wolvercote', 'Cwm Rhondda', 'Jerusalem' and the 'Carmen'. Since the Great War, Sunday Evensong had become more elaborate and was more prominently advertised in the termly calendars. It was increasingly a parade of the school and choir in front of visiting preachers. Sung Eucharist and the frequent taking of communion, which had been the achievement of the Oxford Movement, suffered in comparison. At the Sung Eucharist itself it was on the anthem and the singing, not on the sacrament, that attention now centred. In that respect 'the School had not kept up with modern liturgical developments', writes Richard Madeley (Roll No. 4112), a new boy in 1946. 'The best part of Evensong was the anthem. I liked Choral Eucharist because there was more music.'

In the school's early days most of the teachers were in holy orders. After the appointment of Leslie Styler in 1931, only two of Kendall's forty-three appointments to the Common Room were priested: Canon Vincent, a wartime stopgap, who taught from 1941 to 1945, and Tom Williams (1946–57). Madeley writes: 'I remember Wally Vincent set a record for the fastest Choral Evensong at 18 minutes when his wife was in labour!' OSE remember Williams as a figure of fun. After the retirement of Macnamara and Menzies, Kendall, who liked to control everything, was in effect single-handedly in charge of the Chapel. An OSE who became a schoolmaster-priest offered a balanced assessment of Kendall's Wardenship. Warm in praise, he adds: 'I believe that his main fault – a very serious one – was that he sought to be both headmaster and chaplain. This was especially noticeable when he, and he alone, prepared boys for Confirmation, in the course of which each boy had a private interview with him, when the question of sexual activity was always raised. No school nowadays would dream of combining headmaster and chaplain, even if the headmaster is ordained.'

Anselm Kuhn has a criticism too, a common one among OSE: 'In one way or another the School was successful in obscuring all that is good and important about religion and reducing it to a tedious and meaningless ritual.' Kuhn suggests that what he remembers as a 'dichotomy' at St Edward's 'between the important valuable message of the Church' and the outlooks of 'many of those in authority in the School' left many of the school's products with an incoherent religious outlook. Diccon Masterman (Roll No. 5042), who arrived just after Kendall's departure, writes: 'The School was, of course, founded as an institution with the express aim of furthering Christian beliefs. Interestingly enough, 15 doses of chapel per week did nothing to reinforce the belief which had been instilled into me as a child and my doubts about all religion were ignited during my time at the School.'

Guy Charter remembers the 'lasting effect ... of being away from home for two-thirds of the year from the age of 14 to 18 ... I suppose I became very self-contained; learning to curb my temper and not to show my feelings. That has had advantages and disadvantages in later life.' In the more open emotional world that has followed, some reminiscent OSE have been ready to confront the question of sex in their schooldays. Freedom to explore one's body and ponder one's new self was difficult if not impossible in a world so lacking in opportunities for solitude. One OSE remembers the difficulty of adjusting to his early 'wet dreams' and recalls the challenge of masturbating unobserved in a crowded dormitory. Another recalls that 'The testosterone imperative became more urgent as we grew through the teens. The School's official view was of course one of total disapproval .... Onanism was specifically deprecated in the Bible and therefore was sinful: sins were to be punished. "Unnatural feelings" between boys, particularly of different ages, were held to be dangerous to both body and soul; even to contemplate a desire for the opposite sex was horrific; lust was the deadliest sin of all. Friendship between boys in different years (and indeed different houses) was actively discouraged and even visiting another house to see a contemporary was frowned upon. Entering another day room was forbidden, though going for walks was permitted .... Of course masturbation was universal, perhaps daily in the majority. No attempt was made to stop it except that team members were abjured to abstain on the day before a match .... Mutual masturbation was also widespread but this was usually between friends of the same year; unlike many other schools there was never any enforced sex with seniors nor, would I say, coercion of any sort. However, new boys were visually appraised and some picked out as particularly attractive. Older boys, even prefects – in my own case no less an eminence than the captain of cricket – would gain their acquaintance and write notes in varying degrees (but not generally intense) of passion known as "tartnotes".... Such relationships seldom gave rise to sex except in the same house where the total blackout enabled dormitory prefects to leave their beds on moonless nights to "have one off". But as for buggery I never heard of even a single occurrence at Teddy's while I was there, nor was it ever spoken of, which it would have been even if only as stories from the past .... I recall travelling home at the end of my last term with a friend, once a "lusher", who told me he did not expect or intend to have any relationship with women; but [I have] often met him since with his long-term wife and four children'.

One OSE admits that 'I found homosexual practices, to which I was introduced early on, rather enjoyable.' Another writes: 'I assume that a much more enlightened approach now has to be taken over the problem of dealing with the cauldron of sexual tensions which prevail in an institution full of adolescents in the throes of puberty. In the Fifties there was no sex education which meant there was much speculation based on frightening ignorance.' Condoms, though becoming more common, were regarded as sleazy and there were no easy cures for sexually transmitted diseases. 'There was,' writes the same OSE, 'continuous experimentation with one's own body and with the bodies of one's peers which was, needless to say ... inevitable.' But as the jaunts to Summertown suggest, sexual initiatives were not confined to the same gender. At least one boy was expelled for getting one of the young 'Annies' pregnant. In so confined a world, nature had vindicated her rights.

34

KENDALL'S CLOSING YEARS

In 1951 the OSE paid for a portrait of Henry Kendall to mark his twenty-five years in charge. The painter was the former soldier Aubrey Davidson-Houston (Roll No. 1739), a pupil under Ferguson, who would paint four later Wardens. Kendall, dressed in his customary cassock, is given knowing eyes and an enigmatic smile. His spectacles lie on his desk together with his pipe and the box for his cigars. He smoked incessantly and many old boys remember the smell of tobacco as he approached. Kendall was presented with the portrait at a special Jubilee dinner attended by 227 OSE. In accepting it he explained that 'any inaudibility on his part would be due to a new set of dentures making their first speech'. His girth was spreading and he was ageing.

The year 1951 saw the fall of the Attlee government and the Festival of Britain. Two editorials in the *Chronicle*, the first in January, the second in April, glance at the trends of contemporary society and contemplate, in troubled vein, the school's place within them. The January editorial is an unexpected plea for 'individuality'. It notes the anonymity, and the danger posed to 'the thinking powers', of the life of the factory hand, 'the inauspicious cog-wheel in the engine of industry'. The 'personal significance' of a member of the crowds that gather at football matches or in bars and cinemas 'must perish as a leaf in the autumn'. The author applies the lesson to the school, where boys 'are crowded together. We eat, if not from the common dish, in the common dining hall. We work as a swarm of bees packed together in the various partitions of a bee-hive. We roost like so many starlings on a winter's night .... When we watch a rugby match, we are constrained to do so *tout en bloc* – Sixth Forms on one side and *hoi polloi* on the other. It is, in fact, a concentrated community in which we exist.' 'Man,' the editorial protests, 'must sometimes live alone. Team spirit is a menace if it becomes an obsession. We must be allowed a relief, and we find it in the solitary pursuance of our own interests. The bug-hunter may seem ridiculous ... the scholar must meet the scorn of cynics when he retires into his shell of study and the aero-modeller as he slowly rotates upon [the playing-field] Corfe 1. But they are right, these "freaks", and even more so if they can meet the contempt of their critics with stolid indifference. Their lives are wider and fuller than those of the idlers who cling together in inconsequential groups and admire their own shadowy excellence. Let us by all means enter into our common life wholeheartedly but let us also seize the fleeting opportunities for individual recreation, and gather our engine-numbers, bus tickets, brass-door knockers and elephant hawk-moths while we may.'

The April editorial carried a different message. Accepting Britain's declining status as a world power, it argued that there was no reason for the Public Schools to decline with it:

> The British civilisation has realised more fully than any other since the time of the Greeks that the greatest pursuit of man is the art of life .... Knowledge and art are indeed wonderful, and should be studied by every civilised being, but nothing is finer then the life of a good man. It is this that the Public School attempts to produce, and it is more successful than perhaps any similar system has ever been. It should therefore neither be thrown away nor modified out of existence without long and careful deliberation.

Noting, as 'a mark of the age', that some schools are proposing the abolition of fagging and that 'a few of the tougher traditions have been disappearing', the writer tries to draw a line:

> The foundation of the Public School rests upon boarding, compulsory games, the House, prefectship, and religious worship in the Chapel. Boarding teaches self-reliance; games develop the physical basis so necessary for character; the House instils loyalty; and from the prefectship comes the experience of authority and command.

The contribution of Chapel is not explained.

The *Chronicle* had expanded again after the war, as had the coverage of games. The editorial of January 1953 inveighed against 'useless but persistent criticisms we receive' about the magazine, of which 'we have had more than our patience can stand'. The main attacks criticize the *Chronicle* for being dull and also for catering too much for OSE. After the First World War the editors had tried to reclaim the magazine from the dominance of OSE news. Now the editorial defended the space given to it. 'There are nearly three thousand OSE .... For every one boy at the School there are six OSE.' The magazine blames 'the deplorable lack of any literary works or paintings or photographs' by or of the boys themselves. 'Surely among the mass of the apparently uninspired and insensitive, there are a few capable of allowing the Muse to enter and guide their pen .... But of pointless carping we have had more than enough.' If the Muse was failing, at least there was a modest increase in the number of societies after the war, though as always they depended on the initiative of a master or senior boy. There was even a Medieval History Society. Other new societies offered their members escape from the school grounds: the Young Farmers Club (established in 1950), encouraged by Jack White; the Piscatorial Society (1951), established by Roger Northcote-Green with the help of Pat Brims; the Sailing Club (1951); and the Golfing Society, which played at the North Oxford Golf Club from 1953. The Arts Society continued, with the support of Jack Tate and John Alexander. So did the Scientific and Engineering Society, though we read that it 'would cease to function' but for the help of Jack Gauntlett.

The Debating Society flourished in the 1950s. The star pupil was B. T. Fell (Roll No. 4305), known to all as George, who was full of lively confidence and humour. But debates were often led by masters rather than boys. A succession of motions set the dapper, bow-tied Mervyn Evans, who had been Librarian of the Oxford Union and had debated there when Edward Heath was president, against the conservative Charles Mather, who appeared in a college or Sports Club tie. In April 1951 Evans proposed the motion, daring at the time, that 'This house considers the Communist challenge should be met by peaceful means rather than by armed force'. Mather in reply attacked a 'creed based on hatred and class war', but his side prevailed by only three votes. The two masters and others who also spoke helped to bring the outside world into the boys' consciousness, and by now a majority of motions before the House had a political content. There was the largest attendance for twenty years – 134 – in October 1951, just before the general election that would bring down the Labour government and begin thirteen years of Conservative rule. Evans proposed, as a Liberal, that 'this House hopes for a change of government on the 25th'. Jack Scarr opposed, but the motion was carried by 107 votes to 18.

In the next month only the chairman's casting vote defeated the motion that 'in the opinion of this House the Welfare State is sapping the individual's sense of responsibility'. Unusually Kendall was present, perhaps to keep an eye on the boys' behaviour in front of one of the speakers, a member of the Wolvercote Boys' Club, which the school now supported in place of the Bermondsey Club. In March 1953 Evans and Mather crossed swords again on the motion, carried by 16 votes to 9, that the 'interests of Great

Britain lie more with the Commonwealth than with Europe'. The reintroduction of corporal punishment for crimes of violence was supported by 27 votes to 10. Discrimination against coloured peoples was condemned by 24 to 18, but not before Mather had declared 'that absolute equality was out of the question'. In April 1951, 83 members and 'four welcome lady guests' attended the debate on the motion that 'this House is in favour of co-education'. John Armstrong, opposing from the floor, portrayed coeducation, tongue in cheek, 'as a gigantic feminine conspiracy to obtain equality. Standards in school would fall and the Common Room would be dominated by "gimlet-eyed gorgons".' Recounts were necessary before the chairman announced the defeat of the motion by one vote.

Edward 'Ludwig' Manning and Jack Scarr ran the music and the plays respectively. Music figures little in OSE memories of the time, and there is irony in the later creation of a music prize in Kendall's name. But some old boys do remember learning something from the playing of gramophone records at meetings of the Musical Society and from small musical soirées organized in Houses by Macnamara and Styler. No reminiscences comment on the ten or twelve anthems, a standard fare of Bach, Haydn, Stanford, Farrant and so on, which were performed each term in Chapel; they were taken for granted. At a typical Gaudy summer concert of 1953 the choir of forty-six sang three testing madrigals, which were followed by less exacting fare, such chestnuts as 'John Peel', 'Bobby Shafto' and 'The Poacher'. The last earned an encore, and the performance ended with 'Rule, Britannia!' The only contribution from the orchestra, which now consisted of 20 boys and 14 adults, was Walton's 'Crown Imperial'. 'This cannot be said to be one of his most successful compositions,' ruled the *Chronicle*.

Back in the Thirties, Styler had produced plays and Brims had assisted him. Their productions had included two Sheridan plays, *The School for Scandal* in 1936 and *The Rivals* in 1937. There were no productions during the war, when the only stage shows were the Radley Masters' Annual Cabaret and the Rag Revue, the annual show given by the prefects and other sixth-formers which had been instituted in 1930. Kendall preferred its innocuous and inward-looking lampoons and satire, which reinforced the school's collective sentiment, to strenuous or searching drama. In 1932 Keith Grimmond (Roll No. 2315) was described as 'the best form of imitator, for he mimics without malice'. The Revue was subject to censorship and from 1941 was suppressed after traversing acceptable boundaries in its mockery of the teaching staff. It was back by the 1950s. After Styler's departure in 1947, Scarr, a pillar of the Oxford amateur dramatic community, was the only master willing to take on the burden of the school play. He was a most accomplished director, among whose productions was Pinero's *The Magistrate* in 1953, which led the *Chronicle*'s reviewer to remark that 'the advance of the quality of acting in the School is the result of a lot of hard work and able coaching by Mr Scarr. The cast were natural and always fully audible; restrained and yet fully alive .... In fact one Old Boy said that it was a performance which could have filled the New Theatre; one parent said that there were many repertory companies which would have been glad to have presented so finished an entertainment; and one member of a junior day room said it was better than doing prep. Even the masters liked it.'

The reviewer revealed his own and the audience's preferences by admiringly describing Pinero's comedy as 'gay and fanciful, and untroubled by life's problems'. Scarr's choice of plays was not adventurous. Other productions of his in the 1950s included James Bridie's *Tobias and the Angel* and Shaw's *The Devil's Disciple*, though the modern linguist Scarr also directed English translations of Molière's *Le Bourgeois Gentilhomme* and *The Barber of Seville* by Beaumarchais. Shakespeare was represented by *The Taming of the Shrew* and *The Merry Wives of Windsor*. Though he preferred comedy, Scarr produced in 1955 a stage version of the very popular film directed five years earlier by John Ward Baker, *Morning Departure*. It suited the school's image of itself as a cradle of war heroes. It also seemed very modern at the time, but Scarr would not be in sympathy with the new wave of drama announced only six months after the production by John Osborne's *Look Back in Anger*. His distance from the new mood is unlikely to have dismayed his audiences. Cowell had made the school play an annual ritual, not a mere staged entertainment. Though his prologues, with their commentaries on the past year of the school's life, had gone, the main performance of the play was tightly fitted into the gap between the rugby match against the Martyrs and the sherry before the OSE dinner in Oxford. Two hours was the maximum permitted.

In sport, the golden era of the 1930s had passed: despite vigorous activity and many successes, the glow had dimmed. There were now seven or eight settled fixtures against strong schools. Northcote-Green coached several good XVs and introduced House Senior and Junior Leagues. Between 1947 and 1960 the XV played 94 matches, winning 44, drawing 9, and losing 41. Rugby continued to be prominently covered in the *Chronicle*. Emmet, Mather and Hill greatly strengthened the rowing, though it was covered much less fully by the magazine. The VIII came second to Winchester at 'the Schools' Head' (of the River) in 1953. The formation of the Martyrs Boat Club in 1936 provided some funds for equipment, though development was hampered by a shortage of money, and a £1 levy had to be imposed on members of the Boat Club. Cricket was thriving again by the mid-1950s. There were now inter-school fixtures in athletics, though they were slimly covered in the *Chronicle*. There were fencing matches, squash matches and the cross-country running of the Harriers. Kendall frequently watched boxing matches; it was reputedly his favourite sport. St Edward's competed against Radley and lost by four fights to two. Inter-House sporting competitions abounded. A report in the *Chronicle* of 1953 listed forty-three cups for them.

In the 1930s Kendall had reluctantly agreed to the introduction of hockey, which lacked the manly aura of rugby and rowing. At least it was a team game. It was now played in the Easter Term, with three or four fixtures, though progress of the game was frequently hampered by drenched pitches. In 1951 the school competed for the first time in the Public Schools' Hockey Festival. The following year a blizzard forced the cancellation of the competition, but in 1953 St Edward's was one of twenty-eight schools participating, among them 'nearly all the best hockey schools in the country', as the *Chronicle* reported. 'The festival is essentially non-competitive, the games being played in the proper spirit of friendly rivalry .... Our results were disappointing, one game being won and three lost.' Injuries were partly to blame and 'we hope that future aspirants will not be deterred by the fact that both the First and Second goalkeepers went home encased in plaster of Paris'. But in the same year the First XI managed to win half of its eight fixtures, though the Second XI won only two of six. The Colts won three and lost four. Bromsgrove, Radley, Pangbourne, Magdalen College School and Bradfield were the schools most frequently played at hockey, as, together with Stowe, Eastbourne and Oundle, they were at rugby. There were still sports fixtures against university teams. Between 1952 and 1956 the XV always played the Oxford University (OU) Greyhounds, the OU Occasionals, and Lincoln College. The Cricket XI played the OU Authentics and Trinity and Oriel Colleges.

This was not a period of high achievement on the academic front. Exemption from the Common Entrance examination, as a means to sustain the numbers, seems to have been quite common. Performances at A level and GCE were not strong, though such exams counted for less than they do now. In the Summer Term of 1953 there were 77 boys in the Sixth Form. Only 16 passed in all three subjects; 35 more in just two. Of the 105 O-level candidates one boy passed in seven subjects; 25 passed in five subjects; 20 in four; 12 in only one. In a second sitting in December four boys passed in three subjects, 18 in two, and 45 in one. The figures for 1954, the year of Kendall's retirement, are no more impressive.

What of the future of the 69 boys who left in the same year? We know what 68 of them did. Seventeen went on to Oxford and Cambridge, ten to other universities, six into colleges of technology or agriculture, three to medical schools. The other 32 proceeded directly into their careers, seven of them military, the remainder in such occupations as accountancy, banking, the law and farming. So more than half of the leavers in 1954 went on to higher education. These figures are not untypical of Public Schools of the era before the expansion of higher education in the 1960s. At Tonbridge, which was much the same size, the proportion of the 195 entrants was almost exactly the same. In April 1955 the *Chronicle* published lists of the 33 OSE resident at Cambridge and the 17 at Oxford. Twelve of the Oxonians were at St Edmund Hall, of which Emden had until recently been principal, and where the Geography tutor, Charles Gullick (Roll No. 1741), was vice-principal. It was not an intellectual powerhouse. Yet in his final report to the Governors Kendall was able to record that the school had won 51 scholarships and 49 exhibitions at Oxford and Cambridge during his tenure. If not a distinguished figure, at least it was not discreditable. The award-holders did not let the school down, for 45 of the 100 got Firsts.

At Kendall's farewell dinner, which 347 people attended, the Chairman of the Governors Bob Mortimer, whose bond with Kendall had been demonstrated in badinage at dinners and other occasions across the years, summed up Kendall's reign. 'The Warden's supreme achievement has been to transform the material circumstances of the School (adding acreage, buildings, numbers, reputation) whilst retaining the inward spirit.' The bishop recalled the Warden's advice to him given many years previously, just before the former's ordination: '"Don't be a spike [an unworldly Anglo-Catholic]. What matters is people." The Warden has proved in his twenty-nine years' service the truth of his own advice.' In his reply Kendall's mind tellingly reverted to memories of his golden years in the 1930s. He quoted at length a depiction of school life entitled 'These I Have Loved', which had appeared in the *Chronicle*. It was by Eric 'Budge' Dixon (Roll No. 2479), the Captain of Cricket in 1935, who was killed in action in 1941:

> The congregation bursting forth with renewed vigour after a sketchy verse by the trebles: the ebullient rapture which greets a winning try: the distant noise from Hall, as it were a million bees: frantic but unavailing efforts to produce a sound from the dinner bell: a classic remark from the instructor: the terrible uncertainty of the ancient cinema projector: the efficiency of the School Shop: the happy abandon of Camp: the confused murmur of diving and laughter in the outdoor baths: the "College dogs". A timely word of encouragement or appreciation: the sense of security created by true friendship: sympathy: the songs of the birds, and especially that of the skylark: cool freshness in the air after a storm: the flowers by the Shop, and the hospitable Jungle: shadows, cast by the setting sun, lazily climbing the Memorial Buildings: the joy of a homecoming. The satisfaction of something achieved.

Kendall had outlasted almost all of his predecessors, almost all of his initial governors, and most of the teachers he had inherited. He had also, as the *Chronicle* remarked, 'outstayed three architects and 3,000 boys – three fifths of the total roll of the School – and he leaves with us a memorial in material prosperity and human personality which entitles him to an honoured place among English headmasters'. Alongside the army of devotees of 'the porp' [porpoise] or 'the old cock' or 'the old man' there were always critics, especially of the second half of his reign. For all his dexterity in getting to know boys he could hardly be as close to them, at least when his energy had waned, as Simeon had been to a community of a hundred or so boys. To Anselm Kuhn, one of his sharpest critics, Kendall was a distant figure. 'The Warden at that time was HEK, a standing joke amongst most of the boys and known as "Ezz-pouf", an onomatopoeic allusion to his mode of speech. What contribution he made to the running of the School, other than conferring upon it the assumed respectability of an ordained clergyman, was never clear. I have no idea how old he was at that time, but with his rubicund complexion, his corpulence and his sedate, not to say lethargic gait, accompanied by his faithful dachshund, he was a widespread figure of fun. Anything less inspirational, one could hardly imagine.' Kendall loved relaxing and Kuhn is one of several OSE to remember that 'he would watch the swimming in the outdoor pool, his gaze visibly following the anatomy of us unclothed boys as we mounted the diving board and jumped'. One of the first acts of Warden Fisher was to introduce swimming trunks. Anselm ends: 'In the four years, I don't think I met (or spoke with him) once – what does that say? Maybe there were good things too, achieved by or in the time of HEK. But in my perception, the many positive things owed nothing to him.'

Another critic is Giles Hunt (Roll No. 3622), who left in 1945: 'Henry Kendall had got Teddies on the map. But he lacked the brio (is that the word?) that he must [once] have had: and from the little I saw of him I think, in retrospect, this was because he was so affected indeed by the constant news of Old Boys he had known being killed.' Most forthright of all is Antony Barrington-Brown: 'Many have spoken and written eulogistically of the Revd Henry Ewing Kendall, to the extent that he is widely remembered both as the founder of the School in the modern age and personally as a saint. This is so far from my own memories of him that I consider it necessary to voice a contrary opinion .... He had done great things in modernising the School – through his building projects and the development of the grounds – and one wonders how the School had managed to operate at all without him. He changed the emphasis from adult authoritarianism from above (including the Almighty's) to a more boy-centred ethos – but one which brought with it its own brand of authoritarianism and control .... Physically and in manner he was somewhat repulsive. He always wore a cassock which, though black from a distance, close up was seen to be smeared with cigar ash, food, and other stains of indiscernible origin. It gave the impression of never being washed. His paunch was restrained by a greasy black leather belt and his largely bald head revealed a somewhat flat top to his skull, over a broad face. A cigar was seldom from his lips – which was an advantage in presaging his approach.' Barrington-Brown too recounts the outdoor pool stories. 'He would pay particular attention to the stripes on boys who had been beaten (bruises lasted for several days, so there were always plenty on view), sometimes enquiring for what they had been earned. He had a seaside villa [actually a cottage] at Mevagissey (known to us as Mevagreasy) whither he invited a coterie of favourite boys (myself not among them, as you may guess) to stay in the summer. It was certainly the quickest path to preferment (sour grapes do I hear?) and some unexpected choices for school prefects.'

'The fact is,' writes Antony Lowe (Roll No. 3242), 'that some of my contemporaries were something less than enthusiastic in their adulation of Henry Kendall. Such a one was John Anderson [Roll No. 3020], and another was Arthur Banks.' John and Antony were both assistant editors of the *Chronicle*. Antony remembers how, being strapped for contributions, he composed a poem 'designed as a send-up of Henry Kendall'. The first letters of the lines, taken together, read 'The Old Cock'. The sequence was half concealed by the indentation of alternate lines, but came back from the printers without it. Leslie Styler, who supervised the magazine, spotted the acrostic at once, two hours before the magazine went to press. 'After sweating blood with the assistance of Mickey Styler we were able to come up with an appropriately sanitised version.'

A balanced view of Kendall comes from the old boy whom we heard criticizing the Warden's assumption of the role of a chaplain. He acknowledges Kendall's generosity in converting his £50 Scholarship into a £70 one. 'My family needed the extra to be able to send me to Teddies. I am grateful to Henry Kendall for all he did for me, but he DOMINATED the School and I was frightened of him – in a sense that I was not frightened by Bim Barff [his housemaster] whom I obeyed out of love and respect .... It was only after I left Teddies that I began to see HEK in a more mature light. As a headmaster he had a wonderful sense of vision for the School. For this I thank him.' He offers, tentatively, an interesting psychological judgement. 'His basic fault, I believe, was lack of self-confidence, and, like many such, he sought to remedy it by domineering.'

Kendall is one of four men discussed by George Mallaby in his memoir of 1972, *Each in his Office: Studies of Men in Power*. The Warden, he remembered, was 'warmly encompassed in the embrace of fun and good fellowship .... He believed strongly in the public school ideal ... and he wanted his school to be the best. If you had asked him what he meant by "best" he would have brushed the question aside as rather silly and unnecessary ... he would have had recourse to some vague and mumbled definitions – "Best? Well, service, good fun, awfully brave and happy, help each other, no nonsense or pretence, natural, think only of good of school," each halting phrase preceded by a preclusive murmuring, consisting usually of a protracted letter E, and by a slight turning and shaking of his corpulent frame. The man was dedicated, single-minded, emotionally devoted .... In a very few years he had acquired immense power within the School, hardly ever disputed and never successfully, and a persuasive influence over his governing body, [which was] stimulated and captivated by his exuberant confidence and single-minded devotion.' The world of headmasters 'is a small world perhaps but within it they reign supreme and they exercise their absolute authority with complete assurance .... They can go ahead with their cherished schemes, the way is clear .... Kendall had the power and he liked it', and though 'he liked his fellow men more ... he did not give his power away ... reserving always to himself, in the last resort, the power of decision'.

One of Kendall's greatest admirers was Derek Henderson. He records idyllic days he spent at the cottage at Mevagissey as a boy and later as a master. In the 1920s, at the suggestion of Bayford Stone, Kendall had purchased the cottage for £125 plus £25 for its furniture. It was set in 'Beaks' Bay', the area of Devon and Cornwall where headmasters and other teachers got away from 'the shop' and lived cheaply near each other in the holidays. They walked and swam and played golf, and invited family and friends to stay. Some invited senior boys to join informal house parties. Derek describes the setting. 'It was an old fisherman's cottage, with a porch in which was always kept a large barrel of beer, one main room containing a large table (seating 12 with a squash) and few if any comfortable chairs, a small cubby-hole for HEK only – he wrote umpteen letters there, talking all the while. Janet Snow, his niece, was the power behind the throne and organised meals etc. Philip, her husband and a housemaster at Eton, was a great sailor and had a superior yacht.' Bridge was played every evening before and after supper. 'It was very nearly a sufficient reason for not being invited if you did not play Bridge. Imagine the scene. At least 12 to 16 people playing racing demon [a card game] – nobody excused. A bridge four consisting of HEK, the Bishop of Exeter, Philip Landon and Philip Snow [a friend of the Kendall family]. A lot of noise and a lot of whisky being consumed (on one occasion I was sent down to Mevagissey to replenish supplies – it got me off racing demon.'

Henderson remembers that Marion Gierlicki, a male Polish émigré who was factotum to six Wardens, served the food. The table was cleared, the Ideal boiler fed with coke and the open fire with logs. 'A huge fish pie or a turkey or a steak and kidney pie was brought in plate by plate. Slowly the bridge players joined, the noise awhile deafening. We all drank beer, and then there was the washing up which took an age. The ladies began to disappear, all within the house. One or two guests departed. The house next door, owned by Bayford Stone, was used by masters and some wives and the huts outside housed most of the boy visitors.' Sometimes

Henderson and Stanley Tackley fished for mackerel for breakfast. There were shopping expeditions by boat into Mevagissey, where Kendall was always known as 'HEK'. 'They also called him "Reverend", with a Cornish accent.' Then came huge picnics at local beauty spots. Often there were four boatloads and a car for the elderly. 'Everyone came to the picnic, be they headmasters, bishops, admirals or generals. All welcome. HEK was in complete charge. A fire was lit and sausages, chickens etc. cooked. If the fire was reluctant to burn, he used his old trilby to fan it, talking all the time and conspicuous in his appalling old clothes. A proper Cornish tea, splits, cream and raspberry jam and then the clear up and journey home. An evening very like day one.' Derek lists bishops and top brass officers whom Kendall drew to the cottage. 'The greatest occasion was one Sunday evening when there were 28 to supper. HEK went to take Evensong and came back with the vicar, his wife and two children. Janet blew a fuse but was brushed aside and somehow 32 ate and were filled.'

Henderson remembers a lot of walking, as well as energetic beach games, which were followed by more cream teas on the walk home where that beer barrel awaited in the porch. Visits to pubs were not encouraged, perhaps on moral grounds or perhaps because Kendall's writ did not run in them. Golf was played locally, or Kendall would organize a trip to play at St Enodoc, usually with Stewart Pether, Philip Snow and Derek himself. There they would call on Joc Lynam, the legendary headmaster of the Dragon School. 'One or two gins were consumed with Joc.' There was frequent sailing in Philip Snow's boat, which was always full. Katie Kendall had a boat too and Derek remembers having 'the greatest sail of my life' in it. Also in the boat was 'Tim' Fisher (Richard Temple Fisher, Roll No. 3823), who arrived at the school in 1943. He was the youngest son of Archbishop Geoffrey Fisher and a brother of Kendall's successor Frank. Kendall knew all the Fisher family well. The family of the archbishop's wife, the Formans, which supplied a dynasty of Repton masters, were distantly related to the Kendalls.

Another of the Fisher brothers to visit Mevagissey was Charles, who presumed to organize a rock-climbing party. 'HEK was not amused. He let his views be known to Charles who left early next day. HEK was in charge: he arranged the entertainment for the party. Charles had caused a considerable upset. Such a pity because in my humble opinion Charles was a really lovely man.' Sometimes boys wondered why they had been invited to Mevagissey. 'They seemed such nondescript and characterless boys. At the end of the fortnight one knew why they had come. One of the really lovely things about HEK was his ability to find out the good qualities in people and to use these to conquer their other characteristics. In my humble opinion,' concludes Henderson, 'he was a very great headmaster.'

Following the announcement in February 1953 of Kendall's forthcoming retirement, five governors met to produce a shortlist of possible successors. The sub-committee of Mortimer, Emden, Andrew Gibbs, Philip Landon and Graham Cooper were all devoted to Kendall, who might as well have been in the room during their deliberations. Kendall wrote: 'Some of the Governors, in their lighter moments, used to suggest that I had something to do with their election. I should like to think that there was a modicum of truth in this because of the wisdom they have shown in the choice of Frank Fisher as my successor.' There were five short-listed candidates but there cannot have been much doubt that the 35-year-old Francis Forman Fisher – a year younger than Kendall on his own appointment – would become the seventh Warden of St Edward's.

35

THE NEW BROOM

Robin Ball (Roll No. 4301) was Senior Prefect on Frank Fisher's arrival. Writing home, he described a lunch party given by the Warden for his prefects. 'He seemed perfectly at home and soon made known his confidence in us and the school.' 'Confidence' is a hallmark of Fisher's Wardenship. Outwardly, at least, he exuded it. Robin wrote: 'We are starting dancing lessons for the senior boys who cannot dance – about thirty of us will be taught by a lady coming up from Oxford. Otherwise there has been nothing new or different to our life here yet.' In January 1955 the *Chronicle* reported an end-of-term Prefects' dance in the Warden's House. 'From all accounts this was a tremendous success. We are somewhat astounded at the rapidity with which the Warden has found out all the answers – too quickly, one senior boy was heard to say.' The holding of the dance was a clever initiative, attention-catching and suggestive of moving with the times yet without confrontational change. Fisher was full of ideas, born not of intellectual abstraction – he was no academic – but of intuition and of thirty-five years of practical experience in male environments: Repton, the army, a POW camp, and Cambridge where, in a shortened wartime course, he had secured a third-class degree in History. He felt he understood institutions and knew where they should be heading. He was to prove right about many things, only failing, as did most of his contemporaries, to appreciate the scale and force of the social revolution that was changing the young. In 1954, two years before 'Rock Around the Clock', it was barely visible, and its extent was not fully evident even when he left for Wellington in 1966. The steps the boys learned at classes and performed at the dance, where Fisher reportedly stood near a light switch to prevent the opportunities of darkness, would soon be superannuated by jive and rock 'n' roll.

Fisher revered his father, Archbishop Geoffrey Fisher, formerly Headmaster of Repton. At first sight Geoffrey looks a dyed-in-the-wool conservative. Roald Dahl blighted the archbishop's reputation by accounts of the beatings he had administered at Repton. Coming from a rural vicarage in Leicestershire Geoffrey

Fisher spent much of his life in boarding schools and episcopal palaces, yet he was taken up by the Christian Socialist headmaster and archbishop, William Temple, whom he succeeded at Repton. Were they the last two headmasters to become primates? Geoffrey allowed Victor Gollancz to teach far from conservative ideas at Repton, and permitted boys to read Alec Waugh's *Loom of Youth*. As a bishop he took an active interest in working-class conditions and in economic distress, even though he had no direct experience of them. He had three Firsts but believed he would have more to offer as an organizer and administrator than as a professor. As archbishop he carried out the first comprehensive review of canon law since 1604 and led the way in ecumenical initiatives. He was active in the World Council of Churches and made the first real contacts between the Anglican Church and the Papacy in modern times. For all his air of rigorous efficiency he had an easy informality and humour, a gift for self-deprecation, and a captivating approachability. Frank inherited these qualities. The Fishers were not 'silver spoon' conservatives: they were products of the manse and the world of the schoolroom, with a strong sense of public duty and social obligation.

Desmond Hill tartly describes 'the indefatigable and immaculate miniature dynamo that was their new Warden'. With his fiercely starched collars and slickly combed hair – which, together with his way of sliding his fingers but not thumbs into the side pockets of his jacket when he addressed assemblies of boys, perhaps explains his nickname, 'Sid', a name with spiv connotations at the time – he was a formidable physical presence, wholly in command of any gathering he held or attended. He handled the Governors as authoritatively as Kendall had done, though in a quite different style. Kendall's reports to the Governing Body had been short, often scarcely filling one side of foolscap and conveying as little as possible. He had no time for formalities: personal influence and character and decision-making were what mattered to him. Fisher's reports were short too, but unlike Kendall's were crisp and concrete. He thought in bullet points and 'boxes'; his agenda was clear-cut; his decisions unambiguous. His reports, which were bases for discussion, rarely exceeded two to three sides of foolscap. His first, in October 1954, runs thus:

1. Numbers in the School (479).
2. Academic (GCE results summarised: numbers in the VI Form taking entrance scholarships to university: possible reallocation of money for Entrance Scholarships).
3. Staffing (2 new appointments to ratio of 1 to 15 masters to boys: B. G. Segar's retirement: Eardley's term away: Gauntlett retires from Segar's: Toynbee to get a rise).
4. The Memorial Library is open.
5. Musical instruments to incur a hire charge.
6. February 1955 will see a School Inspection.
7. The Senior Prefect is praised.
8. The CCF attended camp and the BBC recorded a chapel service.
9. The School's health is good.
10. The Warden thanks the governors for his carpets and curtains.

The report is an epitome of swift perception and action on Fisher's part. He had spotted a weakness in the Entrance Scholarship system. He had effectively removed one of his most elderly teachers, B. G. Segar, and had retired another two, Gauntlett and Eardley, from their Houses, where they would be replaced by Armstrong in Apsley and Veitch in Segar's. There were initiatives large and small. A small one was the addition of an 'extra' to the school bill for music. A large one was Fisher's decision to arrange for a major Inspection to be held early in his second term. In January 1955 he strengthened his hold by securing the Governors' permission to appoint 'any Assistant Master to the office of Second Master or Housemaster and to determine the period of any such appointments'.

His reports were supplemented with papers of equal incisiveness and directness. Those of October 1954 tackle the number and value of the entrance scholarships and bursaries, the registration and entrance fees, the Library Grant and the stocking of the new Memorial Library. Further advances followed in the remainder of his first year. He investigated the practices of other schools in giving awards and in spending on books; he revised the rules of the school's Scholarships so that day boys might compete for all of them; and he raised the prestige of the Music and Choral Awards. A new house-purchasing policy for married staff resulted in the acquisition of 214 Woodstock Road for £3,750 in June 1955. Fisher submitted a study comparing the Burnham scale of pay for teachers in state schools with the scale at St Edward's. Aided by the careful bursar Hubert Beales he appraised the school's indebtedness (the Barclay's Bank loan stood at £22,500), worked out that the farm trading profit stood at £627, discovered that the school buildings were grossly under-insured against fire, and diverted £1,500 of the School Shop profits from games to the new Library, whose book grant he doubled. He helped negotiate the purchase of a refurbished Staines plate dish-washing machine for the kitchens, which would have cost £1,000 new; the acquisition saved the wages of £338, plus their keep, of two pantry staff. He ended evening dish-washing by boys, which had survived the end of the war. His attention to detail was as impressive as the cogency of his policies. He would interest himself in the polishing of tables in Hall and in details of redecoration. The Governors supported his initiatives as readily as Kendall's. Andrew Gibbs, benefactor and frequent creditor of the school, was a key figure, not least as Chairman of the General Purposes Committee, the body most closely involved in the running of the school and especially in its financial affairs. Important too was the eminent libel lawyer Peter Carter-Ruck (Roll No. 2367), a governor from 1951 to 1980, who supplied regular legal advice to the bursar and to his fellow governors. His son Brian (Roll No. 5304) would die in a sailing accident in 1973 aged 30.

A paper Fisher wrote for the Governors in January 1955, running to two sides of foolscap, was an exhaustive list of the changes to the buildings and grounds that had been effected since 1937. It ranged from new buildings and house purchases to new equipment for the vegetable kitchen and the renewal of lawnmowers. The Governors, as he had wanted, responded by instructing him to 'prepare a report on the further development of the buildings of the School'. The meeting of the General Purposes Committee of May 1955 was extended to two days so that he could guide the Governors round the school's 110 acres. For Fisher saw scope for a new phase of building. He craved a purpose-built Music School, a new House, and a spanking new science extension. But he had to be patient. It was not merely that planning regulations remained restrictive; as so often, the demands for refurbishments or adaptations of existing buildings took priority. It was estimated that the refitting of the changing rooms would cost £3,000, a gym floor over the indoor baths £2,000. School House and the Masters' Common Room needed makeovers estimated at £10,000. The building of a hut for £1,500, to serve as an additional laboratory, was contemplated. When Stewart Pether was appointed to succeed Barff as Housemaster of Field House in 1957, £4,500 had to be paid for larger family accommodation. An extension of the Chapel gallery cost £1,200. Also needed was a refurbished heating plant at £5,500. In his first seven years Fisher had to spend £80,000 on additions to and adaptations of existing buildings.

Still, the Tories were in power and numbers were holding up, so perhaps a new phase of architectural expansion need not be long delayed. Alas, the one recent building, the Memorial Library (designed by the firm Dodd and Stevens), was too small – or would have been if boys had been induced to use it. There was no professional librarian. Boys were charged a paltry shilling a term for new purchases, though the charge constituted another of those irritating extras on the termly bill. Even when Fisher raised the grant to £150 it lagged behind Radley's £180, Stowe's £240 and Rugby's £225. The tiny pottery facility in the art room above the Library indicated the status of the activity as a hobby or handicraft rather than as a feature of visual education. The Library did house the handsome Hugh Easton window, which was installed in 1955 to commemorate the RAF heroes of the war, though later it would be moved into the Old Library beneath Big School. It portrays a young RAF pilot gazing skyward with hope and resolution. No one now remembers that the building was a memorial to the fallen of the Second World War, or Tilly's to those of the First.

Fisher's plans were always based on a careful knowledge of the independent sector of education. He saw that society at large was becoming more fluid and meritocratic, more respectful of individual advance or attainment than of collective values. The Public Schools, he sensed, might need to temper the harshness of their environments. He knew that parents, especially mothers, were beginning to balk at the practices of fagging and beating. Academic improvement would be necessary, too. Degree courses were becoming less of a playground for the well-off, more a necessary qualification which state grants were opening to a wider constituency. More and more products of Grammar Schools and the new Direct Grant Schools were competing with Public School boys both for university entrance and in the job market. Fisher was probably aware of the *Survey of Social Conditions* conducted by A. M. Carr-Saunders, D. C. Jones and C. A. Moser that was published in 1958. It showed that 94% of leavers from Direct Grant Schools and 84% from Maintained Grammar Schools were staying on at school at 16, and that the proportions were rising. Only 45% stayed on from Public Schools until the age of 17 or 18. Many of these schools had weaker sixth forms than that of St Edward's, where 67% stayed on into the Upper Sixth (the post A-level forms) in 1957–58 and 70% in 1958–59. Even so, Fisher knew that the academic standards at St Edward's would have to rise. Athletic distinction might still impress some Oxbridge dons, but A-level marks would count for much more. At 'redbrick' universities they would be almost the sole criterion of admission. In any case was it right for so much time and energy to be devoted to games? Would not the school's societies, if properly nourished, foster communication skills and personal interests? Each boy, Fisher would tell them, needed an 'enthusiasm', in whichever of the many activities available in school life he found it. Could St Edward's, which had a long musical tradition, continue to depend on the few practice rooms attached to Tilly's? Ought not art to be given the status of a GCE subject? Ought not drama to move with the times?

One of Fisher's most important papers for the Governors was submitted in November 1956. Soon, he wrote, 'I would like to present a full development plan.' For the moment he offered a strikingly wide-ranging set of interim proposals. He observed that the Chapel, the changing-room, the dining hall and the School Shop were all too small, as was Big School whenever there were visitors. The masters' accommodation was insufficient and there were too many huts serving as classrooms. A building was needed for music. In the Houses day rooms were overcrowded and there was a lack of games rooms and reading rooms. To this last problem Fisher proposed a bold solution. Because the necessary improvements to School House would make it impracticable for both the Houses that occupied it to remain there, a new one would be built across the road near to Corfe House. Ideally, indeed, two new Houses would be built there. On another front Fisher achieved a coup in the housing of the science teaching. Having initially been content to propose a new laboratory hut, he secured a grant of £17,500 from the Industrial Fund for the Advancement of Scientific Education in Schools. It paid for four new science labs, which were completed by January 1958, before rising building costs, which would impair the other building plans, had taken hold. The incongruous plaque of St Edward on horseback was added in 1959.

There were nonetheless financial impediments to ambitious

expansion. Beales' bursar's reports were ominous. In October 1955 he noted the consequences of inflation. In the past year 'the cost of catering has increased very heavily', to £22,485, 'and it appears that a further increase of some £2,000 in expenditure is to be expected this year'. Over the last twelve months the cost of milk had risen by nearly 20%, that of beef by 25%. The daily budget for feeding each boy had risen in the past year from 2s. 9¼d to 3s. 1¾d a day. The total bill for provisions had risen by £1,835. Salaries and pensions were a constant headache. The salaries bill had risen by £1,676, other wages by £1,280.

There had been no serious consideration of the structure of teachers' salaries at St Edward's since the war, despite the setting up in 1945 of the Burnham Committee, which annually fixed teachers' salaries in the state sector. Fisher analysed the problem in a paper for the Governors in December 1955. Burnham rates, he warned, posed a serious challenge to Public Schools, for they had got ahead of Public School salaries. Yet pay increases would mean fee rises, and low fees had been the keystone of Kendall's success. Fees, which stood at £275, had increased by about 50% since before the war, but increases at comparable schools had been higher. Repton's had doubled and were now £321. Fisher might be tempted towards a similar course, but if so, how would parents respond?

In his eyes the need to raise salaries was paramount. The master at a Public School, he reckoned, put in more hours of work over the year than his counterpart in the maintained sector. He usually retired at 60, whereas his counterpart worked until 65. True he had valuable perquisites. He might have free lodging and a number of free meals and pay no taxes on rents and no rates. He might have free or subsidized schooling for his children. These privileges, Fisher acknowledged, must be taken into account. But Burnham had developed a system of Special Responsibility Allowances (SRA), scarcely known in Public Schools except to housemasters, though at St Edward's annual increments, and supplements for having undertaken teacher training (£18) or been a graduate (£60, or £90 if the degree was a strong one), were paid. Fisher calculated that to receive parity a master at St Edward's would need to start on £687, rather than the present £582, though he recognized that there should be reductions for men living in school accommodation. At the same time extra payments equivalent to Special Responsibility Allowances should be paid to men running the CCF and the laboratories, to the chaplain, the Secretary of the OSE, the masters in charge of the timetable and the *Chronicle*, and maybe to all heads of department. The complexity as well as the cost of such arrangements would be daunting. Then there were the costs and administrative burdens of pensions. There were thoughts of a health insurance scheme too.

A new salary structure embodying Fisher's recommendations went through. The salary of a new teacher would be £636, a little below the Burnham equivalent of £651 – a useful point to make to parents ready to protest that money had been thrown away on greedy teachers. Fisher had learned that three other Public Schools were paying £603, £630 and £650 respectively. Money was certainly not thrown away on domestic staff. The bursar, who had worked at the school since 1946, was paid only £576 p.a. He ran the finances with an accountant, Howard White, who served from 1930 to 1957, and with three secretaries who each earned £6 a week. Walter Dunn, after 26 years in the labs, earned £8 6s. a week, and the notoriously grumpy porter, Stan Barnes, £8 7s. 6d after 29 years. Osborne, the chef, of 14 years' service, earned £9 10s., but had to pay for his own meals. Bill Honey, who had served in the school's gardens and greenhouse for 51 years except for the interruption of the First World War, earned £6 12s., as did the much-lampooned gardener Geoffrey Cornelius. These rates could not last. It was becoming harder to run the domestic side of the school on a basis of cosy deference. The domestic Oxford wage market was picking up, and in October 1955 there were only 1,373 job vacancies in the city. But even after increases achieved by Fisher, ranging from 5s. to 15s., the wages at St Edward's were below those of Radley.

The inevitable fee increases came. In September 1956 a boarder's fees rose by £30 a year to £305, a day boy's by £18 to £180. Other schools still charged more. In 1956 the boarding fee was £410 at Harrow, £402 at Stowe, £375 at Oundle, Wellington and Marlborough, £336 at Radley. Generally, however, the Woodard schools were in the same range as St Edward's. Their leading school, Lancing, charged £316. The problems of inflation and national wage scales would persist, placing continuous pressure on the level of fees. Fisher's adroit handling of the issue was not the least of his achievements. By 1961 the boarding fee stood at £405. Fisher was sympathetic to requests for fee reductions and managed to increase the value of scholarships. Bursaries for the sons of clergy still amounted to 25% of fees and there were scholarships for the sons of serving officers. Scholarships and bursaries accounted for £11,000 of the school's annual income. The Barclay's Bank scholarship scheme continued to develop.

In 1955 another financial challenge arose. The school approached Barclay's for a loan of £30,000 so that work could start on the building programme, after which there would be some sort of development appeal to meet its costs. But the government's attempts to curb inflation produced a 'credit squeeze', and for the time being Barclay's would only lend £5,000. The school had £8,000 in hand to proceed with the refurbishment of the changing-rooms and the indoor bath and for the conversion of the heating, but other plans would have to wait at least until 1957. Still, the physical improvements and the science labs were visible signs of Fisher's swift impact. He was already known as a man who got things done.

Even though the Labour Party was out of office, headmasters were alarmed by its discussion document of 1956 *Towards Equality* and by a speech to the Headmasters' Conference by Michael Stewart, the party's shadow Education Minister. In a paper to the Governors in the autumn of 1955 Fisher declared that 'the whole future of the Public Schools is clearly at stake, and it is practically certain that a Socialist government would take some steps to alter their status'. Though events would prove him wrong, the threat seemed real enough. The schools, Fisher told the Governors, should not stand idly by. They should answer back. Here as elsewhere he was looking ahead. The Headmasters' Conference (HMC) was not yet a political pressure group. There was as yet no Independent Schools Information Service (ISIS). Regional associations of schools such as the Rugby Group had yet to acquire stature. Fisher would play a large part in the development of collective mechanisms among the Public Schools. For the moment he proposed that St Edward's should take a lead in stressing their role in the safeguarding of 'our religious life'; the virtues of educational independence; the right to refuse entry to pupils supported by the state; the national advantages of educating overseas pupils; and the benefits of the boarding system. The acceptance of boys from the maintained sector, Fisher argued, would make the Public Schools 'local instead of national schools'. If it had to happen, at least the schools should remain in control of the selection of pupils and of the teaching. He urged the Governors to take a stand on the right of parents to choose their children's schools, on the need for the independence of governing bodies, on the maintenance of a good standard of entry, on the preservation of the present staffing ratio, on the school's specifically Anglican worship, and on the Anglican influence in the classroom: all features that the threat to independence endangered. The controversy over the autonomy of the Public Schools would continue in the years ahead. What no one envisaged at this stage was the erosion of their independence on other fronts. The state of the 1950s did not impose fire doors, demand police checks on teachers, or lay down a National Curriculum, which a school ignored at its peril. Fisher planned for change, but neither he nor anyone else could foresee its extent.

36

WARDEN FISHER'S SCHOOL

THE report of the Inspection Fisher arranged in 1955 had some critical comments. Academic qualifications were described as 'satisfactory rather than distinguished ... few [teachers] have had professional training ... and only a minority have experience of teaching in other schools .... There is reason to think that as things are the present staff is failing to achieve the full power of which it is capable.' The report remarked on an unimpressive pupil–teacher ratio and observed that teachers had to work exceptionally hard and to tackle subjects outside their specialisms. It complained that expenditure on the teaching staff 'has not risen at the same rate as other costs'. Exam results improved quickly under Fisher, but there was far to go. In 1958, 79 boys took A levels, but 38 of them sat only two subjects and 14 just one. Of the subjects taken, 75.7% were passed. Eighty-seven boys sat O levels, but only 18 passed in all subjects. These figures stand roughly in the middle of those of schools of St Edward's type, but all such schools would need to do better in the face of the competition from Grammar Schools and Direct Grant Schools. The school, Fisher argued, needed more Entrance Scholarships to attract clever boys. There was still less cause for cheer in 1959, when Fisher told the Governors that the A-level results were 'a bit down on 1958'. Maths and Physics had improved at A level, but at O level 'Maths was easily our worst subject .... O-level History results were disappointing', as were the History and Biology results at A level. And 'we have not won a great number of Open Awards at Oxford and Cambridge: 14 in the last four years'. In 1960, fourteen boys were put in for Oxford and Cambridge Scholarship examinations but only four awards were gained.

One trouble was that the brightest boys, who took O level at 14 and A level at 16, had no exams to work for other than the rarefied S [scholarship] level. Michael Fairclough (Roll No. 5574) was just 13 when he entered Sing's in Christmas Term 1959 as a Scholar from The Leas at Hoylake. He was placed immediately in Va, the top O-level form. After A level, he recalls, 'the wheels began to come off'. The school had expected him to progress through his fourth year and sit for a university award in his fifth.

'I "rebelled" and wasted my fourth year (although I successfully sat one S-level subject and another A-level subject in a close but different area of science from my first batch of A-levels). Worse, when I was prevailed upon to go back for the all-important fifth year, I got through the first term, but was such a bad influence that negotiations between my father and Warden Fisher resulted in me getting my way and leaving school aged 17 years and 15 weeks.' He promptly went to New Zealand, where he married before returning to take a degree at Nottingham. Though Michael would have a successful career as an accountant in Australia, he regretted the outcome of his time at St Edwards's.

'Looking back I was a complete idiot of course, to have wasted that time and talent. I always think that my life would have been so different if I had understood what was going on for me and had been able to allow myself to be "processed" by the "plan" that the school had for me, although it's fair criticism to say that the school was not able to "sell" the benefits of the "plan" effectively to me .... I have enjoyed my life as it has turned out so far, so I am not complaining except for the waste of talent!... If [on my arrival] I had been put into the Upper Shells [the second stream, which took O level at 15] I would no doubt have found the academic work far easier, but would possibly have lasted the distance better in a personal development sense and might still have been able to have a reasonable shot at the Oxbridge entrance exams, albeit not perhaps at scholar level, in my fifth year.'

The few teachers who strove to foster a work ethic favoured the existing system, which produced the rapid promotion of able boys. A new generation of teachers would end it, but only after a struggle. The Michaelmas Term of 1962 was the first time that Scholars and Exhibitioners did not go straight into Va. Until then boys who, like Michael Fairclough, took O levels in their first year covered a narrow range of subjects. Jeremy Griggs (Roll No. 5472), a Scholar who entered at Fifth Form level in 1958, was taught no History, Geography or Science in his first year, when Maths, French, English, Latin and Greek were his main diet. He did study some German and Science in his second year but his work in these subjects was not examined. He spent four years in the prestigious Classical Sixth. At 16 he took A levels in Latin, Greek and Ancient History. He sat them again, with different set books and a different period of Ancient History, the next year. Although he always passed, he never achieved a distinction. In the fifth year came the Oxbridge entry exams. For this he was taught

Classics by Pat Brims (whom he remembers as 'erudite but dry'), his housemaster John Armstrong, and Mervyn Evans. As they had the cleverest boys to work with they achieved excellent results, but Jeremy reflects, 'There are those who look back on their time at school and point to a particular teacher who inspired them. I cannot say that was ever my lot during my time at Teddies.' Of the four Classicists in his year, three went on to study Law and one Theology. Jeremy proceeded to Magdalene College, Cambridge and became a successful barrister.

Fisher was set on the school's academic improvement. He was no more an intellectual or aesthete than Kendall. When he moved into the Warden's lodgings a slur was spread that he had sent out for sets of Dickens and the Waverley Novels to fill his yawning bookshelves. But he knew where the wind was blowing and understood that the school must bend to it. He did not want an academic hothouse. In his Gaudy speech of 1961 he told parents that the Sixth Forms of the state schools with which St Edward's must compete spent most of their time in the classroom, though they spent less of it than he supposed. If St Edward's followed suit:

> this would mean removing all non-specialist subjects from the timetable, refusing to allow boys to hold positions of authority, play games or indulge in activities out of school .... But this is not education. We believe, and I hope that you do also, that the great strength of a school such as this is that we seek to provide education in the fullest sense – the development of character, personality, responsibility and a real sense of values as well as training the mind. We cannot depart from these principles.

Nonetheless, academic priorities were asserting themselves. In 1964 around half the boy population – 250 out of 498 – were engaged in post O-level work. Of the 105 boys joining St Edward's in the school year 1959–60, 93 took A levels while at school and two more later at technical colleges. Five others left early for jobs but were judged equipped for A-level work, had they stayed. Only five were thought unequal to it. All A-level subjects increased their numbers markedly except Classics, Maths and Modern Languages. English Literature, which had barely existed as an A-level subject before the 1950s, had twenty-five sixth-formers by 1964. Intellectual life was being accorded a new respect. Membership of the Upper Sixth was acquiring an esteem among the boys comparable to that carried by colours in sport.

Fisher improved the teacher–pupil ratio. It had declined from

1:14½ in 1946 to 1:16 in Kendall's last year. Under Fisher, who enlarged the total of the teaching staff from 31 in 1954 to 41 in 1966, the ratio increased to 1:12¾. As at other schools, the intellectual quality of the staff rose. No longer would a master be appointed to teach only or mainly in the lower forms. Bill Eardley, Bim Barff and Stanley Tackley had been among the last. The appointment of a succession of young masters was key to a range of changes made by Fisher, who wanted to bring in men of his own generation and outlook. He remembered how, when he and eighteen other ex-soldiers returned to Repton after the war, 'we were superimposed upon a group of ineffective wartime appointments and residue of pre-war men, all of whom retained both the attitudes and lifestyle of the Thirties. Our contribution was dramatic. We swept away many of the old-fashioned attitudes that we found unattractive, such as power in the hands of senior boys, the cloistered and introverted life of the school, the sheer squalor of much of the accommodation, the old-fashioned and inefficient arrangements.' He wanted to sweep away much at St Edward's too.

On his arrival 10 of the 32 members of staff had been appointed no later than 1927. He handled the retirements of his older masters skilfully. Macnamara was given work in the new Library, Gauntlett the editorship of the new *Roll* and a place on the Centenary Committee, McMichael and Eardley some occasional teaching. Whitrow and Yorke both left, with their careers amply extolled. Fisher made two important appointments in his first term. Of the previous Wardens all except Sing had been clergymen. As a layman Fisher needed a chaplain, who would be the school's first. He appointed Robert Holtby, an immensely clever historian with a real interest in education, who headed a strong field. The choice maintained the school's ecclesiological tradition, for Holtby was a High Churchman, as the Fishers were not. He was an inspiring teacher who led groups of boys to visit the run-down centre of Middlesbrough. The Inspectors of 1955 praised him for the innovative syllabus he had already created for Divinity classes. When Holtby left in 1958 to become the Diocesan Director of Education in Carlisle he was succeeded by Paul Drake, a less charismatic figure but a man of arresting piety and sincerity who, like Holtby, had a first-class degree and who sought to continue Holtby's work. Drake took boys to St Peter's, Spring Hill, and to Birmingham, and even to the French ecumenical centre at Taizé. Under Holtby and Drake, sermons, often by academic clergy, acquired the instructional character that Kenneth Menzies had unavailingly wanted from them. The distinguished high churchmen Eric Mascall, John Fenton (Roll No. 3002) and Norman Sykes came to preach. So did the future Archbishop of Canterbury Robert Runcie. So did Eric James, who would become the first Vice-Chancellor of the University of York. Lenten courses were led by distinguished visiting clergy who lived in the school for a week. A Chapel Committee, containing some sacristans and representatives of each House, was formed in the Michaelmas Term of 1965 to discuss Chapel policy, services and community service. It was an early initiative in pupil consultation. Courses of sermons were often shaped around a theme, a policy advocated all those years ago by Menzies.

These changes took place against a background of declining religious commitment among the boys. The annual number of boys receiving Confirmation, a practice that could owe more to social convention than devotional zeal, is not a reliable test of faith. Yet a change of spirit is reflected in the contrast between an average in the eighties during the 1950s and the figure of 51 in 1965, and more strongly in the modest proportion of confirmed boys who attended the communion services on Sunday mornings in the 1960s.

Fisher's second appointment was Peter 'Bubbles' Corlett. He bubbled with a variety of enthusiasms, even crazes. A post-war version of an old type, the Public School all-rounder, he moved, always with accomplishment, from flying to music to bell-ringing to computing to motorbikes. His zest took the young by storm. I first met him as he entered the Common Room like a whirlwind in September 1962, having just landed his Chipmunk at Kidlington Airport on a return flight from Denmark, where he had been staying with a pupil and his family. In 1955 came another very influential appointment, Peter Whitehouse. A first-class musician, the youngest Fellow of the Royal College of Organists on record, he was an invigorating presence in the Music Department in Manning's last years and would give sterling support to succeeding Directors of Music. An irreverent and very funny man, his humour ranging from the self-deprecating to the lewd, he was a wonderfully enlivening force in the Common Room of the 1960s and was loved by many pupils.

Fisher appointed a succession of highly qualified teachers in the later 1950s and early 1960s. Paul Drake, David Tawney, Fred Pargeter and I all had first-class degrees or doctorates or both.

John Todd, Colin Pedley and Tony Snell were charismatic and highly intelligent figures. Others, appointed for their prowess in games as much as for their intellect, were no slouches in the classroom: Myles Arkell, John Vernon, Cameron Cochrane, Jim McGowan, Roger Lawrence, Kerry Lyons, David Tinsley, Miles Peregrine, Bob Montgomerie and Robin Alden (Roll No. 4084), and the later arrivals Mike Lewis and David Howorth. Most of Fisher's appointments remained at St Edward's to provide its next generation of leaders or went on to other schools, some of them to headmasterships. In a short period Fisher had created a Common Room that would bear comparison with any in the country.

Three of those appointments may be selected, a little arbitrarily, for further attention. David Tinsley, who came in 1959, was the kind of young teacher Fisher judged the school to need, even though he had been at a maintained grammar school whereas most of the staff were ex-Public-School boys. A capable mathematician when they were few and far between in classrooms, Tinsley also offered hands-on technical skills and coached rowing. He brought talent and enthusiasm to all he did and began to transform the Maths teaching. Encouraged by Fisher, he took delivery of the first computer in the world specially designed for schools, though it arrived in the term after Fisher had left. Made by IBM, with a TV screen as a monitor and a domestic tape recorder as a backup store (both innovations), it had a touch keyboard and a magnetic core memory of just 4,000 bytes. Soon boys were using it to program complex routines and were astounding IBM engineers by the complexity of the problems they solved. Ten more such computers were quickly acquired by schools across the south of England. Several pupils chose Computer Studies at university as a result, and went on to successful careers in industry. With Corlett, Tinsley produced one of the earliest books on the teaching of Maths with computers. He left in 1970 and proceeded to hold distinguished posts in the worlds of computer technology and educational administration. It was said that, not having been to boarding school, he would never have been offered a House.

Another arrival in 1959 was David Tawney, who dominated the sciences until he left in 1967. He and his wife Jill had taught at the Diocesan Secondary School in Mauritius. He had a First from Cambridge, though Fisher may have been as much attracted by the couple's religious commitment as by David's scientific skills. The Tawneys were wheeled out to help entertain visiting preachers after evening chapel. Though there was a swing to Science in national education, to which Fisher was alert, the teaching at St Edward's had been held back, despite the efforts in Physics and Chemistry of Yorke and Gauntlett, who in their heyday had been good teachers. Tawney, a pioneer of the new Nuffield and Schools Council developments in science teaching, reinvigorated the teaching of Physics with the help of Peter Church, an outstanding classroom teacher, and of the young enthusiast Tony Snell, a man who also had exceptional musical and linguistic skills. Together they introduced 'Extra Labs', times when boys could be supervised for extra work or in pursuing scientific interests. Tawney also transformed the quality of the sets and lighting of plays, and he and Jill were the driving force of the earliest Common Room shows, an initiative that gave him useful credit in the Common Room where he was not universally popular, partly because of his open criticism of the emphasis on games. Finding the right man for the job – as he so often did – Fisher made him Head of Science when Church took over Cowell's from Brims in 1964. Tawney writes of the Warden: 'While I disagreed with much of what he did, I found him highly professional in never holding educational disagreements against me and always being very pleasant.' Tawney went on to Keele University and further successes.

John Todd was a temporary appointment in History in 1957 and became a permanent one in 1958. In 1961 he succeeded Philip Whitrow as Head of Department. A clever but insecure Wykehamist and Scholar of New College, Oxford, he had joined the Intelligence Corps for his National Service and worked in Vienna, a city with which he fell in love and to which he would lead several rewardingly strenuous expeditions of boys and colleagues. He joined the diplomatic service but resigned in protest over the Suez adventure in 1956, and drifted into school-teaching when he might have preferred to be a don. Devoted to his pupils, he insisted that every member of the Upper Sixth should have an individual hour-long tutorial each week, an arduous regime as I, who had to share the work with him, was to discover. Like me, he was not a man for the games field. He could be prickly and was viewed with some reservations by his colleagues. But every morning at break they would see him putting the finishing touches to his preparations for class, where he dazzled the abler pupils with the authoritative lectures he delivered in famously elegant and orotund sentences that were affectionately mocked by the boys:

> I find it exceedingly odd
> That that eminent pedagogue Todd
> Should if you please
> Spell his name with two 'd's
> Whereas one is sufficient for God.

Time brought its stresses, and in 1983 he gave up teaching to become librarian. He masterminded the arrangement and running of the Library on its transfer to Big School in 1976.

The rise in academic standards took place against a background of lively intellectual exchanges in the outside world. The word 'intellectual' came into common use, sometimes as a badge, sometimes as a slur. The status of science was a charged topic after the publication of C. P. Snow's famous Rede Lecture of 1959 'The Two Cultures', the subject of a talk by Mervyn Evans at the Upper School Discussion Group in 1961. Snow complained of the split between the humanities and sciences and of the ignorance of ostensibly educated people about science, even though it was bringing them material prosperity and improved health. A derisive reply from the Cambridge Eng. Lit. don F. R. Leavis provoked a fierce controversy. Academics of Leavis's persuasion associated science with materialism and philistinism. Scientists regarded literary criticism, which in Leavis's hands became something like a religious cult, as vacuous and at best inexact. Controversies raged in the sciences, which were shaken by 'Big Bang' and 'Steady State' theories, and in history, which was animated by debates over the 'rise of the gentry' or the links between Protestantism and capitalism. The new social sciences burgeoned, despite objections to their methods by philosophers. They would be taken up in the universities which were created in the era of the Robbins Report of 1963, and whose arrival raised new questions about the purposes of a university, and about what should be taught in them and how. Sociology became a catchword, alternately hailed and derided. Economics, thriving on the state's acceptance of Keynesian expansionism, rode high.

Theology was being transformed by Paul Tillich, whose three-volume *Systematic Theology*, published in 1951–63, explained faith as a matter of 'ultimate concern' rather than of belief in a personal God. Such views were popularized by Bishop John Robinson, whose *Honest to God*, published in 1963, was anathematized by the Warden's father. Yet the Warden himself – perhaps more from a desire to awaken intellectual life than from any theological sympathy – encouraged boys to read the book. In the Summer Term of 1963 extracts from *Honest to God* were read out by puzzled prefects at House Prayers in Cowell's, and Fisher allowed an article making teasing reference to his indulgence of the new theology to appear in a recently founded magazine, *The Martyr*, where boys were granted a new if limited degree of literary licence. Behind the regimented exterior of his regime Fisher was cautiously permitting wayward spirits to find roles for themselves.

The march of science was saluted by the *Chronicle* in January 1958, but with reservations and anxieties. 'During the last term two important events happened; one in the world's history, one in the School's. We refer, of course, to the Sputnik and the [completion of the] new Science Block. These two symbolise the predominance of science in the modern world. Science is important. Scientists are vital.' The editorial noted approvingly the Warden's recent decision to require all boys to study Science to O-level standard. However,

> some are talking of education in science to the exclusion of all other subjects. This we regard as most dangerous .... A properly balanced and broad-minded man is worth more to the nation than a narrow-minded specialist. Of course there must be specialisation, but a narrow scientist is a bad scientist .... If the Humanities and the idea of beauty become eclipsed in this world, it will have a deadening effect on individual and national life and thought.

The editorial welcomed Fisher's recent introduction, as a counter to specialization, of a system of subsidiary subjects in the Sixth Form, a change assisted by his decision, early in his tenure, to squeeze an extra period of teaching into the timetable.

The teaching staff had to adjust to the new intellectual climate; they also needed to be versatile. By the earlier 1960s there was a range of General Studies courses for the Lower Sixth (Removes), some of them, including a History of Science course, enterprisingly novel in approach. On alternate Mondays a select group of boys were exempted from the hitherto sacrosanct Prep time to take part in a 'Removes Course', led by Pedley and me, which combined, with something of an elitist air, elements of literature, history, religion and philosophy. These initiatives were intended to extend pupils' knowledge beyond the A-level syllabus and to stimulate their minds by cross-curricular reflection. In the lecture room above the Memorial Library, Todd, Joe McPartlin and I offered what became known as 'The Europe Show', which brought the history, geography and economics of the Continent together. It made a mark. In 1964 Fisher followed other schools in introducing the Politics and Economics A level. I was appointed Head of Department of Economics, though I had only an A level in the subject. Whitehouse helped with the teaching of the subject while Brian Gale, a sharp-tongued lawyer who had been appointed in 1951, taught Politics.

When I decided to accept Frank Fisher's offer of a job in December 1961 for the following September, my tutor in Oxford looked a bit worried. 'Hmm,' he said. 'It's a very nice school but when they're not on their knees in chapel they're scrumming down on a field. I should give it no more than five years.' But I was delighted at the £875 that Fisher was by now able to offer. After all, my friend in ICI, with a coveted Science degree, earned only £1,000. The accommodation, a sitting room downstairs and a bedroom upstairs in 214 Woodstock Road, a house otherwise occupied by the Prichards, was not lavish but seemed more than adequate in 1962. My job would be to teach History and, at a time when a 'Use of English' examination had been introduced into sixth forms (partly as a means of bringing 'the two cultures' together), some English. I was in a seller's market and was able to refuse to take games or the CCF, but I promised to commit myself in school activities elsewhere and soon I was directing plays. Before long I belonged, with my superior in History John Todd and with Alexander, Evans, Tawney and the new assistant chaplain Colin Pedley, to a group of masters who sensed that they represented an alternative to the mainstream of school life, a feeling I enjoyed.

My brief encounters with other school common rooms, at Merchant Taylors' and St Peter's, York, had prepared me for stiff formality and a pecking order. In my first term I visited a friend at Uppingham who had just started teaching there. He told me that a few years earlier the headmaster had telephoned a young colleague to ask his wife to wear gloves in the High Street in future. The atmosphere at St Edward's was quite different. It had its restrictions. Masters were shocked when Olwyn Morris, the Art master's wife, entered the Common Room for coffee. But to a new master the Common Room was warmly welcoming. To my surprise, first names were used. The Warden used one's first name too, though only Bim Barff, now Second Master, and Fisher's friend Brian Gale presumed to call him Frank. The Common Room bar played a critical part, especially on Monday, Wednesday and Friday after evening school. The room was small, the atmosphere cosy. There could be no easy formation of cliques. Bachelors could sup nightly in the dining room, and married men could dine at no or minimal cost once a week. Conversation flowed with the beer, wine and often post-prandial port, which tended to be ordered in advance by the irrepressible Peter Whitehouse from the long-suffering Common Room steward, Frank Mutter. The guest nights were especially lively. The conviviality among masters who might disagree on matters of professional judgement or priorities was an asset to the school. When long-serving masters retired they presented gifts of silver cruets or decanters or candlesticks, which enhanced the collegiate atmosphere.

In December 1962, at the end of my first term, I moved as rapidly as possible across the Quad to pack and to point my Ford Popular towards its Yorkshire home. Fisher, as often, was on the white bench in front of his study. He called me over to sit beside him. Had I enjoyed my first term? he asked. Yes, I had. He said he was pleased with my work and the way I'd settled in. I was naturally encouraged, but wondered how he knew. He answered the question for me. 'I have talked to many of your pupils and they like your teaching and they like you. Enjoy your holiday.' It was masterly encouragement and a characteristically crisp and brilliant show of command.

In keeping with the greater emphasis on work, the contents of the Library were much altered and improved, probably on the initiative of such heads of department as Todd, Vernon and Tawney, who overcame the limits of the book grant. Gone, or at least hidden, were the bulk of the Victorian schoolbooks. Now books were arranged under academic headings, and textbooks and monographs were added. September 1958 brought the acquisition of seven books for Science, four for Maths, eleven for History, eleven for Modern Languages, and eight listed as 'General'. If *Wisden* and the *MCC Coaching Book* were among them, so too were Volume XI of *Shakespeare Survey* and David Attenborough's *Zoo Quest to Guiana*. In September 1958, thirteen books were presented as gifts, including John Armstrong's Oxford editions of Keats and Wordsworth. Not all school libraries could boast, for the budding historian of James I's reign, T. L. Moir's monograph *The Addled Parliament of 1614*. When, in 1962, I reorganized the History section under the direction of John Todd, the Head of Department, I was impressed by the quality and quantity of the books; late in the same decade I perused the History section at the University of Warwick and found it much inferior. As well as the main Library there were, by the early Sixties, more departmental libraries and more laboratories. Some classrooms remained in huts and there were inadequate rooms for the teaching of Biology and other subjects and no specialized language rooms, though Biology would soon acquire its own laboratory among the other science labs.

There were fresh stirrings of cultural life, as Fisher gave fruitful encouragement to societies. Some of them he rescued by having their debts paid off. He financed the new St Edward's Press, which was soon producing play programmes, tickets, notices and so on. There were more societies operating in the 1960s than at any time before. Corlett and Whitehouse encouraged the Bridge Club, which arranged fixtures against other schools, as did the Chess Club; Tawney reinvigorated the Science and Engineering Society and with David Howorth promoted a Photographic Society; an Astronomy and a Meteorological Society grew up; David Tinsley got the Mathematics Society under way; Archaeological and Electronic Engineering societies briefly flowered; the older societies which centred on hobbies, such as the Motor Club, Field Sports Society and the Piscatorial Society, continued. The Arts Society, which visited churches, art galleries and country houses, breathed a rather exclusive air. The lively chaplaincy under Holtby and Drake sponsored a Theological Society, at which distinguished speakers might speak on the role of God in a modern society or address such taxing subjects as the nature of Christ's atonement. John Vernon, who arrived as English master in 1955, introduced boys to plays and poems outside the syllabus, and with Peter Corlett took reading parties to the Lake District as well as ski trips to Wengen. The growing passion for travel, aided by newly introduced annual travel scholarships, produced a Travel Society, which had 250 members in 1954 and was guided by Cameron Cochrane after his arrival in 1957.

The half holidays on saints' days were replaced by two Societies' Days in the Summer and Winter Terms and a Societies' half-day in the Easter one. Coaches emptied the school, taking boys on improving visits. The Debating Society, whose motions were now almost all on serious political or social issues, prospered. Evans, Mather, Church and Armstrong were regular speakers from the Common Room. John Todd revived the Junior Debating Society. The arrival of Vernon produced a resurgence of the Literary Society and a new Shakespeare Society. By the early 1960s he was directing abbreviated versions of current O-level plays. His productions, though not always of high standard, did succeed in establishing a link between the classroom and the stage. Other activities prospered, too. The Music Society and the Light Opera Society played their favourites on a machine still called a gramophone.

Intellectual and cultural life started to stir. For a time there was an elitist Senior Arts Society, run with the help of Dr Alexander and the assistant chaplain, Jim McGowan, who came to the school in 1958. David Tawney's appointment in 1959 brought new life to the Scientific and Engineering Society. Edward Manning had nearly doubled the size of the orchestra and had started a military band for the CCF. A major step forward was taken with the building of a new Music School, across South Parade between the former stables (themselves long since converted into the maintenance buildings) and the Hollies, a house which had served a variety of purposes over the decades. The Music School was opened in 1962 by the aged W. K. Stanton, who had run the music with such distinction under Warden Ferguson. The building was designed by Peter Bosanquet, whose firm Brett, Boyd and Bosanquet, which brought architectural adventurousness to the school, had also designed the new laboratories and the Field House extension.

Mervyn Evans began a Film Society in 1962. Having given a talk on modern cinema to the Literary Society the previous year he took its members to the Scala, the art cinema in Walton Street, to watch *Hiroshima Mon Amour* and provided 'cakes and ale' for a subsequent discussion of it. Then came showings at the school, or visits to watch, Eisenstein's *Alexander Nevsky*, Fellini's *The Swindle*, Bergman's *The Seventh Seal*, Karel Reisz's film of Alan Sillitoe's *Saturday Night and Sunday Morning* and Stanley Kubrick's *Lolita*. The last of these, shown in an overflowing lecture room, 'gave the Society a big financial boost'. It was a change from the diet of the school audiences, which from time to time were crammed into Big School on Saturday nights to watch *The Cruel Sea*, *Brothers in Law*, *High Noon* and *Seven Brides for Seven Brothers*. From 1963 there was a Jazz Society. In 1964 there were 89 members of the Music Society, which, while still holding meetings to listen to gramophone records, also now arranged concerts in the school and visits to London to attend professional performances. A successful scheme of subscription concerts, funded in advance by parents and friends, was launched in 1964 by David Pettit, who had replaced Edward Manning as Director of Music the previous year.

Fisher brought many visiting speakers to the school, and sponsored a discussion group, which met in his drawing room. The art master Lawrence Toynbee, the chemistry teacher Nigel Roberts, and the chaplain Paul Drake figured in it, and outside speakers were invited. The prestigious Mackworth Society, whose members Fisher chose, dined in his lodging and then listened to a distinguished visitor or heard a paper from a member. In June 1963 Hugh Trevor-Roper, Regius Professor of Modern History at Oxford, addressed the Society 'on general historical topics, and when he threw himself open to our questions and discussion, we were enlightened by this distinguished intellect'. No one present could know that one of his listeners, Blair Worden (Roll No. 5520), would become his literary executor.

In Pettit's short but exhilarating period of office the Choral Society performed, among other challenging works, Bach's *St John Passion* and *Christmas Oratorio*. The participation of girls from Wychwood and Greycotes Schools was a major innovation. The *Chronicle* recorded that a performance of Handel's *Messiah* 'bore no resemblance to the assembly which has been singing "Old King Cole" at various times over the last century'. Pettit and his young wife, the clarinettist Angela Malsbury who also taught, gave organ and harpsichord recitals. They were a charismatic couple. More than a hundred people attended each of the many informal concerts in the school. In the drama too, there was a new dawn. Like the revival of music it did not come until well into the Sixties. The review in the *Chronicle* by Simon Pleasance (Roll No. 5388) of Jack Scarr's polished production of Anouilh's *Thieves' Carnival* in 1962 had remarked that the play's 'lack of subtlety was appropriate to the various Commem audiences, now well accustomed to the "jollity" of the School plays and to the long succession of comedies ....

> Perhaps it is felt that a light play has more appeal for parents and OSE, but if this is true it is only because the minds of the audiences have been conditioned .... The play should be a showpiece of this particular side of the School's activities, and not something chosen with an eye on the box-office. The audience will enjoy a serious play, believe it or not.

The same 'lack of subtlety' characterized the choice of the annual House plays, held in all Houses by 1959.

But by 1963 experimental or radical modern drama was making its mark. That year saw my production of Christopher Fry's verse play *A Sleep of Prisoners* and my production of the British amateur première of Brecht's epic *The Life of Galileo*. OSE and others complained about its length but not, apparently, about its Marxist politics. There were mutterings when Jeremy Lane (Roll No. 5490), playing the title role, was allowed to take a personal bow. Thereafter Fisher would liberate the school play from the constraints of the Commem weekend and make it an event of its own. At first he was unwilling to let girls take part, but in 1964 Fred Pargeter was allowed to cast girls from Milham Ford School for his innovative staging of Dylan Thomas's *Under Milk Wood*. A cluster of successful productions followed, among them Colin Pedley's moving production of Arthur Miller's *The Crucible* and my own rendering of Aristophanes' *The Frogs* as a musical set by Whitehouse (who appeared in the programme as Petros Leukoikos). After Fisher's departure, new directors, notably Simon Taylor, Robin Alden and Nick Quartley, would keep the drama thriving in the years ahead. Acting had become enormously popular, and not only as a way of meeting girls.

One housemaster, Stanley Tackley, refused to attend *Under Milk Wood* on the ground that a performance with girls could not be a true school play. As a rule the housemasters were not enamoured of change. The lives of the boys were focused more on the Houses than on the classrooms. When, in my first year, I suggested to my Upper Sixth that they go to see *The Cherry Orchard* at the Oxford Playhouse I was met with incredulous laughter. If I wanted them to see it, they said, I would have to organize it and take them myself, securing the permission first of the Warden and then of each housemaster. Fisher encouraged me to proceed but several housemasters looked for reasons why their boys could not go. The Warden overruled them, which revealed to the boys, as it did to me, the existence of tensions between him and his housemasters. There would be more such battles, one of them over the holding of Removes courses, which Colin Pedley and I arranged with the Warden's support, during Prep.

There was awakening in Art, too. David Morris, who taught the subject from 1961, was succeeded in 1963 by Christopher Ruscombe-King, whose wife Mo assisted him in the pottery. Under them Art attained a status almost equivalent to that of Music and Drama. Chris riveted the pupils by his pregnant silences, Mo by ebullience. They acquired something like a cult following as the Art room became a social centre, even a therapeutic one, for boys alienated from other areas of school life. George Foster (Roll No. 6198) thinks of Chris as 'the inspiration for my arty career in advertising'. Chris and Mo 'took huge delight in teaching those that really wanted to learn'. There was a significant moment in the Common Room's life when Mo was given permission, if on tightly restricted terms, to take tea there. The move was welcomed by the formidable Yvonne Evans, who with others resented the exclusion of wives from the end-of-year Common Room dinners, when they were confined to a separate festivity in the Warden's House at which Renée Barff, as wife of the Second Master, would preside.

In Fisher's time the new academic priorities and ventures into cultural experiment did not impair traditional or conventional activities or affect the underlying structure and character of the school, though that would change under his successor. Nor did sport suffer. The Boat Club enjoyed enormous success and popularity under John Vernon. It increased its participation in regattas, and in 1958 the VIII won the Junior–Senior Event at Reading and then the first of two consecutive and famous victories in the Princess Elizabeth Cup at Henley. Also in 1958 the Second and Third VIIIs won at Reading and Wallingford and the Colts won the Schools' event in Oxford. Success continued, though not quite at that level, in the remaining years of Fisher's Wardenship. In rugby, after some shaky seasons, Brian Gale and Derek Henderson produced in 1960 an undefeated XV. Cricket had no such spectacular achievements, though the team of 1959 had a remarkable run and beat the MCC for the first time. Hockey, hitherto a poor relation of the major sports, climbed in esteem under Myles Arkell and Miles Peregrine. In 1957 Fisher, himself a keen hockey man, introduced colours for the sport and arranged the first of what became regular fixtures against the Martyrs, who formed their own club in 1959. By 1961 there was a Senior House League hockey cup. The XI of 1964 was unbeaten by any school. Fisher did a lot for 'minor' sports, to encourage diversity and choice. The status of squash was enhanced; and 1961 saw the first unbeaten teams in fencing and tennis. New hard tennis courts were opened in 1963, and judo was introduced in 1964. The Harriers, the cross-country running team, won the Parrish Cup in three successive seasons from 1961 and had their first unbeaten season in 1962. A self-coached group, whose activity took them away from the school into the neighbouring countryside, the Harriers acquired a distinctive identity and camaraderie.

All three services of the Cadet Force – Army, Navy, and RAF – prospered. They were encouraged by Fisher, who saw that the phasing out of National Service was in danger of reducing the supply of potential officers. The RAF Section under Corlett was the most dynamic. As boys knew, there were some masters who muttered against the CCF. Yet most of the teaching staff, having themselves been officers in wartime or in post-war National Service, enthusiastically took part, the irreverent Whitehouse among them.

In 1962 the very tall Dick Bond succeeded the diminutive Sam Tero as RSM. All three services of the Cadet Corps continued to thrive. From 1960 links with the armed forces were strengthened by the award of two 'Services Scholarships' each year to the sons of serving officers. In 1965 Fisher persuaded the War Office to provide a purpose-built CCF Headquarters and Armoury on the fields. House competitions in platoon drill and shooting continued, and there were shooting matches in the indoor range against other schools. These were conducted 'postally', the scores achieved on an agreed day being exchanged with the opposing teams. In 1962 seven such matches involved 24 schools. There were 24 matches in 1966, of which the school won 21. CCF Arduous Training provided expeditions which many boys enjoyed, and the CCF also offered opportunities to learn vehicle maintenance. In July 1962 St Edward's joined the Duke of Edinburgh's Award Scheme. Immediately, 170 boys volunteered, and later all younger boys were required to take the Bronze Award. By the end of 1963 the number of participants had risen to 251, just over half the school. Soon there were many Silver and Gold Awards, and trips to the Palace became common. The duke himself visited the school in November 1963 and laid the foundation stone of the new boarding Houses. The Award was incorporated into the CCF, with whose Outward Bound scheme it overlapped.

Fisher made changes that quietly reduced the place of religion and the Chapel in the timetable. It was in his second term that he ended the half holidays held on every major saint's day. Later he reduced compulsory Chapel attendance on weekdays to four services, and for a fifth substituted House Prayers. The two compulsory services at Gaudy and Commem were reduced to one. By now the physical prominence of the Chapel building had come to seem an intrusion. Although an extension to the building appeared on all development plans, it was always at the bottom of the list.

37

WINDS OF CHANGE

David Miller (Roll No. 5697), who had been at the Dragon Preparatory School in Oxford, well remembers his first day at St Edward's in September 1960.

> [It] started with a talk from FFF (never my favourite man!). I think there were 30-odd Old Dragons coming to Teddies that year. At the end of the talk he asked all the boys to leave except the Dragons; he then proceeded to tell us we were a bit of a cocky bunch that should not stay in cliques, and that we had been deliberately spread around houses so we could make new friends. He then shook each boy by the hand as we left and asked our names. I believe he knew everyone's name after that day (including the non-Dragons) and never had to ask again. Astounding.

Few OSE express warmth towards Fisher, but almost all admired and respected him. Like Kendall, he had the personal touch, even if it might seem more calculated. He seemed to be everywhere and he always addressed boys by their names and had an apposite remark about their work or games or family. He looked them in the eye and appeared to give them his undivided attention. Like many bright pupils, David took A level after three years. At the end of his fourth year the Warden's report read: 'I have just come off the First XI pitch watching David make a faultless 100 – I only wish he put so much effort into his work.'

Cameron Buchanan (Roll No. 5627), who arrived in 1960, had a close chum in Peter Barrow (Roll No. 5656). 'We rather fancied ourselves,' Buchanan recalls, 'as literary scribes and indeed wrote the Rag Revue of 1965, our leaving present to the School.' Frequently the two friends, who were in different Houses, would converse while walking round the Quad – a change from the days when friendships across the Houses had been discouraged. 'We would meet in break time or the evenings after the Lit[erary] Soc[iety], Deb[ating] Soc or whatever and engage in deep, erudite (or so we thought!) conversation with many gesticulations. On one occasion passing the Warden's study, FFF opened the window, leaned out and in his usual modular tone which he used for chidings or blessings he said – "What I want to know is, Barrow and Buchanan, when you are talking who listens to whom?" He then had us in for a glass of something and asked what we always seemed to talk about .... He always gave a wave and a shake of the head every time he saw us from then on.' Barrow also recalls his first 'fag', when he was required to tie the laces of the 'highly polished brown Oxfords' of Michael Stanfield (Roll No. 5163), who that term was captain of the unbeaten First XV and is the present Chairman of the Governors. By the time Peter left, Fisher had abolished fagging.

Michael Fairclough, a year ahead of Buchanan and Barrow, remembers 'Warden Fisher in his black suit and black gown' – so different from Kendall's shambolic dress – 'calling me over publicly in the Quad to say "I know you are behind the latest escapade [whatever that might have been] but I can't prove it ... yet", and he never did!' Fisher enjoyed the power that knowledge brings. William Wallace (Roll No. 5062), now Lord Wallace of Saltaire, recalls that in his last year, 1959, when he was a school prefect, he spent a weekend visiting a girl at Malvern Girls' College. 'On Monday, in the middle of lunch, the Warden made a joke about it (how on earth had he found out?) in front of the other prefects. I felt deeply embarrassed and confused – had I done something improper?'

It is a relief to know that he did not know quite everything. 'Birds, beer and baccy were all off limits!' recalls Robin Ewbank (Roll No. 5244), who arrived in 1956. But he got his beer. He recalls cycling to the pub at Thrupp after Sunday morning chapel, sunbathing by the Cherwell afterwards and returning for a quick one before the ride back for Evensong. Fisher took a fierce line against smoking and, still more, drinking, but he could not stop them. The pubs in Jericho are recalled lovingly by Richard Evans (Roll No. 5784), an arrival in 1961, though when a boy who drank with him on a trip to the Oxford Playhouse gave the game away by bragging of the exploit in the wrong company Richard was beaten by Fisher, who kept hitting the back of his elbow and cutting the skin. Nicholas Rollin (Roll No. 5709) recalls a surreptitious trip to Oxford with his contemporary Geoffrey James (Roll No. 5689) to enjoy a curry in Ship Street. Smokers remember listening to music in Taphouse's and then smoking while drinking tea at threepence a cup in the Cypriot Cafe. Fairclough's memories include 'the first joyous puff of the first cigarette' when term ended. Memories divide over whether it was on the Girls' High School or Headington School that an organized 'raid', which is said to have led to expulsions, was conducted. Within the grounds the tradition of midnight swims in the outdoor bath sometimes attracted more than thirty boys. 'Crasher' White's old Norton, with its flat tyre, was appropriated for spins on the Upper Fields.

Those larks would have been recognizable, at least in spirit, to boys of earlier generations. What was new in Fisher's time was the 'rise of the teenager'. Until the economic recovery of the 1950s adolescence was little studied, except by a few psychologists. Children were expected to conform to their parents' tastes in dress and behaviour. A high proportion of teenagers were in work by the age of 15. The rise of what J. K. Galbraith's study of 1958 called 'The Affluent Society' produced profound changes. Wages rose by 34% between 1955 and 1960 and a further 20% between 1961 and 1970. Prices of a range of consumer goods, many of them newly available, fell in relation to earnings. Middle-class parents had more to spend on cars, kitchens and school fees. They also passed on some of the new wealth to their children, who spent it on cappuccinos in the new coffee bars, on denim jeans, and on pop music records and magazines. The affluent working class enjoyed the same pleasures, so that there arose an increasingly classless youth culture with a common argot, including Americanisms, a common taste for rock music, and the sense of a generation gap between adult and teenage worlds. Colin MacInnes's novel *Absolute Beginners* (1959) portrays a new world 'of real splendour in the days when the kids discovered that, for the first time since centuries of kingdom-come, they'd money ... we'd loot to spend at last, and our world was to be our world, the one we wanted and not standing on the doorstep of somebody else's'. Before this revolution there were 'not any authentic teenagers at all. In those days, it seems, you were just an overgrown boy, or an under-grown man, life didn't seem to cater for anything else between.'

By the late 1950s pop music was making itself heard in the school. Radios were now allowed in day rooms, where on Sundays boys might listen to *The Navy Lark* or pop music. Blair Worden remembers listening with his contemporaries in Cowell's in 1961 to *The Top Twenty* on Radio Luxembourg, that flag of freedom from the institutionalized conformity of the BBC. The programme, in which the current leading pop songs were played in ascending order of popularity, ended on the hour on Sunday when Evensong began. The boys would wait to the last moment, and if possible hear the start of No. 1, before racing to get across the Quad to Chapel before the bells stopped. They faced severe punitive consequences if they did not make it, but they always did. Some pupils, recalls

Jeremy Griggs, 'had record players, another means of keeping abreast with what we called "The Hit Parade". Armed with a pass into Oxford, and sometimes without one, boys annoyed the shop staff at Messrs Taphouse by monopolising the headphones to listen to the latest rock 'n' roll hit under the pretence of being about to purchase the record.' A Dansette, a popular brand of record-player, could be bought for a few pounds. Radios crossed barriers of class as well as age.

In 1958 the *Chronicle* touched on an anxious national debate about class consciousness. The controversy centred on the categories of 'U' and 'non-U' defined by the linguist Alan Ross in 1954 and popularized in an article by Nancy Mitford the same year. Another lively term of social description was 'square'. 'Today,' declared the *Chronicle*,

> we are ruled by two words: 'square' and 'non-U'. A 'square' is one who has the ability to appreciate the value of culture, and 'non-U' is a term applied to one who thinks differently from a particular community. These terms however have become ones of abuse and scorn. It is 'non-U' to read *The Observer*, only the *News of the World* must be read on Sundays, therefore whoever reads *The Observer* is a 'square'. Whoever prefers Chopin's 'Etude in C Minor' to Elvis Presley's 'Hound Dog Rock' is a square'.

It was in June 1961, under John Todd's tolerant supervision, that senior boys founded *The Martyr*, which carried original compositions. The *Chronicle* described it as 'an excellent innovation', but remarked that 'one can't pretend that the first issue of the magazine was an unqualified success'. As such magazines go *The Martyr* had a reasonable run, but after the issue of Summer 1964 the *Chronicle* regretted that 'it is no longer either penetrating or provocative'. Its irreverent streak, which incurred some suspicion among the more conformist masters and boys, aped the new public wave of satire which had been announced by Michael Frayn's articles in the *Manchester Guardian* in the late 1950s. *Beyond the Fringe* reached the London stage in 1961; *Private Eye* began in the same year; and in 1962–63 the televised show *That Was the Week That Was*, described by Mary Whitehouse of the 'Clean Up TV Campaign' as 'anti-authority, anti-religious, anti-patriotic and pro-dirt', brought satire into the home. The subscription of the Masters' Common Room to *Private Eye* was reluctantly accepted by older members once they were assured that *Country Life* and *The Field* would still be taken. The subversive mood of the new satire had a modest but prophetic impact on the Masters' Common Room and in prefects' studies, though in the latter case the energy of the early Beatles was perhaps a stronger emancipating force. In 1963, the year when according to Philip Larkin sexual intercourse began, a change of atmosphere could be sensed inside the school as outside it.

To Fisher there were already trends that were worrying enough. His Gaudy speech two years earlier painted a grim social picture. Boys were growing up in an atmosphere 'which is frankly alarming'. 'You are all aware of the growing figures of teenage crime. Violence is on the increase, highway robbery is reported practically every day; the press is full of reports of crime, perversion, murder and corruption of one sort or another; the bookstalls are flooded with pornographic literature; and the moral standards among young people have declined and are declining very rapidly.' No one was speaking out against it and 'we have been told in what must surely be one of the most unfortunate sentences of all time that "We have never had it so good": we all welcome the increasing material prosperity but I could wish that the politicians would be prepared to bring home to the nation that in many ways our standards have declined to a frightening extent .... I would not want you to think in what I have said that I am condemning the young people of today, rather I am criticising my own generation for allowing these things to come about.' The phrase 'the permissive society' would come into general use only in the late Sixties, but the alarm that produced it had already struck. The year 1964 produced the Dangerous Drugs Act. Cannabis, which the public mind associated with coloured immigrants, was the subject of a Home Office investigation into nightclubs. Britain, hitherto low in the alcoholic league table, climbed in the 1960s. Legislation of 1967 largely decriminalized homosexuality and permitted abortion in loosely defined circumstances. The National Health Service, still regarded in some quarters as a sop to socialism, began to hand out free contraceptives. The 1969 Divorce Reform Act loosened marital ties. The school would have to adapt to an altered social world.

On 10 November 1960 Foyle's, London's largest bookshop, took just 15 minutes to sell its 300 copies of D. H. Lawrence's *Lady Chatterley's Lover*. A Selfridge's spokesman said 'It's bedlam here. We could have sold 10,000 copies if we had had them.' At the six-day trial which had begun on 27 October, thirty-five leading literary and cultural figures testified to what was called the book's 'redeeming social merit'. John Robinson, the controversial Bishop of Woolwich, stated that Lawrence showed sex as 'an act of holy communion' and that 'Christians ought to read' the book. The trial was a test of the Obscene Publications Act of 1959, which had been introduced by Roy Jenkins as a Private Members Bill. Mervyn Griffith-Jones QC, prosecuting, asked the jury: 'Would you approve of your young sons, young daughters – because girls can read as well as boys – reading this book? Is it a book that you would have lying around in your own house? Is it a book that you would even wish your wife or your servants to read?' The prosecution lost. A mother with a teenage daughter at boarding school wrote to the Home Secretary expressing her fear that 'day girls may introduce this filthy book'. Fisher spoke about the book in the Chapel after Evensong, asking the boys, as one gentleman to others, to hand in any copies they had got hold of. Several OSE recall being moved by his account of the volume to a new commitment to the twentieth-century novel. Two years later, alarmed by the fad for 'drainpipe' trousers, Fisher suggested to the Masters' Common Room that a minimum width at the bottom of boys' trousers be imposed by tape-measuring, but behind his back the Common Room laughed at the idea. The episode was just one of a series of tussles over the boys' appearance. Should hair be allowed to reach the back of the collar? How high up the knee might elastic-sided boots reach? An inflexible school would look silly, but a flexible one risked the taking of ever greater liberties.

The real struggles over appearance and behaviour would come after Fisher's time. The cult of the teenager, if it encouraged some boys to test limits, had not eroded the underlying conservatism of the majority. In the prelude to the general election of 1959 a motion in the Debating Society that 'This House would welcome a change of government' from the Tories was lost by 31 votes to 9. The previous year a motion to support the encouragement of racial integration was lost by 44 votes to 14, and the Society judged it better, though only by three votes, to get to the moon than feed the poor. Perhaps there is a sign of changing attitudes in the defeat by eleven votes, in another debate of 1958, of a motion, which again set the conservative Mather against the liberal Evans, calling for sterner punishment for criminal violence. But in 1959 the motion that 'There is no education without co-education' was lost by 36 votes to 15, and one in favour of a Channel Tunnel was firmly rejected. Conservatism is equally conspicuous in the results of a self-styled 'Gallup Poll' of 1964, whose results were published in the *Chronicle*. It revealed that 66% of boys approved of capital punishment and that 92% approved of the use of corporal punishment in schools. Eighty-four per cent did not wish to see the voting age lowered; 87% supported the Conservatives, compared with the 8% who favoured the Liberals and the 6% of Labour supporters. Seventy-six per cent were staunch monarchists. Only 24% supported Mods, 32% Rockers; 32% hated both. Sixty-one per cent liked the Beatles, but only 38% the Rolling Stones, while 78% wanted the preservation of some restrictions 'on the style and length of hair'.

In Field House, remembers Chris Sprague (Roll No. 5328), 'many boys were quite reactionary' and resented the changes introduced to the House when Stewart Pether succeeded Barff as housemaster in 1957. Until then Field House's distance from the main site had protected it from 'the reforms that were being brought in by Warden Fisher, although a reminder of things to come was a particularly ugly extension to the house ... nearing completion that summer. The daily routine in the House was probably much as it had been before the Second World War .... In a way this was reassuring for a new boy. Everyone knew exactly where he should be and what he should be doing at any time of day .... Barff left the Prefects and senior boys to run the house.' It was in Sprague's second term that Pether took over. 'He took a more active hand in running the House ... and to our amazement called us by our Christian names, something that few of us had experienced in our school careers ... Pether also made it clear that he did not wish boys to be caned ... though, his patience tried, he did occasionally do so. Pether introduced a regime that was clearly more humane than hitherto, but that very humanity was a source of resentment.' There were similar relaxations in Cowell's under Church, in Segar's under Evans, and in Apsley under Armstrong.

For Fisher was quietly adjusting the mores of the school and softening its rigours. Gradually he divided day rooms into study spaces, here and there adding a games room or a reading room with books, newspapers and a television. Doors appeared on lavatories. Boys sharing surnames, who until now were distinguished from each other by 'major', 'minor', 'minimus', 'IV', etc., were henceforth identified by their initials. Boys' shirts, hitherto washed once a week, made way for more frequently changed ones with attached instead of detachable collars. A charcoal grey suit for Sundays and special occasions replaced the navy blue one, which, Fisher told the school, reminded him of 'miners out in their Sunday best'. The black ties commonly imagined to have been introduced in mourning for Queen Victoria gave way to dark blue ones sporting ersatz heraldry. For the time being 'bashers' survived, but few boys wore them once out of sight of the school. Fisher took benign note of an attack on boaters by Richard Peel (Roll No. 5501) in *The Martyr* entitled 'The Last Straw' in July 1963. Eight months later they ceased to be compulsory in Summertown, where local youths had taunted the wearers with the song 'Where did you get that hat, boy, Where did you get that hat?', though only in July 1966 did they cease to be required wearing in central Oxford. Thereafter they quickly disappeared from the scene.

One day in his last year, 1965–66, Fisher arrived for the weekly Common Room break meeting carrying, as usual, a small piece of paper with the headings he intended to address in his brisk way. The meetings were hardly discussions, more an issuing of decrees by the Warden. On that occasion he produced a bombshell. He announced that personal fagging had become out of step with society and unacceptable to an increasing number of parents, and declared its instant abolition. Church and Evans crossed the Quad and implemented the decision by the end of Break, in spite of protests from their startled prefects. Other housemasters did little or nothing. In Mac's the performance of 'duties', in effect indistinguishable from personal fagging, was enjoined for some years afterwards. The boys were dismayed by Fisher's move. 'It only served,' wrote the *Chronicle*, 'to create a gulf across the House', an institution 'which has rapidly broken down over the last few years.'

Despite the changes he brought, the character of much in the daily life of St Edward's, at least for most of Fisher's Wardenship, would have been familiar to Victorian schoolboys. Early in my time, unaware of the rule that new boys must keep their jacket buttons fastened, and finding a bright Shell form unresponsive in a history lesson, I told them to undo them. As the bell rang for the end of the period the boys rapidly refastened them in case they met a prefect outside. Jeremy Griggs (Roll No. 5472) describes himself as 'small and awestruck' on his arrival in Apsley in 1958. He was 'perceived as both a swot and no sort of jock on the sports field .... For the most part I was able to escape to music rooms .... In those five years I certainly experienced my fair share of teasing, descending at times to outright bullying.' He became an accomplished musician, especially on the clarinet. Other boys too may have found music, which could be practised in something like privacy, an escape or solace. Jeremy overcame his diffidence and became Head of Apsley. But his appointment, he says, 'was much to the chagrin of my immediate contemporaries, who, true to their form of earlier years, seized hold of me on learning of my appointment and forced my head into a lavatory pan and pulled the flush. It was of course ignominious for me. I still get a sick feeling in the pit of my stomach as I recall it. But I had learned not to react to such incidents.' During his two terms as Head of House he administered 36 strokes of the cane, the exact total he himself had received, 'so in one sense a measure of parity prevailed'.

Chris Plumridge (Roll No. 5426), who arrived in 1958, recalls: 'The regime was harsh: early morning runs, cold showers and fagging, bullying, beatings, sometimes administered by older boys, all of which created a climate of fear. The food was execrable ... the system was inflexible and made no allowances for individual needs ... and the Swinging Sixties were just around the corner.' He adds: 'My four years at St Edward's were probably the most miserable of my life: correction, make that definitely the most miserable.' Charles Orwin (Roll No. 6148), who arrived seven years later, found his time 'indubitably the unhappiest of my life .... During the first couple of years I dreaded the end of each school holiday and the return to school. My parents said I should stick it out to the end ... that this was something every boy had to endure, that it would be social death should I fail to complete my time at public school.' Orwin's contemporary George Foster (Roll No. 6198) states: 'My parents, bless them, gave a lot so that we should go to Teddies .... To this day I wish that they had saved their money. I hated my time there, the place scared me with its constant bullying and stupidity. I didn't have the wit to really let on to my parents how much I felt trapped and lost. Bullying and "ragging" were rife. 500 repressed and hormone-filled boys were a recipe for that. Fagging had been officially abolished but there were still "duties" to be performed.' Another OSE of Fisher's time writes: 'I do not look back with any great fondness on my four years there .... Boys were supposed to be cool and sarcasm was embedded. Bullying on all sorts of levels was common and destructive. The teachers seemed to abandon the school culture to the boys who replicated some deeply unpleasant behavioural patterns.'

The food is a common complaint among OSE of the era. Adrian Goldring (Roll No. 5981), a boy from 1963, remembers himself as one of the few who scarcely missed a single sitting of the only optional dining-room meal, tea at 4 p.m. Junior boys served food and collected dirty plates and often went without sufficient food themselves or were left with the worst cuts. Yet the eating arrangements were to be transformed by changes made by Fisher and implemented by his successor. After a conversion of the kitchens in the autumn of 1966 a cafeteria was introduced in the following January. It operated both in the dining hall and in the old Big School, which became an additional eating area. Visitors from fifty schools came to see how the cafeteria system worked.

I learned something of life in the Houses only in 1964, when, on the sudden death of Bill Veitch, Mervyn Evans was moved rapidly into Segar's and I was given temporary charge of Corfe House, then a sort of waiting room for the new boys of Apsley and Sing's until the building of the new house would leave School House to Apsley alone. In my first term or so at St Edward's I entered a House only once, when I had occasion to visit Pat Brims in Cowell's on some matter of business. A knock on the door brought in the prefect Robert Wilson (Roll No. 5725), whom I knew as a Sixth Form pupil. He exchanged words with his housemaster on some matter of House business and then left, firmly closing the door behind him. I was struck by the formality of the exchange. The two seemed scarcely to know each other. An account of life in Cowell's by Nicholas Derbyshire (Roll No. 5239), at the school from 1956 to 1961, might almost have been written in the Victorian age. 'The day to day life of the School was run by the prefects, and beatings and fagging were both alive and well .... The housemaster (Pat Brims) was never seen in the House and [his] door provided a one way communication only.' Blair Worden remembers being a new boy in the House in 1958:

> After a few days we were summoned to the Senior Day Room, lined up, and ordered to look at the ground. We stood for several minutes while the president hurled abuse at us – 'You're absolute dirt!', etc. – until at last he ordered us to 'Get out!'. What seems strange in retrospect is that, far from resenting our humiliation, we interpreted it, as we did all our ritual afflictions, as laudable character-training, hallowed (we assumed) by tradition.

Down the corridor Bill Veitch's Segar's was very different. Several OSE recall the energy and humanity he brought to the House after the retirement of the ageing and unmarried Gauntlett in 1955. 'He was friendly, warm, gregarious, and enjoyed practical jokes and general good-natured banter. He could be strict and no one had any desire for a caning from someone with the physical attributes he still possessed. He was extremely fit and agile and often joined in cricket nets and rugby training sessions, where his sporting prowess still showed.' He entertained pupils to family meals and afterwards would turn on a television for them to watch sport. Under him Segar's was the supreme sporting House. Will Sykes (Roll No. 5713), who was Head of Segar's, remembers: 'We were proud to be in Segar's. Bill Veitch's style somehow suited and welded the sometimes weird mix of people and generated an indefinable "house spirit".' He was not much in Common Room, spending his time in the House during evening prep, but at 6 p.m. he would appear just when Frank Mutter was setting out the drinks and spend ten minutes enjoying a whisky. We had little in common but I grew to like his easy manner and friendly demeanour. He seemed to me then, as he does now, to epitomize much of the best in the traditional St Edward's, sporting, straightforward, rather hearty, but also sensitive to others and with the capacity to create informality and friendliness. His premature death was a blow to the school.

One of the innovations by Fisher to be recalled by OSE was the sex education talk conducted by the dour Scot Alastair Henderson, school doctor since 1947. He was not at the forefront of modern guidance on the subject. William Wallace recalls the lecture he gave to leaving boys. 'The gist of his talk was that there were good girls and bad girls; good girls don't want you to do anything; bad girls did but might well infect you with dreadful diseases, the nature of which was not spelled out.' Chris Plumridge gives a similar account: '"Well boys," he said, "you are about to go into the wide world where you will come across girls. You may feel some strange urges when you encounter girls." We waited with bated breath, sniggering. "I want you," he continued, "to always remember to keep a sense of values." No further information was forthcoming: sex education over.'

Peter Bond (Roll No. 5657) gives an account of his medical induction as a new boy in 1960, when Henderson was assisted by the Sanatorium sister, Miss Monica Grimwade, known as Bloody Mary on account of her vigorous administration of injections. Boys were weighed and measured and were told to cough as their private parts were inspected. Then Henderson spoke. Bond had assumed 'that a sex talk for thirteen-year-olds would be about the facts of life' and was a little mystified when the doctor spent several minutes talking about something which seemed to be called 'master-baiting'. 'I had no idea what this was .... Was the doctor telling us not to annoy the masters and not to misbehave in lessons? Henderson's strong Scottish accent with its madly rolling "r"s didn't help.

'Bloody Mary had noticed that most of the boys looked completely baffled. "Doctor," she said, "I think some of the boys don't know what masturbating is." The Doctor stopped for a moment.

'He asked how many boys didn't know what it meant. About ten boys put up their hands and the phenomenon was explained, accompanied by threats as to its moral dangers .... For the next two years I believed that touching myself in that area was a mortal sin.

'Henderson's advice was not finished. "Maybe an older boy will want to be friendly with you," he suggested. This seemed an implausible hypothesis ... but Dr Henderson knew that temptation took on unexpected forms. "Perhaps he will offer you a piece of cake." This seemed a fairly innocent scenario but I hadn't appreciated the villainy involved in a Battenberg or a Victoria sponge. The Doctor's voice became emphatic: "If he does, say no, I don't want it." I have to say that I don't recall ever being offered a piece of cake throughout my entire time at Teddies.'

Housemasters did not always add much enlightenment. In the Christmas Term of 1958 Fisher, vigilant as ever against vice, received indications that boys were doing rather more to each other than offering cake. Investigations and warnings were launched across the Houses. In Cowell's the Classicist bachelor Pat Brims addressed the new boys. 'Now I mean, if any older boy should come to you and I mean, if he should suggest you do something which I mean he ought not to suggest you do, you must come and tell me about it, I mean you must.' When in their perplexity two of the boys went to see him in hope of clarification, he mistook their stumbling question for a request for instruction in the facts of life. 'Ah yes,' he said, wrapping his right arm, as he usually did at awkward moments, round the back of his neck, 'well I mean it's the entry of the um, the um, of the penis – which is a Latin word! I mean it's a Latin word – into the um, into the um, into the vagina – which is another Latin word! Which shows, I mean, what a wonderful language Latin is.' Again no further information was vouchsafed.

Yet boys have positive memories of many teachers of this era. There was a gentler tone in the classroom. Few masters would now have resorted to Arthur Tilly's practice of telling an unhappy boy to 'pull himself together' and that 'you're not going to die'. In music boys responded to the teaching of Peter Whitehouse and Peter Corlett. George Howe (Roll No. 5949), who later achieved fame as the composer George Fenton, would offer a moving tribute to Whitehouse's teaching on *Desert Island Discs*. Mervyn Evans taught with humour and with an infectious liberalism of outlook. William Wallace writes of him as 'an extraordinarily good and sensitive teacher with a strong sense of values: I think he was one of the influences that made me a Liberal in politics and life'. Fran Prichard's 'Morning Men!' 'seemed to get us off on the right footing,' writes Nicholas Rollin (Roll No. 5709). 'As with some masters, he made everyone feel they had some potential to develop and treated his pupils in a straightforward and reasonable manner.' Eccentricity or colour of personality, if allied to good nature and carried off with conviction, always endears masters to boys. Pupils enjoy recalling John Alexander talking animatedly as he crossed red lights while driving members of the Art Society to theatres and exhibitions.

Another hazardous driver was Eric Reid in his racing-green Jaguar. In 1957, when Emmet suddenly retired pleading ill health, Fisher had needed to replace him quickly with another bachelor. He appointed the evergreen Reid, who had already been Housemaster of Sing's from 1936 to 1940. To boys in Tilly's he seemed incredibly old, coughing and spluttering through his tobacco. Once, beating a boy, he paused after the second stroke to 'have a little rest'. No one ever found out if he really had been a 'spook' during the war. 'Have you had a successful day?' he would always ask. Courteous to a fault, he nonetheless took offence at a production of John Barton's Shakespearian compilation, *The Hollow Crown*, which he thought unpatriotic. Fred Pargeter's 'Bangs' lectures in Chemistry were famous. So was the jollity of Derek Henderson's lessons. 'This isn't Room 6 at the Ritz, this is Room Six in the Work Block,' he would intone to the signature tune of *Rawhide*. He would stress the refrain *Rollin', Rollin', Rollin'* for the entertainment of Nicholas Rollin and his peers. Pupils knew how hard Jack Scarr worked for them. His 'police raids' (extra tests) would be followed by 'coffee and liqueurs', work out of school which was in effect free extra tuition.

Stanley Tackley ('Tackles'), in the later stages of his housemastership of Sing's, taught Ve, the form for boys who had failed O levels, and inspired warm and widespread affection. He warned one pupil not to go to the LSE in case they 'turn you into a Socialist'. Stanley occupied two rooms with his pungent ageing Labrador, Brandy. John Gowland (Roll No. 5633) recalls the ritual of Tackley's attempts to get the dog to remove a handkerchief from his pocket. '"Er, er, come Brandy, er, come, Brandy," he would repeat as he bent ever closer to the carpet for the dog to perform the trick. Once, having lost track of the animal on its late-night walk, he stopped by the Red Lion to call Brandy, Brandy. "I'm sorry, sir," a passing policeman told him, "but I think you'll find they're closed."' He became Second Master in 1964 but was a distant figure during his tenure and not a happy one. Gowland recalls visiting him in his damp retirement cottage at Flushing in 'Beaks' Bay' in Cornwall, where Tackley had so often stayed with Kendall at Mevagissey. He never returned to Oxford.

Dogs became extensions of their owners' personalities. Another Labrador, Honey, was as gentlemanly as its master Fran Prichard, and the dog Fausta as forthright as its owner Mervyn Evans. In Field House boys heard Leo, the ageing and weighty retriever of the ageing and weighty Barff, staggering up or down the stairs. Mather's constant walking companion was his dachshund Otto. The story of Charles on his knees for fifteen minutes near the pavilion, calling out 'Now Otto – you know you are there, I know you are there – so stop buggering about and come out this instant or there will be serious trouble!' may be apocryphal.

38

CENTENARY

In Fisher's first year a Development Plan was promulgated on his initiative. Four years later, in November 1958, with the school's 100th birthday five years away, he proposed to the Governors a new version of the plan, a Centenary Appeal. In 1959 he submitted to them three sheets of foolscap headed 'The Centenary, 1963'. The document proposed the writing of a history of the school, a new *Roll*, a new appeal, a royal visit. The celebrations would show off the school to visitors ranging from vice-chancellors to local tradesmen. There would be floodlighting, fireworks, bonfires, displays, garden parties and chapel services. A Centenary Committee should set it all in motion and masters should be involved in the planning.

Fisher saw the Centenary as an opportunity for fund-raising and to provide the endowment the school conspicuously lacked. But there were already a number of appeals. The Endowment Fund and the War Memorial Fund from before 1945 both survived, though the latter was closed in 1956. There was also another Development Fund, which had invited donations from all OSE, and whose progress was still regularly reported in the *Chronicle*. In 1963 it was renamed the Improvement Fund. Over the years the school's coffers had been enlarged by mostly small contributions from OSE, governors, masters and other well-wishers. The combined total of these gifts stood at £33,000 in the late 1950s, but most of the money was invested and it was a bad time to sell. In 1957, when the school needed £4,250 to purchase 236 Woodstock Road, there was only £1,250 in hand. The Endowment Fund was administered by the Governors, who the following February agreed to take a loan (not a gift) from it. In June 1959 stock was sold, and a further loan was made from the Endowment Fund to help purchase 50 Oakthorpe Road. But the Funds could only do so much, and anyway the Trust Deed of the Endowment Fund allowed expenditure only from income, not from capital. The school received occasional windfalls, such as the will in 1957 of Mrs Woodward, who honoured the wishes of her late husband Henry Woodward (Roll No. 613), a governor. It left more than £4,000 before tax. But larger sums were needed. The Governors contemplated, though in the end did not take out, a further loan of £60,000 from Barclay's to cover house purchases and other planned expenditure.

How could more money be raised? The St Edward's Society had never been more buoyant. Its dinners were held across the land and the performances of its teams were copiously reported in the *Chronicle*. In 1959 it donated £40 to set up two travelling scholarships for boys, a scheme dear to Fisher. It gave £1,500 towards the Centenary celebrations. But it was not going to be a major source of revenue. There were no longer such OSE as Harold Rogers and Bayford Stone, who in earlier times had been heavily involved in the school's finances and politics. OSE seem to have had no role in determining the goals of the Improvement Fund or of the Centenary Appeal.

Fisher's plans for development met a new snag. The playing fields, designated as part of the Green Belt, were the subject of correspondence in October 1960 to and from the school, central government and Oxford City Council. It resulted in the approval of the proposed development of three buildings, firmly within the Green Belt, for school use. But in the same month the threat of an inner ring road, which would slice the fields in half, raised its head. Fisher, who relished a fight, was not deterred from his plans. The threat receded, though it would return in a heightened form under Fisher's successor.

Fisher persuaded the Governors to appoint Rich and Co., who had already raised funds for Charterhouse, Bradfield and Tonbridge, to run the Centenary Appeal. A charming former soldier, Colonel Gilkes, moved into the school for a year to run it with Bim Barff, as Centenary secretary, and with Fisher himself. It was the start of the professionalization of fund-raising, which has been controversial ever since. It was also in 1960 that a great new opportunity arose. In October the Governors noted the interest of the property company Span Developments in purchasing the Field House estate for development. Fisher seized the chance. He got the Governors together again for a quick decision and the sale went through.

The target of the appeal was £150,000, of which the school aimed, successfully, to raise two-thirds by the time of the Centenary. By 10 July 1963, a fortnight before the celebrations, £90,123 14s. 8d, most of it from parents, had been raised or promised, £82,352 9s. 3d by covenant and the rest by single donations. When the celebrations began the target of £100,000 had been reached, as Fisher was able to announce during them. So the programme of physical improvement could continue. Tilly's and Cowell's, where

Fisher was preparing for the departure of Reid and Brims, would both have married quarters by the following year. The work in School House was to go ahead, although the Chapel extension received no more than its customary mention. In January 1963 the *Chronicle* published plans for two new Houses to be built on the fields by September 1964. The architect, Johnson Marshall, 'has designed a fine building which will make a significant contribution to 20th Century school architecture'. The opportunity was taken not just for the largest expansion since the 1870s but for the creation of a new landscaped Quad in a landscaped setting. Fisher's approach to the interiors of the new buildings shows him caught between two worlds, the old one of communal living and a future which would bring single studies, a privilege hitherto accorded only to the Head of House. Most senior boys were placed in studies for three, while day rooms remained for juniors, an arrangement that would not be easy to convert when the emphasis on individual privacy grew. The new Houses acquired a measure of self-sufficiency by having their own changing-rooms and drying rooms. The housemasters' quarters, often inconveniently placed in the old Houses, were now designed to allow them and the boys easy access to each other.

For the Centenary two huge marquees were erected on the Corfe fields for worship, speeches and eating. Four golden days followed an initial downpour. At one point there were more than 3,000 people in the Quad, and probably a larger number watched the firework display on the fields. Communion and Evensong took place on the Friday and Saturday. On Sunday the Bishop of Ely celebrated communion in the Chapel at 7.15 a.m.; there were two communions at 8.15 a.m., one in the Chapel celebrated by Bob Mortimer, Bishop of Exeter, the other in the marquee by the Bishop of Oxford; and 2,000 filled the marquee for the Sunday morning service, when Bob Mortimer preached. A *Son et Lumière*, a fashionable medium at the time, was performed three times in the Quad, to a mixed reception. Robert Gittings wrote the script. Recordings were played of a reading by Laurence Olivier of Gittings's poem 'September 3rd 1939' and of extracts from the soundtrack of Olivier's filmed performance as Richard III, though the absence of Olivier himself from the proceedings was noticed. Edward Manning conducted two performances of his last concert and, said the *Chronicle*, 'came out triumphantly'. There were five outdoor displays of gymnastics, swimming and diving, cricket against the Martyrs, and bumpers for OSE House IVs. Classrooms were filled with exhibitions of work. Three huge dinners were given on three nights, a concluding luncheon on the Sunday, three garden parties, a firework display, the Beating of the Retreat by the Band of the Royal Marines, and perhaps most impressively of all a fly-past by nine boy pilots led by Peter Corlett.

In his speech Mortimer addressed criticisms of the Public Schools. 'So long as the parents themselves desire this kind of education for their children,' he insisted, 'they should be allowed to have it.' Douglas Bader, speaking off the cuff, maintained that the pendulum of education had swung too much towards academic achievement. He hoped it would revert to 'the centre'. 'Some of us,' he declared, 'would not have got into St Edward's today.' The great thing,' he added, 'the great value, of a school like this is that the pattern continues. As we sit around here today during this week we see the boys doing the same things that we were doing thirty years ago, forty years ago, a hundred years ago possibly.'

There was a shadow over the celebrations. Kendall, on a voyage around the world, had died at sea three months earlier, on 26 April. Bader's speech ended: 'I would like to say, on behalf of all of us who were taught in the School by Henry Kendall as Warden, that the School is extremely lucky to have had Frank Fisher to follow Henry Kendall. To follow Henry Kendall was impossible and Frank Fisher has done it.' The closing speech, by the Governor Sir George Mallaby echoed him: 'Mr Warden, it is your triumph.'

Fisher had his devotees outside the school too. He is one of the heroes of John Rae's book of 1981, *The Public School Revolution*, where he is described as having 'his father's grasp of administration, together with a mind open to new ideas and a talent for getting things done. He bothered about detail without ever letting himself become immersed in it.' He was also 'an astute operator in the public relations field'. Fisher was a driving force behind the Public Relations Sub-Committee, set up in 1963, of the Headmasters' Conference (HMC). From 1964 to 1979, the period covered by Rae's book, 'he was probably the most influential headmaster on the Conference'. In 1973, when he was Chairman of the HMC, he launched its trade magazine, *Conference*, and started the institution's Political Sub-Committee. In 1979 he was made Chairman of the Independent Schools Joint Council Advisory Committee. Though most of that work was done after he left St Edward's for Wellington, his commitment to the promotion of the Independent sector had been formed earlier. No other Warden has been so prominent on the national educational stage.

The year after the Centenary, and after thirteen years of Tory rule, Harold Wilson's Labour Government came to power. What would it do about the Public Schools? Though there were outright abolitionists, they were unlikely to prevail. If private education were forbidden then why not private healthcare? – a prospect Labour shunned. But there were alternatives: the removal of the charitable status of the schools; a return to the proposals of the Fleming Report of 1945 for state-assisted places; or the government might divide and rule the many categories of private and boarding schools and pick off some of them for its own purposes. In 1964 the government set up a Public Schools Commission under the chairmanship of Sir John Newsom, which revamped the Fleming proposals and proposed the allocation of half the boarding places to pupils paid for by the state. Some saw the Commission, a merely departmental and not a Royal Commission, as an attempt to kick the issue into the long grass. Its report in 1968 was not even discussed in Cabinet. Still, Fisher knew the need for robust and organized defence. He found in Graham Kalton's factual survey of the Public Schools in 1966 a reliable compendium of useful facts and statistics. Though not a founding father, Fisher was a keen supporter of the Independent Schools Information Service, which was founded in 1972. With others he persuaded the schools to describe themselves as 'Independent' rather than 'Public', a deft act of re-description which presented them as friends of autonomy rather than of privilege.

On 27 November 1965 Harold Macmillan, robed as Chancellor of the University of Oxford, opened the new Sing's and Field Houses. With the eloquence and nostalgia that marked the speeches of his old age, Macmillan, a product of Edwardian Eton, looked back to the Great War in which he had fought. 'I wish sometimes our critics would spare a moment to loiter in the memorial cloisters or quadrangles of our schools and read again the list of our names – the proudest roll-call in the world.' No one realized the extent to which, as a result of new building to the west of the subway, the focus of the school would be redirected there. Six houses, a sports centre and two pavilions now lie on that side of the Woodstock Road.

In June 1965, in response to proposals by the Newsom Commission, the Governors restated the intentions of the Founder in words of the original trust. 'The object of St Edward's School, which is founded to the glory of God and for the furtherance of the faith in Christ as it was held and taught by the primitive church before the division of East and West and hath been received by the Church of England, shall be to supply a liberal education in accordance with the principles of the Church of England. In the Chapel of the School divine service shall always be conducted and the Sacraments administered according to the rules and rubrics of the Church of England as set forth in the Book of Common Prayer, unless through God's mercy the use of the first Prayer Book of King Edward VI or of some equally Catholic form of liturgy should be restored by lawful authority.' The references to the Edwardian Prayer Book and Catholic liturgy had once been explosive. Now their resonances had been lost. The original 'object of St Edward's School' was increasingly hard to recognize in the outlook and conduct of boys or masters. Ever fewer masters attended Chapel.

In the previous year Fisher had appointed Williams, Church and Evans as housemasters of Tilly's, Cowell's and Segar's. He also raised eyebrows, and provoked some bitterness, by announcing that Brian Gale, the master to whom and to whose family Fisher was closest, would take over Mac's when Mather retired, a full three years in the future. Gale was a talented man but not an uncontroversial one. Did Fisher already expect to be gone by 1967? At all events the appointment tied the hands of his successor, who would not find Gale easy. Rancour also arose, though farce came with it, after the Warden, in the summer of 1965, had given money to the Common Room for a gift of its own choice to mark his departure. A committee of three – Tackley (as the senior master), Todd and Ruscombe-King – was appointed to select the gift. During the holidays, when Tackley was safely away at his Cornish cottage, the more freethinking Todd and Ruscombe-King spent a day in Bloomsbury and returned with a framed set of Aubrey Beardsley's 'Salomé' prints, which were based on Oscar Wilde's play of that name. The purchase included a blown-up version of one of the pictures, that icon of Aestheticism *Peacock Skirt*. Older members of the Common Room were outraged by this reminder of *fin-de-siècle* Decadence. Younger ones, even those who did not care for the pictures, saw a chance to taunt the old guard. Tackley, on return, was appalled to learn of his exclusion from the decision. Fisher, kept informed of the proceedings by Gale, was amused by the affair, or anyway purported to be. There had to be a vote. The Beardsleys were rejected by a majority of only two.

The episode revealed the absence of procedures for decision-making by the Common Room, which by tradition had the character of a gentleman's club where disputes were not expected to arise. Mather and I were commissioned to devise a Common

Room Constitution to which Todd, a Liberal ardently committed to proportional representation, appended a complex system of single transferable voting. Henceforth the termly meetings would have motions, votes and minutes. Most of the Beardsleys were sold to the coach of a visiting team from Belfast and the money was spent on a rather flimsy Sixties bureau which thus constitutes Fisher's gift to his masters. Todd himself bought *Peacock Skirt* for his sitting room. Gale purchased one of the more arousing prints and gave it to the Warden, who placed it in his lavatory.

At their meeting of March 1966, which Fisher's impending successor Richard Bradley attended, the Governors received a seven-page résumé by Fisher of his Wardenship. The Governors of this era were an imposing body. Three of the most influential, though none of them could be present at that meeting, were Peter Carter-Ruck, Sir Roger Mynors, and a more recent appointee, E. T. 'Bill' Williams, the Warden of Rhodes House in Oxford. He had joined the body in 1960 and would be knighted in 1973. His skills in man-management equipped him to liaise between the Governors and the Masters' Common Room, to many of whom he became a familiar figure. Bob Mortimer, the long-standing Chairman of the Governors, could remember Simeon. Nine of the governors had been appointed under Kendall, the first of them being Lt. Col. H. T. Birch-Reynardson who joined the body in 1936. Graham Cooper had been appointed aged 30 in 1947. The eleven appointed under Fisher had preserved the balance achieved by Kendall of the Church, academic life, the services and the business world. They included Basil Guy, Bishop of Gloucester; the Oxford lawyer Teddy Burn (Roll No. 3027), a member of the General Purposes Committee; the Professor of Chemistry J. W. Linnett, another of the committee's members; the Eng. Lit. don Graham Storey (Roll No. 2970); the businessmen Geoffrey Palau (Roll No. 2961), who would be chairman from 1985 to 1992; John Davies (Roll No. 2476), a rising politician; the academic General Sir Ian Riches; and Major-General Sir John Winterton. There were two weighty additions in 1960: the former master at St Edward's Sir George Mallaby, diplomat and former First Civil Service Commissioner; and Aubrey Davidson-Houston (Roll No. 1739), a former soldier and a tireless society portrait painter who painted several Wardens. An assiduous governor, he too served on the General Purposes Committee. All the governors appointed in Fisher's time had been educated at Public School. All had performed some kind of military service, though in subsequent times there have been only three professional military appointments, Admiral Sir Frank Twiss in 1969, General Sir Antony Read in 1972, and Commodore (later Vice-Admiral) Mike Gretton in 1984.

From Fisher's résumé the Governors learned that there were now 508 boys, 31 of them day boys, a rising proportion. Staff changes were noted, and a proposal to extend Jack White's two-year secondment to Uganda was eagerly agreed. 'I think,' wrote Fisher, 'it is in the best interests of everybody that he should stay away.' The meeting noted that brown shoes, hitherto the preserve of school prefects, could now be worn by all boys, and that prefects might 'wear shirts of a quiet kind of their own choice on weekdays'. It learned that a boy had been rusticated for misconduct on Field Day; that nearly £38,000 had been set aside for renovations in the Main Buildings; that a new metal workshop had opened; and that the school teams were doing well. Fisher's document also claimed that the boys now enjoyed a greater degree of personal freedom, though he exaggerated it. He observed that the presence of girls in musical performances and plays had 'helped to break down the feeling of a cloistered society' – a fashionable phrase at the time. It was certainly a start. When the sociologist Royston Lambert and his team visited the school to conduct research for their book *The Hothouse Society* (1969), they were pleasantly surprised by the relative liberalism of the school and remarked on the informality of relationships between staff and pupils, a virtue which Ferguson and Kendall had in their own time sought to foster. But Fisher exaggerated again when he wrote that 'artificial divisions between age groups have become blurred' and that 'any form of uncontrolled new boy tests and any form of physical bullying seem to be things of the past'. Some years later, when speaking of his time at St Edward's to John Rae, Fisher claimed he had eliminated beating by boys. He had not, even if it had become less frequent, not least because in some houses the prefects themselves had reacted against it. In such matters Fisher was a less forward-thinking headmaster than he thought. Or perhaps he knew less about what went on in the Houses than he thought.

By 1980 he was a governor of seven schools – but not, to his disappointment, of St Edward's, even though he returned to live in Oxford. One of the governors reportedly said that they had been ordered around by him often enough for one lifetime. He nonetheless remained devoted to the school. In the months before his death in 1986, when he knew he was dying, he worked for the appeal. Only a day or two before his death he presided at an appeal meeting. He prearranged his funeral service in the Chapel and the scattering of his ashes in the burial ground. He is the only Warden other than Simeon whose remains lie there.

39

WARDEN BRADLEY

THE Governors searched long and hard for the right successor to Fisher. The days of fixed appointments were over. Richard Alan Bradley, the successful candidate, who served for five years, was nearly 40 on his appointment. He had a salary of £2,750 per annum plus £350 towards additional expenses; a car mileage allowance; and the Lodgings free of rent and rates and with free heating and electricity. The Governors, having come to realize, as other schools had done, what an asset to a school a headmaster's (or housemaster's) wife could be, wanted a married man. Bradley was married with two children. As the *Chronicle* said in announcing his appointment, 'Mrs Bradley will have to look back 62 years to Mrs Hudson for guidance as to the role of a Warden's wife.'

Bradley came with an exceptionally rounded and accomplished record. He had been Second School Prefect at Marlborough, where he was deputy to Fran Prichard. He played rugby, hockey and athletics but had wider interests too, and had edited the *Marlburian*. He won a Scholarship to Trinity College, Oxford, where he read History. Intellectually, he was much abler and more engaged than his two predecessors. He had a service record, which ever fewer candidates for headships possessed. He was commissioned in 1945 into the Royal Marines, with whom he served for two years in India and Java. A friend wrote: 'I do not doubt that he would have had a distinguished active service record had the war not finished when it did.' At Oxford he played rugby for the Greyhounds and the Occasionals and, some thought, should have gained a blue. He climbed with the Mountaineering Club and was elected to Vincent's, the select undergraduate club. He supported the Oxford and Bermondsey Club (an East London boys' club), 'the strength of whose undergraduate link at the time owed a great deal to his enthusiasm and example', as one of his referees for St Edward's wrote. In 1949 he was its club manager and assistant to its Warden. His father had been a Prison Commissioner and Director of Borstals, and Richard himself, a naturally thoughtful and sensitive man, had a pronounced social conscience.

After Oxford he spent a year teaching at Dulwich, when he played rugby for Blackheath and Surrey. He then taught for sixteen years at Tonbridge, where at various times he ran the hockey, the rugby, and the History Department, in which his many innovations included an annual night pilgrimage to Canterbury Cathedral. He produced plays, founded a Literary Society and a literary magazine, wrote light verse and reviews and a pageant. He was second in command of the CCF and a pioneer of Arduous Training. As a housemaster from 1961 he made Ferox Hall the most popular House among applicants for Tonbridge. He developed contacts in the States, where he taught for a time at the Gilman School, Baltimore, and which in 1963 he toured on a lecture circuit. His Headmaster's reference described him as 'a devout Christian, a regular communicant [as, by the School's Articles of Association, Wardens of St Edward's had to be], a good stimulating preacher'.

Bradley's was a complex personality, which at St Edward's was to be sorely tested by exhausting work and difficulties in his private life. Serious-mindedness, and a moral earnestness that some found deterrent, mingled with delicious, quietly self-deprecating wit. The seriousness is reflected in his termly reports to the Governors, which, rather than prescribing courses of action as Fisher's had done, explored problems of principle and invited open discussion of them. In an era when the bureaucratic aspects of headmastership were growing, he was no administrator and had too few secretaries to help him. He was no financial manager either, and had to lean on Gibbs and Beales for guidance. He had proved himself as a housemaster, an essentially pastoral skill, and in the classroom, where he had excelled in the guidance of individuals. Headmasters need other gifts. He had little taste for the political battlefield over Independent Schools in which Fisher had engaged. Some masters, used to being ruled by edict, were surprised when in his first week the new Warden came into the Common Room to demonstrate the workings of a simple duplicating device called a BANDA machine, which he claimed would improve teaching. Wardens did not normally descend to such detail or offer their staff technical instruction.

His great strength, though it could also be his problem, was his thoughtfulness. In his very first term, having encountered disciplinary problems among some senior boys and had intensive discussions with one of them, he wrote a short but penetrating essay entitled 'An Apparent Conflict', which he circulated to the housemasters and Sixth Form arts teachers. He was responding earnestly to an earnestness he had identified in the boy himself. His first paragraph reads:

> One of the problems that I have often confronted as a Sixth Form teacher is the danger of an apparent conflict between the clearly defined Christian values, for which a school like this stands, and the liberal intellectual adventures of the classroom. In the course of one term, it is not impossible that a clever Sixth Former might be exposed, as a result of lively teaching, to the philosophy of Nietzsche, the morality of D. H. Lawrence, and the drama of Sartre or Pinter. While such things are whirling round in his head, we shall be requiring him to attend compulsory Chapel; and perhaps we shall be overlooking the sense of paradox with which he will be moving from such intellectual adventures to the relative banalities, in his mind, of St Paul's moral exhortations.

There was, the Warden added, a 'real danger' that conventional injunctions to right conduct 'may seem quaint after contemplation of the casual approach to sexual intercourse which is implicit in [Pinter's] *The Homecoming*'.

Bradley's paper declared his support for intellectual adventure in the classroom. 'I want to re-affirm that I do not believe education is a matter of clapping pious blinkers on willing horses.' 'A number of people,' he added, 'have commented that Christian teaching and practice (in general and in the School)' bore blame for the 'apparent conflict' he had identified. 'This is an assumption that I already held.' Nonetheless, 'it seems essential that we should offer a critical apparatus with which to offset the headiness of such things .... I wonder if we should introduce them' to Sartre or Pinter 'if we cannot subscribe to correctives'. A few readers of the document privately scoffed at it or wondered whether such morally elevated discourse was the proper business of a headmaster. Some science teachers asked why they had been not been on the circulation list, and were duly sent copies. Some masters worried lest, despite Bradley's assurances, the recent liberalizing trend might be reversed. But he had raised fundamental educational issues and asked his staff to think about them. At least they now had the measure of the man.

His sense of humour was sparklingly displayed at the OSE Yorkshire dinner in May 1969. Three cars drove to Worksop College carrying the Warden, Fran and Pat Prichard, Pam and Duncan Williams, me, the Prichards' and the Williams's Labradors, and Bradley's diminutive poodle. We were warmly greeted by Roger Northcote-Green and what seemed packs of gun dogs and retrievers, which romped with the Labradors while the poodle was left to look on. The sight inspired Bradley to an impromptu comic turn on his ownership of a dog lacking the social credentials of a headmaster's pet. There was pathos in the wit, for there was always something of the outsider about him.

He had an advantage in his relations with his staff. Four of the housemasters, Prichard, Williams, Armstrong and Church, had been friends or acquaintances of his at Oxford. With Evans and Pether they made up a strong team still in their prime (the seventh housemaster, Mather, being about to retire). The Second Master Bim Barff, who had held the post since 1957 and had stood in for Fisher when the Warden had taken a sabbatical for the Easter Term following the Centenary. The second-mastership was a largely honorific post, for neither Kendall nor Fisher had had a taste for delegation. It remained one under Barff's successor Tackley, who held the post for two years. Only under Tackley's successor John Armstrong did it begin to acquire the substance that the increasingly taxing duties of the Warden made necessary. Bradley trod warily in his dealings with the older members of the staff. He accurately warned the Governors that Pat Brims would not welcome the popularization of Classical Studies which was being adroitly pioneered by the Classical Association in a bid to preserve Classical teaching. Likewise, the stern Continental rigour of Alexander's German teaching was at odds with the move, which was dear to Bradley's heart, towards the use of machinery and language laboratories in Modern Language teaching. In 1969 Jack Tate finally retired to the archives, which he looked after until his death in 1988. Another veteran was Hubert Beales, who had been one of Kendall's Mevagissey set. He had returned to the school after the war, in which he was wounded at Dunkirk. He was bursar from 1946 to 1975. His reserve and self-effacement concealed the enormous importance of his skilful financial management. From 1959 to 1970 he had as an assistant Jack Butterworth (Roll No. 2471), his contemporary as a boy, who was succeeded by Gordon Fuzzard. Otherwise he had only an office junior and a single secretary. Masters respected him, as did the Governors, whose Minutes praised the 'accuracy and clarity of the bursar's budgets and financial statements, which they have been receiving continuously over a number of years'.

Bradley saw that with only seven housemasterships, each with a fifteen-year tenure, too many able and energetic masters had too little hope of preferment and were likely to look elsewhere. There were departures that the school could ill afford. The year 1966 brought the departure of Vernon, who left for a prep school headship, and of his fellow English teacher Cameron Cochrane, later headmaster of Fettes. David Pettit's departure for Clifton in the same year was a major blow, for although high standards were maintained by his two successors the music ceased to fizz. The sciences suffered from the departures of David Tawney in 1967 and of Roger Lawrence and David Tinsley in 1970. Robert Montgomerie, a Classicist, left in the same year; he would become Rugby's Second Master. Robin Alden (Roll No. 4084), who had arrived in 1965 and contributed substantially to the teaching of English and to the drama and rowing, also left in 1970, to become a housemaster at Rugby.

Colin Pedley left too, in 1968 after six years. If anyone represented the two faces of Bradley's 'apparent conflict', it was he. A clever and inspiring teacher, he added enormously to the intellectual life of the school. Yet his cerebral honesty led him to lay bare doubts, and nuances of belief, that were painful for the chaplain Paul Drake, who was struggling to sustain the life of the Chapel in the face of mounting criticism from boys and of questioning from some masters. Drake himself left for a parish in 1969 after eleven years' service. He was succeeded as chaplain by the Ulsterman John Fielding. Pedley himself was not replaced as assistant chaplain. Instead a number of lay masters helped out and were drawn into the life of the Chapel.

Some of Bradley's appointments to the staff, including some very good ones, stayed for a short time: David Oxley, Richard Oliver, Claude Evans, Paul Cheetham and Robin Murphy. Some stayed longer. He found dedicated language teachers in Chris Lane, John Donald, Malcolm Nock and Michael Boswell; first-class English ones in Simon Taylor and Malcolm Watson; and a mathematician of national stature in David Cundy, who would be a pillar of the school's academic life for more than thirty years. As Head of Maths he became a figure on the public stage of mathematics education through his role in the introduction of the Schools Mathematics Project. Bradley could spot talent.

What of the pupils in Bradley's time? As at other schools, reminiscences of old boys tend to be written in advancing years. The supply of written recollections dwindles from the 1960s. George Wilkinson (Roll No. 6357), whose career exactly spanned Bradley's tenure, feels that his generation is alienated from the school. Unusually for a former Head of School he has unhappy or uncomfortable memories of St Edward's. Yet his suggestion is hard to test. Bradley's was the time of the 'Swinging Sixties', the 'Age of Aquarius', the world of 'student protest' and 'flower power', though the labels can lead us into exaggeration or simplification. A few OSE of the era see themselves as having belonged to a great movement for change, but the demonstrations of discontent came later, during Henry Christie's Wardenship. No more than Fisher's tenure were the Bradley years a time of pupil rebellion.

The school did produce its crop of student protesters. Jon Snow (Roll No. 5816), the television presenter, left at the same time as Fisher. Having improved his A levels elsewhere, and having worked for Voluntary Service Overseas in Uganda, he went to Liverpool University where he was rusticated for his political activity in 1970. But while he had had his dissatisfactions at St Edward's his radicalism was not born there. Another OSE student activist at Liverpool, where he studied from 1969, was Christopher Graham (Roll No. 6032), who while an undergraduate became the youngest ever local government councillor, and who is now the UK's Information Commissioner. Unlike Snow, and unlike most boys at St Edward's, he did develop his political commitment while at the school, though he probably owed it more to his home background than to the environment at St Edward's. Nicholas Emley (Roll No. 6084) joined the infamous demonstration in February 1970 at the Garden House Hotel in Cambridge against the regime of the Greek Colonels. In the mêlée he accidentally removed a policeman's helmet. The result, a spell in Borstal, has generally been seen as a travesty of justice. A character reference by his former housemaster Mervyn Evans failed to move Mr Justice Melford Stephenson. Nicholas had been no dissident at school.

The Colonels had an eye out for trouble. When Nicholas's brother Miles (Roll No. 5878) holidayed in Greece in 1970 he and his friend were inveigled into making some indiscreet remarks to a group seemingly consisting of fellow Greek students. They were arrested and deported. Alan Muir (Roll No. 6456), who was no incendiary, was arrested on holiday in South Africa just after leaving St Edward's in 1971 and was interrogated by the security service, BOSS, who knew all about him. They accused him of having consorted at school with his contemporary in Field House, Stephen Hayward (Roll No. 6443), the son of a major-general, who indeed had some left-wing opinions but was a rebel neither at the school nor subsequently at Cambridge.

The decisive changes were in youthful lifestyle, not in political outlook. Over the 1960s the word 'boys' gradually disappears from the *Chronicle* as a description of the pupil population. 'Boy' had come to mean 'child', the condition from which teenagers declared their freedom. Another change came with it: the use of first names, rather than surnames, by masters addressing boys. In the early 1960s it grew common among the boys themselves, indeed was described by one of them, Stephen Winkley (Roll No. 5412), a future Headmaster of Uppingham, as 'flourishing like the cedars of Lebanon'. Later in the decade, in its official reporting the *Chronicle* began to call boys by their first names as well as surnames. At home teenagers had become less deferential to their parents. They dressed differently, listened to different music, insisted on their own social arrangements and bedtimes. As Fisher had seen, they wanted to bring the freedom and autonomy they knew in the outside world into the school. In any case adults themselves were increasingly stating that education was about the discovery and development of the individual, not about the imposition of intellectual or social norms. Yet boys did not rush to embrace that ideal. Alongside their teenage instincts there was the sense that new freedoms and emphases were undermining the collective spirit that had thrived on the hierarchies and discipline of the Houses. In 1968, a high point of the student protest movement, the *Chronicle* betrayed nervousness about the new mood of liberty: 'In broad terms the modern trend is from regimentation to free choice. How much we get out of living at St Edward's depends more and more on each individual. As more freedom is handed out, the possibility that he will waste the opportunities afforded by such a school becomes greater.'

In the following year the magazine viewed with mixed feelings the 'spectre of Pupil Power', which seemed certain to 'reveal itself with increasing frequency in many of our schools. It continued:

> The Sixth Form version of the Student Power movement in the universities is strongly entrenched in London and parts of the South-East, and claims to have established footholds in some leading independent schools. Chief amongst its aims it numbers the abolition of uniforms, the abolition of corporal punishment especially of one boy by another, a complete re-appraisal of the prefect system, and the establishment of close communications between the Sixth Form and the management of the school.

How should St Edward's respond?

> It would require the thickest of reactionary blinkers for one not to recognise the present urgent need to allow intelligent young people a greater voice in affairs that affect them deeply, and the folly of preaching the virtues of individual responsibility and the fruitful

use of leisure time without providing either the occasions or the conditions where these virtues might be exercised.

Yet the editorial warns 'against the immature posturing and political sloganeering of the more extreme proponents of Pupil Power', such as the advocates of a recent proposal that sixth-formers in Leeds should sit on school governing bodies. The mood at St Edward's was very distant from the atmosphere of the universities, and the concerns of most boys far removed from student stances on the Vietnam war, unilateralism, civil rights or Apartheid.

40

THE LOST LEADER?

THE reference for Bradley written by his headmaster declared that 'although essentially a traditionalist by nature he is far from opposed to changes in the life and curriculum of a Public School'. He proved to be restless for change and pursued it with gusto. He bombarded the Governing Body with proposals and turned it into a kind of think tank. Fisher had occasionally trailed his policies in informal meetings with masters or prefects, but Bradley wanted formal and extensive consultation.

He tried to raise academic standards, chased up heads and their departments, and reported their performances to the Governors. By the autumn of 1967 he had made substantial changes to the teaching arrangements. The Lower School was reorganized and pupils' first terms were set aside for assessment of their O-level choices and prospects. Pupils were given more flexibility in the combination of A-level subjects. He increased the number of weekly teaching periods from 32 to 35 and added to the teaching time spent on non-examination subjects. He introduced a system of three-weekly reports on boys' work, which would survive with few adjustments for more than thirty years. Physical Science was introduced, and videotapes and other technological advances were encouraged in the classroom. He brought in an 'audio-active room' for Modern Languages, though not the full-scale language laboratory he would have liked. He urged the provision of more classroom space, and lamented the inadequate size of the Memorial Library, which could seat only 10% of sixth-formers and was needed for the increasing number of study periods.

Distinguished literary figures such as Iris Murdoch, John Wain and Stan Barstow were brought in to lecture, as part of Bradley's plan to improve the school's image in the neighbouring university, where in his words 'too many dons regard the School as a hidebound muscle factory just opposite the BMC Radiator Works'. Yet the academic record of his tenure, which was too short – here, as in other matters – for his policies to be properly tested, was not striking. The early 1960s had seen Oxbridge awards and places running at between 24 and 30 a year. In December 1966 the number was 25, but it dropped thereafter, to 17 in 1968, 16 in 1969 and 18 in 1970. In 1966, 84.9% of A levels taken were passed, but only 45.8% of them with grades of A, B or C. Over the following four years the percentage of passes ranged between 80.5% and 82.4%, and the A–C grades varied between 41.6% and 54.3%.

In December 1968 came a shock. Oxford City Council, beset by the city's mounting traffic congestion, proposed a spinal road, parallel with the railway, which would prevent any future development of 15 acres of school property across the canal. That was bad enough; but, far more alarmingly, the scheme provided for a spur road to provide a link from the spinal road to the Summertown traffic, which would slice the school's grounds in half by crossing them opposite the Lower II pitch, immediately to the south of the area that would later constitute the Kendall Quad. It would have been a devastating blow to the school. Soon it transpired that the Council had drawn up its plans in ignorance of the existence of the new Sing's and Field House buildings in the same area, but the exposure of the Council's ineptitude did not dispel the threat. Bradley quickly spotted the danger and moved fast. Throughout the alarming episode which followed he displayed unfailing vigilance and shrewdness. His first step, taken with the Governors, was to hire as a consultant Professor Colin Buchanan, the acknowledged expert on road planning, who swiftly spotted flaws in the scheme. By June 1970 Buchanan and the QC Desmond Wright were hard at work on the school's case. In November a stinging letter from Bishop Mortimer reached the Lord Mayor. How, he asked, could boys be expected to cross a busy road at least eight times a day? The main rugby and cricket grounds would become unusable.

Buchanan produced telling arguments, and Bradley himself submitted an eloquent document. It addressed the practical problems for the school, among them the prospect that it would have to build an expensive bridge to join a now mutilated estate, and confronted broader issues:

> The traffic relief problem is a result of a mounting and uncontrolled tendency of 20th Century life. We are being asked to surrender vital educational amenities for the solution of a problem which may conceivably have changed its nature by the end of this present century. By contrast, the requirements of education will continue quite unabated. I submit that it is in direct contrast to all civilised standards and all sensible priorities that so distinguished a school and so noble a vision should be sacrificed to a utilitarian contemporary need.

In 1961, he pointed out, the school had accepted that its playing fields would become part of the Green Belt. Now the authorities were going back on assurances they had then given. In the cause of the larger issue the school reluctantly confined its attack to the spur road and conceded that the land across the canal might have to be sacrificed. In the event neither the spine nor the spur road was ever built. The public inquiry was begun in the last two weeks of June 1970 and resumed in November. Wright presented the case for the school and called on the written submissions of Buchanan and Bradley. The inquiry cost the school £1,503.41, of which £791.25 went to Buchanan and £386.55 to Wright. Bradley's exertions had saved the school, or at least had preserved it in a recognizable form.

Prices rose by 49% in the 1960s. Fees and salaries had somehow to keep up. In Bradley's second term the Governors agreed to raise the fees from £486 to £522. They were still about £40 below the average for such schools, and demand was not affected by the rise. But Bradley recognized that the 'extras' which were customarily charged were an irritant that might deter boys from activities on which they were levied. When he withdrew the charges for learning musical instruments and for using the Art Room the numbers rose, though the increase was also indebted to the popularity of the teachers of music and art. He did what he could for masters' salaries. They rose by 7% at the end of 1967 and there was a flat-rate increase of £120 in 1970. After the recent fund-raising and building this was not a time for further physical expansion, but Bradley made sure that the Centenary Appeal did not lapse.

Fisher had allowed boys occasionally to be taken out by their parents between morning and evening Chapel on Sundays. The emptiness of Sunday afternoons had become more oppressive with the rise in the proportion of married masters, who liked to give the day to their families and were less and less disposed to arrange play rehearsals or other activities instead. Adrian Hatt (Roll No. 6142) wrote in the *Chronicle* in 1967 of the 'dreariness, boredom, depression' of wet Sundays, when 'a boy slouches lazily ... head resting in his hands' in his horse-box. Parents wanted to see more of their sons, and a growing proportion of them lived in the Thames Valley catchment area, near enough for visits to be easy. In the long term, indeed, the main geographical base of the school would become more regional than national. In his first year Bradley introduced Parents' Evenings, to be held three times in a boy's career. Parents of 70% of boys in the Removes attended the first meeting. In time each House would hold meetings for the parents of all its boys, arranged by year groups.

The days when families despatched their sons to St Edward's at the beginning of term and left the school to get on with their upbringing were over. Gaudy, shortened by the bringing forward of GCE exams earlier in the term, had become almost entirely an occasion for parents. OSE now had the other annual gathering, Commem, more or less to themselves. It too was abbreviated.

Traditionally the rise of boys to seniority had brought them power and hierarchical ascendancy. What senior pupils now increasingly wanted was not so much ascendancy over their juniors as a degree of independence, appropriate to their years, in the running of their lives. In recognition of that trend Bradley continued Fisher's policy of enhancing the status of membership of the Sixth Form, and pursued some enterprising if risky initiatives. Occasionally he allowed a pupil to become a 'Mature Student' who attended school only for tuition, had no affiliation to a House, and was directly supervised by the Warden. He also introduced the category of Senior Schoolboy (though he might have been wiser to avoid the word 'boy') to allow pupils to withdraw from their accommodation in the Houses and, if they were prefects, to relinquish their duties. The few who took up the offer were allocated bed-sitting rooms in the houses of married masters while continuing to belong to their Houses, where they were allowed what Bradley termed 'a certain degree of detachment'.

In February 1969 the Warden told the Governors of his plan for a 'Sixth Form non-residential centre', to be housed in the old Isolation Block once the building of the new Language Centre had freed its space. 'It is envisaged that a Club should be started on these premises, in which VI Formers could both work and meet for relaxation.' As far as possible it was to be self-governing. A committee of masters and boys was at work on the scheme and by September, when the Centre had been completed, the premises were ready and a licence, the first for under-18s in Oxford, had been granted by Oxford magistrates to allow the sale of beer and cider. Other schools would soon try similar experiments. Some masters were sceptical, sometimes for what proved good reasons. The club attracted boys for drink, not for work. Though it did not produce the reckless drunkenness some had foreseen, equally it did not stop illicit expeditions to Oxford pubs. The notion that boys could largely supervise the project themselves was unrealistic. There was sloppy accounting and even embezzlement, until adults were brought in and a professional barman employed. A compromise between adult and pupil authority would persist in later years, when the club was twice moved to new premises.

At the same time as the club an Upper School Committee was formed. Boys elected two representatives from each House and met with a supervising master to discuss matters of school policy. Tony Snell bravely took on the supervisory role. Soon the boys were allowed to elect a master representative. They chose Michael Rutland, a young scientist with a risqué air, though his service was short for he left in 1970. The committee pressed for a school dance (Fisher's brief experiment on that front having been long forgotten). It demanded hot meals on Sunday evenings and claimed the credit for the introduction of fluorescent lighting in Big School to improve examination conditions. It persuaded the Warden to allow corduroy jackets, though few chose to wear them. It sponsored a regular news-sheet, *Info*, which published essays on matters of school policy and advertised activities in Oxford as well as in the school. But the committee was not popular with the boys. *Info* itself criticized it as 'a waste of time', 'much the same as the House of Lords' or 'like the House of Commons in 1600'. One boy wrote that he might stand for election 'so that I can get it abolished', another that 'There are better things to waste time grumbling about' than dirty trays. The prefects, who anyway had more power than the committee, already provided an effective medium of consultation, or so boys felt. One member of the committee, Colin Irving-Bell (Roll No. 6280), put up a reasoned defence. At least policy issues had been discussed and the Warden had listened. But he acknowledged the difficulty – one the Warden had not fully faced – of ensuring that the members represented the views of their constituents, not merely their own. Colin thought there was 'far too little discussion between boys on any subject. Boys' attitudes are very typical of the general attitude of the world. Too many people are content to accept what others say and not to question. They are too apathetic towards the world around them.' When the committee arranged for an Economy Lunch one day to make a contribution to aid for Biafra (the breakaway province of Nigeria), it transpired that it had failed to communicate its decision to its constituents, who in large measure opposed the plan.

The committee was formed just after the Chapel Committee, that pioneering exercise in consultation, had disbanded. Its scope had been confined to the allocation of collections to charities, a matter that could easily be handled by the sacristans and the chaplain. It was dissolved on the ground that there was not enough to discuss. Issues of Chapel policy were evidently off limits, for had consideration of them been allowed there could hardly have been more to discuss. Long-standing problems persisted. As church attendance and religious knowledge declined in the home, the institutional conventions of Chapel attendance and Confirmation seemed ever more remote from faith and spiritual experience. Confirmation now normally took place at the young age, some said too young, of 13 or 14. An essay in the *Chronicle* in 1968 identified 'a great need in the School at present for an end to apathy, and a need for a solid core of "religion" to build on, or even to try out and choose to reject. These two needs are complementary. Apathy would end, I reckon, with the emergence of a vital, even if negative, interest in religion.' The author advocated Confirmation at a later age and an eight-month course which would link worship to religious instruction. A pupil must be provoked into 'thinking on his own ... and given ample time for both comprehension and decision'.

Many grumbled at compulsory Chapel. Even some devout boys thought religion was demeaned when placed on the same footing of compulsion as the other obligations of school life: rugby, the CCF and so on. There were no anti-Chapel demonstrations, but there was a growing sullenness. Still, the choir liked the obligatory services and there remained some affection for the lusty singing of hymns at the weekly Congregational Practice, 'Congregagger Pragger' as it had been known down the decades. Chapel was one of the issues the Warden was determined to grasp. Finding the school prefects to be against the compulsion but not against the promotion of faith, and believing that a majority in the Common Room thought the same, he set out to strengthen the boys' faith while reducing compulsion. From January 1968 he made suggestions for change to the Governors. As a first step he raised the possibility of a choice of services on Sundays and a division between senior and junior boys to allow for their different outlooks and simultaneously to relieve the pressure of space on the building. In January 1968 he tackled the complaints about compulsory attendance on weekdays by introducing Junior and Senior chapels on alternate days, half of them, he hoped, to be conducted by volunteers from the Common Room. By September 1970 a new structure was in place for Sunday services. There would be four of them, and all boys except those in their last year would be required to attend at least one: Holy Communion at 8.15; two simultaneous services at 10.30; and Evensong at 6 p.m. One of the 10.30 services would be Sung Eucharist (or sometimes Matins), the other an essentially secular theme service with readings or reflections on moral or spiritual concerns. The theme service, devised each week by one of the Houses, was usually taken by a lay master, sometimes with the help of pupils. The innovation would have a long life, thanks partly to the handful of masters who kept it going. The exemption of final-year pupils, who henceforth would not be obliged to attend any Chapel services, breached the compulsory principle which until recently had been taken for granted through the school's history.

There was a second prong to Bradley's policy. He aimed to stimulate interest in religion in the classroom, a move which had the drawback of adding to the congestion of the timetable and to the teaching load of masters. Boys in their first year were to have three periods of study based on the New Testament. There would be no religious instruction in their next two years, when the demands of O level would monopolize the timetable, but in the following year there would be a two-period course on the place of religion in life. In the Sixth Form there was to be a weekly period of general discussion when some philosophy and theology would be addressed.

Inroads into compulsory Chapel risked prompting the inference that worship was now regarded as of limited importance. Bradley saw that they might also lead boys to question compulsion in other walks of the school's life. His general policy was to offer diversity of choice within a framework of compulsion. Just as boys could choose which service to attend on Sunday mornings, so in the CCF the introduction of a Civil Defence section and later a Community Service option provided more choice within an activity that remained obligatory. Likewise boys had to play games but had a greater number to choose from than their predecessors. Though Bradley saw his alterations to the Chapel regime as 'the most important and most controversial' of his changes, they were part of a wider policy of giving boys freedoms and with them responsibility for their own choices. He rewrote the School Rules in a more liberal spirit. Cafés and chemists were no longer out of bounds, the use of radios was more freely allowed, and 'Lock-up' times were reduced.

In assessing pupils' capacity for mature behaviour he divided them into three categories: those in their 'early years', those in their 'middle years', and those in their 'final stages', though he acknowledged the approximate character of the classifications. In the 'turbulent years' of the middle category, he recognized, 'the first attempt at the exercise of choice and discrimination is often very misguided'. But the school should restrict the freedom of a boy in the 'final stages' only if he abused it. It was the sixth-formers whom Bradley did most to emancipate. He arranged for more study periods to be unsupervised, and encouraged housemasters to allow older boys to attend or participate in events outside the school. 'I have attempted,' he explained to the Governors, 'to move forward cautiously towards an emancipation of the Sixth Former, without losing the basic reality of the School's authority.'

The Bradley years were ones of lively discussion among boys, or at least among the brighter sixth-formers. In 1970 the *Chronicle* sprang into fresh life, in a new format. In the mid-to-late 1960s it had been dull, had lost money, and had had to reduce its size. Even the OSE section was shortened, though it did produce a supplement of original contributions to make up for the demise of *The Martyr*. Rapid turnover of the masters who supervised the *Chronicle* had not helped. Now the magazine was placed on a new financial footing, thanks to an appeal that raised £1,000 and to a decision that lifetime subscriptions would from now on be charged to boys' fees. Henceforth, several issues would contain extensive and to some readers provocative essays by senior boys on such subjects as the future of Public Schools.

In the Spring Term of 1971 George Wilkinson, who had arrived in the same term as Bradley, was his last Head of School. In the summer, when Bradley had been given leave to acclimatize himself for a new job in Canada and John Armstrong was Acting Warden, George, who was living with the Barffs, took his A levels as a Mature Student. His illuminating if at times contentious recollections describe a school which, 'on the surface at least', 'must have appeared one of the more successful minor public schools, punching well above its weight and offering a modern and enlightened education'. He refers to victories on the river, successful rugby and cricket teams, fine drama, some outstanding teaching, and the excellence of his housemaster Peter Church. But he also suggests that little had changed in boarding schools since his grandfather's days at Bromsgrove. Most of the teaching staff, he thinks, were 'as perplexed as we were by the changes' in society beyond the 'small enclosed world that was SES'.

Of Bradley he writes: 'My sole memory of him in that first term of his and mine is his address in the School Chapel on the Sunday evening in late October, following the disaster at Aberfan: moving, humane and filled with anger at the injustice of the event. That, I believe, was the man, and that, I believe, is how he intended his Wardenship to be. Looking back I feel he was putting down a marker for the School and him.' Yet Wilkinson's experience as Head of School convinced him that the Warden had become isolated from boys and Common Room alike. He blames masters and prefects for giving him inadequate support, remembers the very disappointing collection raised for him by the boys when he left, and suggests that Bradley has been 'airbrushed out of the history of SES'.

I do not remember any collective dislike of him in the Common Room, where indeed he had a lot of support, but he was not popular with the boys, who reacted adversely to the very characteristic that George recalled admiringly: he wore his heart on his sleeve. He could seem too quick to moralize, and too eager to interpret local difficulties as symptoms of a general malaise. He took endless care over troubled boys. Yet during his time there seems to have been an increase in the number of pupils who left under a cloud, even if the reasons and significance of that development are impossible to assess. In his first term he had to dismiss three boys. In 1971 three more became the first to be expelled for drugs offences. At least two others were removed for breaking the law as distinct from rules. Eight or more left because, as Bradley put it to the Governors, they 'did not want to be here for various reasons'. For the first time we read of boys receiving psychiatric treatment; two of them left the school. These difficulties, and so many others, wore him down. Few knew the extent of his care and compassion. Robert King (Roll No. 6449) died in the Radcliffe Infirmary in 1970 after a drawn-out struggle against a brain tumour. While Robert lay dying, his widowed mother lived with Mervyn and Yvonne Evans, Robert's housemaster. Bradley paid frequent visits to the hospital, often late at night after a hard day's work, and gave support to the mother. He had to give draining attention to a prolonged search for a paedophile who had gained access to boys in several schools in the Thames Valley, and who was eventually caught and jailed. With great skill the malefactor had so planned his predatory forays as to create the suspicion that a member of the school might be responsible. His tactic sowed damaging suspicion and division.

Bradley's personal problems became public when the Chairman of the Governors sent a letter to all parents, which was read to the Common Room and boys at the start of Spring Term 1968. It announced the legal separation of the Warden from his wife, but confirmed the full confidence of the Governors in him. Henceforth Bradley had to live in a community in which his difficulties had been made public. He was left with three children to bring up on his own. Sometimes the pressure told, in tiredness and irritability. Provision of hospitality became a problem for him. The *Chronicle* recorded that the Mackworth Society, the dining and paper-reading society which met in the Warden's lodgings that Fisher had created, was unable to meet in the Spring and Summer Terms of 1968, ostensibly 'because all the members had left'. On the last night of the following Christmas Term there suddenly appeared an alternative *Chronicle*, a slickly produced illicit magazine concocted largely by leaving prefects. A measured editorial welcomed the Warden's plans for further discussions between masters and boys. Other contributions were not measured. There was a hilarious 'Spot the Christian' competition, which carried a photograph of an empty chapel, as well as a witty description of local pubs. Less witty, and merely tasteless, was 'Mrs Bradley's Diary', modelled on 'Mrs Wilson's Diary' in *Private Eye*. It was bound to hurt.

In 1970 the separation became a divorce. Bradley, who had offered his resignation at the time of the separation, offered it again. After lengthy consultations, the Governors agreed to it. For an Anglican school it was difficult to accept the divorce, especially since the chairman was the Church's acknowledged expert on ethics. Bradley would go on to an enormously successful career as a headmaster in Canada and the United States. If he had stayed at St Edward's there would have been, for better or worse, no shortage of excitement. He would have continued to confront the challenging social changes to which the school had to find ways of adapting. As it was, the Governors would have to look, after only five years, for a new Warden.

41

WARDEN HENRY CHRISTIE

RICHARD BRADLEY'S successor, Henry Christie, the ninth Warden, who was chosen from a good field, was the first to have served already as headmaster of an established HMC school. He had been Head of Brighton College since 1963. Born in 1924, he was a King's Scholar at Westminster and an Exhibitioner of Trinity College, Cambridge. He served in the RNVR in the war and was mentioned in despatches in 1945. A mathematician, he had taught for eight years at Eton and been Under Master and Master of the Queen's Scholars at Westminster for six. The Christies were a closely knit family with a son and three daughters. Henry's wife Naida proved an enormous asset, not only as a headmaster's wife but in the classroom, where she was an enthusiastic and talented teacher of English.

When Christie left after seven years the *Chronicle* said: 'He came to a school at odds with itself and somewhat at odds with the world outside .... It was a school which badly needed guidance and a steadying hand if it was to achieve its aims.' That was a questionable statement, but in appointing him the Governors may indeed have been looking for a 'steadying hand' and for a reassertion, after Bradley's precarious experiments in pupil freedom, of tested practices and values. If so, they got them. They also got, in place of Bradley's exploratory documents, the briefest Warden's Reports since Kendall's. And in place of Bradley's soul-searching they got cheerfulness and at times Panglossian optimism. At the end of his first term Christie recorded his first impressions of the school for the *Chronicle*. In his article he admires the spaciousness of the school, its green lawns and playing fields. He extols its friendliness and, selectively citing recent exam results, praises the academic standards. He also lauds the music, games, the woodwork, the printing work, Community Service. And 'never have I been at a school where there is so much drama'. The OSE dinners are marvellous. Teachers and pupils are thanked; the bursar and his staff are thanked; the Head of School (Nigel Paton, Roll No. 6332) and the prefects are thanked; the musicians are thanked; participants in all out-of-school activities are thanked. Games, printing and

Community Service, 'to mention only three' activities, are lauded and their exponents thanked.

Noting the pace and the pressures of school life, he remarks that 'nobody thinks such beaver-like activity is in any way out of the ordinary, so my wonder turns to gratitude to all those who work so hard to produce so zestful a community'. Commitment to the realization of marvellous opportunities 'pervades St Edward's and this is what makes it such a splendid school in which to live and work'. 'Splendid' was Henry's favourite adjective. Everyone – boys and masters – imitated his use of it. His courtesy was boundless, too. No one, however critical of his policies or actions, could resist it. Of the five Wardens I served, no other was so liked, even loved, by the servants and domestic staff. His universal bonhomie nourished the school's traditional sense of community. Though he did not get close to pupils, he won respect even from those who thought his attitudes old-fashioned. When he left in 1978, a banner was draped across the roof of Tilly's with the affectionate, only faintly mocking words 'Bye-Bye Henry'.

Christie never rushed into decisions or initiated reforms; rather he responded to events. It was unkindly said that the Warden's desk had to be approached by a climb up the carpet, so many were the problems swept under it. Yet his sensitive antennae warned him to adjust to change. He knew when to back down. His first report to the Governors noted that, while everything else was 'splendid', the untidy appearance of the boys was 'too informal for my taste'. He summoned a large group of them to tell them so. There followed some enforced haircuts and some resentment. Yet the policy did not last; the team photographs of his Wardenship show locks tumbling down over the collars, even to the shoulders.

His antennae were needed, for soon the school would face more dramatic challenges than long hair. On the morning of the CCF Inspection in the summer of Christie's first year boys donning their uniforms discovered that the fly-buttons of their trousers were missing. While linen-room staff frantically plied their needles to restore them (just in time), the school became aware that the words 'NO CCF', and a CND symbol, had been painted on the roof of Sing's. The Inspection went ahead and the *Chronicle*, reporting the Inspection with unusual brevity, made no reference to the protest. But 'pupil power' had struck. Four years later there was a demonstration against the quality of the food, when only about twelve boys attended lunch and most of the remainder stood in the Quad looking through the windows. Nick Stevenson (Roll No.

7521) remembers that the event had 'a very high level of support'. Both episodes were efficiently organized. After the second, Christie promised to get the food improved but, Stevenson writes, he let the matter drop 'once things had settled down a bit'.

When I was appointed in 1962 I was one of only eight masters, other than the chaplains, not to be or have been CCF officers. The number would soon increase, just as the number of masters not attending Chapel did. Colleagues who had done National Service retired. Yet many young masters with no military experience joined, and all three sections of the Force continued to thrive. A number of boys enjoyed the CCF, even if the chores of spit-and-polish, the discomfort of the uniforms, and the slog of the proficiency exams had become no more popular. But in Bradley's time the CCF and its military ethos had become contentious. Shortly before his departure the *Chronicle* published thoughtful pieces, among them an essay by Iain Bruce (Roll No. 6418) and Ashley Wyatt (Roll No. 6480). Though conceding that the CCF might still foster 'certain human qualities which will always be needed', they asked whether it was 'right that the public' – for the CCF was heavily subsidized by the Ministry of Defence – 'should have to provide money for ammunition regularly used by twenty or thirty boys in the Rifle Range, when the money could be spent on, say, hospital modernisation?... Is it good in these days of juvenile delinquency and student unrest to make a boy shoot at a picture of a man, with a gun that can kill at over a mile, when he does not want to do so on moral grounds?' The article was quoted in a later article by a master in the *Chronicle*, and Mervyn Evans contributed a letter to what had become a wide debate, of the kind which Bradley encouraged but which was less welcome under his successor. Bradley had keenly supported the CCF and encouraged it to broaden its activities and to incorporate or assist the Duke of Edinburgh Award Scheme, first aid, Arduous Training, life-saving, swimming, radio communications and vehicle maintenance. The Ministry of Defence's money was thus spent on an increasing range of non-military activities. There might be limits to the MoD's tolerance of this trend, but it was the survival of military duties and functions that irked many boys.

In the year of the demonstration the MoD's stance changed, and it now asked the schools to aim for a voluntary CCF. Thus government policy now concurred with the desire of boys. Most headmasters ignored the request, for they knew that the government would not just pull the plug. But Christie went along with it; to assuage not the Ministry but the boys he made radical changes. Participation in the CCF would become just one of a variety of options for Monday afternoon activities, including Community Service. The new policy would begin with the senior boys. About a third chose to stay in the CCF, another third to perform Community Service, and the rest to participate in other activities. 'If this arrangement works,' wrote Christie to the parents, 'we plan to extend it to the younger age groups year by year.' The *Chronicle* rejoiced in the change, and the Warden wrote that 'everything seems to be working well and everyone is happy with the arrangements'.

In reality the scheme proved too radical to be practicable. Since most of the staff continued to give their Monday afternoons to the CCF as officers, there was not the manpower to arrange sufficient tasks for Community Service or supervise boys learning car maintenance or printing, or the variety of other options. In 1973 the plans were accordingly modified. Now that the CCF had become voluntary for senior boys the main opposition to it had been neutralized. Shell boys were eased into the CCF by their third term through map and compass work and the Duke of Edinburgh's Bronze Award. They were also introduced, within the CCF arrangements, to 'minor sports' such as tennis, squash, judo, fencing and athletics – 'in order', as Christie told the parents, 'that they might discover some talent which would otherwise remain hidden'. Fourth-formers were fully militarized and took the Proficiency Examination as well as compulsorily attending the annual camp. Fourth- and fifth-formers spent the rest of CCF time in naval, air or army sections or on such other activities as canoeing, signals and vehicle maintenance. Yet the extension of options, far from easing the problem of manpower, added further to the burdens on the teaching staff. There was also the fear, not entirely misplaced, that the new options might be soft ones or take up too little of the afternoon. Boys recalled enjoyable and unsupervised afternoons at the printing press or taking disused cars to bits. Nonetheless, a skilful semi-retreat had been conducted. The element of voluntary commitment brought the CCF a renewed lease of life. It thrives today, as it does at other schools where similar adjustments were made in the 1970s.

The Community Service activities belonged to a tradition that went back to the school's inter-war work at the Bermondsey Boys' Club in the East End. Eric Reid had organized annual visits to St Edward's by the club's members, who played soccer on the hallowed rugby turf. After the war the school turned its attention to the Wolvercote Boys' Club, but with the growing prosperity of the subsequent decades such efforts had come to seem patronizing. Local help for the aged or the young, or for the mentally handicapped, had come to seem more fitting causes. Such activity, it was reasoned, would be good both for the boys themselves and for the school's image. Boys helped elderly people with their gardens or visited local primary schools, where they organized games or encouraged reading projects. They gave assistance at the Cowley Road geriatric hospital. A weekly Seven O'Clock Club was set up within the school for local people with learning difficulties, most of them young. Boys worked with the local Social Services Department, earned its trust, and answered calls for help in such matters as refuse collection.

Such initiatives were not new, but they were enlarged and energized by David Conner, assistant chaplain from 1971 and chaplain from 1973, who handled the complex and delicate staffing problems they posed. But Conner, who wanted the service to be a voluntary commitment on the boys' part and to be independent of institutional obligations, was irritated by its incorporation into the Duke of Edinburgh Award scheme, in which it became a compulsory requirement, and into the new arrangements for Monday afternoons. As Conner explained in the *Chronicle* of November 1972, there were now three categories of boys doing Community Service. The largest group were the volunteers; a smaller number did it as part of their Duke of Edinburgh Award; and sixteen boys in their final year did Community Service in CCF time on Monday afternoons. Community Service trailed off after Conner's departure for Winchester in 1980, and was effectively killed by the health and safety legislation of the following decade.

Conner, appointed part time by Bradley on the eve of the Warden's departure, arrived at the same time as Christie. He proved the outstanding appointment of these years. His inspiration was largely responsible for the impact of the 'theme services' introduced by Bradley as an alternative to the liturgical service on Sunday mornings. About half the school usually attended them, though sceptics called them 'godless Chapel'. In one term of 1974, for example, the themes and events included an examination of long-term imprisonment entitled 'Time Inside'; a discussion of 'The Place of Woman in Society'; a performance by the Water into Wine folk band; and the production of a morality play by Shell C under the direction of Naida Christie. Outside the Chapel Conner transformed the pastoral life of the school. With the Head of English Malcolm Watson he pioneered a minority time course, known as the 'Bull Ring', which, in the face of suspicion from boys and masters, introduced senior pupils to the novel method of counselling known as 'encounter groups'. Boys trying to give up cigarette-smoking could join David and his wife Jayne, who were doing the same, on the understanding that for each cigarette they would place a £1 note in the drains or give it to the National Front.

Bradley had introduced the holding of Chapel services at 8.40 a.m. on every weekday, three a week for senior boys, three for juniors. That arrangement survived Christie's regime. But where Bradley had made the services voluntary for senior boys, Christie quickly restored compulsion, though he retained the 'theme services' and the choice between one of the Sunday morning options and Evensong. If he thought he had solved the Chapel issue he was wrong. This was a time of wide questioning of the place of religion in the Public Schools. A meeting held at Bloxham School, a Woodard school, in 1969 produced the 'Bloxham Project Research Unit', whose directors would produce a series of original papers which sought to bring loving Christian values to personal relationships in schools and so to connect the principles boys heard expounded in Chapel to the practice of their daily lives. Schools were to monitor the progress towards that ideal, a proposal that to many in the schools, including some heads, seemed at once threatening and impracticable. But at St Edward's Conner's advocacy persuaded Christie to set up a working party to respond to the Project's work. It included the chaplains, the Second Master, two Common Room representatives and two senior boys.

A series of intensive meetings of the working party resulted in proposals for change in the patterns both of religious instruction and of worship in Chapel. As things stood, boys were taught Divinity in only two of their years: for two periods in the Shells and one in the Lower Sixth. Now two periods were to be devoted to it throughout each of the five years. A structured syllabus introduced boys to a wide variety of theological and religious questions, Christian and non-Christian. In Chapel the three compulsory weekday services would be replaced by one weekly compulsory discussion for each year group, in which some worship would figure and which would extend into worship the ideas pupils encountered in the classroom. There might be Jewish, Muslim or Buddhist as well as Christian forms of worship.

Christie took the proposals to the Governors, who had difficult decisions to make. Was the scheme compatible with the school's history and with its Articles of Association? Graham Cooper and Bill Williams grilled Conner and me as representatives of the working party before accepting the proposals. No comparable school acted so boldly or decisively in response to the Bloxham Project, even if the changes commanded narrow support in the Common Room and even though they, too, would falter after Conner's departure.

Eight of Bradley's appointments to the Common Room proved to be long-term ones, though six other masters he had appointed left at the same time as he did. Christie made 24 new appointments, five of whom would become headmasters. He chose some able recruits; all but six of the 24 would stay for more than four years, and nine would remain until retirement. Even so, lifetime service to the school had ceased to be the norm. The long queue for housemasterships remained, though Cowell's, Segar's and Tilly's became vacant in Christie's time. Under Christie, Modern Languages teaching was further strengthened by the appointment in 1972 of Elizabeth Weeks, the first woman to become a full-time member of staff, who would be Head of Spanish for nineteen years. On Jeanie Bee's recruitment to the Maths Department in 1977 the number of women reached five. Robert Aldred and John Gidney joined the already strong English team. The chemist Bob Clements, who served for fifteen years, and the physicist Keith Jones, who stayed until retirement, were long-serving teachers. Music achieved fresh life and distinction under Philip Cave. Christie gave his support to a revival of the Classics after Pat Brims's retirement by appointing Nick Quartley, Linda Lyne and John Leach (Roll No. 4710), who was Head of Department until 1987 when he became headmaster of the school Christie had previously headed, Brighton College.

In 1971 John Watkins (Roll No. 6404) wrote a piece in the *Chronicle* entitled 'The School and the Individual', describing the toughness and conformism of day-room life for junior boys. Watkins's sympathies are not with boys who would 'protest against anything' but with those who offer 'rational and sincere' dissent. Were compulsory games, Corps and Chapel, he asked, compatible with individual development? It was not only boys who asked such questions. Countless speeches by headmasters and prize-givers of the 1970s breathe the same spirit. Headmasters joined politicians in embracing the pursuit, alongside team and group activities, of individual skills and talents and self-fulfilment. They gave boys more individual freedom too. Christie permitted coloured shirts, in the hope of improving their appearance 'by allowing them to wear something in which they will take a pride'. It was a vain hope, for as a rule boys do not take pride in school uniform. When Christie allowed informal 'weekend dress', and later extended the provision to weekdays after school, they wore the jeans and T-shirts that were the uniform of their peers and their generation – a conformity chosen by the young rather than imposed on them. There were other extensions of freedom. Pop music, which could now be played more loudly, echoed across the Quad. Leave outside school was more freely granted. Tensions were emerging between two conceptions of the school: one as a cosy self-contained community – the old 'boy-centred commonwealth'; the other, now gaining ground at its expense, as a community which should interact as much as possible with the outside world. The division can be seen in conflicting attitudes of the authorities to the school's proximity to central Oxford, in some eyes a virtue, in others a hazard threatening exposure to drugs and sin.

Such tensions are a background to the rebellions of Christie's years. Yet why were those challenges to authority, vivid as they were, sporadic? The relaxations of rules, the legacy of Bradley's encouragement of debate and his tolerance of diversity of thought, as well as Christie's own unreadiness to retaliate are each part of the answer. Another is the absorption of boys in the packed schedule created by the encouragement of individual talents. Martin Stokes (Roll No. 7402), a clever boy with 'omnivorous musical interests' and many other talents who arrived in 1975, remembers 'a desperate rush to fit things in and get things done, a concert one moment, a play the next, house and school duties and so on'. The overcrowding of activities carried its dangers. There were also inconveniences, as when the growing number and prestige of minor sports, among them golf, which was introduced in 1974, led to competition for the services of versatile sportsmen. Minor sports themselves took their place in a spectrum of wider activities, not all of them athletic. By the 1980s the Representative or 'Rep' Tie, that long-standing award for distinction in minor sports, would be extended, albeit haphazardly, to mark achievement in such activities as music and librarianship.

It was not only variety of activities that caused so much liveliness in the school in these years but a change in the relationship between masters and pupils – another antidote to rebellion. Even when boys and masters had got on well, the staff had hitherto remained for the most part distant figures. Now senior pupils were frequently entertained by masters and their families. Philip Clover (Roll No. 7459) arrived in 1976. He found his early years in Sing's tough, but 'the Sixth Form I loved. I worked hard at the lessons I liked and for the teachers I liked. At last there was a real purpose in life, and the new library under the watchful eye of John Todd was an excellent learning environment. I spent a lot of time in the Music School as well and was treated by the staff more as a colleague and friend, rather than a pupil .... My duties as second Head of House included locking up and reporting to Fran Prichard. Again I felt that I was being treated as an equal and friend as we discussed the day's events over a pint of home brew.' In Segar's, prefects drank coffee daily after lunch with the housemaster. Peter Alhadeff (Roll No. 6649), who left in 1974, says that he and many of his contemporaries remember those discussions 'for the cut and thrust of the conversation, not to mention the daring shift towards a more continental brew, Nescafé Blend 37. Relations with staff in the Sixth Form generally became less rigid as the school became more informal.' Martin Stokes remembers that 'the liberalism of the time was reflected in the way I was taught by my A-level teachers – as undergraduates rather than school kids, expected to think for ourselves as intellectuals and already in the swim of "grown up" debate and discussion .... I got into folk music with Tony Snell; sing-songs around the housemaster's piano in Segar's being plied with booze were also formative.'

Trips abroad brought staff and pupils together in Venice or the Pyrenees. The population of Segar's was transported to Paris, Normandy and Belgium on Leave Weekends. Tony Snell led caving and climbing expeditions, folk song groups and Morris dancers. Staff and pupils mingled on reading parties for A-level preparation. Teams, crews, casts and musical groups thrived on zestful leadership from teachers and banter with them. In the Common Room any danger of polarization of 'hearties' and 'arties' was dispelled by the number of masters, among them Simon Taylor, Malcolm Watson, David Howorth, Fred Pargeter and Nick Quartley, who were active both in games and in the arts. There was a lot of fun in the Sixth Form in those years, when the continued pressures of examinations and of attention to minutiae of the syllabus had yet to prevail. A boy might be coached in rugby by Joe McPartlin and taken on a tour of local churches by me just afterwards. This was McPartlin's golden age in charge of the XV. His reports in the *Chronicle* breathe his forceful personality and his gift for inspiring flair and ability. Chris Jones (Roll No. 6564), who left in 1972, Captain of the XV and later a Scholar of Selwyn College, Cambridge, recalls listening to outrageous arguments between McPartlin and me, conducted in jest but meant to provoke thought, about whether rugby is essentially a homosexual activity. When he got to Cambridge Chris felt that St Edward's had made him more sophisticated in argument than some of his contemporaries.

As the old barriers between masters and boys broke down, so the Houses, where boys ruled each other, lost their centrality in their lives. The change is reflected in the decline, which caused resentment, of inter-House sports competitions. Inter-House leagues evaporated and even the knockout competitions were of declining interest. Apart from the occasional 'regatta', rowing had more or less ceased to be a House sport. Yet at school level these were excellent years on the river. In the decade from 1975 to 1985 the school produced a number of rowers who would go on to win national prestige. In 1977 the British coxed IV consisted entirely of OSE. Five OSE rowers represented Britain in the following year. As Acting Warden before Christie's arrival John Armstrong had pinpointed the shortage of rowing expertise after the departure of Vernon and Alden. In 1974–76 Christie, himself an oarsman, appointed three masters, Mike Rosewell, John Lever and Greg Spanier, who joined Richard Simmonds as rowing coaches.

If the communal identity of the Houses was under threat, it remained true that boys might learn most not from masters but from each other. Martin Stokes's memories recapture the life of a pupil in Tilly's in the Christie years. He was especially influenced by Johnnie Schinas (Roll No. 7428), who arrived in the Easter Term of 1976. He was allocated Martin, who was a year older, as the 'uncle' who would show him the ropes. Soon Martin felt that it was he himself who was the initiate. Johnnie taught him where to smoke, by the canal bridge or in the alley by the Music School. 'As our courage and shamelessness grew, we graduated to the house toilets.' Johnnie introduced Martin to London, to rock music, to worldliness. The two remained friends in adulthood.

Martin 'enjoyed sports but I disliked the sense of coercion and officialdom and was, through music and other things, classified or self-classified as an "'arty'". He was redeemed from that stereotype by soccer. Twice a week he crossed the canal bridge to play it on a makeshift pitch. The footballers were 'a dissident bunch of misfits but these were competitive games, entirely self-policed and refereed which enhanced one's sense of enjoyment.' But rock music was his real interest. 'The route to Corn Dolly, the main pub/rock venue in Oxford, over the bridge and via the canal towpath, was a major undertaking, and a fairly serious disciplinary breach. It was quite the thing to get there, get served, and listen to the band and get back with some tales to tell.' Yet Martin and Johnnie, who looked older than their 15 and 14 years, managed it. Martin thinks that 'quite a complex and interesting story about Teddies's social and recreational life' could be written round rock music: 'what factions gathered round which bands, and the endless debates (Stones or Beatles? Floyd or Genesis? Bowie: charlatan or genius?)...; the surreptitious listening to John Peel after lights out; the circulation of worn and second-hand LPs'. Rock 'was a boyish world', 'one of the ways we managed to conceive of social lives without girls'. By the time Martin reached the Lower Sixth 'drinking in the Dew Drop [in Summertown on the Banbury Road] was more or less an open secret. The drinking permitted in the rather dingy JCR [Junior Common Room] was not really very appealing.'

For all the buoyancy of the school's life, Henry Christie's Wardenship was conducted against a background of economic turbulence and financial anxiety. The cost of Public School education had risen dramatically from the mid-1960s. Figures in John Rae's *The Public School Revolution* reveal the extent of the change. In 1966 the average annual fee to attend a major boarding school was £545. In 1978, when Christie left for Dartmouth, it stood at £2,028. In 1980, two years into the Wardenship of his successor John Phillips, it had risen to £2,744. Between 1966 and 1980 the increase was 503%, almost the same as that over the whole of the half-century from 1916 to 1966. The critical years came in the earlier and mid-1970s. In 1972–73 the retail price index climbed by 8.9%. In the same period the fee income rose from £376,275 in 1972 to £400,417 (only about 6%), whereas the cost of masters' salaries rose from £134,654 to £149,145 (about 11%). In May 1973 the bursar reported further troubling information about the 'explosion in wages'. Despite two recent increases for 'daily women', their hourly pay remained 9d. below the equivalent municipal and hospital rate of 5s. 3d. Superficial exercises in cost-cutting seemed likely to achieve little, though John Armstrong did produce the innovation of a school laundry.

More fundamental economies would mean staff reductions. Christie contemplated reducing the three English literature sets to two and even ending the teaching of some A-level subjects which had few takers, such as Spanish, German, and even Classics. Yet these were all areas of academic strength. Occasionally the prospects of increasing the income from the plant and buildings, to take advantage of the burgeoning market in conferences and holidays, were discussed, but this was before the age when an increase in bedsits and small studies had made the accommodation of visitors practicable. In the oil crisis of 1974–76 inflation spiralled out of control. Between September 1974 and September 1975 prices rose by 26%, and fees in the major HMC boarding schools by 32.91%. When in 1974 the Houghton Report on teacher salaries in the state sector recommended exceptional increases, the Public Schools felt obliged to follow suit, as they did later, after the Clegg Commission on public-sector pay in 1979–80 had brought further increases in state teachers' pay. In 1980 it was widely anticipated by bursars and governing bodies that in the following year the average fees of Public Schools would rise from £2,744 to £3,500. There was also renewed concern that the schools would lose their charitable status.

Pundits predicted serious consequences of fee rises for the Public Schools. They forecast that numbers would fall once boarding fees topped £3,000. Drawing attention to the decline of the birth rate since 1964, they argued that schools would seek to offset growing costs by increasing their numbers and competing with each other in a shrinking market. Three radical solutions to the numbers problem were proposed. The first, encouraged by ISIS, was to make up the anticipated shortfall by admitting foreign pupils. By 1978 there were already 14,400 foreign pupils in the Independent Schools, 4.72% of the total. But would a still higher number of children from alien cultures be easily assimilated into schools with strong, even if now muted, Christian traditions? Might schools not find themselves competing more fiercely for clever and hard-working Hong Kong boys as well as British ones? The second radical proposal was to introduce girls into the Sixth Forms, a move pioneered by John Dancy as headmaster of Marlborough. By 1977 there were 7,000 girls in the Independent Schools. Their arrival added £3 million a year to the revenues of schools previously restricted to boys. The boys could be expected to welcome the girls' arrival, but would it be desirable for a handful of girls to live in an overwhelmingly boys' world? Headmistresses thought not, and said so. A third possibility was to reduce the age of entry from 13 to 11, the stage at which pupils would otherwise enter state secondary schools and at which, it was suggested, they might switch from the state to the private sector. Perhaps parents unable or unwilling to fund an entire childhood of private education would be able to cope if fees had to be paid only from age 11. That proposal, too, encountered hostility, this time from the Prep Schools. Membership of the Independent Association of Preparatory Schools had fallen from 497 in 1967 to 449 by 1977. Yet those figures, like many other gloomy statistics on private education in the period, were misleading. The problem was a regional rather than a national one. The Prep Schools were heavily concentrated in the Home Counties and the South, where competition led to many mergers. Overall, the national demand for Prep Schools remained buoyant. In spite of inflation their numbers rose from 59,000 to 72,000 between 1966 and 1977.

For the pundits were wrong. Independent Schools as a whole continued to grow and flourish, in spite of huge and rapid economic changes. In 1980 ISIS recorded 366,000 pupils in its member schools, and the numbers would continue to rise in the 1980s. Prep Schools weathered the economic crisis of the mid-1970s as they had done the Depression of the 1930s. Demographic factors worked to the schools' advantage. Although the birth rate had fallen in post-war years, the decline had been less marked in Social Categories A and B, the main recruiting grounds of private education. Parents in these groups succeeded in forcing their salaries up in line with inflation, much as they had managed to sustain their salaries during the deflation of the 1930s. The number of middle-class and professional jobs was growing, especially in the burgeoning service sector, which supplied new jobs for mothers as well as fathers. Many women took full- or part-time jobs to help their families pay for private education. Grandparents sometimes helped. Some parents did have to reduce expenditure on holidays, even though the cost of Continental travel was falling in real terms. In 1978, the year of John Phillips's appointment and a year before Margaret Thatcher became Prime Minister, a firm of consultants surveyed 300 clients who were paying school fees. According to the replies, 83% had cut down on other expenses to raise the school fees; 40% had raised more money as a result of wives taking a job; and 29% had been helped by generous relatives. The average income of those surveyed was £12,956, about six times the annual school fees. Tax relief on endowment mortgage policies helped parents who might have struggled. So did the schools' scholarships and the allowances paid by the Ministry of Defence and the Foreign Office to employees.

Nonetheless, the 1970s were anxious times for the school. In June 1974, during the oil crisis, a paper written by Admiral Sir

Frank Twiss for his fellow governors of St Edward's asked gloomily how in such straitened times the school could maintain its numbers without reducing the quality of the entry. Should it not do more to court Prep Schools? Should it look for additional income, for example by holiday letting? Another potential problem was the increasing proportion of day boys, whose numbers steadily grew between 1972 and 1976 to more than 70 out of the total of 500 or so. It was gratifying that local parents, dons among them, wanted to send their sons, but day boys paid lower fees and there were fears that the identity of St Edward's as a boarding school might be diluted. The school held to its insistence that day boys attend for everything except bed and breakfast.

Even the innately positive Christie was worried. Not usually a man prone to extensive discourses, he submitted 'Thoughts on Contingency Planning' to the Governors in October 1976. One problem he noted was that ever fewer boys who had been registered at birth were taking up their places. Registrations were, in any case, declining, which meant that planning around future annual entries had become more difficult. It has remained so. Perhaps anxieties about the cost of fees have played their part. Perhaps, in some phases of national politics, fear of government action against the Public Schools has contributed. But there has been another factor. Parents gradually became more questioning and discriminating about the schools they considered, investigating a wider range of them and keeping their powder dry. The demand side of the market equation was accordingly strengthened. Christie feared that numbers would fall, or that pupils would be withdrawn after O level to save parents money. His concern was not borne out.

Christie's paper identified another important development. Parents, he observed, 'on the whole live within 60 miles of the School and enjoy the opportunity of visiting the School from time to time .... They also seem to like the Leave Weekend .... The present arrangement allows a boy to spend a night at home every three or four weeks.' Christie did fear, though again the fear proved needless, that the increase in the time boys spent away from the school on Leaves and at half-terms might provoke parents to ask for a reduction in fees. In reality the changing attitudes of parents were bringing new opportunities to the school. Not only were fathers and mothers visiting it more often: they were becoming part of its community, developing an appetite for involvement and delighting in the games, the plays, the music and the art. The more frequently parents came, and the more they commented on what they saw, the more conscious the Governors became of a parental desire for improvements in living accommodation and in facilities for games and the arts. Christie's paper also recognized the approaching threat of government regulation. Safety laws and health laws were imposed on all 'public places'. The first development in that trend was the installation of fire doors and fire alarms in buildings not designed for them. Sealed areas within communal buildings are not conducive to communal life. Time and again a heavy fire extinguisher would be used to prop open a fire door in a House to facilitate the habitual movement of pupils.

Numbers and money were more immediate problems. The emollient Christie, unwilling to risk confrontations with Prep Schools or girls' schools, would not countenance 11-plus entry or the opening of the Sixth Form to girls. So would the school have to reduce entry standards to keep up its numbers? It was an alarming thought. St Edward's, though never a narrowly academic school, had a sound though hardly a distinguished academic standing. In 1978, for example, it had an A-level pass rate of 85.6%, of whom 56.3% gained A-C grades. These were better figures than under Bradley. In some years the proportion of A–C grades rose above 60%, though in others it fell below 50%. But at least Prep School headmasters could expect scholarship boys from their schools to reach their potential in the Sixth Form. A reduction of standards at entry would mark a change of policy that would shift the balance of abilities in the boy population and risk deterring heads and teachers looking for academic achievement.

Yet Christie's paper acknowledged that, for all the difficulties, 'the Accounts have always shown a surplus'. They would continue to do so, for the numbers kept up. They did so in spite of above-average fee increases, which marked the end of the policy of keeping the fees lower than the norm. By September 1972, when the school charged £801, only thirteen major Independent Schools were charging more. Bradfield, Stowe, Oundle, Charterhouse, Sherborne and Cheltenham were all cheaper. There were changes, however, in the social composition of the parent body. The registration forms, which asked fathers to state their employment, showed an increasing number of company directors, as well as of investment analysts and management consultants, new jobs generated by a changing economy. How might the values of these parents, to which the Thatcher years gave encouragement, make themselves felt in the school?

At St Edward's as at other Public Schools, fast salary increases, usually pitched a little above inflation, made most teachers happy with their lot. Many of them benefited from subsidized housing and private health schemes and could educate their children freely or cheaply in the schools where they taught. In the 1970s salaries amounted to 30–40% of the expenditure of the Public Schools. Thus in 1976, when the income of St Edward's was less than £900,000, £270,000 went on salaries. The work of bursars was becoming increasingly complex. They had to keep up with complex changes in taxation law and other demanding legal issues. Keeping costs down in an inflationary period took skill. The burden of mounting successive Appeals, and of controlling large building projects, produced a growth in bursarial staffs. There were assistant bursars, school accountants, pay clerks and secretaries. St Edward's had a secretarial staff of seven in the mid-1970s; today the number is 22. It is a tribute to John Armstrong, who succeeded Hubert Beales as bursar in 1975, and to Andrew Gibbs that the school coped so well with this bureaucratic expansion.

Between 1964 and 1978 the Independent Schools raised £60 million for buildings. In 1979 alone they spent £24 million on them and on new equipment. Some headmasters were judged by the bricks and mortar they added to the site, and the term 'master builder' was freely used at prize-givings and speech days. A year into his Wardenship Christie set in motion an Appeal for a multi-purpose hall, an improved library, work on the boathouse, field drainage to resolve the abiding problem of flooded pitches, and, ideally, a Sports Hall. There were unavailing searches among rich OSE, of whom there were few, to find people willing to form a trust to raise money. Approaches to charitable foundations failed. Still, there were many parents ready to contribute to building projects from which their children would benefit. Hooker Craigmyle, the firm which had managed the Centenary Appeal, was hired again. Between 1959 and 1979 it raised some £45.3 million for its various Independent School clients. The Appeal of 1972 set a target of £150,000, which was revised in the light of inflation to £200,000 in November 1974. The appeal raised £196,000 by 1976. Christie was especially thanked by the Governors for his personal involvement, and a report on the appeal remarked that 'without the social charm of the Warden and Mrs Christie who attended every reception ... only a fraction' of the sum would have been raised.

The appeal produced substantial achievements: the transformation of Big School into the Library under John Todd's exemplary librarianship, the conversion of the old Memorial Library into an art and exhibition space, and the building of the multi-purpose New Hall, which was constructed behind Big School with its entrance facing the Quad to the south of the same building. It had stages at both ends for plays and concerts. Yet each of these achievements had its problems or limitations. The Memorial Library building proved inadequate to meet the advancing cause of visual education, which was now rooted in the school's syllabus. Though the conversion of Big School was a triumph in its use of space and equipment, the hope that its imaginative layout would encourage self-motivated study proved unrealistic. And too much was expected of the flexibility of the Hall, which had to accommodate too many uses and proved imperfect for some if not all of them. Was it there for plays and music, or for examinations, or for assemblies and prize-givings? Some wanted the building, which was first used at the Gaudy of 1976, to be called the Olivier Hall, but the characterless term 'New Hall' was preferred. It has become known merely as The Hall.

In the Summer Term of 1978, while the school was holding an academic conference to commemorate the martyrdom of its patron a thousand years earlier, Henry Christie announced his impending departure. He was 54 and had six years to go, but he had the chance to become Director of Studies at Dartmouth and his attachment to the Navy won out. The tribute in the *Chronicle* which claimed that he had had an unstable inheritance remarked on his 'genuine warmth and feeling for people .... Henry Christie is essentially a humble man and a kind man. He has the capacity to listen, which really means the talent for projecting himself into the problems of others' – even if his 'administration is sometimes a little tenuous and stretched' and 'decisions may be a little delayed'. 'And he inspires trust .... His inclination has often been to let well, or even less than well, alone. There is in him, in fact, a strongly conservative sense and a repugnance to interfere or tamper with what is working, even at less than full capacity.' It had been a very different approach from Bradley's. What would come next?

42

WARDEN PHILLIPS

Henry Christie was succeeded by the 50-year-old John Phillips. A bolder Governing Body, confident about the school's standing and condition, might have chosen a younger man, who could be expected to move on after a few years to another school. Fisher, 35 on his appointment, had done so. Though Bradley, appointed at 40, left in enforced circumstances, he was young enough to proceed to two very successful headships in North America. St Edward's gave Fisher and Bradley their first headships. But the pattern was changing. For the first time in the school's history, Wardens were now appointed with less than half their career ahead of them. Christie, in his second headship, was aged 47 on his appointment, his two successors 49 and 46 on theirs.

Phillips had spent the previous twenty-six years at Charterhouse and in many ways fitted the classic Public School profile. Born to a family of Imperial employees in the Far East, he was at school in Malvern. After National Service he took his degree at Magdalen College, Oxford. The last Warden to have had military experience, he had been Commanding Officer of the CCF at Charterhouse. He had also taught at Prep School. But it was the range of his skills that must have attracted the Governors. He had played cricket, hockey, football, fives, and the flute. He sailed, and he painted in watercolour. His artistic interests were soon apparent in the liberal display of oils, watercolours and prints in the Warden's lodgings, some of them daringly contemporary.

There were books, too. Phillips had been a major influence in the academic life of Charterhouse and especially of its very successful History Department. Once more the school had a historian-warden. A pupil of Bruce McFarlane and A. J. P. Taylor at Magdalen, Phillips gave glimpses both of the seriousness and of the puckishness of his two famous tutors. He had promoted the study of local and industrial history in Charterhouse's extramural teaching centre in Derbyshire. He had worked under three distinguished headmasters of Charterhouse, Brian Young (1952–64), the Etonian Oliver van Oss (1965–73), and Brian Rees (1973–81). Van Oss was probably the greatest influence on Phillips's approach to schoolmastering.

He had gathered a galaxy of young teachers around him, many of whom became Phillips's friends. Van Oss was a reforming and innovative headmaster who arrived after stuffy years at the school, and Phillips was invigorated by his liberal and inclusive methods. Phillips had been an outstanding housemaster of the largest House, Gownboys, where, as a colleague wrote, he 'achieved a peculiarly personal mixture of public success and private happiness among the boys for which he will be long remembered'.

He had a personal touch; and he was a family man, his four children ranging from young adult to young teenager. The most influential figure in his life, and a strong and benign influence at St Edward's, was his wife Pat. A graduate of St Anne's College, Oxford, an accomplished Modern Linguist, a natural cook and hostess, she was dedicated, at St Edward's as at Charterhouse, to the support of her husband's work. Like her predecessor, Naida Christie, she taught in the classroom. Sharing her husband's musical skills and interests, she helped the school maintain its high reputation in music. The tenth Warden and his wife were far and away the most hospitable couple to have occupied the lodgings, which rang to the sound of generous drinks and of supper parties attended by members of the Common Room and by a string of outside guests. When the first Sixth Form girls were admitted in 1983 Pat emerged as a powerful educational force. With Linda Lyne she organized the pastoral lives and accommodation of the new girl-pupils with assurance and with a characteristic sensitivity to their inevitable teething troubles.

John Phillips already knew a number of the staff at St Edward's from his teaching career, when, like many masters, he had got to know his opposite numbers through inter-school activities. He was heartened to discover that his Second Master would be Peter Church, whom he had met frequently at Rugby Group meetings. But one thing the Phillipses did miss. On their first weekend in the school I was asked on Sunday morning to drop in for lunch. So impromptu a gesture from the Warden's lodgings was something of a novelty. As I was scheduled to rehearse *Orpheus in the Underworld* at 2 p.m. I thought I would have to refuse, but they would not hear of it, and an informal family lunch followed. But I felt they were rattling around in an isolated house. Were they lonely? It is a measure of their approachability that I felt able to broach the subject. They were, they admitted, missing the life of a boarding housemaster, whose pupils, in Phillips's liberal regime, had always been welcome to drop in. A man whose palpable strengths lay in his pastoral skills, and who was not inhibited from baring his feelings, now had to learn to live at one remove. He would be judged now by the making of school policy; by his responses to pressures and changes in school and society; by his ability to raise money and achieve high pupil numbers; by his diplomatic skills in handling parents or Prep School heads. He had those aptitudes, but they were not his core strengths.

At a Rugby Group meeting held at St Edward's in 1981, Sir Keith Joseph, Secretary of State for Education, addressed a meeting of Heads of History hosted by Chris Danziger, who had become Head of History at St Edward's two years earlier. Joseph was working towards what would become the National Curriculum and the merging of the Certificate of Secondary Education with O levels. Sixth Form teachers feared that the changes would bring excessive standardization, a lowering of standards in the exams taken at 16, and a devaluation of the grades on which applications to universities depended. Very unusually for a minister, Joseph had taken direct control of the content of syllabuses. In History his measures led to a reduction both in the content of courses and in the writing of continuous prose, as well as to a misguided emphasis on process rather than knowledge. He listened to the meeting but was unmoved. The Independent Schools were not obliged to adopt the National Curriculum or the GCSE. In more confident days they might have rejected them.

Pressure from the state would grow, on that as on other fronts. Pressure from parents grew too. Those whose sons were booked for a House at St Edward's were given a preliminary tour of it. From the early 1970s mothers began to protest at the conditions in which their sons were to live. Having in many cases kitted out their boys' bedrooms at home with every comfort and gadget, they were taken aback by the large and spartan dormitories and the crowded and noisy day rooms. At many Public Schools boys had their own studies, but at St Edward's there were only a handful of them, each for three or four prefects. A system of communal accommodation which had sustained Victorian ideals of hierarchy and discipline survived even when the ideals themselves had faded. The modern teenager wanted more privacy.

To alter the living environment, money that might have gone on novel and eye-catching projects had to go on the refurbishing of buildings which had been put up between 1873 and 1936: Apsley, Cowell's, Segar's, Tilly's and Mac's. In 1977 Armstrong recorded that £278,984 had been expended on the New Hall, the Library, the refurbished Art School and the new laundry, all developments financed by the last Appeal. In 1977–78, £60,000 had to be found to modernize the rabbit warren of Mac's, no mean task. Some governors were dissatisfied with the result. There were still thirty-four boys in dormitories. Only two single study-bedrooms were provided; the remainder of the boys lived in shared ones. In January 1979 Phillips proposed that the renovation of Tilly's, Cowell's and Segar's go ahead, at an estimated cost of £150,000, heavy expenditure at a time when a new Appeal was being launched for a new boarding house and other facilities. The work on Tilly's, which included an extension of the building, was set in motion a month later, 'to be financed from revenue and bank borrowing as required'. It was finished within a year, and this time the results were far-reaching. All boys were now in bedsits, the youngest of them in rooms of nine or ten, the age group above them in rooms of four or five, the next in double rooms, and boys in the Lower Sixth and Sixth Forms in singles. The renovation of Cowell's, Segar's and, eventually, Apsley were to follow. Though the changes were welcomed, they brought their challenges and problems. Houses divided up into small rooms are harder to control. Housemasters and prefects had been able to address whole dormitories and day rooms with ease. The alterations hastened the decline both of the prefectorial system and of communal House spirit, while advancing the emphasis on the individual.

To John Phillips, himself so successful a housemaster at Charterhouse, the personal impact of housemasters was the key to successful boarding education. Yet as the communal character of the Houses declined the burden of running them became heavier. Routines of organization and discipline that had hitherto been left to the prefects now fell into the housemasters' hands. Though married housemasters had become the norm, the accommodation for their families sometimes seemed inadequate and to offer too little privacy.

A marriage could be a real source of strength in a House. Bim and Renée Barff, Charles and Biddy Mather, Fran and Pat Prichard, Mervyn and Yvonne Evans, Peter and Josie Church, and other couples, were husband-and-wife teams. Yvonne Evans, Josie Church, Ann Arkell and Sheilah Peregrine acted as House nurses. But more and more wives whose husbands might become housemasters had careers of their own. They did not relish the prospect of returning from work to find their husbands working through the evening. The House tutor system was insufficiently developed to offer much respite to housemasters, who could rarely expect more than one free evening a week. For all these reasons the post of housemaster was becoming less widely coveted. Three members of staff refused Houses in Phillips's time. Although the tenure of a housemastership had been reduced from 15 years to 12 in 1973, the housemasters were an ageing group. I, who had been the first of the twelve-year appointments, was nearly 35 when I took over Segar's in 1973, young by the standards of the time. The housemasters appointed during the Phillips years were all older.

Prefects were becoming increasingly reluctant to enforce school rules, even when they kept them themselves. Another disciplinary challenge was created by the ever more infrequent use of the cane. Without it no school rules could be imposed unless the pupils tacitly consented to them. Unconsciously, the boys were coming to dictate the terms on which the school was run. The doomed attempts to curb smoking illustrate the point. There had long been generally accepted 'rules of the game': clandestine but well-known smoking areas, smoking times, 'busts', and beatings. But without beatings how should smokers be punished? There might be 'gatings', which confined pupils to school, a common punishment but one too easily circumvented. Or a boy might be withdrawn from a games team – but at an unfair cost to his teammates. He might be fined – but how much? Large fines might lead to borrowing, or even theft, while small ones would scarcely trouble the more affluent pupils. Rustication – the sending of pupils home – was thought harsh, could damage the pupil's education, and might provoke parental wrath. At a meeting of the Rugby Group Second Masters in the later 1980s, some speakers suggested tariffs of fines for smokers and, after multiple offences, expulsion. The OSE Stephen Winkley, then Master of the Scholars at Winchester, snorted: 'Rubbish. A tissue of make-believe.' He was right. Heads took tough stances on paper but failed to enforce them. The pupils had won.

The Houses were overcrowded. Phillips set a high priority on the creation of a new House, whose members would be recruited from existing Houses. The Governors concurred. It was one of many capital projects of the Phillips era. There were plans for a Sports Centre, for new classrooms for Maths teaching, for an all-weather playing surface for hockey, and for an innovation on which Phillips set his heart, an Art (or Craft), Design and Technology Centre. With prophetic vision he saw the teaching of Design and Technology as a bridge between the arts and the sciences, and wanted to combine it with twelve new classrooms for Maths teaching. The existing art facilities were too small for that goal, and the activities in the inadequate workshops, housed in the old huts, mere hobbies. After Chris Ruscombe-King's death in 1983 Nick Grimshaw had begun the hugely successful expansion of artwork throughout the school. Project work submitted by pupils for the new Design A level was forwarded for national recognition. Facilities were needed to match and further such achievements.

The combined cost of the initiatives would have been at least £2 million. In 1979, when the covenants entered into under the previous appeal ran out, a new appeal was launched. Again Craigmyle were the fund-raisers. Fran Prichard, a major figure in his generation of teachers at St Edward's and a personality dear to parents and old boys, was to lead the approaches. A novelty was an invitation to some Common Room members to join the Governors in planning the appeal, a step that reflected Phillips's eagerness to consult the staff and widen their involvement. In 1981, at the instigation of John Todd, the President of the Common Room, he urged the Governors to allow the Common Room formally to elect its own representatives on the Governing Body. The initiative was unsuccessful. The Governors did agree to an informal arrangement by which they would themselves elect a candidate for whom the Common Room had expressed support, but the arrangement was implemented just once. Of all the post-war Wardens, Phillips was probably the closest to the Common Room, where there was barely a hint of opposition through his tenure.

Craigmyle, which had spotted the growing parental demand for privacy and comfort, wanted the appeal to focus on the building of an eighth house. They persuaded the school that the Design Centre, which they judged to lack selling power, should not top the list. They saw that its adoption would have expensive implications not only for building but for staffing and equipment, and curriculum development, and that the proposed new subjects were remote from the school's image and traditions. Opinion, both among the Governors and in the Common Room, was divided over the Sports Centre, which was to house a gymnasium and swimming pool, though the latter did not materialize. It was accepted that the Centre would have to earn income as a public sports club, something achievable only if the hours of the school's use were severely restricted. Judging by the experience of twenty-two schools, it looked as if sports centres barely paid their way. Nevertheless, and even though the appeal was moving slowly, in November 1979 the Governors overcame their doubts and set the building of the Sports Centre in motion. An appeal target of £250,000 had been set to cover the three building schemes: a new House, the Sports Centre and the Craft, Design and Technology Centre (CDT). In the event, the first of these was modified and the third eventually postponed. Only £74,000 had been raised when the builders of the Sports Centre moved in. By February 1980 Prichard could report an increase to nearly £170,000, more than half of it from current parents. As yet only twenty-six old boys had contributed. But by November 1980, when the main campaign to attract OSE giving was under way, their contribution had increased to £94,000.

By then, under pressure from donors, the Sports Centre had become the priority of the appeal. The new House was now placed third, behind the CDT Centre. By July 1982 the appeal had reached £392,000, and at the Gaudy of 1983 an anonymous donor gave £10,000 to nudge the figure above £400,000. In 1983, in the presence of an enthusiastic Sir Douglas Bader – the appeal's President, after whom the complex was named – the Centre was inaugurated. The six squash courts built in 1931 were renovated and incorporated into the project. In place of a new House Phillips had to be content, for now, with further refurbishment, new studies, and a new 'service tower' of washrooms and toilets for Segar's (where I was housemaster) and Cowell's, an edifice quickly dubbed 'Oxley Towers', perhaps with the recent TV hit *Fawlty Towers* in mind. The project cost the astronomical sum of £277,000. Of that, £1,000, and a great deal of time, were spent in a battle with the local planning authorities, who, even though the local residents voiced no opposition to the scheme, placed a preservation order on the lime trees between the old buildings and Stratfield Road, which the school had planted in 1936. Obstruction on the planning front was becoming a tiresome fact of life.

Phillips wanted to build on to Corfe House. When that proved too ambitious for the time being, he settled for the awkward solution of a two-centre House, one part in the existing Corfe building, the other in 236–238 Woodstock Road. David Drake-Brockman, who had been head of house in Phillips's Gownboys and had come from Glenalmond to teach Classics at St Edward's in 1979, took over the new House in 1982 and made a resounding success of it. In 1990, two years after Phillips had left and with Drake-Brockman still housemaster, a new annexe to Corfe House would at last create a single site for the House. Phillips's dreams for Design, Art and Technology were also achieved. In his last term, on 27 May 1988, after the last of the huts had been razed, the Craft, Design and Technology (CDT) Centre, built in the Sanatorium Gardens, was opened. It had needed yet another appeal, the last and greatest of Fran Prichard's money-raising campaigns, which had raised £642,000 by the spring of 1988. The CDT Centre did have its teething troubles. A newly appointed Director withdrew at the last moment, and teachers in both Art and Technology departed. But under the direction of Nick Grimshaw and Patrick Morton the Centre soon proved a massive asset to the school's curriculum and reputation.

The appeal funds enabled the building not only of the CDT Centre but of the new Maths classrooms by the north boundary wall. With the Centre, the Sanatorium and the School Shop they formed the new Cooper Quadrangle, named after Graham Cooper, a governor since 1947 and chairman from 1973 to 1985. The Chairman of the Appeal was Frank Fisher. As had become usual, current parents were the main donors. From 1985 there were proposals to replace the succession of ad hoc appeals, which had funded striking projects, with the creation of a permanent fund-raising committee that would have strong parental representation. The school would long be exercised by the choice between the two approaches.

Phillips's hope was always for a new boarding House. By 1982 the boy population had crept up to 536. This expansion had been absorbed without undue discomfort by the existing teaching spaces, dining areas and playing fields. The school had a good teacher–pupil ratio. As in other Public Schools, the introduction of new subjects had increased the teaching staff, which at St Edward's had grown from 31 on Fisher's arrival in 1954 to 48 in 1970 and 52 in 1980. The ratio, slightly below 1:10, was a little better than at most comparable schools. So, provided it could solve its accommodation problems, St Edward's could handle the recent increase in pupils. But would the growth persist? Could building be planned on the assumption that the swelling of fee income would last? And if the numbers continued to increase, might not a new House, which Phillips had envisaged as a means to thin the population of the old ones, absorb most or all of the new pupils and leave the old Houses overcrowded?

Phillips's zeal for the CDT Centre was part of his wider interest in the whole school curriculum. Early in his first year he created the post of Director of Studies, to which he appointed the scholarly classicist OSE John Leach (Roll No. 4710). The post gave direction to the school's academic life and raised its profile. It also enhanced the status of heads of department in relation to the housemasters.

When Leach left in 1982 to become, at Brighton College, the first member of the Common Room to be appointed to a headship since Roger Northcote-Green's departure for Worksop in 1947, I held the role for two years before David Cundy took over. Cundy's quiet decisiveness, his acute intellect, and his grasp of the academic landscape in a time of considerable change in the curriculum, made him a great asset to Phillips and his successor.

Phillips was a pioneer on many academic fronts, even if his initiatives were overshadowed by the arrival of GSCE and the National Curriculum with its prescriptive and intrusive demands, which ate heavily into Cundy's time. At the outset of his Wardenship Phillips ordered reviews of the timetable, of the number of O levels taken, and of the allocation of time between A levels and minority-time subjects. Seeking, like other Wardens before him, to squeeze more teaching periods into the timetable, he found room for two more a week. He created a proper General Studies syllabus for the Upper School and enterprisingly had it run for two years in conjunction with Headington School, though his proposals for a further sharing of the two institutions' resources foundered on practical obstacles, especially the geographical distance between the schools. Another brave move was Phillips's decision to attach the Lower Sixth curriculum to the Oxford Certificate of Educational Achievement (OCEA), a scheme run by the Local Authority. He tried to promote more general reading and thinking within the school by requiring pupils to read, and be examined on, three designated books a term, though his plan did not endure. It won limited backing from the Common Room, which dubbed it 'the Shadow Curriculum'. He sanctioned a very ambitious Study Skills course, which was also short-lived. He provided for A-level teaching not only in Design but in Art History and Business Studies. He welcomed the academic use of computer technology and had an area in the Memorial Library set aside as a Computer Centre. Phillips also increased the number of outside speakers who addressed the Sixth Form, and introduced a four-day course for Oxbridge candidates, who under new university rules had to apply for admission during rather than after their A-level year. He encouraged the creation of the annual Lower Sixth Pastoral Conference, which, unlike some of his other initiatives, would be long-lasting. It exposed pupils to a full day of talks and discussions and invited them to reflect both on their individual aspirations and on their social responsibilities within the community. More and more, the disciplinary powers of senior boys were giving way to pastoral obligations.

Phillips was keen to strengthen links with Prep Schools, especially those that regularly sent pupils to St Edward's. He had the clever idea – which he pursued despite the doubts of some of the Governors and which became the envy of some other Independent Schools – of granting awards to bright 11-year-olds that would give them financial assistance and, by securing them places at St Edward's, spare them the stress of Common Entrance. Twelve Prep Schools joined the scheme, which, together with a separate scholarship for the Dragon School in Oxford, attracted a steady succession of able boys. The school also gained a number of bright pupils from the national competition for the Goodenough scholarships and bursaries, named after the former governor William Goodenough and supplied by Barclay's, which, regarding St Edward's as its 'lead' school, supported about thirty boys at the school at any one time. There was disappointment later, in 1989, when Barclay's chose to phase out its annual awards.

Despite the liking of Phillips in the Common Room and his eagerness to consult and involve it in the running of the school, it was becoming a less contented place. The spirit of questioning among the boys a decade earlier had moved to the staff. The Common Room – no longer a gentleman's club and no longer dominated by bachelors who had no families to return to in the evenings – was losing a little of its conviviality. At St Edward's, as in comparable schools, a basic shift in mentality was occurring which would gather strength in the decades ahead. Though there are a great many exceptions, teachers have come to think of themselves less as pursuers of a vocation than as employees under contract. Where once they would have expected to put down roots in a school community and move schools no more than once or twice in a career, now they readily move on to schools that offer higher rewards or status. Earlier generations of teachers would have been dumbfounded when in 2012 some staff, as members of the Association of Teachers and Lecturers, joined in strike action against changes in teachers' pension arrangements.

The material conditions and rewards of the staff became a contentious issue in the Phillips era and have remained one. The school, mindful of the high house prices in the area, has done what it can to provide married accommodation, both for teachers and for those non-teachers whose duties require them to live close to the school. Houses in or near Stratfield Road that were hitherto single-occupancy now house a number of teachers, and an increasing number of teachers have been accommodated in the Houses. In 1988 the school housed 39 teachers (54%); now it accommodates 60 (51%). Yet it cannot accommodate everyone, and some of those who were disappointed have looked on enviously at more fortunate colleagues. The variable quality of the housing provided, and the issue of time limits on occupancy, have caused further contention. The distribution of financial rewards has been another enduringly unsettling issue. In Phillips's time the school devised a labyrinthine system of 'living in' and 'living out' allowances, which provided endless headaches for the bursar and attracted awkward questions from the Inland Revenue. Another divisive and laborious issue was, and remains, the growth of Responsibility Allowances in schools. Who should get them? If House tutors, why not games masters, or vice versa? Should the growing demands of pastoral care be financially rewarded? Teachers who, rightly or wrongly, believe the burdens and stresses of their jobs to be increasing have looked askance at 'country members' among their colleagues who have involved themselves in fewer extracurricular activities.

During Phillips's Wardenship professional concerns began to be raised at the termly Common Room meeting, which had traditionally been held merely to discuss the staff's social arrangements. The change of mood is evident in an unhappy conflict which began in 1987 — the sharpest in the Common Room since the crisis over the Beardsley prints in 1966 — when Nigel Hamilton (Roll No. 4699), a former teacher and the father of two boys at the school, offered a large sum of money to the Common Room. He had in mind expenditure on the wine cellars and on dinners. But the Common Room Committee was divided. Some wanted to divert the money from the use of the Common Room to a field centre — a rural base, of a kind run by several schools, for weekend studies in Geography, Biology and local history — which was being considered as a memorial for the recently deceased David Howorth, a man with a taste for the outdoor life who had taught at the school from 1964 to 1985. Phillips, who had pioneered a similar facility in the Peak District for Charterhouse, was eager to provide a parallel one for St Edward's, though the Governors, who considered the scheme a year before Phillips's departure, put it off for the next Warden's consideration. It was never implemented. Another sign of change in the Common Room was the emergence of divisions over subscriptions to periodicals. Hitherto, in a spirit of live-and-let-live, members who voted for their own favourites had also supported the purchase of magazines far from their own tastes. Now moral objections to *The Field* deprived it of its necessary quorum of voters. Smoking in the Common Room was also a divisive issue. Could smokers be allowed and trusted to exercise voluntary restraint, or should smoking be banned, as eventually happened in 2000? It was not that the Common Room was a bitter place, but older members talked nostalgically of what they remembered as the 'collegiality' of earlier days.

The passage of generations was brought into relief in 1987 when two of the leading figures of the post-war school were struck down. John Armstrong, approaching retirement, died of renal failure and his friend Peter Church suffered a severely incapacitating stroke. Yet the wholehearted commitment of powerful personalities, on which all schools depend, survived the transition of generations. Rob Hughes, David Wippell and Nick Grimshaw would be stalwart Common Room figures throughout the 1980s and 1990s. Charles Neill, who succeeded David Conner as chaplain in 1991, had none of his predecessor's innovating instincts, but he was a steadying force and a great support to the Warden. He made aesthetic and practical improvements to the Chapel and had an organ formerly at Magdalen College, Oxford installed. Even so, the profile of the teaching staff presented problems for Phillips. More than half the full-time teachers were over 50, and only six were under 30. Another challenge concerned the coaching of games. Just one top sportsman on the staff was under 30. For three years Phillips tried and failed to find a young teacher equipped to coach rowing. Would the school have to make a practice of appointing coaches who had no role in the classroom? The dilemma highlighted the numerical decline, in an era of expanding extracurricular opportunities, of the all-round schoolteacher committed to a wide range of activities.

Perhaps it was the misfortune of the cultivated Phillips to become Warden in an era when the job of a Public School headmaster was perforce becoming ever more managerial. Symptomatic of the change was the creation of a Warden's Committee, which was snidely referred to as 'the Senior Management Team' and on which the Second Master, the bursar, the senior housemaster, the Director of Studies and the chaplain sat. As in other institutions, management came to seem an end in itself. Staff spent more of their energy on responding to it; less on spontaneous initiatives of their own. Broad issues concerning the character and direction of the school retreated from discussion. When in 1988 the Governors canvassed the opinion of the teaching staff on the choice of

Phillips's successor, a number of voices argued for the appointment of a man committed to firm principles and with clear ideas about the future of education and of the Independent sector. Pressures not only from within the school but from parents, central government, local planners and pupils were, it seemed, making the running of the school reactive rather than proactive. Idealism had always had to be tempered by empiricism, but was it now succumbing to it?

Wardens Simeon, Kendall and Fisher had had clear visions for the school. What visions were there now? Bookshelves of the later twentieth century groaned with new volumes on Public Schools. There were at least twenty-six major ones between 1959 and 1985. Some were historical, among them David Newsome's *History of Wellington College* (1959), J. R. Honey's *Tom Brown's Universe* (1977) and John Mangan's *Athleticism in Victorian and Edwardian Public Schools* (1981). Others, such as Graham Kalton's *The Public Schools: A Factual Survey* (1966) and John Wakeford's *The Cloistered Elite* (1969), turned sociology and statistics loose on the schools. But none of the books offered modern ideals for the schools to follow. John Dancy's *The Public Schools and the Future* (1963), Tom Howarth's *Culture, Anarchy and the Public Schools* (1969) and John Rae's *The Public School Revolution 1964–79* (1981) provided notable defences of independent education and robustly answered its critics, but envisaged no new directions other than adjustment to whatever changes society might happen to undergo. The ideological commitment of earlier generations, which at St Edward's as elsewhere had begun as a religious commitment, was lacking. In John Phillips's last year, the 125th anniversary of the school in 1988, the Gaudy Sermon was preached by David Conner, formerly chaplain of the school and at this time Rector of Great St Mary's, Cambridge. He ended with a sentence which casts a troubling shadow over late-twentieth-century private education: 'The School still really does possess the wherewithal, in spite of its privileged position in society, to use its independence to challenge the materialistic mores of the world in which we live – and after all the only point (the only moral point) of independent education is that it should pioneer and challenge rather than simply play the world better at its own game.'

CO-EDUCATION

Recalling her arrival at the school as one of the first of the eleven Sixth Form girl entrants in 1983, Deborah Hynett (Roll No. 8324) writes: 'We were your pioneering experiment! ... I am sure it was a very significant development for the School.' Indeed it was. Yet Hynett and her contemporaries were not the very first of the girls to be enrolled at St Edward's. In the Christmas Term of 1982, Penny Burke (Roll No. 8168), who had a brother in Segar's and was the daughter of Peter Church's secretary, was admitted as a day girl. But that was an exceptional arrangement, not meant as a precedent. It was with the entry of 1983, when eleven girls arrived, that St Edward's became a co-educational school. The second stage came in 1997, when girls were admitted not merely into the Sixth Form but from the age of 13. Today 35% of the school's 670 pupils are girls, and the proportion is planned to increase.

St Edward's was a late starter in the move to co-education. Marlborough had first taken girls into the Sixth Form in 1968, Lancing in 1970. Another early joiner was Charterhouse, where John Phillips welcomed post-O-level girls, his three daughters among them, into Gownboys House. The spread of co-education has been slow and uneven. Charterhouse is one of the schools to have continued to confine girl admissions to the Sixth Form. Marlborough took 21 years, St Edward's 14, to proceed from the admission of senior girls to the recruitment of younger ones. There has been a general pattern, to which St Edward's has conformed. At first a few senior girls are admitted, usually as day pupils or housed with local families. Then, when numbers have grown, a school building is adapted to accommodate girls. In the daytime they are based in boys' Houses, where characteristically two girls share a study. At first the girls' building is merely a hostel. In time it might become a House, as eventually happened to 236–238 Woodstock Road, which became Oakthorpe House after Corfe had vacated it in 1990.

At St Edward's as elsewhere the establishment of girls' Houses ended the presence of girls in the boys' houses. That was a critical change, which some regretted. The Governors had contemplated the creation of co-educational Houses but had understandably backed off. Co-residence, which few schools adopted, was widely regarded as risky and over-experimental by that cautious middle-class opinion to which the schools have tended to defer. At St Edward's the cost of converting buildings that had been equipped for the residence of boys would anyway have been punitive. Yet the separation of the sexes ran counter to the traditional premise of boarding, which obliges pupils of all kinds to learn to live together. Some liberal-minded headmasters were open to the idea of co-residence. John Dancy, the headmaster who admitted girls to Marlborough, recognized as early as 1963, in his book *The Public Schools and the Future*, that the segregation of the sexes was increasingly at odds with teenage culture. He quoted E. M. Forster's remark that Public School boys 'go forth into the world with well-developed bodies, fairly developed minds and undeveloped hearts'. 'The experience of other countries', wrote Dancy, showed that mixed boarding 'is a perfectly feasible proposition'. It was already proving feasible in some English universities. Co-residence would have answered the call of David Conner's sermon of 1978 to 'pioneer and challenge rather than simply play the world better at its own game'.

John Phillips, who was intensely in favour of co-education and expended much anxiety on the issue, had to work hard to secure the Governors' agreement. When in the summer of 1982 a proposal to admit a small number of girls to the Sixth Form was put to the General Purposes Committee, the meeting split five against five. The chairman followed convention in delivering his casting vote for the status quo. In November the committee met again and decided in favour of the change. The Governors deferred the committee's recommendation for three months. In February 1983, however, they voted by eleven to two in favour of admitting a small number of girls. Only one governor was irreconcilable, but there had been doubts and reservations to overcome among the others. Some foresaw a transformation of the school's character if the admission of girls caught on and the numbers became large. In the short term there was the question of how a small number of girls would fare in a community so masculine in its traditions and identity. How responsibly would the boys respond? Who would look after the girls, and how and by whom would they be housed? There were other practical considerations. Boys encountered hostility from time to time from local teenagers in Summertown. What then of girls as they walked back at night to their accommodation outside the school? And how would girls, in a school with no facilities for female sports and with far too few numbers to make up teams, fit into the regime of games and exercise?

The Governors asked Phillips, who acknowledged these difficulties, to consult his staff. In a packed meeting, masters who held high the school's reputation on the games fields voiced concern. One or two teachers with connections to local girls' schools, which naturally felt threatened by the initiative, were also opposed. The few women on the staff were warmly in favour, especially Linda Lyne, who spoke eloquently. But what swayed the doubters was the quiet but firm support expressed by some of the older members, particularly Fran Prichard. The Warden was able to report overwhelming support to the Governors.

The sensitivities voiced on behalf of the local girls' schools reflected a wider concern in the Independent sector. The Independent boys' schools were accused of turning to girls to boost falling entries. That was hardly fair, for in the late 1970s the girls' as well as the boys' schools were experiencing a steady if modest growth in demand. For the present the boy population of St Edward's was expanding, partly as a result of Phillips's cultivation of the Prep Schools. There were 514 boys when John Phillips took over in 1978. In the Christmas Term of 1983 there were 532, as well as 12 girls. In the Autumn Term of 1984 there were 562 boys and 18 girls. A year later the figures were 570 and 18; by 1988 they were 569 and 21. When in 1982 they considered co-residence the Governors envisaged a total population of 536. In Phillips's time the annual girl entry never exceeded ten. Gradually, however, the number of girl pupils in the school crept up. There were 20 in 1985, 27 in 1986, 31 in 1987, 37 in 1988, 37 in 1989, 44 in 1990. Even so, anxiety about the school's overall numbers persisted. Again there was concern, though again it proved unfounded, that fee rises might increase the number of boys leaving after O level or its successor GCSE, which was introduced in 1986. Phillips tried to counter the threat with a scheme of Lower Sixth scholarships, but they attracted few applicants and still fewer academically gifted ones.

Why did girls want to come to St Edward's? Some reached their decision on academic grounds. The school offered A-level subjects, especially in science and technology, which were not available at many girls' schools. But the spirit of teenage emancipation was at work too; and headmistresses had made fewer concessions to it than headmasters. St Edward's, on the edge of a city full of educational and social opportunities, had made more concessions than most male schools. There was the risk that the school would take on difficult girl pupils who had rebelled against tight restrictions at single-sex schools. But in general girls responded gratefully to the greater trust accorded them in a freer environment. Olivia Brown (Roll No. 9694), who joined the Sixth Form in 1993, remembers 'being so excited at getting in'. She had found her previous school 'rather rigid and stifling – St Edward's was so much more relaxed. If you behaved with maturity you were treated with the appropriate respect, and given the freedom to go with it.' Freedom brought its challenges. One of the first girls, Emma Bigland (Roll No. 8287), 'having come from a very strict boarding school', found that 'the freedom went to my head'. She did however gain a sense of stability from her membership of a St Edward's dynasty. She was the daughter of Robert Bigland (Roll No. 4681), the niece of John Bigland (Roll No. 4682), and the granddaughter of Ernest Bigland (Roll No. 2295), who was a governor. Ernest's brother Anthony (Roll No. 3388), her great-uncle, had also been at the school. OSE families which sent their daughters to St Edward's recognized the changes in the school's culture since their own generations, which had endured the privations and the harsh mentality of the Houses and day rooms.

For the boys, the arrival of girls was not a transformative event. They were used to the presence of girls in music and drama, where they had done so much to raise standards. Boys were used to keeping company with girls not only in the holidays but on the growing number of exeats and leave weekends. In October 1986 the Debating Society discussed the motion that 'This House believes there is no place for girls at S.E.S.' Rightly expecting a large turnout, the Society held its meeting in the Hall. Yet the motion signalled no male backlash, and the speeches in favour were light-hearted. On the other side Linda Lyne was joined by two girls who had entered the school in 1984, Rebecca Petrie (Roll No. 8500) and Karen Kilkenny (Roll No. 8485). They spoke confidently and were at ease before the male ranks of the audience. The motion was lost 'by a considerable majority', reported the *Chronicle*. Even so, the school did not trumpet the change to co-education. The *Chronicle* tersely announced it in a sentence placed below news of the completion of the refurbishment of Cowell's and Segar's and of Corfe's new wing.

In the summer issue of the *Chronicle* in 1984 Jonathan Back (Roll No. 8002) contributed an article of two short columns entitled 'In a Minority. A Girl's Eye View of the School'. An accompanying photograph showed five girls and seven admiring boys strolling across the Quad. Back quoted one of the girls:

> The first term as a new girl here at St Edward's is mainly taken up on the many social rounds that have to be made before one can find a niche in the community. This can be difficult as at times one can feel rather insecure, unsure of who one's true friends are and uncertain what to expect and what is expected in return. It is hard to distinguish between those on whom you can rely (those who like you for yourself) and those on whom you can't (those who like you for your status/popularity). The second term is where the main process occurs of becoming accustomed to the life and ways of the community.

In the same issue of the *Chronicle* another girl felt that she had to prove to her teachers that she was there to achieve academic success and not just for fun. 'I think,' she wrote, 'it is now time for the staff to stop worrying about us.' Several appreciated the range of opportunities on offer, but saw the small numbers of the girls as a drawback, a feeling shared by some of their teachers.

Pat Phillips, who took so many pains on behalf of the girl entrants, found and supervised the women, some of them members of the Common Room, who housed the girls. She and Lyne held weekly meetings with the girls. Several girl OSE remember the care shown them by the House nurses. Georgina Pelham (Roll No. 8765) recalls: 'Pat Phillips and Jane Haddock [the House nurse of Mac's and Tilly's and mother of four boys at the school] were very much the people looking after the girls though we pretty much looked after ourselves (or at least thought we did!). Thursday Break was the race for the Trio biscuits in the Phillips's drawing room and a chance for Pat to talk to us and to try to gauge any potential problems.'

Georgina too had the advantage of belonging to a St Edward's family, as the daughter of the prominent OSE Mike Pelham (Roll No. 4836) and the sister of Hugh, the Captain of Boats and Head of School in Easter Term 1985 (Roll No. 7972). But nothing prepared her for a question she was asked at interview: 'What would you do if a boy told you you had fat legs?' Other prospective girl entrants were asked how tough they were. 'If you couldn't take the often tactless, teasing boys,' Georgina remembers, 'you weren't going to have a happy time.' The boys could be hurtful when they thought they were being funny. At St Edward's as elsewhere boys held up cards giving scores to the looks and clothes of passing girls. The practice persisted for some years, together with such unpleasant behaviour as the writing of mysterious messages in girls' books. David Alexander (Roll No. 8282) remembers that when he reached the Sixth Form in the summer of 1988 'we had only got up to four girls in Apsley, so it was obviously a slow start and I can't imagine how awful it was for those girls to put up with the habits and growing pains of so many teenage boys'. Rebecca Petrie sums up her first term: 'It was a baptism of fire. The boys holding up scorecards as we filed into the refectory was a low moment (in a Laura Ashley pinafore and a mop of uncontrollable red frizzy hair). I did not score highly and a group of boys insisted on barking at us as we walked from Field House to the Quad, which also became really unpleasant.'

Yet Rebecca also recounts a much more positive side to the story. 'There were also really wonderful boys there who were thrilled to have girls amongst them. I think it taught both sexes a great deal.' 'We were needed in all sorts of things,' she recalls, 'such as the choir, all sports, and plays and as School and House prefects. I remember not only featuring in our House play but being borrowed by Tilly's next door for theirs as they had no girls.' Sport was a problem for Georgina Pelham, who had to convert from lacrosse to hockey. Emma Bigland, being 'very sporty', also 'really missed' girls' sport. But in her second year she and other girls formed a rowing IV, 'which I loved. We trained really hard and were very successful, in fact unbeaten in that year, and it gave me a great sense of purpose as I was made captain and it kept me out of trouble.'

Helen Cook (Roll No. 8701A) arrived at St Edward's in September 1986, the third of three siblings to attend the school. She was Head Girl in the second of her two years. Her elder brother James (Roll No. 7694), who had arrived in 1978, at the start of Phillips's Wardenship, was an early member of Corfe House. He would take a First at Oxford and become a research biologist and worldwide explorer. Another brother, Stuart (Roll No. 8174), arrived in 1982; in later life he would be a distinguished Professor of Cardiology. On her arrival Helen was one of fourteen girls. Helen recalls Joe McPartlin's various forms of address to her in the classroom: 'Stuart's sister', 'Lassie', 'Cook'. She recalls, 'I seem to recall finding a loo a challenge at times.' In Segar's the girls had to use my downstairs loo, an arrangement that would now be illegal. In adapting to a mostly male environment Helen was helped by the experience and knowledge of her brothers. Other girls, she suggests, may have faced steeper challenges. She herself remembers 'trying to find clothes that blended in rather than stood out'. But 'my overall memory of the two years is very positive'.

In 1980 Nick Quartley took over as supervising editor of the *Chronicle*, a burden he would carry for twenty-five years. In the autumn of 1984 he published two poems next to each other. One had been written exactly fifty years earlier by John Virr (Roll No. 2601), who in adulthood was a poet and writer as well as a company director. The other was a new piece by the 17-year-old Matthew Higham (Roll No. 7943). The juxtaposition illustrates changes not only in literary taste but in English boys' perceptions of girls. Virr wrote:

> A kiss, a smile, a fickle maid;
> With few, but with how splendid stars
> The highways of the world are laid
> Between their shining bars.
> A star beside the stars she lay
> A fairness in the foulest fray.
> But in this young maid's heart of gold
> A true love – as the mirror told –
> Put forth its great and cherished light;
> But this to lonely men was ... night.
> And still a maid but for this ban;
> The kiss and the kisses Cyprian,
> Went wandering on, ill used by fate,
> But still there lived the heart so great
> A broken love without a mate.

Higham's poem, 'Description', reads:

> Turquoise hair
> Flecked with black night
> Graduating to
> Undulating purple and blue.
> Rust-blusher.
> Space-black eyes
> Let nothing escape,
> But blink,
> Occasionally.
> White throat,
> Pouting orange beak.
> Joseph's dreamcoat
> Cascading from your shoulders
> Down your thighs

To your love-red
Pixie-booted
Feet.

I thought you were
A kingfisher
As you strutted down
The High Street.

To judge from the educational language of the decade, the 1980s were the age of stress. Teachers were allegedly stressed. Pupils were allegedly stressed. The school, anxious about anxiety, brought in psychiatrists, not only to help individual pupils but for termly sessions to advise housemasters. Chaplains bore an increasing burden of secular pastoral care, which they discharged superbly. In interviews conducted for an A-level research project reported in the *Chronicle* of Autumn 1988, Helena ('Hena') Thomas (Roll No. 8794) questioned 150 lower- and upper-sixth-formers, using tests devised by the Stress Clinic at the Maudsley Hospital. 'Few', she concluded, found the school itself 'a stressful environment'. But she did find an inverse correlation between participation in sport and such manifestations of anxiety as perspiration, palpitations, panic attacks and breathlessness. Of those who spent no more than four hours a week on sport, 32% had such symptoms, but only 16% of those spending eight or more hours. In the latter category, 35% recorded sleep problems compared to 70% of the former.

There were certainly new pressures on the teaching staff, some of whom began to talk of early retirement, though in the event none seem to have taken it. As well as the new and ever more closely monitored exams and syllabuses, there was the growth of assessment by coursework. Increasingly, teachers felt that they were on trial. The Thatcher government urged the clearing of dead wood from the profession. Parents, worried about their children's exam results, took a growing interest in teachers' performance. The Governors pressed for a system of teacher evaluation and commissioned annual reports by the Director of Studies and heads of department, which were scrutinized by the Warden, and by the Governors themselves.

The timetable, and the lives of pupils and teachers were crowded by the expanding range of extracurricular activities. Yet the flourishing of so many non-academic pursuits did not damage the school's academic reputation. Examination results improved, albeit not dramatically, during Phillips's Wardenship. The A-level pass rate rose from 86% in 1978 to 93% in 1986, a figure comparable with those at Abingdon, Radley and Oxford High School. In 1978, 39% of A-level results were As or Bs; in 1984 the figure was 43%. Even so, applications to Oxbridge met with varied results. Though 13 awards and places were achieved in 1981, the number did not reach double figures again until 1985. With the arrival of such new subjects as CDT and Physical Science, and with such older subjects as Religious Studies and Politics becoming A-level ones in the 1980s, A-level pupils now had far more subjects to choose from. They also had many more universities to apply to. In 1991, the first year when the *Chronicle* supplies such figures, 102 pupils went on to universities, only 15 of them to Oxbridge. The expansion of higher education, the centralization of the national admission process, and the growing preoccupation of parents with their children's university prospects called for informed advice from the staff and added to the workload.

Despite such pressures this was an age of great vitality and achievement in the school's sporting and cultural life. It was an outstanding era for the Boat Club. Mike Rosewell and his successor Bill Sayer, much liked by their crews and by supportive OSE, made St Edward's one of the top three or four rowing schools in the country, maybe even the top one. In 1984 the school won the Princess Elizabeth Cup for the first time since 1959. In 1985 the rowers won five 'Victor Ludorum' awards and 45 open regattas, and nine of its crews won Head of the River events. The same year saw the first competitive entry of a Girls' IV. Coached by Graham Wells and captained by Emma Bigland, they won four regatta finals. By 1992 there would be a Girls' VIII. The boys produced a regular supply of oarsmen, perhaps three or four a year, who gained selection at national level. Those exploits rested on the strength of the school's rowing community in depth and numbers. The Rugby XV of 1982, coached by Ian Wright, joined the unbeaten sides of 1960 and 1975. In rugby and rowing alike, success at the top rested on the strength in depth supplied by large numbers of enthusiastic participants. Joe McPartlin resumed his charge of the XV in 1984, his famously deflating wit in coaching sessions undimmed. Knowing the value of a broad base, he reinstated House matches and House senior leagues. David Wippell, another coach of magnetic character, produced a series of unbeaten Third XVs. Hockey, where Myles Arkell now worked with Robert Aldred and Peter Badger, continued to prosper, despite the continued absence of an all-weather playing surface. Cricket thrived under Badger, who was in charge from 1981 to 1985 and again from 1987 after he had spent time in New Zealand on an exchange. He was aided by the Kent and Glamorganshire cricketer Brian Edrich, who had assisted the coaching, to warm admiration, since 1964. Alastair Cane (Roll No. 7805) achieved a school record with a score of 170 in 1984. In swimming, which was coached by Wippell, Andrew Moore (Roll No. 7848) broke all the school's records. He would go on to represent his country. Swimming, cross-country running, tennis, sailing and canoeing acquired a new standing, even though they were still categorized as 'minor sports'.

Some coaches in the traditionally 'major' sports looked askance at that development, as they did at the arrival of the Sports Centre. They also complained that the pattern of new teaching appointments, in which more attention was given to academic than to athletic prowess, was undermining the status of their sports. Unless St Edward's altered its priorities, they asked, how could it keep up with other schools proficient in traditionally popular games: Eton, Marlborough, Harrow, Bedford, Cheltenham, Wellington, Oundle, Radley? The appointment of women to the Common Room reduced the potential number of coaches of boys' teams. Grumbles surfaced in coaches' reports in the *Chronicle*. The recently created Games Committee, chaired by Arkell, pressed the coaches' case.

There was vitality in the arts. Music reached new heights of quality under Philip Cave and Robert Hughes. Large orchestras and talented soloists performed in ambitious concerts at Commem and Gaudy. At the 1985 Gaudy, for example, Jonathan White (Roll No. 7995) played in Mozart's Flute Rondo, Chris Knight (Roll No. 7951) in Rachmaninov's Second Piano Concerto, and Richard Morris (Roll No. 7896) in Fauré's *Élégie* for Cello. Then came Arnold's Suite for Orchestra, followed by what the *Chronicle* called the 'crisp, tidy and effervescent' performance of Rob Hughes's Concert Band. Hughes brought to instruction in music the dynamism and conviviality that others brought to games coaching. His innovations included pop concerts and visits to popular musical shows.

The era of Christie and Phillips saw a staggering amount of activity on the stage. There were two or three major productions of plays by masters each year, as well as frequent Drama Group presentations by boys of plays by such writers as Beckett, Pinter, Ionesco and Stoppard. House plays prospered and an annual drama festival of plays performed by Shells was introduced in 1982. Pupils put on their own performances. Lower Sixth boys, with local girl friends, achieved exceptional standards of acting and directing in such productions as *Requiem* (a show devised by the cast), Brian Clark's *Whose Life Is It Anyway?*, Edward Albee's *The Zoo Story* and David Halliwell's *Little Malcolm and his Struggle against the Eunuchs*. Nick Quartley, Simon Taylor and I directed school stage productions, as did John Trotman after the departure in 1985 of Taylor, who went first to Deerfield Academy in Massachusetts and then to Winchester. His outstanding productions of Shakespeare included *Hamlet*, *King Lear*, *Much Ado about Nothing* and *Twelfth Night*. He also directed Robert Bolt's *A Man for All Seasons,* Peter Terson's play about football hooligans *Zigger Zagger, Nicholas Nickleby,* a shattering production of *West Side Story, Kes* (the play adapted by Lawrence Till from Barry Hines's novel), and Peter Shaffer's *Equus.* There was always a whiff of danger and excitement about Taylor's productions, especially those of plays with a contemporary edge. A Segar's parent telephoned me to question the appropriateness of staging *Equus*, in which the leading lady strips (though in the school's production the actress merely mimed the action). 'I can tell you one thing,' he said of the play. 'They gave it the thumbs down in Windsor.' Quartley, who was in charge of the stage and of the New Hall, handled competing demands for their use with unobtrusive tact, and himself directed memorable productions such as *The Comedy of Errors*, Arthur Kopit's *Indians*, and Brecht's *Arturo Ui*. Trotman made his striking debut with *The Duchess of Malfi*. Malcolm Watson's productions included *The Canterbury Tales* and *Tom Thumb*, mine *Julius Caesar* (my 30th production at the school), Tom Stoppard's *Jumpers*, Peter Shaffer's *Amadeus*, and an experimental rendering of the screenplay of Ingmar Bergman's *The Seventh Seal*. Thanks to the skills of Philip Cave, the Director of Music, I was able to direct *The Mikado, Orpheus in the Underworld*, and, with Robert Hughes, *Godspell*. Later the school would move on to opera and would stage *Nabucco*, *Attila* and an outdoor *Cavalleria Rusticana*.

A number of professional actors of the future performed, among them Teddy Kempner (Roll No. 6789), Roger Wood (Roll No. 7292), and Andrew Jones (Roll No. 7485). Their forebear Laurence Olivier appeared in the Quad on 25 and 26 June 1981, based in a caravan next to the Warden's house, to film some sequences for John Mortimer's *A Voyage Round my Father*. William Pugh (Roll No. 7629) remembers a contemporary's encounter with the veteran of Cowell's *A Midsummer Night's Dream*:

'Boy', said Olivier sharply to the startled pupil.
Boy: Yes sir.
Olivier: Do you like this school?
Boy: Not really sir.
Olivier: Good. I hated it too. Come in and have a drink.

The boy was plied with wine in the caravan and exited tipsy.

In the Easter Term of 1984 the *Chronicle* conducted a questionnaire inviting (i) assessments of the school's facilities and (ii) suggestions for improvement. The Sports Centre was the facility that was most appreciated; the Library came second; the New Hall third (though Sixth Form pupils also placed the Junior Common Room high). The proximity of Oxford was ranked 11th. The toilets came bottom. Top of the features in need of improvement came the House buildings, followed by the food and the dining facilities. Pleas for the admission of more girls and for the provision of weekly boarding came much lower, 11th and 14th respectively. No one mentioned the Chapel on either list.

In the memories that pupils have sent me to aid in the writing of this book, the 1960s are a dividing line. Until then, recollections are dominated by hierarchies, beatings, fagging and deprivation, however indulgently they are sometimes recalled. From the 1960s onwards pupils found the practices of that earlier world wrong, even laughable. In September 1979 Phillips proposed that housemasters observe a self-denying ordinance not to cane for a term. One housemaster was opposed to the proposal, but he went along with it. At the start of the next term the Warden announced to the school that corporal punishment had been abolished. Its use had become so rare in recent years that the news made little impression. Caning was outlawed in state schools in 1987 and in private schools in 1999. Poland had outlawed it in 1783; no wonder the practice was known on the Continent as the British disease. In 2009 a survey by the *Times Educational Supplement* of more than 6,000 teachers found that only one in five would support its restoration.

However much stress was felt, the atmosphere among the pupil population of the 1980s seems happy when set beside the school's long earlier history or beside the discontents of the 1970s. Something else had changed over the decades. Helen Cook judges that 'the life-skills I learned' at St Edward's were 'the perfect grounding for a career in a profession dominated by males'. That may sound a mixed compliment, but many other pupils of this time, male and female, describe their education at St Edward's as a good preparation for life beyond the school. In the 1920s and 1930s St Edward's had turned in on itself, with lasting consequences for its character. By the time of John Phillips's departure in July 1998 it had again come to terms with the outside world.

44

WARDEN DAVID CHRISTIE

THE closer historical writing gets to the present, the less historical it can be. Written amid unfolding developments, it inevitably struggles for perspective. In the history of an institution it presents special problems, for a high proportion of the participants in the story will still be working in it or retain attachments to it. I have two further difficulties to face. The first is the challenge of separating history from autobiography. For almost the first century of the existence of St Edward's I knew next to nothing of the school. I worked in it from 1962 to 1999, with seniority playing an ever more prominent part. In 1985 I became Second Master, a post re-titled Sub-Warden the year before I left. I forged a close working relationship, though always as his subordinate, with David Christie, who became the eleventh Warden on John Phillips's retirement in 1988. My second difficulty is that, having been in the midst of things until my retirement, I have subsequently been remote from the life of the school and am bound to have a weaker feel for it.

In these last chapters there will be rather less about personalities. Yet there is one that cannot be bypassed, so influential a Warden was David Christie and so high is his stature in the roll of the school's leaders. He was Warden for sixteen years, from 1988 to 2004. It was the longest reign since Kendall's, even before the Governors extended it two years beyond the expected retirement age. Before drawing up the shortlist from which he was chosen the Governors do not seem to have had particular criteria in mind, though they consulted Common Room opinion about the qualities they should be looking for. Their choice of Christie broke a mould. All the Wardens since Kendall had been southern Englishmen from Public Schools and Oxbridge. They played team games and had shared at least some military experience; they had an English outlook and were committed Anglicans. Christie was a Scot, educated at Strathclyde and Glasgow Universities as an economist, a subject in which no previous Warden had been proficient. He did not have an Anglican background. Though a keen and accomplished golfer he was not a particularly enthusiastic player of team games. After six years' teaching at George Watson's College, the independent school in Edinburgh, under Roger Young, a formative influence on his educational values, he had spent five years at Moray House College of Education in Edinburgh, where he trained teachers and conducted research into curriculum development and the economics of education. He had moved to England in 1983 and before coming to St Edward's had had a very successful period teaching at Winchester, where he was Head of Economics.

In England academic interest in education was looked down on. Postgraduate teacher-training, and the qualifications it brought, commanded little respect in the Independent Schools. David Christie, with his European perspective, brought fresh thinking and new ideas. He had taught in Sweden for a year after graduation and in 1977 had joined the European School in Luxembourg, where he stayed until leaving for Winchester in 1983. He had examined for the baccalaureate, a school-leaving examination system likewise not respected in England. He possessed intellectual stature too. He had published a book and scholarly articles on the Scottish Enlightenment, and was a driven bibliophile.

There was another way in which Christie's appointment was a departure. Few Public School headmasters of the previous era had taken a stand on matters of educational philosophy. Intimidated by media scrutiny and by government policies, they used speech days not to expound principles but to trumpet their successes and to mouth slogans about 'the pursuit of excellence'. Henry Christie and John Phillips were caring and intelligent men, but fundamental educational thinking was not on their agenda. They rarely produced policy papers for their Governors, as Frank Fisher and Richard Bradley had done. David Christie resumed the practice.

Under his guidance the reputation of the school flourished. He built up a formidable standing among fellow heads, as he did in Prep Schools, which he assiduously cultivated. Many expected him to be head-hunted away. An accomplished speaker, combining a light touch with transparent seriousness, he was beguiling to parents, to whom he gave unstinting attention. He was a forceful and decisive figure, if a less confident one than he seemed. He had a moral earnestness worthy of his hero Adam Smith, and a short fuse in the presence of indifference to right conduct. Some found his censoriousness irksome. Some felt threatened by the playful irony of his humour or his taste for intellectual abstraction. Occasional displays of mild pomposity were punctured by his wife Elsa. Yet James Quick, Housemaster of Apsley, knew where Christie's professional instincts lay: 'What I found most endearing about him was that when it came to the crunch he was always on the side of the individual boy or girl. He certainly showed immense care and compassion in one or two difficult cases that I had to deal with as a housemaster and to me personally on occasions.' The chaplain Andrew Wright, who remembers Christie with warm personal affection, noted conflicting traits in him: impulsiveness and yet a habit of procrastination; a taste for 'dramatic and hard-edged change', yet also 'a more conservative and establishment streak'. He remarks on the Warden's 'instinct for all those things which made St Edward's what it had been'. He also recalls the sense of authority he imparted: 'There was no doubting who was in charge.' And 'at heart, for those who could see it, he was a man of deep humanity.' There was a private side to the Warden, which few knew. It centred on his loving relationship with his wife and his three children, who were aged 14, 12 and 5 on his arrival. In 1992 the family vacated the upper floors of the Warden's lodgings and moved into a house on the Woodstock Road, leaving their previous quarters to Apsley's housemaster.

Christie's tenure produced one fundamental transition: the move in 1997 to co-education throughout the school. In other fields his aim was rather to preserve and develop existing features of the structure and ethos of St Edward's than to change them. He was concerned to maintain a broad spread of abilities among the pupils and to enhance the school's pastoral skills. He gave a new emphasis to anti-bullying policies and appointed a permanently attached school counsellor. Assertive though he was, he never shunned consultation, either with the staff or with the Governors. He appointed committees and ad hoc gatherings to ponder policy issues and gather information on them, though some staff complained that decisions took too long. The Warden's Committee was enlarged to include the two teachers who had overall supervision of all sporting activities and games (David Drake-Brockman) and cultural activities (Anthony Kerr-Dineen).

Christie arrived just as a healthy period in the nation's economy was ending. It had achieved post-war records of growth, at over 2% a quarter. The rate started to fall in the third quarter of 1987, and in 1990 the economy shrank by 1%. Inflation reached 10.9% in 1992. Retail prices, including house prices, were falling. Also in 1992, 1,200 businesses collapsed. As so often before, an economic downturn produced fears about the school's numbers. As many as seventy-eight private schools closed in 1990, though most were small and weak ones. In 1991 the Headmasters' Conference forecast a 3% fall in boarding numbers, at a time when the schools were having to award salary increases of 11–13%. Entry at 11 was discussed, not for the first time, but there was little evidence of demand for it. In 1992 St Edward's budgeted for a fall in numbers from a figure in the low 580s to 565. Fees, which currently stood at £3,450, were increased by 6.5% that year and by a further 3.4 % in the following one. The bursar David Bramble argued for a measure of prudent retrenchment, on the assumption that the fall in numbers had come to stay. The annual salary increase toppled to 1.5%, to dismay in the Common Room, which had become used to salary rises above inflation. There also were fears of an end to the practice of annual increments (in addition to pay rises) and even fear of redundancies. Yet by 1993 recovery was on the way. In 1994 inflation came down to 4% and growth was up by 4%. To sighs of relief in the Independent Schools, prosperity had returned. It would persist through the administration of Tony Blair of 1997–2007. Expensive as Public School education was, there were enough parents who could afford it.

Christie's Wardenship produced a striking rise in the number of pupils, so striking that the question was sometimes asked as to whether the school should fix a limit to its size. There were 583 pupils at the time of Christie's appointment. By 2000 the figure had grown to 609, and by 2006 it had reached 660. It was the girl intake that swelled the numbers. Whereas at first girls had been a small addition to an expanding boy population, now their large numbers compensated for a sharply declining one. On Christie's appointment there were 33 girls. There were 197 by 2000, and 230 in 2006. Meanwhile the number of boys declined from 569 in 1988 to 412 in 2000 – although the latter figure would rise to 430 in 2006 and has remained at about that level. In attracting pupils to the school Christie had an invaluable associate in Anne Brooks, formerly Warden Phillips's secretary, who from 1991 to 2006 held the new post of Registrar, which carried responsibility for admissions. The widow of an OSE, Robert Brooks (Roll No. 5003), and the mother of three children educated at the school, Tom (Roll No. 8811), Will (Roll No. 8968) and Katie (Roll No. 9084), she had an invaluable knowledge both of St Edward's and of the local community and achieved wonders with her Open Days, prep school visits and vigilant running of the machinery of entry. She became the first resident housemistress of the transformed Oakthorpe House in 1995 and was heavily involved in the launch of full co-education at the school.

The continued prosperity of the Independent Schools was

aided by the poor reputation of Local Authority Schools, where academic and disciplinary standards were thought to be low, and by the hazards, trumpeted by the press, of knife-wielding and drug-taking in the teenage world beyond the school gates. But no Independent School could expect to benefit automatically from those perceptions. Parents were becoming increasingly open-minded and discriminating in their choice of Public School, a tendency which made future numbers – the basis on which financial calculations and architectural plans had to be made – hard to predict. Of 7,500 boys who entered private Secondary Schools through Common Entrance in the autumn of 1992, 2,300 (more than 30%) had changed the school of their choice since March of the same year. But once their children had arrived at a school many parents developed a sense of personal commitment to it. They frequently attended school events and welcomed consultations about the children's progress. If parents liked the boarding schools, a poll conducted by the Association of Governing Bodies of Independent Schools in 2001 suggests that pupils liked them too: 61.5% said that the decision to attend boarding school had been theirs; 69% rated the experience 'good' or 'excellent'; 66.5% said it had shaped and helped their social lives; 92.3 % said it had helped them to learn to live with others. The figures indicate the success of the Public Schools in adapting to the demands of the teenage world.

Christie brought a proposal for full co-education to the Governors in 1994. He knew there were risks. Would enough parents of 13-year-old girls want to submit them to the distractions, even dangers, of a predominantly boys' school? The building of expensive boarding houses might be a gamble, but he did not want St Edward's to fall behind other schools which had taken or were considering the same step. In any case he believed he could attract a niche market, for among the few co-educational boarding schools none were in London, the Thames Valley or the Home Counties. Christie heard parents of boys at the school, and old boys, asking hopefully whether the school planned girl entry at 13. As when girls had been admitted to the Sixth Form, the restrictions of single-sex girls' schools encouraged some girls to seek a co-educational environment.

Christie's tenure was marked by extensive building and by ambitious improvements of facilities. During the recession of the early 1990s, which saw a national decline in the number of pupils boarding, ISIS warned that the fall would not be reversed when prosperity returned. Yet at St Edward's there was no marked increase in the ratio of day pupils, which has kept within the range of 20–30%. Boarders had to be housed. In 1997, when full co-education was introduced, Oakthorpe House became a full boarding house for girls and Mac's another. In 2000 Corfe House was handed over to girls, and the boys who had occupied it moved to a new building, Kendall House, which adjoined Field House and Sing's in the Kendall Quad. There were other substantial developments west of the subway. The Fisher Field, an all-weather playing surface which opened in 1991, was made possible by a hugely generous donation, though the school had to find £130,000 to complete it. Another all-weather surface was created in 2001. Initially called the Bader Field, it was renamed the Chris Lawless Field in memory of the former Captain of Hockey (Roll No. 7263) who died in 2003 at the age of 42. The Douglas Bader Sports Centre had been demolished in the previous year, to make way for a new health and fitness centre, run by the company Esporta, with whom the school shared the facilities, though the old outdoor pool had to be concreted over to make way for it. Its disappearance provoked barely a protest. A newly designed six-hole golf course on the Lower Fields came into use.

There were continuing refurbishments, in the Houses and out of them. The Sanatorium was moved into 277 Woodstock Road (Angle House), which had formerly been occupied by the Second Master. The expanding Bursar's department moved into the old School Shop building. The Common Room took over the original Big School – latterly the small dining hall – as its sitting room, with a bar on a mezzanine. Outside inspections had marked effects on the school's facilities and housing arrangements. New fire regulations and an inspection in 1996 resulted in costly changes in the houses. Following a critical report on the kitchens by the Health Inspectors in 1989, substantial alterations were made to the eating arrangements, at a cost of over £1 million. New kitchens offered pupils a wide choice of good food. The old dining hall was renovated, and pupils now ate at staggered times. In 1996 the school, having previously employed an outside company for catering, decided to do it itself. Steps were taken to ease the pressure on space and accommodation, and nearby houses were bought when they became available. Four houses were acquired in Oakthorpe Road in the early 1990s, at a cost of £442,000. Two further house purchases, in the Woodstock Road, claimed another £507,000. Such opportune acquisitions could easily hold up planned ones, which themselves might be thwarted by the planning authorities, who refused the school permission to build six accommodation units for teachers on the old piggeries site.

Like all Wardens, Christie needed to raise money. Since the Centenary Appeal, appeals had identified two or three building projects for support. For donations, usually made in seven-year covenants, the school had relied largely on current parents whose children would benefit from the improvements, though OSE would always give something, especially for sporting facilities. Schools were turning to rolling programmes of fund-raising, the model favoured in the United States. The days of external professional fund-raisers were ending too. Instead schools appointed their own development directors and development offices. In 1990 Roger Ellis, formerly Master of Marlborough and now the school's Chairman of Governors, proposed a move in this direction, and a sub-committee, chaired by the publisher and future Lord-Lieutenant of Oxfordshire Hugo Brunner, was set up to take it forward, though only in 2003, with the arrival of T. D. G. ('Tim') Edge, would the post of Development Director be made permanent. The new approach was slow to bear fruit. An appeal in 1996 to raise money for scholarships and for new science laboratories fell flat. The difficulty with scholarships was that parents, though glad enough to contribute to projects from which their own children would benefit, were less eager to subsidize the education of later generations.

In November 1993 Christie told the Governors that 'all members of the School community feel the increasing weight of bureaucracy, regulations and inspection.' The Inland Revenue (subsequently Her Majesty's Revenue and Customs) increased its scrutiny. A struggle by Malvern College to preserve favourable educational terms for teachers' children was seen as a test case by the Headmasters' Conference, whose schools contributed to the legal costs of a case which reached the House of Lords, where the schools won. Subsidized housing was another target.

The trend of external scrutiny had a direct effect on three areas of school life. The Protection of Children Act of 1989 (known as the Children Act) brought a new inspection regime, though David Christie prudently established a pattern of cooperation with the local Social Services before the Act came into force. The legislation immediately increased both work and paper. It is hard to argue against any laws that seek to further the protection of children, but the machinery of inspection was heavy and cumbersome, as I, who was given responsibility for the implementation of the Act, can ruefully testify. Any suspicion of 'inappropriate behaviour' would activate Social Services and the police. Schools were prohibited from conducting their own investigations into cases of possible sexual abuse. In an institution which set great store on good personal relationships and trust, the Act brought many losses. Teachers were advised not to be alone with an individual pupil. A comforting hand on the shoulder of a distressed youngster might have repercussions, as might an invitation to drop in for a cup of coffee. Newly appointed teachers waited months for police checks on their suitability to be completed. The Inspectors' insistence that waist-high panels be introduced in the open showering areas in boys' houses united teachers and pupils in derision. It was a far cry from the tin baths of the old Apsley and Sing's or from the nude bathing in the outdoor pool.

A second source of intrusion was the Independent Schools' Inspectorate, to whom Ofsted devolved the inspection of the Independent sector. Its machinery of wholesale inspections replaced the occasional and less searching visitations of the less powerful body, Her Majesty's Inspectorate, which had previously had responsibility. No one could sensibly argue that schools should not be subject to public inspection, any more than that children should not be protected, but here too a massive increase in bureaucratic labour was imposed. Towers of paperwork and of forms for box-ticking preceded the visits. When I last took down the book of the regulations prepared by the school to meet inspection requirements I could scarcely lift it. Parents understandably looked to see whether an Ofsted inspection of the school had been 'successful'. But how was success to be measured? The Inspectors' reports had a way of mixing formulaic conclusions drawn from the completed forms with transparently subjective judgements. There were also puzzling inconsistencies. The first Ofsted Inspection marked St Edward's 'Very Good'. The second said that the school had improved since the first – and marked it 'Good'.

Thirdly there was the growing bureaucratization and intrusion of state examinations. In 1989 the newly introduced GCSEs, whatever their merits, were seen as less challenging to the brighter pupil, and the GCSE system's stress on intellectual process rather than on knowledge reduced not only the body of pupils' knowledge but the development of skills in its deployment. Many teachers thought GCSE a poor preparation for A level. The growth of coursework at A level created a new raft of rules and uncertainty about the degree of help a pupil might be given. Modular A-levels added to the complications. So did A/S levels, the examinations, introduced in 2000, taken after a pupil's first year in the Sixth Form. There was growing dissatisfaction with the marking of exam scripts by the boards. Requests for re-marking became common and often resulted in changes of grade. 'Our views and those of the Board clearly do not coincide,' wrote the St Edward's Geography Department on one of the occasions when the Board produced a surprising set of grades. So much concern was there that the Headmasters' and Headmistresses' Conference (HMC) was moved to declare that schools 'were losing confidence in the examining bodies'. Long-standing examiners, opposed to the new marking systems or wearying of accumulative bureaucracy, started to resign.

The education of pupils became ever more dominated, and more restricted, by syllabuses. In the cause of a broader education, pupils took, and had to be taught, an increasing range of subjects, with the ironic result that General Studies courses, which had been taught outside the syllabus, were squeezed out of the timetable. Exam League Tables heightened the concentration on exam results. Headmasters had constantly to explain the shortcomings of the tables or point out that a tiny swing in performance could send a school shooting up or down them. Newspapers, in their annual coverage of exam results, puzzlingly derived conflicting league tables from a common set of statistics.

It was 'with the academic life of the school', remembers Andrew Wright, that David Christie 'felt most at home'. 'His dearest wish was to see a big improvement in the learning culture.' Determined to get the best out of teachers and pupils, he cared more for what he called the 'intellectual climate' of the school, and for 'academic sparkle', than for the arithmetic of exam results. Yet the results held up well. In every year of his Wardenship A-level passes topped 90%, with A–C grades usually between 65% and 75%. In 2001, a representative year, two-fifths of the candidates obtained As and nearly two-thirds As or Bs. At GCSE an average of 85% A–C grades at GCSE was achieved over the period 1988–2001. The figure of 29% A grades can be set beside overall HMC figure of 27%. The standards stood up at university entrance, too. In 2001 there were seventeen offers from Oxbridge, a figure comparable to those achieved by Radley, Harrow and Oundle.

'Are we trying to do too much?' Christie once asked his Governors. If so, his own drive was responsible. The minutes of the General Purposes Committee of the Governors in March 2000 remarked on his 'sustained energy and constant restlessness with the status quo'. He was open to experiment and change in the classroom.

He was alert to special academic needs and made everyone take dyslexia seriously. He worked hard at raising the status of Heads of Department, and annually discussed each department's results and problems with its Head. He launched a 'curriculum audit' to examine the whole structure of the curriculum, and rethought the pattern of the school day, which had scarcely changed since the war.

In September 1999 an eight-day working cycle was introduced, as were such new subjects as Drama and Sports Studies, although they added to the crowding of the schedule – a problem that would have been exacerbated if the school had yielded to the public pressure for health education in the classroom. Equipment for information technology was constantly updated, at considerable expense. Field trips, reading parties and educational holidays proliferated. Self-assessment by pupils was introduced into all the internal reporting systems. Much of the drive came from David Cundy, the Director of Studies, and then from the combination of his successor as director, Sarah Kerr-Dineen, and the Senior Tutor Ian Rowley. A new kind of academic report card was introduced. One period a week was set aside from the crowded timetable for a new tutorial system, which gave tutors time to discuss the progress of pupils' work and to encourage academic interests. The previous tutorial system had been based in the Houses, but its replacement was organized around the classroom, a further encroachment on the traditional centrality of the Houses in pupils' lives, though subsequently the tutoring of senior boys was restored to Houses; their running had become a team effort, less reliant on the single exertions of an overworked housemaster or mistress.

The hard work of the Governors, a body about twenty strong, is reflected in the large volume of their papers in the David Christie years. Their job was becoming more complex, more burdensome and more answerable to outside pressures. One committee of the Governors, chaired by Peter Oppenheimer and attended by the Warden and the Director of Studies, addressed matters of educational policy; another oversaw financial investments; and so on. The Warden and his bursars, David Bramble and Stephen Withers Green, worked closely with the Governors, especially Michael Stanfield, the then Chairman of the General Purposes Committee, to enable the school to adjust to new outside pressures and new legislation.

Over the generations the composition of the Governing Body had evolved in character. Once it had been common to have three or even four retired military officers on the body, but Commodore Mike Gretton, appointed in 1984, was the last. During the chairmanship of Bishop Robert Mortimer from 1951 to 1973 there had been five bishops or deans on the Governing Body. That constituency declined too. In David Christie's time, when the body always had twenty members, the world of business and commerce had the highest number of representatives, though the number dropped from nine in 1988 to six by 2004. Academics were the second-largest group: there were six in 1988 and five in 2004. In both years there were two retired Prep or Public School headmasters. One of the latter, Roger Ellis, was chairman from 1992, though the other four of the last five chairmen have been businessmen. The gender revolution and the move to co-education made their gradual impact on the body. In 1992 the first women, two of them, were appointed governors. By 2004 there were four.

45

DAVID CHRISTIE'S SCHOOL

Charles Neill, the chaplain, left St Edward's in the summer of 1991 after eleven years at the school. A Public School boy himself, he had taught at three independent schools before his arrival. When he became a schoolmaster, in 1957, 'it was like going back into the world of my own school .... People seemed to accept the structures, customs and priorities of school life without question .... Nobody seemed to object to the terms Christian, scholar and gentleman.' When, now a priest, he moved to a different school in 1966, 'Everything seemed to have changed .... Pupils claimed to have rights. All the corporate and compulsory elements in the system were under attack .... It was an uncomfortable time', though 'it could also be refreshing and stimulating'.

At St Edward's, Neill, who held immutable religious beliefs, found that patterns of religious observance which had long been taken for granted had evaporated. Weekday services and Theme Services had been made 'acceptable to every pupil' by becoming 'less specifically Christian', a development in tune with the advice of senior churchmen who were urging the message of Christian love and of humanitarian obligations rather than the doctrinal content of faith. Neill found 'genuine and deep social concern' among the pupils and plenty of good works, but less interest in the Chapel. The teaching of a 'superficial knowledge of world religions' pandered to the notion that religious truth was merely 'a matter of opinion'. As chaplain, Neill strove to 'restore a sense of holiness, wonder and awe to the worship and to the place of worship'.

Neill's successor as chaplain was Andrew Wright (Roll No. 6948), who came from parish work in Liverpool, Carlisle and Wigan. He preserved Neill's inheritance as well as making Religious Studies an A-level subject. With the help and support of David Wippell a line was drawn against the devaluation of Christian observance. David Christie, temperamentally suspicious of institutional religion, might have welcomed less emphasis on the liturgy, more adaptability to modern trends. But he respected the place of Christianity in the life of the school. He also knew that those Common Room members who were most committed to the Chapel believed that the Eucharist should be the cornerstone of its services.

Wright, who became Housemaster of his old House, Segar's, remarked on a 'period of remarkable change' in the Common Room between his arrival at the school in 1991 and his departure in 2007. When he joined the staff 'there was still a nightly formal table, served by a steward', with a number of teachers regularly attending. The bar was 'homely, snug', and 'packed in the early evenings', with 'a great buzz about the place and a great sense of community', something Wright treasured after his parish days. In retrospect 'it seems extraordinary that the bar was often open at lunchtime' and that 'some teachers prepared for afternoon lessons with a glass or two of red wine'. Julian Macnamara, first an assistant director and then Director of Music, remembers the Common Room of Christie's time as 'exceptionally convivial', with 'a tremendous sense of fun about everything we did'. On one occasion in the bar after supper, he recalls, the Warden and Joe McPartlin were sparring as usual:

DC: Joe, have you prepared your lessons for tomorrow yet?

JM: Warden, I prepared them in 1963.

DC: Well, don't you think you should bring them up to date?

JM: Not really, Warden, the Alps haven't moved very far since then.

Even so, the tradition of nightly conviviality was waning. The number of teachers living far away, a decrease in the number of unmarried teachers, and the piling up of evening duties had their effect. Formal dinners were reduced to one a week, which was poorly attended. The bar life evaporated. Physical changes to the Common Room brought improved facilities, but at the cost of the intimacy of the hitherto cramped conditions. Still, something of the old spirit survived. The introduction of a Common Room pantomime revived a theatrical tradition among the staff, and a termly 'Safari Supper' (for which staff ate one course at one colleague's house before proceeding to another's), inspired and run by the Maths master Charlie Baggs, was very well supported. But the spirit of enjoyment among the teaching staff was not furthered by the external pressures on them. James Quick, son of a distinguished Public School headmaster and himself a man of excellent teaching and pastoral skills, had been appointed to the staff by John Phillips at the age of 22. He warmed to 'the unity, friendliness and freedom from cliques in the Common Room', but with time came to sense that the school was 'losing its glue' as the demands of procedure imposed by the National Curriculum, League Tables, the rules of coursework and modules and so on, intensified. He also noticed a new readiness of teachers to stand up for themselves over the salary system and allowances.

Phillips had made 71 appointments to the Common Room, of whom almost half, 34, were brought in as full-time classroom teachers, the rest being part-timers, music teachers, graduate assistants, sports teachers or short-term appointments. David Christie made 325 appointments in his fourteen years, a heavy demand on his time even though he had the help of appointment committees. The proportion of appointments to full-time posts during his tenure was little more than a third. The readiness of teachers to stay at the school was declining. Of Phillips's 34 full-time Common Room appointments 19 stayed for more than fifteen years, a large enough number to sustain a sense of stability, if also to create queues for promotion and to curb momentum for change. Around two-thirds of Christie's Common Room appointments left within ten years, a proportion roughly double that of Phillips's. More and more teachers were viewing their appointment as the first step on a ladder of promotion. Ever fewer were committed to teaching in the independent sector, let alone in a boarding school. Increasingly, teachers prized their professional skills of instruction more than any pastoral goal. Some balked at evening duties that took them away from their partners or families. Some advocated weekly boarding.

Christie made some strong appointments: eleven of his choices have gone on to headships. By now the teaching staff represented a much wider range of social background than in earlier generations, both in the number of teachers who had themselves not been to independent or boarding schools and in the proportion of those recruited from outside Oxbridge. In 1965 Frank Fisher had broken the near-monopoly of Oxford and Cambridge graduates by appointing the biology teacher John Tree, a graduate of London. Five of the next 21 appointments to permanent posts, made by Fisher and Bradley, were non-Oxbridge men (one of them, Guy Rigault, a Frenchman). The proportion increased. Almost a third of Henry Christie's appointments to permanent posts, eight out of 25, had graduated outside Oxbridge, and more half of John

Phillips's, 24 out of 43. By 2003–4 the proportion of non-Oxbridge appointments on the permanent staff was nearly two-thirds.

Like Phillips before him, Christie created or strengthened committees providing for consultation and coordination between the school's leadership and its staff. These processes did not dispel discontent. In the earlier and mid-1990s a newly critical tone entered the staff's comments at the termly meetings of the Common Room Liaison Committee, on which a representative of the Governing Body, first David Conner and then Derek Roe, sat, sometimes together with the Chairman of the Governors' General Purposes Committee or the bursar. In 1990 the Governors, feeling they were not engaging sufficiently with the staff, proposed a 'getting-to-know-you' exercise. Dinners were arranged at which governors and staff would mingle, but they were not apt occasions for business and the representation of staff at them seemed arbitrary. The initiative did not last. Another development was the division of the Common Room into four constituencies of age, each of them electing a member to the Liaison Committee. The effect was to highlight the anxiety of younger teachers about their low salaries, at a time in their life when many of them were starting families, and the worries of older staff about their finishing salaries, on which their pensions would be based.

Teachers and housemasters came under increasing pressure to keep parents informed of the progress of their pupils. Some parents frequently phoned or emailed. Some demanded that their children be given extra help with coursework, which the examination rules forbade. The mood of the Common Room sank during the recession of the early 1990s. The questioning of benefits in kind by the tax authorities upset the school and its employees, especially when in 1992 the Liaison Committee was told not to expect salary increases beyond the rate of inflation. The threat to school numbers brought by the economic downturn threatened jobs. Rocketing house prices added to the strain on the limited accommodation the school could provide for its staff. There were awkward questions. Should accommodation be granted for the rest of the occupant's working life? Should it be awarded on the basis of school duties that required staff members to be close at hand? Had the school an obligation to housemasters when their tenure ended? Christie and his bursars worked away to try to provide a coherent housing policy, but it proved impossible. Besides, any Warden would want to use the system to attract or retain outstanding staff, to the inevitable disappointment of others. The provision of free or subsidized education for the children of staff was another difficult area.

The salary system came in for criticism, too. Traditionally, Independent Schools had operated salary structures in parallel with each other, even if the rates of pay varied. There had been few Special Responsibility Allowances, which produce complexity and confusion. But by 1993, thirty-two teachers had responsibility allowances. Some staff wanted there to be more, particularly for games coaches, who were hard to recruit. Yet increases in payments to staff would have meant cuts elsewhere. Science teachers worried not only about the ageing condition of their laboratories but about safety in them. The salary structure, with its 35-point increments, looked cumbersome and outdated. Yet by 1996, when the economy had recovered and pupil numbers were again rising, the tensions in the Common Room had eased. The Liaison Committee now found little to discuss. The Common Room was never a militant body.

In 2005 there came a blow. Bursars at HMC or Rugby Group meetings had formed the habit of discussing the current economic climate and of reaching a common understanding of each other's intentions in setting the next round of fees. A school that broke from this arrangement might price itself out of the market or, if it set low fees, arouse suspicions about its quality. Until the Competition Act of 1998, which came into force in 2003, competition law did not apply to charities. But in 2005 the Office of Fair Trading gave notice to fifty schools, St Edward's among them, that their recent discussions had been unlawful, even though it is doubtful that the levels of fees would have been significantly different without them. The Chairman of the Governors Sir Bob Reid, formerly Chairman of Shell Petroleum and British Rail, led negotiations with the Office on behalf of the fifty schools and achieved a settlement which allowed them to state that they had broken the law unwittingly. The schools agreed to pay a manageable amount of money into a trust from which to make payments to pupils who had been at the school during the period of infringement since 2003 and needed funding for further studies.

Under Christie the school, with its growing fee income, was putting up buildings; it was also looking neater and sprucer. There were shrubs in tubs, manicured lawns, pot plants. Pupils were more uniformly and tidily dressed. The school was also becoming physically more security conscious, a place of keypads and fobs. What of the pupils in this era? As always, teachers fretted about them. Were they working enough – or working too hard? Were they spending too much time on extracurricular activities, especially drama and music? Did they have sufficient intellectual curiosity? Were they drinking too much? One girl OSE recalls that 'The best thing about SES was the JCR and the ability to buy beer legally' – in 1999 – for £1. The pupils 'looked forward to these evenings so much', and tried to get served by prefects who might let them exceed their quota. Other girls recall the giggly practice of hurling oneself against prickly bushes in the Quad on the way back to the house after the bar had closed. The national drinking culture had taken hold. Olivia Cooper (Roll No. 9694) remembers that the King's Arms in Summertown was 'a favourite haunt, with a very kind landlord who would give us a nod if any of the teachers came prowling'. Simon Mills (Roll No. 10222) recalls that 'we cut our drinking teeth in shady pubs in Jericho or around the Westgate'. Parents sometimes returned pupils in an inebriated condition after a leave weekend or day out. Drinking habits were moving down the age groups. Local off-licence retailers unscrupulously sold drink to those below the age limit, and there was a cottage industry in the manufacture of false ID cards. The staff organized patrols in Summertown or 'busts' on drinking sessions, but pupils usually anticipated them. Like smoking, drinking was occasionally punished by 'gating', but rarely with anything worse.

Drugs were a different matter, as in most HMC schools. Possession might lead to expulsion: dealing and distributing certainly would. In 1993 six pupils were expelled for smoking cannabis. But the government's indecision over the status of the drug made for awkwardness. Given the prevalence of drug-taking in society at large, and the proximity of Oxford, it may be surprising that the school was not hit by more incidents, though we can only guess how much consumption went undiscovered. The police, when they learned of drug-taking by pupils, were content to leave matters to the school. They did however visit housemasters to help them recognize the symptoms and equipment. Parents, tending to overestimate the power of adult authority to affect the behaviour of teenage peer groups, keenly supported the school's warnings against drugs.

The coverage in the *Chronicles* of David Christie's years testifies to the extraordinary energy of the school's life, to the variety of talents and experiences it fostered, and to the range of the institution's successes. If we take as an example the edition of autumn 1999, we find one headline celebrating the return of the Princess Elizabeth Cup to St Edward's after fifteen years, another the achievement of seven boys in representing their country in rowing, another the school's best-ever GCSE and A-level results. Seven boys and one girl had Oxbridge offers. Ninety-five of the 139 Sixth Form leavers of 1998 had moved on to higher education.

In the same issue the female chaplain, Hilary Benson, recalls a walk to Cambridge, with a camel named Chloe, to raise money for the Gabbra tribes of northern Kenya. An exchange pupil from the Doon School in India gives an account of his impressions. The 20th anniversary of the priesting of David Wippell is celebrated. There has been a Prep Schools activity day based on the study of German. There are reports on the Junior Debating Competition; on the second edition of another pupil-magazine, *SES Who*; on a peripatetic concert in the school's grounds; on a performance of *West Side Story* in the Chapel quad by GCSE pupils after their exams; on the Gaudy Concert, when the programme ranged from the Blues Brothers and *Evita* to Elgar's *Serenade for Strings*, the sextet from *The Marriage of Figaro*, and Sibelius's *Finlandia*; on a Common Room concert; on talks to the Book Club by celebrated writers; and on meetings of the Kenneth Grahame Society. The magazine reproduces artwork and design posters. The forthcoming creation of the Esporta Sports and Leisure Centre is announced and there is an article on the old outdoor pool, which is to be bulldozed to make way for it. There has been the regular Politics trip to Washington, DC. The autumn term has seen productions of plays by two Houses and the German Department. 'The school's first major co-educational tour', a hockey tour to Australia led by Charlie Baggs, is described, as are an expedition to Barcelona, a ski trip to Torgon, an A-level reading party in Patterdale, Duke of Edinburgh Award expeditions, and a canoeing trip on the Wye. There are reports on cricket, swimming, golf, tennis and clay-pigeon shooting. Two St Edward's girls, Polly Dick (Roll No. 10483) and Vicky Croll (Roll No. 10592), are Oxford's under-14 tennis champions. Girls in general are making their mark on the sports pages.

The move to full co-education was a challenge to the Sixth Form girls already at the school, who in one sense had had the best of the previous arrangements. In the daytime they had spent time in boys' houses and shared studies with them. At night they had had bolt-holes in Oakthorpe House or digs, sharing toast and hot drinks away from double-sex pressures. Now, living and working in separate houses, girls had a less 'co-educational' experience than before. Olivia Cooper, one of many to recall the previous system with affection, thought the transition a shame: 'sharing a study and common room with the boys' had 'produced some wonderful friendships and memories'.

Perhaps the Children Act would have made fully integrated co-education impracticable. Perhaps parents would not have accepted it. Certainly they liked the school in its new form. Christopher Northcote-Green (Roll No. 6001), whose daughter Libby (Roll No. 11068) left in 2006, judged from her experience that characteristics of the school which he admired – 'not being stuffy and arrogant and producing well rounded and decent students' – had survived the change. As in all schools, co-residence raised anxiety about sexual relations. The pupils received clear instructions about 'inappropriate behaviour' and 'overt displays of affection'. They were advised to make a wide range of friends and not to become too involved in individual relationships. A solemn document was issued warning against the risk of pregnancy, though most pupils were wiser about such matters than their teachers knew.

Like the sixth-formers before them, younger girls new to the school were impressed by its readiness to allow pupils to make their own way. One of the initial Shell entry, Elizabeth Yarrow (Roll No. 10436), who had never boarded or changed schools before, found that at St Edward's 'you learn to become more independent and responsible for yourself. You are suddenly treated a lot more like adults.' Boys sensed that they had more liberty than they might at other schools. For David Alexander (Roll No. 8282), a pupil in the last years of John Phillips's Wardenship,

> perhaps the overarching memory of my time at St Edward's was the enormous amount of freedom we were granted and trust that was put in us. Even in the junior year I think we were allowed pretty free access to Summertown, and at the weekends we were always in Oxford watching films, shopping or sightseeing.

Alexander left in the year before the Children Act and the avalanche of Health and Safety restrictions that accompanied it, but the pupils' appreciation of freedom survived. They welcomed permission to attend the May Morning celebrations in Oxford, though each year the school hesitated before granting it. The presence of girls had not raised the level of pupil behaviour. They smoked more cigarettes than boys. Leonie Roberts (Roll No. 10108) recalls inventing a family crisis and forging a note from her mother asking permission for her daughter to go home. Instead she went to the theatre in London, joining an audience which turned out to include Stephen Fry and John Major. Next morning every noticeboard in the school carried photographs of her in the *Daily Mail*.

Georgina Pelham 'never felt disadvantaged in a predominantly male situation', and is now surprised when she finds female colleagues at work struggling in one. She took Maths A level, the only girl to do so, 'to prove that girls can do Maths'. She writes to me: 'French was fun and history lively. I will never forget your bursting into Cole Porter in the middle of teaching Charlemagne ....' She appreciatively remembers my 'equivalent of pre-season training' when I organized trips and talks intended to widen the minds of Oxbridge History candidates. Other girls stress the significance of the noisy socializing in the Quad in the gathering dusk. Holly Branson (Roll No. 10460), who arrived as a Lower Sixth pupil, remembers that 'once the conversation did start flowing it was difficult to prise us all apart to get back to bed and from then on boys and girls were friends'.

At least among the senior pupils, and especially in their last year, a new focus of identity was emerging: the Year Group, which took on increasing importance as the competitive teams, disciplinary structures and corporate feeling of the Houses declined. From the mid-1990s there was an annual Leavers' Photograph, and soon there was a Leavers' Year Book on the model of those of American high schools. In previous generations many OSE had sustained school friendships in adulthood, but had not normally forged bonds so extensive as those which now persisted across year groups. Olivia Cooper 'made some wonderful friends at Teddy's, many of whom have become friends for life. Two are now godparents to my own children. Whenever we manage to get an extended group of us together it's as if 15 years have not passed at all .... I could not have chosen a better place to study – I certainly worked harder and got far better grades when enjoying myself at Teddy's than I would ever have done elsewhere. I believe it helped to produce some of the most rounded, friendliest, most confident and loveable people I know. And I wouldn't change a minute of it.' Simon Mills has happy memories too, even though he thinks he was 'close to expulsion several times' and was saved only by the lobbying of his housemaster Geoffrey Boult and of Ian Rowley. He is grateful for the school's tolerance of his 'truculence' and remembers the good sense of his housemaster in accepting 'sneaking out' as a fact of life. He thinks of the school during his time, 1996–2001, as undergoing rapid transition, with constant building and the arrival of co-education, the Internet, and the Sports Centre. The old guard, he notices, was passing. He recalls that those elder statesmen, the physically imposing Joe McPartlin and Paul Kitovitz, 'had adjacent classrooms on the top floor of the Work Block, their doors at right angles to each other. As pupils gathered on the landing before class, each man would impose himself in his respective portal', their 'embonpoints nearly touching, jostling even'. But the coaching of rugby, McPartlin's forte, had passed to a new generation, to 'enthusiastic young men with laptops and degrees in sports science'. Mills wonders whether the free flow of wine when staff entertained pupils would be permitted 'in today's climate'.

For the most part the teaching staff is admiringly remembered. Ida Severin (Roll No. 9054) bumped into the Music master Mark Sellen seven years after leaving and was touched that he remembered her and her playing of the oboe. For her that 'summed up the school', of which she has 'such fond memories'. It was on 'the long walk between the Quad and my study', which 'allowed for lots of chats', that she got to know James Ashworth (Roll No. 8553), whom she would marry. Theirs is one of at least eight OSE marriages to date.

46

EPILOGUE

This book has a somewhat notional ending in 2013, the 150th anniversary of the foundation. Yet David Christie's departure in 2004 has to bring the curtain half-down. Up to that year the Governors have given me free access to their papers. But no institution can encourage the inspection of such documents from its very recent past – in this case so recent that it can hardly be 'history' at all. For the years since 2004 I have rightly seen only a limited range of sources and have not sought to trespass on documents that properly remain confidential. Any archival cut-off point will seem arbitrary, but the year 2004, about a decade before the end of our story and a date which marks the end of a long Wardenship, seems as apt as any. It is a point from which to look back briefly over the story we have followed, before returning to the present.

The school which Algernon Barrington Simeon founded in 1863, and which ten years later he moved from central Oxford to the Summertown site, sprang from the ideal of 'godliness and good learning' that reflected a powerful religious impulse in Victorian Britain. Yet soon the advance of secularism, which has permeated the school's history ever since, reduced the appeal of a semi-monastic community of the kind Simeon had built. By the late nineteenth century the expanding scope of the state, and the swelling of Imperialism, were making new demands on the middle classes from which the newer Public Schools recruited their pupils. There arose a new kind of idealism, devoted to public service and focused more on this world than on the next. Alongside their religious obligations the Public Schools fostered a concept of 'manliness', built on team games, Houses and cadet forces, which subordinated the individual to the group.

Though the claims of godliness and manliness were placed in competition with each other, both aspirations corresponded to broad impulses of society. It was after the Great War that the Public Schools turned in on themselves. The terrible and perplexing loss of life in the war, the weakening confidence of the ruling class, the new hedonism of young high society, and the post-war economic distress reduced the self-assurance of the Public Schools, even though their numbers boomed. Under its longest-serving Warden, Henry Kendall, when St Edward's prospered in numbers and reputation, a new ethos emerged, one I have characterized as 'the boy-centred commonwealth'. The life of the school and the experience of the boys became more an end in itself than a preparation for adult responsibilities or fulfilment.

The Second World War, in which OSE became national heroes, for a time reconnected the school to the wider world. Yet the aftermath of the second war, as of the first, brought changes in society to which the school would have to adapt. One was the growth of the state, which has risen with the decades. Over the later twentieth century the proliferation of state regulation and inspection regimes, and the rising status of national examination, reduced the autonomy of the Public Schools. Perhaps a still more fundamental alteration, one which has been a motor of change in the school ever since, was that of social mores. By the 1950s the rise of egalitarian social policies, the decline of Empire, the new affluence, the erosion of hierarchies by increased social mobility, the new middle-class jobs in a service economy, the 'rise of the teenager' – all those developments were altering the outlook of the families from which the school recruited its pupils. Parental demands ended the frugality and the tough disciplinary regime remembered by older pupils. The concept of manliness, and the emotional buttoning it enjoined, came to seem dated. The 1960s brought new opportunities and new freedoms to boys' lives. Cultural pursuits began to thrive alongside athletic ones. Over the ensuing decades the disciplinary and collective emphases of school life yielded to pastoral ones and to the goal of individual fulfilment, which thrived on the expanding variety of the school's facilities and activities. Instead of living in a boy-centred commonwealth, pupils were encouraged to look outwards and acquire a wider sense of social responsibility. Then, in 1983, came the most radical of the adjustments to post-war social change – the move to co-education, which has become as transformative a step as any in the school's history. It is barely too much to say that over the past half-century St Edward's has reinvented itself.

That process has continued under David Christie's two successors, the twelfth and thirteenth Wardens, both of whom came to St Edward's after successful headmasterships elsewhere: Andrew Trotman, who moved from St Peter's, York; and Stephen Jones, who arrived from Dover College to succeed him in 2011. For the reasons I have indicated, I shall not attempt a close account of the events of their tenure. Yet the era since 2004, which has been as alive and significant as any other in the school's history, and is the one remembered by the highest number of living people, cannot be left blank. In conclusion I attempt three things. First I sketch some broad developments of the years from 2004. Secondly I try to give a flavour of the life of the school over that period through snapshots of its activities in two randomly chosen school years, 2007–8 and 2011–12. Thirdly I survey some recent issues and challenges that face the Public Schools in general, and say something about their bearing on the distinctive history and character of St Edward's.

The physical transformation of the school continued apace after Christie's departure, with the completion of projects on which he had embarked. In 2004 Segar's moved into a new boarding house, just to the south of its old site, near Oakthorpe Road. Cowell's, which had been the neighbour of Segar's, expanded into its former building, which it shared with the English Department. Also in 2004 yet another girls' house, Avenue House, was established on the avenue alongside Corfe. The innovative North Wall Arts Centre was completed in 2006. In the following year it would win both Civic Trust and RIBA awards for the architects Haworth Tompkins and the builders Benfield & Loxley. The Centre radically adapted the Victorian buildings on the northern boundary of the school, which had accommodated, at various times, the indoor swimming bath, the gymnasium, the Armoury, the careers department, the laundry, the Junior Common Room and the lavatory block 'the Crystal Palace'. Housing exhibitions and performances from outside as well as from within the school, the Centre symbolically has one entrance from the school side, one from the street. The Inspection report of 2008 commended the school's readiness to engage with the local community, something the Charity Commission presses on institutions claiming charitable status. No such tribute could have been paid half a century earlier.

Further building projects followed. There were notable additions to and refurbishments of Sing's, Field House, Mac's, Tilly's and Oakthorpe between 2007 and 2010. Field House was extended in 2010. In 2009 the architecturally dominant Life Sciences building, subsequently renamed the Ogston Building in recognition of its benefactor the Yorkshire businessman Hamish Ogston, father of Digby (Roll No. 11564), Isabella (Roll No. 12049) and Patric (Roll No. 12050), was erected to the east of the older laboratories. In the same year the cricket pavilion, the fourth in the school's history, made way for the award-winning fifth (The Martyrs'

Pavilion), though its predecessor, which had come to be flatteringly described as art deco, was preserved and impressively restored. More accommodation for girls was provided by the opening of Jubilee House in 2013. The construction of Avenue and Jubilee added to the buildings to the west of the Woodstock Road, where a majority of the houses, six out of eleven, were now situated. Kendall's underpass, built to connect the school buildings to the playing fields, now links two architectural settings. An appeal launched in 2012 envisages further physical expansion through the funding of a new Music School and even of a thousand-seat concert hall, buildings that would perhaps be situated on the site acquired in 2010, just to the north of the school on the Woodstock Road, of the former Lemon Tree restaurant (previously the Red Lion pub) and the Jack FM radio station.

With physical expansion has come numerical expansion. The number of pupils in 2012, 667, marked a 14% increase since David Christie's arrival. In the same period the number of girls had risen sevenfold, to 233. The school plans to increase the proportion of girls and, in line with the trend in comparable schools, to enlarge the school's overall numbers. Despite its growth, St Edward's has begun to look relatively small. A survey of the twenty-eight schools in the Rugby and Eton Groups in 2011 set the 654 pupils at St Edward's against an average of 790. In 2012 Uppingham had 995 pupils, Marlborough 872, Rugby 831, Stowe 754, Marlborough 872, Clifton 720, Radley 687. Growth in a school's numbers has its challenges, notably the preservation of a sense of communal identity, but the scope it offers for economies of scale and for the funding of new or improved facilities is a powerful argument for enlargement. Debates about the optimum size for the school's educational or communal welfare have yielded to economic considerations. Growth is imperative, one insider has explained to me, because the market respects the 'bigger battalions'. The language of the marketplace has permeated the educational process itself, with the expectation that schools will provide 'value added' quality for its pupils.

The readiness of so many parents to pay fees of more than £30,000 a year to send their children to Public Schools is an indicator of the views of middle-class parents about the condition of the state sector of education. More strikingly, it also reflects a long-term economic trend which, despite recurrent crises and gloomy projections, has greatly enlarged the disposable income of prospective parents. Since 1970 the fees at St Edward's, which have been more or less in line with those of comparable schools, have increased around forty-fold. Inflation over the same period has been around thirteen-fold, so that the school's real income from fees has more than trebled. It is from 1980 that the gap between inflation and fee increases becomes striking. Because of the swelling of pupil numbers, by about 24% since 1970, the total income from fees has increased still further. The building programmes, the expansion of facilities, and the diversification of pupil activities on which the school has thrived are all indebted to what, in earlier and more frugal days of St Edward's, would have seemed an economic miracle. Those developments have in turn magnified the resources the school has been able to offer and the attractiveness of a boarding education. The increase in the teaching staff, which surpassed that of the pupil population and has helped to enhance the variety of activities inside and outside the classroom, has been made possible by the same economic trend. In 1988 there were 63 teachers. In 2012 there were 117, a growth of 86%. The seven women on the staff in 1988 had risen to 48 by 2012, when they comprised 41% of the staff. Though the turnover of staff has continued to be rapid, the school has remained a recruiting ground for headships elsewhere, for five teachers have been appointed to them since 2004.

The full Inspection of the school in 2008, and the Boarding Welfare Intermediate Inspection of 2012, produced almost wholly favourable reports. There was much to commend. The excellent Information Communication Technology facilities reflected a consistency of development since Warden Phillips's pioneering endeavours. The Inspectors approvingly remarked on the provision of 500 music lessons in the weekly timetable and on the high number of concerts and other musical events every year. In 2008 the impressive total of twenty-five subjects was offered at A level. The proportion of A and B passes had risen from 64% in 2004 to 75% in 2007. The report of 2008, which noted this striking improvement, also approved the school's readiness, which would have surprised previous generations, to encourage pupils to assess the effectiveness of their teachers. It was also in 2008 that the school was granted baccalaureate status, so that its pupils now had an alternative to the A-level syllabus; the introduction of the baccalaureate was probably the most important single academic development in secondary education of the decade. The first batch of pupils from St Edward's took the baccalaureate exams in 2010.

We can turn now to some highlights of the first of our two

selected years, 2007–8. The North Wall was home to a range of theatrical and musical activity. An adaptation of Dickens's *Great Expectations* was followed by Pinter's *The Hothouse*. In September the school's Modern Jazz Sextet performed such favourites as 'Tequila', 'Black Orpheus', 'Goodbye Pork Pie Hat' and 'My Funny Valentine'; a performance of Mozart's Mass in C Minor and his *Exsultate Jubilate* followed in October; and a lieder masterclass and recital came in January. Musical activity outside the building saw three choirs of St Edward's combining with two visiting American choirs in the Chapel; a visit by the Chapel Choir to sing Evensong in Gloucester Cathedral; and, in the single month of February, performances by the Concert Band and no fewer than three school jazz bands. In March 2008 forty pupils were involved, with pupils from two other schools, in a charity show, attended by the ambassador of El Salvador, to raise money for a hospital in his country. There were expeditions by the German Department to Berlin, by a Religious Studies group to Rome, and by a climbing party to the Alps. There was also a visit to Auschwitz.

The Woodstock Group, consisting of the school's ninety scholars and exhibitioners, visited the Bodleian Library to view, on the centenary of its publication, the manuscript of *The Wind in the Willows*; it was later addressed at the school by Bodley's Librarian. There were meetings of the Kenneth Grahame Society, a body wryly described by the *Chronicle* as 'the school's oldest society which has, over the years, left few stones unturned in the search for imaginative interpretations' of Grahame's book. The Sports section of the magazine reported on the matches of ten girls' and ten boys' hockey teams, 13 boys' rugby teams and 13 girls' netball teams. There were four soccer teams, and the Harriers had a highly successful season. A distinguishing feature of the year was the tenure of David (now Sir David) Lewis (Roll No. 5797) as the 680th Lord Mayor of London. The school participated in the Lord Mayor's Show and was represented at the dinner in the Guildhall which inaugurated his period of office. Subsequently many OSE attended a dinner at the Mansion House facilitated by the Lord Mayor, who during his period of office took every opportunity to talk about the school and his own debt to it.

The year 2011–12, the first year of Stephen Jones's tenure, was no less crowded with activity. National attention was again drawn to the school when Cameron MacRitchie (Roll No. 11878) took part, with Sir Steve Redgrave, in the torch ceremony of the London Olympic Games. Preparations began for the 150th anniversary and for fund-raising initiatives to complement it, with a view to financing the proposed Music School and concert venue as well as new scholarships and bursaries. The girls' hockey First XI completed its fifth successive season as unbeaten County champions. Selections from the impressive Gaudy art displays filled six pages of a massive edition of the *Chronicle*. Sport occupied 76 of the 256 pages of the publication, but there was also an emphasis on academic attainment. There were extracts from Shell and Fourth Form Essay Prizes. Throughout the year there were twenty-seven formal musical events. On the stage there were productions of James Phillips's *The Rubenstein Kiss* and Sondheim's *Into the Woods* as well as the annual Shell plays. A trip to Cracow and Auschwitz again remembered the Holocaust, and the *Chronicle* published a thoughtful piece on how the subject might be taught.

The 140th year of the *Chronicle* was marked by a lavishly illustrated 35-page history of the magazine, published in its pages, by the school's archivist Chris Nathan, who devoted six pages to 'spoof' *Chronicles* and to unofficial magazines that had been published over the generations. Only two of them emerged with much literary credit: the long-deceased *Martyr* and two recently founded ventures, *Quill* and *Quad*. The Summer 2012 issue of *Quad* was withdrawn on the ground that it might give offence. There were some protests at the size of the 2012 issue of the *Chronicle*, which because of publication delays covered two years and was judged 'too big to handle or to work through', though the length was also a tribute to the range of school activities described in the magazine. The numerous photographs, many uncaptioned, and the variations in presentation might have impressed the designer of a travel brochure. The flavour of commercial enterprise was enhanced by the inclusion of a new feature of the OSE section on 'OSE in Business'. There was also a section on the Friends of St Edward's, a body founded in 2008 that welcomed parents and their relations and friends, and which testified to the appetite outside the school for association with it and for encouragement of the institution's development. The *Chronicle* of 2012 recorded that during the year the Friends had held two London drinks parties, arranged a TV-style interview with the new Warden, and organized a Quiz Night.

So vibrant a record tells its own story. Yet every generation in a school's life experiences its particular pressures. The present-day application of such terms as 'customers', 'consumers', 'accountability' and 'transparency' to an educational context would have been unintelligible to earlier generations. Parents make ever more considered and more calculating choices about the education of their children, keep a closer eye on it, and want to be ever better informed about it. They give attention – though not slavish or uncritical attention – to academic league tables and Inspection reports. Parents from affluent homes want schools to provide the creature comforts of home life. If one boarding house offers better amenities than another, a cry of unfairness goes up. Inspection reports, by commenting on variations in facilities, encourage this mentality. So does the 'arms race' of the Public Schools, which seek to outstrip each other in the amenities they provide, or in the 'trophy buildings' that figure prominently on their websites, or in the facilities they offer for such subjects as Drama, Design and Technology, and Sports Science. Bursars, though they may balk at expenditure on expensive accommodation, spot the lucrative demand for holiday courses from 'customers' who may expect hotel standards. There has nonetheless been some unease about the provision of single en-suite accommodation, with its scope for unsociability or isolation. En-suite rooms were provided in Mac's in 1996 when the House was converted for girls, and, in 2001, in the Sixth Form bedrooms in Kendall House and a few of the Corfe bedrooms. But in the new Segar's (2004) and in Avenue (2006), washrooms are shared by groups of pupils. In 2013 there was a return to en-suite accommodation in the provision for sixth-formers in Jubilee. Which course will the school favour in the future? In such matters Public Schools have not only the wishes of parents to consider but the inclinations of the pupils. The demand of teenagers for greater liberties, individuality of dress and opportunities to leave the school grounds is much greater than a generation ago, and is harder for a school to contain. There is pupil pressure; even pupil power. At St Edward's it is due to the initiative of boys that soccer has been transformed from a hobby for enthusiastic dropouts from the rugby field, played on the neglected Canal Fields, to a sport fielding four teams.

A school exists for its pupils. In the face of the public measurement of success in examinations, St Edward's has adhered to its traditional aim of combining excellence at the top – a cohort of particularly able pupils and teachers – with a rounded education for pupils of a range of abilities. It knows, as it has always done, that there is more to education than exams. The founding mission of the school was a Christian one, centred on the Chapel and on doctrinal faith. Those priorities have long retreated. And yet, in other forms, idealistic aspirations still blossom. The argument is sometimes made that the tolerance, respect and understanding enjoined on pupils in their relations with each other, and the flourishing of charitable fund-raising, are closer to the message of the Gospel than was the hierarchical and unyieldingly tough and masculine school of earlier generations. Whether the school will retain a specifically Christian character is one of the open questions for its future. However it answers them, the Public Schools, whose existence has repeatedly come under threat, now look as secure and prosperous as ever. For all the challenges St Edward's faces, its current buoyancy and vitality entitle it to look confidently ahead.

POSTSCRIPT

MALCOLM OXLEY AND ST EDWARD'S
by Chris Jones and Blair Worden

On Malcolm Oxley's retirement in 1999 the Warden, David Christie, wrote in the *Chronicle*: 'When a new history of the School comes to be written he will bulk large in its pages. Unless, of course, he writes it.' That prophetic allusion to Oxley's invincible modesty, a trait that has compounded the difficulties facing all historians who write on subjects of which they have been part, has been borne out. Oxley, who taught at St Edward's for about a quarter of its 150 years, from 1962 to 1999, had an influence on the school perhaps as great as that of any member of the Masters' Common Room through its history. Only Wilfrid Cowell, a dominant figure in the earlier life of the school who like Oxley served as Second Master, is his obvious equal. Readers of Oxley's narrative could not guess at his stature. They get glimpses of his activities, but gain no sense of their scale. The book gives a strong sense of the values he brought to his work for the school, but scarcely chronicles their impact.

We have written this appendix, without his knowledge, in the hope of doing something to rectify the omission. Neither of us has anything like his intimate acquaintance with the subject matter of his book, and anyway our account of his place in the story will have to be lopsided. Both of us have compelling memories of the charismatic impact of his teaching on our lives and on the school. Blair Worden was in the History Sixth in Oxley's first year, Chris Jones nine years later. So our first-hand knowledge of him from a boy's perspective is confined to the early part of his career. Very many of the pupils who likewise think of him as a formative influence on their lives belonged to later generations. Jones became a governor in 1995, when Oxley had been Second Master for ten years, and so has witnessed his contribution from an angle different from a boy's. But it is easier to recall the sense of excitement generated by a dynamic young teacher than to penetrate the processes of strategic decision-making and assessment in which, in his senior years, he was so prominent, but which inevitably were often conducted behind closed doors.

He came to St Edward's with a strong First in History from University College, Oxford. He was recruited by Frank Fisher, who was eager to raise academic standards, though Fisher is unlikely to have sensed how much else Oxley would bring to the school. With John Todd he formed a formidable, even legendary partnership in the teaching of History. He also taught English and other subjects and was the school's first Head of Economics. He was Housemaster of Segar's from 1973 to 1985, when he succeeded Peter Church as Second Master, a post he held first under John Phillips and then, from 1988, under David Christie. In his final year he stood in for Christie while the Warden had a sabbatical term.

On his arrival at St Edward's, Oxley's effect on its intellectual and cultural life was immediate. The prevailing mood of the school, among masters and boys alike, was conservative, conformist, and class-bound. Prowess on the games field, a sphere of activity at which he liked to poke genial fun, enjoyed far higher esteem than achievement in the classroom or in drama or music. It is a merit of this book that it does not underestimate the virtues of that environment. But his own priorities were different. So was his demeanour. In a community that took its norms of principle and behaviour for granted he seemed to question everything. To the boys it was a startling approach, though it found its moment in the irreverent mood which spread in the outside world in the early 1960s and which was peeping through the gates of St Edward's. He was an unconventional figure in another way too, for his Yorkshire vowels set him apart from the standard accents to which the boys were used. It was to the brighter boys that his cast of mind appealed most. The edge and vitality and voraciousness of his intellect were a novel experience for them. With time he made working hard and intellectual curiosity what they had never been: fashionable. On his retirement a volume of essays by former pupils was printed in tribute to him, an honour normally reserved for distinguished dons.

Though Cowell's teaching methods were less bracing than Oxley's, there are a number of parallels between the two careers. Both cared deeply for the Chapel and were conscious of the school's founding Christian purpose. Both were polymaths of learning and the arts. Both stood back from the tradition of muscularity and manliness and gave confidence to pupils who sought fulfilment outside it. Both made a speciality of the stage. From the outset Oxley began to replace the school's safe and dated repertory with excursions into the avant-garde. Over the decades he would produce countless plays and musicals, ranging from Aristophanes to Brecht, from medieval mystery plays to the Victorian music-hall entertainments that he and his casts performed in old people's homes. Developing an abiding interest in the history of art and architecture, he took boys who were often unaccustomed to leaving the school premises on weekend expeditions to historic houses, churches and galleries. There were more ambitious excursions in the holidays. Adventurous visits abroad included one in 1968 which found him and a party of boys in a camp-site outside Prague when the Russians invaded. Later he took his House to Belgium for half-term. If there is a founding influence in the development of academic and artistic life in the school over the past half-century or so, it is he.

Wit and a playful tone of iconoclasm were his pedagogic style. Yet he was never a dissident figure. His irreverence was harnessed by firm principles, and by a Christian faith, which made him no less a stabilizing than an enlivening force. One reason he was able to make so large a mark on the school was that even while encouraging fresh thinking he possessed qualities – amiability, integrity, trustworthiness, responsibility, conviviality, a gift for teamwork – that fitted well with the traditional characteristics of the Common Room. He was an indefatigable and outstandingly successful housemaster who pioneered pastoral methods and communal enterprises that are vividly recalled by countless pupils and parents. He was a strong influence in the life of the Chapel, where he was a powerful preacher. And behind everything he did there lay the historical perspective on the school's purpose and character which informs this book. He organized the exhibition to mark the school's 125th anniversary and wrote the accompanying handbook.

Traditionally the post of Second Master had carried few administrative burdens. Under the bureaucratic pressures of the later twentieth century its responsibilities expanded beyond recognition, so much so that not long before his retirement a new post, Sub Warden, was created, into which he moved. He did not care for the title, which reflected a trend towards formal hierarchical demarcation in educational institutions, but it gave a truer indication of his role. Over his fourteen years as the school's number two, whole areas of the community's life came under his direction. Study skills; school rules; the school's safety and security; all manner of regulations and rota and liaison activities; the guidance of new staff; the production of guiding documents; preparations for the array of school inspections: these are only some of the ever-enlarging duties which he performed with cheerful efficiency and through which he shaped policies and practices. The authority and respect he commanded from the Common Room, from the Governors, and from two very different Wardens gave the school an invaluable thread of continuous purpose and aspiration. With Christie in particular, with whom, especially as a bibliophile, he found common interests, he formed a close working bond.

Like Cowell, he did not become Warden. In both cases there was a moment when that might have happened, in Cowell's case in 1904, in Oxley's in 1988, though by Oxley's time an appointment from within the school would have been surprising. Instead the stature acquired by both men, which gave such authority to their initiatives and judgements, was a creative force among the teaching staff rather than from above it. Perhaps that was the right outcome. Neither man had an appetite for the financial planning and management that are essential to a headmaster's role. Neither had a taste for personal supremacy. Besides, Oxley, a firm believer in the independence of the school, would not have enjoyed the challenge that has fallen on all headmasters of adjusting to the state's inroads on educational autonomy and to the intrusion of the artificial modern vocabulary of educational discussion.

The extensive administrative commitments of the later part of his career never overlaid his creative instincts. He was at the centre of the school's intellectual and cultural life up to his retirement. 'It is barely too much to say,' he writes in his last chapter, 'that over the past half-century St Edward's has reinvented itself.' His readers should know, what he would never claim and may not even realize, how largely that achievement is his own.

SOURCES

Anyone writing on the past of St Edward's will be indebted to the pioneering *A History of St Edward's School* by Desmond Hill, published in 1962 for the centenary of the school. Though historical fashions change, his book remains a firm foundation.

PRIMARY SOURCES

THE ST EDWARD'S SCHOOL ARCHIVE
The archive contains not only the official papers of the Wardens, Governors and Bursars and administrative material but also letters and scores of reminiscences. The documentary sources are supplemented by printed ones such as the school prospectuses and the *Chronicle* and the successive editions of *The Roll of St Edward's School*, which are listed below. I have not footnoted my text, for material in the archive which I quote and cite can be easily identified and consulted there.

THE ROLL OF ST EDWARD'S SCHOOL
1. ed. A. B. Simeon and W. H. A. Cowell (1890)
2. ed. W. H. A. Cowell and H. S. Rogers (1898)
3. ed. W. H. A. Cowell (1907)
4. ed. W. H. A. Cowell, J.F.W. Eardley and J. C. Hyde (1927)
5. ed. R. J. Northcote-Green (1939)
6. ed. R. J. Northcote-Green and R. A. O. Clark (1951)
7. ed. J. M. D. Gauntlett (1963)
8. ed. F. H. Prichard (1992)
9. ed. C. L. Nathan and D. A. Roe (2013)

OTHER PRINTED DOCUMENTS
In placing St Edward's within the broader movement of the Public Schools I have found the following sources especially useful.

Reports of Public Bodies:
The Clarendon Commission (Public Schools) (1864)
Schools Enquiry Commission (Endowed Schools) (1868)
The Fleming Report (Public Schools and the National System) (1944)

College Registers:
Balliol College Register 1832–1914, ed. E. Hilliard (1914)
A Register of the Alumni of Keble College, Oxford 1870–1925,
    ed. O. C. C. Nicholls (1927)

School Registers:
Charterhouse Register 1870–1900, ed. A. H. Todd (1900)
Clifton College Register, ed. E. Borwick (1911)
The Eton Register 1893–99 (1901)
Haileybury College Register 1862–1900, ed. L. S. Milford (1900)
Harrow School Register 1801–93, ed. R. Courtenay Welch (1894)
Merchant Taylors' School Register 1871–1900, ed. W. Baker (1907)
Radley College Register 1847–1904, ed. W. Legg (1905)
Repton School Register 1537–1905 (1905)
Rossall School Register 1844–94, ed. T. W. Ashworth (1894)
The Lists of Rugby School (printed for the school, 1901–5)
A Companion to the Rugby School Register from 1675–1870,
    ed. T. L. Bloxam (1871)
Sedbergh School Register 1546–1909, ed. B. Wilson (1909)
Sherborne School Register 1823–93, ed. H. House (1893)
Tonbridge School Register 1900–65, ed. C.H. Knott (1966)
Uppingham School Roll 1824–94 (1894)
Wellington College Register 1859–1923, ed. C. T. Hunt (1923)
The Commoners of Winchester College 1836–90,
    ed. C. W. Holgate (1891)

SECONDARY SOURCES

WORKS CONCERNING ST EDWARD'S SCHOOL
Hinchcliffe, T. *North Oxford* (1992)
Hopkinson, T. *Of This Our Time* (1984)
Mackarness, C. C. *Memorials of the Episcopate of John Fielder Mackarness, Bishop of Oxford 1870–1888* (1892)
Mallaby, G. *Each in his Office: Studies of Men in Power* (1971)
Menzies, K. *Addresses to 'Christian Minor': Some Sermons addressed to Public Schoolboys* (1934)
Olivier, L. *Confessions of an Actor* (1982)
Simeon, A. B. *A Short Memoir of the Rev. Thomas Chamberlain* (1892)
Simeon, B. *A Short Memoir of Algernon Barrington Simeon M.A.* (1929)
Squires, T. W. *In West Oxford* (1928)
Whitehead, J. *The Church of St Thomas the Martyr* (2003)

HISTORIES OF OTHER SCHOOLS

Of the many school histories old and new I have found the following particularly useful:

Blumenau, R. *The History of Malvern College* (1965)
Boyd, A. K. *A History of Radley College* (1948)
Bradley, A. G. *A History of Marlborough College* (1893)
Carleton, J. *Westminster School* (1965)
Cust, I. *A History of Eton College* (1899)
Firth, J. d'E. *Winchester College* (1949)
Furness, W. *The Centenary History of Rossall School* (1946)
Hope Simpson, J. *Rugby since Arnold* (1967)
Leach, A. F. *A History of Winchester College* (1899)
Leach, A. F. *A History of Bradfield College* (1900)
Newsome, D. *A History of Wellington College 1859–1959* (1959)
Roach, J. *A History of Secondary Education in England 1800–1870* (1986)
Tyerman, C. *A History of Harrow School* (2000)

BACKGROUND AND GENERAL

Archer, R. L. *Secondary Education in the Nineteenth Century* (1921)
Bamford, T. W. *The Rise of the Public Schools* (1967)
Barnard, H. C. *A History of English Education from 1760* (1970)
Burnett, J. *A History of the Cost of Living* (1969)
Curtis, S. J. *History of Education in Great Britain* (1968)
Dancy, J. *The Public Schools and the Future* (1963)
Fraser, G. M. *The World of the Public School* (1977)
Gardner, B. *The Public Schools* (1973)
Gathorne-Hardy, J. *The Public School Phenomenon* (1977)
Graves, R. *Goodbye to All That* (1957)
Greene, G., ed., *The Old School* (1934)
Heeney, B. *Mission to the Middle Classes: The Woodard Schools 1848–1891* (1969)
Honey, J. R. De S. *Tom Brown's Universe* (1977)
How, F. D. *Six Great Schoolmasters* (1904)
Howarth, T. E. B. *Culture, Anarchy and the Public Schools* (1969)
Kalton, G. *The Public Schools – A Factual Survey* (1966)
Kirk, K. E. *The Story of the Woodard Schools* (1937)
Mack, E. C. *Public Schools and British Opinion 1780–1860* (1938)
Mack, E. C. *Public Schools and British Opinion since 1860* (1941)
Mangan, J. A. *Athleticism in Victorian and Edwardian Public Schools* (1891)

Mitchell, B. R. and Deane, P. *Abstract of British Historical Statistics* (1962)
Newsome, D. *Godliness and Good Learning* (1961)
Ogilvie, V. *The English Public School* (1957)
Otter, J. *Nathaniel Woodard* (1925)
Parker, P. *The Old Lie* (1987)
Percival, A. C. *Very Superior Men: Some Early Public School Headmasters and their Achievements* (1972)
Rae, J. *The Public Schools Revolution: Britain's Independent Schools 1946–79* (1981)
Vaughan, C. J. *Memorials of Harrow Sundays* (1889)
Wakeford, J. *The Cloistered Elite: A Sociological Analysis of the English Public Boarding School* (1969)
Waugh, E. *A Little Learning* (1964)

FICTION
Benson, E. F. *David Blaize* (1916)
Browne, M. *A Dream of Youth* (1918)
Campbell, M. *Lord Dismiss Us* (1967)
Farrar, F. W. E. *Eric, or Little by Little* (1858)
Lunn, A. *The Harrovians* (1913)
MacInnes, C. *Absolute Beginners* (1959)
MacInnes, C. *City of Spades* (1957)
MacInnes, C. *Mr Love and Justice* (1960)
Vachell, H. *The Hill* (1905)
Waugh, A. *The Loom of Youth* (1917)

INDEX

Abbots Bromley girls' School, 38
Abingdon, Montague Peregrine Bertie, Earl of (11th Earl of Lindsay), 146
Abrahamsen, Theodor, 271-2
Acland, Sir Henry, 31
Adams, Sergeant (gymnasium instructor), 163-4, 174, 186, 200
Agnew, Herman, 184
Agnew, Percy, 184
Alden, Robin, 337, 346, 376, 399
Aldenham, Alban George Henry Gibbs, 2nd Baron, 249, 252
Aldenham, Henry Hucks Gibbs, 1st Baron: supports school, 85, 88, 95-6, 103-4, 113-14, 129; death, 115
Aldred, Robert, 396, 429
Alexander, David, 425, 451
Alexander, John, 284, 293-4, 341, 344, 361, 375
Alhadeff, Peter, 398
Allen, Sir Hugh, 216, 260
Ancient History: teaching of, 333
Anderson, John, 318
Angus, R.L., 113-14
'Annies' (maids), 164, 271, 308
anniversary (1933), 246
Anouilh, Jean: *Thieves' Carnival*, 345
Appeals: (1972-6), 403, 405; (1979), 412-13; (1988), 412-14
Apsley House, 238, 240, 248, 257, 324, 326, 355, 358, 409-10
Apsley Paddox, 237-8, 244, 248, 257-8
Archaeology Society, 343

Archer-Houblon, Ven. T.H., Archdeacon of Oxford, 206, 215, 228, 242
Ardingly School, 38, 263
Arithmetic, 123
Arkell, Ann, 410
Arkell, Myles, 337, 347, 429
Armoury, 248, 255, 456
Armstrong, John: as housemaster of Apsley, 295, 324, 355; debating, 312, 343; teaches classics, 334; donates books to Library, 342; friendship with Bradley, 375; as Acting Warden, 387; installs laundry, 400; as bursar, 405; on building expenditure, 409; death, 418
army: entry to officer class, 193
Arnold, Matthew, 13, 149
Arnold, Thomas, 12, 45, 128, 145
Art: teaching, 346
Art History, 415
Art School, 410
Articles of Association, 117
Arts Society, 311, 343
Arundel, Bob, 293
Ashworth, James, 453
Assistant Masters' Association, 113
Association of Governing Bodies of Independent Schools, 437
Association of Teachers and Lecturers, 416
Astronomy Society, 343
athletics, 148, 154, 234, 314; 'Standards', 239
Avenue House, 456-7

baccalaureate: introduced, 457
Back, Jonathan, 423
Bader, Sir Douglas, 217, 245, 259, 268, 284, 288, 366, 413
Bader Field *see* Chris Lawless Field
Badger, Peter, 429
Baggs, Charlie, 445, 450
Baker, John Ward: *Morning Departure*, 313
Ball, Robin, 322
Banks, Antony, 318
Barclay's Bank, 250, 252, 284, 296, 325, 329-30, 416
Barff, Bim: joins staff under Kendall, 236, 292; dines by candlelight, 248; pupil's respect for, 318; as housemaster of Field House, 326, 355; teaches in lower forms, 335; addresses Fisher by first name, 341; pet dog, 362; as Centenary secretary, 364; friendship with Bradley, 375; as married teacher, 410
Barff, Renée, 248, 305, 347, 387, 410
Barnes, Stan, 329
Barrington-Brown, Antony, 285-6, 298, 301-2, 317
Barrow, Peter, 349-50
Barson, Reg (woodwork instructor), 285
Barstow, Stan, 380
Barton, John: *The Hollow Crown*, 361
Bates family, 133
Bates, William, 84, 133
bathrooms: shortage, 124
Battersby & Co. Ltd (London outfitters), 235
Bayzand, P.J., 91

Beales, Hubert, 236, 269, 278, 291, 295, 325, 327, 373, 375
Beardsley, Aubrey, 103; 'Salomé' prints, 368-9
Beasley family, 303-4
Beasley, T.W., 100
Beatles, The (pop group), 353
Beauchamp, Frederick Lygon, 6th Earl, 37, 42, 57, 62-3, 83, 86, 88, 95, 129
Becket, Edward, 14
Becket, St Thomas, Archbishop of Canterbury, 10
Bee, Jeanie, 396
Beechey, Canon St Vincent, 37
'Beehive' (prefect's base), 223, 257
Bell, Dudley, 276
Bell, John, 273
Belson, Louis, 47
Belson, Rev. W.E., 47
Belson, William, 47
Bencraft, Russell, 142-3
Benfield & Loxley (builders), 456
Benson, Edward, 54
Benson, Hilary, 450
Berger, John, 275
Bermondsey Boys Club, 281, 311, 393
Betjeman, Sir John, 36
Bickley, George, 178
Big School, 36, 48-9, 70, 74, 169, 208, 227, 256, 405-6, 438
Bigbury, Devon, 89, 104
Bigland, Anthony, 259, 423
Bigland, Emma, 259, 423-5, 428
Bigland, Ernest, 258, 423
Bigland, John, 259
Bigland, Robert, 259, 423
Biology, 343
Birch-Reynardson, Lt. Col. H.T., 369

Bird, Christopher, 158
Bird, Rev. J., 158
Bird, John, 158
Bishop, Miss (matron; 'Popper'), 163-4, 218
Blakiston, Alban, 171, 175
Blakiston, Felix, 171
Bleadon, Cyril, 122
Blencowe, 'Mother', 163
Blencowe, Oswald, 187
Blomfield, Arthur, 35
Bloxham Project Research Unit, 395-6
Bloxham School, 16, 155
Blyth, Reginald, 93
Boarding Welfare Intermediate Inspection (1912), 458
Boat Club, 119, 155-6, 195, 217, 243, 347, 428; *see also* rowing
Boer War *see* South African War
Bond, Dick, 348
Bond, Peter, 359
Booth, Charles, 164
Bosanquet, Peter, 344
Bossom (boat builders), 155-6
Boswell, Michael, 376
Boult, Geoffrey, 452
Bowra, Maurice, 232
boxing, 227, 314
Bradfield School, 16
Bradley, A.G., 32
Bradley, Mrs R.A., 372
Bradley, Richard: as prospective successor to Fisher, 369; appointed Warden, 372; background and qualities, 372-5, 387-8; salary, 372; teaching staff, 376, 396, 446; policies and reorganization, 380, 382-3, 385-6, 434; opposes Oxford City Council's road proposals, 381-2; and religious observance, 385-6, 395; resigns and leaves, 387-9; personal problems, 388-9; pupils' view of, 388; encourages CCF, 392
Bramble, David, 436, 442
Branson, Holly, 452
Brasenose College, Oxford, 32
breaking-up suppers, 44
Brett, Boyd and Bosanquet (architects), 344
Brewer, John, 294
Brewer-Williams, Edmund, 198, 283-4
Bridge Club, 343
Bright, William: runs Brotherhood of the Holy Trinity, 26; preaching, 28; sponsors St Margaret's Church, 35; attends breaking-up supper, 44; on academic standards, 50; at dedication of Chapel, 57; on supporting council, 83; death, 103
Brims, Pat: bachelorhood, 194; recruited as Classics teacher, 268, 284; teaching, 271, 285, 334; serves in World War II, 278; returns from war service, 291; as housemaster of Cowell's, 304, 358; and Piscatorial Society, 311; co-produces plays, 312; on sexual subjects, 360; retires, 365, 396
Broderick, Cuthbert, 34
Bromsgrove School, 152-3, 214, 217
Brooks, Anne, 436
Brooks, Robert, 436
Brooks, Tom, Will and Katie, 436
Brooks's (estate agents), 237, 241, 256

Brotherhood of the Holy Trinity, 26
Brown, Olivia, 423
Browne, Martin: *A Dream of Youth*, 167
Bruce, Ian, 392
Brunner, Hugo, 439
Buchanan, Cameron, 349-50
Buchanan, Colin, 381-2
Bull (clergyman), 33, 38
bullying, 123, 167-70, 176, 201, 220, 305, 356-7
Burborough (groundsman), 154
Burgon, John William, Dean of Chichester, 61-2
Burke, Penny, 420
Burn, Teddy, 369
Burnham Committee: and salary rates, 328
bursar: appointed, 213
bursarial and secretarial staff, 405
Bursey, Henry (coachman), 66-7, 134, 162-4
Bursey, Mrs Henry (nurse), 47, 83, 134, 163
Burton, George, 286
Business Studies, 415
Bussell, Dorothea, 204
Bussell, Rev. F.V., 183
Bussell, John G., 112, 153, 157, 185, 187-8, 204-5
Bute, John Patrick Crichton Stuart, 3rd Marquess of, 30
Butler Act *see* Education Act (1944)
Butler, Richard, 164
Butterfield, William, 58
Butterworth, Jack, 375

cadet corps (CCF), 185-6, 347-8, 391-3
cafeteria, 358

Callender, Geoffrey, 242
Calvary, 206
Camp, Peter, 270-2, 274
Cane, Alastair, 429
canoeing, 429
Carroll, Lewis *see* Dodgson, Charles Ludwig
Carter, Bernard, 200-1
Carter, Brigadier-General Francis, 235
Carter, Howard, 193
Carter, Rev. J.O.H., 174-5
Carter (organist), 174
Carter, Canon Thomas Thellusson, 61
Carter-Ruck, Brian, 325
Carter-Ruck, Peter, 325, 369
Cash, Stone & Co. (Chartered Accountants), 159, 213
Cass, Leonard F., 112, 187-8
Castleden, John, 220-1
Cave, Philip, 396, 429, 431
CCF *see* cadet corps
Cecil, Lord Hugh, 114
Centenary (1963): celebrations and Appeal, 363-6, 405
Central Committee (boys and masters), 101, 156, 195, 259
Chamberlain, Thomas: at Christ Church, Oxford, 7, 9-10, 15; founds St Edward's School, 7, 13, 56, 128; at St Thomas the Martyr, 9-11, 13; character and career, 9, 11, 13, 15; and Thomas Arnold, 13; appoints Fryer headmaster, 15; and conditions in New Inn Hall Street, 18; dismisses Fryer, 21; Simeon meets, 25; appoints Simeon headmaster, 27-8; disapproves of move to Summertown, 41; payments

from Simeon, 43; attends breaking-up supper, 44; religious practices, 55, 127-9; demoted by Wilberforce, 56; founds churches, 57; Simeon's relations with, 65; death, 88; memorial window, 289
Chambers, Trant, 43
Chapel: building, 38, 54, 56, 58; use of incense, 48; additions and changes, 59, 209, 255-6, 365; services, 62, 64, 126, 133, 395; funding and costs, 81, 137, 161; liturgy, 130-1; choir and organ, 132-3; stained glass windows, 133-4; described, 136-9; decline in use, 139-41; Douglas on, 178; memorials, 189-90, 206; Fisher declares too small, 327; compulsory attendance, 348, 385-6; Committee, 384-5; theme services, 394-5, 444; *see also* choir; religious practices
chaplains, 335
Chard, John, 182
Charter, Guy, 282, 304, 307
Cheetham, Paul, 376
Cheltenham School, 37
Chemistry, 338, 396
Chess Club, 343
Chesshire, Arthur, 43
Chesshire, George, 43
Children Act (1989) *see* Protection of Children Act
choir, the school's, 49, 52, 53, 58, 65, 84, 100, 122, 123, 126, 131, 132
cholera, 11
Choral Society, 345
Chris Lawless Field (*earlier* Bader Field), 438

Christ Church, Oxford: Chamberlain at, 7, 9-10, 15; character, 7; Simeon at, 7, 10, 24, 26; Tom Quad, 36
Christie, David: moves to Woodstock Road house, 240, 435; background, 433-4; Wardenship, 433; on educational principles, 434; qualities, 434-5; aims and accomplishments, 435; and economic downturn, 435; promotes co-education, 435, 437; and rise in pupil numbers, 436; fund-raising, 439; and academic standards, 441; reforms and innovations, 442; and religion, 444; appoints teachers, 446; and teachers' concerns, 447-8; departure, 454; tribute to Oxley, 463; sabbatical term, 464
Christie, Elsa, 434
Christie, Henry: and demonstrations of discontent, 377, 391-2, 397; background, 390; reports to governors, 390-1, 403-4; Wardenship, 390-1, 400; popularity, 391; introduces voluntary participation in CCF, 393; and religious practices, 395; and economic-financial difficulties, 400-1, 403; building proposals, 405; resigns and moves to Dartmouth, 406; and stage performances, 430; and educational fundamentals, 434
Christie, Naida, 390, 394, 405, 408
Chronicle (school magazine): founded, 43-4; on academic standards, 50; on dress and style, 53; on school rules, 53; on

Chronicle (school magazine) *continued*

contributions to school Chapel, 57; on opening of Chapel, 58-9; prints Simeon's sermon, 61; on consecration of Chapel, 62; obituary of Bursey, 67; and Dalton's Wardenship, 69; on teaching staff, 69; on departure of Watkins, 70; on physical development of school, 74; Sayer edits, 83; Cowell revives and oversees, 87, 110, 122; obituary of Chamberlain, 88; Wynne-Wilson edits, 91; and Set system, 92; summarizes Hobson's address, 93; Cowell pays tribute to 200th issue, 100-1; praises W.C. Stocks, 100; on departure of Hudsons, 104; subsidized, 108; and old boys, 109-10; contents and contributions, 119-22, 179-81, 218; on sport and games, 119, 121-2, 142-3, 147-8, 152-5, 180, 217, 239, 313-14, 459; on liturgical celebrations, 120; requests incense in Chapel, 130; on religious practices, 133, 180; reports organ unpaid for, 133; on ignoring Patron Saint's Day, 140; poems, 142, 179-80, 192, 196, 276, 426; on compulsory games, 151; finances sports, 156; OSE contributions to, 180-2; reports Debating Society, 183, 219; on Boer War, 184, 185; on cadet corps' field exercises, 186; on Chapel panelling, 189; Jubilee numbers (1913), 192, 196; on abstaining from alcohol during Great War, 199; Great War issues, 201; on Armistice (1918), 206; on increased costs of boating, 207; on changes to building, 209; reports on music concerts, 216; on lectures, 218; post-Great War changes, 218; praises Ferguson, 229; regrets Gillett declining Wardenship, 231; 400th issue (1925), 242-3; Diamond Jubilee number (1933), 246-7; on outbreak of war (1939), 276; in Second World War, 278, 282; reports Second World War casualties and awards, 282, 288; on atomic age, 289; on contemporary society, 309; criticized, 310-11; on OSE residents at Cambridge and Oxford, 315; on Warden Fisher, 322; on march of science, 340; on class consciousness, 352; on *The Martyr*, 352; on abolition of fagging, 356; on loans for new Houses, 365; drops word 'boys', 377; on new freedom for young, 378; on religious apathy, 385; reforms under Bradley, 387; alternative publication (1968), 389; on CCF, 392; tribute to Henry Christie, 406; on girls at St Edward's, 423-4; Nick Quartley edits, 426; on university entrants, 428; sports coaches' reports to, 429; on music, 430; questionnaire on school facilities and improvements, 431; on David Christie's Wardenship, 449; on Holocaust, 460; shows Gaudy

art displays, 460; size of 2012 issue questioned, 460
Church of England: and Oxford Movement, 5-6; parish stipends, 17; Oxford church buildings, 35; ritualism and liturgical practices, 55-6, 61, 130; and state, 62-3; and public schools, 330
Church, Josie, 410
Church, Peter, 294, 338, 343, 355, 368, 375, 387, 408, 410, 418
Church Times, 106, 162
Churcher, George, 69
Churchill, (Sir) Winston, 297
Clarendon Commission on Public Schools (1861), 19, 54, 232
Clarke, William, 189
Classics: teaching, 71-2, 83, 91, 107, 123-4, 211, 246, 334, 400
classrooms: named, 125, 224
Clegg Commission on public sector pay (1979-80), 401
Cleland (Clerk of Works), 57
Clements, Bob, 396
Clerk, E.M., 203
Clewer, Berkshire, 61
Clifton College, 16, 37
Clover, Philip, 397
clubs *see* societies and clubs
Clynes, J.R., 218
Clynes, William, 218
co-education: in independent schools, 420; *see also* girls
Cochrane, Cameron, 337, 343, 375
Coles, Rev. Starkey, 183
Collins, Grenville, 304
colours (award), 92, 148, 347
Combe, Thomas, 57-8
Combe, Mrs Thomas, 57, 96
Commeline, Archibald, 181

Commeline, Charles, 181-2
Commems, 58, 120, 122, 128, 133, 206, 219, 243-4, 252, 265, 269, 278, 283-4, 288, 345-6, 348, 383, 429
Common Room: Dalton's low view of, 69; divisions and factions, 69; view of Hudson, 196; respect for Kendall, 266; ageing members, 292; physical changes, 325, 444; informality, 341-2; women in, 341, 347; life in, 342, 446-7; Fisher's gift to, 368; Liaison Committee, 369, 417, 447-8; represented on Governing Body, 412; meetings, 417; strong members, 418; *see also* teachers
Common Room Magazine, 167, 175-6
Competition Act (1998), 448
Computer Centre, 415
computers, 337, 415
Confraternity of St Edward, 44-5, 108-9, 139, 198
Conner, David, 394-5, 418-19, 421, 447
Conner, Jayne, 395
Conservative Party: government (1951-64), 311
Cook, Helen, 425, 432
Cook, James, 425
Cook, Stuart, 425
Cooke, Paul, 281-2, 284
Cooper, Graham, 276, 321, 369, 396, 414
Cooper Lodge, 115
Cooper, Olivia, 449-50, 452
Cooper Quadrangle, 115, 414
Corfe House, 113, 209, 239-40, 358, 413, 438, 461
Corlett, David, 273

Corlett, Peter ('Bubbles'), 336-7, 343, 347, 360, 366
Corn Dolly, Oxford (pub/rock venue), 399
Cornelius, Geoffrey (gardener), 329
Cornish, George death, 119, 327
Cornwell, Frederick, 39-40
corporal punishment: abolished, 431-2; *see also* discipline and punishments
Cory, William Johnson, 42; *Ionica*, 263
Cotton, George, 145
Council, 103
Cowell Gates, 170, 263
Cowell, Wilfrid: on teaching staff, 69, 71, 78, 83, 92, 99, 104, 191, 203-4, 222, 262; as peacemaker, 78; salary, 82, 161-2, 212; directs *Chronicle*, 87, 110, 122; management and innovations, 87; theatrical productions and prologues, 87, 92, 100, 184, 206, 218, 244; and Set system, 92; and old boys' society, 109; returns and preaches sermon, 121; contributes to organ fund, 133; encourages Harold Peake, 147; not considered for Wardenship, 191, 466; receives tribute at 1913 Jubilee, 195; on Great War, 204; and memorial buildings, 206-7; regrets change in curriculum, 211; nicknames, 222; runs Set A, 238; proposes names for music rooms in Memorial Buildings, 242; modifies duties, 251; death, 260, 262; achievements and influence, 262-3, 463; portrait, 262; cold-shoulders Shuffrey, 263-4; qualities, 464; teaching methods, 464
Cowell's House (*earlier* Set A), 238, 294, 304, 355, 364, 368, 396, 409-10
Cowell's-Segar's Block, 257-8
Cowie, Arthur, 30, 44, 49, 51, 61, 135
Cowie, Benjamin, Dean of Manchester, 42, 83
Craft, Design and Technology Centre (CDT), 115, 311-14
Craig, John, 204
Craigmyle *see* Hooker Craigmyle
Cranbrook: Queen Elizabeth's School, 98-9
Cranmer, Arthur, 291
Cranswick, Alec, 300
cricket, 101, 107, 119, 121, 147, 150-1, 153-6, 217, 245, 314, 429; professional coach appointed, 148, 150, 154
Croll, Vicky, 450
cross-country running, 347, 429
Crum, Canon John Macleod Campbell, 181
'Crystal Palace' (illicit venue), 299
Cuddesdon Theological College, Oxford, 6, 25, 28, 56, 88
Cundy, David, 376, 415, 442
Cunningham, Admiral of the Fleet Sir John, 295
Cunningham (sergeant-instructor), 188, 211
Cunninghame-Grahame, Herbert: death, 119
curriculum *see* individual subjects
Currie, Sir Edmund, 96

Dahl, Roald, 322
Dalton, Arthur E. (Herbert's brother), 69, 180

Dalton, Rev. Herbert Arthur: rebukes Harold Peake, 11; later career, 68; Wardenship, 68-72, 85, 170; differences with Simeon, 73-9, 80; resigns, 73, 79; criticizes excessive holidays and distractions, 74, 76; marries Simeon's sister Mabel, 75-6, 80; salary, 75, 77, 80-2; and classroom discipline, 78; conflict with Common Room, 78; cricket-playing, 154; in charge of New Buildings, 233; death, 251; accommodation, 295

Dalton, Mabel (*née* Simeon), 75-7, 79; birth of daughter, 80

Dancy, John, 401, 421

Dangerfield, Grahame, 301

Dangerous Drugs Act (1964), 353

Danziger, Chris, 409

Davidson, Madgwick, 24-6, 38, 43, 47, 127

Davidson-Houston, Aubrey, 309, 369

Davies, Eric Wynne, 261

Davies, John, 369

Davies, Leonard, 199, 201

Davis, F.W., 19

day boys: numbers, 403, 438

Debating Society, 180, 182, 183, 219, 260, 262, 272, 275-6, 311-12, 343, 349, 354, 423

de Denne, Alfred, 275

Denstone School, 38, 214, 245

Derbyshire, Nicholas, 358

Design Centre *see* Craft, Design and Technology Centre

Development Director, 439

Devereux, Arthur, 243

Dexter, Cecil, 220

Diamond, Anthony, 272

Diamond Jubilee (1933), 246

Dick, Polly, 450

Dickinson, George, 142-3

Dingwall, Walter S.: joins staff, 207; as bursar, 213, 256, 268; administrative talents, 236; as housemaster, 238; relinquishes bursarship, 249; marriage, 258; career, 267; Sowby on, 268

Director of Studies: post created, 414

discipline and punishments, 78, 102, 177, 201-3, 221, 223-4, 235, 272-4, 286-8, 298-302, 411

Disraeli, Benjamin, 56

Divorce Reform Act (1960), 353

Dixon, Eric ('Budge'): 'These I Have Loved', 316

Dizer, John, 293

Dodd and Stevens (architects), 326

Dodgson, Charles Ludwig (Lewis Carroll), 24

dogs (pets), 361-2, 374

Donald, John, 376

Dore, Hayward, 209

Dore, Mrs (Hayward's mother), 209

dormitories: refurbished and modified, 208, 409-10

Douglas, James Sholto, 100, 102, 124, 167, 177-8

Doull, Alexander, 109

Dowling, Alfred, 63

Dragon School, Oxford, 416

Drake, Paul, 335-6, 343-4, 376

Drake-Brockman, David, 413, 435

drama *see* theatre and drama

Drama Group, 430

Drama Studies, 442, 461

dress and appearance (pupils), 45, 53, 102, 173, 235, 286, 306, 354, 355-6, 370, 391, 397
drinking *see* smoking and drinking
drugs, 353, 449
Duke of Edinburgh's Award Scheme, 348, 392-4
Duncan (butler), 171
Duncan, George S., 203, 207
Dunn, Alastair, 301
Dunn, Ian, 248
Dunn, Walter, 285-6, 303, 329

Eaglesim, Rev. T.A., 50
Eardley, John ('Bill'), 217, 219, 236, 292, 305, 324, 335
East, Rupert, 158, 202
Easton, Hugh: designs memorial window, 326
Economics: teaching, 341
Edge, T.D.G. ('Tim'), 439
Edmonds (dairy), 162
Edmund, St, of Abingdon, 144
Edrich, Brian, 429
Education Act (1944; Butler Act), 296
Edward the Martyr, King of the English, 13-14, 45, 58-9, 120
Edward VII, King: death, 121
Edwards, Arthur Morris, 66
Edwards, Miss (matron), 164
Egerton, Wilbrahim, 1st Earl, 103
electric light: installed, 208
Electronic Engineering Society, 343
Eliot, Lord *see* St Germans, 3rd Earl of
Ellis, Roger, 439, 443
Emden, A.B., 252, 257-8, 295-7, 315, 321

Emley, Miles, 377
Emley, Nicholas, 377
Emmet, Maitland, 236, 245, 291, 294, 304-5, 361
Endowment Fund (1928), 233, 256-7, 262, 363
English Chronicle, 138-9
English Church Union, 43
English (subject), 107, 123, 333
Esporta (company), 438, 450
Eton College: Chapel, 12
'Europe Show', 340
Evangelical Movement: 18th century, 11
Evans, Claude, 376
Evans, Mervyn: appointed to staff, 293; married, 293, 410; debating, 311, 343, 354; teaching, 334, 341, 360; talks on 'Two Cultures', 339; founds Film Society., 344; as housemaster, 355, 358, 368, 375; keeps dog, 362; gives character reference for Emley, 377; accommodates dying Robert King's mother, 388; on guns and shooting, 391
Evans, Richard, 350
Evans, Yvonne, 347, 388, 410
Ewbank, Robin, 350
examinations: by early visiting examiners, 50; by Oxford and Cambridge Board, 72-4, 85; Higher Certificate, 72, 211, 267; results, 74, 93, 267-8, 315, 332-4, 404, 428, 441, 450, 458; Common Entrance, 314-15; and coursework, 428
Eyres, Lawrence, 131, 178, 231

fagging, 223, 274, 299-300; abolished, 350, 356-7

Fairclough, Michael, 332-3, 350
fees and charges, 16-17, 43, 84-5, 87, 107-8, 212-14, 254-5, 284, 296, 328-9, 382, 404, 436, 457-8
Fell, B.T. ('George'), 311
fencing (sport), 347
Fenton, George *see* Howe, George
Fenton, John, 336
Ferguson, Arthur, 228
Ferguson, William Harold: on teaching staff, 91; religious practices, 138, 232; succeeds Sing as Warden, 191, 197; ill health, 196, 229; speech at 1913 Jubilee celebrations, 196; financial appeal, 197-8; appointments to teaching staff, 199, 203, 207-8, 212; announces war casualties, 200; takes in Serbian refugees, 203; reforms and initiatives, 210-11; salary, 212; and approach to Woodard Society, 214-15; introduces surcharges, 214; music and hymns, 216, 220; cricketing, 217; cultural interests, 217-18; and night rioting, 222-3; reputation, 224; leaves to be Warden of Radley, 228-9; praised by Board of Education Inspectors, 228; leaves private notes for Kendall, 234; and Shuffrey, 263-4; attends OSE dinner, 266; in Great War, 277
Festival of Britain (1951), 309
Field Club, 127, 180, 262
Field days, 187-8
Field Fund, 262
Field House: purchased, 113; Tom Hopkinson in, 225; Set C occupies, 238-40; sold, 240, 364; renamed Apsley House, 248, 257; moves to Apsley Paddox, 257; Barff at, 292, 326; matron, 295, 303; Chris Phillips at, 299; Bosanquet designs extension, 344; isolation, 355; enlarged and refurbished, 456
Field Sports Society, 343
field trips, 442
Fielding, John, 376
Film Society, 344
Fisher, Charles, 320
Fisher, Edwin, 284
Fisher Field, 438
Fisher, Francis Forman (Frank): dominance, 240; and Tom Williams, 293; teaching staff, 294, 324, 335-7, 446; introduces swimming trunks, 317; succeeds Kendall as Warden, 321; character and qualities, 322-3; concise reports, 323-4; reforms and administration, 324-7, 330, 355-6, 358; and building developments, 325-6, 363-5; and salary structure, 328-9; on academic standards, 332, 334-5; subject and curriculum changes, 339-41; informality with staff, 341-2; encourages societies and activities, 343-8; differences with housemasters, 346; pupils' view of, 349-50; abolishes fagging, 350, 356; discipline, 350; on social changes, 353; and sex talks and practices, 359-60; Centenary proposals and ceremonies, 363; reputation and offices outside school, 366;

Fisher, Francis Forman (Frank) *continued*
and Beardsley prints, 368-9; presents résumé of Wardenship to governors, 369-70; death and funeral, 370-1; reduces beatings, 370; sabbatical, 375; chairs appeal committee, 414; policy papers, 434; appoints Oxley, 464
Fisher, Geoffrey, Archbishop of Canterbury, 320, 322-3
Fisher, H.A.L., 215, 255
Fisher, Richard Temple ('Tim'), 320
Fisher, Robert, 50
fives (game), 145
Fleming Report on Public Schools (1945), 296-7, 367
Fletcher, John, 222-3, 224
Flower, Sir Cyril, 90-1, 96, 98-9, 167
food and drink, 19, 30, 51-2, 161-3, 199, 226-7, 248, 328, 357
football *see* soccer
Forbes, Alexander, Bishop of Brechin, 26, 31, 127
Forbes, Horace Courtenay Forbes, 19th Lord, 83, 86
Forman family, 320
Forster, E.M., 421
Fowler, R.C., 175
Frayn, Michael, 352
French, 71, 107, 123, 262, 333
Friends of St Edward's, 460
Froude, Hurrell, 5
Fry, Stephen, 452
Fryer, Frederick, 15, 19-22, 27, 29
fund-raising committee: formed, 414

furnace: installed, 208
Fuzzard, Gordon, 375

Gabbitas-Thring (educational agency), 96, 203
Gale, Brian, 341, 347, 368-9
Games Committee, 429
games and recreations: early, 20, 29, 43, 70; fixtures with outside bodies, 43, 101, 152-5, 217, 245, 313; organized sports, 101, 119; compulsory, 107, 151; role, 119, 147-52; national interest in, 148-9; regulated and organized, 149-50; expenses and payment for, 152-3, 155-6; coaching by teachers, 157, 217, 236, 245, 293; professional coaches, 216-17, 313, 429; Kendall encourages, 245; activities after World War II, 313-14; Fisher on, 326 347; minor sports, 397
Gaudies, 93, 110, 122, 127, 131, 133, 137, 183, 189, 197, 246, 265, 273-4, 278, 290-1, 297, 306, 312, 334, 348, 353, 383, 406, 413, 419, 429, 460
Gauntlett, Ambrose, 291
Gauntlett, J.M.D. ('Henry', 'The Grocer'): appointed, 207; teaching and character, 268-9, 285, 303, 338; serves in Great War, 277; leads harvesting parties in Second World War, 279; long service, 292, 294; Vaudrey asks to take photograph, 305; retirement, 324, 358; post-retirement duties, 335
GCSE, 409, 415, 440
General Purposes Committee, 325

Geography, 123
George V, King: accession, 121
German: teaching, 246, 400
Gibbard (butcher), 161
Gibbs, Andrew, 295-6, 325, 373, 405
Gibbs, Edith, 117
Gibbs, G.H.B., 242
Gibbs, Henry Hucks *see* Aldenham, 1st Baron
Gibbs, Vicary, 115-17, 256
Gibson, Guy, 280-2, 288
Gidney, John, 396
Gierlicki, Marion, 319
Giffen, Sir Robert, 164
Giggleswick School, 33
Gilkes, Colonel, 364
Gill, Henry, 74
Gillett, Rev. Charles, 104, 153, 157, 167, 230-1, 242
girls: servant seduced by older boys, 170; at St Edward's, 258, 408, 420-6, 436-8, 450-2, 455, 457; admitted to Public School Sixth Forms, 401; and sports, 425, 428, 450, 460
Gittings, Robert, 276, 365
Glee Club, 121
Godley, General Sir Alexander John, 244
Goldie, B.M., 203, 220, 238
Goldring, Adrian, 367
golf, 397, 438
Goodenough, Sir William, 250, 253, 284, 296; scholarships and bursaries, 416
Gore, Charles, Bishop of Oxford: attends 1913 Jubilee celebrations, 194; (ed.) *Lux Mundi*, 130
Goss, Sir John, 84, 112
Gover, Geoffrey, 306

Governing Body: established, 60; during Kendall's Wardenship, 295; composition, 442-3
government regulations, 188, 404, 439-40
Governors: during Fisher's Wardenship, 369; work increases, 442-3
Gowland, John, 361-2
Graham, Christopher, 377
Graham-Hodgson, Harold, 253
Grahame, Kenneth, 20-1, 30, 50, 110, 143-4, 146, 152, 192, 242, 321; *see also* Kenneth Grahame Society
Grahame, Roland, 21, 50-1
Grahame, Tom, 21
Graves, Robert: *Goodbye to All That*, 270
Great Depression (1930s), 255
Great War (1914-18): school casualties, 112, 187, 199-201, 204; effect on school, 199-203, 205; honours and awards, 204; ends, 206
Greek, 222, 285, 333; *see also* Classics
Green, Charles, 107, 167, 173
Green, Claud, 158
Green, Peter, 21
Gretton, Vice-Admiral Mike, 370
Greycotes School, 345
Griffith-Jones, Mervyn, 354
Griffiths, Rev. J.W., 199, 221, 238
Griggs, Jeremy, 333-4, 352, 356
Grimmond, Keith, 312
Grimshaw, Nick, 412, 414, 418
Grimwade, Monica ('Bloody Mary'), 359
Grotius, SS, 197
Grove House, 233

Guardian, The (Tractarian periodical), 74
Guest, Aubrey W.K., 207, 277, 292
Guest (financial supporter), 38
Gullick, Charles, 315
Gurney, Rev. Alfred, 83, 103
Guy, Basil, Bishop of Gloucester, 369
Gwatkin-Williams, Captain, 218
gymnasium and indoor swimming bath, 151, 163

Haddock, Jane (House nurse), 424
Haileybury School, 16
Halcomb, Ronald, 192
Haldane, Richard Burdon, Viscount, 185, 1867
Halifax, Charles Lindley Wood, 2nd Viscount: as Patron, 42; serves on supporting council, 83; as school's trustee and owner, 85-6, 88; and Simeon's departure, 89; supports school financially, 95-6, 103, 116-17; intervenes with Duke of Marlborough over lease of land, 114; in High Church Movement, 129; attends 1913 Jubilee celebrations, 195; and Ferguson's financial appeal, 197-8
Hall, Rev. Arthur, 174
Hall, E.G., 85
Hall, S.E. (baker), 162
Hamilton, Nigel, 417
Hammond, Edward, 99
Hammond, N.W., 200, 207
Hankey, Tom, 278, 285, 288
Harding, Kenneth, 280
Harper, Herbert: 'The Football Match' (poem), 142-3
Harrison, Sydney, 282

Harrow School: compulsory games, 150
Hartley, L.P., 166
Hartley, W.R., 278, 291
Harvey, Lawrence, 194
Hatt, Adrian, 382
Haughton, Thomas, 204
Havergal, Henry, 224
Hawkins (accountant), 86, 95, 115, 159
Haworth Tompkins (architects), 456
Hayward, Stephen, 377
Hayward, Tom, 145
Headington School, Oxford, 415
Headmasters' (and Headmistresses') Conference (HMC): St Edward's admitted to, 92; Michael Stewart addresses, 330; Public Relations Sub-Committee, 366
Heald, Rev. B., 112, 186-7
Heath, (Sir) Edward, 311
Heathcote, Sir William, 5, 129
Henderson, Alastair, 359-60
Henderson, Derek, 258, 293, 319-20, 321, 347, 361
Henly, William, 50
Herington, Sydney, 69, 78
Herschel, Sir William, 129
Hervey, L.F., 112
Hewetson, Edward P., 245, 258, 267
Higham, Matthew, 426-7
Hill, Desmond, 80, 154, 178, 203, 245, 293, 304, 323
Hill, Air Chief Marshal Sir Roderick, 295
History: teaching, 123, 340-1, 409
Hitler, Adolf, 275
Hobbs, Eric, 204

Hobson, Thomas Frederick: character and background, 90, 95; as Warden, 90-3; teaching, 91-3; troubled relations with Simeon, 93-6; personal finances, 94; resigns, 96, 105; Flower praises, 98-9; Hudson criticizes, 98; attends old boys' dinners, 110; changes religious practices, 138; death, 251
hockey, 156, 314, 347, 429, 450, 460
Holdcroft, Henry, 158
holidays, educational, 442
Hollies (property), 209
Holtby, Robert, 335, 343
Home, Rev. J., 21
Home, James, 21
Home, John: suicide, 21, 27
Honey, Bill (gardener), 329
Hooke, Walter, 7
Hooker Craigmyle (fundraisers), 405, 412
Hope, Rev. B., 112
Hopkins, Gerard Manley, 149
Hopkinson, A.S. Stephan, 223-4, 280-1
Hopkinson, John and Paul, 224
Hopkinson, Sir Tom, 224-5
Hopton, Harry, 204
Hopton, William, 49
'horseboxes' (desks/cupboards), 68
Houghton (of St Peter's Hall), 278
Houghton Report on teacher salaries (1974), 401
House, Alan, 260, 274
housemasters, 304-5, 410-11
Houses (*earlier* Sets): character, 52; system and organisation, 92, 106, 220, 224, 233, 236, 238-40, 259, 399, 410-11; inter-House competitions, 239, 239-40, 399, 429; plays, 345-6; tutorials, 442; *see also* individual Houses
Howe, George (George Fenton), 360
Howorth, David, 337, 343, 398, 417
Hudson, Mrs Thomas, 104
Hudson, Rev. Thomas William: Wardenship, 90, 96, 98, 103, 177; background and qualities, 98; and pupil numbers, 99, 103-4; encourages games, 101; caning, 102; and finance, 103, 161-2, 165; leaves St Edward's for Great Shefford, 104; issues prospectus, 106-7; appeals to old boys, 109; attends old boys' dinners, 110; keeps pigs, 162, 241; presents Union Jack in tribute to Boer War casualties, 184; reluctance to form rifle club, 185; appoints Ferguson, 191; Ferguson on, 196; clerical teaching staff, 208; death, 251
Hughes, Marion, 11, 13, 35, 127
Hughes, Robert, 418, 429-31
Hughes, Thomas: *Tom Brown's Schooldays*, 169
Hunt, Giles, 305, 317
Hursley, Hampshire, 5-6
Hurstpierpoint School, 38
Huskinson, T.L.B. (Tom), 291
Hutchinson, R., 121
Hutchison, Rev. Robert, 50
Hutton, W.H., Dean of Winchester, 219-20
Hyde, Edward, 224
Hyde, James, 204
Hynett, Deborah, 420

Iliffe, Frederick, 69-70, 133
Imperialism, 181-3, 192
Improvement Fund (*earlier* Development Fund), 363
Independent Association of Preparatory Schools, 402
Independent Schools Information Service (ISIS), 330, 401-2, 437
Independent Schools Inspectorate, 440
Independent Schools Joint Council Advisory Committee, 366
Industrial Fund for the Advancement of Scientific Education in Schools, 327
infirmary (and sick nurse), 47
Info (news-sheet), 384
Information Communications Technology facilities, 457
Ingles, David, 50-1
initiation rites, 274
Inspections: (1911), 122-5; (1926), 245; (1955), 332; (2008 and 2012), 458
Internet, 453
Irving-Bell, Colin, 384

Jackson, William, 164, 167, 173
James, A.D., 267
James, Eric, 336
James, Geoffrey, 350
James, S.R., 215
James, Trevor, 245
Jeffrey, Arthur, 67, 163-4, 278
Jeffrey, Mrs (housekeeper), 163
Jellicoe, Frederick, 69-70, 82, 133, 154, 160, 174, 242
Jenkins, Roy, 353
Jermyn, E.A., 185-8
Johnson, Lizzie, 163
Johnson, Mrs (Shop manager), 163, 291

Jones, Andrew, 431
Jones, Brian, 286
Jones, Chris, 398-9, 463
Jones, David Osborne, 189
Jones, Keith, 396
Jones, Stephen, 455, 459
Joseph, Sir Keith, 409
Jotcham, Charles, 163, 167, 170
Jubilee (1913), 192-4
Jubilee House, 457
Junior Common Room, 431, 449
Junior Debating Society, 276, 343
Junior Training Corps (OTC renamed), 278

Kalton, Graham, 367
Keble College, Oxford, 33, 35, 47, 50, 60, 88
Keble, John, 5-6, 24-5, 57, 63, 127
Keith, Geoffrey, 287-8
Keller, A.H., 225
Keller, Cyril, 225-7, 229
Kempe, C.E., 133, 138, 189
Kempner, Teddy, 431
Kendall, Henry Ewing: teaching staff, 207, 235-6, 268, 284, 294-5; introduces House system, 220, 232-3, 236, 239-40; appointed Warden, 230-2; background and career, 232-3; salary and allowances, 232, 252; relations with boys, 235, 272, 273-4, 287; and school dress, 235; policies and aims, 236-7, 259; acquires Apsley Paddox, 237; acquires property from 9th Duke of Marlborough, 240-1; dominance, 240; quits Woodard Society, 241-2; encourages games, 244-5; and opening

ceremonies for Memorial Buildings, 244; reorganizes form structure, 245-6; praised in 1926 Inspection report, 246; building modifications and developments, 248-52, 255, 257-8; and construction of underpass, 249, 457; financial management, 249, 252, 256, 284, 295; character, 251, 266; achievements, 253, 258, 266-7, 297, 316-17, 455; forms links with armed forces, 253; and inter-war social-economic conditions, 255; lacks cultural-intellectual interests, 260, 291; writes letters of recommendation, 261; and religious practices, 264-6, 306; maintains academic record, 268; replies to Gauntlett's application for leave, 269; Abrahamsen on, 271-2; beatings and punishments, 273, 302; effect of Second World War on, 277-80; service in Great War, 277; holiday cottage at Mevagissey, 279, 319-21; announces names of war casualties, 280-1; disapproves of Hopkinson's conciliatory attitude to Germans, 280; offers spaces to other schools in Second World War, 280; keeps in touch with families of dead boys, 282; on new War Memorial Fund, 283; Barrington-Brown dislikes, 285; mistreats staff, 285-6; issues chits for outings, 287; defers retirement, 292; Menzies on, 292; celebrates 25 years at school (1950), 297; portrait, 309; smoking, 309, 317; attends Debating Society, 311; theatrical preferences, 312; watches boxing, 314; retirement, 315, 321; criticized and praised by former pupils, 316-19; bridge-playing, 319; relations with governors, 323; death on world cruise, 366

Kendall House, 438, 461
Kendall, Katie (Henry's sister), 273, 320
Kennedy, Benjamin, 131
Kenneth Grahame Society, 272, 450, 459
Kerr-Dineen, Anthony, 435
Kerr-Dineen, Sarah, 442
Kerry, Rev. W.T., 91
Kidd, Canon Beresford, 242, 265-6
Kilkenny, Karen, 423
Kinch, E.G.N., 112
Kinch (poulterer), 161
King, Edward, Bishop of Lincoln, 28, 57, 77-8, 83, 128, 140-1
King, Robert, 84, 388
King-Lewis, Arthur, 91
King-Smith, Charles, 298
Kinnaird, Angus, 27
Kinnaird, George William Fox Kinnaird, 9th Baron and Frances, Lady, 27
Kitcat, Cecil, 83
Kitcat, Walter, 109
kitchens, 438
Kitchin, Brook, 249-50, 255-7
Kitovitz, Paul, 453
Knight, Chris, 429
Knight, C.S., 153
Kuhn, Anselm, 301, 303, 305, 307-17

Labat, Rev. Christopher L., 99-100, 115, 153, 157
Labour Party: government (1945), 289, 296-7; government falls (1951), 309, 311; regains power (1964), 367
Lacey, Patrick, 200-3
Lambert, Royston: *The Hothouse Society*, 370
Lambourn, John, 286-7, 302-3
Lance, Canon E.M., 215, 232, 242
Lancing College, 38, 150, 215, 329
land acquisitions *see* property and land
Landon, Philip, 295, 319, 321
Lane, Chris, 376
Lane, Jeremy, 345
Langdon, C.B., 20
Language Centre, 380, 383
language teaching, 343, 396
Larkin, Philip, 353
Latin, 123-4, 246, 333; *see also* Classics
latitudinarianism, 128
Laud, William, Archbishop of Canterbury, 219
laundry, 400, 410
lavatories, 202, 225, 299, 456
Lawless, Chris, 438
Lawrence, D.H.: *Lady Chatterley's Lover*, 353-4
Lawrence, Roger, 337, 376
Leach, John, 396, 414-15
League Tables, 441, 446
Leavers' Year Book, 452
Leavis, F.R., 339
Lee & Perrins Company, 37
Lee, James Prince, 45
Leeds, Howard, 44
Legat, Alfred, 49

Letts, Rev. Ernest: helps with *Chronicle*, 44; joins staff, 49; musical activities, 49, 58; departs, 50, 71, 75, 120; in Grove House, 63, 66, 233; attends Simeon's wedding, 80; deputizes for Simeon during sabbatical, 87; builds outdoor swimming pool, 151, 157
Lever, John, 399
Lewis, Sir David, 459
Lewis, Mike, 337
Ley, John, 201
Library, 180, 233, 255, 324, 326, 339, 342-6, 405, 410, 431; *see also* Memorial Library
Liddon, Henry: meets Simeon, 6-7, 25; and Chamberlain, 9; preaching at St Edward's, 28; supports Simeon, 41; dismissed as vice-principal of Cuddesdon, 56; and Public Worship Act, 56; at dedication of Chapel, 57; opposes consecration of Chapel, 59; and Simeon's differences with Dalton, 77-8; on supporting council, 83; death, 87-8; religious practices and beliefs, 129-30, 141, 183
Life Sciences Building *see* Ogston Building
Light Opera Society, 344
Lindsay, Sir Coutts, 136
Lindsay, James, 136
Linnett, J.W., 369
Literary Society, 260, 272, 343-4, 349
local tradesmen and services: dealings with, 160-2
Lock, Walter, 90, 183, 215, 242
London Life insurance company, 256

'Long Earnie' (boilerman), 285
Longley, Charles Thomas (*later* Archbishop of Canterbury), 7, 10
Loscombe, Frank, 175
Lowder, Rev. Charles, 24, 36, 127
Lowe, Anthony, 285, 317
Lower School: reorganized, 380
Lower Sixth Pastoral Conference, 415
Lucas, Rev. H., 112
Lund, Alfred, 184, 189
Lunn, Arnold: *The Harrovians*, 166-7
Lynam, Joc, 320
Lyne, Linda, 396, 408, 422, 423-4
Lyons, Kerry, 337
Lyttelton, Edward, 167

Mace, Arthur, 193, 242
McFarlane, Bruce, 5-7
McGowan, Jim, 337, 344
Machin, B.W., 211
Machin, Mrs B.W. (*née* Ferguson; W.H.'s sister), 211
MacInnes, Colin: *Absolute Beginners*, 351
Mackarness, John Fielder, Bishop of Oxford, 41-2, 56-7, 59-62, 64, 130, 335
Mackworth Society, 345, 389
McMichael, Jack, 236, 277, 292
Macmillan, Harold, 367
Macnamara, Arthur: appointed to staff, 203; in holy orders, 207; and levelling of playing fields, 209; Rawlinson complains to of son's conditions, 210; manner, 222, 226-7; and Laurence Olivier, 223; gives lanternslide lecture, 227; accommodation, 230; as housemaster, 236, 239; on sex manuals, 271; dislikes beating boys, 273; pays for Chapel screen, 280; gives up housemastership, 294; long service, 297; retires, 306; musical soirées, 312; works in Library on retirement, 335
Macnamara, Julian, 445
Macnamara's House (Mac's; *earlier* Set D), 40, 239, 268, 294, 409-10, 456
McPartlin, Joe, 340, 398-9, 425, 429, 445, 453
MacRichie, Cameron, 459
Madeley, Richard, 306
maids *see* 'Annies'
Major, John, 452
Mallaby, H.G.C. (Sir George), 207, 245, 257, 267, 366, 369; *Each in His Office*, 318
Malsbury, Angela, 345
Malvern College, 37, 214, 439
Manning, Edward ('Ludwig'), 236, 291, 292, 312, 344, 365
Mansfield, Robert, 23
Marlborough, Charles Richard John Spencer-Churchill, 9th Duke of, 241
Marlborough, George Charles Spencer-Churchill, 8th Duke of, 103, 113-14, 117, 157, 240
Marlborough College: fees, 16, 214; founded, 37; 'Great Rebellion' (1851-2), 145; girl pupils, 401, 420-1
Marris and Norton, Messrs (Birmingham furniture suppliers), 39
Marsh-Allen, Bob, 302
Marsham, Hubert, 174
Martin, W.M., 19, 32

Martyr, The (magazine), 340, 352, 356, 460
Martyrs Boat Club, 314
Mary, Princess Royal, 263
Mascall, Eric, 336
Masterman, Diccon, 307
Masterman, Sir John, 295
Mathematics, 49, 107, 332-3, 337, 396, 414, 452
Mathematics Society, 343
Mather, Biddy, 410
Mather, Charles: rowing, 292; appointed to staff, 294; debating, 311-12, 343, 354; pet dog, 362; retires, 368, 375; as married teacher, 410
Maths Centre, 115
Matthews, Elsie (nurse), 305
Meadmore, Geoffrey, 221-3, 225, 232, 273-4
Medieval History Society, 311
Memorial Buildings, 125, 207-10, 227, 234, 239, 242-3, 249, 277
Memorial Chapel, 289
Memorial Funds, 206-7, 209, 243, 256-7, 283, 363
Memorial Library, 206, 283, 324, 326, 342-6, 380, 405-6; *see also* Library
memorials: to war dead, 189-90, 206, 256, 289
Menzies House (*earlier* Set C), 239, 292
Menzies, Rev. Ken: appointed to staff, 207; teaches Greek, 222, 285; Ferguson praises influence, 234, 239; teaches Divinity, 234; as housemaster, 236; resigns housemastership over fracas, 239-40; and Paul Cooke's death, 282; classroom manner, 285; activities, 291-2; retires, 291, 306; and sermons, 356; serves in Great War, 377; *Addresses to Christian Minor*, 292
Merivale, Philip, 163, 167, 175
Merritt, Alfred, 148, 150, 154
Merry, Company Sergeant Major, 216, 258, 300, 303
Meteorological Society, 343
Mevagissey, Cornwall, 279, 319-21
Michie, Charles, 264
Milham Ford School, 346
Miller, David, 349
Miller, Miss, 38, 405
Mills, Simon, 452-3
Mitford, Nancy, 352
Moberley, Edward, 269-70
Moberly, George, 6-7, 23-4, 29
Montauban, E.H., 91
Montgomerie, Robert, 337, 376
Monthly Magazine, The, 186
Moody, Brian, 225
Moore, Andrew, 429
Moore, Wilkinson, 35
Moreton, John, 271-2
Morrill, Miss, 38
Morris, Alfred, 17
Morris, David, 346
Morris, G., 17
Morris, Olwyn, 341
Morris, Richard, 430
mortgage: liabilities, 81-2, 86-7, 95, 103, 116-17, 256, 284; transferred, 118
Mortimer, Bob, Bishop of Exeter: denies decline in discipline, 203; performs in sketch and plays, 216, 219; career, 219, 244; on Olivier at school, 223; prayers, 225; and Kendall's jokes, 266, 315; on Board of

Governors, 296, 315; bridge-playing in Mevagissey, 313; and appointment of Kendall's successor, 321; at Centenary celebrations, 365-6; opposes Oxford Council's road proposals, 381; chairs Governing Body, 443
Morton, Patrick, 414
Moss, C.B., 167-9
Moss, Herbert, 167-9
Motor Club, 343
motto (*Pietas Parentum*), 197
Moxon, T.A., 231
Muir, Alan, 377
Murdoch, Iris, 380
Murphy, Robin, 376
Murray, Athole, 99
music: Letts teaches, 49-50, 58; participation in, 69-70, 174, 312; religious, 133; performances, 216, 312, 345, 429-30, 450, 459; Ovenden directs, 291; building for, 327, 457; under Stanton, 344; pop, 351-2, 399-400; under Philip Cave and Robert Hughes, 396, 429
Music School, 325, 344, 398-9, 457, 460
Music Society, 344
Mutter, Frank (Common Room steward), 341, 359
Mynors, Sir Roger, 295, 369

Nathan, Chris, 460
National Curriculum, 409, 415, 446
National Provident Institution, 118
National Society for the Education of the Poor, 22

natural history: interest in, 146-7
Neill, Charles, 418, 444
Nethersole, Michael, 177
Neville, Roger, 301
New Buildings, 75, 81, 102, 114, 125, 175-6, 209, 233, 239
New Hall (The Hall), 125, 406, 409, 431
New Inn Hall Street, Oxford (Mackworth Hall), 15, 28-30, 33, 43, 45
Newhouse, Robert, 221-2
Newling, Edward, 262
Newman, John Henry, Cardinal, 5-6, 9-10, 55, 63, 127
Newsom, Sir John, 367
Nock, Malcolm, 376
Noel, F., 133
Norrington, Sir Arthur, 295
Norris, Edmund, 224
North Wall Arts Centre, 456, 457-8
North-Cox, Wilfred, 204
Northcote-Green, Christopher, 451
Northcote-Green, Joan (*née* Greswell), 295, 303, 305
Northcote-Green, Libby, 451
Northcote-Green, Roger, 236, 245, 267, 278, 291, 294, 303, 374, 415
Nunn, Bernard, 192

Oakthorpe House *see* Woodstock Road, Oxford: Nos.236-238
Obscene Publications Act (1959), 354
Officers' Training Corps (OTC), 122, 187-9, 200, 278
Ofsted, 440
Ogilvy, Frederick, 58
Ogilvy, Gilbert, 58, 62

Ogilvy, Sir Reginald, 58
Ogston Building (Life Sciences Building), 456
Ogston, Digby, Isabella and Patric, 456
Ogston, Hamish, 456
Old St Edwardians (OSE; old boys): association, 108-10; sports clubs and societies, 109-10, 153-4; Rogers' secretaryship, 110, 171; Boer War volunteers, 184-5; war dead memorial, 189-90; gifts and contributions to school, 243, 256, 363-4, 413, 439; reported in *Chronicle*, 243; regional dinners, 252; and Endowment Fund, 256; service in Second World War, 278, 288; casualties in Second World War, 281, 288; and new War Memorial Fund (World War II), 283; dominance in *Chronicle*, 310; appeals to for development funds, 363
Olive, Rev. Carlton, 83
Oliver, Richard, 376
Olivier, Laurence (*later* Baron), 223, 365, 431
Oppenheimer, Peter, 442
Orchard's (Banbury builders), 38
orchestra, 92
organ, 133
Orwin, Charles, 357
Osberton House, 234
Osborne (chef), 329
Osborne, John: *Look Back in Anger*, 313
Osney House School for the Sons of Gentlemen, 13, 18, 154
Osney, Oxford, 9-10
OTC *see* Officers' Training Corps

Ottley, Herbert, 69
Ovenden, Lionel H. ('Bertie'), 207, 260, 286, 291
Owen, John Michael, 302
Oxford (city): building and road development, 34-5, 381
Oxford and Bermondsey Club, 372
Oxford, Bishops of: as Visitors to St Edward's, 42
Oxford Guardian, 47, 56, 128
Oxford Movement, 5-7, 9, 26, 48, 54-6, 61, 127, 129, 140, 306
Oxley, David, 376
Oxley, Malcolm: appointed at St Edward's, 341; early years on staff, 342, 358, 359; made housemaster, 295; as Director of Studies, 415; directs stage productions, 430, 431, 464; school career, 433; and implementation of Children Act (1989), 439; achievements and influence at St Edward's, 463-6

Paget, Francis (*later* Bishop of Oxford), 67-8, 90
Palau, Geoffrey, 369
paperchases and steeplechases, 157, 216; *see also* cross-country running
parents: involvement and financial support, 382, 403, 405, 455
Pargeter, Fred, 336, 346, 361, 398
Parker (fishmonger), 161
Partington, J.B., 112, 199
Patrons, 42
Peach, Cyril, 158
Peach, Rev. P.H.W., 158

Peake, Harold, 70-3, 145-7, 167, 169-70, 242
Peake, Walter, 146
Pearce, Clifford, 99
Pearson, John Loughborough, 58
Pedley, Colin, 337, 341, 346, 376
Peel, Richard, 356
Pelham, Georgina, 424-5, 452
Pelham, Hugh, 424
Pelham, Mike, 424
Penny, Bernard, 158
Percival, Major, 188
Peregrine, Miles, 337, 347
Peregrine, Sheilah, 410
Perkin, Bernard, 273
Perkins, Rev. J.H.T., 91
Perse School, Cambridge, 29
Pether, Stewart, 293-4, 320, 326, 355, 375
Petrie, Rebecca, 423, 425
Pettit, David, 344-5, 376
Philip, Prince, Duke of Edinburgh, 348
Phillips, Chris, 299
Phillips, H.E.W., 112
Phillips, John: teaching staff, 406, 410, 414-15, 418, 428, 446-7; background, 407-8; succeeds Christie as Warden, 407; hospitality and sociability, 408-9; and housemasterships, 410-11; reforms accommodation, 410; initiatives and reforms, 411-12, 415; promotes Design and Technology Centre, 411, 413-14, 457; closeness to Common Room, 412; and building projects, 413-14; favours co-education, 421-2; and cultural activities, 429-30; abolishes corporal punishment, 431-2; departs, 432; and educational fundamentals, 434; and academic achievements, 438
Phillips, Pat, 408, 424
Phillips (wine and beer merchants), 161
Photographic Society, 343
photographs: group and individual, 45#
Physics, 332, 338, 396
Piper, Miss (cook), 164
Piscatorial Society, 343
playing fields, 113-14, 117-18, 121, 157, 438; threat to, 364
Pleasance, Simon, 345
Plowman, A. (blacksmith), 162
Plumridge, Chris, 357, 359
pneumonia and deaths: cases, 46
Pogue, Cecil, 201
pop music, 351-2, 399-400
Potter, John, 29
Potter, Michael, 29-30
Potter, Rev. R., 29
Prag, Dr ('Tooley'), 286
Preedy, Charles, 142-3
Prefects, 43, 53, 170, 173, 177, 223, 239, 257, 299-300, 411
Prep Schools, 402, 416
prices (cost of living): rise (and fall), 212, 246, 328, 400, 435
Prichard, Francis ('Fran'): appointed to staff, 293; coaches games, 293; house in Woodstock Road, 341; teaching, 361; pet dog, 362; at OSE Yorkshire dinner, 374; as housemaster, 375; Clover reports to, 398; as married teacher, 410; appeals for development, 412, 414; supports admission of girls, 422

Prichard, Pat, 374, 410
Prioleau, Richard, 83, 160
Private Chapels Act (1871), 59-60
Private Eye (magazine), 352
property and land: acquired (1924-34), 240-1; purchases under Fisher, 363-4; acquisitions (1990s), 438-9
prospectuses, 83-4, 106-8
Protection of Children Act (Children Act, 1989), 439-40, 451
Prudential Insurance Company: holds school's mortgage, 116-18
Public Schools Bursars' Association, 268
Public Schools Commission (Newsom, 1964), 367
Public Schools (independent schools): development and ethos, 12-13, 111, 310, 419; pupil numbers, 16, 457; and Classics, 19; finances, 32, 37; location, 32-3; and university entrance, 50; and sex, 54, 270; interchange of teachers, 112-13; games, 113, 144-5, 150, 153; gain outside awards and scholarships, 124; Simeon on antipathy to, 127-8; and religious practice, 140-1; unruliness, 145; and morality, 149; novels on, 166-7; Officers' Training Corps, 187; post-Great War fortunes, 205, 214; House system, 233; inter-war success, 254; salaries and allowances, 254, 328, 401, 448; types, 259; and Labour governments, 289, 296-7, 330, 367; adaptation to modern life, 326; Sixth Forms, 326-7; fees, 329, 401, 448, 457; selection of pupils and schools, 330; and state interference and regulation, 330-1, 403-4, 409, 439-41; Mortimer defends, 366; costs increase from mid-1960s, 400; foreign students, 401; girls admitted to Sixth Forms, 401; flourish, 402; building funds and costs, 405; E.M. Forster on, 421; caning abolished, 432; and economic fluctuations, 435-7; success and popularity, 437, 462; favourable terms for teachers' children, 439; recent issues, 456; competitive endeavours, 461

Public Worship Regulation Act (1874), 55, 61
Pugh, Peter, 301
Pugh, William, 431
punishments *see* discipline and punishments
pupil numbers: under Simeon, 86-7; decline, 94; under Hudson, 99, 103-4; under Sing, 115; under Ferguson, 198, 208, 213-14; under Kendall, 233, 248, 255, 296; under Fisher, 370; under Phillips, 414, 422; under David Christie, 436; recent (2012), 457
pupil power, 378-9
pupils: deaths and funeral services, 47, 63, 84, 106, 210; Common Room, 102, 431, 449; later careers, 108, 125, 192-3, 221, 267, 315; age range, 122-3; social origins, 125; life and conditions, 166-78, 356-9; solitaries, 309; use of first names, 378; staff relations

relaxed under Christie, 397-9; freedom and independence, 451; friendships and continuing contacts, 452; recollections of school, 452-3
Pusey, Edward, 7, 9, 43, 67
Pusey House, Oxford, 35, 183
Puxley, Kay (nurse), 305

Quad (magazine), 460
Quartley, Nick, 346, 396, 398, 426, 430, 460
Quick, James, 434, 445
Quill (magazine), 460

radios: listened to, 290, 351
Radley College, 16, 38, 90, 94, 214, 228, 329; Masters' Annual Cabaret, 312
Rae, John, 370; *The Public School Revolution*, 366, 400, 419
Rag Revue (annual), 275, 312, 349
Randolph Hotel, Oxford, 34
Rawlinson, Leo, 210
Rawlinson, Peter, 210
Rayson, Thomas, 210
Read, General Sir Antony, 370
Redgrave, Sir Steve, 459
Rees, Brian, 407
Reform Act (1832), 5
Reid, Sir Bob, 448
Reid, Eric ('Peggy'), 236, 271-2, 291, 292, 361, 365, 393
religious practices: under Simeon, 28, 41, 127-9, 131-2; routines, 51; services, 74, 103, 120, 125, 130-1, 219, 305-6, 368, 394-5; under Hudson, 102-3, 107; outside suspicion of, 138-9; Hutton on, 220; decline in interest, 264, 385-6; and doubts, 307; under Fisher, 335-6; under Bradley, 394; Neill and, 444; *see also* Chapel
Religious Studies, 123, 444
Repton School, 322-3, 335
Rhodes, Cecil, 182
Rich & Co. (fundraisers), 364
Richards, Sylvia, 203, 207
Riches, General Sir Ian, 369
Rifle Club, 107, 185-8
Rigault, Guy, 446
rituals and conventions, 299-301
Robbins Report (1963), 339
Roberts, Field Marshal Frederick Sleigh, 1st Earl, 185, 187-8
Roberts, Leonie, 451
Roberts, Nigel, 344
Roberts, Thomas, 134
Robinson, John, Bishop of Woolwich, 353; *Honest to God*, 339-40
Roe, Derek, 154, 245, 447
Rogers, Harold: termly bill as pupil, 108; career, 109, 170-1; as secretary of OSE, 110, 171; describes Chapel, 134-6; Tractarianism, 136; on Matron Bishop, 164; recollections of school life, 166-7; as school's chief architect, 170, 206, 209-10, 248-9; draws for school magazine, 176; wealth, 198; proposes memorial effigy for Simeon, 251; converts Chapel, 255-6; designs Cowell Gates, 263; on religious practices, 264-6, 278; designs memorial screen for World War II dead, 289; generosity, 364
Roll, Geoffrey, 221
Rollin, Nicholas, 350, 361
Rooke, C. (carrier), 158-9

Rosewell, Mike, 399, 428
Ross, Alan, 352
Rossall School, Lancashire, 16, 37
rowing (sport), 101, 150, 155-6, 217, 245, 256, 259, 303-4, 314, 399, 428-9, 450; girls', 425, 428; *see also* Boat Club
Rowley, Ian, 442, 452
rugby football: at school, 44, 101; poem on, 142-3; rules, 149; dominance, 152-3; fixtures, 152-3, 217, 245, 313; resumes after Great War, 217; under Fisher, 347; under McPartlin, 398-9; successes in 1980s, 429
Rugby Group (shools association), 330, 408-9, 411
Rugby School, 12-13, 45, 145, 152
rules and regulations, 52-3, 102, 287, 298-9, 301-2, 411; defied and broken, 303
Runcie, Robert, Archbishop of Canterbury, 336
Ruscombe-King, Christopher, 346, 368, 412
Ruscombe-King, Mo, 346
Russell, Rev. Thomas, 13
rustication, 411
Rutland, Michael, 384

sailing, 429
Sailing Club, 304
St Anne's girls' school, Oxford, 13, 30, 38-9
St Barnabas church, Oxford, 11
St Bede's School, 180
St Edmund Hall, Oxford, 315
St Edward's Press, 343
St Edward's School, Oxford: founded (1863), 7, 13, 128, 454; name, 13; early pupil numbers and length of stay, 14, 16-17, 22, 29, 54, 63, 74; early years described, 18-21; moves to Summertown, 33, 35; Wilkinson designs, 34-40; recognized as Public School, 38, 92, 103, 117; communal activities, 43-4, 71; aims and values, 45, 461-2; capacity, 47; organization and classes, 48-9; academic standards, 50-1, 85, 93, 267-8, 285, 314-15, 327, 332-3, 404, 441; daily routine at Summertown, 51-3; Tractarianism, 54, 74, 94, 136, 183; staff salaries and wages, 63, 82, 160-1, 212, 325, 328-9, 404-5, 436, 448; expansion, 74, 81; accommodation and facilities, 81, 124-5, 208-9, 233-4, 257, 409-10, 461; shows profit under Simeon, 82; admitted to Headmasters' Conference, 92; old boys' association formed, 108-10; financial arrangements under Sing and Vicary Gibbs, 115-16; room names, 125; outside condemnation of religious services, 138-9; solitary and independent boys, 145-6; stock holdings and investments, 156; transport to and from, 158-9; domestic costs and life, 159-65; balance sheets and account books (1888 and 1890), 160-1; moral standards, 178; militarized, 179-80, 183-9, 198; social concerns and Community Service, 180, 392-4, 450; in Great War, 199-202; takes

in Serbian refugees in Great War, 203; Swedish drill introduced, 211; post-war inflation and expenses, 212-13; celebrates 50th anniversary of move to Summertown, 219; conditions under Ferguson, 224-8; praised by Board of Education Inspectors (1921), 228; building modifications and additions under Kendall, 248-52, 255-8; inter-war position, 255; ethos and values under Kendall, 259-60; staff move on to headships in other schools, 267; and world affairs (1930s), 275-6; in Second World War, 277-9, 283; archives, 286; Catholic teachers, 293; married accommodation, 295, 324; school life under Kendall, 298-308; smells, 298; excursions outside school, 302, 350-1; building proposals and developments under Fisher, 325-6, 330, 364-5; catering costs, 327-8; trips abroad and outside visits, 335, 338, 343, 398, 450, 459-60, 465; and social changes (1950s-60s), 351-3, 389; conservative views, 354-5; Development Plans (1954 & 1958), 363; objects restated (1965), 367; demonstrations of discontent and activism, 377, 391-2, 397; Oxford's road scheme threat to school grounds, 381-2; stress among pupils and staff in 1980s, 427-8; and economic downturn (1980s-1990s), 435; accommodation reorganized (1990s), 438-9; physical appearance and security, 448; achievements and character, 454; developments and activities since 2004, 456-9

St Edward's School Society, 108-10, 171; *see also* Old St Edwardians

St Frideswide church, Osney, 11

St Germans, Edward Granville, 3rd Earl of (*earlier* Lord Eliot), 42

St John's College, Oxford, 39

St Mark's School, Windsor, 155

St Paul's church, Oxford, 11

St Paul's College, Stony Stratford, 152, 1555

St Peter's Hall, 278

St Thomas the Martyr church, Oxford, 9-11, 25, 41, 55, 127

St Thomas's Church Mission Clubs, 186

Salters (boatyard), 156

Sanatorium, 170, 210, 213, 248, 414, 438

Sandell, Joseph, 107, 134

Sankey, John, Viscount, 242, 257, 270

satire, 352-3

Sawyer, Canon H.A.P., 250

Sayer, Bill, 428

Sayer, George, 83, 91-2

Sayer, W., 14

Scarr, Jack, 284, 293, 312-13, 361

Schinas, Johnnie, 399-400

scholarships and awards (outside), 72, 85, 93, 100, 107-8, 124, 211, 267, 332, 380, 428

scholarships, bursaries and exhibitions (internal), 69, 87, 124, 195-6, 250, 284, 318, 329

School House, 325-6
School Shop, 52, 101, 152, 154, 156, 161-3, 248, 256
school song ('Carmen'), 120-1, 306
Schools Mathematics Projects, 376
Schoons, George, 285
Science: teaching and laboratories, 72, 326-7, 330, 337-8, 340, 344
Science Block, 249-50
Scientific and Engineering Society, 260, 311, 344
Scivyer (head gardener), 163
Scott, Gilbert, 34
Scott, Sir Walter, 31
Sealy, Arthur, 49
Second Master, 375
Second World War Memorial Fund, 257, 283
Sedbergh School, 33
Segar, B.G. ('Binks'), 199, 222, 236, 277, 292, 294, 324
Segar, Gerald H., 229, 236, 238, 270, 277, 279, 292, 302
Segar's Block, 249
Segar's House, 208, 257, 355, 358-9, 368, 396, 398, 409-10, 456
Segar's Navy Club, 302
Sellen, Mark, 453
Senior Arts Society, 344
Sergeant, G.M., 112
servants, 66-7, 163-5, 271, 308
SES WHO (magazine), 450
Sets: system, 106; discipline, 201; A, 195; B, 115, 195; C, 115, 220; D, 109, 203, 225; E, 100, 213, 220; *see also* Houses
Severin, Ida (*later* Ashworth), 453
Sewell, William and Henry, 30

sex: dangers, 53-4; activities and awareness, 270-1, 307-8; education, 359-60
Shackleton, William M.W., 199, 203, 222
Shakespeare Society, 343
Sherborne School, 167
Shop *see* School Shop
Shrewsbury School, 231-3
Shuffrey, Oswald, 202-3, 263-4
Shuttleworth, Rev. Edward, 69-71, 78, 133, 242
Simeon, Algernon Barrington: at Keble's funeral, 6-7, 25; at Winchester, 6, 23-4, 172; attends Christ Church, 7, 10, 24, 26; on Chamberlain, 9, 11; and early years of St Edward's, 15, 454; on Fryer, 15, 21-2; succeeds Fryer as headmaster, 21, 23, 27-8; behaviour and character, 23-4, 29; directs school, 23-4, 28, 32, 41-3, 45, 63-4; relations with Liddon, 25; religious principles and practices, 25-6, 28-9, 55-6, 61-2, 126-8, 130-1, 138-9, 183; early teaching and tutoring career, 26; relations with Chamberlain, 28, 32, 41, 65; birching, 30; meets Felicia Skene, 30-1; suffers from stress, 31, 67; moves school to Summertown, 33; raises and borrows money for school, 33, 38, 43, 47, 63; and design of St Edward's, Summertown, 35-7, 41; and building costs, 39-40; concern over teaching standards, 45, 50-1; diphtheria, 46-7, 63; publishes list of donors, 57; and completion of

Chapel, 58; and consecration of Chapel, 59-61, 63; conflict with Burgon, 61-2; sermons, 61; granted payments, 63, 86, 103, 116-17; hands-on management, 63-4, 81; disputes with adults, 65-6; relationship with pupils, 65, 172-3, 235; rift with Letts, 66; servants' devotion to, 66-7; appoints Dalton headmaster and becomes Warden, 67-8; differences with Dalton, 73-9; and expansion and development of school, 74, 75, 81; and classroom discipline, 78; and teachers' complaints, 78; autobiography, 79; achieves appointment of trustees for school, 80-1; marriage, 80, 133; retirement stipend, 80-1; and school finances, 81-2; and school governors, 85-6; financial management, 86, 94; sabbatical (1889-90), 87; resigns, 88-9; appointed to living at Bigbury, 89; appointed to school's new governing body, 89, 96; co-appoints Hobson as Warden, 90; relations with Hobson, 93-6; forces Hobson's resignation, 96; Hudson's attitude to, 98-9; demands departure of Hudson, 104; attends old boys' dinners, 110; owns Field House (Corfe House), 113; Sing's dealings with, 116; toasts school, 120; on antipathy to public schools, 127-8; on lack of organ, 132; and payment for organ, 133; employs Trevor-Battye as secretary, 147; helps fund gymnasium, 151; and payment for sports, 152; and domestic arrangements, 159, 161; receives Moss's complaints of bullying, 167-9; Charlotte Yonge praises, 171; birthday parties, 172; attends 1913 Jubilee ceremonies, 194; gives blessing at 1923 celebration, 219; and House system, 233; moves to Davenant Road, 238; death, 251

Simeon, Beatrice (*née* Wilkinson), 80, 87, 133, 171-2
Simeon, Captain Charles, 6
Simeon, Cornwall, 38
Simeon, Geoffrey, 30
Simeon, Hugh, 69, 77, 81, 95, 116-17, 197
Simeon, Sir J.B., 57
Simeon, Philip, 23-4, 27
Simeon, Violet, 171
Simmonds, John, 289
Sing, John Millington: on teaching staff, 82-3, 91-3, 99; succeeds Hudson as Warden, 104; background and character, 111-12; regime, 112; and prospective loss of playing fields, 113-14; and school finances, 115-17; relations with Simeon, 116; arranges school inspection, 122, 124; and financial crisis, 129; walking, 149; referees rugby matches, 153; encourages rowing, 155; and domestic management, 159, 161-2; payments to, 162; and maids ('Annies'), 164; punishments, 177-8; and school morals, 178; and international crises, 179;

Sing, John Millington *continued*
  reluctance to form rifle club, 185; retires, 191, 196; speech and tributes at 1913 Jubilee celebrations, 195-6; takes world cruise, 197; on Great War casualties, 204; temporary teaching at Winchester, 204; clerical teaching staff, 208; fails to persuade Gillett to accept Wardenship, 230; and successor to Ferguson, 231; as Bursar of Woodard Schools Southern Group, 237; and House system, 239; serves on reconstituted Governing Body, 242; character, 251; resigns as chairman of governors, 251-2; obituary tribute to Cowell, 263; attends OSE dinner, 266; keeps in touch with families of boys killed in war, 282; death and memorial window, 289
Sing's House (*earlier* Set B), 239, 257, 270, 295, 299, 324, 358, 361, 398, 456
Sixth Form, 78, 106, 267, 327, 386-7, 398, 415; candidates for Senior School Certificate, 72-3; club, 383-4; girls, 401, 404, 408
Skene, Felicia: influence on and support for Simeon, 30-2; background, 31; attends sick pupils, 46; nurses Simeon, 47; intervenes in Dalton-Simeon quarrel, 79; Hudson's attitude to, 98; Chapel memorial window, 134
Skinner (furniture supplier), 39
Slessor, Arthur, 72, 79, 85, 183
Smith, Irton, 17-21, 23, 28-9
Smith, Richard, 17
smoking and drinking: by pupils, 350, 411, 449, 451
Snell, Tony, 337-8, 384, 398
Snow, C.P.: 'The Two Cultures', 339
Snow, Janet (Kendall's niece), 225, 319-20
Snow, Jon, 377
Snow, Philip, 319-20
soccer (association football), 149-50, 461
social changes (1950s-60s), 351-3
societies and clubs, 43-4, 71, 260, 272, 311, 343-4; *see also* individual bodies
Solomon, Gerald, 265
South African War (Boer War), 182-6; old boy casualties, 134, 141, 184
Southwell, Henry, Bishop of Lewes (and Provost of Lancing), 252, 256, 266
Sowby, Rev. Cedric W., 258-9, 266-8
Sowby, Mary, 268
Sowby, Rose Mary, 268
Spanier, Greg, 399
Spanish, 396, 400
Spanish Flu (1918-19), 207
Sparrow, Anthony, 302
Spooner, Edwyn, 17
sports *see* games and recreations, 1939
Sports Centre, 411-13, 429, 431, 438, 453
Sports Studies, 442
Sprague, Chris, 355
Spurling, Alfred, 184, 189
squash, 347
Squires, T.W.: *In West Oxford*, 9-10

Stanfield, Michael, 350, 442
Stanton, Cyprian, 17
Stanton, Cyril, 17
Stanton, Edward, 17
Stanton, Rev. L.W., 17
Stanton, Rev. W.H., 17
Stanton, William, 17
Stanton, W.K., 112, 197, 199, 212-13, 216, 228-9, 241-2, 344
Stephen, Fitzjames, 13
Stephenson, Mr Justice Melford, 377
Stevenson (undergraduate), 65
Stocks, G.G., 100
Stocks, Rev. W.C., 100
Stokes, Martin, 397-400
Stone, Edwin, 196
Stone, William Bayford, 213, 233, 242, 249, 251-2, 255, 284, 319, 364
Storey, Graham, 369
Stowe School, 231
Strange, Louis, 200
Street. David, 288
Street, George Edward, 35, 58
Stubbs, William, 56
Styler, Leslie, 236, 268, 272, 284-5, 293-4, 302, 306, 312-13, 318
subway: constructed, 249-50, 457
Summertown: St Edward's moves to, 33-5; foundation stone laid, 41; opening delayed, 47-8; boys' outings into, 287
Sumner, B.H., 295
Sutton, Rev. R., 38
Swatman, Philip, 220-1
swimming, 119, 429
swimming pools: indoor, 151, 168, 325; outdoor, 151, 157, 438
Sykes, Norman, 336
Symes & Co. (builders), 39, 58

Tackley, Stanley ('Tackles'), 236, 279, 294, 320, 335, 346, 361-2, 368, 375
Tait, Archibald Campbell, Archbishop of Canterbury, 55
Talbot, Edward, Bishop of Rochester, 42
Tamplin, Robert, 70, 72, 134
Tate, Jack, 236, 284, 286, 291, 294, 304, 375
Taunton Commission (on Public Schools, 1868), 54
Tawney, David, 336-8, 341-4, 376
Tawney, Jill, 337-8
Tawney, R.H.: *Equality*, 254
Taylor, A.J.P., 407
Taylor, Algernon, 99
Taylor Loughborough (bell founders), 133
Taylor, Simon, 346, 376, 398, 430
teachers: and curriculum, 19, 48-50, 68, 71-2, 123, 211, 228, 284, 340, 415, 427-8; married, 49, 63, 79, 257-9, 266, 293, 295, 305, 324, 342, 365, 372, 382, 410, 416; staff and recruitment, 49-50, 69-71, 82-3, 91, 99-100, 122, 199, 207, 236, 268, 284, 292-4, 335-7, 446, 458; untrained, 49, 332; salaries, 63, 82, 160-1, 212, 325, 328-9, 404-5, 436, 448; women, 203, 396, 429; pension scheme, 213, 416; wartime ancillary staff, 285; Catholic, 293; remoteness from pupils, 304; ratio with pupils, 334-5; status of wives, 347; styles and personalities, 358-62; depart, 376; represented on Governing Body, 412; growing

teachers *continued*
  independence and activism, 416-18; housing, 416-17; concerns, 447; education for children of, 448; *see also* Common Room
teenager: rise of, 351, 354, 377, 461
Temple, William, Archbishop of Canterbury, 322-3
Tenant, William, 49
tennis, 145, 156, 216, 347, 429
Tero, Sam (PT instructor), 303, 348
Territorial and Reserve Forces Act (1907), 187
theatre and drama: Cowell initiates and produces annual plays, 87, 92, 100, 206, 218-19, 240; Shakespeare productions, 223, 318-19, 343; Styler and Scarr produce, 312-13, 345; Vernon produces, 343; Drama Group presentations, 430; at North Wall, 459-60; Oxley produces, 464-5
Theological Society, 343
Thomas, David, 290
Thomas, Helena ('Hena'), 427
Thornton-Duesbery, Rev. Julian Percy, 278
Thring, Edward, 111, 263
Thursfield, R.S., 256, 277, 291, 295
Tibbs, James, 69
Tillich, Paul: *Systematic Theology*, 339
Tilly, Arthur: appointed to staff, 207; starting salary, 212; as rugby coach, 217, 236, 245; as disciplinarian, 221, 235; catches Tom Hopkinson mole-hunting, 225; as housemaster, 238; befriends Sowby family, 268; debating, 275; Great War service, 277; and celebrations at World War II's end, 290; health decline and death, 292; gives up housemastership, 294; brusqueness, 360
Tilly's House (*earlier* Set E), 170, 234, 294, 326, 364, 368, 391, 396, 399, 409-10, 456
Times Educational Supplement, 189, 432
Tindall, Mark, 245
Tinsley, David, 337, 343, 376
Tod, Alexander, 202
Todd, John, 337-43, 352, 368-9, 398, 405, 412, 464
Tollemache, Leo, 99
Tollemache, Leone Sextus, 99
Toynbee, Lawrence, 293, 344
Tractarianism: and Oxford Movement, 6; Chamberlain and, 9; opposes liberal ideas, 13; at St Edward's, 54; on Church and State, 62; doctrines and practices, 127-8; Simeon embraces, 127; and liturgy, 129-30
Tree, John, 446
Trevor-Battye, Aubyn, 70-1, 147, 192-3
Trevor-Roper, Hugh, 345
Trotman, Andrew, 455
Trotman, John, 430
trustees: appointed, 80-1, 85-6
Tuke, Rev. R.M., 115
Turner, A.E. & Son (clockmakers), 260
Twiss, Admiral Sir Frank, 370, 402
Tyrwhitt, Rev. Cecil, 50

INDEX

'U' and 'non-U' speech, 352
Underhill, Percy C., 183
universities: entrants to, 42, 85, 93, 108, 221, 246, 267, 315, 428, 460
Upper School Committee, 384
Uppingham School, 111, 150, 341
Ussher, Beverley, 184

van Oss, Oliver, 407-8
Vaudrey, David, 299, 301, 303-5
Vaughan, Charles, 45, 131
Vaughan, Rev. E.J., 133, 153
Veitch, Bill, 292, 295, 305, 324, 358-9
Vernon, John, 337, 342, 343, 347, 375, 399
Vincent, Canon W.A.L. (Wally), 267, 306
Virr, John, 426
Visitor: appointment deferred, 42
Vowles of Bristol (organ builders), 133

Wain, John, 380
Wakeman, H.O., 103
Walker, Ernest, 216
Wallace, William (*later* Baron Wallace of Saltaire), 350, 359, 361
Wallis, Neville, 99
War Memorial Fund, 256, 262, 288, 363
Warden's Committee, 418, 435
Warden's House, 172, 244, 256
Watkin, David, 299
Watkins, James K., 69-70, 78, 81-2, 153
Watkins, John, 396
Watson, Malcolm, 376, 394-5, 398
Waugh, Alec: *The Loom of Youth*, 167, 323

Weeks, Elizabeth, 396
Weeks, Willy, 286
Weller, Arthur J., 112, 187-8
Wellington College, 53
Wells, Graham, 428
West, Dr Frankland, 291
Westwood, John, 71
Wetherall, Arthur, 99
Whalley, Herbert, 57
Whalley, Rev., 57
Whatley, Norman, 278
Wheeler, Cuthbert, 106
Whigs, 5, 55, 63
White, Harold, 329
White, Jack ('Crasher'), 292, 298, 351, 370
White, Jonathan, 429
White, Mrs (laundress), 159, 161
Whitehouse, Mary, 352
Whitehouse, Peter, 336, 342-3, 346, 347, 360
Whitfield, J.O., 231
Whitrow, Philip, 257, 275, 277, 285, 292, 294, 335, 338
Whitrow, R.B., 207, 236, 239
Wiblin (pork butcher): Battle of Wall, 66-7; sells field to school, 114-15
Wilberforce, Samuel, Bishop of Oxford, 10, 56
Wild, Commander, 218
Wilde, Oscar, 103
Wilding, L.A., 267
Wilkinson, Cyril and Wilfred, 134
Wilkinson designs, 34-40
Wilkinson, George, 376, 387-8
Wilkinson, William, 34, 36, 38-40, 56, 58, 126, 135
Williams, Duncan, 293, 374-5
Williams, Sir E.T. ('Bill'), 369, 396

Williams, Oliver, 115-16
Williams, Pam, 374
Williams, Tom, 293, 306, 367
Williamson, Harold, 204
Wilson, Rev. R.J., 43-4
Wilson, Robert, 358
Winchester College: Moberly retires from, 5; Simeon attends, 6, 23-4, 172; Chapel, 12; length of pupils' stay, 16; school slang, 23; as model for St Edward's, 41, 68; Warden, 68
Winkley, Stephen, 378, 411
Winnington-Ingram, A.P., Bishop of London, 194
Winterton, Major-General Sir John, 369
Wippell, David, 418, 429, 444, 450
Withers Green, Stephen, 442
Wolvercote Boys' Club, 311, 394
women: teachers, 203, 396, 429; as governors, 443; *see also* girls
Wood, Hon. Charles *see* Halifax, 2nd Viscount
Wood, Roger, 431
Woodard, Nathaniel, 12, 21, 38, 127, 138
Woodard Society, 32, 80, 94, 96, 214-15, 219, 237, 241-2, 252; school joins and leaves, 214-15, 219, 241-2
Woodstock Road, Oxford: No. 195 (Bishopstone), 209; No. 214, 341; Nos.236-238 (Oakthorpe House), 363, 413, 420
Woodward, Mrs Henry, 363

Woodward, Henry, 363
Worden, Blair, 345, 351, 358, 463
Work Block (*earlier* 'The Work House'), 249, 255, 258, 303, 453
World War I *see* Great War
World War II (1939-45): outbreak, 274, 276-7; school activities in, 277-80; evacuees from other schools accommodated, 280; OSE casualties, 281, 288; ends, 288-90; effect on school, 455
Wright, Andrew, 435, 441, 444-5
Wright, Desmond, 381-2
Wright, Herbert, 100, 161
Wright, Ian, 429
Wyatt, Ashley, 392
Wyatt (spirits and oil firm), 159
Wychwood School, 345
Wylie, (Sir) Francis, 83, 85, 107, 242, 252
Wynne-Wilson, D.A., 82, 91-2, 115, 161

Yarrow, Elizabeth, 451
Yonge, Charlotte, 5, 171, 206
Yorke, A.F. (Freddie), 207, 236, 238, 250, 277-8, 285, 292, 294, 335, 338
Young, Brian, 407
Young, Roger, 434
Young, Walter, 67, 163-4, 251

Zulu War (1879), 181-2